Jacob Wilson

Phrasis

A Treatise on the History and Structure of the Different Languages of the World

Jacob Wilson

Phrasis

A Treatise on the History and Structure of the Different Languages of the World

ISBN/EAN: 9783337812874

Printed in Europe, USA, Canada, Australia, Japan

Cover: Foto ©Thomas Meinert / pixelio.de

More available books at **www.hansebooks.com**

PHRASIS:

A

TREATISE ON THE HISTORY AND STRUCTURE

OF THE

Different Languages of the World,

WITH A

COMPARATIVE VIEW OF THE FORMS OF THEIR WORDS,

AND THE

STYLE OF THEIR EXPRESSIONS.

BY

J. WILSON, A. M.,

AUTHOR OF ERRORS OF GRAMMAR AND NATURE OF LANGUAGE.

———

ALBANY:
J. MUNSELL, 78 STATE STREET.
1864.

Entered according to Act of Congress, in the year 1864,

BY JACOB WILSON,

In the Clerk's Office of the District Court of the United States for the Northern District of New York.

TO

TAYLER LEWIS, LL. D.,

THAT

EMINENT LINGUIST AND PROFOUND SCHOLAR,

THIS WORK

IS MOST REVERENTLY INSCRIBED,

BY

HIS ADMIRING PUPIL,

THE AUTHOR.

PREFACE.

We shall hardly be contradicted, when we say that the study of language, as a science in itself, has attracted, so far, but very little attention in this country. Indeed, it would be quite impossible for the student, however great his interest in the subject might be, to find the means with which to prosecute his inquiries. The study of philology, at the present time, presupposes the ability to read, at least, French and German works. There are very few works published in this country which are devoted exclusively to this subject—we know of not a single general or comprehensive work similar to the one before the reader; nor do the works of English authors present us with anything like a complete view of the subject.

There is, then, a want, which is every day felt, of a work which shall give a fair view of the present state of philological science, which shall initiate the inquiring student into the mysteries of language, and inform him of its wonders and its beauties, of a work which shall be complete in itself, and which shall not imply anything else than a knowledge of the English and a disposition on the part of the learner to study and reflect, a work which shall be simple and plain enough for anybody to read, and yet thorough and philosophical enough for even the experienced philologist to study with advantage. It is to be hoped that this may be found the work desired.

No effort, no expense, has been spared by the author to render this work deserving of the attention and confidence of the student, and to make it complete, accurate, and intelligible. To name the number of years, long, weary years, that the author has spent in slavish toil upon this book, or to tell the number of books he had pored upon in order to render him familiar with the subject, and, especially, with the character and structure of the different languages of the world, or to state the amount it had cost him in collecting those books, nearly all of which were imported, many being rare and costly, would seem mere boasting; and hence the silence upon that point. Suffice it, for the present, to say that he never suffered this work to go to press, until he felt that he had mastered the subject, and was able to take the responsibility.

Some credit is claimed for the general plan and conception of the work — one which is entirely new. It remains to be seen whether there is a better design for imparting a thorough knowledge of the nature of language. How well the work has been executed, we leave the reader to judge.

To make the work complete in itself, a brief sketch of English Grammar is given; this is followed by a sketch of the Latin, a very different language and grammar. This is given to enable the student to understand or recognize the new features which he will continually meet with in the languages he is about to consider. This is followed by a critical examination of the nature of nouns, adjectives, cases, numbers, genders, comparisons. Much light is thrown upon the nature of pronouns, prepositions, adverbs, and conjunctions — showing what they are, and the forms they have in other languages. There is a thorough review of the forms of the participle, and a consideration of its development — the more particularly, because it is the basis of the verb. The nature of the verb, and the growth of moods and tenses, will be well illustrated in the comparative view that is given of it.

The most important part of the whole work is the comparative view of the history and idioms of the principal languages of the world. It is believed that nothing can so well instruct us in the true nature of language, as the manner in which the different classes of people, or nations, express their ideas. Here, the selections have been very copious, and no pains have been spared to render their character and meaning easily understood. The subject of Etymology has, also, been thoroughly treated of, and the rules by which we may trace the connexion of words, have been carefully set forth. The large lists of words under this head must prove very instructive to any one who carefully examines them.

The main object of the work has been to present a comparative view of the different idioms of the world, and, besides, such facts as would best instruct the student in the nature of language. But, to make the work complete, we have sometimes felt it necessary to discuss, philosophically, some of the questions in philology. These discussions, however, occupy but a small space in the treatise, and are not expected to be particularly interesting to the general reader.

It will be noticed that there are no references in the work, and it is for the reason that it is in no sense a compilation; the only instances in which we are willing to admit that we have extracted from other works, are in the occasional selection of words and sentences for illustration. We have considered them as common property, and have always felt at liberty to take them when we had nothing better at command. But there are several works to which we are greatly indebted for our instruction in this science; we have made constant use of many of them—but only as instructors. It may not be amiss to name them, partly to acknowledge our obligation, and partly to suggest to the student the names of desirable works. They are as follows: Bopp's Comparative Gram. (3 vols.); Prichard's Eastern Origin of Celtic Nations; Garnett's Philological Essays; Latham's Ethnographic Essays—and Handbook of English Language; Wm. Humboldt on the Kawi (3 vols. Germ.); Rapp's Physiology of Language (4 vols. Germ.); Eichhoff's Comparison of Languages (Germ.); Sulzer's Origin and Nature of different Languages (Ital.); Grimm's German Gram. (5 vols. Germ.); Grimm's Hist. of Germ. Languages (2 vols. Germ.); Tooke's Diversions of Purley (2 vols.); Harris' Hermes; Dobrowsky's Slavic Etymol.; Müller's Survey of Languages.; Dictionnaire Linguistique (Fr.); Bock on the Structure of Languages (Germ.); Arndt on the Origin of Europ. Lang's.; Jameson's Hermes

Sythicus; Diefenbach's Celtica (2 vols. Germ.); Latham's Russian Races; Prichard's Nat. Hist. Man (2 vols.); Adelung's Mithridates (4 vols. Germ.); Pott's Etymological Inquiries (2 vols. Germ.); Schleicher's Compendium (Germ.); Donaldson's New Cratylus — and Varronianus; Michel on the Argot (French); Bernhardy's Sprachlehre (2 vols. Germ.); Diefenbach on the Roman Lang's. (Germ.); Julien on Chinese Syntax (French); Rask's Researches (Dan.); Drival's Comp. Gram. Sem. Lang's (Fr.); Benfey on the Egyptian Language (Germ.); Portal's Symbols of the Egyptians (Fr.); Grotefend's Rudiments Umbricæ (Lat.); E. Renan on Sem. Lang's.; Huschke's Osk. and Sabel Language-monuments; Spohn on the Language and Letters of Ancient Egyptians (Lat.); Jenisch Comparison of Lang's of Europe, — besides other minor works, of which little use has been made. To enumerate the grammars, treatises, and specimens of text, which represent nearly every language treated of in this work, besides the lexicons for a large share of them, all of which have been examined by the author and studied by him for years, would require more space than we have to spare here.

We have, as said before, taken great pains to make the work plain, as well as complete and accurate; but yet no one, we hope, will expect to find it so easy that he is to learn the science of language from it without effort, without earnest and unceasing study; no such book has ever yet been printed — none ever will be. We must add, finally, that the author's little work, published in 1858, on the *Errors of Grammar and Nature of Language*, must be taken in connexion with this. It contains an explanation of many theories which lie at the foundation of this work; it will show, too, the road which the author has traveled to arrive at his present position.

To Dr. Lewis, of Union College, who has spent several weeks, even while in declining health, in carefully examining, criticising, and improving, the manuscript of this work, the author is under the greatest obligations, and he knows not how to express the gratitude which he feels for a service which so few could perform, and which has been so kindly offered and so ably done.

PHRASIS.

PART I,
THE ELEMENTS OF LANGUAGE.

CHAPTER I.
ENGLISH GRAMMAR.

1. In discourse or composition, the first and leading divisions are sentences. It is merely the sum of these sentences, perfect and distinct individuals in themselves, that constitutes all that is spoken or written. Grammar, at least, has nothing to do with anything but sentences, either simple or compound.

2. If we regard language as the medium by which we express or indicate thoughts, feelings, and facts, we may denominate a sentence *the simplest and most elementary form of language.* Every sentence is an expression indicating that something exists or is, or was or will be. It may have more than two parts, but it cannot have less. It must contain not only the word indicating the doing, or being, or existing, but the name, also, of the person or thing which does, or is, or exists; as, *men walk, the moon shines, Cicero spoke, the town is old, the base was broad.*

3. In every sentence, then, besides the word which indicates what is done, or what is or was or will be, i. e. the *verb*, as it is called, there is found the name of some person, or thing, or place, or of some property or quality. We call these names *Nouns;* as, *men, moon, Cicero, town, base,* in the examples just given. Two divisions of nouns are usually recognized, those which are *common*, and those which are *proper;* common names are such as apply equally to all of a large class, as *man, tree, book,* while proper names are applied to some individual of a class to distinguish that one from the others, as *Joseph, Albany,*

Europe—or, in other words, one is a family, and the other is an individual name. It is impossible to draw any nice line of distinction between common and proper names, but the above will answer in practice. *Collective* nouns are also sometimes spoken of; they are names of bodies or collections, as *army, assembly, company, nation*. There are also *abstract* nouns, names of qualities, as *length, wisdom, goodness;* and *verbal* nouns, names of acting, doing, being, as *the speaking, the seeing, the becoming.*

4. To a certain extent, nouns have different forms according to the sex they represent; they are said to be of different *Genders;* as, *lion* and *lioness, poet* and *poetess, emperor* and *empress, hero* and *heroine, testator* and *testatrix*. But a very large class of names are applied to individuals without marking the distinction of either sex ; as, *friend, sheep, servant, worker, lover*. In some instances, the male of a class is known by a name very different from that which applies to the female of the same class; as, *brother, sister ; lord, lady ; son, daughter ; boy, girl; gander, goose; drake, duck*. In some of these instances, as in that of *goose* and *drake*, the words are clearly related in origin, and in none of these cases were the words, as *boy* and *girl*, originally used for gender distinction.

5. Persons and animals alone, with us, have gender—things are *neuter* (the Germans call it the *sächlich*, thing-ly gender). In Latin and Greek, gender is conceived to extend to things, on the basis of their possessing masculine or feminine qualities, and, hence, they speak of them, often, as *he* and *she*, while we would say *it*—just as we, again, say of the ship, *she sails, the moon casts her shadow, the sun sends his rays.*

6. Nouns denoting males are said to be of the *masculine* gender, and those denoting females of the *feminine* gender. Nouns denoting things which are lifeless, or which we do not speak of as having sex, as *book, box, tree, rock, crowd, time, water*, are said to be of the *neuter* gender. We should prefer to apply the term gender only to nouns which distinguish it by their form, but, in grammar, the practice is to call all nouns masculine which denote males, and all feminine which denote females. In other languages, as the Latin, gender is much better marked.

7. The variation of forms of nouns to indicate unity or plurality, is much more common ; thus, we use the term *books* for more than one, and *book* when a single one is referred to, and so *boxes* and *box, trees* and *tree, affection* and *affections, valley, valleys, sky, skies.* We call *plural* the form indicating more than one, and *singular* the form indicating only one. The plural form is generally made by adding *s* or *es* to the singular, but not always; as, in *ox, oxen ; child, children ; brother, breth-*

ren; man, men; foot, feet; goose, geese; woman, women. There are some nouns which have no plural; as, ten *sheep,* ten *cattle,* ten *deer.* In many cases, where we adopt the word of some other language, we adopt also its plural; as, *datum* (from Lat.), and plural *data, cherub* (from Sem.), plur. *cherubim;* so, too, the above plural in *en* is rather after the German manner, *en* being for *s* or *es.* The forms *foot* and *feet, man* and *men,* etc., will stand as proof that the plural is only a variation of the singular and contains nothing foreign or in addition to it.

8. CASE. In the words which are called pronouns, as, *I, thou, he,* and *she,* we notice two different forms, according as they come before the word expressing doing or being, and hence are subjects, or follow this word, and are objects; thus, we say *I strike,* but not *strike I,* rather, *strike me;* so, *he strikes,* but not *strike he,* rather, *strike him;* also *thou strikest,* and *strike thee, she strikes,* and *strike her.* When these pronouns are placed before nouns to indicate *whose* or *for whom,* that is, possession or origin, they assume still another form; as, (for *I*) *my book,* (for *he*) *his book,* (for *thou*) *thy book,* (for *she*) *her book;* so, again, we say *his language,* i. e. language coming from him.

9. These different forms are called *case forms,* and the form before the verb is called the *Nominative;* that after the verb is called the *Objective.* (Not only is this form taken when following such verbs as *strike,* but also after prepositions, such words as *to, by, before, with,* etc.; as, *to him, with her, before thee, by me*). The third forms, as, *his, her, thy, my,* are called *Possessives.* In other languages, as in the Latin, they carry out this system of varied forms for cases not only in the pronouns, but also in the nouns; they have *puer,* boy, for the Nom., *pueri,* boy's, for the Poss., and *puerum,* boy, after verbs or prepositions. (They have even other case-forms, which we will notice elsewhere). The German, in this matter, holds a sort of middle place between us and the Latin. They have endings peculiar to certain case-forms in very many instances where they have long since disappeared with us, thus, they say *der Sohn,* the son; *des Sohnes,* the son's, or (of) *the son; dem Sohne,* (to) *the son; den Sohn, the son* (objective). Notice that the article has four forms, while our *the* has but one (the Germ. *der* is more like our three case-forms of pronouns; as, *he, his, him; they, theirs, them.*). Even the Anglo Saxon, or old English, had more of these forms than we; thus, *thaet word,* the word (Nom.); *thaes wordes,* the word's, (of) the word (Poss.); *thaet word, the word* (Obj.); and besides these, they had a peculiar form for our objectives when found after the prepositions *to* and *for;* as, *tham worde,* (to) *the word,* and in the plural, *tham wordum,* (to) the

words (this case-form is called the Dative). All their nouns did not vary in this manner, or to this extent; thus, *sunu, son* (N.); *suna, son's* (Poss.); *suna,* (to) *son* (D.); *sunu, son* (Obj.); *sunena,* (of) *sons* (Poss. plur.); so *mann, man* (N.); *mannes, man's* (P.); *men,* (to) *man* (D.); *mann, man* (Ob.); *syn, sin; synne, sin's; synne,* (to) *sin; synne, sin* (O.); *synna, sins* (pl.); *synnum,* (to) *sins* (plur.).

10. In English nouns, there cannot be said to be more than one case-form, or two, if we count the nominative, and that is the *possessive;* as, *man's* authority, *boy's* book, *hand's* effort—regularly formed by adding *'s, s* and apostrophe. Plural forms, which already end in s, add only the apostrophe to form the possessive; thus, *boys' books,* i. e. books of the boys. Still, it is the practice of grammarians to treat the noun as having three case-forms, adding, only, that the nominative differs from the objective form simply in the place it occupies—the nominative being the doer or subject of the verb, and the objective representing the object of the verb or preposition. Sometimes the order of words is inverted, and the objective comes before the verb; thus, *him they slew* (*him* object of *slew);* so, the nominative often follows; as, *there stood the man* (the man stood, *man* nominative).

11. Such verbs as *is, was, are, will be, become,* may have a nominative after as well as before; as, *he is the man*—*man* is called *predicate* nominative.

ADJECTIVES.

12. Nouns are not always used as names of things spoken of, that is, as subject or object; they are often placed before other nouns to indicate the kind of thing; as, *wood-*car, *house-*work, *iron-*mine, *forest-*tree. Such words as *wood, house, iron,* and *forest,* are joined to the nouns to tell what kind, or to form with the noun a new name, that of a subdivision of cars, mines, trees. Nouns so used, or any other words so placed, are called *adjectives.* Speaking generally, adjectives are words joined to the noun to tell *what kind, how many,* or *what thing.* In our language, and more generally in German, nouns are joined as adjectives to other nouns without change of form, and this on the principle that the noun may be used in one and the same form both as subject and object. But, more commonly, a new form has grown up for the noun used as adjective; as, *joyful* man, *joyous* mirth, *humane* man, *tolerable* success, *amusing* story. In many instances, the original noun on which the adjective has grown up is entirely lost sight of, or is to be found in some other language;

as, in *genuine* logic, *wicked* men, *happy* men, *shrewd* men, *great* men, *mortal* men, (from Latin *mors*, death), *corporal* punishment (from L. *corpus*, body), *physical* powers (Greek *phusis*, nature).

13. It is very common to find these adjectives used not only before the noun as above shown, but following the verb and closely connected with it,—especially after *is, was, be, been;* thus, he *is happy*, this *seems excellent*, some men *are great*, he *becomes a soldier*. It is common to call these words adjectives, and to say they belong to the subjects of the verbs which they follow. But, in the opinion of the author, this is a very unnatural way of disposing of them; they are certainly adjectives in form and nature, but they have not the place of the adjectives. They are no more adjectives than one noun placed before another noun, without varying its form, is a noun. They certainly do not belong to the noun or pronoun before the verb, but, if at all, to some noun following them, and implied; as, *he is happy*, i. e. a happy one, or person. Our preference is to treat them as adjectives which belong to the verb and unite with it to form a new verb.

14. But it must be borne in mind that every adjective has the nature of a verb (or, at least, of that form of a verb called a participle), and that in many languages the adjectives are treated as real verbs, that in such expressions as *is walking, is wise, is prevalent, is excellent, is here, is black, is a man*, the very essence of a verb lies in these adjectives—so much so, that *is*, being a mere auxiliary, is left out entirely, in many languages, by which suppression the whole verb is seen to lie in these adjectives; or, in other words, the adjective holds the place and performs the office of a real verb. It is true, that every adjective is a noun in its origin, but it is that form of the noun, the objective, which is found following the verb and connected with it, either directly or by means of prepositions, and uniting with it so closely as to form with it a new verb—at the same time ceasing to have any of the real characteristics of a noun, which is known as being the name of a person or thing. (*See Errors of Grammar on objectives and adjectives*).

15. Adjectives have different forms to indicate degrees of quality; as, *hard, harder, hardest;* or *hard, more hard, most hard*,—or, taking the descending order, *hard, less hard, least hard*. The first or simplest form is called the *positive;* the second, made by adding *er* or prefixing *more* or *less*, is called *comparative;* the last form, made by adding *est* or prefixing *most* or *least*, is called the *superlative*, or highest degree. Some adjectives are compared irregularly; as, *bad, worse, worst; little, less, least; much, more, most; good, better, best*.

16. A particular kind of adjectives are *numbers*, as, *ten* men, *five* books; they are called *numerals*, and are again divided into *cardinals*, as *one, two, three*, etc., and *ordinals*, as *first, second, third*, etc.

17. Adjectives of very frequent occurrence, and which may be regarded as marks of the noun, are the words *a, an*, and *the*. They are called the *articles*—*a* and *an* being called indefinite, and *the* being the definite article.

PRONOUNS.

18. The oft occurring words *I, thou, he, she*, and *it*, are called the *personal* pronouns, or the *personals*. The first, *I*, represents the speaker, and is said to be of the *first person; thou* is used to denote the person spoken to, and is called the pronoun of the *second person; he, she*, and *it*, are personals of the *third person*, and they always stand in the place of the name of the person or thing spoken of.

19. The first personal has, for the three case-forms of the sing., respectively, *I, my* or *mine, me* (Nom. Poss. Ob.), and for the plural, *we, our* or *ours, us;* in the same way, *thou, thy* or *thine, thee*, and plural, *ye* or *you, your* or *yours, you;* and for the three personals of the third person, *he, his, him* (masc.), *she, her* or *hers, her* (fem.), *it, its, it* (neut.); the plural is the same for these three, *they, their* or *theirs, them*.

20. What is called a compound personal is formed by adding *self* to the objectives of these pronouns; as *himself, herself, itself, themselves*, except that in the case of *I* and *thou*, the possessive form is taken; as, *myself, thyself*.

21. The words *who, which, what*, and *that*, are called the *relatives*, as referring back to some person or thing already spoken of. They have no peculiar forms when they represent plurals. The first has the case-forms *who, whose, whom; whose* is also used as the possessive of *which;* beyond this, there is no variation in the forms of relatives.

22. To all of them, except *that*, the word *ever* may be joined to form what are known as compound relatives; as, *whatever, whichever, whoever*, besides *whatsoever, whomsoever*.

23. *Who, which*, and *what*, are used in questions, and are called *interrogatives*—or, if we may judge from some other tongues, it is rather the interrogative that is used as relative. All pronouns are adjective in their nature, and become independent individuals by the suppression of the noun to which they should belong. Every adjective used without its noun is, properly, a pronoun; as, *this* is so, *all* walked, *each* spoke, *none* spoke, *one* said, *some* said.

24. Our own relatives, *which, what,* and *that,* are used as adjectives, as, *which man,* as well as relatives, as, in *the man which said.* And in other languages, as in Latin, the personals of the third person are used as adjectives too, just as if we said *he man, she girl, it thing,* as we do say *this man, this girl, that thing.*

VERBS.

25. We have already anticipated, necessarily, to some extent, the office and meaning of a verb, and we have only to repeat, here, that verbs are used to tell what *is done,* or what some one or some thing *does,* or what *exists* or *is* (in time either *past, present,* or *future);* as, *he walks, he is struck, he seems, he becomes.* Bearing these characteristics in view, verbs are easily distinguished from other words.

26. Verbs fall readily into two very important classes, or divisions, those which take objectives immediately after them and are *transitive,* as, *James struck him,* and, on the other hand, those which cannot have an objective attached to them, except through the connexion of a preposition, and are hence *intransitive;* that is, the action is not looked upon as passing over to an object; thus, *James is writing, James speaks, James looked for him.* Transitives are regularly followed by nouns or pronouns in the objective case; no other verbs are transitive, save, if you will, those cases where it is assumed that the object precedes; as, *him he slew.* But, even here, it may be questioned whether or not *him* is not thrown out independently, and another *him,* the real object, suppressed.

27. The nouns that follow *is* or *be* in its different forms, are said to be nominatives; as, *he is a man, he will be an officer,* but they are certainly not subjects like other nominatives, otherwise the verb would have two subjects, one before and one after (In Arabic, among others, we find acc. after *be.*). As before intimated, such nouns are pure adjectives, and adjectives are allied to objectives. There are other cases where verbs are followed by nouns which are not properly objects, and the verbs are hence not transitive; thus, *he seems a man,* (*to be* implied), *he became a man* (came to be), *he was elected prince* (to be prince).

28. But, it is well to bear in mind that intransitives taken with the preposition are as much transitive as any other verb, that is, they may and do have objects. We understand transitives to differ from intransitives only in the suppression of the preposition; so, *to write* you is transitive, but *to write to* you is intransitive; *flee* the land is trans., but *flee from* the land is

intrans.; we may say *seek him* or *seek for him*—the same verb being transitive or intransitive according as we use or do not use the preposition *for*. The verbs, in many instances, which we must use with a preposition, we find in other languages used without them. Verbs which may have objects, but yet do not have them in the particular case in question, are called intransitive; thus, the expression *he writes* is intran., but *he writes a letter* is transitive. (*See Errors of Gram. on reflexive verbs.*)

29. Another important division is into *regular* and *irregular* verbs; thus, those that form their past tense and past participle (that form of verb which follows *have* and *had*) by adding *d* or *ed* to the verb, are regular, and those which do not are irregular. Thus, the verb *walk*, past, *I walked*, and part., *have walked*; the verb *love*, past, *I loved*, part., have or had *loved*; but not so with the verb *see*, past, *I saw*, part., have *seen* (not *seed*); so of *speak*, *spoke*, and *spoken*, of *be*, *was*, *been*, of *make*, *made*, *made*, of *go*, *went*, *gone*, *do*, *did*, *done*, *come*, *came*, *come*, *strike*, *struck*, *struck*. This last or irregular form, which does not need the new element *ed* to form pasts, is sometimes called the *strong*, and the other is called the *weak* tense.

30. There are still two other forms of the verb, or rather of the transitive verb, which are uniformly recognized and are of great importance, the *active*, and the *passive* form. When we say *John strikes James*, or *John loves James*, we use the active form of *strike* and *love*, since John, the subject of remark, is the actor or doer; when, however, we use another form, and say *James is, or was, struck by John*, or *is, or was, loved by John*, there the subject, James, is not the striker, the lover, but the one struck, or loved, the object, the one who suffers. The compound form *is struck*, *was struck*, and the like, is called the passive of *strike*, etc. But, really, as to form, *is struck* is no more passive than *is happy* or *is striking*, for both expressions denote simply a condition, or state, without reference to the action which produced that state, but it so happens that, in the passive form, the *is*, *was*, *will be*, *have been*, etc., are practically suppressed, and the whole force is thrown upon the participle, now become a verb, as in the case of *struck*. Every transitive expression may thus be reversed and put in the passive form, with the object as subject. (*See Errors of Gram. on passives.*)

31. Every passive expression is intransitive in its character, and we shall continually find it difficult to distinguish it from other intransitive forms, whenever *is*, *was*, etc., are used; thus, *he is celebrated* is passive, if you understand that some one celebrates him, but it is intransitive, if he is simply a celebrated man. All that is passive in the form lies in the participle after *is*, *was*, etc.; *has struck*, in form, is as much passive as *is struck*, but *struck* is, in sense, active in the former and passive in the latter.

32. TENSES. Verbs have different forms, or marks, by which they indicate whether an action or being is present, past, or future. These forms are called *tenses* or tense forms.

33. The *present tense* denotes a present or continuing doing or being, as *walks, speaks, reads, is reading, are saying, is struck*.

34. The *past tense* denotes a doing or being that is finished, or one continuing in past time; as, *walked, read, spoke, was reading, was saying, was struck*. The *future tense* indicates what is to take place, or what will be taking place, and the mark of it is *shall* or *will*; as, *shall read, will read, will speak, will be reading, will be struck*. A second future, or *future perfect*, is made by using *have* after *shall* or *will*; as, *shall have read, will have been spoken*.

35. By the *perfect* it is indicated that something is just now or recently completed, and it is known by the mark *have* or *has*; as, *has read, have spoken, have been reading, has been read*. And, lastly, the *pluperfect* is known by the sign *had*, and it indicates a completion some time since; as, *had spoken, had read, had been reading, had been read*.

36. MOODS. There are certain other forms, or combinations of forms, to indicate some condition or circumstance about the doing or being. These forms are called the *moods*. The simple form of the verb, which has no condition or qualification attached to it, is called the *indicative;* all those tense forms above given are of this mood. If we place before them *if, though, unless*, or other words indicating doubt or condition, we have what is called the *subjunctive* form; as, *if he walk, unless he walks, though he laugh, if he walked, that he speaks*. Whenever we use the signs *may, can, must, might, could*, and *should*, before the bare verb, as, *may go, might go, must go*, we have what is called the *potential* mood — indicating that something is possible or necessary. In orders or requests, we use the bare verb; as, *go away, return now, see him, give me*; verbs used in this manner are called *imperatives*. That form of the verb which is uniformly found with the preposition *to* before it, is called the *infinitive;* as, *to write, to speak* — in a few instances the *to* is omitted, after *see, hear, feel, need, help, let, make, bid, dare, may, can, will*; as, may (*to*) go, hear him (*to*) speak, I saw him (*to*) go.

37. PERSON. There is a variation also in the ending of the verb according to the person of the subject; thus, we say *I speak, thou speakest, he speaks, we speak ;* so, *I am, thou art, he is, we are*, and we call these different forms the *persons* of the verb. Verbs in English can hardly be said to vary for number, since the three persons of the plural are regularly like the first singular; as, I *write*, we, you, they *write* ; I, you, we, they *wrote*. The verb *be*, as it is called, however, seems an

exception; thus, (sing.) *I am, thou art, he is;* (plur.) *we are, you are, they are;* past tense, *I was, thou wast, he was; we were, you were, they were;* the other tenses are regular, as fut., *will be,* 2d. fut. *will have been,* perfect, *have been,* pluperfect, or past perfect, *had been.*

38. PARTICIPLES: Every verb has three other forms, known as participles; one in *-ing,* as, *walking, speaking, reading, being* (called the present participle); another ending in *ed,* as has *walked,* and for irregular verbs having various endings; as, has *struck,* has *gone,* is *hit,* is *bent,* has *been,* a man *seen* there (called the perfect, past, or passive participle). There is a third, called the compound perfect, made by prefixing *having* to the perfect just noticed; as, *having read, having gone, having seen.*

39. These participles are never connected directly with subjects, or nominatives, but through some form of the verb *be* (*is, was, will be,* etc.), or by *have, has, had;* thus, he *is walking,* he *is struck,* he *has walked, has gone, has seen, has heard, will be known.* These connective verbs, as well as *may, can,* etc., signs of the potential mood (besides *do, did*), are called auxiliaries.

40. The present and past, or perfect, participles are often used as pure adjectives; as, a *walking* giant, a *broken* reed, a *celebrated* man. They, as well as the compound, often stand as if independently; thus, the man *walking* by the sea heard the roaring; the man *impressed* with this, said; the man *having heard* it, said. The present part. in *ing* is often used as a noun; thus, *the walking.* Participles and infinitives, besides other derived forms of the verb, are called *verbals.* A verb not of the infinitive mood is said to be *finite.*

ADVERBS.

41. Of the different kinds or classes of words which go to make up a sentence, there remain three others usually named in grammar; namely, *Adverbs, Prepositions,* and *Conjunctions.* These three are not well separated from each other, and we often term them, taken together, *Particles.* They are generally small words, and often play the part of simple connectives.

42. Speaking generally, adverbs may be termed adjectives which have ceased to belong to nouns, or, in other cases, as nouns in the objective case which stand independently in the sentence. They are found either referring to the expression of the whole sentence; as, *then* the torrent rushed with terrible roarings, or to the verb alone; as, to speak *fluently,* or to an adjective; as, *extremely* great, or to another adverb; as, *very*

violently. Generally, they tell the *how, when,* or *where,* of a fact or doing, or they tell *how much.* Many of them are of pronominal origin (that is, adjective without noun), as, *how, here, there, now,* etc., etc.

CONJUNCTIONS.

43. It is often hard to distinguish the conjunction from the adverb, since there is no real difference in their origin; they are that kind of adverb which never belongs to any word in the sentence, but they stand independently, or they connect one sentence, word, or phrase, with another. There are several words which you may call, indifferently, either adverb or conjunction; as this is so, *therefore* that is so; he did *as* I ordered him to do.

44. There are so few conjunctions that we give the following list, by which they may be known: *and, also, if, or, either, neither, though, although, but, nor, that, for, as, because, unless, whether, yet, than, lest.*

PREPOSITIONS.

45. They are easily distinguished from the other two classes of particles, not in their origin, for they, too, are adverbs, pronouns, or nouns, but in their use. A *preposition* is such a particle (not being a verb) as is always followed by an objective noun or pronoun; as, *to* him, *with* us, *along* the shore, *behind* the car, *instead* of that. All, or nearly all, prepositions may be found without an objective following; as, he was spoken *to,* he ran *along,* he fell *behind,* and they become adverbs, just as adverbs used with an objective become and should be called prepositions; as, *near* us, *down* the road, *up* the hill, *like* me.

46. Here we give a list of prepositions: *at, in, on, of, from, for, by, with, among, against, before, behind, till, during, toward, about, up, down, out of, upon, along, under, between, after, above, over, round, through, to, across, below, without.*

47. The classes of words which we have now named are called the *parts of speech*—they are usually reckoned at ten (counting in participles, articles, and those exclamatory words, called *interjections*).

48. Let the learner be cautioned that the rules given for the distinction of parts of speech are not infallible—no such rules can be given in grammar more than elsewhere. Nature has put no landmarks to separate one class from another.

49. We have given all that the student of language will need, but, of course, we cannot pretend to have written a complete grammar. Let it be borne in mind that the main object of this grammatical sketch was to enable the common student to understand the meaning of grammatical terms, without being compelled to refer to any other work.

CHAPTER II.

LATIN GRAMMAR.

50. The English language is a modern language, and it possesses the usual features of modern languages; but the Latin, as well as the Greek and the Sanscrit, represents a class of ancient languages that presents many features which differ from those of modern idioms. We will take a brief survey, here, of those features in Latin.

51. The first thing that we remark as strange in Latin, is the six case-forms. Here, the endings of the noun and of the adjective (which is a form of the noun), have developed themselves into the representatives of our prepositions, or prepositions with the article; as, *of the, to the, by the;* thus, *puer*, a boy, but *pueri*, of the boy, *puero*, to the boy, or with the boy.

52. But it is not only in these prepositional cases, that we find an ending distinct from the base of the noun; the nominatives, too, have common endings. There is a large class with the common ending *a;* as, *al-a,* wing, *cur-a,* care, *silv-a,* wood, a large class in *us,* and *um;* as, *vent-us,* wind, *man-us,* hand, *regn-um,* kingdom, *mal-um,* evil, *don-um,* gift—besides other endings. In the adjective, they have, for their office, to distinguish gender; thus, take the three nominative forms *bon-us, bon-a, bon-um* (for which we have the single, unvarying, form *good*). Of these, we use *bonus,* when we say *good man* (a male), *bona,* for good woman (a female), and *bonum,* for good thing (a neuter). And, in the noun, too, these endings vary with the gender; so, *a* is for them generally a *fem., us* a *masc.,* and *um* a *neuter* ending. Further, we may remark, that there is no doubt that this *us, a, um,* is the equivalent of our *a* and *the*, suffixed (i. e., joined to the noun at the end). The Latins have no other article. Besides, this *us* and *um* are clear variations of one ending—and *a* is a weaker form of the same.

53. We have certainly the germ of this common ending of Latin, in our final *e*, and perhaps in *d*, and others; thus, for the Latin *caus-a*, we have *caus-e;* *tub-a, tub-e*. There is but a slight

difference between *e* and *a*. We might compare also *son-us* and *soun-d*, *jug-um* and *yok-e*, *tot-us* and *tot-al*, *riv-us* and *riv-er*, *hort-us* and *gard-en*, *corv-us* and *rav-en*, *man-us* and *han-d*. The German endings *en*, *l*, *er*, *es*, belong to this family. Besides these remnants of endings, it may be said, in many cases, that the change of vowel in the body of the word compensates for the gender endings lost; thus, *soil*, for L. *sol-um*, *vel-um*, sail; *hor-a*, hour, *turb-a*, troop, *bon-us*, good, *mit-is*, meek, *pac-e*, peace, *can-is*, hound.

54. The cases found in Latin, are the *Nominative*, *Genitive* (sign *of*, our poss.), *Dative* (sign *to*, *for*), *Accusative*, (our objective), *Vocative* (the person addressed), and *Ablative* (sign *with*, *from*, *by*, *in*). The endings of these cases are by no means uniform for all nouns. The changes in the original endings of the nominative must produce a corresponding change in the other cases. Thus, the nouns which have the nominative in *a*, have their cases, in the sing., in this way: *penn-a*, *penn-æ*, *penn-æ*, *penn-am*, *penn-a*, *penn-a*; and for the plural, *penn-æ*, *penn-arum*, *penn-is*, *penn-as*, *penn-æ*, *penn-is*. (The cases just given, correspond in order with the names above given). In English, those forms would be expressed (in the sing.) by pen, of the pen, for the pen, the pen (obj.), the pen (voc.), with the pen; so, in the plur., pens, of pens, etc.

55. *Vent-us*, *vent-i*, *vent-o*, *vent-um*, *vent-e*, *vent-o*, (plural) *vent-i*, *vent-orum*, *vent-is*, *vent-os*, *vent-i*, *vent-is*, — wind, of wind, etc.; plur., winds, of winds, etc. *don-um*, *don-i*, *don-o*, *don-um*, *don-um*, *don-o*; plur., *don-a*, *don-orum*, *don-is*, *don-a*, *don-a*, *don-is*, — gift, of gift, etc.; plur., gifts, of gifts, for gifts, etc. *rup-es*, *rup-is*, *rup-i*, *rup-em*, *rup-es*, *rup-e*; plur., *rup-es*, *rup-ium*, *rup-ibus*, *rup-es*, *rup-es*, *rup-ibus*, — rock, of rock, for rock, etc.; plur., rocks, of rocks, etc.

56. In many cases, the nominative ending is entirely lost; as, *puer*, *puer-i*, *puer-o*; boy, of boy, to boy. In other instances, this ending is not lost, but blunted; thus, *pars* (for *parts*, *partes*); gen. *part-is*, a part; so, *dens*, (for *dents*, *dentes*), tooth; *serm-o* (for *serm-on*, *serm-ones*), gen., *serm-onis*, of speech.

57. A moderate inspection renders it very evident that all these case-forms are variations of those forms with gender endings. We find *is* often in the genitive, but it occurs also in the nominative in the place of *us*; as, *classis*, a fleet. In the plural, we have the ending *es* or *i* combined with the gender ending *us*, *a*, *um*, or, existing as a mere variation of it. Those case-forms which end in *i* and *o*, are plainly shortenings of this *is* and *us*. The uniform endings of the accusative are *um*, *am*, *em*, which are forms of the neuter *um*.

58. The changes of these noun and adjective endings are not

so much prepositions as forms to correspond with the nature of the verb, or verbal, which governs them; thus, *caret omni culpa*, he wants (in) all blame (*culpa*); *caret* is followed by an ablative, or *in* case, because it means *wanting in*; *ortus regibus*, risen (from) kings; *ortus*=risen from, and, hence, has with it the *from* case, or abl; *natura animalibus tribuit*, nature (to) animals has given (*tribuit*, has given to—hence the dat. case with it); *curis vacuus*, (from) cares free (*vacuus*, free from—hence the abl. case); *hostis virtutibus*, (an) enemy (to) virtues (*hostis*, opposed to, *inimical*); *amor nummi*, love (of) money (*amor*, love, to be fond of); *memor fragilitatis*, mindful (of) weakness. No principle seems better established, in all languages, than that the preposition is a growth of the verb and belongs to it. Whenever found, it always belongs with some verb, or verbal, expressed or implied. When standing alone, it represents the verb and its participle.

59. In concluding our remarks upon the cases of Latin nouns, we may observe that all the cases following the nominative are known as *oblique* cases. It is to be observed, also, that the acc. (obj.) case, in neuter nouns, is always like the nom.; and that the ablative plural of all nouns is like the dative.

ADJECTIVES.

60. The Latin adjective has nothing peculiar in its character, save its varying form to correspond with the gender, number, and case, of its noun. Thus there is, as said before, a form *bonus* for mas., as *bonus vir*, good man, a form *bona* for fem's, as *bona filia*, good daughter, and *bonum*, neut., as in *bonum telum*, good dart. (In short, the form of the adj. is a repetition of that of the noun). And these three, *bonus, bona, bonum*, have each their six case-forms in each number, like so many independent nouns; thus, (sing.) *bonus, boni, bono, bonum, bone, bono*; and (fem. sing.) *bona, bonæ, bonæ, bonam, bona, bona*; and (neut. sing.) *bonum, boni, bono, bonum, bonum, bono* (*bonus*, like the noun *ventus, bona*, like *penna*, and *bonum*, like *donum*). Thus, we have *boni viri* (of good of man), of a good man — treating the two as a unit, a compound; *bonæ filiæ* (of good of daughter), of a good daughter; *bonarum filiarum*, of good daughters; *bonis donis*, for good (for) gifts. It is clear you must consider the adjective as lost in the one compound, or, that the two are individuals unconnected. The requirements of science seem to be, that each is independent; that *good*, in any of these cases, does not so much belong to the noun, as, for instance, *man*, as, rather, to some general term, as, *one, thing*, included in the adjective itself; so, *a good man*, a good one a

man, i. e. a good person or thing of the man class. There is much proof to sustain this position, which will be given, some of it, elsewhere.

61. The comparative in Latin generally ends in *ior, ius,* our *er,* and the superlative, in *issim-us* (*us* is an adj. ending), our *est;* as, *dur-us, dur-ior, dur-issimus,*—hard, hard-er, hard-est. We look upon these endings as a growth of the ending *us.* It strikes us as somewhat peculiar, to find in Latin that the comparative is followed by the ablative (the *with* case); as, *dulcior melle,* sweeter than honey (in Lat., *sweeter with honey*), i. e. the comparative is a real positive; and we also have *sweet by the side of honey,* or *compared with honey.*

PRONOUNS.

62. All the Latin pronouns are real adjectives, (of a particular kind, it is true)·sometimes used with a noun and sometimes alone—we have only to except *ego*—I, *tu*—thou, and *se*—self; these latter ones do not vary for gender, and they have only one set of case-forms. The other pronouns, like adjectives, have each three sets of forms and cases, for the three genders; as, *hic*—this (mas.), *hæc*—this (fem.), *hoc*—this (thing, neut.); so, *ille*—that (mas.), *illa*—that (fem.), *illud*—that (neut.); *is*—that (m.), *ea*—that (f.), *id*—that (n.). These three pronouns, *hic, ille, is,* mean this, that, when used with the noun, as *that man,* but they mean *he, she, it,* when used without the noun, as, *ille dixit*—he said (that (one) said). There is also *ipse*—himself, *ipsa*—herself, *ipsum*—itself; so, *qui*—who, *quæ*—who (f.), *quod*—which (n.); and *idem*—he the same, *eadem*—she the same, *idem*—it the same.

VERBS.

63. The Latin verb furnishes us with many peculiarities. The first we notice, is the growth of endings representing nom. personal pronouns; as, *I, thou, he;* thus, *am-o,* I love, *am-as,* thou lovest, *am-at,* he loves; *am-amus,* we love, *am-atis,* ye love, *am-ant,* they love. This is precisely as if we should use *loves* for he loves, *lovest* for thou lovest—*loves* being the form proper for *he, she, it,* and *lovest* the form for thou; so, we might use *am* for I am, and *is* for he is, *art* for thou art. These few cases are about the only instances of verb forms in English to correspond with the personal pronoun, and these we never use as equivalent to the verb and pronoun, i. e. without the nominative. Those Latin person endings extend, in slightly varying forms, to all the tenses and moods (not inf.).

64. In English, we have only one tense, the past, ending in *ed*, which shows the tense by the ending, and we use the auxiliaries *have, had,* and *will,* to supply the place of endings. But in Latin, save in exceptional cases, the tenses are all after the manner of our past in *ed;* as, walk-ed lov-ed.

65. The mark of the Latin past is *ab, eb,* corresponding exactly to our *ed* in lov-ed, lov-edst (2d. per.), and to which *ab* is joined the ordinary person endings already shown in the present, thus: *am-abam, am-abas, -abat; -abamus, -abatis, -abant.*

66. The mark of the perfect is *av, iv;* thus, *am-avi, am-avisti, am-avit; -avimus, -avistis, -averunt.* This tense, in meaning, and perhaps in construction, corresponds more with our past than with our perfect. But *amabam* is usually translated *I loved,* while *amavi* is put down as *I have loved, amavit, he has loved.*

67. The pluperfect, *I had loved,* runs thus: *am-averam, -averas, -averat; -averamus, -averatis, -averant.* The future, *I will love,* is *am-abo, -abis, -abit; -abimus, -abitis, -abunt.*

68. The 2d. future is *amavero amave-ris, -rit,* etc. The present subjunctive (potential) is *am-em,* I may love, and has no tense element besides *em: ama-rem, -res, -ret,* etc., I might love (past subj.); *amave-rim, -ris -rit,* etc., I may have loved (perf. sub.); *amavissem, -isses, -isset,* etc., I might have loved (p. perf.).

69. We thus see that in the subj. (pot.) mood there are not those auxiliaries which we find in English. The infinitive has a common ending *are, ere, ire,* for one form, our *to,* and *avisse, isse,* for another form, our *to have;* as, *amare,* to love, and *amavisse,* to have loved.

70. If we use the present participle as a noun, as *the walking,* we use the simple participle form which is found also in the different application, a man *walking* by the sea. But, in Latin, we have a distinct form (both grown up from one form, however) for each case; thus, we would have *ambulandum* in the first instance, and *ambulans* in the next. The forms *ambulans,* ambling, *amans,* loving, are pure adjectives, with very little variation, however, in the cases of the three genders; thus, *viro ambulante,* to a man walking (dat. form, to agree with *viro*). These are called *present* participles.

71. The form in *andum* is a true noun, and has its case forms *andi* (gen.), *ando* (dat.), *andum* (acc.), like other nouns, while we would have one and the same form, of *walking,* to *walking.* This is known as the *gerund.*

72. There is still another form, grown on the same base as the others, to which we have nothing in English that precisely

corresponds. We refer to those forms, known as *supines*, which end in *tum* and *tu;* as, *ama-tum*, to love, *ama-tu*, to be loved. It answers most nearly to our infinitive; it is not often used.

73. The *passive* in Latin presents us with a new set of endings and combinations. Our own passive is regularly made by using some tense of the verb *be* (*is, was, will be*), and joining to it the perfect or passive participle of a transitive verb.

74. We use *is loved* for our present passive, but the Latin *amatus sum*, loved I am, is a perfect, and is translated *have been loved;* and *amatus erat*, loved he was, is a pluperfect, *had been loved.*

75. The present is a simple form, thus: *amor, amaris, amatur; amamur, amamini, amantur*—I am loved, thou art loved, etc.

76. The past passive is also a simple form: *ama-bar, -baris, -batur; -bamur, -bamini, -bantur*—I was loved, thou wast loved, etc. The future is *amabor*, I will be loved. The 2d future, *amatus fuero*, shall have been loved. Prest. subj., *amer*, I may be loved. Past., *amarer*, I might be loved. *Amatus sim* (loved may be), I may have been loved; *amatus essem* (loved might be) I might have been loved. These two tenses are the perf. and pluperf.

77. The participle in *tus, ama-tus*, lov-ed, corresponds to our regular past participles. It has, as it is a true adj., a *fem.* and *neut.* form, as well as *mas.*; thus, *amatus, amata, amatum.*

78. Another participle, called the future pass., as, *amandus* = to be loved, must be loved, is a variation of the *gerund* already noticed.

79. But the peculiarities of the Latin idiom will be best understood and appreciated by means of some selections from its composition, to which we now turn our attention.

80. *Tenuere* (held)· *tamen arcem* (fort) *Sabini*—they-held still (the) castle, (the) Sabines (did). It is generally claimed that words placed like *Sabini*, are nominative to the verb, as, *tenuere*, but it strikes the author differently; *Sabini* is thrown in, as we often find in Latin, parenthetically, as a sort of adverb or explanatory term. *Jupiter inquit, tuis jussus avibus hic* (here) *in Palatio prima urbi fundamenta jeci*—O Jupiter, he-says, by-thy-own (*tuis*) being-commanded, by-birds (*avibus*), here in Palatium first to-the-city (of the city) (the) foundations I-have-laid (*jeci*) (i. e. here first I laid). Here *tuis* = thy, and *avibus* = birds, are words which are claimed to belong together, though we find them separated by *jussus;* they certainly agree in number and case. Still we do not think they properly belong together, i. e. not as the adjective belongs to the noun when it is joined to it as in *tuis avibus;* we think every word belongs

where it is found. The point here lies in the question *by whose* or *by whom* he had been ordered—*by thy own* (and this comes first, as being the most prominent); farther on, he puts in *avibus* as explanatory, or as if in apposition with *tuis; prima*, too, in form agrees with *fundamenta* (both neut. acc. plur.), but yet it is clear that *prima* is an adverb=*first*, and quite independent of the noun.

81. *Arcem jam* (now) *scelere emptam, Sabini habent*—the castle now, by-treachery gained (as it was) the Sabines have (it)—*emptam* (got) is a part. (adj.) agreeing with *arcem*, and yet it is in every way isolated from it. Quite generally, the Latin acc., or obj., and everything used as objective and belonging to it, comes before the verb; but there are frequent instances where the object follows the verb also: *tuum est, Servi, si vir* (man) *es, regnum*—thine (it) is, Servius, if (a) man (thou) art (*es*), (the) kingdom (thine is the kingdom): *regnum* is usually taken as the subject of *est*, but, in its place, it is independent of the verb—kingdom (*regnum*) is emphatic.

82. *Ea quæ ad* (to) *aures suas.* (his) *pervenissent*—those (things) which to (the) ears, his own, had come—ears his, *aures suas*, for *his ears; frater Antigoni, regis Macedoniæ*—brother (of) Antigonus, king (the king) (of) Macedonia; here, *regis* agrees with *Antigoni*, but yet no one calls it an adjective, rather, a noun in apposition, i. e. separate from the other noun and distinct, yet agreeing with it and denoting the same individual; *ora modis attollens pallida miris*—(her) countenance (in) manner bearing, pale wonderfully, i. e. having a countenance pale in a wonderful manner, or wonderfully pale; *pallida* agrees with *ora*, but it is evidently connected with the participle which it follows—she was pale as to countenance, not necessarily *pale countenance;* so *miris* agrees with *modis*, but hardly, in this sentence, belongs to it—it is used in the sense of an adverb, she bore a countenance pale in a manner that was wonderful (*miris*).

83. *Ignotum argenti pondus* (weight) *et auri*—unknown (the) silver's weight and (the) gold's (gen. sing.); *ignotum* agrees with *pondus; fugam Dido sociosque parabat*—flight Dido and (*que*) companions (she) prepared; the meaning is that Dido prepared for flight (*fugam* is acc.), but it is not so expressed; *Dido* stands independently, *she* is nom. of *parabat*, or it has none; *-que* is the suffix *and*, and *-bat* is the past ending, 3d sing. *Imoque trahens a* (from) *pectore vocem*—(from) lowest, also (*imoque*=and from the deep) drawing from breast (a) voice, i. e. drawing from depths of (his) breast a voice; *imo* (*que*=and) agrees with *pectore* (abl.), but it is used adverbially or independent; and drawing *from below* a voice.

84. *Si vestras forte per aures*—if (to) yours perhaps to ears (it has come), i. e. if perhaps (it has come) to your ears; *vestras* agrees with *aures*, but it is not so placed as to belong to it directly; it is parenthetical—if perchance to ears (that is to yours).

85. The Latin preposition uniformly governs what follows and not what precedes it.

86. *Italiam quæro patriam*—Italy (I) seek (it) (my) country (my native country); here *Italiam* and *patriam* agree, and yet, one is not an adjective belonging to the other; *vani docuere parentes*—vain (they have) taught, (the) parents (have). Here *vani*, adj., agrees with *parentes*, but it does not belong to it—it is an adverb in force, meaning *in vain, vainly*, as we also so often use the adjective without change of form in the place of an adverb; *et vera* (true) *incessu patuit dea*—and true (in her) gait was-manifested (the) goddess (*dea*), i. e. she was plainly a goddess by her walk; *vera* agrees with *dea*, as if it were *true goddess*, but it has the force of *truly*, and does not belong to *dea*.

87. *At Venus obscuro gradientes* (the walkers) *ære sepsit*—but Venus, (in) obscure, (they) walking (in the) air (she) buried, i. e. she concealed them walking, the walkers, in the air; *obscuro* agrees with *ære*, but it is an adverb belonging to what follows; *Obscurely she buried the walkers in the air*; *gradientes* is present part., in the plur., the walking (ones); *ac veniendi poscere causas*—and (of) coming to-ask (inf.) (the) causes; to ask the cause, here, is one verb, and *coming* (the gerund), in the genitive, is its object, i. e. to ask the cause (of) coming; *lucus in urbe fuit* (was) *media*—(a) grove in (the) city was (in the) middle (of it): *media* agrees with *urbe* in the abl., but is independent of it.

88. *Quem si fata virum servant*—whom if (the) fates (the) man preserve, i. e. if the fates preserve him, this man; *quem* agrees, as an adj. pron., with *virum* (acc.) but cannot be joined to it (rather, standing independent); *totum vulgata per orbem*—whole (wholly) published through (the) world, i. e. through all the world; *totum* agrees with *orbem*, yet it is an adverb, in the sense of wholly, belonging to published, with which it is found; so, too, in *clara-que in luce refulsit*—clear also in light (he) shone, i. e. and clearly shone (*clara*, an adj., but in place of adv.).

89. We have given these examples chiefly to prove that Latin words, especially the adjective, belong where they are found, that, at least for the Latins themselves, the order of words was a natural one, and needed no transposition, that it does not follow that every adjective must have a noun to which

it may belong; that it neither follows that every verb must have a nominative outside of it, and every nominative a verb, or every objective a transitive or preposition to govern it.

90. Farther examples will illustrate other features: *Multis cum* (with) *lacrymis vicinos orare cœpit*—(with) much with tears (his) neighbors to-beg (he) began (obj. before the verb, as we usually find it); *multis* agrees with *lacrymis*, but it has the force of *much*, i. e. much with tears he begged; *venatum iverant*—to hunt (they) had gone (supine=inf.); *leo asinum* (acc.) *illam* (acc.) *partiri jubet*—(the) lion (the) ass that (i. e. it) to divide (he) commands; to divide it, the lion the ass orders (orders the ass): first, we have *divide that* as a verb, and, next, we have *ass divide that*, as another verb, depending on *commands*, of which *leo* is the nominative, and having, hence, its place before the real verb, i. e. all that follows it; *asinum* is acc., as the subject of infin. always is; *partes poneret æquales*—(the) parts (he) placed equal (or equally); *æquales* agrees with *partes*, but belongs to the verb.

91. *Sibi vix minimam reservans particulam*—(for) self scarcely (the) least reserving, (a mere) particle (*particulam* is independent); *hujus me calamit* *docuit*—his me (the) calamity (has) taught (me); either *his me* is independent of the rest, or *his* is subject of the verb, and *calamity* is parenthetical; *his has taught me*, i. e. *the calamity h*..; *effusa mellis copia est*—poured (of) honey (an) abundance (there) has (is); poured, *effusa*, a past participle, is used here as the verb, and *est, is*, is simply added at the end, i. e. *it poured, the honey did* (*est*); *Græci autem* (but) *quum audivissent*—(the) Greeks, but when (they) had-heard, i. e. when the Greeks had heard. Yet *Græci* is not, most clearly, the nom. of the verb—it is independent; *eum ibi occultari* (pass. inf.)—(they heard) him there to be concealed, that he was there concealed (they heard that).

92. *In eodem quondam prato pascebantur grues*, in same, once, (in a) meadow were-feeding cranes (were). Not *in the same meadow*, necessarily, though *eodem* agrees with *prato; in eodem* =together, an adverb; *legendum est mihi*—reading is to me, i. e. I must read; *est mihi voluptati*—(it) is to me (for a) delight, while we would say *it is a delight to me: peritus belli*—skilled of war (skilled in war); *dignus honore*—worthy in honor (of honor); *Cæsar misit suos*—C. sent his-own (or his), i. e. sent his soldiers (one case surely where an adjective has no noun to which it may belong). Such a use of the pronoun and adjective is very common in Latin; the point lies in the *whose*, or the *which*, the *what*, and the thing or person need not be named; *is homo erat ut*—he (a) man was (so) that, he was a man that, such a man.

93. The use of adjectives, especially adj. pronouns, as adverbs having no noun to which to belong, is very common in Latin; thus, *eo pervenit ut*—to-this (there) he came that, i. e. so far (*eo*) he came that; *sunt quos juvat*—(there) are whom (it) delights (those whom); *ex doctoris imperitia*—from (the) teachers unskillfulness; *earum ope*—(by) their help (*ope* is abl., but *earum* = of them, is gen. plur., and yet, *earum* has the force of an adj. belonging to and agreeing with *ope; quod quum ille cerneret*—which when he saw (it); *quod* is another independent word, and not, as is often said, the object of the verb; so, too, *quam quum duceret*—whom (fem.) when (he) lead (her), i. e. when he led her.

94. *Nuntiatum est classem* (fleet) *devinci*—announced (it) is (the) fleet to be beaten, i. e. that it was beaten (pass. inf.)— an infin. pass. being used where we put a subj. or indic. with *that. Cæsar venit, vidit, et vicit*—Cæsar came, saw, and conquered; neither in the Latin nor the English form, has *vidit* and *vicit* any nominative; *quis fecit*—who did (it); objective pronouns are often implied, like *it*, in the verb, as the article and pronouns are often implied in the noun; *vides-ne*, seest thou not, i. e. see thou? *ne* is a mere interrogative mark (not) suffixed or added (see interrog. = negative); so, too, *num venit*— (has he) come, or came he? *num* = non, whether, not, a mere question sign; *ea cum ita* (so) *sint*—those (things) since so they are; *pater amat liberos et tamen castigat*—(the) father (he) loves (his) children and still (he) chastises (them) (see the pronouns included in the verb and noun).

95. *Cæsar in Asiam profectus est*—C. into Asia gone (he) has (is), i. e. has gone to Asia; the noun with the preposition, as *in Asiam*, is treated in Latin as the true object of the verb, and hence comes before it; *quo mihi hanc rem*—(for) what to-me this thing, i. e. of what use, *quo* used as adverb, one of those many cases of pronouns, as well as adj's, without the noun; *si nihil aliud nisi*—if nothing other unless, i. e. if nothing else than; *maxima minima*—greatest least, i. e. greatest and least.

96. Many prepositions here, as in English, are used as adverbs, that is, have no objectives following them.

97. *Hoc est preceptoris*—this is preceptor's (genitive), i. e. it belongs to the preceptor; *post Æneæ* (gen.) *mortem*—after Æneas' death; *eum secutus est* (is) *Silvius*—him followed (he) has Silvius (has); *ut civium* (gen.) *numerum augeret*—that (the) citizens' number (he might) increase (it); *Marius consul creatus* (est)—M. consul made (was), i. e. was made consul; *in cornu tauri parvulus quondam* (once) *culex consedit*—on (the) horn (of a) bull (a) little (one), once, (a) gnat sat, i. e. a little gnat sat; *Hanibal navali prœlio victus*—H. (in a) naval

battle (being) beaten; *ut ex Europa recederet*—that from Europe (he) should-depart; *Europa* is treated as object of the verb, though governed by *ex* the preposition.

98. *Hanc* (hence) *ob causam* is usually considered as if written *ob hanc causam*, for this cause, but it is clear that *hanc* does not belong to *causam*, with which it agrees, but it is rather an adverb like the others we have noticed; or, we may take *hanc-ob*=here-of, in which case *causam* would stand absolute or independent—at least *ob* cuts off *causam* from *hanc;* so *hac in re*—(in) this in (the) thing, i. e. here in the thing; *secundo quo-que anno*—(in the) second also (in the) year, i. e. also in the second year.

99. *Scipio dicere solebat*—S. to say used, i. e. used to say; *ea quoque res*—that also (the) thing, i. e. this thing also; *Albæ ruinis*, (of) Alba (from) ruins, from Alba's ruins. *Thales interrogatus an facta hominum deos laterent*—Thales (being) asked if (the) deeds (of) men (the) gods (acc.) escaped, i. e. were hidden from the gods. *Pythagoræ philosophi tanta fuit apud discipulos suos auctoritas*—(of) P. (the) philosopher such was, among (the) disciples his (own), (the) authority; such was P's authority among disciples, his own. *Schœnus Atalantam* (acc.) *filiam formos-issimam dicitur* (said) *habuisse*—S. Atlanta (a) daughter most-beautiful is-said to-have-had (one), to have had a most beautiful daughter, Atalanta; *quæ cursu viros* (acc.) *super-abat*—who (in) running (even) men (she) surpassed; *ut ejus* (his) *voluntate id* (it) *sibi facere liceat*—that (by) his will (abl.) that (thing) (to) selves to-do (it) may-be-permitted, i. e. to permit (license) them to do that; *sibi* is object of *facere liceat*, and *id* is the object of both together. (*See Errors of Gram. on objectives.*).

100. *Ille petiit ut quidquid tetigerat aurum fieret*—he asked that whatever (he) had-touched gold (it) might become (past. subj.); *Cæsari quum id nunciatum esset*—to C. when it told might be (*esset*), i. e. when it was told to C.; *qui dicerent sibi esse in animo*—who should say (that) to selves (it) was in mind, i.e. they intended; *esse*=inf., to be, but infin's after verbs are treated as subjunctives or indicatives; *obsides-que uti* (that) *inter sese dent*—hostages-also (*que*) that between themselves (they) may-give (them), that they may give hostages between them; *obsides* is acc., plur., independent; *hac oratione ab Divitiaco habita, mittit*—(with) this oration of D. (being) had, (he) sends. This form of expression is very common in Latin, where we find the abl., generally with a participle, but sometimes alone or with nouns, used entirely independent. We observe that the independence of the parts of the Latin sentence is its prevailing feature.

101. *Cæsar Gallorum* (gen. plur.) *animos verbis confirmavit,* C. (the) Galls' minds (with) words (he) strengthened (them); *his responsis ad Cæsarem relatis mittit*—(with) these answers to C. (they being) related, (he) sends; so, *his rebus gestis*— these things (abl.) done, being done.

102. The examples thus far given, illustrate most of the peculiarities of the Latin idiom. In order to prepare the student for what he will meet with elsewhere, we have given this large number of examples; they will illustrate features which we shall continually meet with in other languages, and which seem strange to us, because not found in our own. We find the order of words often far different from ours, but we see that it is a natural or reasonable one after all. We find, among other things, a beautiful illustration of the truth, that all the parts of the sentence are complete in themselves, and that they do not really lean upon or belong to others; we find the verb, here, containing its own nominative, and its own objective pronoun, and that the noun implies its own adjective, its own verb.

103. To carry the principle to extremes, each word contains the point, the expression, of the whole sentence, this being made up of repetitions of like terms. We may add, besides, that it can be shown that identity or similarity of forms of words does not prove common origin or connexion, since, viewed through a proper glass, all words have a common form and like marks.

104. Upon the Greek, it is unnecessary to dwell here, so little there is in it that is not English, or German, or, especially, Latin. Among the variations from Latin, we notice the development of a true article, '*o*, '*e*, *to* (three forms to correspond with the genders). It has, besides the plural and singular forms, one that is called *dual*, a form peculiar to nouns where two things are intended. The Lat. ablative case is absent, its place being supplied by the genitive and dative—there are, hence, but five case-forms in Greek. There are in Greek several new tense-forms, especially new forms of the past, called *aorists*, besides an abundant growth of participle and infinitive forms. Besides the active and passive forms of Latin, there is in Greek what is called the *middle* form of the verb, one in appearance substantially the same as the passive; but in meaning it is confined to cases where *self* is concerned; as, *love myself, strike self, act for self.* In other languages, this application of the verb is known as the *reflexive.* Beyond these, the Greek grammar is chiefly Latin.

105. But the idiom, while it has much in it that is Latin, has some in it, too, which is German, even English. The object we find, often, as in Latin, before the verb. The independence

of the adjective from the noun, is far clearer here than in Latin. The use of those long adjectives which so much distinguish German, is found here to some extent; as, a mark (of) *the for you friendship*, while we would say *of my friendship for you;* (a) token (*of*) *the* (*my*) *for Hipponicus friendship*, i. e. my friendship for Hipponicus; the for the gods (things), i. e. the (things) of the gods. The genitive is often a pure adjective before the noun. In Latin, we have *hic munitissimus* habendi senatum locus — this most fortified (for) holding (the) senate place, i. e. this holding senate place, most fortified; all the words before *locus* constitute one adjective, and they belong where they are found.

106. We must notice, finally, on this branch of the subject, the constant occurrence of participles and infinitives, in Latin and Greek, which hold the independent place of pure verbs — always, however, depending upon some verb, or verbal, as a sort of object; thus, *vi coacturos* — by force '(they) would compel (them by force) (dependent upon the idea *they thought that*); *coacturos*, in form a future part., acc. mas. plur., meaning *about to compel*, is so much a verb, as to include in it sub. and obj. pronouns; it is generally assumed in such cases that *esse* = be, is, was, is implied, but this is simply unnecessary; *se* (self) *patribus suis didicisse* — themselves (from) fathers, theirs, had learned, (*they said*) that they had learned; *didicisse* = to have learned, perf. inf.

107. Some languages, as the Sanscrit and Finnish, have more than six cases, i. e. they have varied the forms more than the Latin has. In Sanscrit, there is a *Locative* case form, by which *place* is indicated, and an *Instrumental* form, denoting the *cause*, or *means*, or *instrument* — they may both be called variations of the ablative, which again is a form of the dative.

108. It may be necessary to define the term *root* or *base*, which we shall often meet with. It is used to designate that imaginary, undefined, part of a word which remains after divesting it of its prefixes and suffixes, its *initial* and its *final* letters — precisely, as if we should speak of what was left of a stick after cutting the *ends* off. That part of a word which is common to a class of words, is called its *ending*, as the *ing* of walk-ing, speak-ing, the *es* of Lat. rup-es, sermon-es — what is left after striking off this ending is the *root*.

109. Prefixes are sometimes called *preformatives;* prefixes less individualized are called *augments*, as the *ge* of Germ. *ge-sehen* = seen, *ge-sicht* = sight, *g* of *g-lück* = luck, our *a* of a-live, a-rise, the *e* of Greek *e-lip'* = left. Prefixes and suffixes taken together may be called the *fixes* of a word.

CHAPTER III.

HISTORY OF NOUNS.

110. Of nouns as a class, we have little that may be said in addition to what has already been stated under the head of English Grammar. They are, of course, intimately connected with the adjective first, and the verb afterward. Nouns are, apparently, unmeaning names of things, but, on close inspection, we find them rather names of qualities and actions, which distinguish things; and, hence, they readily identify themselves with the two classes named. Nouns, adjectives, and verbs, are alike in each having shoots grown out of them, which we call endings, and which are not so much marks of those classes, as representatives of whole words that seem thus to adhere, as parasites, to the main stem. It is the philosophy of these endings of nouns which we propose to consider, and it is their comparative view which we intend to present—beginning with those of case.

Case Endings.

111. The farther back we go, in the history of the German languages, the more we see of case and person ending; thus, in Gothic cases, we find the broad *us* and *a* of Latin; as, *sun-us*, a son; *flod-us*, flood; *fot-us*, foot; *hand-us*, hand; *arm-s*, arm; *gard-s*, yard; *mat-s*, meat; *hveil-a*, while, hour; *saurg-a*, care, sorrow; *band-i*, bond; *ded-s*, deed; *knod-s*, kind, kin; *blom-a*, bloom; *fauh-o*, fox; *vard-o*, ward; *tugg-o*, tongue; *rath-jo*, L. *ratio*, reason; *faurht-ei*, fear. These all have reference to the Greek and Latin nominative endings *us*, *a*, *um*, *os*.

112. In old German, we again find these endings, but, generally, not so long and full; thus, *sun-u*, son; *ah-a*, L. *aqua*, water; *mond-a*, L. *mundus*, Germ. *welt*, world; *mur-a*, L. *murus*, wall; *stunt-a*, Germ. *stund*, time; *tual-a*, L. *mora*, dwell, delay; *war-a*, L. *cura*, care; *red-a*, L. *ratio*, Germ. *rath*, reason; *kiloub-a*, belief (*ki=ge* of Germ.); *sel-a*, soul; *erd-a*, L. *terra*, earth; *minn-a*, mind (love); *heil-i*, L. *salus*, health; *hert-i*, hardness; *chu-o*, L. *vacca*, cow; *tub-a*, L. *columba*, dove (*clb=tb*); *wis-a*, wise, way; *avar-a*, image (after); *witaw-a*, L. *vidua*, widow; *herz-a*, L. *cord-e*, heart; *oug-a*, Germ. *auge*, eye; *sam-o*, seed.

113. Old Saxon *erth-a*, earth; *forth-a*, fear; *fold-a* field; *gib-a*, gift; *rast-a*, rest; *kunn-i*, kin; *gi-wirk-i*, work; *gi-siun-i*, vision, sight; *rik-i*, L. *regnum*; *gum-o*, L. *homo*, man (*gm=hm =m*); *man-o*, moon; *tog-o*, L. *dux*, duke. There is, we observe, a great resemblance between Gothic, old German, and old Saxon.

114. Anglo Saxon *luf-u*, love; *sac-u*, Germ. *sach*, case; *stig-u*, stage, step; *vrak-u*, weak; *cynn-e*, L. *genus*, kind; *nett-e*, net; *gum-a*, L. *homo*, man; *pleg-a*, play; *eordh-e*, earth; *fold-e*, fold, field. Thus, in Ang Sax., we find these endings less prominent, and yet, much stronger and more common than in the present English. The old Friesic is much like the A. S. in this respect.

115. But, in place of these, the old North, and its descendants, shows the prevailing r ($=s=us$); as, *fisk-r*, fish; *hëst-r*, horse, "hoss"; *hring-r*, ring; *laekn-ir*, doctor ($l=d$); *end-ir*, end (Germ. *-er*); *hiort-r*, hart; *lim-r*, limb, Germ. *lied*, leg; *kiol-r*, keel; *æf-i*, L. *ævum*, age; *and-i*, L. *animus*, mind; *bog-i*, bow; *daudh-i*, death; *man-i*, L. *luna*, moon; *ux-i*, ox; *skugg-i*, shade, shadow; *thank-i*, thought, mind; *nagl-i* ($i=ir$), L. *clavus*, nail, claw; *ask-a*, ask; *vind-r*, wind ($-r=a=e$).

116. In middle German, these endings are less and lighter, in many instances, the final *e* appearing, as in A. S., where we and modern German have left it out—this *e*, like ours, being the *a* of Latin; thus, *und-e*, L. *und-a*, wave; *mur-e*, L. *mur-us*, wall; *sag-e*, say; *reis-e*, ride; *wund-e*, wound; *bett-e*, bed.

117. The modern German shows these endings in the adjective very prominently; thus, the mas., fem., and neut. forms of *blind*, in Germ., are *blind-er, blind-e, blind-es*, as in Lat., *bon-us, -a, -um*, good. These endings, $er=es=e$, are changed, in the other cases, into *en, em; er*, in different Germ. dialects, we find as *re, aro, earo, jaro* (L. *turus, ture, tura*), *rar, rer*, and *el*. The Swedish adj. *blind* is (m.) *blind-er*, (f.) *blind'*, (n.) *blind-t*—this *t*, which we see at the end of the neuter, is for *en, et*, which appears at the end of nouns; as, *pris-et*, the price, *ark-et*, the bow (L. *arcus*), *ed-en*, the oath. Nothing is clearer, than that this suffixed article (so called), is a development of the very endings we have all along been considering, and that the L. *us, a, um*, is just such a suffixed article; also Wall. suffixed *il, lu, le, a, i*, and the Alb. *i, e*, Bask *a*—proof that the article is a development of an ending. That neut. *t, et*, of Swedish, appears in Gothic as *ata* (*blind-ata*), and *jata;* this is the same as L. *atum*, just as *ands* equals *andum*. It is the same, too, as the suffixed Per. *ra* of acc. case, Marathi *la*.

118. No truth is easier to demonstrate, than that the endings of all cases, and of both numbers, are simple variations of one and the same type, and nowhere is that truth more evident, than in the German languages. In Gothic, as we have seen, the nom. sing. had an ending *s, is, us*, like the *us* of Lat., and the *er, en, es*, of Germ. adjectives. This nominative ending continually tends to disappear, in the modern Germ. languages, by withering away; yet, its roots are never lost, but always lie hidden in the body of the word. In these languages, some

nouns have one form through all the cases, and, over and over again, do we find the ending of one case common to the others. The ending *am, em*, may be taken as the base for all noun endings; in that form it is dat. in Germ., and acc. in Lat.; in the form of *en, um*, it prevails as dat. plural; *er, ar, es*, are other forms of this *em*, and are found prevailing in the gen. and nom. plural—though other endings for them are common. It is common to find these endings soften down to mere vowels; as, *an* = *a, um* = *u; en, es, er* = *e*—the L. *am*, acc. end., is known to be merely a developed *a* (= *e*). This is the case almost wholly in English, where we have *tub-e* for all cases in which the Latin would have *tub-a, tub-æ, tub-am*; and, in the plural, we have *tub-es* = L. *tub-æ, tub-arum, tub-as, tub-is* — observe *tub-æ* (tub-e) = *tub-es*, i. e. a sing. form for the plural.

119. It is hardly necessary to say that the Lat. and Gr'k cases can all easily be identified with those of Germ.; the L. gen. *æ* = our *e*, gen. *i* = *is, ir; gen. is* = *es* is also nominative; and we have often met with them in Germ.; the acc. *am* we have already noticed, and the abl. *a, e* (*ad*), is only a modification of this *am, em*—the dat. belonging with the gen. (= nom.); the *is*, in the plural of the 1st declension, is simply the *es* of our plur. *speech-es*. The *um* of L. gen. plur., we have often found in Germ.; *orum* (gen. plur.) is a development of this *um*, and is properly double—its correspondent being the old North *ar*, old Sax. gen. *aro, ero, jero*, old Friesic *era; ibus*, dat. plur., is also a development, of *is, es*, and double—the *b* in it pointing to the *m* (dat.) of Germ.; it is not different from the Gothic (nom. and gen.) plural *eis* (G'k *ees*), *gis* (*g* = *e*), *gos, jus* (*j* = *g* = *d* = *b*).

120. The Greek cases are much nearer English; in the 3d decl., gen. *os* (L. *us, es, is*), dat. *i*, acc. *a* (our *e*); nom. plur. *es* (our *es*), dat. *si* = *is, es*, gen. *on* = *um*, acc. *as* = *es*. In the 2d decl., nom. plur. *oi* = *i*, dat. plur. *ois* = *oi-es*, acc. plur. *ous* = *oi-es*, L. *os, us*—*ois* = *is*, is another form of the L. *ibus*.

121. Another positive proof of the identity of these L. cases with each other, is the fact that, in the modern Latin languages, those variations found in the old tongue wholly disappear, i. e. one ending is found in all cases, as is the case with us.

122. The Slavic languages will furnish us with some instructive features in this connexion; *om, em*, is a common ending in Russian, instrum. in the sing. and plur., and dat. in the plural also—in the adjective, it is found in the dat. sing., as well as in the instr. and prep. cases. In some instances, it is reduced to a mere vowel; it is precisely the L. *am*, Germ. *em*. In the plur. prep. case, we find *ach* or *ak*, for the ending of nouns—it is found also in the gen. plur. of adjectives. For animate beings,

the acc. sing., here, is like the gen., and for inanimate beings, it is like the nominative. Russ. adj's have gen. sing. in *ago*; this is no doubt the prepo. ending *ak*—and both are identical with the old Lat. abl. *ad* (Hung. acc. *at*, and plur. *ak*), just as in some of the Slavic we find *ech, ek,* in the perfect tense, while we have *ed*.

123. In Pol., we find substantially the same endings—adding that here, as in Russ., they are often reduced to mere vowels. We find in the dat. sing. *owi*, gen. plur. *ow*, Russ. gen. plur. *ov* (*ob*), L. *bi* of *ibi, sibi,* and *bus* of the plural; but *ow, ob,* is evidently $=om$. To give the full forms of Pol. cases, we have, for the name John: N. *Jan,* G. *Jan-a,* D. *Jan-owi,* A. *Jan-a* V. *Jan-ie,* In. *Jan-em,* Loc. *Jan-ie;* plural cases are *Jan-owie, Jan-ow, Jan-om, Jan-ow, Jan-owie, Jan-ami, Jan-ach.*

124. In the Bohemian nouns and adjectives, we shall find similar endings; the *ago* is *iho* ($g=h$), which may be reduced to *a, e;* and the *owi, ov,* appears here as *u* (*uv*), *i* (*owi*). In the adj., the dat. sing. is *imu, emu,* while in the noun it is *ovi,* showing *imu* $=ovi$. In Illyrian, we find nothing particularly new. The *g, h, j,* and *ch,* which we find running through the Slavic languages, is the *ch* of Germ. dat. *mi-ch, di-ch, si-ch,* as the *em* is that of *d-em, ein-em, welch-em.*

125. From the fact, which we think is now made evident enough, that the case forms are produced by a simple change in one and the same ending, and from the fact, too, that one case form, under certain conditions and in certain cases, may be used to perform the office of any other, we infer that the expression of case does not lie in the ending, but that it lies, rather, in the body of the word, or in the context. Those endings are indeed growths to represent the prepositions, which may be considered as developments of just such suffixes, but they have only grown out to represent what was already a force in the word, given to it by virtue of the context. They add nothing to the word, for they have grown out of it. A noun in the dat. case was dative always, dative long before it ever developed its proper ending, dat. long before it was governed by a preposition. Words with endings, all words with prefixes and suffixes, are not compound, they are simple, single. Nor does the preposition put a noun in the dat. case, for example, (as said before, it was dative always); it adds nothing to the word; if it was not already dative, it could not take the preposition which belongs with datives. So, again, we see the dative may be considered as having its force all reserved in itself, or, as getting that force from the whole sentence—it is immaterial which view we take.

126. Let us not be surprised to find the apparent inconsistency, that the word and the ending, or the word and preposition,

both express the same thing; the whole sentence, when critically examined, is found to be only a multitude of repetitions. Do we not continually find such repetitions as these — *a son of his, extract it from, to which he was directed to, a senatu,* by the senate, (wherein we find *his* = of him, *extract* = draw from, *senatu* = by the senate).

127. So, we see plainly that the prepositions add nothing, that it is a simple case of duplication; and yet, these are simply illustrations of a principle that is at work in all languages, and in all parts of them. Every time the Latinist says *ego amo,* or *puer amat,* I love, the boy loves, he uses nominatives which are already represented in the verb by *o* and *at* (for, *amo* means I love, and *amat,* he loves); and it is really as if said *I love-I, the boy loves-he*—and to go still further, those endings indicate only what must be contained in *am',* the root. You never can put the preposition *ab* in Lat., or *from* in Eng., before a word which is not ablative, which does not contain *from* or *ab* already; so, it is not *man* that is good, it is only the *good man* that is good—*good* can only be applied to that class of men who are *good men* (if it properly applied to other men, they would be *good* too), and the word *man* must be used to represent that class of *good men.* We see, thus, what must be the result of all philosophizing, *the part expresses as much as the whole, is equal to the whole.*

128. We notice here a principle which we shall have occasion to advert to more than once; any oblique case (one not nom.), in fact, any form that appears in language, may be taken as the base of some new form. Any case form may, under suitable conditions, perform the office of another; thus, in Latin, *caput* means head, and *capitis* (gen.), of the head, and this form *capitis,* still gen., becomes, as an adjective, *capital;* it is now treated as a new base, and as such receives the adjective ending *is,* as *capit-al-is;* as such new form, it may now go through all the list of cases as if it were a noun—we find, among other forms, *capit-al-ib-us,* dat. plur., which we might treat as a noun meaning to-capital (ones), or to-the-capitals. So, every genitive may go through a new set of cases as the base of an adjective; every adjective becomes, thus, merely a genitive run through the cases as a new noun. We, too, take the L. *capital,* and, forgetting to observe that it was ever gen., forgetting that it is anything else but a nom., or base form, we treat it as such, and we get the adjective (called adverb) *capital-ly;* we do more, we treat it as a verb = to (have) capital, and get the derivative *capital-ist* (a pres. part. for a noun, like *serv-ant*); and, again, we take it as equaling to (be) capital, and we get the other participial form *capital-ness* (called noun). If capitalists

were like fish to be caught, we might then say again *capital-isting*, wherein the same ending, somewhat varied, occurs three times. Behold the origin and mode of all repeated endings.

129. Further, we may notice that case endings are to be identified with the personal endings of verbs. Thus, it is noticed that *at* of the Latin supine *amatum*, is allied to *at*, *ad*, endings of old ablatives, and this is the *at* that appears in the 3d person sing., as *am-at*. It is well understood, that the case endings are varied articles or demonstratives; the person endings must be such also, for they represent pronouns, and hence, the two classes are related. Again, we shall show, hereafter, that the verbal and part. endings are to be classed with those of the persons, but the identity of those verbal endings with the noun and adj. endings of Germ., for example, has already been hinted at, and can easily be proved. Not only these, but all adj. and adverb endings, such as L. *-tim*, *-ter*, G'k *-then*, *-de*, *-thi*, belong with the endings of case.

130. We see, then, the same class of endings applied to several very different purposes; this is not alone a law of language, but a law of the creation. In the animal and plant kingdoms, we everywhere see this working of one thing into very different results; thus the nose of the elephant becomes his trunk, and his tusks are only teeth; the shell of the turtle, and its protection, is the internal skeleton of other animals; the beautiful rose flower is only a bundle of leaves; we might go on thus to infinity—*everywhere one thing only differs from another in being more or less transformed.*

131. In the Finn. and Tart. languages particularly, we have the case endings developed into full suffix prepositions; as, Hung. *fa*, tree, *fa-bol*, out of the tree—showing the origin of prepositions following the noun.

Plurals.

132. The identity of the plural with the genitive singular has been noticed elsewhere (*Err. of Gram.*); just as much as the genitive is a form of the nominative, so much, again, is the plural a form of it also. Both the gen. and the plur. have, often, endings where the nom. has not, and are in so far different from it, but we often find them both either like the nominative, or varying from it by only an internal vowel change (as *man* and *men*), proving that in fact the three are not essentially different, and are only apparently so by developing, in some cases one more than the other, elements which all have alike.

133. In many languages, the plural scarcely differs from the sing., at least, only as our *this* and *these*, *goose* and *geese*, and in

all tongues there are numerous instances of the identity of the two; as we say, ten *sheep*, ten *fish*, ten *head*. The Gr'k and L. nom. plural. (-*es*) has no element not found in the gen. sing., (-*is*). In G'k, neut. plurals are treated as singulars, mere collectives. Every gen. really indicates a plural; there can be no *of a thing* unless it has parts—it must be a minuend which contains the subtrahend and the remainder. Such words as *money* (much (of) money), as *water* (a pint of water), as *land* (an acre of land), are as much plural as *boys*, ten (of) boys—*ten* indicates simply a certain quantity of the class denoted by *boys*, the words *much, pint, acre*, do no less. They are plurals which have no singulars.

184. But the plural has other connexions besides this; its agreement in different languages with the features of the feminine, is too striking to be passed by as unmeaning. In Latin and Greek, the fem. ending is *a*, but *a* is the ending also of the neut. plur.; as, *bon-a*, good, both fem. sing., and neut. plur.; *es, is*, a fuller form of this *a*, is also a fuller form of the plurals *a, i, ai, oi*. Our *ess*, as in *lion-ess* (fem.) is clearly a variation of that plural ending *es*, as we see in the L. *leon-es* = lions, and the fem. ending *ina*, G'k *aina*, San. *ani*, Germ. *in*, A. S. *en*, is the same as the Germ. plur. ending *en*, Per. *an*. The Slavic languages, and indeed many others, could furnish us proof in the same direction. The plural ending of Arabic and Persian, *at*, Ethiop. *at, an*, is also a fem. ending slightly varied. The Syr. *tha, ta*, is both a plural and a fem. ending. But it is unnecessary to go further to prove a truth so manifest.

135. [It is true *oth, at, ta*, are supposed to be endings peculiar to the plur. of nouns which are feminine, but it is true, too, that some masc's (and in Per., neut's also) have this fem. plur. ending. Note that, in Sem., to the plur. in *oth* (*at*), *im* (the mas. end.), is also added—and we have the plur. of a plur., precisely like *ox-en-s* for oxen].

Genders.

186. One thing is at least certain; in the earlier stages of language gender-forms were not used to distinguish sex. What the precise meaning of the variation in forms for gender was, is not so plain. There are uncultivated languages, we know, where the distinction is simply of the animate from the inanimate, and many others again, where no gender-forms are developed at all. To go back even no farther than the Greek and Latin, and the modern languages of Europe, we find the gender-forms do not indicate sex, and seem to have no reference to it

at all. Thus, in L., *sermo*, a speech, and *liber*, a book, are mas.; but *pars*, a part, and *rupes*, a rock, are fem.; and in Russ., *dom*, a house, is mas. also *korabl*, a ship, but *kniga*, a book is fem.— while in Germ., *book* (buch) and *house* (haus) are neuter.

137. In Russ., as well as in Lat., and elsewhere, fem. nouns have (for inanimate objects, abstracts) a common ending *a*, *ia*, and for the mas. *e* and *y* mute. But that all gender endings are modifications of one and the same thing (and that the ordinary ending) is clear enough. There is no ending of any gender but which appears in some form or case of another gender; thus, L. *bon-um* is nom. neut., but it is acc. mas. also; *a* is fem., but neut. plural also, and, in Greek, it is acc. sing.— having in Germ. languages even other offices. The difference in gender-forms is even less in the oblique cases than in the nom.—after the nom., the neuter commonly runs parallel with the masculine.

138. The neuter seems to be objective in its nature; it certainly often agrees in form with the mas. acc.—in German, *es* is neut. adj. ending, but also mas. gen. The common Slavic neut. ending *o* is undeniably a condensed *ego*, *eho*, *eo*, *o*, of the gen. mas. The conclusion to be arrived at, is that the neuter is, in its origin, an oblique case of the masculine, taken as the base of a new form—it is in this fact, that we find the explanation of that universal phenomenon, the neuter nom. never differing from the neuter acc.—i. e. its nominative is already accusative. Neuters, referring as they do, to inanimate objects, can hardly be regarded as subjective, as acting, thinking—they can be objects alone. They are now assuming a nom. or subjective character, just as the infin. and subj. moods, known to be objective and dependent, get to be independent, i. e. indicative.

139. The coincidence between the fem. and the plural has already been noticed. The coincidence, too, between fem. nouns and abstracts, such as *goodness*, *harmony*, *justice*, is equally striking and general. It is a uniform feature in language, to find abstracts feminine. The nouns of the Latin 1st declension end in *a* and are fem.; as, *vita*, life, *hora*, hour. There is a class of fem. nouns in Lat. which end in *ia* (a Russ. fem. end.); as, *justit-ia*, justice, *concord-ia*, concord. There is a class of L. fem's allied to these, those in *tas* (our *ty*, the *ta* of so many, the *heit* of Germ., our *ness*, *n = t*); as, *brevitas*, briefness, *celeritas*, celerity. The real ending here may be taken as *as* (the original of fem. end. *a*); the *t* is a developed element latent or suppressed in the adjectives *brevis*, *celer*, but appearing in the abstract noun based on it—just as we have *t* grown up in verbs. Indeed, it appears before *ia* also, as *tristitia*. There are feminines in *tudo*; as, *magnitudo*, magnitude, from *magnus*—where the real ending

is *o*, the *t* being repeated in *d*. (Is not *magnitud* a pure ablative? that is its form). In the Semitic languages, we find strongly this coincidence between the marks of fem's and abstracts, it being *t* and *a* in both cases.

140. We find also Latin *prudentia*, prudence, and *audacia*, boldness; but they are precisely the neuter plural forms of the adjectives *prudens* and *audax*, i. e. they denote prudent (things), bold (things). There can be no doubt that such nouns are neuter plural adj's, and that they are nothing else — save that they are feminines also. In brief, we should call the fem. a neut. plural taken as the base of a new form — it is an adjective used as a noun in this case.

141. The agreement of the pron. 2nd person with the fem. marked words, must not pass unobserved. In almost all languages, the letters that mark the fem., also mark the 2d person. In Semitic, we find *t* used both for fem. and for *thou;* so, in L., *tu*=thou, and *tas* is fem. ending; *as, es, is,* are the marks of the 2nd person sing. of verbs, but also of fem. nouns. Our *est* of *walkest*, Russ. *esh*, is the same as our *she*. *Thou* is properly a feminine pronoun.

CHAPTER IV.

HISTORY OF ADJECTIVES.

142. This subject we have already considered in some of its phases (*Err. of Gram.*); there are other points of view to be taken, and these we will proceed to consider here. Not only is every adjective in origin a noun in the genitive case, it is equally true, that every noun in an oblique case may be considered an adjective or adverb. Again, every case of an adjective with its noun is a real compound of two nouns, just such a compound as *woodhouse*, where *wood*, though a noun, performs the part of a true adjective. When the union is close, as we find it in the Indian and Tartar languages, then the adjective does not vary to agree with the noun. When it has gained more independence, it has case and number endings, and it becomes an independent word, a case like nouns in apposition; the more it assumes the character and form of a noun, the greater its individuality.

143. The Latin and Greek adjectives have far more individuality than those in German and English. Our adjectives must stick close to the noun, like a true parasite; their adjectives are not subject to such unvarying conditions; they are often found

remote from the noun, playing a part on their own responsibility; we say *good man's*, but they say *good's man's*; we say *of good men*, they say *of good of men*, i. e. they use forms which make it equivalent to such an expression.

144. We are prepared to advance still another idea with regard to the rise of adjectives, one which goes still farther back into their origin; it is this, that in principle, adjectives are growths or developments of *noun endings*; it is certain that a large class of them, namely, *pronouns, articles, demonstratives*, have such a source; and that adjectives are developments of these elements (pronouns, etc.), we do not doubt. The class of nouns called *diminutives* are important in this connexion—such as the Germ. *Lottchen*, little Lott, *fräulein*, a little woman, *chen* and *lein* having the force of *little*. There are abundant instances in all, or nearly all, languages; in the Italian, they exist in great variety, so also in Persian. So, in Ital. we find *libr-one*, large book (*libro*), and *libr-accio*, a large ugly book, *uccell-etto*, poor, dear, little bird (*uccello*). This proves two things; first, that endings may be developed, in nouns, to represent two, and even three, adjectives; and, second, since those suffixes are evidently variations of other noun endings, that the noun alone embodies the idea of the same noun with the adjective.

145. In regard to the compound that arises out of the adj. and noun, we mark, here, that all compounds are cases of duplicates—nothing can be black except *black* things, nothing shady except *shady* things. We find, in the Indian languages, abundant instances of these doubles, sometimes identical, as *going-going*, sometimes slightly varying, as *issuing-going*. Whenever we say *he came running, he went going, he ran leaping*, we have cases of repetition. (It is just such participles, we think, that give rise to adverbs; in Russ., such participles, or gerunds, are treated as adverbs). There are several absurdities arising from the assumed connexion of the noun with the adj., but we must omit to notice them here; suffice it to say, there are no things without qualities, there are no mere men, mere books; they must be bad men, good men, white men, new books, good books, these books, blue books.

Comparison.

146. Comparison is by no means peculiar to adjectives; to say *more* (of a) *bridge, more* (of a) *city, mostly men, mostly wheat*, these are comparative expressions, just as *more black, most black*; thus, we see in the Bask language, *gizon*, man, *gizon-ago*, more man.

147. Nor are those comparative endings, as our *er*, L. *ior*, G'k *ter* (and *iŏn*), Slav. *ejsi*, *si*, peculiar or anomalous; *er* we have often met with before, and *si*=*is*, *es*, is a form of *er*; the G'k *ter*, Pers. *tar*, is also a development of *er*—it is the L. *tur*, *tor*. That the comparative is simply a form of the positive, is seen by the frequent use, in all languages, of the positive as a comparative; thus, speaking of two boys, we call John the tall (one), the taller; again, many of our comparatives are formed by associating the positive with *more*, *less*, but we must observe that the adj. is, in this case, (as *more beautiful*,) comparative aside from the *more*—for, if *more-beautiful* alone was comparative, then, *beautiful* could not be so, and we should be reduced to the dilemma of having no comparatives but those in *er*, an absurdity which cannot be admitted for a moment; once more, every expression treating the adjective as having a degree, is comparative; such as *so great as*, *so small*, *round like a ball*, *it was white as snow*. So, it is clear that adjectives are compared without the adverb; it is clear, too, that it is compared without the ending *er*—so many instances occurring where it is such without that suffix. Besides, to show the identity of pos. and comp., we have many comparatives which are used as positives; as, the *latter* one, the *former* one, the *better* man, the *senior* editor, i. e. they are relative, comparative terms, but not more so than many or all adjectives.

148. We might say with truth, that every adjective is a comparative term—nothing is good, or white, or black, by itself alone. A thing is sweet only by something which is not sweet, or which is sour. There are no absolute qualities; A may be tall by B (a very common form of comparative in many languages), i. e. taller than B, but short by C who is very tall (a common superlative), i. e. tallest by A and B. It is on this principle that we so often find the ablative, or the *by*-case, following the comparative, as in Latin, for example. The gradation of these three degrees into each other, is one of the commonest things in language.

149. Besides, if we think, we shall see that there are really no degrees in qualities; a thing is more round, or square, or black, or crooked, only as one bridge is more bridge than another, or as one boy is more boy than another. We might say, too, that all qualities are really superlatives, for when a thing is really black, or really square, or really crooked, is not that the extreme, can it ever become *blacker*, or *squarer*, or *crookeder?* No more than when a thing becomes a house, can it ever become *more a house*, or be *the most house*.

150. Again, we must see that there can be no degrees beyond a comparative. In no way can the mind compare more than

two things, that is, one thing with another. When we say *A* is the best of the three, or the good or better one, we mean the best of the group three (a unit). All we mean is, that he is better than the rest, which reduces it to a comparison. The history of the comparative in all languages, fully sustains the above doctrines; it is only by remembering them that we can understand the form in which we often find it.

151. Our superlative ending is *est*, plainly a form of *er*, the Lat. *tim*, *ssim*, G'k *ist* and *tat*. In Illyr. and Boh., we find the superlative existing as a comparative prefixed by *nej*, *na* (= the); as, Illyr. *bolji*, better, *najbolji*, best, the better — in Russ., it is also expressed by the compar., and sometimes *na* is prefixed; so, in French and Ital., we say *the more beautiful* for *the most beautiful*; in Hebrew, we find *the good* for *best*, i. e. the good one of the group, the best.

152. Adjectives, we must add too, are very much in the nature of verbs; a noun never becomes a verb, until it first becomes an adjective. One of the forms of the adjective (the adverb) is always joined to the verb, directly or indirectly. In the more uncultivated languages, the adjective scarcely ever differs in form from the noun, and in character from the verb. The adjective belongs to the noun just as much as the verb belongs to its nominative, but not more, and as, in principle, every verb has its own pronominal nom. (as, *the man he-reads*), so, the adj., too, belongs not to its noun but to its pronoun; as, *the good* (one) *man, the being-good man, the man the one* (who is) *good*.

153. In those other languages where the adj. uniformly follows the noun, as *the man* (the) *great = great man*, it is clearly the representative of a complete, though dependent, sentence; thus, *man wise* (as in Fr.) = the man (being) wise, who-is-wise (= wise), i. e. *wise* takes the place of a full sentence. The adjective following the noun is more of an adverb, and is far less closely connected with the noun, than when placed before.

154. All the agreement that lies between the noun and adj., arises from both representing the same thing in the same manner; both are adj's or nouns, and complete in themselves; as, to the good man, (as in Lat.) to the good (one) to the man.

155. [As well here as elsewhere, we may, by way of note, defend ourselves against the critic who will be sure to see that by the theory of this work everything is reduced to nothing, all dividing lines are destroyed, etc., etc. We confess that our main effort through all the work is to show that things which, heretofore, have been thought to have nothing in common, we now find to be really much alike, perhaps even identical in character; but still, we should by no means deny that they are

yet distinct. Thus, we show that adj's are, in origin, nouns, and that pronouns are adjectives—but they are nouns and adj's of a peculiar kind; they hold places and develop forms foreign to ordinary nouns and adj's. Their connexion with the parent stock is obscured—it requires such an effort as we have been making, to render that latent connexion evident. In practice, the classes are very different, and we so treat them. Things may have the same origin, the same elements of character, and still belong to very different classes. When we say that two classes usually considered distinct are not different, we mean, be it always understood, only as to their origin, only when we examine them philosophically; just as *price, praise, prize*, Lat. *pretium*, known to be forms of one word, are not different, so (and in no other sense,) all things are not different.]

CHAPTER V.

HISTORY OF PRONOUNS.

156. Pronouns, in their connexions, extend through every department of language; they may, with propriety be regarded as affording the basis of all the forms which we find developed as adverbs, prepositions, and conjunctions; they are, undoubtedly, the original of a large class of primitive verbs, as, indeed, they are represented in all verbs by the personal endings; in many languages, they are grown as possessives at the end of nouns, in others, they appear as the suffixed article, while the endings of all nouns, in all languages, must, in the end, identify themselves with pronouns. It is a favorite idea of the author, that pronouns have arisen as a growth of these noun and verb endings thrown off, and it may be well for the student to keep this idea in view. We shall learn much of the pronoun in every class of words of which we treat, and to give its history in full here, would involve much which we should have to repeat under other heads, and, hence, we will omit so much as would properly come elsewhere. We shall content ourselves, principally, with presenting the new and various forms in which the same pronoun appears, in different languages. We shall thus discover to the learner, relationships which will often surprise, and always interest him; it is by tracing the connexions of words, that we shall most successfully learn their nature and use.

157. We may observe, by way of note, that we use the following abbreviations to denote the different languages: *Germ.* German; *G'k*, Greek; *Dan.*, Danish; *Sw.*, Swedish; *Du.*, Dutch; *Slav.*, Slavic, i.e. Russian, Polish, Bohemian etc., *Rus.*, *Pol.*, *Boh.*; *Sem.*, Semitic, i. e. Arabic, Hebrew, Syriac, and Ethiopic, *Ar.*, *Heb.*, *Syr.*, and *Eth.*; *Cel.* Celtic, i. e. Welsh, Irish, Gælic, Cornish and Celt-Breton, *Wel.*, *Ir.*, *Cor.*, and *C-B.*; *L.* Latin; *Sp.*, Spanish; *It.*, Italian; *Fr.*, French; *Per.*, Persian; *San.*, Sanscrit; *Go.*, Gothic; *Lith.*, Lithuanian; *A. S.*, Anglo Saxon, and others which will need no explanation. In comparing the forms of pronouns and particles, the student should have constantly in view, the sections under the head of Etymology — especially those on letters.

Personal Pronouns.

158. *I:* our personal of the first person is reduced to a single vowel, while in Latin it is *ego*, in Germ. *ik*, *ich*, and *ih*. It is clear that our simple *I* arises from the quiescence, or vanishing, of the *g* and *ch* into a silent *h*, thus $ich = ih = i$. In Dan., this pronoun is *jeg* (L. *ego*); Fr. *je*; Sp. *jo*; Slav. *ia* and *ga*; Lith. *asz*, and San. *ah*: but in Celtic, it is *mi* (Fr. *moi*), Per. *men*, Hungarian *en*, Semitic *ana* and *ank*.

159. Bear in mind, that the forms above given are nominatives, and that even in those languages which are characterized, in this pronoun, by *g*, *ch*, *k*, *j*, and *z*, we still find in the accusative (obj.) the mark *m*, as in our own *me*, Germ. *mich*, Slav. *me* and *mne*; and we thus see clearly that all the various forms of *I*, above given, readily identify themselves with each other, *g*, *k*, *j*, and *z*, being not only equal to each other, but to *n* and *m* also. In Sem., we find those two apparently unrelated letters, *n* and *k*, united in *ank* (or *anok*), just as we see in the Germ. *mich* (mk), our me. It only proves that *n* (aud m) $= g$ is also $= k = ch$, *h*; we may look upon *ank* (nk) and *mich* (mk) as doubled, or as a case of elements repeated (nk, kk).

160. The plural of this pronoun, which with us is marked by *w* (in *we*), in Slav. is *mi* and *my*, Wel. *ni*, Per. *ma*. The *es* of the Lith. form *mes*, the *s* of L. *nos*, the *eis* of Go. *weis* and G'k *'ēmeis*, the *s* of our *us* (ws), the *an* of San. *vayan*, are all, substantially, marks of the plural, for these forms. We easily see how this plural is only a variation of some of the cases of *I*; thus, $me = we$ (m = w), Germ. *mir* (me) $= wir$ (we), and G'k *me* (me) $= noi$ (we), and the like. The difference between *we* and *me*, when it exists, consists chiefly in the former developing a plural sign.

161. *Our* is another form of *we*, showing the *r* lost in our *we* but appearing in the Germ. *wir;* we find these forms of *our;* viz., Dan. *vor;* Go. *uns-ar;* Du. *ons* (Germ. *uns*, our *us*); L. *nost-er*, Fr. *not-re*, and Port. *nosso*. The *r, ar, er*, are clearly growths of adjective endings; the *-erer* of Germ. *uns-erer*, and also *-eros* of Gr'k *'ēmet-eros*, are cases of double endings, or, they are adjectives formed upon an old one as a base, the Germ. form being grown upon *unser*, the genitive of *we* (our); our *mine* (my-en), and *theirs* (their-s) are of the same kind, and, no doubt, also L. *nos-t-er* (*noster* and *'ēmeteros* are, also, clear comparatives — *ter*, *eter*, other).

162. We have only to remark on this pronoun *I* in conclusion, that the *n, m*, and especially *s* and *z*, which we find the base of it, are clearly demonstrative letters, and its origin may thus be traced back to the pronoun *this*, or its cognate adverb *here; I* denotes *the one here*, or *this*, as opposed to *that* person *there*, *thou* or *he*.

163. *Thou:* this pronoun has very little that is peculiar or striking in the forms it presents; its leading letter is either *t*, as in Lat. and Per. *tu*, or *s*, as in Gr'k *su*, *d* in Germ. *du*, *th* in our *thou*, or *nt*, as in Sem. *ant* — all showing that *thou* is a clear demonstrative, like *that* or *there*.

164. But the forms which we find this pronoun assume when it appears in the plural, are decidedly curious and interesting; thus, our own *thou* (th) becomes with us, *you* (y), in Go. *jus*, Iceland *thér*, Dan. *i* (=y), A. S. *ge* (=ye), Germ. *ihr* and *ir*, Slav. *wy*, Wel. *chwi*, Per. *shuma*, L. *vos*, San. *yuyan*. The *er* of *ther*, *r* of *ihr*, *s* of *vos*, and *un* of Sem. *chun*, are clearly plural endings. The letters which mark all these forms given, are unquestionably alike; in the Germ. *ihr*, the *th* of *thou* and *ther* has softened into *ih* or *h;* in Dan., the plural mark *r* disappears, and *ih* becomes *i*, which again departs little from *y, g, j;* the *w* of Slav., and *v* of L., are forms only of *y* (=*u* and *v*) which we find in *ye* and *you* — The Wel. and Sem. *ch* is a variation of the *th* and *g* sound, seen above.

165. *Your* presents also some peculiar forms; thus, Go. *izv-ar;* Icel. *yd-ar;* Sw. *ed-er;* old Sax. *iuw-er;* old Germ. *iw-ar;* Germ. *euer;* the *d* of *eder* has the place of *j* (=y), as we see by the Dan. form *jer* (yer); so Go. *izv*=*iv, iw, ju*, you. The *d* of *eder* also represents the *h* of German *ihr*, which is always a softening of *th*, in these pronouns; both point to the *th* of *thou*. That *eder*=*ihr*, we see by the other Sw. form *er*, for *eder*. The Dutch has *uw* and *uwe* (you) for *your* and *thy*, i.e. the adjective part *er* is not developed; the Slavic *your* is *wasz* and *wass* (Latin *vos*), Latin *vos-ter*, French *vo-tre*.

166. The pronouns of the 2d person are, unquestionably, in

origin, the same as those of the 3rd; the Germ. *ihr*, you, is the same as *ihr-er*, their, and *ihr* her; Germ. *sie*, they, is also used for *you*—indeed, the use of *they* for *you* is common the world over; the *th* of our *thou* is the *th* of *the, that, them*. The student will also notice, that not only are the different pronouns alike, but also, that the different cases of the same pronoun are identical, one having no element which the other has not; thus, Germ. *ihr*, you, corresponds to our *your*, and to the form *iwar, iuwar*, and we have already noticed how the Dutch use *us* for *our*; so, again, Germ. *wir*, Icel. *ver*, is our *our*, though used by them for *we*; *our* scarcely differs from *your*, as also L. *vor*, you, from *us*; again, the Dan. *han*, he (Slav. *on*) is our *him*—indeed, there is no end to such comparisons if we choose to pursue them.

167. The personals of the 3d person are far more extensive in their connexions, and in the variety of their forms, and we shall have to proceed with less regard to order than we observed in treating of the others; let it suffice that we give a complete and comprehensive view of them. And, first, take *He*; our form is equal to *the*, as we see by its plural *they*, *th* softening to *h*; in Gr'k, we find only *e*, acccompanied with a mark partially representing our *h*; in the Latin tongues, *s*, as in *se* (self), takes the place of *h*—the German shows this *s* in its *sein*, his, and *sie*, they, *sich*, self; in short *sin* (=him) runs clear through the German languages for *his*.

168. In German, the *s*, *th*, and *h*, entirely disappear, and we find *er* (*ir* in old Germ.) for *he*; all we have here is that common ending noticed above. It is the same as German *der*, the, and *ihr*, their and your, the *d* and *th* vanishing in *h*, and thus becoming silent; our *here*, Germ. *her*, is also a near relative of this *er*. There is a Gothic form *gains*, or *jains*, equal to Danish *hans* (his), Gr'k *ekein-os*, Germ. *jener* (that), Slavic *on*, Fr. *son* (his), Welsh *hon*, Semitic *hun*, *ain*, Persian *an* (this), our *him*.

169. The Latin has more than one form to represent *he*, *she*, and *it* (or what is the same, *this* and *that*); in the form *ille*, Fr. *le* and *il*, Sp. *el*, Sem. *el*, (the), the *l*, always equal to *d*, *th*, has taken the place of the usual *t* sound, so that *ille*=*le*, *de*, the; in *hic* the *c*, no doubt, is for the common Lat. ending *-que*, and related also to the Germ. *ch* in *ich*, *dich*, *sich*, so that we have *hi*=he, they; indeed, *hi* (these) is the plural form used for *they*—the other cases of *hi-c*, the gen. *hujus* and acc. *hun-c*, easily identify with *his* and *him*; *is*, *ea*, *id*, (he, she, it), another form, is a variation of this *hic*, the *h*=*th* quite disappearing, and the *s*, *a*, and *d*, being adjective endings; we have, in this form, *ejus* for *hujus* (his), *eum* for *hunc* (him), *ii* for *hi* (they); that there is a suppressed *s*=*th*=*h* here, is abundantly proved by its derivative *suus* (his), by the old Lat. *sum* for *eum*, *sam*

for *eam*, and Go. *si* (she), and *sa* (the); *id* is plainly our *it*, and *ea* is our *she* with *sh* suppressed; the corresponding Greek is *o, e, to,* (*o* and *e* with *h* breathing), the characteristic alone appearing in the neuter *to*—this is the Greek *the*.

170. *She* and *It*, it is hardly necessary to add, are only variations of *he* and *the;* in A. S., *heo* is she, and *se* is the; in Germ., *sie* is she. In A. S., *it* is *hit*, in Sw., *det* (Germ. *das*), showing that *t* is not radical, but belongs to the ending as the *d* in Lat. *id* and *illud*. In Danish, *he* and *she* differ only as *han* and *hun* (L. *eum* and *eam*); in Slav., he, she, it, is *on, ona, ono,* and in most languages the change is no greater.

171. Of the plurals *They* and *Their* little need be said. The former, in Latin, is *hi* and *ii;* Dan. *de*, Germ. *die* (our *they* and *the*); Germ. *sie;* Icel. *their, thaug,* and *thetta* (the forms of our *their* and *that*); Slav. *oni* (Germ. *jener*); Welsh *hwy*, Ir. *siad*, C-B. *hi;* Sem. *hem* and *hum* (our *them*, in form). The other Lat. form *illi*, they, Fr. *ils* and *elles*, It. *eglino*, has the *ill* to represent the usual *th*, or *h*, and *i* final for plural mark, i.e. *illi*= *li, di, thi, they;* so, we see *illorum* (of-them, their), in Fr., *leur* (their), Sp. *les*, It. *loro*. Besides these forms of *their* just given, there is yet to be noticed the A. Sax. *hira;* Dan. *deres,* Germ. *ihrer* and *ir;* L. *eorum*. The Welsh affords the form *eu* for *their,* Cornish *aga* (also *agan,* our, and *agas,* your); when we take in connexion the Welsh forms *eich*, your, *ein,* our, *ych,* you, *ei,* his, her, him, we can readily see that this *eu* and *aga* (*g*=*ch*) are to be referred back to the Germ. *euch,* you.

172. For the article, we will simply give some of its different cases, as found elsewhere, to show what various applications have been made of them in English. In the Ang. Sax. nominative, we find mas. *se* (the), fem. *seo* (she), neut. *thaet* (that, it); gen. mas. *thaes* (these and this), gen. fem. *thaere* (their, there); dat. *tham* (them, him); in Germ., nom. mas. *der* (their), fem. *die* (the, they) and neut. *das* (that); gen. *des* (these); dat. *dem* (them). In Welsh, the article is *yr* (and *y*), Germ. *er,* he. In Latin, the nearest corresponding pronoun to our *the,* is *ille,* Fr. *le*.

Demonstratives.

173. The usual demonstrative letters are *th, d, s,* and the like, but *l* is often met with in such pronouns, (as we saw in *ille*), and we shall find *m* and *n* common letters for a like office. Our own *this* and *that* may be regarded, we need hardly observe, as modifications of *the*. The plurals *these* and *those* are only slight variations of *this;* the Germ. *dieser*, this, is in form our *these*.

174. In Slavic, we find these forms: Boh. *ten,* this; Pol. *on*

(Boh. *onen*), that (German *jener*, our *one*); there is also the doubled Pol. *ten-to*, this-here (Greek *tou-tos*); Illyr. *ti*, these; Hung. *ez*, this, and *az*, that, and *emez* (*em-ez*, double) this-here, *ez-az*, this (the-that); Alban. *ata* (also *ai*, *agio*), it and this; Sem. *ze*, *dhu*, *d*; Go. *sa* and *thana*, and San. *sas*, *sa*, *tan*, *tat*; all these forms are easily placed in one and the same class.

175. Another class is one which apparently departs from this, but which still is undeniably only a variation of it—it is the class marked by *m*, and the like; thus, in Welsh, *hwn*, *hon*, *hyn*, are used for *this* (*hyn* = *these* also), and *hyny*, *hono*, *hwnw*, for *that*; *this* is identical with the Dan. *han* and Slav. *on* (he); C-B. *hen* (he) and *ann* (the); Sem. *hon* or *hun*, and *ain*; Per. *an* and *shan* (them); Ir. *sin*, Dan. *hin* (that), and Go. *gains* (he).

176. In Hung., *eme'* and *ama'* are used for *this* and *that*; in Cornish, *ma* and *na* are used as suffixes at the end of nouns, in place of *this* and *that* (besides *hom*, this, and *hon*, that). In Manchu, *ere* = this (Germ. *er*), and *tere* = that (Germ. *der*); in Mongolian, *ene* = this, and *tene* = that.

177. In French, *this*, and *that*, is *ce* (*the*, Sem. *ze*, Pol. *ci*); we find also *ces* (these), *cet* (that); it has also *celle* and *ce-la*, for *this* and *that* (L. *ille* and *qualis*, Wall. *a-quel*). For *cet* and *cette*, the Ital. has *questo* (L. *iste* with *q* prefix), and for *celle*, it has *quello* (L. *ille*); Fr. *ce* = It. *che*.

Relatives.

178. That the relatives are simply a development of the personals and demonstratives, as *who* of *he*, and *what* of *that*, is proved beyond a doubt; in other languages, the Latin for example, they are used as adjectives (demonstratives), as our own *which*, *what*, and *that*, so often are. In Germ., *wer*, who, is a form of *er*, he; *welcher*, which, is a variation of Fr. *celle*, Lat. *ille*, Ital. *quello*, (our *which* is the same word, *l* suppressed, see Scotch *quhilk* (*qu*, *vv*, *w*)—so L. *quod*, *wod*, *wot*); the Germ. *der*, the, is very commonly used as a relative, and our own *that* is a pure article (see Anglo Saxon *se*, *the*, *thaet*).

179. The Fr. and Sp. *que* (which, what) is the It. *che* (*q* = *k*, *c*), and this readily leads us back to Fr. *ce*, our *the*, *that*; this *que* is our *who* (Aug. S. *hwa*), *qu* = *kv*, *hv*, *hw*. The Wallach. has, for *who*, the forms *quare* (where), *quare-le* (suffix article), and *quine* (him, whom).

180. The Pol. *kto*, who, agrees nearly with our *what* (Latin *quid*, *kid*, *kt*), while *co*, what, is more like *who*; *komu* whom (him); in Rus., in place of *kto*, we find often *ko*, for who, and *chto*, or *tchto*, for what; in Boh., *koho* and *cheho*, for whose (L. *cujus*, Germ. *wessen*). The Latin *qui*, who, easily identifies

itself with our *who*, *qu* being equal to *qw*, *hw*, and, hence, to A. S. *hwa*; *cujus* = whose, *quem* = whom, *c* and *q* = *k*, *h*; so *quod* = what, San. *kim*, Alb. *ke*, *kous*, Mong. *ken*, Turk *kim*.

181. In the Irish, we find *cia*, *ce*, *ci*, for who (It. *che*, Fr. *que*), *ciad*, *cad*, what, (L. *quod*); there is also Ir. *da*, (that), and this is reduced again to *a*, who, what. In Welsh is *pwy*, who, and whom, (*p* being used for L. *q*); the form *yr hyn*, the-this, is also used as relative. In Cor., also, *py*, *pa*, who and what; also *nep* (*pen*). In C-B., *piow*, who, and *pe*, what (Fr. *que*), Greek *pos'* (and *kos'*, *tis'*, *tos'*).

182. In Semitic, we find *ma* and *min*, for what and who; in Heb., we have *asher*, shortened *she*, (Go. and San. demon. *sa*); in Arab., the form *the-this* is used for relative. Hungarian has *mi* and *mik*, what, *melly*, which (Germ. *welcher*) — besides *ki* and *kik*, who. In Manchu, this *m* is *w*, as *we*, who (German *wer*); what is *ai*, Celtic *a*.

183. In Dan. and Swed., *som* is used for *who*, *that*; it is our *some* and *same*, *so*, *as*, *such*, Greek *'oi-men* (some).

184. Other languages have developed a class of pronouns from these relatives which we have not; thus, there is the L. *talis*, such, Germ. *solch-er*, Go. *swaleiks*, Russ. *tolik* and Lith. *toley*, G'k *telik-os*, Pol. *tak-i*, Welsh *sawl*, Aug. Sax. *swilc*, Hung. *olly-an*; all connected with *that*, L. *ille*, Fr. *cel'*. This is demonstrative, and the relative form is L. *qualis*, what, or *what-kind*, G'k *kelikos*, Russ. *kolik*, Go. *hweleiks* (how-like), Du. *welk* (which) Hung. *milly-en*. This pronoun is identical with Germ. *welch-er*, and hence our *which*; it is, too, the L. *quis*, who, with the *l* of *ille* appearing. *Quantus*, how great, and *quot*, how many, in Latin, are other variations of *quis*; leave off *us*, the adjective ending, and *quani* = *quot*, *quod*, our *what*; there is, also, L. *tot*, so many, our *that*; Hung. *quot*, and *quant*, is *hany* (our many).

We might observe that our *like*, Germ. *gleich*, G'k *elik-os*, is identical with *qua-lis* (what-like), the *q*, lost with us, appearing in the Germ. *g*, — the Ang. Sax. *ylc*, same, and *hw-ylc*, which, belonging to the same order.

185. The student may learn from this relative class, how easily *p*, *q*, *k*, *t*, *ch*, *c*, *h*, *w*, and *m*, change for each other.

Interrogatives are identical with relatives, and hence need no separate consideration.

Indefinite Pronouns.

186. Our *every* is in Danish, *hver*, showing that it is the same as *where*, with which we often find it, as, in *every-where*; in

Gothic it is *wazuh* (was, what). The identity of this *every* with the relative, is proved by the frequency with which we find *ever* = *every* following it, as, *who-ever, what-ever;* this *ever* in L. is *cun*, or doubled, *cun-que* (*quem*, whom), as in *qui-cun-que*, who-ever; the L. *quis* is often used for *some, any*, and hence = *all, every*. The German *every* is *jeder*, in form our *either*, but also *whether*, and hence *which*; we use *either* for *both*, which refers us back to *all* = *every*. In Pol. it is *kazdy*, the *k* pointing to *kto*, who; in Hung., *minden*, every, each (*melly*, which); in Welsh, *pob* is every, but *pwy* is who; Cor. *myns*, all, ever, but *ma* = that, *pup*, all, and *py*, who.

187. *Each* and *any* must be taken as variations of *every;* the three easily replace each other; *each*, in Ang. Sax., is *aelc*, (Du. *welk*, which); in Fr. it is *chaque; cha* is *ce*, that, and *que* is suffix; the Asiatic *eka*, one, is also equal to *each;* so we often find *each-one*.

188. *Any* is the same as our *an, one, a*, and *many* belongs with it also; so do *all,* and *some*. In Italian, *qualche* (*qual-che*, which-that) is used for *some*, as *quis* is in Latin. The Latin *aliquis*, some-one, is simply *else-who, other-who, which-who, ille-who*. The Spanish *cada*, each, any, is the Latin *quot, quant*, and Germ. *jeder;* it is also the Slav. *jeden*, one.

189. *Many*, in German, is *viele* (full), which refers back to *welcher*, which — the L. *multus*, our *much*, belongs to the same family. That *many* is the same as *any, an, one*, is seen by the Germ. *man*, Fr. *on* (old Fr. *hom*), for our *one*, and by the G'k *mia*, one.

190. The word *other* may also be classed with these pronouns; in Latin, it is *alius* and *alter*, Gr'k *allos*, our *else*, Fr. *autre;* it is plainly, in form, connected with *ille* (and *all*), as the *ther* of *o-ther*, and *der* of Germ. *o-der*, point to the article *the*. *Either* is identical with *other*. That *some* is a relative in origin, is seen by the use of Danish *som* for *who; some* is equal to *same*, and both refer to Germ. article *dem*, and L. *i-dem*, same, Fr. *meme*.

191. In concluding our chapter on pronouns, we may dwell briefly upon their component parts. We notice particularly in pronouns, what is observable also in all classes of words, the repetition of one element in the same word, as in Lat. *quis-quis* (who-who) some one, Greek *tou-tos*. But, most commonly, the elements slightly vary from each other, yet never so much as to leave their identity questionable; thus, Fr. *le-quel*, which (*the-which*), Fr. *ce-la*, that (*the-that*); L. *ille*, he (*the-that*); Fr. *quel-que*, some (*which-that*); It. *qual-cuno*, some (*which-which*), and *qu-esto*, this (*which-that*); Wall. *a-qu-est*, that (*the-which-that*), and *in-sami*, the-same (L. *i-dem*); Dan. *hvord-an*, how (*where-then*); Pol. *tam-ten*, this (*the-this*), and *k-to*, who (*who-*

that); Ang. Sax. *aeg-hwa*, whoever (*each-who*), and *hwae-ther*, whether (*who-there*); G'k '*os-tis*, and '*o-ti*, who, what (*who-who*); Germ. *den-selbe*, the-self, same, and *der-jenige*, he (*the-that*); Ar. *el-la-dzi*, which (*the-the-this*).

192. It is hardly necessary to multiply examples where they are found so numerous; not only may we separate these words into elements, as we have, but those elements again, and so on indefinitely; thus, our *that* is plainly double, and our *what* also, as we see by its G'k equal *o-ti*, L. *ut*—in brief, we may say that *every consonant, every letter, represents this element which is repeated in the word*. It may be noted, too, that every case of one pronoun following another, as *he who, that which, this here, which one*, is one of double pronouns.

CHAPTER VI.

HISTORY OF PARTICLES.

193. Under the head of Particles are included what is usually known in grammar as Adverbs, Prepositions, and Conjunctions; particles we will again divide into two classes, putting adverbs and conjunctions together, as there is no real difference between them, when properly considered. (We every where find the purest conjunction replaced by the common adverb).

194. In investigating particles, we must constantly bear in mind one very important rule; that two or more words which come together in text, belong together, that they are parts of one compound, just as much as there are such in any compound; and that, as such elements, they are duplicates, repetitions, and the one may be considered as a form of the other, or both as forms of one type; it is a matter of no importance, that in some cases we find the elements separated, and in others printed together.

195. [We may mention here, by way of note, that in comparing words together, as we do under the head of Particles, equality, denoted by the sign =, or by words, generally has reference to the meaning; it will be easy to separate the words which are mere definitions from those which are considered to be etymological forms of the particle in question.]

We will consider first the class of adverbs, which includes also conjunctions.

Adverbs.

196. All adverbs are more or less connected, in their origin, with pronouns (except those which are cases of nouns, and they are not particles, i. e. they are not small words whose original form and meaning have become obscured); but a certain class of adverbs are more decidedly pronominal in form, that is, differ less from pronouns, than others; such adverbs, and indeed others, may be looked upon as presenting new forms of the pronouns. Thus, we have *where, when, whence, whither, whether,* from relatives, *what, which;* and *there, then, thence, thither,* demonstratives, from *this, that,* besides the other forms, *how, why, while;* in many instances, we can find these very forms as pronouns; so, *when,* Germ. *wann,* is Go. *wana,* acc. of who, and *thana* (then) is acc. of the, this; *where,* in Icel., is *huer,* who, old Germ. *wer* and *huer;* so, Go. *wathar* (whether), is who, Germ. *wer; hither,* Germ. *hin* (be-hind), is Go. acc. *hina,* of *his, hita,* this; *while* is A. S. *hwile,* who, Germ. *weil,* old Germ. *huilon,* A. S. *da-hwile* (the while); old Germ. *wanan,* whence, and its equal *wenan,* is *whom; there* is German *der,* the, and *da,* there, Ang. Sax. *thaer* = of the; *how* (our *who*), A. S. *hu,* Germ. *wie,* old Germ. *wic* and *wis* (wise), *hus, wiose; why* (which), A. S. *dy* (the), Gr'k *ti,* Lat. *quia,* Ang. Sax. *hwi,* Lat. *quid* (what), Germ. *warum* (was-um)— Latin *quare,* wherefore, why, is our *where,* L. *cur,* Illyr. *jer; now* is also demon., like *how,* but in it is used the *n* (so often found) for *t,* as Lat. *nunc* = *tunc,* in Go., *gu* (L. *jam, eam*), A. S. *iu* and *geo* (he, the,) (our *yet*), besides *nu* (g = n) — it is after the form of old North *inn* (Germ. *jener*) that, it.

197. In Latin (and Greek), the pronominal form and character of these adverbs is unmistakable; thus, *quo* (by-what), whether, wherefore; *quod* (what), that, as, since; *qua,* where, how (by-what); *quam* (acc. of *which*), how, and *quum,* a form of same, when, since; *hic* (he), here, then; *dum,* while, and *tum,* then (like forms), point to the Greek *ton,* the, an article lost in Latin—*jam,* now, then, is a variation of *tum,* but more nearly agreeing with the pron. *eam; nun* and *nunc* (*nov,* new, L. *nov-us*), is a modification of *dum : tunc,* then, thence, corresponds in character with *hune* (acc. of *he*); *utrum,* whether (either), a form of *uter,* which, points also to *uti,* that, Lat. *id; an,* also, whether, is the *inn* of old North, and related to *when,* Germ. *wann*— that *an* is related to *nun,* now, is seen by *num,* used like *an,* also by *ne,* not, and whether; *ubi,* where, there, is the dat. case *ibi,* to-that; *ita,* so, is a form of *id,* so is *ut, uti,* that; *ideo,* therefore, is made up of two parts, this-that, or this-for-that.

198. By the way, the student, in looking over the list of particles, in any language, cannot but be struck with the numerous cases of doubling or repetition, a subject we have spoken of before; and these instances where the repetition is evident, are only very few compared with those where it is latent—it gives us the secret of the growth of all words. So, we find *quo-que*= also (where-as, which-what); *nunc-nunc*, now-now = sometimes; *qui-dem*=indeed (which-the); *nam-que*=for (for-that); *vel-ut*, like (which-that, or-that).

199. In the German languages, we can see it in an even stronger light; as, Gothic *this-quaruh-thei* is where-ever (this-where-that); *swa-swe*=so as, L. *sic-ut* (so-so); A. S. *tha-tha*= then (then-then, the-the); *on-this-healfe*=by-this (L. *hac*, Germ. *des-halb*); *swa-hwaer-swa*=where-so-ever (so-where-so); *for-hwy*, wherefore, why (for-why); *swa-gelice*, like (so-like); and all our own cases where two or more particles come together; as, *now-then*, *as-well-as*, *so-that*, *never-the-less*.

200. We might go farther and find the same state of facts existing in all languages; that this class, at least, of adverbs presents new forms of pronouns, is as true in Asia as it is in Europe—it is true, too, in Africa. But we have done enough fully to illustrate the law; we will now proceed to consider some of the leading adverbs and conjunctions more in detail.

201. *And;* this *an* equals a relative, just as *ne* equals *whether;* and equals *ad, at, hence, also, that*. In Latin, *and* is *et*, Greek *kai;* judging by *kai, et* may be a transformed *te;* L. *que*=and (but *que* is *which*); Fr. *que* (ke)=how, that, what, but; *et* has another form, L. *ac* (*t*=*q, c*); *what* is another form of *et*, that; so we find A. S. *hwaet* (what) for *et*, and, Lat. *aut-em, ita-que;* Germ. *auch*, Lat. *ac*, Fr. *que;* in old German *ge, gie, ja* (*jam, tum*, L.) Icel. *og*, Celt. *ag, agus*, A. S. *eac, and*, and *kai*, but; in Ang. S., *ge*=*c-um, t-um* (*g*=*c*); Go. *ak, akei*=but, Germ. *aber*, so *b-ut* is *et;* Goth. *ith*, Lat. *autem* (if, L. *si*), *et*, Greek *de* (the)=but; old Germ. *bethiu* (b-et)=but and *et*, and; so *but* is *et*, with *b*; Fr. *car* (gar), for Latin *quare*, hence *kai, et;* Illyr. *i* and *a*= but, and (*ith*=*i, ac*=*a*); *gar* is found in the Tart. languages, slightly varied, meaning *but;* C-B. *e-get*=Fr. *que, et*, yet.

202. *As; as* is clearly a transposed *sa*, A. S. *se* (the), Go. *sa;* it is same as *so* (and *that*); in Germ., *as* is *wie* (how, who); it is the same as Fr. *que*, L. *ac*, also L. *ut*=that; in Germ., *als* (else, L. *alius*) is *as;* Fr. *comme* (L. *quum*)=how as; Welsh *can* (Fr. *comme*, Per. *chun*)= as—also *fel, felly* (Germ. *welcher*) Cor. *a-vel* (*f*=*p*, Cor. *pa*=what), Lat. *avec*, with— Cor. *ma mar, maga*=as, that (*ma* is demonstrative).

203. *So* has a variety of forms also; thus, old Germ. *sus*, is

one of them, L. *si-c*, *si-c-ut*, *ita*, and our *same;* we find *al-so*, hence *so* equals *al*, *als*, *all*: C-B. *kent*, *ker*, *ken* (Fr. *comme*) = so, L. *tant* (*k* = *t*); Cor. *ages* (Irish *agus* = and, Welsh *ag* = as, with), *es* = so, than; Fr. *ain-si* = so (this-so).

204. *That* is another form of *as* and *so*, and it is often used in connexion with them; that it is a form, too, of *what*, is seen by L. *quod*, what and that; Go. *ei*, *thi*, *thei*, *thatei*, *unte*, (and) mean *that*, German *dass*, and *weil;* Swedish *at* (to, too, two) = th-at, Latin *ut*.

205. *Again*: the idea of this particle is based on that of repetition, hence we find it connected with *other*, *and*, (Irish *agus*); in Germ., it is *wieder* (whether) L. *iterum*, G'k *eteros*, other; the *a* is prefix, as we see by A. S. *on-gean*, Du. *te-gen* (*to-gen*), Germ. *ge-gen*, so that *gain*, *gen*, is the true form, equal to Go. *gains*, (G'k *ekeinos*), Celt. *gan*, as, and with, (Lat. *cum*, *quum*, *quem*); also Latin *jam* = now, Gothic *ju*, Germ. *je*, ever, Latin *con*, with.

206. *After* is intimately connected with *again;* it is often pronounced *ater*, a form found in other tongues, and as such, we see it related to *other*, L. *iterum* = again, Du. *agter;* Germ. *n-ach* is near, next, and after, Dutch *echter* = yet, German *noch* (after) — so, we say *yet-again;* L. *infra* (*inf*, *ifr*), Fr. *apres;* Lat. *post* is *after*, It. *poi*, Fr. *puis*, It. *do-po* (*p* = *f*), Cor. *wose*, *woge;* C-B. *arre*, yet, after; Illyr. *polag*, near (below), L. *post*, Slav. *prez*, our *-proach*.

207. *Back* is related to *post* and *again* (b-ack), San. *a-paka*, a-back, a-fter, old North *aptr* and *eptri*, after, posterior; Slavic *paku* = again, G'k *palin*, Illyr. *ka* = near, to, also *pod* = under; Greek *apo*, after and away, back, by — we say *near-by*, hence *near* = by, and *by* = back; Greek *epi*, *epei*.

208. *But*: this we have already seen equal to *et* (and), *ut*, and *yet;* Dutch *maar* (more, o-ver), French *mais*, Per. *magar* (L. *magis*) = but — this is also Cor. *ma*, *mar* (ma is *that*, *what*); hut, yet, German *doch* = *noch*, and *nach*, Fr. *donc* (*dum-que*); Germ. *sond-ern*, Lat. *sed*, our *sunder*, means *but* — we use *but* in the sense of *except;* but may be taken as *b-out*, *without*, in old Germ., *uzan* being equal to *but*, *sed* (out); Go. *alga* = but, G'k *alla*, L. *alius*, other; Germ. *aber* = but (over, after), old Germ. *afur*, *auor* (o'er); in Illyr., *a* = but (Germ. *aber*, *auer*, *a*), also *al* (Greek *alla*), our *else*, German *als;* Ital. *mai* = never (but, more); Corn. *mes* = but, G'k *men*, Russ. *no* (G'k *min* = him, that); Welsh *ond* = but (German *sondern*, our *and*); so, A. S. *and* = but, L. *autem;* also Wel. *pe*, *ped* = if, is L. *sed*, our *but*, as well as *what* (*pe* = what).

209. *Even, ever*: *even* is same as *ever*, *like*, *as*, equal (*v* = *q*) Cor. *avel*, C-B. *evel*, as, like, equal, even-as, level; Cor. *kepar* =

as, like, and *kettep* = every (Cornish relative *nep*, also, = any, every; also relative *kemmys*, Latin *quantus*).

210. *Ever* (every), Germ. *immer*, Du. *immers*, L. *s-emper* and *imo*; L. *ibi*, *ubi* (*ebber*), *ubi-que* (where-as) = everywhere, and *ubi-ubi* = wher-ever; Mod. Greek *pote* = ever (relative); Latin *un-quam* (two pron's) = ever, and *nun-quam* = never (two pron's), L. *ævum*, G'k *aiōn*, ever, age; G'k *pãs*, all, every, is a relative like *pos'*, hence *pantes-'osoi*, all-such, all-who (who-who); Germ. *je* (the) = ever; Cor. *avar* = early—ever, eer, ere, early; Germ. *sehr*, very, ever, Per. *har*, old Germ. *sar*, Tart. *gar*, old German *war*, Latin *vere*, German *wahr*, true.

211. *If*: It. *ove* (where, L. *ubi*, *ibi*), Germ. *ob* (whether, or), Germ. *wenn* (when), all show how *if*, Goth. *iba*, Ang. Sax. *gif*, old Germ. *of*, *ob*, *jof*, are relatives in origin; Lat. *si* = if (the, this, Latin *is*), Sanscrit *chet*, Greek *ei*, Gothic *ith* (Lat. *ut*) and *thau*; Gothic *gau*, *g-abai* (Greek *kai*) = if, Latin *s-ive* (that-which) = whether, if; Welsh *o*, *os*, *od* (Latin *si*, and *ut*) = if, also *pe*, *ped* = if (but *pa* = what); in Russ., *esli* is *if*, German *als*, *else*, Russian *li*; in Russian, *bude* equals *if* and *be*—we find the same form used for *if* and *be* in many languages; thus, we say *be this so*, for if this is so—so, Fr. *soit* = may it be, or be it, is used also for *either*, *or*, *whether*, *as*, indirectly *if*. (It only shows, among other things, that *be* is pronominal also).

212. *Or*: Fr. *ou* is *or* and *where*; It. *ovvero* is or, and *ove* is where; Germ. *oder* is or (other), L. *vel*, *ve* = or, Germ. *welcher*); the Greek *ē*, *ē-pou*, or, are also relatives; Icel. *eda*, *edur*, (either), and *ella* (else) = or; A. S. *aegther* and *outher*, or, A. S. *hwae-ther*, either, Go. *aith-thau*, L. *aut* (*alter*, other), or, old Germ. *eftha*, or, *aut* (after = other, or), also Go. *other* = or; see what compounds we find—who-else, else-where, A. S. *elleshva* (Lat. *aliquis*); Germ. *et-was*, *et-lich* (*et*, what); old Germ. *aegh-wider* (either-whether)—and, remember that words with which we find *else* = or, either, associated, are like it; Cor. *py* is or, but *py* is also a relative.

213. *Nor* is a form of *or*; it is *or* with *n* prefixed; in Latin, *nc-que* (*nec*) = nor (not-which), i. e. it is a form of *que*, which; in Germ., *noch* = *doch*, yet, now, is used for *nor*—Germ. *weder* (whether and neither) also = nor; it is plain that *nor* is a form of *neither* = either; in Welsh *na* is nor and than, words which are alike—the vulgar say, better *nor* that (Swed. *end* (and) = than); so, in Greek, *ē* (which, that, as) = *or* and *than*—as we hear, better *as* that

214. *Not*, in the form in which we have it, is identical with *neither*, though generally it is an ordinary demonstrative; as, the G'k *mē* (*men*, but), L. *ne*; L. *nun* is now, and *non* is not, so our *now* is like *not*; Ang. S. *ne*, *noht* and *nocht* (Germ. *noch* is

yet) = not; Gothic *nithau* (neither) = not, Germ. *nicht;* in old German, *els* (else, German *als,* as) and *nalles* mean not—*nalles* develops, with us, into *none-less, not-else ;* the Greek has a form *ouk* (*ou,* or), Icel. *ecke,* Danish *ikke,* for *not;* and Danish *ingen* (any) means *none,* Germ. *kein* (Goth. *gains,* Greek *e-keinos*)— German *einigen,* Greek *enioi* (some), Danish *ingen.*

215. *Soon:* Du. *haast* is *soon* (haste); Germ *bald* (bold) is *quick, short, soon* (Icel. *ballr*); old Germ. *san* and *sane,* Goth. *suns,* mean *soon, quick* (then, than)—it is often found as suffix, as *hera-sun,* here-soon; Celt. B. *kent* (Lat. *tant*) is *sooner,* Cor. *whare* is *soon* (where)—*soon* is, like the rest, clearly pronominal. *Rather,* though connected with *soon,* seems more immediately identified with *ready.*

216. *Often:* this word is connected first, in form, with *after;* it is the Ital. *s-ovente,* Fr. *souvent,* Lat. *sæpe;* old Germ. *thicco* (our *thick*) means *often,* so in Dutch, *dik-wils* (thick-whiles) is *often.*

217. Our *only,* in form, is *one,* but in other languages, it is more clearly pronominal; so, in Lat., *tantum* (so-much)is *only ;* so, Russian *tolko* (Latin *talis*), German *nur* (Latin *nun*), Gothic *that-ainei* (that-one).

218. *Since* is connected, in form, most intimately with *soon* and *then,* and is clearly pronominal; in Lat., and in many other languages, it takes the form of *as* and *when* (a relative); A. S. *sith-than,* since, Germ. *seit-dem* (since-then)—A. S. *sith,* means *late;* L. *post-quam* (after-which), It. *poi-che,* Fr. *puis-que* and *de-puis,* It. *do-po,* L. *post-ea* (after those); G'k *epi, epei* (after) = since—so that *since,* here, is a form of *post,* after, which is a relative like Greek *pōs, pote,* meaning *when.*

219. *Yet:* Germ. *noch* means *yet* and *nor;* Du. *nochte* means *neither ;* thus, we see *yet* = *nor;* It. *an-che,* Fr. *ain-si* (German *au-ch* and *no-ch*), this-that, yet, Germ. *jedoch;* L. *tamen* (so), G'k *toi,* our *though, tho',* Germ. *doch,* Lat. *quam-quam* (which-which) = al-though, G'k *kan* for *kai-an* (and-if). (Such words as *kan,* which we may properly consider as the union of *kai-an,* but which is still equal to our Latin *quom,* prove what we have claimed, that two words coming together, as *and-if,* are really elements of one compound); Ital. has *pur* = yet, even, German *a-ber* = but old Germ. *a-fur, a-bur;* Welsh *eto* is yet (Latin *et,* Germ. *doch*); Goth. *thauh-gaba* is *yet* (that-if), old Germ. *thoh-thoh* (tho-tho, that-that), and *tho-widar* (tho-whether).

220. *Though* has the form *chotia* (It. *che*), Germ. *s-chon,* It. *gia,* Latin *tam* (then, German *denn*), Cornish *ken* (Corn. *ytho* (tho) is *now, then*); Welsh *er* is *tho,* and *yr* is *the.*

Till: this is identical with our *to, too, two* (so); German *bis* is *till, to,* and L. *bis* is *twice,* C-B. *beta ;* Go. *unte,* our *unto* and *until* (Germ. *und*, and, as, so)—again, we see that what we call two words, as *un-to*, corresponds with our *and*, which we now see has its elements too—witness also *u-t*, that, Greek '*o-ti* (which-that), our *what;* in L., *till* is *ad* (to) and *ante* (ad, and, as), also *us-que* (so-that, *ut-que*), *ante-quam* (to-which), *do-nec*, *d-um*, *quo-ad*, and *prius-quam* (fore-that), Gr'k '*ōs* (as, so) and '*eōs* (what, that). *Still* is *till* with *s* prefixed; Lat. *clam* is our *calm*.

221. *Together* has the forms: Germ. *zusammen*, It. *in-sieme*, Ang. Saxon *aetgaedere* (at-gather)—all identical with *the-same* (Lat. *simul*), to-same; in *together*, *to* is of course prep., and *ge* is a common prefix; and *ther* is the pronominal part, with which *same* often identifies; Greek '*omou* (same), Persian *hem*.

Prepositions.

222. We can identify prepositions with pronouns as easily as we have adverbs, indeed, the line between prep's and adv'bs is by no means strongly drawn, the one being often used to perform the office of the other. Prepositions are a growth out of pronouns, and, through pronouns, a growth out of the endings of nouns and verbs also. The case endings, it will be remembered, represent not the prepositions only, but the preposition and the article, or the preposition and demonstratives, which are articles. But pronouns are all clearly developments of the endings of nouns and verbs, proof of which is found in the fact, among others, that in almost, if not all, languages, they are found in some of their forms, inseparably connected with nouns or verbs, or both. In many languages, in the Semitic and Celtic, for example, the preposition and the pronoun, and article, readily unite into one word, as German *beim* for *bei dem*, which proves the intimate connexion of the two classes. It is well known, too, that a large class of prefixes to verbs, in the various languages of the world, are unmistakably prepositions—some of these have been thrown off, as the *ab* of the L. *ab-stract*, while others exist only in the inseparable state.

223. We find so many of our prepositions identify themselves with each other, after we proceed a short distance in tracing their origin, that it is almost impossible to make any just division among them; we will use, however, a few leading prepositions as heads, under which, with very little regard to order, we will include all the most interesting and instructive forms of prepositions. Nor do we confine ourself solely to prepositions, but we notice, incidentally, the origin of certain other words which come in the connexion, thereby showing what remarkable vari-

ations some words have, and what unexpected applications they are found in.

224. *With:* We find the following forms; Germ. *mit*, G'k *meta* and *meth*, Sem. *min*=in, Dan. *mod* and *i-mod*, meaning against, Germ. *wider*, and Go. *withra*, against (whither), A. S. *to-weard*, (toward) and L. *versus*, against, A. S. with, against, Sw. *vid*, by (L. *quid*=what), Corn. *worth*, meaning to and against, Hung. *vel* (l=d, Germ. *welcher*) and *ve*, Russ. *bez* and Pers. *bi*, for without; it has its forms in *middle, medium, mean* (Per. *miyan* and *der-miyan*, amidst, between), *com-mon* (*com* is prefix)=mean, Germ. *ge-mein*, low, a-mong, San. *madya*, Zend. *mat;* there is another class of forms, as the G'k *sun, sum* (s=w), Lith. *su*, Russ. *so* and *su*, San. *sa* and *sam*, Pers. *ham*, L. *cum* (*quum*), with and when, Lat. *con, co* (c=s), Welsh *can* (and *gan*)=as and with, Fr. *chez*, at and with (Italian *che* equals when), our a-gainst, Germ. *ge-gen* (*gen* is rel. like Celt. *can*, Pers. *chun*, how and as)—L. *contra*, G'k *ka-ta*; as *without* is only one of the forms of *with*, the following connect with *sun, con;* as, Fr. *sans* (and *dans*, in and with), G'k *aneu*, Russ. *vnya*, Germ. *ohne*, Go. *inu*, old Germ. *ana, aane*, and *ano* (in, on), Germ. *sondern* meaning but, L. *sed* (with equals but).

225. The branch headed by *sun* has very extensive connexions outside of the list of prepositions; our *same* is identical with San. *sam*, with, Pers. *ham*, our *sim-ilar*, G'k *'ama* = German *zu-sammen*, L. *idem* (= with), .to-gether (geth equals with); from the sense of *with* and *together*, taken with the etymology, we connect L. *omnis* equal to all, Illyr. *vas, sva*, Lith. *wissas*, Boh. *wsse* (with) = all, whole, full, G'k *'olos*, Oskish *sollos*, our sole, solid; San. *sarva* is every, whole, Latin *salvus* (l=r), our safe, sound, Per. *har*, Germ. *jeder*, Germ. *ganz*=all (*g*=c, s), our even—all these point to San. *sa* (ha)=with; (in Lat., we found *qui*=any, all, and, and *que*=al-so (both relatives); so, now, we find *with*, related to *qui*, also connected with words denoting *all, whole, safe;* there is also L. *semi* and *hemi*= half, which point to San. *sam* (halves are equals, same)—and many other cases which we cannot notice here.

226. *With*, as we hinted above, is connected with *betwixt* (G'k *meta-xu*) and *between*, being identical with midst, t-wixt, L. *inter* (a form of *in*)=between, and German *unter* (a form of *inter*)=be-neath and amid, and German *hinter* (a form of *inter*, inner)=behind and down, under; we have the connexions *with-out* and *with-in*, and in A. Sax., *with-aeften* equals behind, after, and *withforan* equals be-fore, and hence *with* equals out, in, after, fore, since it unites with these words.

227. *Out:* Germ. *aus, ausser* (out-er), Per. *az*=of, Lith. *uz*, Lett. *is*, G'k *cis* for in, Go. *ut* (L. *ut*=that), Per. *ex*, Lat. *e* and

ex, our of, off (we say *out-of*),San. *ut*, old German *af* and *aue ;* this preposition is plainly the same as *to, so, that,* the letters being transposed.

228. *Up* and *under :* San. *upar* and *upa*, G'k '*upo* and '*uper* meaning under and a-bove, Lat. *super* and *subter* meaning over and under, San. *upari*, our upper (outer), Germ. *über*, Fr. *sur*, Cor. *war ;* Per. *bar* (*u-par*) is on, and upon ; L. *supra* is above and up-on ; old German *u-bar* (German *aber* for but, bout) and *uffa, upha* for ab-ove, ab-out ; A. S. *bufan* (butan, but)=*super* and a-bove, o-ver (*aber*, other, *oder*) ; A. Sax. *up* and *uppan*= *super, de-super ;* Gr'k *peran* meaning above and beyond ; Gr'k *para*, our *from ;* G'k *peri*, our *for ;* Dan. *paa* is up-on ; Russ. *po* means a-bout, a-fter (L. *post*) ; Illyr. *pak*, our back ; Germ. *auf* is up, on, of and off ; Greek *apo* and *epi*=of, up, and on ; Alb. *mpi* (Latin *ambi*, Germ. *um-bei*), and *per*=*su-per ;* Alb. *a-pher* (after), by; Ital. *fra* (from) equals *in-fra, in-ter, in-tra,* our by; Cornish *dre* (un-der), through (Latin *trans*), and *a-dre* meaning around, Celtic Breton *tro*, French *tour*, our thro'.

229. There is no end to the connexions of such words. The student will particularly notice here, what he will observe in every branch of language, that, from the full form Lat. *su-per*, for example, some languages use *per* and vary it as *ber, bar, ter ;* others use *uper*, upper, up, while the Fr. throw out the *p*, and have *sur ;* this shows that it is as true in words as it is with animals, that every part is complete in itself, and has the capacity, under certain conditions, observable chiefly in the lower orders of life, *of becoming itself a whole ;* and we observe, too, that a word may be divided, as to its elements, very differently; thus, *in-ter* (*in* and *ter, per, sur*) or *int-er* (*int*=and, *ad*); and ab-ove (over, of out), or a-bove (bout, but, by). So that we find representatives for parts of words, or for two words uniting together, in other simple (so considered) and complete words. These points, well kept in view, will enable the student to proceed much easier in tracing the lineage of words.

230. *By ;* G'k *e-pi*, Germ. *bei*, Lat. *ob* (over), Lith. *pi*, San. *abhi* and *api*, G'k *opiso* (=a-fter), our back, Gothic *bi*, in and around, A. S. *be*, in and to, Fr. *de*, L. *de*, *e* equals of (our to); A. S. *emb* (em), *em-be, ym-butan*, Gr'k *am-phi*, Lat. *amb* (and L. *am-bo* meaning both, as Germ. *bei-de* equals both ; *by* equals and, and both), Russ. *o-b, o, ob-o*, old Germ. *um-bi*, Welsh *am*, Irish *im-m*, Latin *circ-um*.

231. (We see by this *am-bi, um-bi*, the growth of a preposition by doubling, while the elements *am* and *by* are both used alone, with the sense of the full form *um-bi ;* and observe, too, those elements *um* and *bi* (*m-bi*) may themselves be conceived of, as made up of elements again like themselves ; Russ. *ob* is clearly

double, as much as *amb*, and even the *o* equal to *ob* has its parts, undistinguishable, as *o-o*. Such facts as these, in language, we find patent everywhere.) The L. *a-pud* meaning *at* and *with*, belongs with *epi*; *among* is to be classed with *ambi*; *to* and *at* are other forms of *by*, *pi* (p=t), as they are also of *the*, *that*.

232. *For:* the connexions of this particle are very extensive; the identity of orthography proves its relation with the following: *fore*, *be-fore*, *former*, *forth*, *ere* (fore), *early*, Latin *prius*, *first*, Germ. *früh*=*early* and *fore*, San. *puras*, G'k *prin*, Lith. *pirm* (all denoting *fore*, *first*, and marked by *fr*, *pr*, *er*); *far* and *from* (Go. *fruma* for first, Germ. *erst*), *further* (Germ. *vorder*, fore)—our word *prince*, Germ. *fürst*, belongs with *for*, *fore* (a fore-man); there is the German *frau*, *froh*, *fromm*, and our *force*, *frost*, *fresh*, and very many others which we might name, also connected with *fore*, *first*, *for*.

233. These are the variations *for* undergoes: Gr'k *pro*, *pros* and *proti* (=for), Latin *præ* meaning for, and before, Rus. *pra* and *pred* (=before), Rus. *pro* for of, and about, and *pre* for beyond, and *pri* for near; Go. *faura* and *faurth*, L. *præter* for before, and above, Fr. *pour*, Fr. *proche* for near, L. *prope*, Rus. *protiv*, against, Illyr. *pored*, near, and *potlam*, after, Welsh *ger* meaning near, and *er*, for, and *er-byn*, against, Corn. *rag*, (gar) equal to for, and from, and *a-rak*, before, Cornish *re* (*rag* and *er*), by.

234. *Of* and *off*; *of* (ov) is thus connected: L. *ab*, and, L. *e* and *ex* (=*from* and *of*), G'k *apo* and *aph* (off), San. *apa* for off, away, and far, our *afar*, San. *ava*, away, off, Goth. *af*, Pers. *az*, Rus. *ov*, *ot*, and *o*= of, against, and from, Illyr. *od* and *oda* (our *to*), and *van* (German *von*, of, from)=outer, extra, (the Hebrew *min* meaning from, is to be compared with the German *von*, of); The Germ. *v-on*, of, shows the *on* equal of; Welsh *o* and *odd* (same as *a* and *ay*, with) equal of, and from—it is *a*, meaning *of*, in C-B.; *e*, which in L. equals of, from, in C-B., is seen with the forms *enn*, *el*, *er*, for in, Fr. *d-ans*. If we bear in mind the G'k *apo*, we shall easily connect *after* and its family with *of*. In Alb., *nte* and *mpe* (into) is in, and of, and *mpi* is by; in Fr. and L., *de* is of (to); in Wal., *de* and *dela* (*la*=the); in Hung., it is *tol*, while *nel* (*t*=n) is by; old Germ. *ir* (*is*, *aus*, *out*) means of, from; Slavic *iz* (*aus*) means out, Latin *ex*, of.

235. *To*, *at*, *in*, and *on*: *to* equal to *at*, shows easily how the letters of a word transpose; Lat. *ad*, Wal. *la* (*l*=*d*)—showing *to* equal *the*; Sem. *l* and *d*, Fr. *a* and *de* (*at* and *to*), Germ. *zu*, Rus. *do* and *za*, Gaelic *do*, Goth. *and* is in, and *und* is to, till; A. S. *oth*, old Germ. *ant* (at), at, and *ana*, an, in (hence in-to); also *nah* (*ana*) means *to* and *from*, and *v-an*, *f-ona* (Germ. *von* —*on* with *v*) is used for *from* and *of*; Lat. *ante*, French *avant*

(on-to, in-to) meaning before, is a form of *at, ad, and;* so is L. *apud,* with, and G'k *ana,* on. The pronominal nature of these four particles is very evident.

236. *Through* and *across: through* is thus represented: Lat. *trans* for over, across and beyond, Gaelic *thar* and *trid,* Welsh *tros* for over, Sans. *tiras,* Russian *cherez,* Illyrian *srez* ($s = ch$), *sez, kroz* (cross), all meaning through (cross is *tros, trans*), old Germ. *thurg, thuru* (thorough), Germ. *durch,* A. S. *thurh,* Goth. *thairh,* Per. *dar,* in, G'k *dia,* L. *per* ($p = t$), G'k *peri* for about, above, around, beyond, and hence over and across, through; Polish *przez* equals through ($p = t$) and *przy* equals by, *procz* equals out, outer; and for outer, out, out of, we find Pol. *krom* and *o-krom* (a-cross), *krom* for *trom* ($k = t$); the *cr* of *cross* is the *tr* of *trans,* and the *pr* of *per;* so, too, it is the *vr, pr,* of o-ver, *su-per,* the *ar* of around (*ard, dar*), Germ *herum* (Polish *krom*). (Door and all its class connect with *through,* German *durch.*)

237. We may, as well here as elsewhere, state definitely, what we have before only touched upon, viz., the following law: Every case-form, tense-form, person-form, or form of any kind, is just as much a proper representative of the word, as that which we call the word itself, and which, as *amo* or *ama,* we erroneously conceive to be the *root,* the *base,* the *original.* Every abbreviation of a word is one of its forms, every combination of it with some other element is also a form of the same. And all this arises from the fact that one form may be more condensed or more developed than another; to illustrate, *amabant* (past tense) is one of the forms of *amo,* (it is *amo* in one of its developments, not *amo* of the present, but that imaginary thing which we call the verb *amo,* that thing which is made manifest by its forms); *whom* is a form of *who, lovest* is a form of *love, loving* is another form; *before* is a form of *fore, attract* is a form of *tract, pretend* is one of the phases of *tend.*

238. It is only by remembering this law, that we shall understand how it occurs, that what we find used in one case, in one number, or in one tense, is found, in another language, in another case, number, tense, or application; as, what we have for *these,* the Germans have for *this* (*dies-er, dees*).

239. We may remark, farther, that verbs are named from the 1st person, sing. prest., but there is no reason why the verb should not be named as well from any other person, or tense, or mood—so the verb *amo* we might call *amare* (inf.), or *amabat;* and so the noun may be called from any of its case or number forms, as well as by its usual name, the nominative. The verb or noun itself is an imaginary thing, and is only represented by the forms, called words, from which it is itself distinct, as the

soul is from the body. So *amo* is as much one of the forms of what we call the verb *amo* (but which might be called *amare* as well) as *amat* or *amavi* is. We discard the idea of any form, or word, being the root or original of a class — we may use the term for convenience, but it can never stand testing. Where are the root or base-forms of the human race?

CHAPTER VII.

HISTORY OF NUMERALS.

240. That at least three of the numerals, the first three, are pronouns, is beyond all doubt. In almost all languages, the numeral *one* is used as an article, or as a sort of demonstrative pronoun — it belongs to the family of our *a, an, any, none, some*. We have seen under the head of pronouns, that *an* is demonstrative as well as *the*. The Fr. *on*, German *man* (Russ. *on*, he, *oni*, they, Sw. *han*, he), is used as we employ *ðhe*, in *one asks, one says*, and as *they*, in *they ask, they say*. In Dan., we find *eet* (it) as well as *een*, for one. The Germ. *man*, one, the Gr'k *monos*, al-one, only, and *mia*, one, shows *many* = *one*.

241. The related forms of *one* differ from it very materially in form. Even its own adjective *first*, Germ. *erst*, Gr'k *protos*, L. *primus*, Rus. *pervi*, is apparently far removed from it; but, that these superlative forms are in the end identical with *one*, is seen by the Turkish *bir*, one, and Per. *bar*, once. The Lat. *semel*, is once, our simple, single, similar (same, even), L. *semi, demi* (half), (middle, with, G'k *sun*), sole. Our each, Per. *ek* or *yek*, one, Gr'k '*apax*, once ($p = k$,) and Gr'k *eka-teros*, each (San. *eka*, one), is another form of *one* — *either, whether*, Lith. *katras*, San. *kataras*, G'k *poteros*, is also a remote form (G'k *elk* (from, apart, alone) is *eka*, each, one (al-one), Latin *ex*).

242. We will now dwell briefly on some additional forms of *one* as they appear in different languages. Thus, in Slavic, we find such forms as, *jeden, eden, gheden*; this *d* does not appear in our *one*, L. *un-us*, Gr'k *hen*, but it is clearly the *r* of *protos*, first — strike out this *d*, and *eden* becomes *een*, one; other Slavic forms are *ains, weens, wienas*, our one. The Semitic has *echad* or *ehad* (San. *eka*, Slav. *gheden*), also *had, and, ante* — the Per. class, besides *jek, yek*, has also *ju, yuo*. The Finnish class has *egy* (*eka*), *aku, akt, ogy* = *ot, it* (Danish *cet*), *wait* (*w-one*), *ykss* and *odyk* (Slav. *eden*, d = k). Old Germ. has *cyn* for *egen, een*

(G'k *'eis*), Alb. *gna* equal to *una*—so, we see we have suppressed the *g, k, d, y, t*, which appears in other languages, or we have only *n* to represent it.

243. *Two*: The identity existing between some of the forms of *one* and *two*, is easy to be observed; thus, the Turk. *bir*, our *first*, is the Latin *bis*, twice, and the *either*, *each*, and *whether*, which we have just connected with *one*, are also connected with *other* = *second*, *two*; so, too, the *k* and *d* marks of *one*, seen in so many languages, are not different from the *t* and *d* of *two*.

244. The numeral *two* is plainly identical with the demonstrative element *ta*, Gr'k *to*, our *the*, as well as with the adverb *too*, prep. *to*. In Latin, *alter*, other, is often used for *second*—in short, it is a prevailing feature in language, to find *other* equal to *second*. We can easily connect our *two* with L. *bis* (bs, bt), by taking *tw* equal to *tb*, reversed *bt, bs*.

245. We will now give some of the forms of *two*. In Germ. class, we have *twei, zwa, zween* (*een, ein, eins*, one), *zuene, tu, tov*, and *bais* (Gr'k *beta*, L. *bis*). In Slavic, *two* is *dva, doua, du, diwe*; Sem. *dou, ith, aeth* (leaving off some of the endings) —there is also *chl, quil, kill, haul*, and *ter* (less the endings of the plural), where *chl, ql, kl*, and *hl* identify with *kl, tl, tr*, and point to our *three*, Lat. *tres* (See the forms of Sem. *three*). The Heb. form for *two* is *sena-im* (*aim, im*, is plural ending); this reminds us of the Malay forms for one, *sa, sat, sar, isa, do, taha, tika*. Of the Tartar languages, those which have *emu, omin*, for one, have also *djuo, djur, dsur, chojur* (*chj* = *dj*), for two— and those which have *bir* equal to *one*, have *iki, oke* (*k* = *t*), for two. In Finn., two is *kak, kyk, kit, kwekt* (*k* = *t, w*), in Malay, *lor, kal, dua, row, nou* (*l, d, k, r*, and *n* = *t*, and *tw, du*) — *lr* = *tr*.

246. *Three*: That *three* is not essentially different from *two*, must be evident on the slightest reflection—they are as nearly identical as *this* and *that*, or as *here* and *there, here* and *the;* Germ. *der*, the, three.

In the Gr'k, Slav., Germ., Celt., and Lat. class of languages, *tr* is the prevailing mark for *three*. In Sem., it is *sel, tel, toul, tl, se* (all = *tr, tl*); in Malay, we have this same *tal, tel*, but also *tig-a, tor-ho*; Finnish *kol', kor'* (*k* = *t*), also *kwiu, kuim, kolm*, like our *two* (*k* = *t*); in Tart., it is *il'* (Sem. *t-el*), also *gur* (*g* = *d, t*)—and for such dialects as have *bir* for one, we find *utsch, uss, wisse*, for three (this we may divide thus, *ut-sch*).

247. *Four*: The variations which the number *four* exhibits, in the different languages, are these:

Tartar; *duin, digin, dort, dorb'*.
Sem.; *arb', har', ub', arr'* (*arb* = *bar*, f-our).
Slav.; *chetyr, seter, chtir', zetter* (*ch* = *z*).
Per.; *tchetr, djahar, zippar* = *zittar, tsulor* (*l* = *d, t*).

Finn.; *nel', negy, njul.*
Malay; *papat, ampat, pat, opat, wutu, haa, ra, fa, efar, hpat, wati* ($w=p$).
Gr'k; *kattr, tessar, pessar, catre, quatr, bator* ($b=q, f$).
Germ.; *fiar', vier, fidwor, feower* ($dw=w, u$).
Celt.; *ceithir, pedwar, pevar, peder* ($p=f$).

248. That all these forms can easily be connected, is a matter that does not admit of question; in Tartar., *du* equals *dg, dr*, which is the *tr, ter* of G'k and Slav. four; the Slav. *chetyr*, L. *quatuor*, our *quarter* (fourth), Greek *kattr*, *catre, quatr*, Persian *tchetr, djahar*, have all developed an internal *t* which does not appear in our *four*, but which does appear in the German form *fidwor*, and in the Celtic *pedwar* for *pevar* ($=fevar$, *feower, four*)—those letters *t, k, q, c, tch, dj, b*, are all equals of our *f=p*. In Finn., *nel, neg, njl* equal *nr, wr, fr*. In Malay, we see how forms reduce; thus, *papat, opat, efat, pat, wat, fa, haa, ra*; these easily go with *peder, pessar, four*.

249. That this numeral might, as a matter of etymology, be identified with any one of the three which precede it, is something quite evident. The Tartar points clearly, in its *duin*, to the L. *duo* and its own *djuo*, two; the Finn. *negy* points to the San. *eka* and its own *egy, aku*, one, while the *tr, dr*, prevailing in the Slavic, Greek, and German classes, indicates *tres*, three. There is indeed little question, that the different numerals are all allied, and are merely the different application and development of one element. But about the precise history of this *four* further than this, there is nothing demonstrable—though something may be said as probable.

250. It has been supposed by some, that *four*, in such forms as Celt. *peder*, Gr'k *pessar*, Slavic *chetyr*, our quarter, is a compound of *one* and *three*, the *pe, qua, ch*, representing *eka*, one, and *ter*, three, yet we cannot say that we have found any evidence sustaining this theory. The resemblance between *four*, in its different forms, in the course of languages, and *two*, is greater than that between *four* and any other numeral. The strongest evidence in this direction, is found in the Tartar class, already noticed, and in the Caucasian class which we may notice here; thus, we find, there, the forms *di* and *tchor* equal to four, and *tu, schi, jer* ($=cher$) equal to two. Besides, the *ch, t*, and *p*, so common as the initial element of *four* in the European languages, also points to the *two*, as does the *dw* of *fidwor*.

251. It is supposed, again, but without any positive proof that we know of, that *four* is a compound $= 2 \times 2$, or the 2d two. We can only take this proposition as nearly certain, that four stands in a closer relation with two than with any other numeral, in a word, that two is the element, or fundamental element, of four;

taking etymology alone for evidence. There is no history on this point. There is, besides this, another theory, of which we can only say that it presents what is barely possible, that *four* equals one from five, on the Rom. system of notation, IV ; *four* and *five*, it must be said, often resemble each other in form.

252. There is some evidence to show that four has at times been treated as the base of the number system, being designated by a word signifying *whole, all, end*. Taking this as true, and remembering that *four* is probably a form of *two*, we should be finally brought to the conclusion that two is the base of the numerical system. In our opinion, two is the beginning and the end of all numbering—beyond *this* and *that*, *here* and *there*, we have no numbers—all must come under the category of one or the other. To number is to compare, but we can compare only two things, or one with one.

253. *Five :* There seems to be not so much doubt about the number *five*. It is a fact not to be questioned, that numeration, in the earlier stages of society, was carried on with reference to the fingers; and we still find the child involuntarily resorting to the fingers in his first lessons in counting and calculation. It seems to be well established, that there are tribes who in their system not only count in the fingers of both hands, but after this count also their toes.—for instance, some of the Am. Indians. The Greenlanders can count with their numbers only to five, one hand, and when they go beyond that they must repeat, as we do when we get beyond ten—thus, six is *one-on-2d-hand*, eight is *on-2nd-hand-three*. After ten, the toes of both feet are counted also; thus, for 13 they have *on first foot three*. When they have twenty, they have, in their terms, "a whole man", and to get beyond twenty, they must use a 2d man.

254. In several languages, is easily discernible the identity between the term for *five* and that for *hand;* thus, Per. *panchan* means *five* and *pentsha* means *hand*, and there are several instances of the like in the Malay class of languages. In some of the African tongues, not only is *hand* equal to *five*, but seven is expressed by *hand and two*, and *fifteen* by three hands. Alex. Humboldt tells of American tribes where four is used as such a base, six being *four with two*, and eight being *five with three*.

255. Some of the forms of *five* are the following :
Tart. ; *tunj', ton', tub'* ($t = $ G'k *p*); many of the Tart. tongues have *bash, besch,* equal to five, but this is precisely the word for *head*, while *hand* is *kal, gal, gar.*
Slav. ; *pett, pent, pink, piatt.* (G'k *pente*, L. *quinq'*, Germ. *fünf*).
Per. ; *pendj, pinz, lons* (in Ossete) ($l = p$).
Finn. ; *wiss, wjet, wit, uet, at, ot* ($w = p$, $at = p\text{-}at$, $p\text{-}ent$).
Malay ; *lima, rima, dimi* ($l = f, p$)—*lima, rima = hand.*

Gr'k; *pes, pend, quing, sing, cinq*—p, q, s=f of *five*.

We notice in many instances, that *hand* and *foot* agree in form; notice in Gr'k also *pes, pend* equals five, and *pes, pod*=foot.

Germ.; *fünf, fyf, fimm, five*; Celt. *cuig, pemp* (c=q, p, f).
Sem.; *kham'* (p=k, kh), *ham', am'* (for *kam, pam, ham*).

256. *Six:* We can ascertain nothing decisive about the history of *six*. The Greek '*ex* is practically equal to *ex*, out of, beyond, over, and we notice something of this coincidence in some of the Tartar languages; moreover, *ex=eks* may be identified with the *eka*, one, and we might thus take *six* as one after or over (taking 5 as the basis or end), i. e. 5 and one more, or one in the 2d hand, or series. There are many instances of a coincidence between six and one, also between six and two=one; notice also L. *sex=seks, sequor, secutus, secutive* (the one after or following). Some, again, have supposed six to be 2×3; two threes.

257. We may notice these forms:

Tart.; *ning', njun', dsurg', surg* (*ng, nj*=*dj, ds*, s of *six*)'; many Tart. tongues have *alt, alty* (*alt=at, as, sa*, six).
Slav.; *chest, se, sest* (ch=s).
Sem.; *sis', seth', schash, sedest, soas, sita* (six).
Pers.; *shess, shesch', achs', spuz* (*sp=sh, s*).
Finn.; *kuss, kot, kud, kwet, kut* (*k=s*).
Malay; *sad, daou, anom, ono, nel, ol, houn, elen—nam, anam*, appears in many of the Malay tongues; it resembles the Tartar *six* and our *nine*.
G'k; *giast* (*gi=si*), *ex, hex, sex, fiess* (*f=s*), *sie, seje, cheie*.
Germ.; *sex, sechs, segs, zies, sess, seks, saihs, six*.

The Tart. *alty* is connected with our *all, whole, heap*.

258. *Seven:* There is often a remarkable coincidence between *six* and *seven*; we even see it in the Lat. *sex* (6) and *sept'* (7)—but this is perhaps the very coincidence of *one* and *two, this* and *that, a* and *the*. It is quite possible, even probable, that six and seven are 1+5, 2+5, just as 11=1+10, 12=2+10; in one case 5 being the base, and in the other 10. We know the Roman numerals are made after that manner, as VI and VII. The forms of seven are these:

Tart.; *nad, dol, jedi, edi, sett* (n, d, j=s).
Slav.; *sedm, sem, sept*.
Sem.; *sib', tab', sub', 'aft*.
Pers.; *hapt, heft, 'aaft, 'awd, 'owu* (*aaft=saft, sept*).
Finn.; *kjet', ssis, ssat, het, la-but, la-ssat, ja-get*.
Malay; *pit', tudj, het, fil, it, fit, pitt*, (see *s-ept*).
Gr'k; *state, hept, sept, set, siet, cheapt* (*set=*Malay *fit*).
Germ.; *sebn, sibn, simm, sojn, san, sio, sov* (sev-en).

Celt.; *seachd, saith, seih.*
All these forms are easily identified.

259. *Eight:* This is another number about whose history there is much that is doubtful. It has been maintained that with 8 and 9 we enter upon a subtracting method of notation, that 8 is two from 10, and 9 one from 10. Considering the great resemblance, often found, between the forms for eight and two, and between nine and one, the proposition is plausible. Indeed in the Rom. method, 9 is IX, one from ten. It is, we think, more probable, however, that the system applies to the *nine* than to *eight*, as we find the fact in Roman.

260. It has been claimed, again, that *eight* is two *fours*, as we imagined *four* to be two *twos*, and, considering the oft recurring coincidence of *eight* with *two* and *septem* (which we believe to be accented on *two*, with *five* for a base), we regard this theory as the most probable. In Tartar and Finn., we find *eight* pointing most undoubtedly to *two*.

261. Here follow the different forms of eight:
Tart.; *djak, djapk, naim' (nm = dp), ssek, ss-egis (dk, sk=st).*
Slav.; *osm, ossam, vossom, aszt, akt' (sm=st, ct).*
Sem.; *semoun, tem-on, sem-ent (snn=stn, st).*
Pers.; *hasht, hasch, ast, utu* (eight, ate, oct).
Finn.; *kadekssan, kattesa, kykamyss, nilonou, nuul, nillach, niglach (kdk, ktt=oct, ott, Slav. akt, kyk=nul).*
Malay; *wolu, balu, qual, arrou, afa, de-lapan, salapan (wl, bl, gl=wr, ar; af=akt, oct).*
Greek; *tete, okto, oict, uit, vot, ott, vuit, huit, opt.*
Germ.; *acto, acht, ahtan, atta, eight.*
Celt.; *ochd, wyth, ciz, eith.*

Behold the variations that *pt, kt, tt, ct, ch, ck,* undergoes. In Mal., *lua, rua, dalua* equal two, and *papat, apat, ampat* equal four, hence *de-lapan* equals two *fours*.

262. *Nine:* very little is to be said of *nine*, save what was mentioned in treating of *eight.* In Tamil, *nine* is clearly *one from ten.* The initial of Malay *nine* agrees with *one;* the endings of all Finn. *nines* are like *ten.* It will be observed, also, that some forms of nines equal *novus*, new, and it has been claimed that those words have the same origin.

263. The following are the forms:
Tart.; *ujun, jegin, jissun, jessu, dokus (jeg=dok=nv).*
Slav.; *devett* (Tart. *dok, nov, n=d*).
Sem.; *tisch, tis, tasa, nouh, zet, tse (ts=ds, dv, nv).*
Pers.; *nouh, nah* (*n=*Slav. and Sem. *d, t*).
Finn.; *ydekssan, ygoksse, uttesa, ykmyss, ontolon.* Here we have *ydek=ygok, ykmy, utt, ont* (*=dev, nov, dok*).
Malay. *songo, nawa, siwa (s=n), sira, ea, tiwa (s=t, n).*

Gr'k; *nande, ennea, cnar, egnia, nou, nef, nov* ($nd = dn, dv$).
Germ.: *neun, onun, negen* ($ng = gn, dn$), *nio, ni* (*ein* = one).
Celt.; *naoidh, naw, nao* ($nd = dn, nw = wn, dn$).

We may notice here, without difficulty, great resemblance between some forms for *nine* and those for *one* and *ten*.

264. *Ten:* We will lastly give the forms for *ten;*
Tart.; *djan, men, arb, on.*
Slav.; *dessett, desymt, desmith, zassech.*
Sem.; *asro, gasrh, assir, ascher* ($asr = das$, *dec-em*).
Pers.; *desme, deh, des, lus* ($l = d$, $des = d\text{-}es$).
Malay; *dasa, pulu, rouru* ($rr = pl$), *seik.*
Gr'k; *djett, thiet, deka, dez, deu, de, des, dix, deci.*
Finn.; *kmn*, ($km = dm$), *das, lu, jon* ($j = d$).
Germ.; *tehan, zehn, tein, tigen, taihun, ti, ten.*
Celt.; *deich, deg.*

Behold the forms into which *dc, dg, dt, dk*, develops itself.

265. That the basis of *ten* is *two*, is evident enough — referring, without doubt, to two hands, or fives. It is even possible that *cem*, in L. *decem*, represents *five, quinq, cinq*. Ten, Greek *deka*, is no doubt, too, connected with *dexter*, the right, which again connects with *deiknumi* (Greek), to show, and with *digit*, finger or pointer, shower; *toe* belongs to the same family, as well as Germ. *zahl*, number, *tell, count, show*, say, in-dicate. Not only does *the right* agree with *ten*, but in some languages also *left* agrees with *five*.

We will notice briefly some of the numbers after ten.

266. The uniform practice in the different languages, is to go on, after ten, adding to ten, as 13 = three and ten (thirteen). This position is clear for all except *eleven* and *twelve*, which differ considerably in character, so far as appearance goes, from the other combinations. That the initial part of *twelve* might be *two* is possible, but the *lv* has little to do with *ten.*

267. The following forms will illustrate *eleven.*
Fries.; *andlova, alvene, elleva.*
A. S.; *endlufon.*
Icel.; *ellifu.*
Goth.; *ain-lif* (one left).
Fries.; twelve is *twiliva, tolva, tolef.*
Old Sax.; *twelif.*
Icel.; *tolf.*
Goth.; *tva-lif* (two left).

268. That this *lv, lf, lif*, represents our *leave, left*, Go. *leiban*, G'k *leipō*, admits of little doubt; so that 11 would be *one-left, one-over*, or *one-more;* and twelve equals *two-left, two-over*. The use of this *over*, or its equivalents, in numbering in this way, is common with us and elsewhere. In Wall., 11 is one over 10, or *one*

HISTORY OF NUMERALS. 71

and *ten*, as *unu-spre-dece* (this *spre* equals *supra*, *over*, *and*)—so, *twelve* is *two-over-ten*. In Lithuanian, 11 is *wieno-lika*, and 12 is *dwylika*—and with the same *lika* up to 20. This *like*, can, it is true, be identified with *deka*, *ten*, as *ten* is remotely connected, again, with *and*, *over*, *one*, but that *lika*, in Lith., represents directly *ten* or *deka*, does not seem probable. It seems preferable to refer it to *lif*, *lv*, which we have been considering, or to *super*, *over*, and besides to the *ly* of *only*, thirdly.

269. By the way, in French, 11 and 12 are reduced to *onze* and *douze*, not different from our *once* and *twice*—and even in our *eleven* and *twelve*, the *one* and *two*, being accented, prevail almost to the exclusion of the other element; this calls to mind, too, the form of some of those numbers which we have before been considering, simple in appearance, while in fact we know them to be compound (as *eight*)—the accented element prevailing to the exclusion of the other.

270. But we do not find such irregularity or ambiguity, in these numbers, in many other languages. Thus, in Persian, 11 is *yazdah*, 12 is *duwazdah* (*yak* = 1, *du* = 2, *dah* = 10). The *dah* is plain, and is found so in all the rest of the *teens*, but the *z*, which is found in no others, save 19, seems to be a third element equal to *az*, by, with, and. In Gael., we find *deaz* in all the teens and in 11 and 12, without connexion, as *aon-deaz*, *do-deaz*. This system prevails in Celtic. It is the one of L. and Greek, *un-decim*, *duo-decim*, *tre-decim*. The connective is not developed in the Latin languages generally, though we do find *y* = *and* in Spanish. In Polish, commencing with 11, the numbers are connected substantially as in Latin—the copulative is scarcely developed—though in Russ., we see it appearing in a strong light; as, *na* = on, over, and; thus, *odin-na-dzat*, one-and-ten, eleven.

271. The number *twelve* is often represented by *dozen* (same as San. *dasan* = *ten*)—*dozen* (Germ. *duzend*) is connected also with *thousand*, Germ. *tausend*. So that *thousand* is only a *ten*, and *hund* (-red) is not perhaps different. Gothic *tai-hun* is ten (2 fives?), our *teen*, *teh-en*—here we see the *hund*. It is easy to see that Fr. *douze* (12) is our *dozen*; Lat. *cent* (-um), *hund*, equals Fr. *cinq*, *five*; in some of the Tartar dialects, the same word is used for 3 and 100. Twenty is a developed *two* (Latin *viginti*, twenty, is not far from *quinque*, *five*).

272. In Goth., we find for 20, 30, 40, *tvai-tigus*, *thrija-tigus*, *fidvor-tigus*—*tigus* another form of *ten*. In Lat., for these they use *viginti* (*bi-ginti*), *tri-ginta*, *quadra-ginta*—the *ginti* here plainly representing *ten*, and yet agreeing in form more with *centum* (100), and with *five* (*quing*)—furnishing more proof of ten = *hund*, five (200 is *du-centi*). In Irish, the case is still

plainer, as 30 is *trio-cad*, and *cead* = 100 (*cead* also is *first*); in Cor., *i-ganz* = 20, and *cans* = 100. In San., *vin-sati* = 20, *sata'* = 100, and *pancha-sat* = 50.

273. In Celtic, by the way, we do not find the same regular system of twenty, thirty, forty, as we do in other European languages, but 30 is ten and twenty, 40 is two times twenty, 80 is 4×20, 50 is 10 and 40, 300 is 15×20. We notice in Pers., that these numbers have scarcely developed enough to render the latter element distinguishable; thus, 30 is *si* (and *sih* = 3), *shast* equals 60 and 6.

274. In Latin, besides the forms *decem et octo*, and *decem et novem*, there are also *duo-de-viginti* (2 from 20), *un-de-viginti*, for 18 and 19 — so the usual forms for 28 and 29 are *two-from-thirty*, *one-from-thirty*. This lends credibility to the position that 8, as well as 9, is made by subtracting one from 10, two from ten. In the teens of Mod. Greek, we find *dekatreis* (ten (and) three), but 11 and 12 are *en-deka*, *dō-deka*. In Alban., the connecting *mpe* = of, and, over, is developed, commencing with 11; as, *nie-mpe-dgiete* (11), *tre-mpe-dgiete* (13). We notice also in Alb., 20 is *nie-dzet*, 40 is *di-dzet*, while 10 is *dget* — so that they stand *one-ten*, *two-ten*, so far as form goes, making ten equal twenty, as it really is. The Greek *eikosi* (20) points the same way (*deka* = 10).

275. In some of the dialects of Samoid, we find that 8 is 2 from 10, and 9 is one from 10. It is claimed that in others, however, it is different, that 8 is 2×4. It is true in this case that *det*, the last element, is like *det* = *four*, but it is also not unlike (Jurak) *kot* and *bied* = *ten*. It is probable, we think, that 8 is formed in the Jurak dialect as in the Ostjak; in *nine*, the *ju* = *ten* is plain. In these dialects, 11 and 12 are formed just as 8 and 9, with only *over* in place of *from*. It is clear that these two sets of numbers are really the same on different sides of the zero mark. It is worthy of note also that in Jurak, 9 is called *Samoidish-ten*; by the way, we find the very same word used for 10 as for 9 — in other cases, 9 is called *Ostjak-ten*; twenty is called *two-tens*.

276. *Mille*, in Latin, is the same as our million in form, but is used for *thousand*. It may be remarked that many words denoting numbers, such as G'k *muroi*, *chilioi*, are simply indefinite terms, as our *heap*, *lot*, *host*, *multitude* — and even *five*, *hundred*, and *thousand*, may be proved to have connexion with such terms.

277. It is well known that in many languages, letters are used to indicate numbers. There is at least one language ("Rothwelche") where names of letters of the alphabet are used to denote numbers also. The first 9 letters of the G'k alphabet

denote units (counting in, for 6, an ancient letter not found at present), and the next 9 represent the tens (including an ancient one not used now, representing 90)—the last 9 being used for the hundreds (with an extra one for 900). In Hebrew, the first ten letters are used to denote the 10 numerals, units; 20, 30, etc., up to 100, are denoted by the next nine in order—the remaining four being used for 100, 200, 300, 400. The same in Syr. and Arm. There is evidently a close relationship between the names of letters and the names of numbers.

278. It is clear to any one who inquires into the nature of numbers, that they are only marks of order; so, we found the first two numbers denoting only *former* and *latter*, and that *three* was allied to them, and *four* to be the one before *five*, or the latter or second *two*; we found 8 and 9 to be either the 2d and 1st (latter and former) before *ten*, or the 8 to be the latter or second *four*; we found 11 and 12 to be the one or the two after *ten*—ten being the former or first, the basis. This is the secret of the system; *twenty* is only the latter or 2d *ten*, *thirty* the *ten* after 20, *forty* the latter or 2d twenty. So we find them proceed by steps, by comparisons. There can be no doubt hanging around this position. So much, at least, is certain about the nature of numbers; and it is by virtue of this system of order, that, in Semitic and European languages, the alphabet is used to denote numbers. We repeat it, *number is based on order; every number is a mere relative mark, or mark of relation.*

279. Twenty, for example, denotes only *one*, it is the latter or 2d *ten*—it is still only one thing, one *ten*—so, *ten* is the 2d fifth. Hence, we frequently hear it said, *he has reached his twentieth year* (=20 years). Observe that all ordinals, as 25th, point only to one thing, the 25th—the same must be true, too, of cardinals, as 25. It is on this principle that the German (and others) says *third-a-half* (the 3d one being a half), for the number 2½, showing that in numbering, regard is had alone for *the last thing* numbered.

280. The Arabic characters, or figures, can, without doubt, be identified in their forms with letters. Of these, we notice particularly that 2 and 3 resemble each other, while 7 and 8. have precisely the same character (v), only differently placed.

281. We notice in many languages, that the numerals are made to apply to things in the singular, and that where they do belong to the plural apparently, it is really to the genitive sing.; thus, 20 men is twenty of the quantity or class *men*. Every number, bear in mind, is a unit. Hence, too, a coefficient, a number or a name, never belongs to a thing, but to something of it, as 20 (heads of) men, as we say head of horses, 20 pieces of silver, for 20 silvers—5 is always 5 one, 5ab is 5 ones of the

ab kind. Every plural is a collective noun in the genitive case, it is the quantity, the denomination and the denominator. And as the denominator of a fraction never has reference to number, so it is with the plurals. We must repeat it, *no number is plural; all, many, every, each,* used with a plural application, are yet singular, and are properly followed by a genitive. It is certain that every nominative plural is a genitive, for it is the quantity. We can have no number, unless it be a number or quantity of something.

282. Six of a thing, or number, is the same as six from it, but every subtraction implies a remainder; hence, you never can take the whole of a thing, or from a thing, or, if you do, something must still be left. You have a heap of 12 apples, a pile, a quantity; you may take from the pile until the last one — when you come to the last, there will be no taking *from* or *of,* but simply a taking. Hence, there is no such thing as one of a thing or from it, if it be the last or the whole; *one* and *whole* equal *nothing*.

CHAPTER VIII.

HISTORY OF PARTICIPLES.

283. The participle, and under this head we will include all kinds of verbal nouns and verbal adjectives, may, with propriety, be taken as the basis of the verb, and as such its forms will first come under consideration. We will give a full comparative view of the participles of different languages, that the student may learn how they are marked, and may observe, also, the curious changes which is undergone by the final syllable which thus characterizes them.

284. We will commence with the participles and verbals of the German languages. The Swed. infinitive is *bind-a,* Danish *bind-e,* A. S. *bind-an,* Germ. *bind-en,* our bind; so, the endings all reduce to *e,* and that, even, with us, disappears. The Gr'k *ein,* L. *ere, er,* belongs with them. That the Dan. *e* represents the L. *er,* is seen by the pres't ind., where the *er* appears; as, *bind-er.*

285. The present participle has the following forms; Gothic *bind-ands;* old Germ. *bint-anter;* Icel. *bind-andi;* Germ. *bind-end;* Eng. *bind-ing;* Dan. *bind-ende; ant, and, end, ing* (g=d), are all modifications of one form, as, again, they are all a strengthening of the infin. *en.* The final *s, er, i, e,* noticed in these forms, are adjective marks.

286. The corresponding past participles, of these languages, are as follows; Go. *bund-ans;* old Germ. *bunt-aner;* Icel. *bund-inn;* A. S. *bund-en;* Du. *bond-en;* this participle, it will be seen, tends to identify itself with the infinitive, marking the tense rather by the body of the word than by the ending. We have, for this participle, both *bound* and *bound-en.* The *en* of this part. often appears as *ed, et, t,* as in our own *lov-ed, brough-t,* Germ. *ge-lieb-t* (from *lieben,* love)—the *ed* showing the identity of this part. with that in *end.* The Gothic has a form of this part. in *ths;* as, *salb-onds,* sav-ing, *salb-oths,* sav-ed—the *oth* is our *ed,* with the adjective mark *s.*

287. With these German participles, those of Latin readily compare; the present ends in *ans (ants);* as, *am-ans,* loving (Gothic *bind-ands);* the past ends in *atus;* as, *am-atus,* lov-ed (Gothic *salb-oths, -ots),* the Go. *s* corresponding to the Lat. *us.* The Anglo Saxon has a gerund in *anne* (with prefix *to),* from *ande;* as *writ-ende,* writing, gerund *writ-anne,* L. *scrib-endum,* writing—the *e* of the one and *um* of the other, being the noun ending.

288. It should also be remarked, that the German past participle has the prefix *ge* (varying in some of the family, and disappearing in others); as, *schreiben,* to write, and *ge-schrieben,* written.

289. The French, Italian, and Spanish participles afford little that is peculiar, when compared with those already given; in French, however, the *et, it,* of the past part. is reduced to *e, i;* as, *parler,* to speak, *parl-e,* spok-en (for *parl-et)*—but in old French, this *t* appears; as, *done-it,* given (French *donn-e), ost-et* for *ot-e.*

290. CELTIC PARTICIPLES: The Celtic languages have not developed the part. endings so strongly as the Germ. and Latin have, still, such as do exist are easily ranged along-side of those already noticed.

291. The Welsh has no uniform infinitive mark, yet the ordinary endings *od, ed, yll, u, i, o, aw,* may be taken as the representatives of it. In Gaelic, we find the more regular *adh* (Welsh *ad);* as, *leagh-adh, lav-ing;* it takes, also, the form, in Irish, of *amh, ail.* In Irish, the infin. has prefix *do,* the *to* of ours; as, *buail,* strike thou, *do bualadh,* to strike; the infin., in Irish, differs from the imperative not only by adding inf. mark, but also by a change in the body of the word; as, *righ,* reach, inf. *do-rochtain.* This *adh* of Gaelic is the *at* of Latin supine *am-atum,* and the *tas* of *brevitas.*

292. In Celtic, the present participle agrees more with the infinitive. In Irish, this part. has the prefix *a, ag* (our *a* in go *a walking,* also German *ge* of past part.), thus, *teidh,* go, *do*

dhul (infin.), and *ag dul* (part.); *tabhair*, give, *do thabhairt* (infin.), *ag tabhairt* (part.). In Cor., this *ag* is *ou*; as, *care* (inf.), *ou care* (part.), loving; in Celt. Bret., it is *o*; as, *kana*, to sing, *o kana*, singing (French *chant-ant*).

293. The past participle in Celtic is marked by the usual *t*; thus, in Irish, struck is *buail-te*; *dean*, do, *dean-ta*, done. In Cornish, this *t* appears as *s*; thus, *care*, love, *kyr-ys*, lov-ed; *ry*, give, *re-ys*, given. The Welsh uses its passive part. only for the persons of the verb; thus, *car-ir*, (he) is loved; *cerid*, (he) was loved; *cer-ir*, (he) will be loved; *car-wyd*, (he) has been loved; *car-asid*, (he) had been loved—all these forms going through all the persons of the tense without change. The inf. is here also used for this participle, and it shows well how the two are equal; thus, I am *wedi-dysgu*, I am *after-learning*, i. e. have learned. It has, too, another adj. form for this part., in *ed-ig*; as, *car-edig*, loved, the *ig* being an adject. development; *dysg-edig*, learned (teached). In C.B., *dalea* (and *daleout*), to delay; *dale-et*, delayed; *kana*, to sing, *kan-et*, sung; *kavout*, to find, *kav-et*, found—from which we see how this part. and the infin. agree. It is seen most clearly, in Celtic, that all the participles are based on the infinitive.

294. SLAVIC PARTICIPLES: The Polish infinitive is marked by *c=s*, *z*, Russ. *t*; as, *pis-ac*, to write. The part's and verbals of Polish are as follows:

Imper. *pisz*, write.   P. Part. *pis-an-y*, written.
Part. Pr. *pisz-ans*, writing.   Past T. *pis-al*, wrote, written.
Ger'd *pis-anie*, the writing.   Past. act. *na-pis-awszy*, hav. written.

Pisz-ans has also the declinable form *pisz-ans-y*, Germ. *schreib-end-e*, L. *scrib-ent-e*, from *scribens* (*ans=ens*); *pis-an-y* is like *scrip-t-us*, Lat., our writt-en: it is the precise form of Go. *bund-ans*; *pis-an-ie* is the A. S. *writ-anne*, L. *andum*; *pis-al=pis-an*; the past active has the common prefix *na*. All these forms of Polish verbals show very prettily how such forms may gradate into each other.

295. The Russsan imperative is *pali*, burn; infinitive *pal-it*, to burn; the other forms are as follows:

Pr. Part. *paly-ash-i*, burning.   Past act. *pal-ivsh-i*, hav. burned.
Pr. Pass. *pal-im-i*, being burned.   Pr. gerd. *paly-otch-i*, in burning.
Past Pass. *pal-enn-i*, been burned.   Past gerd. *pal-iv* (*sh-i*), hav. burned.

296. The Pr. Part. *ash-i* is Pol. *ans-i*; *im-i* is Pol. *any* (Gr'k *pot-im-os*, to be drunk); *enn-i* is a variation of this *imi* (as we find *anne=ande* in A. S.)—other forms of this participle are given in *t-i* (L. *t-us*, our *ed*); as, *ter-ti*, rubb-ed, *kalo-ti*, pricked; *-ivsh-i* is P. *-awsz-y*. The gerunds are simply the present and past part's, differently applied; thus, while the part's are

HISTORY OF PARTICIPLES. 77

adj's belonging to the noun, the ger'ds are used independently; as, (while) *walking* on the banks of the river, I mused, (in) *serving* our country, we do our duty, *having received* your letter, I answered; *otchi* is found shortened to *a, ia,* and *ivshi* to *iv.* There is, too, the past tense *pal-il,* identical with *palim,* and inf. *palit.*

297. The Bohemian infin. is *piti,* to drink, imper. *pi,* (*pij*), drink, *vóla-ti,* to call, *volej,* call.

pij-ici (*pije*), drinking (R. *-ashi*).   *volaj-ici,* calling.
piv-shi, hav. drunk (R. *-ivshi*).   *vola-vshi,* hav. called.
vol-ani, the calling (ger'd).   *volan,* being called (Pass.).

As we saw in Russian, so here *pivshi* has the form *piv,* which again equals *pil,* drank, hav. drank; so, also, *volav* equals *volal, volan.*

298. The Slovensh has little that is noticeable; *del-ati,* to do, *del-at* (supine), *del-ajoc,* doing, and ger'd *del-aje* (Polish *ans*), and *del-anje,* the doing (A. S. *anne,* Lat. *andum*) Serb. Wend. *pal-ic,* to burn, *pal-acy,* burning, *pal-il* (*pal-iwsi*), hav. burned, *pal-eny,* burned (pass.); there is also a condensed ger'd, *pal-o,* Russian *pali-a.*

299. The Illyr. is almost identical with those already noticed; *vid-eti* (*videt*) to see, *vid-es,* seeing, *vid-evshi,*, hav. seen, also *vid-el, vid-jen,* seen (Pass. L. *vis-um*), *vid-jenje,* the seeing (Polish *anie*)—just so in Latin, *andum* is gerund mark, and *andus* passive participle.

300. It remanis yet briefly to consider that past active part. in *iwsi, ivshi, awszy.* In origin, it is plainly only a growth of the pres't part. *ans, yashi, ici;* its identity, too, with the past in *il, al,* is seen by its common reduction to *iv=il.* With its prefix *na,* as in Polish, it corresponds exactly with German *geschrieben.* But, in form, the ending is double, and it is as a present based on the past part.; as, Russ. *paliv-shi* on *palil;* it is like the L. *dic-to* from *dic-o,* the *t* representing the ending of an infin.; this *v, iv, av,* is used very generally, in Rus., to represent the infin. ending in these forms upon forms; thus, we find, there, a pluperf. tense of *pali, pali-v-al,* which is the past of a new form of *pali, paliv* for *palit,* it is the *av* of *am-av-ere,* the base of *am-av-eram* (Lat.); the G'k perf. part. *tetu-ph-ot-os,* may, no doubt, be compared with it.

301. The old Prussian infinitive ends in *int, it,* pres. part. in *uns, ons* (Go. *ands*), and the past or pass. part. in *its, int-s* (Go. *iths*). The Lith. has a pres. and fut. pass. in *mas* (R. *imi*), and a past act. in *d-amas* (*dams*), Russ. *iv-shi,* Sans. *t-avan,* also a future *s-es* (*sens*), G'k *s'as.* s-ōn, Sans. *s-yan.*

302. HUNGARIAN PART'S: In Hung., the infinitive ends in *ni,* as *var-ni,* to wait; *var-o,* waiting (short as in Boh.); *var't*

(past part.) waited, (active and passive); *var-and-o*, a part. indicating one who will wait, or one to be waited for, and corresponding exactly to the Ger. *zu lobend*, to be praised (to praising), and the Lat. *a-mand-us*, (one) to be loved. The parallel between these part's and those of Latin is unmistakable — the present in *o* being a condensed form, as the Dan. *e*, infin. for L. *are*. Not only are the past and fut. part's used with both an active and a passive force, even the present part. is often used passively also.

It has also a gerund *var-van*, shorter *var-va*, corresponding in form with the Slavic, and used like it. It is to be compared with Russ. short ger'd *iv*, Lith. *dams*, Sanscrit *van*.

There is also a pass. infin. *var-at-ni*, to be waited (for), *var-at-o*, pres. part. denoting *the waited (for)*. Here is another case of a verb formed upon a new base — *at-ni* is a double inf. ending. With *varat* as the base, it takes the full set of part's; besides *var-ato*, there is the past *var-atot*, fut. *var-atando*, ger'd *var-atvan*.

303. FINNISH PART'S: The verbals of the different dialects of the Finn. family, present some interesting forms; thus, in Suomi, *ole-man*, the being (Gr'k *men*); *ol-eva*, being (part.); *oll-u*, been; *san-ova*, saying (*va*=ing); *san-onu*, said (past. act.), *san-ottu*, been said.

Syrian. inf. ending *ny* (Hun. *ni*); as, *ysty-ny*, to send, sending; *yst-an*, the sending; *yst-yg*, sending (our ing); *yst-oma*, sent (G'k, -*omen*, -*men*); as, *me em yst-oma*, I am sent.

Wotjak inf. ends also in *ny*; as, *kary-ny*, to do; *kar*, (imper.) do; *kar-en*, do-ing (*em*, Germ. *en*) and do-ne; *kar-ysj*, doing (see Illyr.); also *kar-yku*, the doing; in the latter we find the usual endings change into *k*, a letter which we will see again in the Turk. infin. -*mek*; we find also *kar-on* and *kar-ono*, doing (Pol. *anie*.)

In Sheremis, we find for *coming* these variations, *tol-em*, *tol-as*, *tol-sa* (*sa*=as); *tol-ema*, hav. come (*ge-kommen*, Germ.), also *tol-mynga*, (-*muka*), pointing to Turk. -*mek*.

In Ostjak, for *ver* (*kar*), make, we find *ver-dai* (-end), *ver-do*, *ver-men*, making, and *ver-em*, made.

In the Lapp. form, we find *et* as inf. ending; as, *aell-et*, to live; *aellem*, living, and having lived.

304. TURKISH PARTICIPLE: Following the Finn. and Hung. we may properly speak of the Turkish verbals. The infin. here ends in *mek*, *mak*, and *ma*, *me* — pointing to the *men* and *ma* of Greek verbals, and the *ma* of Finn.; for the verb *love*, we find inf. *sev-mek*, *sev-mich* (-mish) and *sev-duk*, hav. loved — the former being a form of infin., and the latter to be referred to the past act. of Slavic; *sev-er* and *sev-en*, lov-ing, the *er* com-

paring with Alban. *are* = ing (that *er* is used for *en*, is seen by L. inf. *are* = Germ. *en*). There is a far longer list of verbals in this tongue, but it will not be of use to review them here.

305. ALBANISH PARTICIPLE: The present participle ends in *s, se* (L. *ans*); as, *mount-es*, conquering; *pene-se*, making; *divio-s,* hearing; *divion-are*, heard; *dasou-re*, loved — the past ending *are, re* (Latin *-urus, -ari*); we find also *de-ne*, given, and *thene*, said.

306. PERSIAN PARTICIPLE: The Persian offers the following; *perest* is the imperative form, meaning *adore*.

perest-ende, the adorer.   inf. *perest-iden*, to adore.
perest-an, adoring.   *perest-ide*. hav. adored.
perest-a, (shorter form).   *perest-ide buden*, to hav. adored.

It is easily seen that *ende* = *an, a;* even this *a* is also sometimes dropped, making part. = imper. The form in *ide* is identical with inf. *iden*, also with Turkish form in *duk*. The inf. in *d-en, t-an*, often, is double, and to be compared with Turkish *mek*, if not with Latin supine *-atum*.

307. In this connexion, we might briefly refer to the Hindostani part's; for the verb *mar*, strike, we have *mar-na*, to strike; *mar-ta*, striking; *mar-a*, struck; *mar, mar-kar*, hav. struck. The inf. mark *na* is Hung. *ni* and *ani*, Germ. *en;* the *ta* is our past sign, *a* is a shortened *na;* *kar* is genitive sign.

308. And here we may also introduce the Bengali verbals. The inf. and pres't part. have the same form, and end in *ite* (Rus. *it*); as, *kar-ite*, making and to make; past act. *kar-iya*, hav. done (Hind. *a*, Rus. *iv*); there is the verbal noun *kar-an, kar-na, kar-ana* (Pol. *anie*), doing; there is, too, a form, like Slavic gerund, *kar-ile*, on doing, being done (the precise Slavic past *il;* and like Slavic it is also found in the past tense), and another gerund *kar-iba*, doing, to do (Russ. *iv*, Hungarian *va*), besides a passive in *ta* (Latin *tus*).

309. MANCHU PARTICIPLE: The infinitive of this tongue ends in *me* (G'k *men*, T. *mek, me*); as, *khoach-ame*, to nourish; the participle ends in *ra, re* (L. *are*, T. *er*); as, *khoach-ara*, nourishing (used also for present and future tense); there is the form *khoach-afi* (Greek *sas*, Turkish *iser*).

In Mongolian, the infinitive ends in *cho, ku* (Turk. *mek*); as, *abu-cho*, to take; there is a gerund *abu-su*, taking (Man. *afi*), a supine *abu-ra*, to take (Manchu *re*).

We might here present some of the Thibet verbals; infinitive *byed-par* (var), to make; *bya-rou, by-ar*, to make (gerund); *byed-pa* (va), making; *byas-pa* (va, ta), made (past part.); *bya-va*, to make, L. *facturus*. The endings *ar, rou, re, va,* are such as we have often met with.

310. SEMITIC PARTICIPLE: In Semitic, the participle endings

have not developed so strongly as we have seen in the languages so far treated of. It will be observed that such endings keep pace, in growth, with common noun and adjective endings. With us, as in Semitic, the *us, a, um*, of Latin adjectives and nouns almost wholly disappears; we have lost, too, as in Semitic, the ending of the infinitive, using with it only a prefix; we have only the ending *ing* for all the part's and verbals found in Lat., for such irregular verbs as *run, set, strike*. The Semitic participles are formed after the manner, principally, of the German *ge-schrieben*, from *schreiben*, to write, and our *strike* and *struck*; that is, they do not develop new endings, but rely upon changes in the body of the word, adopting more or less generally, such prefixes as *m, a, l* (Germ. *ge*, Celt. *a*, our *be, to*). But all the Semitic languages show this last participle ending very strongly as a development in the personal endings, which are variations of the verbal endings. The Syriac shows it, too, very clearly in the common noun or verbal ending *ath, an* (Latin *tas*, Germ *en*, Greek *ma*, Ethiopic *ot, o, t*).

311. Thus, in Hebrew, we have:

qatel-ah, she kills.
qatal-etta (eth), thou killest.
qatal-etti, I kill.
qetol (inf.). to kill.

Part. act. *qotel*, killing.
Part. pass. *qatul*, killed.
me-qattel, ma-qetil, killing.

And in Arabic:

qatal-at, she kills.
qatal-ta (t), thou killest.
qatal-tu (t), I kill.

inf. *qatal-un*, to kill.
Part. act. *qatil-un*, killing.
Pass. part. *ma-qtul-un*, killed.
imper. *a-qtul*, kill (root, *qtl*).

So the verb *a-nsur*, aid (imper.), also *l-insur*; *naser-un*, aiding, fem. form *naser-atun*; *nasr-an*, aiding, ger'd and inf.; *ma-nsur*, aided (part. pass.), (root is *nsr*; *a, l, ma*, are prefixes).

We notice here very plainly, in the persons, the *t* of our loveth, L. *am-at* and *am-atum, am-ant*; and the scarcely developed *un* of Arabic, points to the Latin ending *um*.

312. Here we may introduce the Malay participles; they too, like the Semitic, are marked by prefixes. For *diabat*, touch, we find *men-diabat*, to touch; *ada-diabat*, touching and touched; *telah-diabat*, having touched; *tur-diabat* (and *te-*), touched (pass.). The prefix *men* is very common; it is the Semitic *ma*, and it has the form also of *pen*; as, *pen-diabat* (verbal noun); *ada* and *telah* have also, as separate words, the value of *is* and *being*.

313. GREEK PARTICIPLE: We will first consider the infinitives and participles of the Greek active, bringing into the comparison those of Sanscrit and Latin as occasion may require The ordinary Greek infinitive ending is *ein*, as *leipein*, to leave (our *ing*,

leaving, Germ. *en*, *bleiben*, to leave); in modern Greek, this *ein* becomes *ei* (Dan. *e*); as, *graph-ein*, G'k, *graph-ei*, mod. G'k, to write. It has, also, the forms occasionally, of *men*, *mein*, also *s*, *is*, a growth or form of *ein;* there is the infin. ending *ai*, (mod. G'k *ei*), peculiar to one of the past tenses (aorist); as, *eleips-ai*, to have left, and a form *enai*, peculiar to the perfect tense, *le-leiph-enai*, to have left. This *enai* is a growth of *ein*, so as to become double; it is practically an infin. of an infinitive, such as we saw in treating of the Russian participle; it is like the *isse* of *am-av-isse*, to have loved, and the *t-are* of *can-t-are*, to chant. As it is past and double, it is also passive, and equal to *-om-en* of Greek participle ending *-omen-os*.

314. The regular passive infin. ending of Greek (also ending of middle, i. e. active) is *esth-ai*. We do not regard this as essentially different from *enai*, indeed, we find *enai* also used for passive; *esth* equals *est*, *eth*, *en*, *ein*, *et*. The Latin passive infin. ending *ar-i*, *ar-ier*, is also double, it is hardly necessary to add.

315. It might be matter of interest to the student to point out the connexion between Greek and Latin (especially old Latin) infin. endings and those of cases, but we must pass the subject by, simply reminding him that all verbal endings are to be identified with case and noun endings.

There is also the Latin supine ending *tum*, Greek *ton*, which, in Sanscrit *tun*, marks the ordinary infinitive; in old Latin, the infinitive ends in *um*, and *tud* is an old supine ending.

316. The Greek ending for the present participle is *ōn*, *ous-a*, *on*; San. *an*, *ati*, *an;* Lat. *ans;* Lith. *as*, *anti;* as, G'k *leip-ōn*, leav-ing; it is the same as infin. *ein*, our *ing*. In the gen. case, it developes into *ont-os;* as *leip-ontos*, of leaving. In the aorist, it assumes the form of *as*, *asa*, *an* (mas., fem., neut.), gen. *ant-os* (Polish *ans*, *as*);' the full form of this participle is *leip-s-as* (leaving off augment of the tense), i. e. it is an ordinary participle on the new base *leip-s*, itself representing an inf. or verbal. This *sas* is precisely the Slavic past act. part. In the perf. part. *ōn* becomes *ōs*, and *ontos* (gen.) becomes *otos*. In San., *ōs*, *uia*, *os*, is *van*, *usi*, *vas*—*sas*, *sasa*, *san*, is *tavan*, *tavati*, *tavat*.

317. For the passive and middle participles, *om-en-os* is the usual ending in Greek; as, *leip-omenos*, leaving self, or being left. Leaving off the *os* (fem. *ē*, neut. *on*) as the adj. ending, we have *omen*, *men*—in Sanscrit, *an-as*, and *aman-as;* so we see by San., that *men = an*, German *en*, *t*, Lith. *am-as*, Russ. *mi*, *emi*, Greek *ma*. There is no more doubt that *omen*, *men*, is a growth of inf. *ein*, than there is that Lat. *atus* (*am-atus*, lov-ed) is a form of supine *tum*, which is active. We find, in the aorist, *eis*, *ent-os*, an active ending, in place of *omen-os*.

318. The student will not fail to observe in the Gr'k partici-

ple forms, how beautifully they illustrate that feature of language by which new forms arise out of old ones, and how the endings become thus repeated. It is one of the most interesting phenomena of language, and it affords us one of its most important laws. To illustrate the nature of it, we might refer to such forms as these, common among the illiterate; *bestest* (superl. of a superl.); *less-er* (compar. of a compar.); *worstest* (sup. of sup.); *lec-tur-ing* (a part. on a part.)—the *tur* is itself a part.' ending; so thru̱-st-ing—the *st* being a past participle mark.

319. PARTICIPLE IN URUS: We will use this as a general head, under which to bring, in a manner somewhat disconnected, many leading and important points in the history of the participle; this participle is connected with all other verbal forms, and we can hardly say anything of those forms which will not, directly or indirectly, have a bearing upon the character of the one in *urus*. While we have in Latin *am-ans*, loving, *ama-tus*, loved, *ama-ndus*, to be loved (fut.), *ama-ndum*, the loving, *ama-tum*, (and *-tu*), to love, the loving (supine), we have also *ama-turus*, about to love (future), and what we wish principally to show is, that this participle is a development of the forms just given, containing no element that they do not, that it is an adj. with infin. or part. as basis; and, again, that it is identical with the passive form *ama-tur*, he is loved.

320. In old German, bind-ing is *bint-anter*, Germ. *bind-ende*; and in German, this same participle *-end*, *-ing*, is used for just such a participle as that in *urus* (and *endus*), i. e. both are future (with the difference however that *urus* is active, while the other is pass.); thus, *er ist zu lob-end*, he is for praising, to be praised, while we would use, in a similar case, the infin. or ger'd; as, *so much there is to praise, to be praised*. In Hung., the future in *ando* (Lat. *andus*), a form of Germ. *end*, is used both for future pass. and fut. act.; thus, we find *ir-ando level*, Germ. *zu-schreibender brief*, to-be-written letter, a letter which will be written (pass.); one *about-to-write* (a letter) is also designated as *irando*, the precise L. *scripturus*. Still further, in Hung., the common pres't part. is used precisely as this fut. *ando*; thus, *clad-o bor* (*o* = ing) = *elad-ando bor* (*ando* = *turus*), Germ. *zu-verkaufender wein*, for-selling wine, selling wine, wine *to-be-sold*.

321. In the Vedas, this same form *tar* is used both as pres't part. and present indicative. The Lat. forms *do-nor* (n = t) and *da-tor* (G'k *do-tēr*, Sans. *da-tar*), our giver, belong to the same class; so, *rap-tor*, rob-ber (from *rapio*), *scrip-tor*, writ-er (from *scribo*). That these forms *tor*, *ter*, are the Lat. *turus*, is seen by the fuller forms *scrip-tura*, a writ-ing; *fac-tura*, the mak-ing; *rup-tura*, a breaking. These forms, it will be seen, are purely active; the *or* is precisely the *er* of *giv-er*, *serv-er*, *speak-er*, and

this *er* we know is identical with *ing* (speak-er = the speaking one), as we see by the corresponding L. forms *ten-ant, serv-ant, prud-ent* (*ant* = Latin *ans, ens,* ing), and we have two ways of regarding this *tor*, both amounting to the same thing, namely, either from *turus, tura*, or as a present part. form (as *serv-ant*, serv-er = L.*serv-ans*) of a new verb, as *scriptor* from *scripto*, or *scriptere*, just as we see *do-nor* from the new form *dono*, from *do*, to give. This ending *tor, ter*, of nouns, is seen in many languages, and assumes a great variety of forms; thus, in our *murder* (a killing); blun-der, tim-ber, thun-der; junc-ture, fracture; *sepul-crum* (-trum), *mira-culum* (-tulum, -turum), *ful-crum, mons-trum, spec-trum*, G'k *bak-tron* (-trum), and *lektron*; master, fa-ther, laugh-ter; nee-dle (dl = tr), hal-ter,—and so on without limit.

322. In the Wallachian, *lauda-toriu* (as well as *laud-andu*, L. *andus*) equals Lat. *laud-ans*, praising (i. e. *toriu* = ans, ing), while to express the Lat. *turus* they need this form, *a fi lauda-toriu*, to be praising = *laud-aturus*, about to praise. To be more precise about it, *toriu* rather equals *tor* than *turus*, and the above form is properly *he is to-be-prais-er*, i. e. he will praise, exactly as we saw in German and English.

And we must observe, too, that in none of the modern Latin languages do we find a future part. in *urus* (if we count not the above *tor-iu*), but we do find Span. *canta-dor*, Rhat. Rom. *canta-tur*, Fr. *chan-teur*, Wall. *canta-toriu*, Eng. *chant-er* or *sing-er;* so, we are left to infer that those languages supply the place of this *urus* by using the pres't in *ens* (as we saw above, a compound *to-be-praising* (praiser) for *about to praise, laudaturus*). (By way of note, we may remark that the *t* of *chanteur, chanter*, belongs with the root as well as with the ending *t-er; er* here = *tur*).

323. If we bear in mind, in connexion with the above, that Turk. *ur* = *ans, ing*, pres't part., we shall find it proved beyond question that *turus* is only a modification, an application, of the present *ans*, and hence of infinitive *are, ar*. We may prove its identity with inf. *are* by a stronger way than such an inference. In Latin, the imperative has not only the form *am-a*, love, but also the longer form *am-ato*, showing that *a* at the end of verbs is a condensed *ato, ao*, as in Danish *a* = *are, ar*. So that we might expect the infin. *am-are* to be really *ama-tre* (-*tur*). Now in French, we find these very endings for inf's; as, *e-tre*, to be (old Fren. *es-tre*), also *repai-tre, sui-vre* (*v* = *t*), *nai-tre, join-dre* (*d* = *t*), *ven-dre*.

324. It only remains now to be shown that *turus* is passive as well as active, since we have already shown that it is present as well as future. In old North, we find the past (and pass.) part's *fall-inn*, fall-en; *tel-dr*, tol-d; *bren-der*, burn-ed. Here we find

dr (=*inn* in some verbs, German infin. *en*), which becomes *dir*, *bren-dir*, in some of the persons of past tense, as the mark of past (and pass.) part.; it is hardly necessary to say this is *tur* of Latin. In Icelandic, we find *elska-dur*, lik-ed, loved, Latin *ama-tus*, and we find the same form -*ader* in the past active, but shorter in the compound tense; as, *hefe elskad*, have liked. (We find also *thier elsked*, you like (pres't indicative), but *hann elskar*, he likes, so that *ar*=*ed*, *edr*). So, we find here, clear enough, that *dr*, *dur*, Fr. *tre*, Lat. *turus*, is used in the passive

325. Besides reminding the student of the precise L. *amatur*, he is loved, let us refer more particularly to the Lat. *tura*, our *ture*. We find *tura* constantly used in Latin as an equivalent of *tus* and *tum*, noun endings, which are applications of the passive participles; thus, we find *posi-tura*=*posi-tus*, position, which is identical in form with the pass. part.; so, *scriptura* = in-scription, something written, and *factura*=*factus* (pass), the making. We can easily see how our part. (or ger'd) in *ing* is used passively in similar cases; *to strike a man* is simply *to make him be struck*, which converts it into a passive idea; that which is *spoken* is a *speech*, a speaking, the *being loved* by God is called the *loving* of God; a man desires a *hearing*, i. e. *to be heard*, he expects a *scolding*, i. e. *to be scolded*. We continually see our gerund in *ing* thus used as a passive: everything that is finished becomes passive, becomes something done; a doing itself when finished becomes *done* (passive); so, all our verbal nouns, such as *fight*, *thrust*, *draught*, *speech*, *depth*, *rent*, *wreck*, *bond*, *song*, and scores of like forms, are *true passives*. The endings *t*, *th*, *k*, *d*, *g*, *ch*, and the like, are the very *t* of L. pass. *tus*, our *ed*.

326. We have certainly gone far enough in this discussion to enable the student to fully comprehend now the nature of this participle in *urus*. We find it simply a gerund, infin., or verbal noun, used just as we use our gerund in *ing*, and our inf., and getting its future force, and passive also, only by its expressed or implied connexion with the verb *be*; thus, just as we say *he is to come to day, he is coming to day*, i. e. will come, should come, just so the Latins constantly use *urus* for a future verb, suppressing *be*; as, *he promised that he would come, is to come, se venturum*. The Danish affords the best illustration of the gerund in *ing* used as pass.; as, *blæs-ende instrumenter*, blow instruments, blowing ones, and *den udgiv-ende Bog*, the outgiving book, book given out; these forms are based on the more original form of expression *the instruments are for blowing*, where *blowing* is exactly equal to a Latin verbal noun in *tura*.

327. There are other points of importance than those so far noticed, in the history of verbals of the German languages, and

we may as well consider them under this head, as they have a bearing more or less direct upon the verbal in *turus*. In Icelandic, we find *ad elska*, to like, and (past tense) *eg var ad elska*, I was to like, a liking, liking—inf. used as ger'd and part. In Swedish, we have *vi hafva kall-at*, we have called (Perf. act.), and *vi hafva kall-ats*, we have (been) called (Passive), also *vi varda* (German *werden*, are) *kall-ade*, we are called. We see, here, three different applications of one form, having a corresponding change in appearance which is unknown to us, as we use *called* for all the cases. In the first place, it is very evident that *kallat* equals *kallad'*, evident from the fact that we, and others, use their equivalents without distinction of form; the identity of *kall-ats* with them will become evident too, after a little consideration. In Danish, so nearly equal to Sw., those three applications of the past part. have no change in form to mark them; thus, *være skrev-et*, be written; *haft skrev-et*, had written; *have været gjore-t*, have been done (chor-ed); *erfund-et*, is found, has been found.

328. So, it is already proved, clearly enough, that *kall-at* (act.) is the same as *kall-ats* (pass.). This is enough to convince us also that the whole Dan.-Swed. passive system is not different from the active. In the Swed. infin, this *kall-ats* above takes the form *kall-as* (ats=as), to be called; so, too, *kall-as* is used in five of the persons of the pres't; as, *du kallas*, thou art called, but also *j' kallens*, ye are called (this is the Latin *ens = ats, as*). If we bear in mind that *kall-ar* (*ar* being L. passive ending) is used in the persons of pres't active, as *han kall-ar*, he calls, we shall have further reason to believe *as=ar* to be identical with active.

Again, in the Icel. *ad elskast*, to be lik-ed, the *ast* (Sw. *ats*, and *as*) is our active *est* of lov-est, as Dan. pass. *es* is our act. *es* of giv-es, i. e. what we use for *lik-est*, they use for *to be liked* (inf. pass.), and what we have for gives, they take for *is given*.

We are thus brought to the conclusion that the Dan.-Swed. passive in its different persons is based on the passive participle (which we have often found to be equal to the act.), that indeed it is that part. varying in the different persons of the sing. and plur., often but slightly, and sometimes not at all.

329. VERBAL ENDINGS: We come now to consider some of the forms which these participle endings assume when marking certain kinds of nouns and adjectives.

We often find several of these endings joined to one root, but by no means all of them; thus, in Greek *po-tos*, a drinking, a draught, (*tos* is L. *tus* past part.)—it means also drinkable, to be drank, and *potimos* has the same meaning; *po-tikos*, pertaining to drink; *po-tēs*, a drinker (es=er); *po-tisma*, a drink;

po-tisis, giving to drink; *po-ton*=*potos*, potion; *po-tamos*, drinkable water, river. For nearly all these forms we may use the simple term *drink*, even drink-water (as Germans would say) = drinkable water, showing, thus, that endings are equal, or do not vary the meaning of the base word. The ending *ikos*,=*itos*, *tos*, our *ic* of graphic; *ros*, *mos*, *inos* (=*men*, *omen*, Sans. *an*), are also found as variations of *tos*; as, *zul-inos*, wood-en (in= en), *pot-imos*, drinkable, *troph-imos*, nourishing; *nose-ros*, sickly, *phthone-ros*, envious—*tos* is precisely the equal of *mos*; thus, *lek-tos* equals not only spoken, but also speakable, that may be spoken. So, we must consider our *able*, *ful*, Lat. *ilis*, *bilis*, and the like, as variations of this *tos*, L. *tus*, and in the end of *ing*. (Note, once for all, that the *os*, *us*, *a*, *is*, are mere adjective endings, which may be left out of consideration).

330. It can hardly be said that such endings have any force at all, if for no other reason for this, that one is so often used for the others; thus, joyful=joyous, joy-ing, i. e. having joy; hurtful=hurting, that which is hurting, and flexible=bending, that which bends; bl, fl=tl, tr, turus.

331. The ending *men*, *ma* (*men-os*, *tus*), is very common in Latin and Greek (besides Slavic, and elsewhere). It is equal to *ing*; as, *certa-men*, striving, *regimen*, ruling, Sans. *dha-man*, a building, a thing built; it often, too, denotes passives (just as we use build-ing to denote the action and building=house, passive); so *car-men*, a po-em, a work, (a thing) done; Sans. *jan-man*, a bearing, a birth, passive; Greek *ma*, *pragma*, an act, something done, and *gramma*, a writing, something written. It has another development in our *ment*, L. *mentum*; as, our government=governing, *teg-mentum*, a cover, covering, that by which we are covered; in Fren., it equals our *ly* of adverbs, as intensive-ment, intensive-ly, as well as our *ing*, as *etonnement*, stunn-ing (stun-ment). There is, also, the wide prevailing *ta*, *tas*, our *ence*, *ness*, *th*; thus, Rus. *teplo-ta*, warm-th, tepid-ness; L. *brevi-tas*, brevi-ty, brief-ness. We have scarcely yet made a beginning in that long list of Greek and Latin verbal endings, but we have given all that it is proper to give here.

332. We will conclude this part of the subject by noticing some of the endings of Pers. The adjectives here are derived from nouns by the suffix *ane* (*en* of silken); as, *merd*, man, *merd-ane*, man-like, -ly; also by *in*; *ahen*, iron, *ahen-in*, of iron; there is the *mend*, as *devlet*, happiness, *devlet-mend*, happy, *derd*, grief, *derdi-mend*, grievous (Fr. *ment*=ly); *tebah*, corruption, *tebah-kiar*, corrupt-er (*tor* of *scrip-tor*); *nam*, name, *nam-dar*, named, renowned, *garan*, heavy (L. *gravis*), *garan-bar*, loaded, heavy (*bar* of Germ. *denkbar*, thinkable), (*dar*=*tar*, *turus*)— *bar* takes the form, too, of *car*, *yar*, as *bakt*, fortune, *bakt-yar*,

fortun-ate, *dil*, heart, *dil-dar*, loved (*dar*=*bar*); *purside*, demanded, *pursish*, a demand (id=ish); *giriftan*, to take, *giriftar*, one taken, a prisoner (*ar*, pass.)—*ar* is properly *turus* with a passive application.

CHAPTER IX.

HISTORY OF VERBS.

333. If we take merely a surface view of language, it will be very easy for us to divide words into two leading classes,—nouns, and such as belong to nouns, and verbs, together with such as belong to verbs. If we rely wholly upon the appearance of these two classes, and inquire nothing about their origin and history, we shall find little which they have in common, and come to regard them as radically distinct. However, none but a superficial view could bring us to such a conclusion; these classes when critically examined are found, in fact, to have everything in common. All nouns are based upon a verbal idea; and, again, the basis of all verbs are nouns, that class of nouns called verbals.

334. It is generally imagined that verbs have that peculiarity, in comparison with all other parts of speech, by which they express and affirm. And yet it must be observed, that it is not alone in the simpler and less cultivated languages, that we find other parts of speech used in the place of verbs and having a value equal to theirs. In all tongues, we find abundant examples where the noun and the verb (as, I *walk*, the *walk*) do not differ in form. In Tamil, nouns and adjectives are treated as verbs. In Japanese, the adjective is used as verb or adjective, according to where it is placed; as, *yoki fito*, good man (or *yoi fito*), *fito yosi*, man (is) good (or *fito yoi*)—so, a child would say *man good*, for the *man is good*. In this language, the basis of every verb is clearly a kind of noun or adjective.

335. In the Thibetan, among others, person endings are not developed, and the verb is simply a participle or verbal, scarcely differing in character from the noun. In all languages, the infinitive, gerund, and participles, constitute an important portion of the forms of the verb. And yet, verbs as they are, they are also as certainly nouns and adjectives; they have all the cases and qualities that belong to nouns and adjectives. Even the Infinitive and Imperative are known to be only mere case forms.

336. In Latin and Greek, we are particularly struck with the number of participles used as verbs; they not only perform the

office of verbs, they are verbs in fact. Whenever we use expressions like these, *I saw a man walking, hear him speak, hear his speech,* we use *walking, speak,* and *speech,* precisely as verbs. Every word used as a predicate, that is following *be*, is a verb also; as, he is *there,* he was *wise,* he is a *writer;* in some languages, as the Russian, the *is* is left out, of so little force is this auxiliary; in particular cases, we also leave out the auxiliary, and thus the predicate performs the part of a true verb; thus, the one was here and the other *there,* he becomes noisy, and I quiet. Indeed, to be precise about the matter, we may say that all objectives, or other words following verbs, bear the main weight of the verbal expression, and may, hence, be called verbs; thus, we say he catches *fish,* i. e. he fishes, he trims with iron, i. e. he irons, he feeds *grain* to the horse, i. e. he *grains* the horse.

Personal Endings.

337. We have already pointed out the identity between all case endings and the endings of verbals and participles. We shall observe hereafter, when we come to treat of tenses, that those endings of verbs which mark the persons, are modifications only of the endings which mark the participles. But what we wish now first to turn our attention to, is the parallel between the personal endings and those endings which in other languages mark the possessive pronouns.

338. In Hungarian, we have *var-tam,* I have waited, *vart-ad,* thou hast, and *vart-a,* he has waited, or expected. To compare with this, we have *lov-am,* my horse, *lov-ad,* thy horse, *lov-a,* his horse. In Semitic, the parallel is quite as certain, but more remote. In the Finnish, we find the identity exhibited in a still stronger light. But it is the Samoidish that we find most instructive in this matter.

339. We will state the whole case as we find it in Samoidish; it will surely be no harm that we note some things which have a more direct bearing on points discussed under other heads. Here, we find *sawa jale,* (a) good day, but *jale-da sawa,* day-the (the day) (is) good; *sawa,* (it is) good — precisely as we say *good* for him; *jale,* (it is) day. Such expressions as the foregoing are often heard by us, but we regard them as only childish or savage. As we said before, every predicate is a real verb; in Samoidish, this fact is so well recognized, that the noun and adjective, when performing the office of predicate, develop endings equal to personal endings, and thus stand independent as true verbs; thus, *sawa,* good, *sawa-m,* good-I, good-my, i. e. I (am) good; *nisea,* father, *nisea-m,* father-my, father-I, i. e. I (am)

father. Not this alone, that personal ending, by a slight variation, may also indicate past time, or even future; as, *nisea-ms*, I (was) father, *nisej-um*, I (will be) father. To show the identity of passive endings with personals, in Samoid., we give the following: *hyr* = cow, *hyr-m*, my cow, *hyr-l* thy cow, *hyr-t*, his cow; so, also, *ud* = hand, *ud-ou* (my), *ud-ol* (thy), *ud-et*, (his) hand; and *loga* = fox, *loga-u*, *loga-l*, *loga-t*, his fox — for *logau*, we find also *logam* (am = au), and *logad* equal to *logal*. To compare with this, we find the verb *mada-u*, *mada-r*, *mada-da*, I, thou, he cut. So that the verb, here, may be conceived to be what we see it is in all simple languages, a participle base, or verbal, developing possessive pronouns, and the expression, *I cut the wood*, would be, in principle, *the wood* (is) *my-cutting* (cutting-my). We see this clearly when we come to the verbal noun, which may receive these endings and become a true verb; as, *madawy*, cut, hewing, becomes, with the personal ending, *madawae-m* = I was (at) cutting, or was cutting (also is cutting). This is with the ending for predicates, and if we use possessive endings (a form only of the other), we get *madawae-u* = my cutting (i. e. it is or was my), having a power equal to *I have cut*.

340. Not only do we have, here, possessives belonging to the noun, but the new form (noun with ending) may be carried through all the cases, as *tea-u* (my), *tea-r* (thy), and *tea-da*, (his) deer; and genitive, *tea-n* (of my), *tea-nd* (of thy), *tea-nda*, (of his) deer (reindeer).

341. There is a slight difference, as we saw above, in two classes of pronoun endings, those called predicative, which grow upon predicates, as we saw in *sawam*, and those subjective (possessive) endings, which we saw in *madau*, *madar*, *logau*, *logal*; but both are one and the same thing. The difference in their use is very slight; thus, *nan mue-m*, (the) bread took-I, the bread (was) my taking, and *nan mue-u*, I took bread.

342. As a noun in Samoidish can be treated as a verb, can receive endings, and even tense marks, so does the verb, again, come to be treated as a noun and develop the different case endings. We see this in all languages where that portion of the verb embraced by participles and verbals, is declined precisely as the noun is, and with the same number of cases. But, in Samoidish, it extends to other forms of the verb. So it is in Tamil; there, the verb is declined like nouns also; thus, the verb denoting *he walked*, or *he the walker*, by a slight variation takes a case form, and means *through him the walker*, or *by the walk* (one).

343. There is a remarkable and significant coincidence, in this language (Samoid.), between the endings of case and those

endings of verbs denoting pronouns or persons—; thus, *m* is the sign of acc., it is the sign, too, of the 1st person; *d*, *ad*, *da*, are marks of dat. and abl., so they are marks, too, of the 2d and 3d persons. We have long before this identified the case endings with the suffix article or pronoun.

344. We find in many languages, incorporated as endings with the verb, not only such as we have already noticed, and which denote the subject or the possessor, but also such as denote the object. So, in Hebrew, *qatal-ta*, thou-hast-killed, and *qatalta-ni*, thou-hast-killed-me ($ta=$thou, and $ni=$me); so, in Italian, *difendi-amo-ci*, we defend selves ($ci=$self), *procura-te-lo*, procure-thou-it ($lo=$it,), *procurar-se-lo*, to procure-self-it; so, in English, *called-m*, for called them, *heard-er*, for heard her; also we say, there killed-he-him, there gave-he-him-it, i. e. gave it to him. There is, theoretically at least, no limit to this developing a new pronoun on a new base (for it is that and no more).

345. It is true, it may be said of these pronoun endings denoting subject and object in other languages, that they do not exist separately. But not less may be said of the separate pronouns, for they, though printed separate, can only be said to exist in connexion with the verb. In truth, all words are as little independent as suffixes—*no word, more than any living thing, can exist by itself alone, can be separate*. The separation of words from the base with which they are connected, is rather apparent than real.

346. Having given now some general ideas of the original nature of the verb, and having considered also, sufficiently for present purposes, the matter of personal endings, we will now consider more in detail the different person, tense, and mood forms of the verb, as we find them in other languages—selecting only such for this comparative view as we find presenting some new or instructive features, and keeping all the while in sight this main object, *the explanation of the growth and structure of verbs*. And, for this purpose, we will begin with the Turkish, a language which possesses a verb more fully developed, and a system more complete in its parts, than any other we could select.

Turkish Verbs.

347. We will take the verb *deug* (imper.), strike, tap (Greek *tup'*); we will arrange the verb in Turkish, and the same under the other heads, by placing the singular persons at the left, and the plural at the right; we will sometimes, also, perhaps, point off the ending separate from the body or base of the word, but in this case we may give the student the caution, here, which we might have given in many other places, that the separating

of a word thus into parts, that is, drawing such a certain line between them, is always more or less arbitrary; it is just like drawing such a marking line between head and neck, and arm and hand, or leaf and stem, or creek and river; it is clear no such line can truthfully be drawn, and yet the distinction between such things is indispensable; and so in language, such marks are always serviceable, though always, also, open to objection.

348. *Present Tense.*

deugur-um,	I strike.	*deugur-uz*,	we strike.
deugur-sen,	thou strikest.	*deugur-siz*,	ye strike.
deugur',	he strikes.	*deugur-ler*,	they strike.

The verb *be*, present tense, runs thus:

im,	I am.	*iz*,	we are.
sen,	thou art.	*siz*,	ye are.
dur,	he is.	*durler*,	they are.

We must add, too, that *ben* = I, *sen* = thou, *biz* = we, *siz* = ye, you — and *ler* is the usual plural sign; the present participle is *deugur* = striking.

349. We conclude with regard to the forms of this tense, that the present participle is plainly the basis here, as we shall find it, also, in other languages. The endings of the 1st and 2nd persons, both numbers, may be taken as the representatives of personal pronouns, or of the verb *be*, or of both. If we take the analogy of the past tense, where *was* is clearly the element (as it is separate), the pres't part. being the base, we might decide that it is the verb *be*, thus bringing back to us the combination well known to us, in place of the prs'nt, *am striking, is striking*. But, in most other languages, the endings have vanished down to a mere mark of the persons — though in principle, *be* is everywhere a part of the form. The impossibility of deciding the point, arises from the fact that the verb *be* is, at best, only a pronoun, and so often has a form not to be distinguished from pronouns.

350. But we do not in either case look upon the form *deugur-um*, for instance, as a compound, but rather consider that some verbal or part. ending has grown up into such representatives as we have just been speaking of.

351. *Imperfect.*

deugur idum = I struck (striking was-I).
deugur idi = he struck (striking was-he).

Here the elements are separate — *idum* being past of *be* (was). In the 3d plur., we find the elements together, as well as separate; as, *deugur idi-ler*, and *deugur-ler-idi*, = they struck — so we find for 1st sing., *deugur-dum*.

There is a second imperfect (or past), formed with the same *deuger* and *imishem* (another past of *be*)—the two being separate; as, *deugur imishiz*, (we) striking were.

352. *Preterit.*

deugdum, I struck.   *deugduk*, we struck.
deugdun, thou struck.   *deugdunuz*, ye struck.
deugdi, he struck.   *deugdiler*, they struck.

This can be regarded as representing two main elements, *deug*, a base only existing in the imperative, and the *idum* = I was, noticed above. But there is the past act. part. *deugduk* (having struck); we may take this *deugduk* as the basis of these forms, and as having simply developed person endings (indeed it is the identical form in the 1st plural). This would be after the known principles of German, and other languages, where the past participle does constitute the past tense. The *d*, here, is the representative of our past *ed*, *t*, but none the less may it be taken as the mark of *was*, verb *be*.

353. There is another form, the 2d preterit, *deugmishem* = I have struck, which is clearly on the base of the past part. *deugmish* = hav. struck. Or, as in the case before, we can consider that it has the element *mishem*, one of the tenses of *be*, and meaning *I have been*. All this proves at least one thing, that one element, if no more, of participles, represents the verb *be*.

354. Then follow other combinations, but containing no new principle. The pres't and the past participles, above given, are the common bases, and they combine with new forms of the verb *be*, of which Turkish has more than one for the same tense.

The future is either like the present in form, or it makes a new combination of the fut. part. *deugjek* with am, is; as, *deugjekim*, I will strike (also *deugjegim*), and *deugjektur* (*dur* = is), he will strike.

355. In the optative, there is the form *deugem*, I would strike (also *deugeh im*). This may be looked upon as made on the base *deug*, with the verb *be* as element, or as a variation of some part. or verbal, as *deuguen* (which we find) equal to striking. It is precisely like the Latin *amem*, I may be. Then there is also the imperf. optative, as *deugidum* (or separate, *deugeh idum*), with the base as before, and *idum* = was. These tenses are accompanied by the prefix *that*.

356. The pres't and fut. subjunctive has the following form, *deugursem*, I may strike (also *deugur isem*)—present part. and *isem*, I may be. There is, besides, the imperfect *deugsem*, I might strike, which we may consider as on the base of the part. *deugiser* = about striking, or as *deug* and *isem*, I may be (the *deugeh* which we saw before).

357. The Finnish languages, a class related to the Turkish, furnish abundant proof in the same direction. Thus, in the Suomi dialect, we find the six persons of the verb *come, tulen, tulet, tulee* (or *tulevi*); *tulemme, tulette, tulevat,* they come. These are all variations of verbal or participle forms, such as *tuleva*, coming, *tulema*, the coming. In the Esthnish present of verb *love*, we have *armasta, armastat, armastap ; armastame, armastate, armastawad; armasta* is imper.=love, *armastada*= the loving, also *armastama,* and *armastaw,* and *armastawas*= loving (part.). In Wotjak, the pres't of *do*, is *karo, karod, karoz (kara); karom (karomy), karody, karozy (karo),* they do; the past is *kary, karyd, karyz ; karym, karydy, karyzy*. And we find *karem*=doing, deed, *karyny, karon, karysa,*=doing, *karysj,* doer, *karem*, done. In the past, we observe *yd, ym,* which is Turk. *idum,* Greek *ema, ama.* In another dialect, we find for *come*, pres't tense, *tolam, tolat, toles; tolena, toleda, tolat (tolebes);* and past, *tolenam (tolesam), tolenat, tolen (toles); tolenna (tolesna), tolenda, tolenet (tolebe),* they came. With these compare the verbals *tolem, tolas,* and *tolsas,* coming, the coming, *tolsa,* the comer, *tolema* (G'k *-ama*), come (past part.).

358. In Mongolian, another relative of the Turk., we find for *abu-cho,* to take, imper. *ab,* in the pres't *bi abun amui*, I taking am, am taking (*amui*, I am); in the past, we have *bi abubai*, I taking-was, I took (*abai*, I was). The whole Mongol. verb is very plainly built up on the same plan as the Turkish, but we have not time to dwell on it here. We must observe that the inf. endings are *acho, ucho,* and the inf. of *be* is *acho,* showing the identity of verbal endings with *be*. The Persian verb may easily be placed parallel with the Turkish, and we will now examine this more in detail.

Persian Verbs.

359. We will take *nush*, drink, imperative and root.

Present tense.

nush-am, I drink, may drink.   *nush-im,* we drink, may drink.
nush-i, thou drinkest.   *nush-id,* ye drink.
nush-ad, he drinks.   *nush-and,* they drink.

With these, we must take in connexion the isolated forms of verb *be; as, em,* am, *i,* art, *est,* is, *im,* we are, *id,* ye are, *end,* they are. We see the unmistakable identity between the endings of this tense and the verb *be*. It must be noted with regard to *est*, 3d sing., that we find *d* for the same in Turkish, so we find *d* in the Per. 2d plur., which generally is intimately connected with the 3d sing. So, we may look upon this tense as the root *nush* and am, is; or, we can look upon it as a mere variation of the short inf. *nushid*, or the part. *nushan, nushand*.

360. The present, so called, is the same as this, together with the prefix *mi*; as, *mi-nushan*, I am drinking. This element *mi*, which sometimes follows, and again is separate, may be taken as the mark of our *be*, and we consider it as the equal of Germ. *ge*, and the Semitic *m* of part's; *nusham* is precisely like L. *amem*. The future has the same form, save that *mi* is replaced by *bi*.

361. *Perfect*.

nushidam, I drank. *nushidim*, we drank.
nushidi. *nushidid*.
nushid. *nushidand*.

In this connexion, we want to bear in mind that *nushid* is the short future, and *nushidah* is part. = having drunk; it is precisely the Turkish *deugdum*. So, we can speak of *nushidam* as formed on the base of the part. above, with endings to mark the verb *be*, or, on the basis of the short infin., for they do not essentially differ (so *amatum* and *amatus*, inf. and part. in L.). But the former is the method in the German languages. We may suppose, still further, that it is on the base *nush*, as in Turk., with *idam*, a lost form equal to Turk. *idum*, was (we find Pers. *budam* = be). Again, we find the part. endings agreeing with *be* in form. There is besides all these, a part. adjective *nusha*, shortened *nush*.

362. *Conditional*.

nushidami, I might drink. *nushidimi*, we might drink.
nushidi. *nushididi*.
nushidi. *nushidandi*.

In this connexion, we may mark *nushid*, the short infin., and and the past part. *nushidah*; either may be taken as the base — but the former will be found best to agree with the usual formation.

363. *Compound Preterit*.

nushidah-am, I have drunk. *nushidah-im*, we have drunk.
nushidah-i. *nushidah-id*.
nushidah-ast. *nushidah-and*.

This is the past part. and *be*; we find *nushidah* the base of several compound tenses, on the foregoing plan.

364 In Afghan, related to the Per., *bi* is the fut. prefix, *u* or *w* for the past, *ki* before the optative, or conditional tense — *di* is also used as a prefix here, as well as in Malay. As in Persian, the past part. is found used in the place of the perfect tense; so the simple infinitive is often used for past tense (as we have found it the basis of the past in other languages), changing the infinitive endings into personals.

Hungarian Verbs.

365. The present tense is as follows:

varok, I wait. *varunk*, we wait.
varsz.   *vartok*.
var.   *varnak*.

Imperfect,
varek, I waited. *varank*, we waited.
varel.   *varatok*.
vara.   *varanak*.

It is easy to see, at the first glance, how nearly identical in form these two tenses are. The base of the present *varok* is *var* = *varo*, the present part., and the endings representing the verb *be*, in harmony with the system of the related Turkish. And it is a question whether the imperfect is essentially different. Whatever in principle may be the elements, they are in fact only the present part., with its endings grown to represent the person endings of the verb *be*. We shall, in other languages, find plenty of like examples. It is well to bear in mind another form of imperfect, a compound of the present tense, with all its endings, and *vala*, was; thus, *dicserek vala*, I praised, *dicserz vala*, thou praisedst, *dicser vala*, he praised (*dicser* = he praises). This leads us to believe that the past, in Hung., differs from the present only by the implied *vala* equal to was.

366. *Perfect.*

vartam, I have waited. *vartunk*, we have waited.
vartal.   *vartatok*.
vart.   *vartanak* (*vartak*).

The past part. is *vart*; so, we may consider the perfect as a variation of the past part., corresponding with the Persian *nush-idam*, Turkish *deug-dum*.

The pluperfect is made by taking the perfect in all its persons, and adding to each the same *vala* or *valt* = was; as, *vartam vala*, *vart vala*, I had waited, he had waited.

367. *Future.*

varandok, I will wait. *varandunk*, we will wait.
varandasz.   *varandatok*.
varand.   *varandanak*.

This is merely a development of the fut. part. *varando*. Another future is made by placing the infin. *varni*, to wait, before each of the persons of *fogok*, I will; as, *varni fogok*, I will wait, *varni fog*, he will wait—*fog* being no doubt a variation of *vagyon* or *van* = is.

368. *Present Subjunctive.*

varjak, I waited.	varjunk, we wait.
varj.	varjatok.
varyon.	varjanak.

This is substantially the same as the first indicative; it is imperative also.

Past Subjunctive.

varnek, I waited.	varnank, we waited.
varnal.	varnatok.
varna.	varnanak.

This clearly corresponds with the same tense in Latin, *amarem*. It is plainly a development of the infinitive *varni*, with personal endings.

369. The forms of tenses which we have so far given, belong to what is called the *indefinite* side. By a slight variation in the endings, these same tenses assume what is called the *definite* form. Thus, in place of the present already given, we have, for the definite, *varom, varod, varja; varjuk, varjatok, varjak;* and, for the imperfect, *varam, varad, vara; varok, varatok, varak*. This is precisely the case of Samoidish predicative and subjective endings, noticed under the head of personal endings, and which are used substantially to point out definiteness or indefiniteness. So, in Hung., *latom az erdöt,* (I) see the wood; *latok erdöt,* (I) see (a) wood. If we mark the possessive pronouns joined as endings to nouns, *om, od, a,* and *ja, unk, atok, ok,* and *jok* (my, thy, his, etc.), we shall see that they are almost identical with these definite endings. We find the infin. confessedly receiving these very possessives = personals; thus, *varn-om kell*, waiting-my must, it must my waiting. i. e. I must wait; and so *varn-od kell* and *varn-ia kell*, thou, he must wait (*kell* = must, there must).

370. It is to be observed also that this difference of form does not extend to part's and verbals, which do not denote person.

Slavic Verbs.

371. The system of tenses in the different Slavic idioms is substantially the same. We take first, as an example, the Bohemian.

Present.

volam, I call.	volame, we call.
volas.	volate.
vola, (for volat).	volaji.

372. The Polish, Serb.-Wend., Slovenish, and old Prussian,

present nothing different. The endings of the Lith. sing. are a little shorter, as we see by the present *lej-u, lej-i, lej-a; lej-ame, lejate, lej-a* (loose). The Russ. varies from the above as follows:

Present.

dala-io, I make.	*dala-em*, we make.
dala-esh.	*dala-ete*.
dala-et.	*dala-iot* (*-ut*).

The Russ. 3d sing. (and the 2d plur., which equals 3d sing.) shows that *a* in Bohemian is shortened for *at*.

373. It is clear in the forms already given, that the same system prevails in Slavic that we have found in other languages. These presents may be taken as the growth of some present participle or infinitive, or, with equal propriety, as the base *vol*, a shortened infinitive or participle, joined to the element *am, is*. We might call attention to the agreement between the Slavic endings and the Latin *o, as, at; amus, atis, ant* (*an*).

374. *Perfect.*

The perfect in Slavic is compounded of precisely the same elements as in the languages before spoken of. We will take first the Slovensh.

sim delal, I have made.	*smo delali*, we have made.
si delal.	*ste delali*.
je delal.	*so delali*.

This is precisely the Latin *amatus sum* = I have been loved, save that here *amatus* would be used as equal to *having loved*, while in Latin it is *being loved*—besides, also, the verb *be* in Latin follows, as it does also in the Bohemian perfect, as we see by the following:

volal jsem, I have called.	*volali jsme*, we have called.
volal jsi.	*volali jste*.
volal (*jest* = is, left out).	*volali* (*jsou* = are, left out).

375. The Serb.-Wend. has the form of Slovensh. The Rus. is based on the formation of the Boh., but the element *is, are*, which we find slighted but retained in the others generally, is entirely dropped here, and all we have is the past act. part, with personal pronoun before, thus:

ja dalal, I (have) made.	*mi dalali*, we (have) made.
te dalal.	*vi dalali*.
on dalal.	*oni dalali*.

376. The Polish presents still another variation:

czytalem, I (have) read.	*czytalismy*, we (have) read.
czytales.	*czytaliscie*.
czytal.	*czytali*.

In the 1st and 2d persons of this form, we have the element *am, is*, represented by mere person endings, joined to the part.

It is the transition between Rus. and Boh.—the 3d persons are the participles, exactly as in Rus. This explains to us the Slav. present, showing that it differs from the perfect only in the element *t* (infin.) or *l* (part.), and that the endings are for *am, is, are*. We must remark, too, that the Russ. perfect corresponds entirely with our German past, *walked, el=ed*.

377. Let us turn next to the pluperfect, and first the Slovensh.

Pluperfect.

sim bil delal, I had done.
smo bili delali, we had done.

This has the same elements as the perfect, and one more, *bil* =was, or have been; and the form is literally *I-am been done*.

378. And next the Bohemian.

byl jsem volal, I had called.
byli jsme volali, we had called.

This is the same as the Slovensh, with a different arrangement—*been I-am called*. In Serb.-Wend., this element *am, is, are*, is suppressed, and we have *bech wuknyl*, I had learned (*bech* equals I was, I had).

379. And next, the Polish pluperfect.

czytalem byl, I had read.   *czytalismy byli*, we had read.

We have here the *byl*=was following the perfect.

380. The Rus. does not seem to have anything to correspond precisely with any of these pluperfects. Though there is the form *ia bivalo vertal*, I had turned (*bival*=was, or have been, and *vertal*, a perfect part.). The ordinary pluperfect is *vertival*, had turned—on the base of an infin. *vertivat*, from the ordinary inf. *vertet*, or from the gerund *vertev*. It is one of those cases of an infin. on an infinitive—but we may quite as well look upon that *val* as identical with the *vil* or *bil* (was) of the other languages. We have even another infin., *vernut*, and a perfect on that base; as, *ia vernul*, I (have) turned; there is even another pluperfect, *ia bivalo vertival*—both part's being double. We must, in conclusion, call the attention of the student to the fact that the Slavic participle used as perfect or past tense, varies in gender and number to agree with the subject. We will next turn our attention to the Slovensh future.

381. *Future.*

bom delal, I will do.   *bomo delali*, we will do (make).
bos delal.   *bote delali*.
bo delal.   *bodo delali*.

Bom is for *bodem* (Per. *budam*), I will be, I am; we have the part. *delal* in place of an inf. In Serb.-Wend., the inf. is used, as *budu palic*, I will burn (*budu*=will be, and *palic*=to burn)

Polish is like Slovensh; Russian is like Serb.-Wend., in one of its futures; another is a future = present, on the base of a new infin., as *ia vernu*, I will-turn, from the infinitive *vernut*, as opposed to the regular infinitive *vertat*.

382. Our attention will next be directed to the *Subjunctive*. In Slovensh it is *bi delal*, I, thou, he, might do; and plural, *bi delali*, we, ye, they might do. This is the infin. (or part., if you prefer) with the prefix *bi*, one that is common in Slavic, and said to be equal to the conjunction *that*; it is really a prefix, like Per. *bi, mi*. The past subjunctive inserts a *bil* = was, been; thus, *bi, bil, delal*, I might have done. In Polish, which makes its subjunctive after the same manner, the particle *ab* (=*bi*) receives the person endings; as, *ab-ym czytal*, that-I read (may read). Polish has another form, a sort of past subj.; as, *czytalbym*, I would read, *czytali-bysmy*, we might read. This *bym* is the *bi* noticed above and here suffixed—it is identical, too, with *be*. In Russ., it is clearly seen that the subj. is only an infin. or past part.; as, *ia zhelal bi yachat*, I wished that to-depart, i. e. I would wish to depart; *ia bi ne dumal*, I not thought, i. e. I should not have thought—*bi* is a mere prefix, and as such not to be translated. So we say, *I had wished*, for *should have wished*.

383. In Boh., we find *volal bych, volal bys, volal by*, I, thou, he might call—the Pol. *bym*, separate, and pointing clearly to *be*. In Serb.-Wend., *bech* = I was, *bese* = thou wast; *bych palil*, (I would burn) = *bech palil* (I had burned)—again we see *bi* = *be, if, that*.

Bengalish Verbs.

384. The first or indefinite present only differs from the root by the addition, for the persons of the singular, of *i, is, e*, and for the plural, of *i, a, em*. The definite present is composed of the present participle and an element *is, am* (-*chhi*, -*chhe*).

The indefinite past adds *ilam, ili, ilek*, (for the persons of the sing.) to the root. It is the precise counterpart of the Turkish tense in *idum*, and may be looked upon as *was* joined to the root, or as the development of a participle. There is an adverbial part. in *ile*, and *ita* of the pres't part. is not essentially different.

The imperfect tense is formed of present part. followed by *was*. The perfect tense is made by using the past part. of the verb and joining to the end *am, is, are*—and a pluperfect by joining *was* to the same. There is a future made by placing *iba, ibe, ibek*, after the root (as *kar-iba*, I will do). This is the same as the Lat. future *am-abo*, and is no doubt a variation of the infinitive in *ita*.

The conditional, *I did* or *would do*, is a variation of the infin., like the Latin *amare-m*, I would love.

Hindustani Verbs.

385. This language does not vary its verb to distinguish the persons. The present tense is simply the present participle used with the personal pron's; as, I (am) speaking, he (is) speaking. Another form of present is the same participle followed by *hun* =am, *I speaking am*. The imperfect is *I speaking was* (*tha* or *ta* = was). Another past is made by simply using the past part., as, I spoken (=spoke). The perfect *I have spoken*, is *I spoken am* (have); the pluperfect is *I spoken was* (had). To express the subjunctive, *I may speak*, the form *bulun* is used—*bul* = speak, and *un* no doubt is for *hun*=am. The future *bulunga* is equal to *bul*, speak, and *unga* for *hunga*, I shall or will be.

Celtic Verbs.

386. The tenses of these languages have generally correspondents, the one in the other. We will start with the Welsh.

Present.

carwyf, I love.   *carym*, we love.
carwyt.   *carych*.
caryw.   *carynt*.

Cornish present—same verb.

caraf, I love.
keryth.   *keryn*, we love.
car.   *carough*.
                          carons.

Celtic Breton present of *kana* (for *kanat*), to sing.

kanann, I sing.   *kanomp*, we sing.
kanez.   *kanit*.
kan.   *kanont*.

Irish present.

buailim, I strike.   *buailimid*, we strike.
buailir.   *buailti*.
buailid.   *buahid*.

Compared with the languages already examined, we find in the Celtic nothing peculiar. We have the root, as *car*, representing the infinitive, or participle, to which is joined the mark of the element *am*, *is*, *are*.

387. In Irish, these endings are not so developed as to distinguish, so strongly as in the other languages, the ending of

the infinitive or part. (which is *ad, adh*) from the element *be*. *Buailid*, the 3rd sing., is not materially different from *bualad*, the infin., as Latin *amatum = amat*. In the other languages, infin. endings are much lighter, so much so that the 3rd sing., which best corresponds with infin., often has no ending at all,— but, in the other persons, the endings, which represent the inf. and part., are better developed. In Gælic, the inf. is continued pretty uniformly through the persons of the tenses without variation, followed by the personal pronouns separate — an excellent proof that the tenses in their persons are only forms of the inf. and participle.

388. The Welsh present was not formerly used by good writers, its place being supplied by the future, as *caraf* for *carwyf*, or by this better, *I am in loving* (I love), using *am, is*, with the infin., or gerund, governed by a prep. The perfect is formed after the same principle; as, *I am after loving*, differing from the other only in the preposition used.

389. In Celtic Breton, verbs have besides the personal form, already given, an impersonal form, one which has no variation of ending for the persons, using the separate pronouns before a form like the shortened inf., or part.; as, *me a gan* = I sing, *te a gan* = thou singest — *a* being a mere augment of participle for infin. So, in Cornish, *my a gar* = I love, *ty a gar* = thou lovest (using the form of the 3rd sing.). The verb *do* is sometimes inserted; as, *my a wra care*, I do love (*wra* = do).

It may not be amiss to give the present tense of the verb *be* in Cornish; as, *of, os, yu*, (am, art, is); *on, ough, yns* and *ens* (are). These are plainly the same as the endings of verbs.

390. *Celtic Past.*

caren, cares, care (cara); caren, careugh, carens, (loved).
car-wn, car-it, car-ai; carem, carech, carent (loved).
kan-enn, kan-ez, kan-e; kanemp, kan-ech, kan-ent (sung).

The first line is Cornish, the second Welsh, and the third C.-B. In this connexion we may notice the C.-B. past of *be*.

oenn, oez, oe; oemp, oech, oent.

So, with these kept in view, we can, with propriety, consider the *car-en, car-wn*, and *kan-enn*, as *car* and *kan* representing the gerund or part., and *en, wn, enn*, = was. If we compare the Celtic Breton *kanenn* of the past with *kanann* of the present, we shall find a close resemblance between them. We noticed such a resemblance in other languages. There should be the same identity between these two tenses that there is between the Lat. supine (inf.) *amatum*, and the part. *amatus*, or the same identity which we find between the inf., or gerund, and the past participle, in the German and Scandinavian languages.

391. We may observe, too, that, from another point of view, *caren*, 1st person Cornish, and *caret* (for *care*), 3rd person, are identical with the past part.—the ending of the part. being *t*, in Irish, and *en* and *et*, in Celtic Breton. So that we find this tense identical with the *deugdum* of Turkish, and the *nushid* of Persian.

392. The Irish past is for *do bualad*, to strike, as follows:

do buaile-as, do buail-is, do buail se, I, thou, he struck.
do buaile-amar, do buaile-abar, do buaileadar, we, ye, they struck.

The prefix *do* which we find in the infin. and part., shows very well that this tense is based on them; and the endings, leaving off the *ar* of the plural, point very clearly to *ad*, *adh*, of the inf. This *do* is identical with all the numerous prefixes found in Celtic, such as *ro, re, o, a*. It is the Slavic *da*, and it is found also in the old German dialects; the prefix *r* is found also in old French, as *r-avoir* (to have), for *avoir*.

There is another form in Celtic for the past, which we will now consider.

393. *Second Past.*

kerys, kersys, caras; kersyn, carsough, carsons (loved).
cerais, ceraist, carodd; carason, carasoch, carasant (loved).
kaniz, kanzoud, kanaz; kanzomp, kanzot, kanzont (sung).
buailinn, buailtea, buailead; buailimis, buailti, buailidis (struck).

The first is Corn., the 2d Welsh, the 3d Celt.-Bret., and the 4th Irish (and it has the prefix *do* before all persons). In this connexion, we must bear in mind the Cor. past of *be, esen, eses, ese; esen, esough, ens* (was, were). So, we may regard these forms of the past as *was* or *has been* joined to the present part., or, which is preferable, as a development of a past participle, personal endings being added. The Irish 2d persons give very nearly the past part. *buailte*; the 3rd persons present the part. ending as it appears in the gerund, or infin. The first persons give the Cornish form of past participle.

We regard this tense as a regular Latin perfect, or as a Greek first aorist (mark the *s* in *ker-s-ys*).

394. Here we will give the *pluperfect*.

carsen, carses, carse (*t*); *carsen, carseugh, carsens* (would love).
caraswn, carasit, carasai; carasem, carasech, carasent (had loved).
kansenn, kansez, kanse; kansemp, kansech, kansent (would sing).
buailfinn, buailfea, buailfead; buailfimis, buailfid, buailfidis (would strike).

In *kansenn* (Celtic Breton), we have substituted *s* for *f*, as it really should be; we find also *kanzenn* and *kanjenn*, and so through all the persons. This tense in form is not essentially different from the perfect, just as in Latin, *amaverunt* (perf.)

equals *amaverant* (pluperf.). You can divide *car-sen*, or *cars-en* — using *sen* = had been, or *en* = was (*cars*, *caras*, for perf. part. *carat*, or *caret*, as in Cornish and Celtic Breton). The student will observe here, as well as elsewhere, how the pluperf. indic. identifies with the subjunctive or conditional. Next we will consider the future.

394. *Future.*

In Welsh, the future runs thus, *caraf, ceri, cara* (*car*); *carwn, carwch, carant; caraf* (*f* = *s*) and *carant* plainly show the inf. ending—the tense is not different from the present. There is, in Welsh, a second future, *carof, carych, caro; carom, caroch, caront*, which is plainly only a form of the other.

The Irish presents a future where the mark is *f*, Lat. *bo*, G'k *s*, Rus. *v* of pluperfect; thus, *buailfead, buailfir, buailfid, buailfimid, buailfid, buailfid* (will strike)—we have here (see the *id* = infin. *ad*) nothing but the infin. of a new base, such as we have so often met with. This puts us in mind of remarking, that *every tense is really a form of its own, and not derived from some other—indeed, so is every person form also.*

396. One single example out of several in Welsh, will show that the principle is unmistakably in the Celtic languages of representing *be* as a suffix at the end of verbs; thus, we have

gwybod, to know.
gwn, I know.
gwybyddwn, I knew.
gwybum, I have known.

gwybuaswn, I had known.
gwybyddaf, I will know.
gwybyddof, I will have known.

Bod (Per. *budan*) is inf. of verb *be; buaswn* = I had been; *byddwn* = I was, *byddaf* = I shall be; *bum* = I have been. It is in the Celtic languages that we find most convincing proof that the auxiliaries, such as *do, be, have*, are practically developments of the endings of verbs; it is there that we find them following the verb, either attached or separate.

397. There are some other combinations which we must yet notice in Corn.; thus, *kared em euz*, loved I have, i. e. I have loved: *me em-euz karet*, I I-have loved, i. e. I have loved — *me* and *em* are both forms of *I*, but the *em* is so closely incorporated with *euz* (have) as to cease to be an independent pronoun, and we have here, as in *ego am-o*, a pronoun separate and one in the verb; so, in the 1st plural, *ni hon-euz karet*, we we-have loved. We find also *karond a rann*, to-love (I) do, i. e. I do love, I love (*a* is an unmeaning prefix); so *karond a reomp*, love we-do, we love; there is also the *beza em cuz*, to-be I have, meaning simply *I have*.

Greek and Latin Verbs.

398. We will next consider, in some detail, the elaborate system of the Greek and Latin verb. What we have already said of other languages will aid us much in obtaining a clear understanding of the system now before us.

399. *Present.*

Lat.;	*amo, amas, amat.*	*amamus, amatis, amant* (love).
G'k;	*leipō, leipeis, leipei.*	*leipo'men, leipete, leipousi* (leave).
Span.;	*amo, amas, ama* (*t*).	*amamos, amais, aman* (love).
Germ.;	*backe, backest, backet.*	*backen, backet, backen* (bake).
Dan.;	*bager, bager, bager.*	*bage, bage, bage* (bake).
Go.;	*skaida, skaidis, skaidith.*	*skaidam, skaidith, skaidand* (Ger. *scheide*).
A. S.;	*gife, gifast, gifath.*	*gifath, gifath, gifath* (give).
Eng.;	*give, givest, giveth.*	*give, give, give* (give).

A mere glance at the above comparative view, will show the identity between those forms and the part. or infin.; *amat* is the supine, less the *um*, and *amant* is the present part., or a form of *amat*. The *amo* is short, for *amam* or *amat*, as we see by Span. *ama* = L. *amat*; Gr'k *leipei* = *leipet*, as we see by the 2d plural; *leipomen* is identical with the middle participle *leipomen-os*.

400. In Germ., we find *et* and *en*, known participle endings; in Dan. and Swed., *er* is equal to L. *are* of inf. The A. S. *ath*, *adh*, is the same as Gælic inf. ending. That those endings are not properly pronouns added, is seen by the number of instances where the same ending occurs in more than one person, and, as in A. S., in more than one number. There is no doubt but that in many languages, as the Lat. and Gr'k, the developments are so strong that they may be considered, from their differentiation, as representing the persons, or, more properly, *the different persons of the verb* be—but the condition must be borne in mind that they are only developments of the one and same verbal ending *en, et, ar*.

401. *The Past.*

There are in the indicative mood of Latin, three forms which perform the part of past tenses. They are, for *amare*, to love, the imperfect (or past proper) *ama-bam*, the perfect *ama-vi*, and the pluperfect *ama-veram;* the endings of the past and perfect, after leaving the 1st person, have forms like the present, i. e. *-am, -as, -at, -amus, -atis, -ant*. It is one of the features of the Latin, as it is of others, that the 1st person sing. of the past tenses differs from that of the present, it being *am* for the former, and *o* for the latter. We observed this, even more strikingly, in Hung. and Samoid., where one denoted possessive endings and the other nominative. And so it is in Latin, the past tenses have accusative endings, such as we should find with an infin., while present tenses have nominative endings. The past tenses are everywhere objective, dependent.

402. The form *ama-bam* corresponds exactly with Turkish *deug-dum*, Persian *nushi-dam*, that is, we have the base *am* or *ama*, for the inf. or part. of the original verb, and *bam* or *abam* representing *was*. There is no form of *be* in Latin which corresponds with *bam* (Germ. *bin*, Eng. *been*), unless we take it as a variation of *eram* = was (or of *fui*); it is clearly identical with Turk. *dum*, *idum*, Welsh *bum*, Slav. *bech*, *byl*, our *was* ($b=w$); *bam* is in form a verb of itself, with base *b* and regular ending. We can, with equal propriety regard it as *amab-am*, taking *am-ab* as a base, some infinitive as *amare*, or *amat(um)*, receiving person endings. In this light, it is the Russ. *v* of pluperf. and other forms. There is no question that *b* of *bam* is the *t* of *-atum* (supine), and of *can-t-o*.

403. But *bam* taken in connexion with the other endings *averam* and *avi*, points more strictly to Lat. *habeo*, have. It is very clear that *have*, which is so common as an auxiliary, in Germ., and in other languages which are conceded to be directly descended from Latin (as Fr., It., Span.), and which appears in later years in Latin itself as an auxiliary for these tenses, may be taken as corresponding with this *bam* and *averam*. It is equally clear that *have* is only a development of the endings of the verb, such as we have in Latin, and which has at last been thrown off or separated.

404. Nearly all writers have treated these elements of Latin verbs as representing tenses of the verb *be*, but this is only true so far as *be* is *have*; and if *have* is not *be*, then this ending under consideration is not *be*. The difficulty arises from the fact that in many languages, perhaps most, *be* is used in place of *have*—so it is in Fr. and Germ., among others. The truth is, they are identical in origin, and we so treat them; *have* is simply later in appearance than *be*. Not only *have*, but *do*, *own*, *mean*, *may*, *shall*, *will* (Slav. *byl*), and perhaps all other auxiliaries, are identical with *be*. The proof of *have* equal to *be* is abundant, and beyond all question; their use in common is of itself evidence enough; etymologically considered, they are not different in most languages.

405. *Greek Past.*

e-leipon, *e-leipes*, *e-leipe*; *eleipomen*, *eleipete*, *eleipon* (left).

The Sanscrit formation is the same. The augment *e* and *a* (Celtic *do*, *ro*, *a*, *aq*) shows the part., or infin., character of the base, as we find augments in other languages uniformly before inf's and part's. The forms *e-leipon, eleipes, eleipe* (for *eleipet*), are not materially different from German *ge-blieben* (left).

406. There is another past, called the Ionic or iterative past; it ends in *skon, skes, ske* (sing.); as, *e-tupteskon*, for *e-tupton* — the augment in this form is generally omitted. This *sk*=*s* is the *s* which we shall find in the aorist, the *b* of Latin past; taking *sk*=*k*, it is also the *k* of the G'k perfect; it is the G'k *z* in *aitizein* (for *aitein*), to ask often, and the *sk* in *methuskō*, I become drunk. So, in Rus., we find *v* (= G'k *sk*) as the mark of the iterative; as, *kidat*, to cast, *kidivat*, to throw often; and, again, we have seen it as the mark of the pluperfect.

407. We can regard *eleipon* just as we have the past of other languages already noticed—either as the variation of the endings of a participle, or the *on, es, e* (for *et*) as the past of *be*. Though the usual form of *was*, in Greek, is somewhat different, there are dialectic forms which often occur, enabling us to assume a form for the persons of *was*; thus, *eon, ees, ee; eomen eete, eon*.

The Celtic presents us with an exact counterpart of these pasts in Greek and Sanscrit. In none is the final element so strongly developed as we find it in Latin, and the cognate languages.

408. The Greek has another form of the past, called 2d aorist, which we will next proceed to notice. It runs thus:

elipon, elipes, elipe; elipomen, elipete, elipon (left).

This is not essentially different from the foregoing in meaning, and it is identical with it in endings. It varies from the past in having the root or base *lip*, in place of *leip*. Just such variations in the body of the word prevail in the German class, and in other languages, in the past tenses; as, German *ich schlage*, I strike, *ich schlug*, I struck; so, our write and wrote, sing and sang. This form compares well with the Germ. part. *ge-borgen*, from *bergen*, to bury, conceal. When we bear in mind that the prefix *e* is not an essential part of the tense, and is often left off, we will the more readily see how it agrees with our *leave* and *left*, *see* and *saw*, Latin *capio* and *cepi* (perf.), *frango* and *fregi*.

409. These changes in the base, and of which we shall find more in Greek, seem to be as if in compensation for the shortness or lightness of the ending, as in *taught* for *teached*, where *t* (for *ed*) is almost silent; so, in the plural, we have *men* for *mans*. It might be remarked, further, that these irregular forms, having lost their tense marks, are reduced to the form of mere presents; as, give, gave, Goth. *giba, gab, stila, stal,* Latin

capio, cepi, ago, egi. There can be no doubt that all such forms as these were originally, and are now, in principle, augmented like this aorist of Greek; so, in Goth., we have *sai-slep*, the preterit of *slepa*, to sleep, and *hlai-hlaup*, preterit of *hlaupa* (German *laufen*, run).

Many verbs have no 2d aorist—it is a new form, wanting in all verbs ending in *azō, ainō, euō*.

410. Aorist 1st.

Besides those pasts already noticed, there is a longer and fuller form, the 1st aorist, running thus:

e-leip-sa, eleip-sas, eleip-se; eleip-samen, eleip-sate, eleip-san (left).

The Sans. endings to correspond with these are *san, sis, sit; sma, sta, sus;* and if, in this connexion, we bear in mind the Sans. *asan, asis, asit; asma, asta, asan,* the past of *be* (was or has been), the Greek *esan,* and Latin *esam* for *eram,* we shall have no doubt about what the aorist endings represent. This tense is also a faithful counterpart of the Latin *am-abam,* Pers. *nush-idam.* The San. *san,* 1st per., shows that Greek *sa = sam,* and Sans. *sit,* 3rd sing., shows Greek *se = set* or *sat;* so that in every respect this tense agrees with the Latin *-bam, -bas, -bat.* In meaning, however, it answers better to our perfect.

411. As we regard this tense in its parts as identical with such tenses as the Lat. *amabam,* it is hardly necessary to repeat here what was said of that form. That this *s* in Greek and Sanscrit, which appears as *b, v,* in Latin, is the same as the *v* of Slavic *vertivat,* the new infinitive on the old infinitive *vertet,* as well as the *t* of Lat. *rogitare* from *rogare,* the *z* of Greek *komizō* from *komeō,* admits of no doubt.

412. As we have said of the others we say of this, that whatever may have been its origin, it has developed an ending which represents an auxiliary verb, *have* or *was.* There are some verbs which have the aorist in *ka* for *sa,* that is, with the augment of the aorist they end in *ka,* like a perfect—being a transition form of the latter.

413. Though the 2d aorist is not so full, it represents the same elements—the ending is shorter, less developed, but this is compensated by the vowel change of the root. There is a striking identity, which we must notice before closing this tense, the 1st aorist, between its endings and those of the participle; as, *as, asa, an* (mas. fem. and neut.). Indeed, we find in mod. Greek imperf. sing., *etimousa, etimouses, etimouse* (I, thou, he honored); but *ousa* is the regular fem. participle ending in G'k. This not only shows the tense equal to a participle, but that the aorist *s* is the same as that of *ousa.*

We will next consider the perfect.

414. *Perfect*.

Closely related to the past of Latin and the aorists of Greek, is the perfect. Its fullest form in Latin is *vi*, as in *ama-vi*, I have loved, from the verb *amo;* a shorter, but nearly identical form, is that of the 2d conjugation; as, *mon-ui* (from *moneo*), I have advised. Neither the *u* nor the *v*, we may remark, is peculiar to the perfect; we find a whole class of verbs with the base ending in *u*, as *acuo, ruo, metuo,* and in *v*, as *moveo, caveo, solvo, lavo*. It is hardly necessary to remind the student that this *v, u*, is the very *t* which we have so often met before in many places.

415. There is in Latin still another and much larger class which includes those that scarcely differ in their base from the present—regarding *i* as the ending of the perfect and *o* that of the present. They are such as follow:

*juvo, juvi; moveo, movi; capio, cepi; facio, feci,
fugio, fugi; farcio, farsi; haurio, hausi; video, vidi.
rumpo, rupi; linquo, liqui; lego, legi; fundo, fudi.*

There are instances where a final letter of the base is represented in the perf. by one of its cognates; such as *augeo, auxi; torqueo, torsi; indulgeo, indulsi; ardeo, arsi; jubeo, jussi; vivo, vixi; gero, gessi; spicio, spexi; coalesco, coalui; fingo, finxi; tergo, tersi; cedo, cessi; sino, sivi.* It is clear here that *g* of the present is represented by *x* of the perfect, *d* by *s, b* by *ss, v* and *c* by *x, g* by *s, sc* by *u.*

416. In more languages than one, we have already found the past participle the base of the perfect tense, with sometimes nothing but personal endings developed, and in some cases even these omitted. It is very natural then that we should consider it the base in Latin also. We have observed this *v* mark of the perf., in Latin, having a strong tendency to disappear as *u* in a large class of verbs, and vanishing entirely in a class still larger. Even in that class of Latin verbs where we should uniformly expect it, often it cannot be found; thus, for *amavisti* we have *amasti*, for *petivi* we have *petii*, and *deleram* for *deleveram*. In the Ital., Fr., and Span. languages, whose tenses are formed on the same principle as those of Latin, these short forms are the prevailing ones, that is, the *v* ceases to be a consonant, as in *petii*, and is lost by harmony with the accompanying vowel. So, in Ital., we find *cant-ai, cant-asti, cant-o,* French *chant-ai, chant-as, chant-a(t)*, both for the Lat. *cantavi, cantavisti (cantasti), cantavit*. In Fr. forms, such as *vendis, vendis, vendit* (I, thou, he has sold), we especially see the identity of the perfect with the old Fr. participle; so, too, in *servis, servis, servit* (has served) —part. *servi*, for *servit*. Such perfects become identical with the German pasts.

417. In L., we find a strong tendency of the perf. to identify with the pass. part., and hence with the supine also; thus, pres. *jubeo*, perfect *jussi*, participle *jussus* (to order); *rideo, risi, risus* (laugh); *parco, parsi, parsus* (spare); *scribo, scripsi, scriptus* (*ps=pt*); *duco, duxi, ductus* (*x=ck=ct*). And there is little doubt that the *v* seen in *amavi* is the *t* of *amatum*; so that, seen from this stand point, it is a mere part. developing endings, and we have *amavi* for *amavim* (as we see by *amavim-us*, 1st plural), *amavisti* for *amaviti*, a double development often found in the 2nd person.

The 3rd plural, *amaverunt*, presents us with an unexpected growth; we have here not only the *unt* =they, and the *av* seen in the other persons, but also the inf. mark *er*. In mod. Latin, the *v* disappearing, we have this form reduced to a mere infin. with personal endings; thus, Fr. *chanter-ent*, Spanish *cantaron* (they have sung), and the infin. *chanter, cantar*. This growth of *amavunt* (*amatunt*) into *amaverunt* (*amaturunt*), is precisely the growth of *amaturus* out of *amare, amatus, amandus*. The Wallach. carries the *r* through all the persons plur., as *laudaramu, laudarati, laudaro* (for *laudarunt*), we, ye, they have praised — while in Latin we should have *laudavimus, laudavistis, laudaverunt* (*laudarunt*). In Tuscan, we find poetic forms for the perf. 3d plural where the person ending is entirely lost, and we have the bare inf.=part.; as, *creder'* for *creder-o=creder-ono*. In the Goth. past (=perf.), we find the same doubling in the plural that we do in Latin 3d plural perfect; thus, *salboda, salbodes, salboda; salbo-dedum, salbo-deduth, salbo-dedun* (saved) — the double *d-ed* being found in the three persons plur. That this *d-ed* is equal to the Latin *av-er*, is very evident from the identity of the tenses in which those elements are found. Both languages have a corresponding tense in the subjunctive, and in both this double element appears in all the persons; as, *salbo-dedjau, -dedeis, -dedi; -dedeima, -dedeith, -dedeina;* Latin *am-averim, -veris, -verit; -verimus, -veritis, -verint* (might have loved, may have loved).

418. If we would consider the Latin perfect as composed of parts, we may say it has the auxiliary have (*avi*) and the perf. or past part., a composition such as we find everywhere; *averunt* of the 3rd plural has grown to represent the infinitive *avere* (*habere*) and the person ending. The past in German is made by suppressing *have* and using the participle alone, even going still farther and suppressing the mark of the participle, as in the irregular verbs (so as to bring it still nearer the present). The same thing precisely seems to have occurred in Latin in a large portion of its perfects.

419. There are in Latin, also, a few scattered remnants of

reduplicated perfects, such as we find prevailing in Greek and in a portion of the Gothic pasts; such as *mordeo, mo-mordi* (bite), *pendo, pe-pendi* (haug), *tondeo, to-tondi* (shear). In some of these reduplicated perfects, the root vowel is also changed, as in our irregular verbs; as, *parco, peperci, tango, tetigi, pario, peperi, cano, cecini, fallo, fefelli.* In that large class of Lat. verbs where the root is changed and the reduplication is not apparent, we may consider it as latent, and they are easily placed parallel with our irregular verbs; as, *cresco, crēvi* (grow, grew), *mitto, misi* (send, sent), *sto, steti* (stand, stood), *sido, sidi* (sit, sat), *lego, legi* (read, read, past), *frango, frēgi* (break, broke), *ago, ēgi* (do, did), *capio, cēpi* (take, took).

420. There is also in Latin the pluperfect *amaveram, amaveras, amaverat* (I, thou, he had loved); the 2d future *amavero, -ris, -rit* (I, thou, he will have loved); and the perf. subjunc. *amaverim, -ris, rit* (I, thou, he may have loved). These are all identical with the perfect as it appears in the 3rd plural—*ram* and *rim* mark the acc. pron., and *ro* marks the nominative. They stand as if made of *averam*, which is the infinitive *habere* (*avere*) with endings, and the root *am*; in the *abam* of the past, the endings are joined to the root instead of to the infinitive.

421. The perfect of Greek will next engage our attention. Of the reduplication we have already found traces in Latin and Gothic; in the Greek, it is a feature more constant, it is one of the most prominent marks of the perfect in that tongue—thus, pres't *leipō*, perf. *le-leipha* (leave), *plekō, pe-pleka*, k=ch (fold). But this manner of regular reduplication is not found in all verbs by any means. In a large class of verbs, namely, those which begin with two consonants (with some exceptions), the augment is *e*, the same as in the aorist and past tenses; thus, *zēloō, e-zēlōka* (z = dz); *speirō, e-sparka; psallō, e-psalka*. The reason of this variation from what we are wont to regard as the regular mode of reduplication is, that this reduplication is really a case of double letters, *leleipa = lleipa, pepleka = ppleka*, and where two consonants come together, as *ds, ps, sp*, they being alike, as we have elsewhere shown, they are, also, *already double*. In such cases as *graphō, ge-grapha, krinō, kekrika, pneō, pepneuka, thlaō, tethlaka*, where we have one of the two initial consonants *l, n, r*, (some exceptions), the augment is regular, because such letters are little more than vowels. It hardly needs from us the hint that the perfect, in its formation, is precisely that of the aorists and the imperfect, that the augment *e*, of those tenses, is only one of the forms of this very reduplication.

422. Having already suggested that all double letters and all cases where two consonants come together are augments, just like

this one of the perfect, we must remind the student that even this Greek reduplication is by no means confined to this tense; it is often found in the present, as *ti-trōskō*, I wound, *pi-praskō*, I sell; it is often found in parts of speech not verbs (as *gi-gas*, a giant, *touto*, this), and in other languages much more clearly than in G'k. This augment has a history identical with that of the Germ. *ge*; this *ge*, too, is a mark not of participles alone.

423. Having considered the initial part of the Greek perfect, let us next consider that which marks its ending. The regular endings which mark the perfect are *ka* and *pha (va)*; as, *peithō pepeika, tupto, tetupha*. Remembering how often $k=t$, we find no trouble in seeing in this *k* the *t* of Latin *amatus*, and the *et, ed*, of Germ. pasts. In some forms of Slav., we have found the usual past sign $l=t$ appearing as $ch=k$; as, *bych, bech*, in place of *byl*, was; so, we find *wuknich (nik)*, I learned, and *wuknyl* (part.) learned—it is only a form of the infin. ending *ic* (is) for *it*, which we often find. The *pha (va)* is only a form of *ka*; the form $v=t$ also appears in the Lat. perf's. We need hardly mention that this *k* and *v* is the *s* of the aorist and of the future.

424. We must observe here, too, that this *ka* and *va* appearing in Greek perfects, is not some new element added to the verb, but simply, as we saw in the Latin perfect and supine a development of what was already in it, a growth of cognate letters from the end of the base or root of the verb. Thus, we have *tuptō, (te)tupha (pt=ph); plekō, (pe)pleka; legō, (le)-leka (g=k); 'aliskō, 'elōka (sk=k); ktizō, (e)ktika (z=k); orussō, ōruka (ss=z=k); 'amartaṇō, 'ēmartēka (n=g=k)*.

425. But verbs ending in *eō, aō, oō*, and the like, really seem to have an additional *k*; as, *phileō, (pe)philēka; timaō, (te)-timēka*. But there is no doubt that there is an undeveloped *n*, *s* or *z*, in this *eō, aō*, just as we find it appearing in *anō, izō, iskō; aō,* may be taken as a transition of *anō* to *ō*. So, *chraō* is for *chravō* (our *grave*, German *graben*), *chaō* for *chavō* (gape, Germ. *gaffen*), *kleo* (Germ. *klaffen*); *thaō* for *thapo, bruō* for *brephō*.

There are also such perfects as *(e)stalka* from *stellō*, and *(e)-sparka* from *speirō*. These are related to the above in their vowel character, and what is said of one will apply to the other. We want to bear in mind that *k* though apparently a hard consonant is really equal to $g=j=i$, and associates well with $v=u$.

We have thus found the Greek perfect to be the exact counterpart of the Latin perfect. As *v* represents *habeo* in Latin, so *k* represents *echō*, have, in Greek (for *ekō*).

426. The perfects in G'k assume another form, a form exactly corresponding with our irregular or strong verbs. It is called the 2d *Perfect*, and is treated as distinct from the perfect proper,

but it is clearly a mere form of it. They are evidently different in age, and one is meant to replace the other. That they both exist together, is no strange phenomenon in nature. Old fashions and new ones are always coeval — but one or the other predominates. Degenerated forms which are represented in nature by others, are only suppressed, they are never extirpated. The forms we speak of are such as *pepoitha* from *peithō*, *leloipa*, from *leipō*, *plekō*, *peploka* (perf. *pepleka*). It is a matter of history in Greek, in the Attic particularly, that the short forms are the older, and that hence the longer ones are the result of growth; so, the *k* and *ph* (*v*) are dropped in the more ancient Greek, and we have the ending *aa* or *a*, the *s* of the future does not appear, and we have *alō* for *alesō*, *kalō* for *kalesō*, besides, *kaō* replaces *kaio*, and *alein* is for *alēthein*.

427. In modern Gr'k, there is no simple perfect tense, unless we consider the 1st aorist as its representative; the aorist, having a form precisely that of ancient Greek, is used for the perfect, and also for the pluperfect and future. The modern Greek has not as many forms for past tenses as ancient Gr'k, for this plain reason, that the elements by age and growth had got to be so strongly developed that the auxiliaries, as *have*, have been cast off from the parent stem, and have become themselves individual verbs. There are as many tenses in later Greek as in the older, but in the later the elements are more frequently separate. Thus, *echō*, *grapsei*, I have written, *echeis grapsei*, thou hast written; literally it is, *I have (to) have written*, as *grapsei* is the aorist (or perfect) infinitive; this is not the only place where we may find the infin. in place of a part. past; so, in Polish, *bede czytal*, will read (past part. where we use infin.) — so in old German, *ist cuman* (inf.), is come, has come. We find also *echō grammenon* (perf. part.) corresponding in form to our *I have written*, though not precisely in meaning. In Greek the use of *have* following the aorist (perf.) part. in place of perfect tense, is very common; as, *thaumasas echō*, wondered I-have (having wondered I-have). The perfect participle followed by *be* is also very common; as, *gegraphōs esomai*, (having) written I-shall-be, i. e. I shall have written; *tetumenoi eisi*, struck (being struck) they-are, i.e. they have been struck.

428. The Greek pluperfects, as *e-le-leipein*, *e-pe-plekein*, *e-te-tuphein*, are only imperfects on the base of the perf. The pluperf., here, is a true infin.; it is just such a form as the Latin *amaveram*, *amaverim*. The developed person endings at the end of an infinitive we have by this time become familiar with. There is, besides, a 2nd pluperfect, based on the 2nd perfect, as *e-pe-poithein*, on *pepoitha*. (We may mention here, by way of note, that the Gr'k aorist inf. as *leip-sai*, is in form the same as

ama-vere, which in Latin, however, we find only in the past tenses with endings added).

429. In Albanian, we find a compound perfect thus, *kam difiouare, ke difiouare, ka difiouare*, I, thou, he, has heard; *kam kapoure*, I-have opened. Here we have the G'k perfect ending *ka* existing separate. It has also a simple perfect, ending in *ba* (G'k *pha*, Lat. *bam*); as, *difio-ba*, I have heard, *scro-ba*, I have written. This *ba* is often reduced to *a*, and has the forms *ze, tze, te*—showing after all that it is the Eng. past *ed*, Germ. *te*. There is a past tense, ending in *ona, ana, na* (Gr'k past ending *on*, Germ. *en* of part.); as, *difi-ona*, I heard, *chap-na*, I opened, *pe-na*, I made.

430. *Future*.

The regular future mark in Lat., is -*bo*, -*bis*, -*bit*, -*bimus*, -*bitis*, -*bunt*, differing from the past -*bam*, -*bas*, -*bat*, etc., in having nominative person endings. But, in the 3d and 4th conjugations, this mark *b* is suppressed, and we have the future identical (practically) with the present subjunctive, as *regam* is both fut. and pres't subj., *I will rule*, or *I may rule; reget*, he will rule, *regat*, he may rule. There is, besides, a 2d future, which differs from the perf. subj. only in being *amavero*, in place of *amaverim*, in the 1st person sing.; its identity, too, with the pluperfect *amaveram* also necessarily follows. This identity of futures with pasts is by no means confined to the Latin. In Greek, too, *s* is both the mark of the fut. and of the 1st aorist, and *leip-s-ŏ* (fut.) differs from (*e*)*leip-s-a* (aorist) only as *ama-b-am* from *ama-b-o*. This mark is often suppressed in the future, as we find it in Latin. To compare all the persons of these two tenses, we have *leips-o, -eis, -ei; -omen, -ete, -ousi* (will leave), and (*e*)*leips-a, -as, -c; -amen, -ate, -an* (left, have left).

431. Here we may introduce the Pol. fut., *bede pisal*, I will write, *bedzic pisal*, he will write, *bedziemy pisali*, we will write. This *bede* (Per. *budam*, Wel. *bod*, Rus. *bit*) is the fut. of *be*, and we have *will be* equal to *will*—*pisal* is the part. in place of inf. We have, in Pol., another arrangement, *pisas bede*, (to-write I will), I will write, where the inf. is followed by (will) *be*. The Slovensh has, for the 3rd persons sing. of *will, bom, bas, bo* (Welsh *bod*), which approaches still nearer the future ending *bo, bis, bit*, of Latin. In Bohemian, we have *be*=will be, will, preceding the infin.; as, *budeme piti*, we-will (to) drink. Persian has also a compound future composed of *will* or *wish* and the infin.; as, *khaham nushid*, I-shall drink; *khahad nushid*, he-shall drink. The Illyr. uses the auxiliary *hosu* (or *su*)=will, with the inf.; as, *ja su pitati*, I will (to) ask; *ti ses piti*, thou wilt (to) drink—and sometimes the *su* is suffixed, as *sitat su* ((to) read I-will), I

will read; *pit su*, I will drink (sounded *pis-u*). We have, here, the Greek *s*, and see what it represents. The Servian has this same auxiliary, in the form of *odshu* (old Slavic *choshtu*), our *wish*, Persian *khash*.

432. The Wallachian presents the following combination:

(*jo*) *voiu lauda*, (I) will praise. *vomu lauda*, (we) will praise.
vei lauda. *véti lauda*.
va lauda. *voru lauda*.

Lauda is without doubt a shortened infin. We are reminded by this of the identity of future ending *bo*, *bis*, *bit*, and Latin *volo*, *vis*, *vult* (will), of which the Wallachian presents a shorter form. The *voru* is our *were*; so the German uses *werde*, were, for will, and the Slavic uses *bil* (will) for was.

433. In Albanish, we have this for the future:

do te difoig, (I) will hear. *do te difiogeme*, (we) will hear.
do te difiotz. *do te difioni*.
do te difioge. *do te difiogene*.

The *te* mark is an augment, sign of infin.; *do* stands for *will*. The modern Greek form is precisely the same; as, *tha qrapsŏ*, I will write, *tha grapsĕs*, thou wilt write, *tha grapsĕ*, he will write, i. e. we have *tha* unchanged and the endings joined to the main verb. This *tha* is to be compared with the *do*, for *dona*, of Alban., with the *va* of Wall. (*v=t*), the Greek *thelŏ = volo*, and the Irish *ta=be*. The form *grapsŏ* used with it, is called aorist subj., but it is properly an aorist infin. receiving endings, as we saw in Albanian, and elsewhere. This language (modern G'k) forms a future also by using *thelŏ* (=*volo*, will) with aorist infin.; as, *thelŏ grapsei*, I-will write, *thelei grapsei*, he-will write—and sometimes the present inf. is used in place of aorist; and, again, we find *na* replacing *ta*.

434. Having gone thus far in showing the various forms which the future assumes, in different languages, and now remarking, incidentally, that the pres't indic., pres't subj., and the future are tenses that everywhere identify themselves, we will now consider more in detail the relatives of our auxiliary *will*, so as to give a still better idea of the future tense. The connexion of *be* with *will* has been already sufficiently discussed. Next to this *have* is one of the most constant representatives of *will*. We have already seen the future placing itself parallel with the past tenses (marked by *have*), and the *s* of the Greek future identical with the *b* and *v* (for *have*) of the past tenses of Latin. It is a constant feature in Slav. to find *have* joined with an infin. to supply the place of the future, as we say, *I am to do*, or, *I have to do*, for *will do*. So, Gothic has *taujan, haba* (to-do I-have)=I will do, and Latin *dicere habeo* (to-say I-have) =I will say, also Polish *mam szytas* (1-have to-read)=I shall read.

435. In Gothic, *munan, mun,* is used for *will;* so we say, I mean (same word as *mun*) *to-do*, i. e. I shall do it, will do it. This *mun* relates to G'k *mellein,* also used for *will,* and identical with it. Our *owe, ought,* is also related to *will,* as we see better by the Greek form for it, *o-pheilō* (*fil,* will) — and Latin *debeo,* ought, is a form of *habeo* = shall : *must, may, might,* are related to *owe, ought,* and in form to *mean,* Go. *mun;* shall. Germ. *soll,* is of course a form of *will.* The Danish has *bor* = ought, and related to *de-beo,* to Wall. *voru,* German *werde,* our *were.* We have noticed so far only a portion of the relatives of *will,* but perhaps the most important portion.

436. It is in the Illyr. and Serb. Wend. that we notice this important fact, that an augment in the shape of a prefix preposition, is the sign of the future; as, *prepisem,* I will prescribe (fore-write), *za-pisem,* I will record, write up (*pisem,* write); so, also, *njesu,* I carry, *po-njesu,* I will carry (and so in other forms of Slavic).

437. The futures in the modern L. languages are marked by *r,* as Span. *ama-re, ama-ras, ama-remos, ama-reis, ama-ran,* will love. When we bear in mind that the perfect 3d plural is *amaron,* which we know is for L. *amaverunt,* we are led to believe that this Span. future is the Lat. 2d future *amavero* = *amaro.* So, in French, *senti-rai, -ras, -ra; -rons, rez, ront* (will smell). There is no 2nd future in these languages.

438. *Passive.*

We will first introduce the passive of Latin, present tense. It runs thus :

amor, I am loved.   amamur, we are loved.
amaris.   amamini.
amatur.   amantur.

The 3d sing. is identical with the future participle, *amaturus,* leaving off the adj. ending *us, a, um; amantur* differs from this form only in the *t* strengthened by *n; amamur* has *m* used for *t* as often occurs; *amor* is for *amatr,* as *amo* is for *amam, amat;* another form, common for the 2d sing., is *amare* (for *amatre*) which is identical with pres't inf. active — *amar-is* = *amor, amar,* with an extra person ending common in this person; and, again, we find in the imperative, which should agree with this 2nd person, the form *amator* (as well as *amare*). So, five of the six person forms above given, are, unquestionably, identical with *amaturus,* and the 6th is not less so, as we shall see on closer inspection. The form *amamini* has long been recognized as a participle similar to the *-menoi* of the Gr'k pass. and middle; this *emen-oi* is not only middle (a kind of active), but it is active in itself, as we see in the infin. ending *cmen* (active).

There is no doubt about *emen=atur*, and hence *amin-i=atur-i*. Again, in the imperative, we find *hortamini* for *hortator*, and *præfamino* for *præfator*, and hence we are led to believe that they are equivalent forms.

439. We must also remember how very plastic we found the part. in *urus*, when treating of its character. We found it used as pass. as well as act., and that it gave birth to a verbal noun in *tura* corresponding to our part. in *ing*, which is used passively as well as actively. And we shall find plenty of examples, indeed we have already under other heads, where the verbal noun is plainly the basis of the passive; as, in Celtic, Slavic, and Scandinavian. We must remember, too, that *or=er, r*, is by no means a constant mark of the passive; it is the ending of infin. in other languages, as Fr.; it marks the active person endings in Swed. and Dan.; it is the *er* of our *speak-er*, and the *or* of Lat. *script-or*, writer. We have noticed, elsewhere, the frequent use of the part. in *urus* as a verb in Latin, as *amaturum esse*, was about to love, and *amaturus est*, is about to love. We find *amaturum*=would love, but *amarem*, a purely past tense, is used with the same force, and the two are perhaps not essentially different. And then we must bear in mind that all the perfect subjunctives are future in their character, as well as form, and we shall see see how the future equals the past, and hence the passive.

440. And there is, besides all this, a large class of verbs which have this pass. ending *-or, -aris, -atur*, but they are still in every respect active in meaning; as, *miror*, I admire, *miraris*, thou admirest, *miratur*, he admires. It is true, they are called deponents, as if they were not a form of the active, but they are act. nevertheless. They are just such actives as those verbs which have the middle form in Greek; there, every verb is conceived of as having one form which is identical with the passive, and which yet, in meaning, is a true active; as, *leipomai*, I leave, and I am left, *leipetai*, he leaves, and is left.

441. But the strongest proof on this point lies in the present passive of Icelandic:

eg er elskadur, I am loved.
thu ert elskadur, thou art loved.
hann er elskadur, he is loved.

Strike out the *am, is*, which may be easily suppressed, and we have only *elsk-adur*, precisely the Latin *am-atur*. But this language has another form for pass.; as, *eg brennest, thu brennest, hann brennest* (in form *burnest*), I, thou, he, is burned. This is a sort of middle or reflexive form, and is identical with the Dan. and Swedish passive, ending regularly in *es, as*—; as, *de tagas* (Swed.), they (are) taken, *elskes* (Danish), is loved. We have already shown, under the head of the participle in *urus*, how evidently identical this form of passive is with the past part., with the pres't infin., with the *er* marking the Dan. pres't act.

442. There are several interesting facts in Gothic, which we may notice, having a bearing on the connexion between the passive and active. Thus, we find *drobgan* = L. *turbare* (active infin.), and *drobnan* = Latin *turbari* (pass. inf.), to be troubled, and *usluhan* = Lat. *aperire* (open), and *usluknan* = *aperiri* (*h* = *kn*), and *fraquistan* = *perdere*, *fraquistnan* = *perdi* (to be lost), (*st* = *stn*) — we thus see what a slight difference there is between the active and passive forms of infin. in Goth., as well as in Lat. We might refer here to our own *whiten* = to be white, *thicken* = to become thick, where we have the real German infin.. ending used for passive infin. So, we find in Gothic, too, *manna haitans Jaisus*, (a) man (who is) called Jesus — where *haitans* = *vocatus* (participle) is used for *vocatur* (is called). It is hardly necessary to say that whenever we use a past part. independently, as *the man captured* = *the man who was captured*, we use a part. as a passive. We find other instances in Gothic of participle for passive; as, *sa reiks this faihrhwaus us-wair-poda*, the prince (Lat. *rex*) (of) this world (is) thrown-out (e-jected); *all bagme usmaitada, gah in fon atlagada*, every tree (shall be) cut-down (part.), and into fire (shall be) cast (participle); *tharei saiada* (sowed) *thata waurd*, where (is) sowed the word; *gah ahmins weihis ga-fullgada* (filled), and (with) ghost holy (shall be) filled (Lat. *replebitur*). It will be observed that this pass. part. alone is used not only for the present passive but for other tenses.

443. The conclusion we thus far arrive at is, that the past (or pass.) participle is the basis of the passive; but the past part. is intimately connected with the infinitive, as the infinitive is with the participle in *urus*.

444. *Slavic Passive.*

In Bohemian, for example, we find *jest hledan*, he-is sought; *jsme hledani*, we-are sought. It will be remembered that this pass. part. *hledan* (sought) is not different from the verbal noun *seeking* (ending also in *ani*).

445. The Polish presents the same history; as, *jestem kochamy*, I-am loved. The reflexive form is used for passive in Polish, as it is in so many other languages; as, *slowo pisze sie*, (the) word writes self (is written). The impersonal form is also used as with us; thus, *one divides* (they divide) the booty, i. e. the booty *is divided*. And it is worthy of note that the form used impersonally in this way, in the sense of *one divides*, differs from the passive part. *divided* only as *ano* from *any*, or as *szyt-ano* from *szyt-any*, or *podziel-ono* from *podziel-ony*.

446. In Russian, we have another instance of a language having a passive part. in place of present passive, as we see by the following:

ia dvizem, I (am) moved. *mi dvizemi*, we (are) moved.
ti dvizem. *vi dvizemie*.
on dvizem. *oni dvizemi*.

The Russian infinitive ends in *at*, the past active ends in *al*, and this ends in *em* — see the identity of the three.

447. *Hungarian Passive.*

The present passive of *varni*, to wait, runs thus:

varatom, I am waited (for) *varatunk*, we are waited (for).
varatol. *varattok*.
varatik. *varatnak*.

Here, we have a new base *varat*, in place of *var*, and probably identical with *vart*, past part., to which are joined person endings. It is not different, in its passive infin. *var-atni* (*at-ni*), from Latin *am-aver* (*av-er*), or the Greek *leip-sai* (*s-ai*), or the Latin *am-atur* (*at-ur*). It is the *il* found in Turkish *deug-iler* (*il-ur* = *at-ur*), he is struck. It must readily suggest itself to the student, that this so called insertion of an element, as *il*, is only such an insertion as we have found the *s* mark of the fut. to be, and the *k* and *v* mark of the perfect, and no more.

448. *Albanish Passive.*

In this language, we find *difion-em*, I am heard; *pen-em*, I am made; *chap-em*, I am opened, and the 3d sing. for these forms is *digion-ete, pen-ete, chap-ete*. In this connexion, we want to bear in mind that *difion* = he hears, and *difiona* = I heard; so that Alban. *-em, -et* = *ur* of *atur*, Greek *mai* and *tai*. The passive is unquestionably here, as elsewhere, the growth of a passive participle. In the past passive, we find *difion-esa, pen-esa, chap-esa*. It is clear that the endings *em* and *esa* have come to represent *giam* = am, and *kese* = was. The pass. tense, called the definite past, differs (in the plural) from the same tense active only by augment *ou* preceding; as, *difiouame*, we have heard, *ou difiouame*, we have been heard.

449. In Wallachian, we may add here, the passive takes the reflexive form, as *jo me laudu*, I me praise, i. e. I am praised, *noi ne laudamu*, we us praise, i. e. we are praised; but the form of *sum amatus*, I-am loved, is also used.

450. *Celtic Passive.*

The Irish passive present for *buail*, strike, is *buailtear*, through all the persons, followed by the personal pronouns; as, *buailtear me*, I am struck — *buailte*, it will be remembered, is the passive part. equal to Latin *amatus*, in form; and, hence, we infer that *buailtear* = *amatur*. The past passive has an unvarying base for all the persons; as, *do buaileadh me*, I was struck, *do buaileadh tu*, thou wast struck. The form *buaileadh* corresponds exactly with the 3rd person imperative active; *do* is an infin. or part. prefix. Hence, we conclude that this is a pure infin., followed by the separate personal pronouns, but as the infinitive is so completely identical with the participles, in Celtic, we may call it the participle also. We have only to call to mind the identity of the present infinitive and the past active participle in Slavic, and of *amatum* (infinitive) with *amatus*, past or passive part., in order to understand this phenomenon. A 2nd past passive is *do buailti*, for all persons. This is plainly and simply the pass. part. *buailte*. The corresponding active tense has the same basis. The future passive is for all persons *buailfear*, which differs from the present only in *f* for *t*. We think them really one and the same. The 1st person future active is *buailfeadh*, and we doubt not *adh* = *ar* ; *feadh* = *fear* = *tear*. There is, in Irish, a conditional for the passive as well as for the active, but we can see in it only a form of the future.

451. In Welsh, the present pass. ends in *ir* for all persons; as *carir ef*, he is loved, *carir ni*, we are loved. This *ir* of Welsh is the *or* of Lat. *amor*. It will be observed that the corresponding Irish is *tear* = *tur-us*. In this *ir*, we have, too, the *ad*, *adh* of Gaelic; the Welsh *cared*, let him love, is not different from *carer ef* (he), let him be loved. The Cornish form is *carer*. The Welsh past pass., for all persons, is *cerid*. This, if we are to judge by the Celt.-Bret., *kared* (loved), past part., as well as pass., besides the Irish past just treated of, is simply a past part., or if you prefer, an infin. In Cornish, *caras* = was loved, is the identical form which we find in the past active; as, *caras* = he loved. The two futures of Welsh passive, namely *cerir*, *carer*, cannot be mistaken. The perfect *carwyd*, and the pluperfect *carasid* can be seen to be substantially the same as the corresponding active tenses, *carodd* (3d sing.) and *carasit* (2d sing.); *carwyd* can scarcely be said to have developed any element more than *cerid*.

452. The Welsh may say also, *mi a garir*, I (am) in loving (being loved), for I am loved; *efe a garir*, he (is) a loved. There is, besides, an impersonal form *yr ydys yn fy negharu*, it is in my loving, i. e. I am loved; *yr ydys yn ei garu*, it is in his loving, he is loved.

It is important to bear in mind that the C.-Bret. uses *karer* (or *kareur*) impersonally for *one loves*, and *kared*, for one loved, *karor*, one will love, forms which are called passive in Welsh and Cornish.

The common passive in Cornish is a compound, the usual one, of *be* and passive participle.

453. Having given so much of other languages to illustrate the Latin passive, we have now only to add that its past pass. is *amabar, -baris, -batur; -bamur, -bamini, -bantur*, that is, it is a present passive on the basis of past active; we have *amabor*, future, on the basis of the *amabo*; so, we have *amer* from *amem*, and *amarer* from *amarem*, present and past subjunctive. The other tenses are compound; thus, *amatus sum* (loved am), I have been loved; *amati erant* (loved were), they have been loved; *amati fuerimus* (loved will-have-been), we will have been loved; *amatus sim* (loved may be), I may have been loved; *amatus essem* (loved might be), I might have been loved.

454. *Greek Passive.*

The present has the following forms:

leipomai, I am left.   *leipometha*, we are left,
leipō (-esai).   *leipesthe.*
leipetai.   *leipontai.*

Making due allowance for insignificant letter changes, we have simply the element *ai* added to the pres't act., which (repeated) is *leipō* (om), *eis* (et), *ei* (et): *omen, ete, ousi*, or *onti*. And we find *ur* or *r* acting the same part in Latin, which leads us to infer that they are one and the same element. This *ai*, in a form sometimes disguised, extends to the other tenses, as the *r* in Latin. We may say, too, that these six persons seem to be merely a variation of *leipomen(os)*, the pass. part.; but *leipomen* is middle (or active) as well, and little doubt is left that *leipomen(os)* = *amatur(us)*, in form. The ending *mai*, and its variation *mi*, and *ma, men*, is in Greek a well recognized active ending. Besides, we must remind the student of the form *amamini* = *amatur* in Latin; and we may add, too, that while in Latin the 2d plural has the ending *amin-i* of a part., the 2d plur. in G'k *leipesthe* is identical with the pass. infin. *leipesthai* (unquestionably the same as *leipomen(os)*). So, the Greek imperative 3rd singular, which should be same as indicative, is *leipesthō*, like the infinitive.

455. Here we give the past or imperfect.

eleipomen, I was left.   *eleipometha*, we are left.
eleipou (-eso).   *eleipesthe.*
eleipeto.   *eleiponto.*

The only real difference between this and the present, is, as in the active, only the augmènt *e*. The first and second plurals are precisely the same, and the 3d persons, sing. and plur., differ only in *o* for *ai*. The reason of this likeness in tenses in Greek, which differ in Latin, is the same for the passive as for the active, namely, that the past in Greek has not developed the *b* mark as in Latin. If the past in Greek really was a tense distinct from the present, it would have, what it now has not, an infinitive and participle of its own.

Viewing these tenses as composed of parts, we might say *ai* equals *be*, *is*, and *ēn* = *was*, having for the base a participle. It is certain these tenses have a tendency to develop such elements.

456. We will next notice the perfect passive:

leleimmai, I have been left.   *leleimmetha*, we have been left.
leleipsai.   *leleiphthe*.
leleiptai.   *leleimmenoi eisi*.

There is no doubt that all these persons are variations of the perf. pass. part. appearing in the 3d plural, and if we find such forms as *leipsai* (leaving off the augment), identical with the aor. inf. act., and *leiptai* not different from *leipetai* (3d sing: pres't), this only shows that the part. (*le*)*leipmenos*, having the form (*le*)*leimmenos*, is not different from the verbal form *leiptos*, which corresponds in form with *amatus*. Hence, we may either regard the first five persons as the simple passive part. used for the passive, with *be* suppressed, or the ending *ai* as representing *be*, which becomes separate in the 3d plural. It is worthy of note in this connexion, that in the subj. and opt. moods of this tense, this form in *men-os* appears in all the persons followed by *be*, as *tetummenos eiēn*, (struck might-be) I might have been struck. In modern Greek, this same participle without the augment, as *grammenos* for *gegrammenos*, is used thus unchanged through all persons with *be*; *eimai grammenos*, I have been written (literally, I-am written), *eisai grammenos*, thou art (have been) written, *ēmēn grammenos*, I was (had been) written, *ēmetha grammenoi*, we were (had been) written.

457. And next the Greek pluperfect passive:

eleleimmēn, I had been left.
eleleipso, thou hadst been left.
eleleipto, he had been left.
eleleimmenoi esan, they had been left.

This tense, evidently, has the same relation to the perfect that the imperfect has to the present. The part. which is at the basis of it is the same as that of the perfect—*am* being an element represented in the latter, and *was* in the former.

458. The future passive is *leiphthēsomai*, with pres't endings in all persons, and the 1st aorist passive is *eleiphthēn*, *thēs*, *thē*; *thēmen*, *thēte*, *thēsan*. The element *leiph*, which is common to both, is, it seems probable, for *leiptos*, with the element *ēsomai* = will be added in the future, and *ēn* = was, in the aorist, i. e. these tenses are real participles which have developed their parts so as to represent such elements.

There is a 2d future *tupēsomai*, and a 2d aorist *etupēn*. We regard these forms as substantially the same as the former, with the parts less strongly developed, or a portion of them latent.

459. The modern Greek varies the 1st and 2nd aorist passive thus, *egraphthēka*, for G'k *egraphthēn*, and *egraphēka*, for G'k *egraphēn*—using *ka* = have, while Greek uses *ēn* = was. We have only to add, to complete the survey, that the G'k has a fut. middle, *leipsomai*, based on the future *leipsō*, and a first aorist, *eleipsamēn*, based on the aorist active, *eleipsa*.

460. It may not be amiss to notice briefly here the Bengal mode of forming the passive. There are two ways, one peculiar to verbs of Sans. origin, where *be* is joined to the past, or pass., part. in *ta*, as is done in Germ., and elsewhere; another, the more usual one, where a sort of gerund or verbal noun is used as the base, and the verb *go* follows it as an auxiliary; as, *it goes to see*, or seeing, i. e. to be seen—like our *it goes to ruin*, *is being ruined*, goes to destruction, is being destroyed; *get* is used in like manner; as, *get ruin*, for *be ruined*, *get hatred*, for *be hated*. The Hindustani passive is made in the same way, save that *go* follows as an auxiliary in all the tenses. Just as the German says *gone lost*, for *is lost*, so the Hind. says *lost go*, *struck go*, for *is lost*, *is struck* (*go lost, go struck*).

461. That we may leave nothing unsaid that may tend to illustrate the connexion between the passive and the active, we will notice a point or two more, before we close the subject. The Greeks use *briaō* in the sense both of *to be strong* (passive) and *to make strong* (act.); so, when we say *the rope is long*, we use *long* passively, but when we use *lengthen*, the verb form of *long*, and say *lengthen the rope*, we use *long* actively. And, too, the most imperfect scholar in Germ. and Fr. knows well how common there the passive form is for the active; as, *is gone* for *has gone*, *is come* for *has come*, *is fallen* for *has fallen*, *is frozen* for *has frozen*, *is disappeared* for *has disappeared*—to say nothing of our *sells* for *is sold*, and *burns* for *is burned*. The connexion between passives and ordinary intransitives is very close, indeed, it may well be said that the passive is a pure intransitive. It is in the Finn. dialects that we see most plainly the identity of Passives, Reflexives, Causatives, and all other derivative forms, with each other. They all have the same formation, and their characteristic mark, moreover, is $t = d$, n, which in its variations is the t and d of German and Roman participles.

462. *Subjunctive.*

The Latin subjunctive, so called, answers to what is usually called the potential in English, and includes the Greek optative and subjunctive. All those Latin subj. tenses (of which there are four) are very properly so named, being all dependent or subjoined, in fact or in principle, to some finite verb. More than this, at least three of the subj. tenses, the past *amarem*, the perf. *amaverim*, the pluperf. *amavissem*, are based on infin's (always known to be dependent); the first on *amare*, the second on the theoretical *amavere*, and the third on the perfect infinitive *amavisse*.

463. All the subjunc. tenses, the three named above and the present *amem*, have endings like past tenses. Their close connexion with the infinitive may be shown by its frequent use for all of them. Thus, *I desired him to do it*, i. e. *that he should do it, that he may do it;* *I expected him at that time to do it*, i. e. *that he may have done it, that he should have done it*. Here, in these two examples, using the same infin. *to do*, we have the four tenses subj., may do, might do, may have done, might have done. And we shall bear in mind, too, that all our futures and subj's (potential) are based on infin's, that is, they are simply infin's with auxiliary *will, may, might, should*. Again, the subj. very often identifies itself with the imperative, but this is known to be only an infinitive.

464. As compared with the Latin, the subjunctives of Ital., French, and Spanish, have considerably changed their form. The Spanish has a tense called 1st conditional, thus:

amar-ia, -ias, -ia; -iamos, -iais, -ian (should love)

The corresponding Italian is:

amer-ei, -esti, -ebbe; -emmo, -este, -ebbero (should love).

The corresponding French is :

sentir-ois, -ois, -oit; -ions, -iez, -oient (would have smelt).

All these forms correspond very nearly with the future; it is evident they are identical with the form *amaverim*, as the fut. is with *amavero*.

There is another form which corresponds, without doubt, to the Latin *amavissem*. It is in Italian thus:

am-assi, -assi, -asse; -assimo, -aste, -assero (should love).

And in Spanish :

am-ase, -ases, -ase; -asemos, -aseis, -asen (should love).

And in French :

sent-isse, -isses, -it; issions, -issiez, -issent (might have smelt).

The past subjunctive of Gothic is also formed after the same principles as *amaverim*. The present subjunctive of this, as well as that of the other languages just named, is substantially the same as the present indicative.

465. Under the head of the Slavic Verb, we have already seen the infinitive, in the form of past participle, the basis and substance of the Slav. subjunctive, accompanied only, or marked, by the prefix *bi* sometimes equal to *if*, sometimes to *that*, but always in fact identical with *be*.

466. But the Celtic subjunctive, under the head of the Celtic verb, was noticed only incidentally, and by far too superficially to permit it to be passed by here.

In Celtic Breton, the present subjunctive is formed thus, *ra ganinn, ra gani, ra gano* (that I, thou, he, may or shall sing). This *ganinn, gani, gano,* is precisely the future indicative, except *g* for *k* by reason of the preceding *ra* (*kaninn*). This *ra* is the augment that appears, in different forms, everywhere in Celtic. It is the *do* of Irish, the *a*, *ag*, of Welsh, the *bi* of Slavic — it is identical also with the Celt.-Breton *ra* ≐ do, make. This is the common augment for the tenses of the Celtic Breton subjunctive, and it may be said to take the place of our *that*, French *que*. While we observe here that the subjunctive tenses are all futures, we may add that the subj's of L. are all futures also, that is, *amem*, the present, has the same form as the futures in the 3rd and 4th conjugations; *amarem*, the past, is in form the French future; *amaverim*, the perfect, is the same as the 2d future, and *amavissem*, the pluperfect, is not different from *amaverim*. The Welsh subjunctive is made by the infinitive with the help of *may*, *could*, *would*, precisely as with us. In Cornish, the subj. tenses are the same as those of the indicative, some of them having the prefix *re* = Celt.-Bret. *ra*. In Irish, as everywhere, the conditional, or subj., is the same as the fut., or it is based on it.

467. *Greek optative and subjunctive.*

The Gr'k subjunctive corresponds in form through its tenses with those of the indicative, save that the personal endings are uniformly *ō, ēs, ē; ōmen, ēte, ōsi*. There is every probability that there exists the same relation between *leipō, ēs, ē* (subj.) and *leipō, eis, ei* (ind.), that there is between Lat. *amem* (subj.) and *amo* (indic.). All the tenses of the Greek subjunctive are present tenses, present on the basis of the different tenses of the indicative.

468. We find the indicative tenses taken as bases for the optative tenses also, but with the endings *oimi, ois, oi; oimen, oite, oien*, for all the tenses except the first aorist, which has *aimi, ais, ai; aimen, aite, aien*. That this optative ending is a development of the indicative is probable, but it has so developed that *oi* stands forth as a new element. These facts we should bear in mind; that verbs ending in *mi* are in their very

-nature past tenses; that for *oimi, ois, oi*, the Attic dialect has *oiën, oiës, oië; oiëmen, oiëte, oiësan;* also, *eia, eias, eie,* for *aimi, ais, ai* (of the aorist); bearing these things in mind, and taking in connexion the undoubtedly related forms of the Latin past subjunctive, we are induced to believe that the Greek optative endings are all past endings, and the tenses all past tenses, corresponding in form, as well as in meaning, with the Latin *amarem, amaverim, amavissem.*

469. But what is this element *oi?* In Sanscrit it is *ya;* but *ya* is used there for other purposes too—it is the passive mark; a class of verbs is formed there distinguished by this element. Our impression is, that *oi* corresponds to the infin. ending, that it is the *re* in *amarem, amaverim.* The *ai* of middle and pass. tenses represents an inf. ending; so does the *ai* of the aorist inf. = *ein;* mod. Greek inf. ends regularly in *ei* for *ein.* We may identify it, too, with the *s* and *b* mark of the fut. In the Finn. languages, we find *si*, the well known fut. sign, as the sign of the subjunctive, coming, as the future *s* in Greek, before the person endings. We find *ka* in these languages representing the Greek *oi;* this is same as *si*, as *ka* = *s* in Greek; it is also the *t* of past participle—*ka* is the mark of denominatives, and of desideratives; it is the mark, too, of imperatives; they are identical with subjunctive, here as well as elsewhere.

470. *German subjunctive.*

In the verb *be*, in German, the apparent difference between the present subjunctive and present indicative is greater than the real one. The present indicative is *bin, bist, ist* (singular), while the subjunctive is *sei, seist, sei*—but the plurals are more alike, *sind, seid, sind* (indic.); *seien, seiet, seien* (subj.). The *b* of ind. = *s* of subj., as we see by the plural, where *s* replaces it, also by the *sum* = *bin* in Latin. The subj. best represents the inf. *sein.* In English, we find this *be*, as we should expect it, in the pres't subj.; but it is infin. and in place of *seien.*

471. In the ordinary and regular verbs of German, the pres't subj. is like present indic.—except the 3rd sing. which differs thus; *singet* (ind.), *singe* (subj.), *liebt*, for *liebet* (ind.), and *liebe* (subj.). There are other unimportant changes in the vowel of the base that occur in some verbs which we will pass over here.

472. The imperfect subj. is also to be identified with the imperfect indicative; *war, warst, war* is sing. (ind. past), and the subj. is *wäre, wärest, wäre* (our *were*); of have, (indic.) *hatte, hattest, hatte,* (subj.) *hätte, hättest, hätte;* so *kam, kamst, kam,* is past ind. (came), but *käme, kämest, käme,* is past subjunctive (might come). In *lieben,* to love, and regular verbs generally, past indicative = past subjunctive. It is very clear that in the

German languages, as in other tongues, the very essence of the subj. lies in the particles *if, when, that,* expressed or implied (the base being like the ind.). The particle *that* may be called the article of the subj., as *to* is the article of the infinitive. The German uses the interrogative form very commonly for subj., saying *is this so,* for *if this is so, comes he here,* for *if he comes here, struck he that,* for *if he struck that;* so, we say *does he speak, all listen,* i. e. *if he speaks.*

The Verb Be.

473. We propose now to give a general survey of this most important verb as we find it in the different languages. No comparative view can be more interesting to the student, or more useful. It will be especially important from its showing the surprising changes which the same word, *be,* may assume in passing through the different persons, numbers, and tenses, forms which are again varied as they appear in other languages. It will be our aim to show how these forms gradate into each other. It will give to the student, too, the general plan or outline of one of the most important verbs in the language where it is found, one which you may call the basis of all verbs, or which enters into their composition as an important element. It will show, too, the tense-forms and person-forms in an entirely new light, one which will serve well to illustrate the character of the forms which we have so far been examining.

And first we will introduce the Gothic.

474. *Gothic Be.*

In the present, *im, is, ist; sijum, sijuth, sind; im*=German *bin,* Latin *sum,* our *am; sijum* for Lat. *sumus,* is only *sum* (*am* for *are*)—*sind,* Latin *sunt* (are). The past is *vas, vast, vas; vesum, vesuth, vesun.* In the plural, *ves* is for *ver,* our *were*—the *um, uth, un,* are only plur. endings. As our *were* (and *are*) is a pure infin., so is *vesum*=Goth. *visan* (infin.), Germ. *wesen* (our *essence*).

The subjunctive is *sijau, sijais, sijai; sijaima, sijaith, sijaima.* Call this *j* an *i,* as it is, and we easily locate it with Germ. *sei, seist, sind,* Lat. *sum* and *sim,* our *be*—it has the form of the Gothic present plural carried through the singular as well. It reminds us of Latin *sim, sis, sit; simus, sitis, sint* (may be).

475. There is a form for *may be,* thus, *visan* (*wisan*), *visais, visai; visaima, visaith, visaina.* This is the Latin *essem, esses, esset; essemus, essetis, essent* (might be); and it is based on the form *visan* (Germ. *wesen*)=*to be;* while the *sijai* is based on

the other infinitive *sijan* (*sigan*), Germ. *sein*. The form *vesjau* (*wesjan*), *veseis, vesi ; veseiina, veseith, veseina*, is only a slight variation of *visan* (*visau*), and means *might be* (past subj.). Here we see Lat. *esse* equals *be* equals *was*, and the subj. again based on the infinitive.

476. *Anglo Saxon Be.*

The Ang.-Sax. has three forms for present ; as,

eom, eart, ys ; synd, synd, synd.
beo, byst, byth ; beoth, beoth, beoth.
weorthe, wyrst, wyrth ; weorthath, weorthath, weorthath.

In the 2nd form, the *b* which we find in *bin*, our *been*, is carried through all the persons. The form *wyrth* is the German *werden*, another form of *were*—the ending *ath* of the plural has come to be a mere plural mark ; it is the *eth* of *speak-eth*, and is not different from the infin. ending. There are two forms for the past, both equal to *were*; as, *waes, waere, waes ; waeron, waeron, waeron*, and *waerth, wurde, waerth ; wurdon, wurdon, wurdon*. Both are forms of the *wyrth* above—so, we see the pres't = past; the form *wurde*, which we find also in Germ., reminds us of *would*—indeed, it is used in German for *would*, as *werde* (were) is used for *will* (see *be* = *will*).

477. With slight variations, those three presents above given are also subjunctive, thus :

sy, sy, sy ; syn, syn, syn (Germ. *sein* = to be), Lat. *sim*.
beo, beo, beo ; beon, beon, beon (been), Lat. *sim, b = s.*

The other form is *weorthe* (sing.), and *weorthon* (plur.).

The past subjunctive is *waere* and *wurde*.

wes, beo, weorth, are equal forms for imperative.
wesan, beon (been), *weorthan*, equal forms for infin.
wesende, beonde, weorthende, for present participle.
wesen and *worden*, for past participle.

See *wesen* = *wesan*, infinitive = participle.

478. Looking over the imperative, and comparing *we-s* (*w-er*) and *we-or-th* with its equal, our *be*, we may observe that *w-er* has developed one infin. element and *we-or-th* two ; *we-or-th-an* has three, and *we-or-th-end-e*, at least four—see how elements are repeated; the Lat. *fu-t-ur-us* has three like Germ. *w-er-d-en*. We may add that the 2d form of the present, *beo, beoth*, is used for future (L. *ero*). There is also *an-weard* (Lat. *prae-sens*) = being, and *to-waerd* (to-ward) = about *to be* (Latin *futur-us*, less the ending, as *fu-t-ur*). These are merely Germ. *werden*, with augments (or prep's) *an* and *to*. If we transpose, as often happens, the letters of *futur*, thus, *furt*, we shall see how it equals *werd*. Indeed, we can regard our *were* as equal to *futur*, the *t* being suppressed, as in Latin *fuero* (will have been, or will be)

for *futero* or *fuvero*. The Latin *fieri* (to be) is another form of *futur*, where *t* is dropped, or otherwise represented.

479. *Old German Be.*

There are few forms here that are new, compared with what we have already seen. In the present plural, however, besides the forms *sin, sun, sind, sit,* already met with, we find *birumes*, we are, *birut*, ye are (but *sindun* is they are). This *bir* is clearly *were*, which again equals *are*; *birumes* is identical with Latin *eramus*, we were (*bir=wir, uir, eer, er*); *sind* also equals *were*, for *sind* is *sid, sir, were* (*s=f* and *w*).

In the imperative, we find *sus, sis, wis, wes* (*ves*), all variations for *be*, L. *sis, esto*—*sis, wes*, is for *si, we,=be*, as German infin *wes-en=s-ein*, L. *es-se.* Swed. has *vara* inf.=*wesen*, i. e. *r=s*.

The forms *ves, var, ver*, are common through the German and Scandinavian tongues for the imperative, showing that imperative equals infin. and the past, and, besides, what development *be* is capable of.

480. *French Be.*

The infin. *etre* equals Latin *futur*(*us*), Germ. *werde*, our *were* (*fut=uut, eet, et*); *etant*=being (part.) is same as Germ. *wesen* (*t=s*); *ete* (been) is same as *was* (*t=s*). The present indic. is as follows:

suis, es, est; sommes, etes, sont (am, are).

The *suis=uuis*, was, is; in *es* and *est*, the *s=b, w, f,* disappears; the 2d plural, *etes*, Lat. *estis* (Germ. *seid*, our *are*), shows what the part. *ete* must have been. And the past tense *etais, etait*, for Latin *eram, erat*, shows *t* equal *r*. We find also:

fus, fus, fut; fûmes, fûtes, furent.
(Lat.) *fui, fuisti, fuit; fuimus, fuistis, fuerunt (fuere).*

This is clearly seen to be our *was, were*, German *wesen*. It is exactly the same as the present, only *f* for *s*; *futes* equal *etes*; one of the plurals of Latin (*fuere*) shows the *were* very clearly (*fuere=vueri, uuere*, were). It is the same also as *etais*, only *fu* for *et*. The future sing. is *serai, seras, sera*, Latin *ero, eris, erit*; the *s* suppressed in Latin appears in French—it is *were* with endings.

The Fr. imperative is *sois*, same as *suis*, am, and taking *s=w*, it is our *was*, the *ves* found in some Germ. imperatives, the Lat. *es*. The pres't subj. is *sois, soit* (may be). There is a past subj. *fusse* and *fut* (Lat. *fuissem, fuisset*), I might be, he might be— this again is our *was*.

481. The Italian presents few things of much importance. The infinitive is *essere* (for *sesere*), Span. *ser*, German *sein*, Fr. *etre*, Latin *esse*. The part. *been* is *sta-to* (to being Lat. *tus*, part.

HISTORY OF VERBS. 129

ending), Fr. *ete* (*et*=*sta*) Span. *sido;* the imperative is *sii, sia* (*s*=*w, b*).
The present indicative is as follows:

sono, sei (*se*), *e; siamo, siete, sono* (are).
era, eri, era; eravamo, eravate, erano (were).

This past is plainly the Latin *eram, erat*, but it is important to observe the *v* appearing in the 1st and 2d plur. It shows that the *b* appearing in ordinary past tenses in Latin, is suppressed in *eram*. The Italian present participle *ess-endo* is the A. Sax. *wes-ende*, Spanish *si-endo*.

482. *Celtic Be.*

Of the Celtic class, we will first turn to the Welsh. The present is thus: *wyf, wyt, yw; ym, ych, ynt*—also the same forms with prefix *yd*; as, *ydwyf*. We want to bear in mind, in this connexion, the imperative forms *bwyf, bydd, boed*, and inf. *bod*, and we shall see that *wyf* is for *bwyf*, relating to Germ. *bin, bist;* the plurals, by replacing the lost *s*, as *sym, sych*, refer also to Germ. *sind, seid*, Latin *sum*.

The past singular, *byddwn, byddit, byddai*, besides *oeddwn, oeddit, oedd*, refers to our *was* (*b* = *w*). It is based on inf. *bod*, imperative *bydd*, Slavic *biti, bede*.

483. The perfect tense is:

bum, buost, bu; buom, buoch, buant, also
buais, buaist, bues; buasom, buasoch, buasant.

The *bum, bu*, is our *been, be*, French *fus, fumes* (*b*=*f*). The second form, *buais*, is our *was*, Latin *fuisse*, French *fusse*. In elements, it is like Italian *era-vamo* (*s*=*va*).

The pluperfect is not materially different,

buaswn, buasit, buasai; buasem, buasech, buasent.

The future is:

byddof, byddi, bydd; byddwn, byddwch, byddant.

It is easy to see in this only the development of the infinitive *bod*, imperative *bydd* (1st plural, here, like *byddwn* of past).

484. *Cornish*.

The Cornish does not vary materially from the Welsh *be*. The present is *of, os, yu; on, ough, yns* or *ens*—which will easily compare with the Welsh. These make a new form by prefixing *as, ys* (the *yd* of Welsh), giving us *assof, yssof, ythof, esof, sof, thof*, (for 1st person)—pointing to *is, was*, Latin *es*, French *sois*.

The past is *esen, eses, ese; esen, esough, ens*—we easily see how this inentifies with Cornish present, our *is* and *was* (*eas*).

17

There is a future=subj. (should be); thus, *bef, bes, bethe; ben, beugh, bens*—and a past tense (was) not different from it; thus, *buf (buef), bus, bue* (be); *buen, beugh, bons.* Here we see repeated again and again *been*, Germ. *bin, be*, and *bus*=was. Both are based on the inf., that which we always find at the base of the past and of the fut.=subj. The imperative is *byth*.

485. *Celtic-Breton.*

In this form of Celtic, the infinitive is *beza*, German *wesen*, French *etre (t=z)*. The participle *been* is *bet*, the French *ete* less the *b*—or you may divide *b-et*, for *et* is part. ending. The imperative is *bez*, Anglo Saxon *byth*, French *sois (b=s)*; the form *bez-et*=French *soy-ez* (be-ye). The tenses are as follows:

ounn, oud, eo ; omp, och, int (present).
oenn, oez, oe ; oemp, oech, oent (past).
bezim, bezi, bezo ; bezimp, bezot, bezint (future).
benn, bez, be ; bemp, bech, bent (would be).

In the present, the *b* and *s*, seen in other languages, as *bin, sum*, are lost in vowels; the past is not different from it—*oes*=was, uas, and *oe*=wa-s. The future is a form of infin., but it agrees with *was*. The last form is like it, but has the *z* suppressed, and it becomes our *be, been*. The Celtic-Breton *weza* is Welsh *bues, buais*.

486. *Irish Be.*

The Irish imperative is *bi, biod*. The present is as follows:

bidim, bidir, bideann (bion) ; bimid, biti, bid.

This *bid* is Germ. *bist*, Celt.-Breton *beza (z=d, st)*. The form *bidim* is the French *etant*, the *e=bi*. The past is:

bideas, bidis, bi ; biomar, biobar, biodar.

So we see by the 3d sing. *bi*, that it is all a development of *be*, the inf.; *bidis*, leaving off *b*, is the Fr. *ete, etois ; biod, biom*, is our *been*. There is another past, *bidinn, bidtea, bidead (biod); bimis, biti, bidis*—*bid-ead* is a double infin., like German *werden*, Italian *ess-ere*. See how the plural agrees with the present plural. The fut. is *beidead*, not different from the second past. The infinitive is *beit*, having the prefix *do* (our *to*), showing its identity with the pasts, which also put *do* before all the persons.

487. The participle with the prefix *ar*, is *mbeit*—where we see the participle mark *m* of Semitic.

We find simpler forms for *be*, as follows: *is, as*, for our *is ; bad, ba* for our *was (b=w) ; bud*, Welsh *bod*, =will be (*bud=bad, ba, be*).

We also find *taim, tair, ta ; tamaoid, tataoi, taid*, for am, is, etc.—this *ta* is the French *ete*.

488. *Slavic Be.*

In Illyrian, the present tense is:

jesam, jesi, jest ; jesmo, jeste, jesu.

This *je* is a prefix like the *as, yd,* of Celt., *e* of Latin *esum,* and as such it is often left off; as, *sam, si,* (but *jest* becomes *je*); then we see the Latin *sum, sumus, sunt.*

The future is:

budem, budes, bude ; budemo, budete, budu.

This is the imperative *budi*, infin. *biti*, with person endings — it is, too, a development of *be.*

There are two pasts, the first *have been,* and the next *was,* thus:

bih, bi, bi (be); *bismo, biste, bise* (*bese*).
biah, biase, biase ; biasmo, biaste, biahu.

We easily see the identity of the former with our *be,* Germ. *bist;* in the latter, we see *was,* Celtic-Breton *beza.* The forms *biv, bil, bit,* are all participial forms, and all variations merely of *biti,* to be ($v=l, t$).

489. *Serb.-Wend.*

The present is like the Illyrian, less the prefix *je*. The past is:

bech, bese (be), *bese* (be) ; *bechmy, besce, bechu.*

This is precisely the Illyrian *biah, biase.*

The future develops an extra *z;* as, plural *budzemy, budzese, budza*—this *z* is the *s* found elsewhere in the future; but even the imperative is *budz,* while infinitive is *bys* (*byc*), *byl*=been, *bywsi* (hav. been), Latin *fuisse.*

The present subjunctive is *bych byl* (I may-be been), I may be — also *budzich byl* (shall-be been), I should be. There is a pass. part. *byty*=been, which is same as infinitive, and like Fr. *ete;* there is the form *sucy,* and *jso* (*so*), German *seiend,* being.

490. *Slovensh Be.*

The present is like that of Serb.-Wend. The perfect is compound, *sim bil* (I-am been), have been; and pluperfect, *bil sim bil* (been I-am been), had been — this tense subjunctive is *bil-bi-bil* (see the elements repeated).

The sing. fut. is *bodem, bodes, bode* (shortened, *bom, bos, bo*). We find for *would* be, the form *besim, bese, be; besmo, beste, beso*—strike off the *be,* and you have the ordinary pres't. We may regard the *be* as a prefix, or the whole as a form such as we often meet with.

491. *Bohemian Be.*

There are few things of interest here, after having already

given so much of the Slavic *be*. The present is *jsem, jsi, jest; jsme, jste, jsou*—showing very clearly that the *js* (*jes*) is only a kind of *s*. We find in the subjunctive, such repetitions as, *byl-bych-byl* (been-may-be-been), I would have been. The participles are (pres't) *jsa, jsouc* (Germ. *seiend*), and (past) *byv, byvsi* (*byl*), L. *fuisse*, our *been*. There is also a fut. part., *buda, budouc*, Latin *futurus*, Germ. *werden*, Persian. infin *budan* and *shudan*.

492. The Polish presents scarcely anything different from the others noticed. The conditional, or subj., is *bylbym-bylabym-bylobym* (I would be), and *bylbys-bylabys-bylobys* (thou wouldst be)—in which *byl*, or *be*, is repeated, or appears, twice.

493. In the Russian pres't, the former prefix *j* and *je* appears as simple *e;* thus, *esm, esi, est* (am, art, is)—showing also that the *e* of Latin *est* may be taken as prefix, making *e-st* = *sunt* (*st*). There is another style of *be* in Russ., as *bivao* (am), *bivaet* (is), where we have *bi* as a prefix, or we may regard it as a mere repetition of *be*. There are part's on this basis, *bivat* (inf.), *bivivat* (to have been), *bivaioshi* (being), *bivavshi* (been)—notice that *oshi* and *vshi*-are pres't and past part. endings respectively.

We may as well notice after this the Albanish.

494. *Albanish Be.*

This appears in the present thus:

giam, ge, este; gemi, gini, giani.
kese, ke, ke; kemi, kete, kene (past, was).

In the *giam*, we may take *gi* as prefix and compare with our *am*, or take *g* = *s* and compare with *sum*, Russ. *esm*, Bohemian *jsem*—the plurals compare with *sumus*, German *sind* (*g* = *s*). When we bear in mind how near *g* is to *k*, we see how near the Alban. past is to the present, especially in the plural. Taking *k* = *w*, *kese* is our *was*, German *wesen*, Celtic *beza*. It is related to G'k *ginomai*, Arab. *kan*, been. In the future, we find *do te giam, do te gemi, do te gene* (I, we, they, will be). The *do-te* may be translated will-that—but, in power, they are no more than augments, the whole verb lying in the present for future. The Alb. shows other forms for the verb *be;* we find a sort of past subjunctive; as, *gese, gesem, gesete* (1st sing. and 1st and 2nd plural)—it is really a past indicative, where the *k* has changed to *g*, corresponding better with the present.

495. *Wallachian Be.*

There are some things to notice in Wallachian. The present is as follows (two forms):

sum (*sunt*), *es, e; suntemu, sunteti, sunt.*
escu, esci, este;

In the second form (sing. only), we find *e* as a prefix.

The perfect, Latin *fui*, is as follows (two forms):

fui, fusi, fu ; furamu, furati, furo.
fusei, fusesi, fuse ; fusemu, fuseti, fusero.

The plural of the first form, as *furo*, corresponds with Latin *fuerunt* (from *fui*); but the *fusero* of the second form is more like the theoretical *fuverunt*, Latin *amaverunt*, the *s* representing *v* as usual.

So the pluperfect (Latin *fueram, fuerat*) is:

fusesem, fusesesi, fusese ; fusesemu, fuseseti, fusese.

This *fusesem, fusese*, corresponds with *fuveram* ($v=s=r$), for *fueram, fuverat*—or with *fuvissem*, for *fuissem*. Infinitive is *fi* (be), or *fire*—part. *fostu*, been, *fiendu*, being (Germ. *seiend*).

496. *Hungarian.*

The present, past, and perfect, in order are:

vagyok, vagy, vagyon (van) ; vagyunk, vagytok, vagynak.
valek, valal, vala ; valank, valatok, valanak.
voltam, voltal, volt ; voltunk, voltalok, voltanak.

The participles are, *valo* (being), *volt* (been), *leendo* (*futurus*). The *vagy* or *van* is our *was, been* ($v=w=b$). The *vol* of the perfect, is the Slavic *byl*.

The Hung. has two forms for *be*, as we find also in so many other languages; instead of beginning with *v*, the second form commences with *l*; as, for the past, *levek, level, leve ; levenk, levetek, levenek*—the infinitive is *lenni* (*len=ben, bin*).

497. *Finnish Be.*

The *be* of the Finnish dialects will somewhat illustrate the character of the Hungarian, besides furnishing us with some interesting forms.

The Wotjak *be* has imperative *lu, ul ;* infinitive *vyl* (Slavic *byl*); present *vanj* (Hungarian *van*); past *vylem ;* luiny (noun), being, (Hungarian *lenni*).

The Suomi *be* is, for the present, *olen, olet, on* (been); *olemme, olette, ovat* (was); the past is *olin, olit, oli ; olimme, olitte, olivat*—in the subjunctive, we find the forms *lienen, lien, lie.* The *ol, lie*, which we see clear through, is the Slav. *byl*, our *will ;* bearing in mind how often in Slavic the $l=v$ and *w, b*, we can see that *le=be, we, was*. In the imper., we find *olkan, olkaat*—that *k* we have noticed already in Albanish. In Lapp., we find infinitive *le*=be, and *lem*=am, *lek*=art, *lae*=is. Syrian *vy, vol*=be (infin.), *voly*=was, *volau*, being.

498. *Mongolian.*

This language presents some interesting forms of *be*. The forms for the persons here are invariable, as they are, too, in

Finnish. The infinitive is *bukn* (be); present is *bui* (*be, bin*); past is *bolai* (Slavic *byl*); perfect *boluge* (Slavic *byl*); subj. *bokessu* (infin. *buku*); the gerund being, having been, is *borun* (our *were*, Dan. *var*, Swed. *vara*). There is another form of *be* thus, *acho* (infin.), *amui* (am), *abai* (was), *asu* (being).

499. *Persian Be.*

The infinitive, here, is *budan* (German *werden, be=were*), and the past tense is *budam, bud* (I was, he was) — change *d* to *l*, and we have Slavic *bul, byl*. The imperative is *bash*, i. e. we have here the two elements together, *be* and *s, sh* (*ba-sh*), which we find *be* alone representing in other languages; it is also our *was*; the pres't tense sing., is *basham, bashi, bashad*.

Then there is the second form *shav* (*sha-v*), imperative, and *shavam*, I am, *shavad*, he is. Here, again, we find double elements, *sh=s* (of *sum, sei, sind*), and *v=b, w* (of *be, was, wesen*).

500. In the Hindustani, the root of *be* is *hu*, infinitive *hu-na*, pres't part. *huta*, past part. *hua*, past act. part. *hu, hukor*. This *hu* is somewhat like Greek *ei* for *be*, and the *u* represents our *b* and *w* of *be* and *was*.

501. In Japanese, *are* equals am, be, is, and *atta* (French *ete*) equals was.

502. In Arabic, we have already noticed that *be* is *kan*, G'k *gin-omai*, our *can*, Germ. *kennen*; in Syrian and Hebrew, it is *ith* and *is*.

503. *Greek Be.*

The present and past tenses are:

eimi, eis (ei), esti; esmen, este, eisi.
ēn, ēs, ē; emen, ete, esan.

The present is easily connected with forms already met with; *eimi*=am; in *esmen*, the *e* is a prefix, as in Slavic. The *ēn* of the past refers to our *b-een*, Celtic *o-en*; the *ēs* and *ēsan* point to our *is* and *was*. The imperative is *eso, esto*, inf. *einai* (b-een, b-eing); present part. *ōn*, (b-eing), and *ousa* (German *wesen*).

504. In the Greek, we see the initial *b* and *s* disappearing in vowels, but in Sanscrit, which is very much like Greek, the *s* again appears; as, the present *asmi, asi, asti; smas, stha, santi*. So, in the optative (subj.), we find, San. *syan, syas, syat* (sing.), but Greek *eiēn, eiēs, eiē* (might be); San. infin. is *as-tun*. So, too, in place of Greek past, we have, San. *asan, asis, asit; asma, asta, asan* — the *a* is an augment here, but no more so than the *a* of present *asmi*. This past is not at all different in character from the present. There is another form of the past, known as the perfect; thus, *asa, asitha, asa; asima, asa, asus* — our *was* and *is* — this has another form, made by the prefix *uv*; as, *uv-*

asa, uvasitha, usima (for *uvasima*). Here, as we have noticed so many times before, there are two forms, at least, of *be;* besides the infin., as, *as-tun,* and *vas, vas-tun* (Germ. *wesen,* Go. *wisan*), there is, also, *bhu, bhavitun* (be, Lat. *fui, fuisse*). To this form belongs the present part. form, *bhavant* (being, *seiend*), contrasting with the other forms *sant* (Lith. *esant*) and *vasant* (Gothic *wisands*). With the usual augment *a,* we find this aorist or past form, *a-bhuvan, a-bhus, a-bhut* (sing.). In the past, which is reduplicated, so called, the doubling is just such as we have found over and over again in the forms of other languages; they are such as, *ba-bhuva, ba-bhuvus.*

Impersonal Verbs.

505. To complete the survey of the verb, we notice yet certain other forms and applications, in addition to the mood, tense, and person forms, which have so far engaged our attention. And first of these, we will notice impersonals.

506. In Latin, as we find more or less in all languages, the 3rd person sing. is used without a nominative, or subject; as, *pluit,* it rains, *tonat,* it thunders, *accidit,* it happens; so, also, in the passive, as *curritur,* it is run (there is running), *vivitur,* it is lived, they live, *ventum est* (coming is), it is come. All these forms are clearly the same as verbal nouns, and they have none of that expression which is conceived to be peculiar to verbs; so, *pluit* = raining, the raining (is), and *vivitur* is simply living, the living (is). But after all, these are as much verbs as any we find, and it only proves again what we have seen long before this, that the verb is, after all, nothing but a pure noun (of the verb kind). And we may say, also, that in our own impersonals, as *it rains, it hails,* the pronoun *it,* so called, is nothing but an article of the verb; we may go still farther, and say that all pronouns used thus before the verb, as *we walk,* are only a development of this article *it.* The Latins, also, use such verbs transitively, as *decet me,* it becomes me, *pudet me,* it shames me (I am ashamed), *miseret me,* it pities me (I pity); we may see by the two last examples, how what we consider a nominative may be conceived to be objective (acc.).

507. That these impersonals are in fact nothing but participles or gerunds, is shown in Greek, where the participle and infinitive are used in the place of just such impersonals as we met with above; thus, *sálpizontos,* it sounding, or being sounded (by the trumpeter) — genitive participle; *eirēmenon,* it being notified — accusative part.; *prostachthen,* it being commanded — accusative neuter participle; *tuchon,* it happening — neuter par-

ticiple; *mikrou dein*, a-little it-wants—*dein*, infinitive, to want; *emoi dokein*, to-me it-seem—*dokein*=to seem, inf., i. e. seeming (is) to me.

508. This shows how such forms may be used in place of verb with nominative; all our cases such as these, *to speak properly this is so, turning this over we shall observe*, are instances where part's and infin's are used in place of verbs and without subjects, and still being as true verbs as any we can find. More than this, all our expressions, as *they say*, *it appears*, German *man sagt* (one says,, they say), German *es giebt* (it gives), *there reigns*, are cases where there is really no nominative or subject, the pronouns *it, they, man, there* (adverb), being scarcely more than articles; it is simply meant to be said that there is a *saying, appearing, giving, reigning*, without indicating *who*—so those verbs, so called, are mere gerunds, or verbal nouns, with a pronoun for article.

509. In Hebrew, the 3d sing. mas. is often used impersonally, as *qara* (he called)=they called, there was calling; so the passive is used impersonally also, here as well as in Sanscrit, as *it is thought by me*, for *I think*. In Georgian, such impersonals are very common. And in Russian, with others of the family, we find many cases of impersonals, and some which are for us rather peculiar. So, we have the neuter passive participle (as in Greek) used impersonally; as, *skazano*, it (is) said, *belyano*, it (is) commanded (*is* being suppressed); so the adjective is also used impersonally, as *legko* (it is) light, easy, *ne mozhno* (it is) not possible—so, again, *emu dolzhno pisat*, to-him (it) must to-write, i. e. he must write.

Frequentatives.

510. This kind of verbs, more or less strongly marked, is found, perhaps, in all languages. In Lat., they are found based on the supine; thus, *clamo*, to call, *clamito*, to call often or quickly; so *rogo* and *rogito*, *volo* and *volito*—the supines being *clamatum*, *rogatum*, *volatum*. Other forms occur which are made by taking the supine of a supine as a base, as *lectito* (original supine *lectum*), *dictito* (supine *dictum*). Some Lat. verbs have two frequentatives; as, for *curro*, we find *curso* and *cursito*, for *defendo* there is *defenso*, *defensito*—showing, thus, very clearly that these new forms are not essentially different from the ordinary verb, as well as that a verb may alone express what we might think could be expressed only by the verb in connexion with auxiliaries and adverbs, or, in other words, that one word expresses as much as several taken in the same connexion.

511. In Greek, what we use as a causative mark, the *z* or *ize*, as in *legalize*, to make legal, is the frequentative mark; thus, '*riptazein* (from '*riptein*), to cast here and there, *stenazein* (from *stenein*), to sigh much and deeply (one word *sigh* = itself and adverbs). There is no supine in G'k which corresponds clearly with the Latin supine in *tum*, but the *z* mark here observed, has its representative in the *t* of the verbals; as, *poteon*, *potos*, *strepteos* and *streptos* (of Greek). So we must give the same history to the *z* of Greek that we did to the *t* of Latin frequentatives — here in Greek, as in Latin, we find this class of verbs to be only infinitives of infinitives.

512. But we may as well observe here, that neither in the *t* of Latin, nor the *z* in Greek, do we find an exclusive frequentative mark. In many instances, the derivatives in *t* and *z* do not differ in meaning from the simple form to which we refer them; and, in other cases, verbs with this mark have anything but a frequentative meaning; as, Latin *poto* (on sup. *potum*), I drink, *canto* (on *cantum* from *cano*), I sing. This is especially true of the Greek verb ending *zō*, as *dikazō*, judge, *distazō*, doubt, *erizō*, strive — verbs with a frequentative form without a frequentative meaning.

513. The Bohemian uses *va* for the frequentative mark (and so does the Slavic generally); as, *delati*, to do, and *delavati*, to do often. But in Slavic, as in Greek and Latin, this *va* or *wa* is used for other purposes besides a frequentative mark — it is identical with the G'k *z* and L. *t*, and has a history in common with them. In the Slov., we find freq's with infinitive ending the same as the common verb has; as, *letati*, to run often, *lamati*, to break often — *ati* being one of the ordinary infinitive endings; we find also in Slovensh, *padem*, I fall, and *padam*, I fall often — showing how slightly the one differs from the other; there is, besides, *strelim*, I shoot, *streljam* (inf. *streljati*), I shoot often — here, we have *jati* for *vati*, showing that the Slav. *va* is the Sans. *ya*, found in so many different kinds of words.

514. We should not pass over, in this connexion, that class of verbs in L. which is rather the opposite of those already noticed; they end in *illo*, and denote that the thing is done slightly or little; as, *canto*, to sing, and *cantillo*, to sing low, *conscribillo*, to write little, to scribble. That this *l* is the *t* and *z* seen before, is little to be doubted. Such verbs are also found in other languages.

• *Inchoatives.*

515. There is a class of verbs in Latin, similar to those found elsewhere, marked by *sc* — as, *calesco*, to become hot (*calea*, to

be hot), *puerasco*, to become a boy, to act the child (*puer*, a boy), *maturesco*, to become mature (*maturus*, ripe). In general, we may observe that an adjective or noun lies at the base of these verbs in *sco*, and we find the usual verbal endings developing so as to represent *be*. It is not, in principle, in the least different from the frequentatives; thus, in form *calesco* = *calito*, *labasco* = *labato* — the latter being an assumed frequentative; s = sc, sk, st, t. It must be observed, too, that this *sc* mark is not peculiar to such verbs; it occurs in verbs whose meaning is distinguished by nothing peculiar; thus, *cresco*, perf. *crevi*, sup. *cretum* (grow); *pasco, pavi, pastum* (feed); *nosco, novi, notum* (know); *scisco, scivi, scitum* (ordain). Compare with these, *amo, amavi, amatum*, and *moneo, monui, monitum*, and we shall see that these presents in *sco* have merely developed the *t* which is latent in *amo*, and which appears as *e* in *moneo*; so we observe that *novi* and *notum*, in their *v* and *t*, mark the *sc* apparent in *nosco*, while *amavi, amatum*, represent the *sc* = *t*, suppressed in *amo*. In our own verbs of this kind, we entirely discard this *sc*, and adopt the form of the ordinary Germ. inf.; as *redden*, to become red, *whiten*, to grow white, or we leave off also the ending *en*, as to *cool* (become cold), to *warm* (become warm), to *polish* (become polished), to *rise* (become raised), *enlarge* (become large), to *improve* (grow better), to *mend* (become mended), *melt* (become melted). (See how near such verbs are to true passives).

516. The Greek has the mark *sk*, exactly corresponding with the Lat. inchoative *sc*, but we rarely meet with any signification, in verbs thus marked, which particularly distinguishes them from verbs not marked with *sk*; generally the difference is of this nature; *didraskō*, I run away, and *draō*, I run; or it is such as cannot be perceived at all. Thus, we see that the Gr'k *sk* belongs more precisely with the *sc* of those Lat. verbs which have lost, or have never had, any inchoative meaning, instances of which we have already given. Many of the verbs in *skō*, in Lat. as well as Greek, are also marked by the reduplication; as, *bi-brōskō, gi-gnōskō, mi-mnēskō, pi-praskō*, and in Latin (more rarely) *disco*, perfect *di-dici, posco*, perfect *po-posci*.

517. This *sk* is conceded to be the identical *sk* in the *skon* which marks some Greek imperfects. This shows that the imperfects of this kind are made, precisely as frequentatives, by taking a supine as a new base, and that they are, beyond that, exactly like other imperfects, such as have not the *sk*. Just as, in Latin, we saw the *sc* identical with the *v* of perfect, and *t* of supine, so in Gr'k, we find this *sk* the same as the *s* of fut., and hence the same also as the *s* of aor., and *k* of perf.; thus, *areskō*, fut. *aresō* (*sk* = *s*), *bi-brōskō*, fut. *brōsō*. It should have been

remarked, of the pasts in *skon*, that they have, also, a meaning of continuance or repetition, thus showing how past tenses are allied with such forms as frequentatives, inchoatives, and the like.

518. The mark *wa* or *va*, which we have noticed before as occurring in frequentatives, in the Slavic languages, is found also in verbs which are purely inchoative; thus, *chory*, sick, *chorowas*, to be, or to become sick (*as* being ordinary infin. ending), *pilny*, diligent, *pilnowas*, to be, or to become diligent; so also *pisas*, to write, *pisywas*, to be busy writing, *bis*, to strike, beat, *bijas*, to be busy beating, *mowis*, to speak, *mawias*, to be busy speaking (*ja* and *ia* = *wa*). But we find other inchoatives where this *wa* is not so clearly developed; as, *siwy*, gray, and *siwies*, to become gray (*es* being infinitive ending), *bialy*, white, and *bieles*, to become white. We have only to add, that the term *denominative* might be used, and often is used, in place of *inchoative*.

519. There is still another class of verbs which we may briefly notice in this connexion, and that is *Desideratives*. In Latin, they seem to be based on the participle in *urus*, or rather to be that part. used as a verb; so, we find the verb *dicturio* (*dico*, to speak, fut. part. *dicturus*), to desire to speak; so also *empturio*, from *empturus* (verb *emo*), *esurio*, from *esurus*, to desire to eat. These verbs express a wish, but a wish is a *will;* so, we see these verbs are pure futures, and no more. In Greek, we also find the desiderative form corresponding with the future; as, *gelasō* (future), I will laugh, *gelaseiō*, I wish to laugh (I would laugh) Another class of Greek desideratives end in *aō* and *iaō* (in the present), and seem to be based on nouns; as, *strategian*, to desire to be a general, *thanatan*, to desire death. It is hardly necessary to remind the student, that *aō* and *iaō* equal the *azō*, *izō*, seen often before this. Desideratives in Sanscrit, are marked by *sya*, Greek future sign *s*.

Causatives.

520. In Gr'k, the marks *sk* and *z* are not only used in forms such as we have before considered, but also as marks of the causative; thus, *methuō*, to be drunk, *methuskō*, to make drunk, *pinō*, to drink, *pipiskō*, to give to drink; *kathizō*, to make sit, *polemizō*, to make war, *thaumazō*, to make or have wonder (to admire), *elpizō*, to have hope (be hopeful), *nomizō*, to make as a law, *erizō*, to have a strife (to strive). (We are constantly reminded how near *make good*, *be good*, and *have goodness*, are to each other — we find all of them marked by this *z*, and by the *sk*).

521. We have such causatives as *harden*, to make hard (as well as *become hard*), *sharpen*, to make sharp; those in *ize*, as *harmonize*, to have harmony, or to make harmonious, *legalize*, to make legal, *culogize*, to give eulogy on, *aggrandize*, to make great; those in *fy*, as *magnify*, to make great, *terrify*, to make terrified, or give terror, *amplify*, to make ample. The *ize*, it is easily seen, is the Greek causative, while the *fy* is the Lat. *fico*, *facio* (= make or do), which we find in such words as *tumefacio*, to make swelled, *satisfacio*, to make enough, *amplifico*, to make ample, *magnifico*, to magnify — *facio = fico, fio, fy*. This *fy* is a common causative mark also in French. The Greek *izo, azo*, is quite identical with this *fio, fy*, (as both are *sk, z*), and may be taken as representing *ago*, to do, act. We are to learn from this, principally, how the ordinary *t* and *s* mark of supine and tenses grows into the representation and form of ordinary auxiliary verbs.

522. But we have also many causatives which are not marked by any ending at all; as, to *lay* (cause to lie), to *set* (cause to sit), to *stand* (cause to stand), *raise* (cause to rise); and all such verbs as to *iron*, to *trim*, to *dress* one, to *paint*, to *indent*, to *shape* — indeed, *all transitives gradate into causatives*. But, it is not alone in English that we find the causative form identical with the ordinary verb; this fact is patent in all languages; thus, in Latin *inflammo* (the causative mark, if any, being the *en, in*, prefix), *loco*, to place, give place to, *termino*, to end, to to cause to end, *terreo*, to terrify, to cause to be frightened, *figuro*, to figure, shape — and perhaps all other transitives which have a noun as the base; precisely so we find in Greek; as, *elpō* (from *elpis*, hope), to raise hopes, *purgoō*, to erect into a tower (from *purgos*, a tower), *timaō*, to honor (from *timē*, honor). All this proves to us again, that *aō, eō, azō, izō, iskō*, are all variations of *ō* alone, *that the causative, and all related forms, has no element not common to all verbs*.

523. Our own *fumigate, navigate, castigate, mitigate, terminate, dictate, celebrate, separate*, and the like, are all causatives, and yet they are only L. supines, in form, used as a new base.

524. The Sanscrit causative mark is *aya* or *ya* (the *ya* which is found in so many other places), as *karayami*, I cause to make. This *aya* is the *eō, aō*, of Greek; in Goth., too, we find it; as, *satya*, I place (*sita*, I sit), *layya*, I lay (*liga*, I lie), *lausya*, I loosen (*liusa*, I lose). In Lithuanian, the causative mark is *in* (our *en* of *harden*); as, *ilginu*, I make long (lengthen). This *in, en*, is the same also as *inō, anō*, of so many Gr'k verbs, and the *nu* of Slavic.

525. In Persian, we find *rasidan*, to arrive, and *rasanidan* (marked *an*), to cause to arrive; *parwardan*, to educate, and

parwarandan, to make educate. The causative mark in Finn. is *t* (as well as denominative). The case of the German verbs is precisely that of English. The Semitic languages are interesting in this connexion, as showing these derivatives without the apparent addition of an element; thus, we have *qatal*, to kill, and *qottel* (double *t*), to cause to kill — a change in the body of the word precisely as the German *wachen*, to wake, be awake, and *wecken* (*wekken*) to wake, awake. (This form, middle letter doubled, is not only causative in Semitic, but also denominative, frequentative, and the like). In Arabic and Syriac, causatives are made by assuming the prefix *a*, as *qatal* and *a-qtal*, our wake and awake — in Syriac, sometimes by the prefix *s*, as in our *s-lay*, to cause to lie, or lay. (In Arabic it is *ast*).

Derivatives.

526. Having treated thus far of some special verbal forms with special meanings, we will now consider, briefly, the accumulation of new forms of verbs which are not marked by any particular application. In G'k *aō*, *eō*, *iō*, *oō*, *uō*, *euō*, *azō*, *oskō*, *anō*, *ainō*, *unō*, *airō*, *eirō*, besides others, all forms of one and the same thing, are common endings of verbs — but mark also, they are not only seen in verbs, but they occur as well in other parts of speech; as, *orcinos*, mountainous (*ein*), *Athēnaios*, Athenian (*aio*), *noseros*, sickly (*er*), *graphikos*, relating to painting (*ik*), *paidikos*, juvenile (*ik*), *paidiskos*, a little boy (*isk*).

527. In Latin, we have also *eo*, *io*, *uo*. These vowels *e*, *i*, *u*, are only representatives of consonants which we find appearing in a large share of verbs; as *g* in *fligo*, *d* in *dedo*, *g* in *lego*, *d* in *vado*, *ng* in *jungo*, *nd* in *findo*, *r* in *gero*, *n* in *sino*, *v* in *juvo*, *h* in *veho*, *ct* in *pecto*, *ll* in *pello*, *rp* in *serpo*, *m* in *premo*, *b* in *scribo*. Observe, here, what different forms the *t*, the same as we find in *dicto* from *dico*, and in *datum* from *do*, assumes in the different verbs, and observe, too, how it doubles in *ct*, *nd*, *ng*, *rp* — the *gi* in *fugio* is a double of the same kind, so the *ci* in *facio*, *de* in *ardeo*, *ce* in *doceo*. We find the same history in Greek, and indeed in all languages; for instance, in our own language, the final letters of verbs are properly this same *t*; as, the *k* in *speak*, *y* in *say*, *e* in *see*, *nd* in *send*, *ng* in *sing*, *l* in *steal*, *ll* in *sell*, *w* in *draw*, *tch* in *catch*, *rv* in *starve*, *t* in *write*, *m* in *come*, *ft* in *lift*, *ld* in *yield*. That these final letters do not belong to the base of the verb, is seen by their entire absence in different languages; thus, the French *dire*, for Lat. *dicere*, *ouir* for Latin *audire*; old North *fra*, Germ. *fragen*, Latin *frango*; old North *fa*, German *fangen*; French *a*, our *have*; Dan. *boe*,

our *abide, abode* — to say nothing of the African and Polynesian languages, where one consonant, with a vowel, represents our longest verbs.

CHAPTER X.
ETYMOLOGY.

528. In the science of separating words into parts, or, rather, of discovering new parts of words, etymology has lately made great advances. It is the course taken by all science; the more intimately we become acquainted with the object of our study, the more points and parts about it we successively discover. It was first learned that sentences were made of parts, or, rather, it was assumed to consider certain parts of the sentence as distinct individuals — just as we are wont to look at the man as made up of head, hands, feet, while to the child or savage, perhaps, he appears as one whole, single and simple.

529. But philology did not rest satisfied with dividing sentences into words; it has divided compound words into their elements, and those elements again into syllables. Not content with that, syllables have again been separated into letters; and there philology apparently halted — but halted only to renew the undertaking. Words have not only been divided into syllables, and syllables again into letters, but it was often observed that one letter is equal to or represents two or more letters; as, $e = ie$ in *field*, $i = ei$ in Germ. *theil*, or *ai* in Greek *pais*, $j = dg$ in *bridge*, short $u = oo$ in *flood*; $s = st$ in *listen*, $m = lm$ in *calm*, $n = gn$ in *sign*, $s = ss$ in *hiss*. So that these single letters which are representatives of the two combined, may be considered as equal to the two, and as practically containing the two within themselves — latent though it be; just so the bud contains the leaf and the flower, and as this bud develops itself into the leaf and the flower, or the branch, so may we say, in language, that one letter develops itself into two or more of its own cognates — as s into *st*, m into *lm*, n into *gn*, k into *ck*, r into *rr*, e into *ai* (in *said*), o into *au* (in *song*).

530. Nothing is more common in language, than for one letter to be the representative of two or more; and though we may not see so much of it in the same language, we shall find more instances where a single character in one language is represented by two or more letters in some other language, as our *tch* for one of the Russian letters, *ds* for one in Greek, *dsh* for one in Armenian, *dschha* for a San. character, *scha* for another and *gha* for another.

531. It is clear that we may regard these as actual equivalents, and one letter may thus represent several others; and, we may either consider the combination of letters, as *tch*, the growth or development of the single letter, as *c*, or that the single letter is really made up of the (invisible) parts represented in the developed combination, and as including in itself, as the whole includes its parts, those different elements, in a latent, unappreciable state. This is no new thing, it is the universal phenomenon of nature. All the different instruments of a band of players, sounding in perfect harmony, produce one single strain, in which the single instruments lose their individuality and become undistinguishable; besides, any one of them may represent the elements of the whole combined, as one letter represents a combination of letters. (It is the leading law of nature, *that the part is as great as the whole, contains as much, and (under suitable circumstances), can do as much. Every whole is but an accumulation of equivalent parts, parts which only apparently differ; every whole is but the repetition of one and the same part. Nowhere is this law better exemplified, than in language*).

The blending of colors furnishes us with another apt illustration; thus, any number of colors mingle and produce a new color — mark, but a single color. So, as we found that every letter may be an equivalent of several other letters, again, every color may be conceived of as made of two or more other colors; and reversed, as every two or more letters combined produce some one sound, which is or may be represented by some one letter or character, so, too, in colors, any number of colors blended will produce some new color, one only, which we do represent, or may, by some new or other name.

But where sounds or colors mingle and produce one, they are by no means lost or destroyed; this new color, this new sound, is really those old colors, those old sounds, acting in harmony, in concert, and so losing their individuality. Two forces acting in concert produce a new force, or new direction — which is only new so far as we have two forces acting instead of one; one force never destroys another, and its own direction is never affected or varied.

532. It is with letters as it is with numbers, every one is part of some combination of numbers, as 2 is part of 4, 6, 30, and it is itself made up of ½, ¼. So we can divide a thing to infinity, with this difference, that for 28 and 2 we have a name 30, and for the parts of 2, as ½, ¼, but not for the combination of letters *str*, or for the unnamed elements that go to make the sound *s*, or *t*, or *h*. That they, too, have their equivalent parts, is just as certain as that the sound *book*, or *str*, has parts. It is the point of philology, now, having divided speech

into sentences, sentences into words, words into syllables, and these again into letters, also to establish the value of the elements which unite to produce the effect of a letter ;— thus, we may take the elements of *o* to be certain values of *a* and *u* (*ah-oo*, spoken quickly), of *e* to be *a* in *ale* and *i* in *it* (*sa-id, sed*).

Letters.

533. Words are not represented in all languages by a combination of separate letters, as in our own. In the old Egyptian inscriptions, we find the figures of men and animals, and other objects besides, wrought up into symbols, hieroglyphics, which have no connexion with letters, or, at least, only a remote one; this part of the subject is too intricate and extensive to be treated of here with any degree of fairness, and we will pass it by. Next is the Chinese system, which we will dwell on briefly under the head of Chinese language. Here, the signs which stand for words appear, at first view, to be single; though made up by a combination, or interlacing, of strokes or lines, the whole presents to the uninitiated only the appearance of one idea. And, lastly, there is what is called the *syllabic* mode, one midway between our single letters and the Chinese word-signs. This we are now about to consider.

534. In the Sanscrit and Thibetan languages, among others, every consonant is assumed to have within itself the force of the vowel *a*. Thus, their *b* has the force of *ba*, and *l* of *la*; other vowels are denoted by affixing some mark to this *b*, *l*; or *ba*, *la*—sometimes above or below (after the Semitic manner), and again after or before the consonant, as in Europe. In these cases, the original *a* sound inherent in the consonant seems to be suppressed — *ba-i* becomes *bi*. These alphabets are called syllabic.

535. That our modern alphabets, and especially the Semitic, are syllabic too, though perhaps not in the same degree, can be easily demonstrated. One of the Semitic class, the Ethiopic, is syllabic in the highest degree. The same letter there, as *b*, slightly marked, is *ba*, *be*, *bi*, *bo*, *bu*. But, are the forms in the other Semitics, the Hebrew for instance, the *b* with its dots and marks above it and below it, for *ba*, *be*, etc., anything else, in reality, than just such marked *b*'s as we have in Ethiopie? It is of no moment that in Hebrew the marks are separate from the consonant, and in Ethiopic attached to it. In both cases, the vowel mark and the consonant constitute one single element. Besides this, the vowel marks in Semitic are of comparatively late origin, and, even yet, they are very commonly left out in

the text; now, in all such cases the consonants act as syllabics, for they, even unmarked, represent an element composed of vowel and consonant, as *b* for *ba*, *mlk* for *melek*.

536. In all our cases where consonants come together, there is no doubt that we may conceive of an undeveloped vowel between them — so *drive* is hardly distinguished from *derive* (*der*=*dr*), *slect* from *select*, *fl* from *ful*, *pretend* and *pertend*, *claim* and *cullaim*. We may see large numbers of instances in Slavic and elsewhere, where they insert a vowel, or leave it out, when we do not — showing that if it is not expressed, it is only implied, and if it is expressed, it is merely not implied. Again, it is well understood that you cannot pronounce a consonant without uttering it with a vowel, showing thus the inseparable connexion of the two.

537. We notice in most of the syllabic alphabets, that there is simply some mark accompanying the consonant, or attached to it, to denote the vowel, but in some instances, for example, the Mongolian and Ethiopic, there is considerable change in the form of the consonant itself, when different vowels are denoted. All this, too, shows the intimate union between the vowel and consonant; it shows too, that the vowels are not only all derivatives from the same base, but that the consonant with the vowel, as *ba*, *be*, .etc., is a mere variation of one and the same thing — just as letters in Semitic vary according as they are initial, middle, or final, — and still remain the same letter.

538. It is evident, too, that these different forms of letters to indicate consonants with vowels, with or without marks, depend entirely upon the consonant they are associated with, and that their assuming the new form, or taking the particular vowel marks, is simply a matter of harmony between them and the accompanying consonant. But it must be borne in mind that there is nothing in these vowel marks, or representatives of vowels, that distinguish them from some or all of the consonants. So, we have *bridge*, where *g* may be considered a mark to denote a particular sound of *d*, exactly as if it were a vowel mark, or vowel; also *laugh* and *myth*, where *h* is used with *g* and *t* in the same way, and *l* and *r* in *able*, *centre*.

539. In all these instances, and many more might be given, the following consonant is merely a mark to indicate a sound of the consonant to which it is attached; it adds nothing to the sound of the fundamental consonant, but merely expresses or shows what force that consonant has; and, in all these cases, we can find, somewhere, instances where the consonant has the same value alone that it has with the consonant attached. Thus *d* is often *dj*, *dg*, *th* is often *t*, so is *bl*, *b*, and *tr*, *t* (in French).

Let it be said, once for all, that *adding letters to a word, in the course of its development, gives it no sound that was not in it before, but it is a mark only to indicate a new force discovered or developed.* Thus, in our spelling books, we find certain sounds of letters distinguished by certain marks, as s =z, and they are precisely in the nature of those vowel marks we have been speaking of. No one thinks those marks give that sound to the letter, but rather that they indicate the sound which the letter has, even without the mark (so s has the sound of z in *rise*, mark it or not, as you like); so it is, exactly, with vowel marks, and with consonants joined to consonants.

540. The Sanscrit family of alphabets, and the Manchu, show all the features of the Chinese and related alphabets; several letters are here united into one character, or, rather, one character possesses the marks of two or more letters; this principle is at work in the Semitic, where letters are varied in form according to their place in the word. In all alphabets, more or less, we find one character representing two or more letters, as the German *ss*, *tz*, Greek *st* — and particularly in the Irish and Slavic alphabets. In the Manchu, the top part of the character is the consonant, and the bottom grows into the representative of the vowel, varying according as that is a, e, i, etc.

541. The Thibetan alphabet, though it does not appear so at first sight, is yet clearly related to the Sanscrit, and both are evidently built on the same basis. They are both equally, as it is called, syllabic, that is each consonant has *a* as its base. And we think it may be discovered that there is a fixed part of this consonant to represent that *a*. The point is clearest in the Sanscrit; here, the consonants, with very few exceptions, have a perpendicular line, like our l, as a basis, and the characteristic portion of the letter is fixed to that stroke. There are, too, leading facts having an influence on this question; first, this perpendicular stroke is used separately as the vowel *a*, and second, when two letters, as *ka* and *la*, unite to form a single character, as *kla* or *kl*, the *a* sound is lost, and with it, also, this stroke in question. Besides, for the other vowels we find appropriate signs fixed to the consonant in some way — indeed it is the prevailing feature, in Asia, to find vowels attached to consonants. We have noticed this as a striking appearance in the Manchu. In Sanscrit, there are a few letters as *t, th, d, dh*, and *r*, where this base stroke is not so clear; but that these are vowels, and even variations of this *a* mark, is certainly undoubted; the first four are forms of *i; r* (and *h*) a form of *a*, related to *i*.

542. But this base stroke of consonants is not confined to Asia; it is found in our own, and in perhaps all others; we see it in our B, D, b, d, l, m, n, t, E, F — it is still plainer in Rus., where

some letters, as *sh*, are formed by the repetition of this *l* mark (like Greek Π). We need not be surprised that it disappears in some letters, when we remember how capital E, with its angles, changes for the rounded small *e*, and how A is changed into its related O. So it is, we see, in the nature of letters, as well as of words, to be made up of elements. *You can find no element so small, that it has not also elements, and as many as the original.*

543. So, we are left to understand, from what has been taught under the head of letters, that words are merely a sign made up of signs, and hence that we do not in principle differ from the Chinese. Their signs of words are made up of parts as well as our own; it is already admitted that most of these have two or three elements and contain a base character or key, just as we have found our alphabets to have a key in their consonants. That they have not developed their word-signs into as many elements as we have, is in perfect harmony with their evident want of consciousness of the division of sentences into words. That their alphabet is built up on the same system as the European, or other Asiatic alphabets, is one of the clearest things in the world. It exists only in a particular stage of advancement, while the Roman, the Semitic, the Sanscrit, represent each another stage of the same performance. The hieroglyphic system of word representation, in its different degrees of development, takes another place and presents still another phase. The Japanese system of characters is interesting as affording the transition between the Chinese and the syllabic arrangement.

544. MARKED AND DOUBLE LETTERS: There are two sources from which the number of characters in an alphabet are increased: one, by marking old letters when they get a new force, and the other by doubling or combining two like letters. Really, all our letters which have two or more powers should be marked to distinguish them, and, thus, our alphabet would be greatly enlarged. This is done to a far greater extent in other languages than in our own. The marks used are unmeaning, and are simply dots, or other marks above or below the letter, or a stroke across it — our own *i* with its dot above it, is a marked letter, so is Q a marked O; the G'k θ and φ are both a marked $o = u$, *v* and *t*; our *k* is only a marked *c* or *g*, the perpendicular line being often found separate from the *c* or *g* part, i. e. from the two lines meeting at an angle.

545. The number of letters which arise from the union of two, like our $w = uu$, in the different alphabets, is considerable, and it includes some we would hardly expect. Our B is a double *o*, *v*; when placed on its back (ꙿ) its identity with W is plain, being crossed by a line at the top (as K is on the side),

and rounded at the angles; one of the Gr'k forms of $p = b$ (ϖ) is this precise form; these resemblances are all not unexpected, for b we know equals p, v, f, w. If we invert our M (ᴍ) we have W; m is clearly a modification of b and w, and hence double; this is not unexpected, for m equals b and is often found for w; n, which is half m, is often hardly distinguishable from u, v (as Greek v).

546. Our s (S) is another double letter, and not only that, it is double o, v, and identical with the b and m; the Greek s (Σ) is only our W placed on its side. In Syriac, s is two o's (ᴂ), Heb. ayin ($=o, v$) is identical in form with its z, s; old Heb. s (shin) was precisely our W, and B on its back unmarked (w); in ancient Greek, s was precisely M, also in Phenician; it is an important fact that in Hebrew (and Greek) an s follows the m, n, group; in the Copt. alphabet, sh, ch, is marked o (Greek ω); s and sh we found in Russian based on $i = u, o, v$; it has long been known that f and s were equal, but $f = v, u, o$.

We may remark while on this subject of o's, that it is to be observed that the base part of p, b, q, d, is o — this is not accidental, they are marked o's. In Russian, we find many cases of united letters, sometimes side by side, sometimes one over the other, sometimes one on the other; in G'k, many instances are found of two or more letters united into one character, exactly as in Sanscrit.

547. ASSIMILATION OF LETTERS: There is a tendency, which we observe, more or less, in all languages, for words (or syllables) and letters coming together to change so as to assume like forms, and thus coalesce so as to produce a single element. So, what would be *tetupmai*, in Gr'k, is *tetummai* ($pm = mm$), *sōmatsi* becomes *sōmasi* ($ts = ss$), *deiknuntsi* becomes *deiknusi* ($unts = uuss$), *to heteron* becomes *thateron* (to-$he = the$, tha); so in Lat., we find *effero* where we might expect *exfero*, and *assisto* for *adsisto* ($ads = ass$). In Celt., the change of words or letters according to what they are associated with, is carried on very extensively and systematically.

548. As an explanation of this phenomenon, we repeat here what we have often touched on already, *that it is only like letters that come together, that all the letters of a word are assimilated, made like each other* — and not alone the letters of the same word, but, also, the letters of two words which are associated together, and hence their tendency to unite and form a single word; as, the Greek *katheudo* from *kata heudo*.

The old North *byggja*, to build (bide), will illustrate the case of like letters; the $j = g$, and $y = j$ and g, hence, the word is *byyyya*; but b also equals v, u, y, hence we have *vyyyya*, or *yyyyya*. It is by this assimilation of letters, that long words may be reduced to single letters; thus, our *have* is, in French, *a*, for *have* equals *aave*, *aaue*, *aauu*, *auaa*, so that the French *a* equal to *have*, contains, or is, four undistinguishable *a*'s. We need not be surprised that the letters of a word should be *like* letters, really repeated letters, and still have such different powers apparently; the two *g*'s in *suggest*, and the *c*'s in *accent*, are double, and yet what could differ more than the former *g* or *c* from the latter *g* or *c*. Indeed, we may say *that every case of double letters presents two letters of different powers;* thus, we have *adjective*, and the Italian has *aggettivo*—its *gg* must differ as our *dj* or *dg*, and its *tt* as our *ct*; so, the Dutch has *boek* where we have *book*, *oe* = *oo*. In conclusion, we may say that since the words of the most undeveloped languages are very short, as *no*, *na*, *ba*, *they really contain latent as many letters as our words*, but they are so much in unison, so little differentiated, that they cannot be distinguished by our ears, though they might be by others more refined.

The Form and Value of Letters.

549. *A*—In the Samaritan, *a* = *t* (we shall use the sign of equality, or the words, to denote that the two letters, both of the same alphabet, are alike in form); in Eth. and Arabic, *a* = *l*, indeed, our A is no doubt a modification of the Greek Λ (and perhaps Δ): in Copt., A can hardly be distinguished from its D, as our *a* = *d*.

550. *B*—In Hebrew, B equals P; in Samaritan, B equals R, and D is only a marked B or R; in Arabic, B equals F (*p*); in Ar. and old Hebrew, B = N; in Syriac, B equals K and P, so Ethiopic B equals K, also Hebrew; Sanscrit B and M equal S. B must be like *l* and *r*, for we find *bl*, *br*, very often, as in *black*, *break*; *b* and *g* are related, as we see by our *go*, Greek *bainō*, and Latin *bous* (*bos*), our *cow* (*gau*); we also find *gladius* (L.), our *blade*, and Lat. *rabies*, our rage (*b* = *g*). B for *be*, is identical with German prefix *ge*, as *bleiben* (for *geleiben*), our *leave*. B equal to *m* and *w* we have noticed before.

551. *C*—This letter, as we have already noticed, is identical with *g*. We often use it for *s*, and that is the only value it has in Russian and Copt. Eth. *c* is a double *k*. C is equal to *h*, as we have *chop* equal to *hack*; *c* is equal to *l*, as Span. *llamar* for L. *clamare* (and *llama* for *flama*, *ll* = *fl*). Our *chore* (work) is Danish *gjör*, Sanscrit *kar*, Heb. *bara*, our *cre-ate*. C is like *d* and *b*, for our *cut* equals *bite*, Greek *daknō*. In German, *c* identifies with *h*, as *sch* equals *sh*; *carry* equals Latin *fero*, our *bear* (*c* = *f*, *b*); *c* for *t*, as Latin *capio* (our *catch*), take, Germ.

fangen. Observe that the different sounds of *ch* are also sounds of *c*.

552. *D* — The Heb. D has the form of Gr'k G, turned (ד); I and R (Hebrew) are only variations of this D; Syrian D=R; Arabian D=R, Z; Ar. D=N; Copt. D equals Roman A. D equals *u* and *w*, for we have L. *duo*, and our *dwell*, also Welsh *dwfr*; we find also devour, define, digest, decamp (*dev* for *dv*, *dig* for *dg*). D equals *t* and *b*, as we see in Greek *deō* equal to our *tie* and *bind*. There is a great resemblance between the character of our *d* and that of our *e*; thus, *mile* is often pronounced *mild*; the Danish uses *d* at the end of words (also *t*) much as our *e*, a sort of mute vowel; as, *mand* for *man*, *langt* for *long*, *godt* for *good*, *frit* for *free*. Again, *d* is often identical in sound with *j*, *i*, hence *d = i*. D equals *p* and *t*, as we observe in German *denken*, Latin *pensare*, our *think*; *d* equals *r*, as in Greek *dikē* = right, just (*d=j*); *d=l*, as in Greek *dakru*, our *tear*, Latin *lachryma*; *d=f*, as Latin *viduus*, French *veuf*, our *widower*.

553. *E, I, Y,* and *O* — It is well known that our E is the same as G'k H (eta); it must be equal, also, to the letters connected with *h* in *history*, as *f, g, d, a, o*. Our F is a form of E, as it is of Greek Γ and D (ד). As *e* is equal to *g*, so it is equal to *y* and *g*, as we see again in *holy*, sounded *hol-e*. E is a form of *c*, as we see by small *e=c*.

The identity of *i* with *y* and *u*, is so often seen that it hardly needs any illustration here. I is the same as *j*, but *j* besides being often *y*, as in German, is in French *z, zh* — hence, we see how *i=z*; *i* being equal to *y*, is also equal to *g* (and *d*), a form of *y*, as we see by Greek *γ* for *g*. I is identical with H, indeed H is really a double I connected. The Sans. *i=e, u, d; i=l=d*, hence *i* equals *d* in power.

Of *y* little need now be said; it is *u*, as we see in Russian; it is *i, j, g,* and *e*; in Goth., *y* has power of *w*. In Eth., *y* (*j*) has the form of *d* and precedes it. As is well known, *o=u, v, w*; it is *h* also, as we see by Eth. *h=*ayin (*o*) — in Eth., *h* has the form of U and *y*. O is identical with Q=P, B.

554. *F* — The identity of *f* with *p, ph*, is very common — one character is often used for both; *f* is same as *v, u, w*; *f* also equals *t*, for we often see the same sign used for *th* and *ph* (*f*). The German *fangen* equals our *take*, Lat. *capio*, seize, so *f=t, c, s*. F equals *d*, for L. *ferio*, our *strike*, French *frapper*, is in old North *drepa* (Germ. *treffen*); *f* equals *g*, as in *furnish* equal to *garnish*, and *find*, German *fangen*, get, gain; *f* equals *r*, as *foot* equals *root* — Heb. *regel* is *foot*, Latin *radius* (root).

555. *G* — That *g* equals *k, c, ch*, is well known; that it equals *n, l, d,* and *r*, we shall find very common; it equals *j*, and hence

z also; its identity with *u, v, w,* is seen by *gu* for *w*, as *guard* equal to *ward*, Fr. *guerre*, war, and *Gwil* for *Bill, Will*. Its identity with *h* is seen by its so often harmonizing with it and becoming silent, as in *sight, night;* see our *mix*, San. *mih*, Lat. *mingo,* Greek *michō*, Lith. *meziu* (x, h, ng, ch, z); *g* equals *z* and *h*, as we see by Lith. *asz*, Sans. *ahan*, Zend. *azem*,· for our I, Germ. *ich*, Lat. *ego*; *g* is for *f, v,* as in *laugh, tough;* $g=h$, as Lat. *hœdus* (kid), our *goat*, Germ. *Ziege*; $g=w$, as in *go=went, drag* and *draw*, A-Sax. *swelgan* and *swallow;* *g* equals *p* and *v*, as in sage, Latin *sapiens;* sergeant, Latin *serviens*. Our *beam*, Germ. *baum* (tree), old North *badm-r*, Go. *bagm, bajms,* shows that *g, j,* of Goth., takes the place of *d, u,* and *e;* Germ. and Sax. *ge, je, ye,* equals our *the; g* with *n* is very common, as in *gnaw*, and the two letters are often found to agree in form in other alphabets; in Greek, *gg* equals *ng*.

556. *H—*This letter has very extensive connexions, but most of them will be noticed under other heads; its most immediate relatives are those with which we find it associated; as, th, ch, gh, sh, ph, wh, ah, oh — that *h* gives birth to such letters, is most evident in Semitic. The Greek *e;* Russian *e, i,* has the form of H; *th* takes the place of our *h* in the Greek alphabet.

557. *K—*The nearest relatives of *k* are *c, g, h, p, q,* and *t*. It equals *t* because *c*, one of its forms, equals *t;* and *g*, another form, equals *d*. It is naturally like *q*, which is really a *k* sound, as in French; and since it is like *q*, it is also like *p*, a form of *q*. Arabian *k* (*q*) equals *f; k* (or *ch*) in Eth. equals *n*, also in Hebrew. French *ch=sh*, but *ch=k*, hence *k=s*. Take the relative pron. forms, and they will show the family to which *k* belongs; as, *ki* (Hung.), *qui* (L.), *ti* (G'k), Osc. *pi*, G'k *pote*, Celt. and Sans. *ma*, German *wer*, our *who* and *that*, Gothic *hwo* (Fr. *ce*, L. *se*), It. *che; k=r*, for Latin *rex* is our *king;* Sans. *srut-as*, Gr'k *klut-os*, Lat. *clutus*, our *heard* (*sr, kl* (*kr*), *cl* (*cr*), *hr*, all equal); *k=w*; as, Germ. *krieg*, Fr. *guerre*, our *war;* it often, in German, takes the place of the prefix *ge;*. as, *k-lein*, little, *k-lotz*, log, *k-lump*, lump — it is here a mere vowel equal to *e, h ; k*, in some forms of German, is in such cases replaced by *h;* as, *hlachen*, Germ. *lachen*, laugh; Gr'k *kuōn*, Lat. *canis*, Fr. *chien*, Lith. *szu*, German *hund*, our *dog—*shows *k=d*, as *g* equals *k, d*.

558. *L—*This is most nearly related to *m, n, r, d, g,* and the vowels. Ital. *bi* equals our *bl*, as *bianco* = blank; French *l* has the power of *i, y;* we find also *oud* for *old*, *goud* for *gold —* in Slav., *l=w, u ;* L. *lect-us.* is our *bed, l* for *b;* look=see, like = seem, l = s.·. French *le* is our *he, the* (she); Germ. *schluss*, our *close, loose, schl, cl=l;* Dan. *alt* for *all, lt* for *ll*.

559. *M—* The connexion of *m* and *n* with *l*, with *b, w, s,* and

the vowels, we have already noticed. The Osc. *m* shows itself to be a double H, or two *n*'s; the Greek *m* is a marked *u* (μ); Eth. *m* is B on its back (ꟽ); *m* equals *h*, as L. *manus* equals hand; our *make*, too, is San. *kar*, L. *facio*, Germ. *thun*, do, m, k, f, th, d; mar = err, where *m* becomes a vowel and vanishes; so, *make* is *ago*, act, and *mars* equals *war*.

560. *N*—The identity, in form, of *n* with H, is too frequent in the different alphabets to pass by unnoticed, or to be considered unmeaning—thus, Rus. N is our capital H, and the G'k small *e* (h) is *n* (η). This only shows in a particular way, what has long been recognized, the vowel tendencies of *m* and *n*. Being so nearly like vowels, these letters have a very extensive connexion; but we most frequently find *and, ing, ent, ence, ens, ln, rn, kn,* which point out the relatives of *n*, i. e. those associated with it.

561. *P* and *Q*—The identity of *p* and *q* has been long known, and that of *r* with *p* and *q*, is not more doubtful. In Samaritan, *q* has the form of our P, the Greek R (Ρ)—so, also, in Heb.; *q* is only found in a few alphabets. Go. *q* is *u*, and its relation to *u, v, w*, we might expect by its always occurring with *u*. Eth. *p* is our T; Eth. *u, w*, is a crossed O, varying so that it identifies with our Q, Greek Φ; Eth. *q* proper is this same marked *o*, Greek Φ; Eth. *j* and *d* have the form of our P. As *p* = *q, k, g*, we can see how the form Γ, Τ, and F (without the middle mark) occurs in the Gr'k alphabets for P — that is, it identifies with *g* and *f*, as we might expect. In Russian, small *p* is *n* of our letters; P (see Gr'k Π) is, like N, (Russ. H), a character of double *i*'s connected at top (Π); *q* = *s*, as in Lat. *quæro*, our *search*; *p* = *w*, as L. *penna*, our *fin, wing*; San. *p* = *j, y*. P is a late letter in alphabets.

562. *R*—This letter has already received, under other heads, most of the attention that is due to it. We will remind the student that its relatives are *s, t, d, l*, besides *p* and *q*. The Chinese had no *r*, but *l* for it, (and the old Per. had no *l*). R, as well as *m, n, d,* and *l*, is closely identified with vowels, and is easily replaced by them.

563. *S*—The true character of this letter has already been shown under the head of double letters. Its changes are principally with *r, t, h, w, f*. It often plays the part of a prefix, like German *ge* and *k*, as Greek *smikros* for *mikros*.

564. *T*—The connexion of this letter with *p, k, s, r, u, v, w, a, i, h,* and others, has already been noticed. In *Christian*, *t* = *ch*; in *mention*, *t* = *sh*. The connexions of *t* may be well seen by taking the article *the, that,* and tracing the different forms it assumes as it appears in different languages, and in different kinds of pronouns. In Rus., we find a form of *t* exactly as if the points at the ends of the cross line of T should extend

down to an equal length with the middle line, making three parallel lines or *i*'s, connected at top like *m* (⊓⊓); this makes *t* a double *p* (G'k Π); our T is not different from E, except that it is placed differently, and the middle line is extended instead of the end lines; there are other reasons, which we will omit here, that go to prove T equal to *e*, *i*, and *u*, besides H, as a consequence.

565. *U, V, W*—These letters, all forms of one and the same thing, as *i* is of *j*, *n* of *m*, or *p* of *q*, *r*, need but few remarks here. The pronouns will best show their connexions. They are beautiful illustrations of vowels which become consonants. In Russian, *u, y,* and *i*, are represented by a letter like our II, another case of double *i*— we knew that *y = i*, and that *u = y*; our own *u* is an illustration of parallel *i*'s (II) connected at bottom. W equals *d*, as German *wer* and *der*, our *will* and Gaelic *toil; w = k*, G'k *kalos*, well, and *kakos*, wicked; wind = round, turn, w, r, t. We have seen *w = g*; it is also equal to *ch, k*; as, German *dich*, Lith. *tawe*, Russ. *tebia*, Sanscrit *tva*, our *thee*.

566. *X, Y, Z*— We have already spoken of X as a form of K; it is nearly related to Z; *y*, too, has been sufficiently noticed already, and *z* needs but a few words. As we consider Z a form of G'k G (Γ), and hence of D also, we do not find it surprising that it often changes with *d, g, j, v, y* — hence, we find G'k *zaō* equal to San. *jivami*, Lat. *vivo*, our *live;* also Gr'k *zeugon*, Lat. *jugum*, our *join, union, yoke*. The striking identity of *z* with *i* and *h* we will again recall to the mind of the student.

567. ORDER OF LETTERS: The number and order of letters in the different alphabets vary. It is said that the original number of letters in the Gr'k alphabet was sixteen, while later Greek, the one of which our own is a modification, has twenty-four. We have great doubts about the number sixteen having anything more to do with the precise limit of fundamental letters than the number twenty-four or thirty. All letters in all languages are closely related to each other; it is very easy to see in letters which appear very remote, that one is only a modification of the other. The number of characters, no doubt, increased in olden times, as we know it to have done in later ones, by a letter gradually assuming a new force in particular words, and, in the end, being marked, or in some way taking a new form to correspond with the place it holds; so with our marked *s* for *z* '(ṣ) the marked *b*'s and *d*'s of Arabic; and, again, by uniting wo letters into one character, doubling, as it is admitted to be the case with our *w* (two *v*'s), of which feature we find so many illustrations in Slavic and others.

568. The Heb. alphabet has twenty-two letters, corresponding substantially with the Greek and Roman, and in the following

order; a, b, g, d, e (h), f (u, v), z, ch (h), t, y (Gr'k iota), ch (k), l, m, n, s (G'k xi), o (a), p, s or z (not in G'k), q (G'k r), r (not in G'k), s, t.

This order is almost identical with that of Gr'k, and it differs from Roman chiefly as the G'k differs from it. The third letter in both is *g*; this not only has the place of our *c*, but is identical with it; one of the sounds of *c* is $k=g$, and by tracing the G'k *g* (Γ) through the various forms which it has assumed, we find the angle made by the perpendicular and cross line, become rounded so as to resemble C. The *f* is the Greek F, digamma (a form of Γ), now lost. The Hebrew *e* has the value of *h* and corresponds better with the Gr'k eta which has the form of H. The Heb. *z*, G'k *dz* (zeta) is plainly a form of *g* and indirectly of *d*; Heb. *z* scarcely differs in form from Heb. *d* or *v*; in old G'k, this *z* has the form of I, and in Phenician it is N placed on its side (Ƶ), a form which shows its connexion with eta (H)— in Russian, it is *s* reversed (ꙅ); in Eth., it has the form of H, which is also the form of *j*; hence $z=j$, *g*, again— Fr. *g* often has the sound of *z*, *zh*. The Heb. *ch* after *z*, is the Hebrew. *e*, G'k eta; *t* is the Gr'k theta — in both cases derivatives of $h=e$, *z* (*t* equals *z* in *them*, pronounced by foreigners *zem*); the Heb. $ch=k$ is our *c*, G'k *k*; the *s* after *n* does not correspond in place or origin with our S; it is the Greek chi$=zi$; in old G'k, it has, like *z*, the form of capital I; the Heb. and Rabbinic forms evidently tend to identify with *m* of the same alphabet (again we see the connexion of *m* and *n* with *z*); the Heb. ayin (o) is almost identical in form with the *s* or *z* following it — in Arab., one of its powers is that of *g*, and in Syr. it has the form of Syr. *g* and *l*; the *s* or *sh* is in form a double ayin or *o* (also double *z*); the *th* or *t* is a form slightly varying from *h* and *ch*.

569. The Gr'k adds to these a *u* and a *v*, and *w* in the character (φ) phi (ph, f, v); it is really a marked *o* or *v*, *w*, and it is not different from theta (th), which in Russian has the sound of *f*, *v* — it corresponds to our *v* and *w*; the next Greek letter is our *x*, called chi, and having the force of *k*—indeed, it is evidently only a modified *k*, as small *k*, in G'k, and *x* are exactly alike in form; the next letter psi (Ψ) has the place of our *z*, and the value of *ps* equal to *s*, *z*; in Russian, it loses its right arm, and has a form mostly like small *y*, and a value like *tch*, *sh*; it may be considered as a marked *c* (on its back), or *s*; it is clearly, too, identical with the Hebrew *sh*, or *s* (shin), which letter in Ethiopic (one of its forms) has the precise form of Ψ. How *p* should be associated with *s* or *z*, as in this psi, need not appear strange, when we bear in mind what the Russian teaches us; there, *p* and *z* have the same form, that of Greek Π, (save that the *z* is connected at the bottom instead of the top, as in *p*);

ETYMOLOGY.   155

again, $p=t$, and $t=s$ and z; in Sanscrit, p equals j and often becomes z, zh.

570. We have, as stated before, the c, a converted g, and we have the k besides, while Greek had only the latter. Slightly varying the i, we have j, not known in Gr'k — comparing i and j, see what different powers the same letter may assume; we have p, q, r (three nearly related), while G'k has only p and r; we have w, which was formerly written two u's, and then vv, and so w. In Rus., two b's are developed, the latter having the value of v, w; after e, in place of Gr'k zeta, Russ. has two z's, one already noticed as s inverted (z); it is evidently connected, in history, with the Greek chi, x, ch; there are two i's, one of which is merely double, like G'k Π; its r is our P; its s and z is our C; its u is our y; after u comes f, v, in form of Gr'k Φ, and then K, being our X, and having its form; and next come four letters, all related, and having the value of z (ts), ch and sh, sh, and sh — they are, the first two, two i's repeated, and hence the same as Π(connected at bottom); and the next two are three parallel i's (⊔⊔) connected at bottom, that is, they are made by repeating one of the two first and uniting the two middle lines; they are related to the Hebrew ch (cheth) and th (tav) — the latter two are identical with the Hebrew sh (shin). The old Heb. furnishes a parallel in its z, identical with i, y; so, in Ethiopic, the sh, and t, is a double H, which equals i.

571. Making allowance for the introduction of additional letters in the Armenian alphabet, and the considerable variation in the name and form of the characters, we may say that it is substantially the same as the G'k. The Arab. has added several letters to the Semitic as it exists in Hebrew and Syriac, making much change in the form and name of the characters, and yet the identity of the two classes is unquestioned. The b has developed into a t, and th, besides a p in Pers., (marked only by dots and without change of form); three letters, not differing in form, are j (dg), h, and k, kh (this group includes the g which here identifies with h); two z's or d's, from Heb. d; an s and d, z, from Heb. z (tsadhe); a t, and a d, z, from Heb. t (teth); an a, h and g, gh, from Hebrew ayin.

Vowels.

572. This subdivision of letters demands still further consideration; we will treat principally of the connexion of vowels with each other. That a, e, i, o, u, and w and y, are intimately related to each other, will not be questioned; we will, however, give the following illustrations. Our a in *late* is precisely the European long e; a in *ah* equals o in *not*, a in *all* equals o in

long, cost; metal, in sound, would not differ if it was *ul, il, ol, el, yl,* instead of *al; pahn,* at a distance, can hardly be distinguished from *pine;* French *i* long is our *e* in *steel;* and *it* can hardly be distinguished from *et;* hence, we hear *yis* for *yes, min* for *men, thim* for *them.* The Greek *u* becomes our *y,* and the Germ. *u* our *i* in *it; but* hardly differs from *bet,* and *bur* not at all from *ber, bir—*and we hear *fur* in place of *for, hum* for *home,* i. e. home = hom = hum.

573. From the diphthongs we have much to learn in relation to vowels, as well as in regard to the union of letters generally. It is hardly necessary to remark that such letters as readily unite into diphthongs are closely related — but all the vowels unite in this way. We notice in regard to these unions of vowels, that they, as well as with consonants, do not arise from the destruction of one of the vowels, but from the two harmonizing together, or from the one preponderating over the other; in no case is the new sound, the diphthong, anything more than the ordinary sound of the two vowels following in quick succession; so, *boil* is *bau-il,* the *o* of *song,* and the *i* disappearing in *il;* so, in *said, sa-id, sa-d, sed—*when the *id* preponderates, we get *s-id, sid;* so, *lo-af, lo-ef, loaf,* and *re-ad, re-ed, read;* we get *break* by *breh-ake,* short *e* in *met* and long *a* in *make,* and *bread* by *breh-ed,* short *e* and short *a;* in *view,* the *i* and *e* are both short (*i* in *mit, e* in *met*), and *w* as *u* preponderates; in *field, fih-eeld,* the *i* is short and *e* long; in *their, theh-ir, there,* the *e* and *i* are both short; in *sound,* we have *o* in *not* and *u=oo,* or *u* in *full—*Germ. *au=*this *ou, ah-oo,* and is the simple union of the ordinary German *a* and *u;* German *ei=*long *i,* and *fein* sounds as *fine —* here, the *e* is short, and it makes the *i* long, just as our *e* in *fine* does; Gr'k *ai=*our long *i,* so *pais, pah-is,* sounds as *piçe;* another German *au* is very much like this Greek *ai,* and arises from the use of German accented *ü,* like our *i* in *mill* (nearly); German *eu* has same sound and on same principle.

574. The following list of words, taken chiefly from the German languages, will better illustrate the connexion and change of vowels.

Old Ger.	English.	Latin.	Old Ger.	Eng.	Latin.
durh	through	per, trans	heim	home	domus
hunt	dog	canis	feim	foam	spuma
sâhan	sow	Go. saian	dheoda	kin	geus, Ger. leute
hrao	raw, rough	crudus	houbit	head	caput, Ger. haupt
fô	few	paucus	troum	dream	somnium
keanc	gone	Ger. gang	guat	good	bonus
feal	fell	ce-cidit			

ETYMOLOGY. 157

Mid. German.	English.	Latin.		
stranc	string	funis		
kol	coal	carbo		
boum	beam	arbor,	Germ.	baum
toum	steam	vapor,	"	dampf
ruo	rest	quies,	".	ruhe
tuot	deed	egi,	"	that

Mid. Nether.	English.	Latin.		
haer	hair	crinis		
scaep	sheep, ewe	ovis		
clet	cloth	vestis,	Germ.	kleid
ghet	goat, kid	capra,	"	ziege
wiel	wheel		A-S.	hvcol
moude	world	mundus,	Germ.	welt
hout	wood	ligu-um,	"	holz
man	moon	luna	"	mond

There is also Go. *dails*, Eng. *deal*, Germ. *theil*, L. *pars*; Go. *tailcns*, Eng. *tolcen*, Germ. *Zeigen*, Lat. *signum*; Go. *mais*, Lat. *magis*, Eng. *more*, Germ. *mehr*; Go. *dauths*, Eng. *dead*, Germ. *todt*; Go. *skeirs*, Lat. *clarus*, Eng. *shine*, Germ. *schein*; Goth. *stiurs*, Eng *steer*, Latin *taurus*; Goth. *giuta*, Eng. *gush*, Germ. *giessen*; Germ. *siegel*, Eng. *seal*, Lat. *sigillum*.

German Etymology.

575.
Ab-halten, hold-off (*ab* = off).
Ab-legen, lay-off, lay-by.
Achten, l-ook, Gr'k *agaō*, San. *ac*, Gr'k *ossō*, esteem
Ahnlich, even-like, like.
Ahnen, ancestors, anticipate; it is the Lat. *ante*.
Als, al-so, as, else.
Amt, office, m, v, f.
Angst, anxious.
Arm, poor, as branch = arm.
Arten, (take-) after (imitate).
Arg, arch, arrant.
Athem, br-eath, Greek *asthma*, Lat. *anima*, Russ. *duch*

Auf-ruhr, up-roar.
Auge, eye, l-ook.
Aus-bruch, e-rupt, out-break.
Aus-dehnen, ex-tend.
Aus-fuhr, ex-port.
Aus-ruf, out-cry.
Bauer,[1] boor, far-mer, 'bode.
Bach, brook, G'k *pēgē*.
Be-fehl, (order), fail, want — the idea of words of command seems based on *wish*, *want*, not on authority; so bid = beg, Germ. *beten*.
Be-gichr, desire, crave, be-g.
Be-quem, be-come, comely, convenient, Swiss *kummlich*.

[1] Note that *ü* is nearer *i* in *it* than *u*; so, *ö* is nearer *a* in *ale* — *au* is like *ou* in *our*; *e* is not silent at the end of words, but is sounded *uh* (*u* in *up*); as, *habe* = hah-buh (*a* = *ah* uniformly) — *See Germ. Lan.*

Be-sitz, pos-session.
Be-such, visit, (be-seek), be = v.
Be-zahl, tell, pay, count, say.
Bild, (shape), build.
Billig, (fair), belle, L. *meli-or.*
B-lott, leaf (*b* is com. prefix).
Blasen, blow, s, w.
B-leiben, leave, (b-leave).
B-lick, look, blink.
Bloss, (bare), plain, bleak.
Böse, (ill), bad, base.
Braten, roast, br, r.
Brauchen, (want), break, Lat. *frui,* use, re-quire.
Brechen, break, San. *dar,* cut, G'k *dero,* strip, bare, but *ge-brechen* = want, frail.
Brief, (letter), write, chart.
Brücke, bridge, breach.
Brünnen, (well), spring.
Brennen, burn, Ger. *dorren.*
Burg, fort, G'k *purgos, polis.*
Bund, bunch, bundle, band.
Dach, (roof), deck, L. *tectum.*
Damp, steam, dew.
Dämmern, dim.
Degen, (sword), dagger.
Dehnen,[1] ex-tend.
Dicht, tight, think.
Dienen, serve, tend.
Dolch, dagger, dirk.
Druck, thring, throng, press, drive, d, p, t.
Dunkel, dim, dunn.
Dulden, dure, L. *tollo,* our in-dulgence.
Durfen, dare, durst.
Durr, torrid, dry, burn.
Ecke, nook, edge, corner.
Edel, noble, d, b.
Eilen, hurry, G'k *elaō,* hie.
Eifer, ire, ardor.
Einzeln, single, once.
Eis, ice, It. *giaccio,* Fr. *glace,* glass, smooth, Ger. *glatt.*

Eisern, iron; *ei* sounds uni-formly as *i* in *ice.*
Endlich, final, end.
Eng, near, narrow, Sans. *ag,* G'k *agō, eggus,*
Erbe, heir.
Er-fahren, ex-pert.
Erlauben, allow.
Erwerb, (gain), ac-quire.
Er-zeugt, be-got, L. *satus,*
Essig, acid (vinegar).
Fahren, fare, ferry, go.
Fang, catch, finger, f, c, k.
Fassen, fast, catch.
Feder, feather, pen, Gr'k *pter-on,* wing, bird.
Fertig, ready, pre-pared.
Fessel, fetter, fast.
Finster, dim.
Flach, flat.
Fleissig, fleet, ap-ply.
Fliessen, flow.
Flügel, (wing), fly.
Fragen, ask, fraction, break, G'k *ag,* L. *rogo.*
Frau, (woman), L. *virgo* (*herr*).
Fremd, foreign, strange.
Freude, mirth, joy; *eu* sounds between *i* and *oi.*
Friede, peace, rest.
Froh, cheer-ful, joy-ful.
Früh, early, fore.
Furcht, fright, fear.
Gabel, (fork), pierce, gore; Cor. *gaval* = get, hold, find.
Gahnen, yawn, gape.
Ganz, all (*g* pref.), whole.
Gar, ready, L. *paro,* very.
Gattung, (sort), cast, class.
Ge-biet, (district), beat, bid;
Ge-fallen, please, fall.
Ge-fahr, (danger), peril, try, risk, ex-periment.
Gehen, go, m-ove, San. *ab.*
Gheist, ghost, gas.

---
[1] Those endings *en* are of the infin., and may drop.

ETYMOLOGY.   159

Gelb, yellow.
Ge-lenk, pliant, link, limber.
Ge-mein, common, mean.
Ge-präge, im-pression.
Ge-sell, fellow, se-lect.
Ge-schlect, sect, class.
Ge-sicht, sight, visage.
Ge-walt, (power), pre-vail.
Gewinn, gain, win.
Ge-wolbe, vault.
Ge-wöhnen, wont.
Giessen, gush, pour, G'k *cheō*.
Glatt, sleek.
Gnade, grace, kind.
Graben, (dig), grave.
Greifen, grab, gripe.
Greis, (old), G'k *geraios*, San. *jarat*, Russ. *stary*.
Grimm, grim, wrath.
Grob, coarse, great, gross.
Gunst, (favor), kind.
Gurgel, gorge, It. *gola*.
Haften, take, cleave.
Hals, (neck), collar, L. *collum*, hill, G'k *gualon*.
Hagel, hail.
Handeln, (act), handle.
Harren, tarry.
Haschen, catch.
Haube, hood.
Hauch, whiff, puff, mouth.
Haupt, head, top, Fr. *tete*, It. *capo*, Fr. *chef*, t, c, h.
Haut, hide, coat, skin.
Heissen, hight, L. *voco*.
Heer, host, army, crowd.
Held, hero, l, r.
Hell, clear, light (hl, cl), brilliant.
Helm, helve, handle.
Herr, sir, lord, Sans. *cur*, Gr'k *kurios*, karl, Lat. *vir*.
Hemd, (shirt), Fr. *chemise*.
Herz, heart, breast.
Heute, L. *hodie*, Sp. *hoy*.
Himmel, heaven, Fr. *ciel*, Go. *kimins*, hell.

Hirn, brain, cran-ium.
Hirsch, hart.
Hobel, level, heaver.
Hoch, high, L. *alt* = auu, G'k *akros*, Go. *auhs*, wax.
Hohl, hollow, hole.
Holen, haul.
Holz, wood, L. *sylva*.
Hülle, veil, husk, case.
Hulse, hull, husk, shell.
Hund, dog, L. *canis*, G'k *kuōn*.
Hurtig, hurry.
Hüsten, cough, husky.
Hüt, heed, guard.
Jagen, chase.
Jammer, lament, whimper.
Junge, young, boy.
Jugend, youth, L. *juvenis*.
Kahl, callow, bald.
Kamin, chimney, channel.
Kampf, combat.
Karg, chary, spare.
Kasten, chest.
Kaue, coop, cage.
Kauen, chew.
Kauchen, squat, crouch.
Kauf, (buy), chap-man, get.
Kehle, (throat), channel.
Kehr, turn, veer, k, t.
Kein, no, none, G'k *ouk*.
Kaum, scarce, rare, sick.
Keck, (daring), quick.
Keichen, gasp, cough.
Keifen, chide, f, d.
Kelch, calyx, cup.
Kennen, know, can, 'quaint.
Keusch, chaste.
Kiefe, jaw, chap.
Kiesel, pebble.
Kind, child, kin, young.
Kippe, tip, edge.
Klage, com-plaint, wail, clamor.
Klappe, flap.
Kleid, (dress), cloth, G'k *kleiō*.
Klein, lean, little.
Klug, skill, sly, 'look.
Klump, lump, clod.

Knabe, (boy), knave, L. *natus*.
Knecht, new, young, G'k *gin*.
Knall, clap, knell.
Knapp, tight, nip, pinch.
Knochen, bone, knuckle.
Knopf, knob, bud, button.
Knorz, knob, snob.
Knospe, knot, knob.
König, king, zarr, reg-e.
Kolbe, club.
Kopf, head, L. *caput*, top, cap, G'k *kar*, *kephalē*.
Korb, (basket), curb.
Korn, grain, kernel.
Korper, body, corpse.
Kraft, force, strong, L. *vires*.
Krähe, crow, rook, raven.
Kralle, claw, craple.
Krank, (sick), grieve, L. *ægre*, Fr. *en-ferm*, Swiss *kum = kaum*.
Kranz, wreath, crown.
Kratzen, scratch.
Kraut, herb, k, h.
Kriegen, reach, ac-quire.
Krieg, war, French *guerre*, cry, jar, quarrel, kr., wr.
Krippe, crib.
Krug, crock, jug.
Küche, kitchen.
Kügeln, roll, hill.
Kuhn, (bold), keen, O. Germ. *kuene*.
Kummer, grief, trouble.
Kunft, (arrival), come.
Kund, ac-quaint, cunning.
Kunst, (art), know, *kennen*.
Kuppe, top, cap.
Kurz, short, curt.
Lappe, flap.
Lassen, let, leave.
Lässig, lazy, Go. *lats*, It. *fiacco*.
Laster, (vice), load, charge.
Last, load.
Laub, leaf.
Lauern, lurk.

Lauf, (run), loafer, elope, Swiss *lope*, San. *ray*, Lat. *ruo*.
Laut, (sound), sound, loud.
Ledig, idle, clear.
Leer, void, clear.
Lehnen, lean, lie.
Leiche, flesh, l, fl.
Lesen, read, lesson, l, r.
Lesen, col-lect, glean.
Liefern, de-liver.
Lied, (song), lid, limb, *mel-os*.
Lob, praise, laud, San. *lap*, *lesen*
Loch, hole, loop.
Löcken, al-lure, e-licit.
Löffel, ladle.
Lohn, (wages), lend.
Loben, L. *laudo* and *lego*.
Los, loose, slack,
Luft, (air), loft.
Lügen, lie.
Lust, (pleasure), de-light.
Mangel, want, m, w.
Mandeln, mangle.
Mark, marrow, k, w.
Masse, measure.
Mauer, (wall), L. *murus*, mort.
Maul, muzzle, mouth.
Menge, many, mix, men.
Messer, (knife), mace.
Mücke, midge.
Mühe, pains.
Mund, mouth.
Muth, (courage), mood, mind.
Nach-ahmen, take-after, (imi-tate).
Nacken, neck, nape.
Nähren, nourish.
Narr, (fool), L. *ignarus*, *margē*.
Nass, wet, moist.
Natter, adder, as we say Ned for Ed.
Nebel, (mist), veil, L. *nubes*.
Nehmen, (take), L. *emo*.
Neigen, bend, kneel.
Neid, strife, need, San. *nid*.
Netzen, wet, n, w.

Nütz, use, need.
Ob-walten, pre-vail.
Ort, (place), corner.
Otter, otter, adder.
Pfaffe, pope, parson, papa.
Pfand, pawn.
Pfeil, dart, bolt, pile, b, d.
Pflegen, (tend), ap-ply.
Pflicht, plight, o-blige.
Pfropf, cork, graft.
Pfund, pound, pf, p.
Plump, blunt, clumsy.
Pochen, knock, beat, p, kn.
Pracht, pride, bright.
Prahlen, brag, brawl.
Predigen, preach, dig, dg.
Prüfen, try, prove, p, t.
Pulver, powder.
Punkt, point.
Putzen, polish, re-buke.
Rach, wrath, wreak.
Rad, (wheel), L. *rota*, *radius*.
Rahm, cream.
Rand, rim, rind, brim.
Rasen, (sod), grass.
Rasen, rave, rant, rage.
Reden = *lesen*, speak, L. *lego*.
Rath, (counsel), *ratio*, reason, L. *ratus*, Ger. *reden*.
Rauch, rough.
Rauchen, reek, quaff.
Redlich, (honest), reasonable.
Reihe, row.
Rein, pure, se-rene, Sax. *hren*, *kran*, Goth. *hrain*.
Reissend, rapid, rash.
Reissen, tear, rent, rip.
Reiz, grace, ir-ritation.
Retten, rid, rescue.
Riss, rent, crack, gap.
Ritz, rift, crack, gap.
Rock, (coat), robe, f-rock.
Rodel, roll, scroll.
Roh, raw, rough.
Rohr, reed, crane.
Rotte, rout, troop, herd.

Rücken, ridge, back.
Rufen, call, *voco*, shriek.
Ruhm, renown, rumor.
Ruhe, rest, quiet, Sanscrit. *ci*, G'k *keiō*.
Rühren, stir, roar.
Rupf, pluck.
Runzel, rumple, wrinkle.
Rustig, lusty, robust.
Rüsten, dress, arm.
Sache, (thing), from *sage* = say, as L. *res*, reason, from *reo* = speak, San. *ah*, G'k *aō*, ask.
Saal, saloon, hall.
Sacht, soft, ch, f.
Satz, sentence, set.
Schaar, (troop), herd.
Schade, damage, scath, the same as *schande*, shame.
Schaffen, (do), shape, make.
Schalig, shelly, scaly.
Schatz, treasure, tax, ex-chequer.
Schauen, shudder.
Schaum, scum, foam.
Scheibe, sheaf, slip.
Scheiden, cut, di-vide.
Schelle, bell, peal.
Schelm, villain, scoundrel.
Schick-lich, (fit), becoming, suitable, con-venient; in all these, come, go, is the base.
Schicken, send, San. *cac*, Gr'k *kēkiō*, go; *ging* (*gick*) is past of *gehen*, go.
Schimmer, glimmer.
Schinden, skin.
Schirm, screen.
Schäker, joker.
Schlagen, slay, slew.
Schlange, long, Latin *anguis*, serpent, snake.
Sch-lecht, (bad), light, low, as *schlank* = lank.

Schluss, conclusion, close, loose, key, Celt. *cloi*.
Schmuck, (dress), neat, from *schmäck* = taste, tasty.
Schnabel, nozzle.
Schnau, nose, snout.
Schnell, L. *celus*, It. *snello*.
Schnitt, cut, S. *ci*, G'k *keiō*.
Schnur, string; the *n* here and above is inserted, or *schn* equal to *sch*.
Schön, (fine), shine, belle, brilliant, bright.
Schreien, cry, It. *gridare*.
Schreck, fright, crack.
Schrift, writ, sch, w.
Schritt, step, stride.
Schuld, guild, fault, L. *scelus*.
Schurf, scrape, cut, San. *ksur*, G'k *zuraō*, shear.
Schutz, shed, sheltor.
Schwach, weak, It. *ebete*.
Schwinden, vanish, dwindle; *sch* is often a mere prefix.
Schwefel, sulphur, Fr. *soufre*.
Schwer, severe, heavy, hard.
Schwing, wing, sweep.
Sehen, see, show, g, h.
Sehr, very, true.
Segel, sail.
Sehne, sinew.
Seide, silk, d, l.
Seicht, shallow.
Seife, soap.
Selig, holy, s, h.
Seltsam, seldom.
Sicher, secure, sure.
Sichten, sift, sight.
Seufzen, sigh.
Sieg, victory, Sax. *sig-or*.
Sinn, sense.
Sitte, (custom), seat.
Sollen, shall, s, sh.
Sonder, sever, nd, v.
Sorgen, sorrow, care, s, o.
Spalten, split, cleft, chop.
Span, bend, bent; a span is a connexion, team, bridge.
Speise, food, sp, f.
Sperr, pinch, poor, press.
Sperren, bar, sp, b.
Spiegel, (mirror), *speculum*.
Spiel, play, sport.
Spiess, spit, spear.
Spitz, peak, top, piquant.
Spinne, spider, spinner.
Spliss, cleft, split.
Spott, scoff, mock, sport.
Sprechen, speak, preach, Sans. *vak*, L. *voco*, spr, v.
Spur, trace, step, spur.
Stadt, town, city.
Starke, starch, stiff.
Stark, strong, sturdy.
Stange, stake, stick.
Starr, stiff, stare.
Staub, dust.
Stauch, toss.
Staude, stalk, bush.
Steil, steep, l, p.
Steigen, stage, step, San. *stigh*, stair, G'k *steichō*.
Stellen, place, put, stl, pl.
Stemmen, dam, cut.
Sterbe, (death), de-stroy, starve.
Stern, star, rn, r.
Stich, prick, bite.
Stiel, stalk, l, lk.
Stift, tack, peg.
Stiften, found, fix, stiff.
Stimme, (voice), tune, say, G'k *stoma*, San. *stu*.
Stirn, front, stern.
Stock, stick, stop, staff.
Stolz, (proud), L. *stultus*.
Storen, di-sturb.
Stoss, thrust, jog, *stut*.
Stossen, push, stave.
Strafen, (punish), straighten.
Strahlen, ray, San. *ul*, G. *eileō*.
Strack, strait.
Straff, strait, tight.

Strang, string, trace.
Strasse, road, street.
Strauch, shrub, bush.
Strecke, tract, stretch.
Strick, string, cord, str, r.
Streiten, strife, struggle.
Streng, strict, strong.
Strich, stroke, strike.
Strumpf, (stocking), trunk, stem, stump.
Stube, (room), step, stoop.
Stück, piece, stick, bit.
Stumm, dumb, st, d.
Stumpf, (dull), stupid and stumpy.
Stunde, time, st, t.
Sturtzen, throw, hurl.
Stutz, shock, stab.
Suchen, seek, ch, k.
Sumpf, swamp.
Sünde, sin.
Süss, sweet, Sax. *suot*.
Sylbe, syllable.
Tadel, chide.
Tag, day, g, y.
Talg, tallow, g, w.
Tand, toy, dandle.
Tasche, pocket, sack.
Thier, deer, L. *fera*, wild.
Tasten, taste, touch.
Tauchen, duck, dip.
Taumel, tumult, (recline).
Taugen, (fit), from which is *tugend*, *tuch*.
Tausch, trick, cheat.
Teich, tank, (pond).
Teppich, tapestry.
That, deed, act, did.
Theil, deal, share, cut, part, San. *da*, *kar*, *vil*.
Thräne, (tear), run, drop.
Thränen, running, train.
Thurm, tower.
Tilgen, ex-tinguish.
Tillen, dig, till.
Tinte, ink, tint.

Tisch, table, dine, dish.
Toll, dull, fool, (mad).
Ton, tone, sound, strain.
Topf, tub, pot.
Tracht, draft, dress.
Tragen, (carry), drag, bear.
Trauen, trust, true.
Traube, grape.
Trauer, sorrow.
Treffen, strike, touch. L. *tracto*, Fr. *frapper*, San. *darp*.
Trennen, sever, *separo*.
Treten = *reden* — *path*, in San., equals *read* and *tread*.
Trift, drove, drive.
Tritt, tread, track.
Trocken, dry, torrid.
Trödeln, dawdle.
Trost, (hope), trust.
Trotz, (dare), scorn.
Trübe, trouble.
Trug, fraud, trick.
Trumm, (wreck), ruins, our *thrum*.
Tuch, (cloth), towel, Fr. *drap*, t, tr = dr.
Tücke, trick, t, tr.
Tugend, (virtue), from *Tüchtig*, fit, tight, also good, strong, equal to virtue.
Tummeln, bustle, tumble, hurry
Um-kehren, re-turn, turn-a-round, *um* = around, *circum*.
Uebel, (ill), evil.
Uebung, use, (practice).
Uhr, (clock), hour.
Um-stand, circum-stance.
Un-gar, not-done, San. *kar*.
Un-gern, un-willing, not-grain, against-grain.
Un-glück, ill-luck.
Un-kraftig, (in-effectual), in-firm, *kraft* = *kar*, form.
Un-schuld, (in-nocence), not-hurt, not-guilt.

Unter-haltung, sus-tenance, en-ter-tain, (*sub* = under), ten, tain = halt, hold.
Unter-schrift, sub-script.
Urbar, arable.
Ur-laub, fur-lough.
Ur-sache, principle—both words are developments of *ere*, *fore*, or-igin, cause.
Uppig, (luxurious), up-y, heap-y, high.
Urtheil, (judgment), or-deal, fore-part.
Ur-wesen, fore-being, or-igin.
Veilchen, violet.
Ver-haft, caption, take.
Ver-kehr, inter-course, run or turn-around, -among.
Ver-lassen, let.
Ver-loren, lose, for-lorn.
Ver-lust, lost.
Ver-nehmen, perceive, take-be-fore, or take-through.
Ver-stand, under-stand.
Ver-werfen, re-ject, re = ver.
Vieh, beast.
Viel, full, very, much.
Vogel, (bird), fowl, falcon.
Vor-fahr, pre-cessor, go-fore.
Vor-gehen, fore-go, pre-cede. *vor-gang* = pre-cedence.
Vor-haben, fore-have, in-tent, design.
Vor-nehmen, pre-eminent, emi-neo = L. *emo*, take.
Vor-rede, pre-face, fore-read.
Vor-spiel, pre-lude, fore-play.
Vor-theil, pro-fit, for-part.
Vor-tragen, fore-carry, pro-po-sal, for-place.
Wach, awake.
Wachsen, wax.
Wackeln, waver, wabble.
Wage, balance, weigh.
Wagen, (risk), wage, hazard.
Wahlen, (choose), cull, *pohl*, S. *val*, G'k *elō*, will, pull.
Wahn, fancy.
Wahr, true, L. *verus*.
Wal, battle.
Wald, wood, L. *sylva*.
Wallen, wallow, walk, G'k *po-leō*, San. *pal*, *pad*.
Wand, wall.
Wappen, weapon.
Wanken, waver.
Wanne, fan, van.
Warten, wait.
Weber, weaver, L. *opero*.
Wechsel, change, L. *vicis*.
Weg, way, L. *via*.
Wegen, move, Greek *agō*, wag, shake.
Weg-stecken, stick-away.
Weg-scheren, shear-away.
Weich, weak, It. *fiacco*.
Weide, food, L. *victus*.
Weisen, (show), *wissen*.
Welk, wilt.
Wenig, few, many, L. *minus*.
Werden, (become), turn, the same as *wenden* = go, wend.
Wesen, essence, being.
Wichtig, weighty.
Wickeln, wind, wick.
Wider-sprach, contra-dict.
Wiese, mead; *Wie*, why, *wi*.
Wimmeln, swarm.
Winseln, whimper, whine.
Winkle, angle, corner.
Wirklich, (actual), from *wirken* = work, as ef-fectual, from *facio* = do, and act-tual, from *ago* = do.
Wissen, wit, L. *vidi*, wisdom, San. *cudh*, *cvidh*.
Wittwe, widow.
Wohl, well.
Wolke, cloud, welkin.
Wucher, usury.
Wuhlen, wallow.
Wünsch, wish, will, S. *av*.
Wurde, worth, honor.
Wurf, throw, warp, wreck.

Wurtz, root, *wurzel*.
Wust, waste.
Wuth, fury, fume, *muth*.
Zahl, (number), tell, say.
Zagen, shake, z, sh.
Zank, wrangle, z, wr.
Zapfen, stopple.
Zart, tender, rt, d.
Zailber, charm.
Zausen, touse, tug.
Zehe, toe.
Zeichen, token, sign, be-to-ken
 = *kennen*, know.
Zeichnung, design.
Zeile, (line), file.
Zeit, tide, time, L. *ævum*, *diem*,
 age, *ætas*, *ewig*.
Zelt, tent.
Zer-stören, de-stroy.
Zer-reissen, tear, rend.

Ziege, goat, L. *hœdus*.
Ziegel. title.
Ziehen, draw, tow, tug, S. *du*.
Ziem-en, seem, come, suit.
Zier, grace, a-dorn.
Zimmer, chamber, It. *camera*,
 room.
Zinn, tin, Fr. *etain*, It. *stagno*.
Zinse, interest, rent.
Zorn, thorn, wrath.
Züchten, e-ducate.
Züchtig, chaste, chastise.
Zwecken, peg, tack.
Zwangen, pinch, press.
Zweifeln, doubt, double, doubt
 = think = L. *volvo*, turn,
 so re-flect = re-turn; med-
 itate equals middle, doubt,
 double.

The parallels we have selected are the most difficult we could find. A vast majority of German words differ far less from English than those do which we have selected. Nothing can be plainer than that Germ. has a representative for every Eng. word. Even in the present state of philology, scarce a word can be found that cannot be traced by plain rules to some like word with us. Not only are the simple words made like ours, but their compounds also — and often when least expected. Thus, German *ver-nehmen* is *per-take*, precisely as *per-ceive* (ceive = capio, take), *ge-walt*, pre-vail (*ge* = pre), *g-lauben*, be-lieve (*g* = be), *un-schuld*, in-nocence, ob-ject, *vor-werp*, (*ject* and *werp* both equal *throw*).

Dutch Etymology.

576. The Dutch has most of its words practically identical with German, making allowance for the replacement of some letters by their nearest relatives. There are, however, many words which bear a greater resemblance for English. Aside from the words which in their form are plainly Germ. or Eng., very few indeed can be found — and even those few can be brought near us by close examination.

We select only a few Dutch words, enough merely to give an idea of the manner in which the Dutch orthography compares with English and German.

Woede, Germ. *wuth.*
Wissel, Germ. *wechsel.*
Wis, Germ. *ge-wiss.*
Winst. Germ. *ge-winn.*
Wet, G. *gesetz*, law.
Week, G. *wach.*
Wasdom, G. *wachsthum.*
Wars, averse.
Wak, wet, G. *nass.*
Wagten, watch, wait.
Waan, G. *wahn.*
Vroom, G. *fromm*, fair.
Vroeg, G. *froh.*
Voeren, ferry, G. *fahren.*
Vlut, G. *fleiss*, fleet.
Ver-pligt, o-bliged.
Ver-keerd, per-vert.
Vergen, urge, press.
Vatten, Ger. *fangen*, take, vat, vessel, hold, fast.
Vak, vacancy.
Uit-loopen, out-lope, elope.
Teken, sign, token.
Stoot, push, G. *stoss*, tap.
Stede, stead, G. *stadt.*
Spaade, G. *spät*, late.
Scheppen, shape, G. *schaffen.*
Rook, G. *rauch*, smoke.
Pligt, G. *pfligt.*
Slot, G. *schloss*, lock.

Sleepen, drag, sledge.
Zoet, sweet, G. *süss.*
Scheelen, ail, want.
Mat, measure, mete.
Keek, look, *keek.*
Schuif, shove, draw, as *push* equals *pull.*
Blink, (shine), blink, look; shine = seem, see.
Laat, leave, let.
Schillen, shell, pare, part, se-parate, de-cide.
Veeg, wipe, sweep.
Vlied, fly, fled.
Ge-niet, (enjoy), use, need.
Braad, roast.
Bezig, busy, 'use.
Kwaad, bad, worse.
Be-leid, be-lead, con-duct.
Rogge, rye.
Eisch, ask.
Er, there, G. *da, daar.*
Op-hoogen, up-high, raise.
Mooi, (fine), pretty (pooty).
Be-loop, be-run, course.
Be-lieven, p-lease.
Hout, wood, G. *holz.*
Erg, irk, grieve, w-orse, Germ. *ärgern*, L. *ægre.*

Danish Etymology.

577.
Aabne, open.
Aag, yoke.
Aager, usury, gain.
Aand, (ghost), L. *anima.*
Aare, artery, ear, grain.
Aarsag, Germ. *uhr-sach.*
Ad-faerd, de-port, *faerd* = fer-ry, carriage.
Ad-gang, ac-cess, to-go, *gang* = cess, both = go.
Ad-skilt, (separate), ad-split.
Ad-vare, ad-warn, warn.

Af-fordre, re-quire.
Af-kraeve, 'quire, crave.
Af-rage, shave, raze.
Af-stige, step-up, (*af* = up).
Af-tegne, de-sign.
Agt, thought, act.
Agtelse, esteem.
Al-meen, common.
Alt, all; *Aldrig*, (never).
An-give, in-dicate.
An-ledning, in-ducement, *led* equals *duce*, lead.

An-namme, re-ceive, take.
An-raabe, call-to, (German *ruf*).
Ar, scar, seam.
Arbeide, work, operate.
Art, sort, race.
Bange, 'fraid, anxious.
Banke, beat, spank.
Bare, bare, mere, pure, but, only, fore.
Barm, breast.
Barn, (child), born, boy, babe.
Be-boe,[1] (dwell), L. *vivo,* Ger. *wohnen,* a-bode.
Be-breide, re-proach, up-braid.
Bede, beg, Germ. *beten.*
Be-drag, fraud, be-tray.
Be-dömme, deem, esteem.
Beesk, bitter.
Be-fatte, contain, vat.
Be-gave, en-dow, g, d.
Be-gegne, meet, engage.
Be-giaere, desire, 'grudge.
Be-gribe, ap-prehend, grab.
Be-greb, Ger. *be-griff,* com-pre-hend, grasp, (idea).
Be-graede, re-gret, grieve.
Be-hör, depend, co-here.
Be-kiende, own, know.
Be-klaede, clothe.
Be-lee, laugh-at.
Be-möie, molest, move.
Be-qvem, be-come, con-venient.
Be-rette, (advise), G. *rath.*
Be-sked, share, de-cide.
Be-skue, view, a-skew,
Be-slutte, conclude.
Be-tiene, at-tend, *be* = at.
Be-troe, in-trust.
Be-tryk, press, t, p.
Be-tyde, be-tide, be-token.
Be-undre, wonder-at.
Be-vant, usual, wont.
Be-vare, pre-serve, guard.
Be-viis, show, device.

Bi-kube, hive, coop.
B-lik, look, bl, l.
B-live, leave.
B-lok, log, block.
Blot, but, bare.
Bo, a-bode, house.
Bolle, bowl, swell.
Borge, borrow.
Brage, crack, crash.
B-rase, roast.
Brede, broad, spread, strew.
Brev, letter, card, G. *brief.*
Bro, bridge.
Brug, use, G. *brauch,* bru, u.
Bruse, roar.
Bryn, brim, brow.
Braende, burnt.
Brök, break, fraction.
Bulder, bustle.
Bund, bottom, soil.
Bytte, (change), L. *muto.*
Baekken, basin, beaker.
Baelg, hull, shell, peel.
Böde, patch.
Bölge, billow.
Bör, barrow.
Bösse, 'buss, box.
Daad, deed.
Daare, (fool), G. *narr.*
Danne, (form), do, G. *thun.*
Deel, G. *theil,* deal.
Digt, fiction.
Diaerv, hard, rude.
Drage, drag, draw.
Dragt, draught.
Dreie, turn.
Dukke, duck, dip.
Dulme, slumber.
Dyd, virtue, good.
Dyrt, dearly.
Dölge, con-ceal.
Dömme, deem.
Eensome, on-ly, lone-some.
Eg, edge; *Egen,* own.
Enig, united, one.

---

[1] We notice prefix *be* in Danish, not appearing sometimes with us.

Er-fare, ex-periment, prove, ex-pert, *erfahren*.
Erindre, warn, wonder.
Faae, G. *fangen*, get, aa, an.
Faa, few, L. *paucus*.
Fad, dish, vat.
Falde, fall.
Falk, falcon.
Falsk, false.
Fare, peril, fare, go.
Fatte, fasten, fetch.
Favn, fathom.
Fegte, fight, fence.
Feil, fault, fail.
Finde, (think), feel, find.
Fiaele, veil, con-ceal.
Flere, more, L. *plure*, pl, m.
Flig, fly, flap.
Flid, ap-ply.
Flyde, flow, fly, fleet.
For-andre, other, *alter*.
Forske, search, in-quire.
For-staae, under-stand.
For-syn, fore-sight.
F-red, rest, G. *friede*.
Fremmed, foreign, G. *fremd*, strange, from.
Fuld, full, ld, ll.
Fynd, force, nd, r, (under═over ═ ver ═ for).
Gal, wild.
Gavn, gain.
Gide, like, choose.
Gierde, hurdle, yard.
Gigt, gout.
Gior, do, kar, chore, 'pare; old North *gera*═*fac*' and *par*'.
Glimre, glitter.
Gloe, gaze, look, glore.
Green, branch, G. *Grenz*.
Grün, grin, L. *rideo*.
Grue, dread.
Grov, gross, coarse.
Guul, G. *gelb*, yellow.
Hals, (neck), hall, channel.
Han, (male), he, one.
Handle, deal, handle.
Hede, (call), G. *heiss*, quoth.
Heelt, wholly.
Heft, hilt, handle.
Hegn, hedge, fence.
Hegte, hook.
Hekke, hatch.
Hemme, stop, hem.
Hen-syn, re-spect, seen.
Hevn, avenge.
Hex, witch.
Hiörne, corner, horn.
Hiul, wheel, Sw. *hjul*.
Hoved, head.
Hoppe, hop. skip, jump.
Hoveri, average.
Hugge, hew, haggle.
Hoi, hill, high.
Hövl, level, heaver.
Idel, only, eet ═ one, *etlich*.
Ilde, ill.
Ild, (fire), zeal.
Ile, hurry, G. *eilen*, l, r.
Jage, chase.
Jorde, bury, earth.
Kaabe, cloak, cape.
Kaas, course.
Kald, calling.
Kalk, cup, chalice.
Karm, frame, form.
Karrig, chary, spare.
Kielder, cellar, cell.
Kiende, known, 'quaint.
Kind, cheek, chin.
Kiaede, chain, G. *kette*.
Kiöb, buy, *kaufen*, k, b.
Klavre, clamber, climb.
Klögt, wit, look, *klug*.
Knap, close, narrow, tight.
Knub, knob, stump.
Koge, cook.
Kogle, juggle, k, j.
Kone, wife, queen.
Knegt, (servant), knave.
Krog, corner, crook, hook.
Krum, curved.

ETYMOLOGY. 169

Kun, (but), on-ly, Ger. *schon*.
Kaemper, champion, combat, camp.
Lade, let, al-low.
Lad, lazy.
Labe, lick, lap.
Led, (gate), lead.
Ledig, lazy, leisure.
Lee, laugh, L. *ris'*, l, r.
Lie, (bed), L. *lect'*, lay.
Lide, (suffer), let, L. *latum*.
Ligge, lic.
Lov, (praise), laud.
Lue, flame, l, fl.
Lure, lurk, lure.
Lukke, c-lose, lock.
Lyde, (sound), loud, lute.
Lyst, de-light, lust.
Laene, (prop), lean.
Löbe, flow, run.
Maal, mete, mark.
Mage, match, make.
Magt, might.
Mandbar, (marriageable), i e. man-able.
Mangel, want.
Mat, faint, G. *müde*.
Maver, meager.
Medlem, member, with, med, mete, end.
Meierei, dairy, G. *Meierei*.
Melden, mention.
Menneske, man, G. *mensch*.
Mergel, marl.
Minde, memory, mind.
Mis-hage, dis-gust.
Mod, (spirit), mind, mood.
Modne, mature.
Mör, mellow, l, r.
Naade, (grace), kind.
Nual, needle, nail.
Naae, near, reach.
Navn, name, renown.
Negte, de-ny, L. *nego*.
Nemme, memory, from *nehmen*, take.

Nidsk, niggard.
Nyse, sneeze.
Naeb, beak, nib.
Naere, nourish.
Nues, cape, (point), nose.
Nöie, nice.
Nöle, de-lay.
Nöde, urge, force, need.
Om-bytte, per-mute.
Om-hylle, en-velop.
Ond, ill, bad.
Op-stille, set-up, still.
Ord, word; *Orm*, worm.
Pant, pawn.
Passe, fit, suit, pass.
Peen, fine.
Penge, coin, penny.
Perse, press.
Pille, pick, cull, pillage.
Pind, pin, peg.
Plads, place.
Pleie, (care), ap-ply.
Plet, blot.
Pose, bag, budget, purse.
Prale, brag, brawl.
Priis, price, praise.
Prygl, club, cudgel, drub.
Pöl, pool, puddle.
Pust, blow, brush.
Raa, raw, crude.
Raage, rook, raven.
Rage, shave.
Rank, right, e-rect.
Ramme, frame.
Rask, quick, rash, brisk.
Reen, neat, clean.
Regne, reckon.
Ret, right, reason, G. *rath*.
Rette, correct, straight.
Rift, rent, cleft.
Ringe, poor, cringe, G. *ge-ring*, little.
Roes, praise, r, pr.
Rude, rue.
Ruge, brood.
Ruu, rude, raw.

22

Ry, rumor.
Rydde, void, rid.
Ryg, back, ridge.
Ryge, smoke, reek.
Ryk, tug.
Ryste, toss, rush.
Red, af-raid.
Raekke, reach, stretch.
Röre, stir, brisk.
Rör, reed, seed.
Röve, rob.
Röst, voice, roar.
Saare, hurt, wound.
Sagte, soft.
Salg, sale; *Sal*, hall.
Salve, volley.
Sand, sure, sound, safe.
Sunds, sense.
Sandt, sound, certainly.
Sige, say.
Sikke, sure, secure.
Sind, sense, mind.
Sinke, hinder.
Skade, hurt, scath.
Skaffe, get, G. *schaffen*.
Skandse, sconce.
Skat, tax.
Skiende, chide, scold.
Skifte, part, shift.
Skin, shine.
Skiaere, carve.
Skiaerpe, sharpen.
Skiaev, (crooked), skew.
Skion, (fair), shine.
Skov, wood, grove.
Skose, scoff, s, f.
Skraa, skew.
Skride, stride.
Skrig, cry, shriek.
Skrive, write.
Skud, shoot.
Skuffe, (cheat), shuffle.
Skugge, shade.
Slag, blow, slay.
Slet, little, slight, light, Germ. schlecht.

Slig, like, such.
Slikke, lick, sleek.
Slug, gulph.
Slutte, close, shut.
Slaegt, class, sect.
Smaa, small.
Snabel, snout.
Snappe, snatch, snap.
Snar, rapid, smart.
Snit, cut, slice, slit.
Snu, sly, cunning.
Snyder, cutter, cheat, $sn = c$ and *ch*.
Sorg, sorrow.
Sove, sleep, L. *somnus*.
Sparke, spurn.
Spedene, dis-patch.
Speide, spy.
Sperre, bar, em-bar.
Spidse, peak, speck.
Spil, play, sport.
Sprog, speech, G'k *logas*.
Spaende, span.
Sted, step, spot.
Stemme, tune, G. *stimme*.
Stik, stitch, stick.
Stille, still, place.
Stoppe, stop, stuff.
Straal, ray, str, r.
Storme, rage, roar.
Strid, strife.
Stunde, tend.
Sturte, hurl, start.
Stöd, stab, thrust, shock.
Suk, sigh, sob, k, g, b.
Stoi, stir.
S-vag, weak, faint, sv, w.
Svare, an-swer, (s)word.
Svamp, sponge.
Svaere, move, hover.
Synes, seem, seen.
Saert, strange, forth.
Söd, sweet, G. *süss*.
Söge, seek, search, ask.
Sölv, silver.
Sömme, seam, hem, s, h.

Sörge, grieve, care.
Taage, fog, t, f.
Taarn, tower.
Tab, damage.
Tag, thatch.
Tapper, brave, stout.
Tarv, (need), dare, dearth.
Tegn, sign, token.
Tigger, beggar, t, b.
Tilfaelde, ac-cident, both =to-fall, fall-to.
Til-rette, a-right, to-right.
Tirre, stir, irritate.
Tot, ton, t, n.
Tour, turn.
Trane, crane, t, c.
Trang, strait, narrow.
Traeffe, hit, strike, f, k.
Traenge, press, throng.
Traet, tired.
Traette, strife, tr, str.
Taekke, (cover), deck.
Tysse, quiet, q, t.

Taet, tight, thick.
Törke, drought.
Ud-drag, out-draw, ex-tract.
Und-tage, ex-cept.
Urt, wort, herb.
Vakker, vigorous.
Vakle, wiggle, totter.
Vanke, wander.
Ven, friend, v, fr.
Verden, world, earth.
Vente, wait, want.
Vide, (know), see, L. *video*.
Vinde, win, gain.
Vise, see, show, v, s.
Vold, force, G. *walt*.
Vred, wrath.
Vride, wreath, wring.
Vaelge, cull, pull, pohl.
Vaen, fine.
Vaev, web, weave.
Yde, yield.
Yngel, (brood), young, en-gen-der.

In Danish, as in German, we have selected for comparison words which vary most from their corresponding English or German; a vast majority of Danish words are either identical with English or German, or they differ from them by unimportant variations. What words cannot be identified with one or the other of these two languages, constitute an extremely small class.

The general cast of the Danish, as of the Swedish orthography, is far more English than German.

Latin Etymology.

578.
Acies, ax, adz, sharp.
Æg-er, sick, grief.
Æstimo, esteem.
Ætas, age, state, (*Ætate*).
Ævum, age, v, g.
Ager, (field), acre.
Ag-gero, heap, herd, crowd.
Ago, do, act, g, d.
Aio, say.

Albus, white, blank, pale.
Ala, fly, wing, fl, w.
A-les, light.
Alius, other, else.
Alter, other, alter.
Alte, (high), loft.
Amo, love, friend, m, l, v.
Am-plus, ample, full.
Ango, strangle, anguish.
Anima, mind, nm, mn.

Annus, year, ring, n, r, — *a* or *an*, *am*, usually prefix.
Aperio, open, cover.
A-pex, point, peak.
A-pes, bee.
Ap-paro, appear.
Ap-pello, peal, call.
Apt-us, fit, apt.
A-qua, water.
Aquila, eagle, q, g.
Arb-or, tree, rb, tr.
Arceo, keep, guard, bar.
Ard-ens, burn-ing.
Ard-uus, hard, high.
Argen-tum, silver, ore.
A-ries, ram.
Aro, ear, till, r, l.
Ars, art, virtue, force.
Arvum, plow (r, l), corn.
Arx, ridge.
Artus, joint, part.
Asper, harsh, hard, sharp, severe; *At* = but.
Ater, black, fatal, dark.
Atr-ox, dark, cruel, dire.
Aud-eo, dare.
Aud-io, hear, ear, d, r.
Augeo, wax, make (*ago*).
Aula, ball.
Auris, ear.
Aur-um, gold, ore, l, r, also yellow.
Barba, beard, b, d.
Beat-us, bless-ed, b, bl.
Belle, pretty, well, bl, pr.
Bell-um, war, bl, wr.
Bene, well, very.
Benign-us, kind.
Bon-um, good, bn, gd.
Bov-e, cow, b, c.
Brev-is, brief, short.
Boo, bellow, low.
Brach-ium, branch, arm.
Bulla, bubble.
Ca-do, shed, fall, go.
Cæcus, se-cret, close, (blind).

Cæl-um, (heaven), hell, Fr. *ciel*, welk-in, cli-mate.
Cal-amus, stalk, quill.
Cal-co, (tread), walk.
Calid-us, scald, bold.
Calix, cup, hollow.
Cal-or, warmth, scald, cl, wr.
Call-us, hard, cl, hr.
Calx, heel, cl, h.
Candeo, shine, c, sh.
Can-is, G. *hund*, dog, hound, as *bon'* = good.
Can-o, sing, sound, sink, chant, sang.
Can-us, (white), shine.
Cap-ax, keep, hold, i. e. large, wide.
Capio, take, catch; *habeo* = *capio*, as G. *haupt* = *caput*.
Caput, head, Go. *haubith*, A-S. *heafod* (heap, high).
Capra, goat, Fr. *chevr.*
Car-bo, coal, r, l.
Car-cer, (prison), bar, *capio.*
Car-eo, (lack), scarce, spare.
Car-men, poem, work.
Carpo = *capio*, carve.
Car-us, dear, c, d.
Casa, house, case.
Caste, chaste.
Castigo, chastize.
Casus, case.
Cauda, tail, d, l.
Caveo, heed, care, v, d.
Caulis, stalk.
Cavo, scoop, cage, coop, v, p.
Cavus, hollow, cave, v, l.
Ce-do, go, yield.
Celer, fleet, Ger. *schnell*, Celt. *kell.*
Cel-sus, tall, (*altus*).
Cen-seo, think.
Cera, wax, seal.
Cer-no, see, cut.
Certe, sure, rt, r.
Certo, try.

ETYMOLOGY.

Cervus, hart.
Ces-so, cease, go.
Cieo, in-cite, stir.
Civitas, (*civitate*), state.
Cla-mo, call, Sans. *kal, kirad,* Sans. *klrap* = sound, rap, strike, clap, (club), cling.
Claudo, close.
Clavis, 'lock, key, close.
Cle-po, con-ceal.
Cognit-us, 'quaint, known.
Colo, till, c, t.
Co-lumba, dove, l; d.
Collum, (neck), G. *hals*, hill.
Co-mis, meek, mild.
Con-or, can, S. *can*, G'k *kon-eo*.
Corn-u, horn.
Corona, crown.
Corpus, corpse, (body).
Cortex, bark, rind.
Cor, heart, cour-age.
Cremo, burn, (*uro*).
Creo, grow, form, S. *kar*.
Crepo, crack, creak, rattle, jingle, rustle, etc.
Cruor, blood, stream, gore, flow.
Crudus, raw, Sax. *hreaw*.
Cudo, beat, cuff.
Culpa, fault, Ger. *schuld*.
Cupio, wish, hope, San. *kup*.
Cuprum, copper.
Curro, run, hurry, Sans. *dra*, Germ. *tragen*, Gr'k *draō*, (draw).
Currus, carriage, chariot, car, cart, coach.
Cursus = *currus*, (course).
Cygn-us, swan.
Demo, take, Ger. *nehmen*.
Dens, tooth, (dent).
Dens-us, thick, dense.

Dexter, right, d, r.
Di-co, say, show, do.
Dign-us, deign.
Dis, rich, d, r.
Do, give, *dab-at*, gave.
Doceo, teach.
Dom-us, home, d, h.
Dos, dowry, gift.
Duco, lead, d, l.
Dulcis, sweet, le, s, G. *süss*, (duce), dear, l, r.
Dur-us, hard, d, h.
Ebur, ivory.
Eo, go, walk, be.
Equus, horse, q, h.
Erro, rove, err, roam.
Esca, eat, meat.
E-veho, con-vey
E-vul-sum, pull, pluck.
Ex-piro,[1] breathe, ex-pire.
Fa-cio, do, make, fashion.
Fallo, gull, slide.
Far, corn.
Ferio, strike, Fr. *frapper*.
Fero, carry, bear, brood.
Ferrum, iron, f, i.
Ferus, wild, fierce, r, l.
Fides, faith.
Fil-um, thread, l, r.
Fin-is, end, bound, f, e.
Flagrum, flog, lash, flame.
Fleo, be-wail, flow.
Flo, blow.
Flos, (*flor*), flower.
Foris, door.
Fortis, hardy, strong.
Frango, (fract), break.
Fremo, roar, fr, r.
Frigidus, fresh, rigid.
Fuga, flight, f, fl.
Fugo, chase, G. *jagen*.
Fundus, land, ground.

[1] The prefix *x* is a form of *s* or *es*; thus, *expiro* = *spiro*, or *espiro*, ex-punge = 'spunge, extent = stent, s-tretch, *ex-ter* = s-trange, *ex-ude* = s-weat. So, we may reduce other prefixes to mere ordinary initial letters.

Funus, pomp,   f, p.
Futilis, foolish,   ftl, fl.
Gallina, hen,   lli, i.
Gannio, whine, moan.
Gaudium, joy, d, y, and glad,
   gl, g.
Gemini, twins.
Gemo, groan, moan.
Gens, kindred, gent.
Genus, a kind.
Gera = *fera*, wear.
Gesto = *gera*.
Gigna, en-gender, gain, get.
Gleba, clod, lump.
Glutina, glue.
Gradus, de-gree, grade.
Gramen, grass.
Gravis, heavy, S. *gur*,   gr, h,
   grave, dear, bear.
Grex, herd, crowd,   g, h.
Hæd-us, kid, goat.
Hala, in-hale, blow.
Hauria, draw,   hr, dr.
Helix, coil.
Hilaris, glad, (hlar, hlad).
Hio, gape, yawn.
Homo, man,   hm, m.
Humilis, mean, small.
Jacea, lie, Sans. *yug*, German
   jagen.
Jacta, = *jacea*, (throw, cast).
Ica, str-ike, sm-ite.
Ignis, l-ight, fire.
Iter, route, road.
Inanis, vain.
Jubea, bid,   jb, b.
Judicium, (*juum*), Saxon *do-
   ma*, doom, judg-ment.
Jugerum, acre.
Jugum, yoke, unite.
Junga, join, yoke.
Juris, right,   jur, r.
Juvenis, young,   jv, yu.
Juv-o, aid,   v, d.
Labor, slip,   l, sl.
La-bor, o-pera, work.

Lapis, (lapid), G'k *laas*, stone,
   lpd = ls = sl, st; lap = sax-
   um, rock.
Lacer, tear, rent.
Lac, milk,   lc, mlk.
Lev-is, light, sleek.
Lat-us, wide, broad, as *bear*
   from *fera* = *lat'*.
Lat-us, side, coast, waist.
Lav-a, wash,   la, wa.
Lega, read, G'k *log'*,   lg, rd.
Lenis, gentle,   l, g.
Leva, lift, help, light.
Lex, (leg), law, lay.
Liber, free.
Liber, book, G'k *biblos*,   lb =
   bl, br, fr.
Liba, lick, slip.
Libra, (weigh), bear; *li, l,* oft-
   en takes place of a prefix.
Lign-um, (*ignis*), log, wood.
Liga, tie, bind,   lg, t, b.
Lingua, tongue, l, d, t.
Linum, linen, flax.
Loca, place,   l, pl.
Lo-quar, quoth, (speak).
Luceo, light, shine.
Ludo, p-lay.
Lumen, light.
Lupus, wolf,   lp, lf.
Luna, moon, month,   l, m.
Lutum, loam,   t, a.
Mac-ula, spot, speck.
Mæl-eo, moist, G. *nass*.
Mag-nus, much, major.
Majestas, G'k *megethas*, might,
   majesty.
Male, ill,   m, i.
Malum, apple, melon.
Man-us, hand.
Mare, water,   r, tr.
Marga, border.
Merces, hire, re-ward.
Mereo, earn, merit.
Meta, mow.
Mi-gro, move.

Mit-is, meek, sweet, m, s.
Mitto, send.
Moles, bulk, mass.
Mollis, mild, plain.
Mora, delay, tarry.
Mos, mode, way.
Moveo, G'k *mogeō*, Sans. *may*, Ger. *wegen*, much.
Muto, change, turn.
Mun-us = donum.
Morior,[1] murder, S. *mar*.
Nidus, nest.
Niger, (ater), dark.
Nox, night, (*nocte*).
Nudus, naked.
Nubes, cloud, G. *Walke*.
Numen, nod, (*nuto*).
Oleo, smell.
Omn-is, all, mn, ll.
O-pera, work, S. *kar*.
O-pes, power.
Orb, circle.
Orior = surgo, rise.
Oro, preach, (speak).
Otium, ease.
Ov-um, egg, v, g.
Os, mouth, oral.
Pab-ulum, food.
Pango, strike, spank.
Par, (even), pair.
Par-cus, spare.
Parlo, bring, bear.
Partus, birth, (brought).
Par-vus, spare, short.
Pa-sco, feed.
Pateo, open; *Pauci*, few.
Paveo, fear; *Pax*, peace.
Pect-us, chest, breast.
Pejor, worse, p, w.
Pellis, felt, pelt.
Pello, drive, pl, dr.

Pendo, weigh, hang.
Pen-na, pen, feather, fin, wing, G'k *ptēnos*.[2]
Penso, ponder, think.
Pet-o, seek, beg, beat, bid.
Pign-us, pawn.
Pingo, paint, picture.
Pinguis, fat.
Pisc-is, fish.
Plaga, blow, flog.
Plebs, folk, people.
Plus, more, pl, pi, r.
Pono, put, place, lay, set.
Porta, door, p, d.
Pot-ens, power, t, w.
Premo, press, San. *parc*, Gr'k *prassō = do*, form.
Prendo, grab, pr, gr.
Pretium, price, worth.
Pro-cul, far.
Puer, boy, born, as *natus* (born) means son.
Pug-no, fight.
Pulso, beat.
Pulcher, Fr. *belle*, *beau*, jolly, beautiful.
Quæro, search.
Quatio, shake, jog, quash.
Radix, root.
Rado, scrape, razor.
Rapio, take, (capio), rob, grab, Ger. *raub*, It. *ratto*, *raptus*, ravished.
Ratio, reason, cause, occasion, It. *cagione = cause*, from *reor = say*, reckon.
Rego, rule, g, l.
Res, (thing), reason, read.
Rete, net, snare.
Rege, king, (r, k), G'k *archos*, San. *raj*, Per. *sha*, queen.

[1] In some of these words, *m* is a mere silent prefix for us, in others it equals *h*, *w*, *s*.

[2] We must here remind the student that the parts of words are like the parts of animals, so intimately connected together, that cut as you will, you are sure to take more or less than belongs to the part.

Rigor, cold, hard, rg, rd.
Ri-deo, laugh, r, l.
Rite, right, *rect-us*.
Rixa, strife.
Robur, power.
Rogo, crave, ask.
Rota, Fr. *roue*, wheel, r. w.
Ruber, red, ruddy,
Rudis, rude, fresh.
Ruga, c-rumple, w-rinkle.
Ruo, rush, run.
Ruptus, broken, burst, and rip, rend.
Sævio, rage, fierce.
Sagitta, shaft, gt, ft.
Sag-um, sack, frock, jacket.
Sagus, wise, w, s.
Salio, leap, skip, sl, hl, l.
Saliva, slaver, spit.
Salve, hail, s, h.
Salus, health, sound.
Salvus, safe, heal, holy.
Sanguis, blood. sap.
Sano, heal, whole, sound.
Sapio, savor, taste.
Sax-um, rock, s, r.
Scalpo, scratch, carve, claw, rake.
Scapus, shank, shaft.
Scelus, villainy, sc, v.
Scio, (know), sage, see.
Sci-tus, skill, civil.
Scribo, write, sc, w.
Sculpo, scalp, carve.
Seco, (*seo*), cut, gnaw, saw, S. *sagh*, G'k *ayō*,
Sella, seat, saddle.
Semen, seed, m, d.
Sero, sow, strew, r, w.
Serp-o, creep, spread.
Servo, save, guard, care.
Severus, serious, sober.
Sider', star.

Signum, sign, token.
Silex, flint, s, f.
Silva, holt, G. *holz*.
Solid-us, It. *sodo*, sound.
Sol-vo, loose, sl, ls.
Somnus, (sleep), dream.
Son-o, sound, ring.
Sop-or, sleep, s, sl.
Sors, lot, fortune.
Spar-go, stre-w, spr-ead.
Species, shape, fashion.
Spes, hope, s, h.
Spero, hope, trust.
Spiro, breathe, savor, Sanscrit *spar*, live, spread.
Spis-sus, thick, sp, th.
Splendid', bright, light, sp = b, spl = l.
Spum-a, foam, sp, f.
Stat-uo, stand, set, sit.
Stern-o, strew, spread.
Stipula, stubble.
Stirps, stalk, stem, root.
Strideo, crack, roar.
Stult-us, fool, silly, sot.
Surgo, rise, grow.
Sus,[1] swine, sow.
Tabella, tablet.
Tact-us, touch, S. *tag*, *thigō*.
Tardus, slack, slow.
Tect-us, hid, deck-ed.
Tectum, house, G. *dach*, Gr'k *stegos*, thatch, deck.
Telum, dart, l, r.
Temp-us, time, mp, m.
Tendo, stretch, spread.
Teneo, hold, keep, t, k, find, bind.
Tento, tempt, try.
Tener, tender, thin, fine, nice, young.
Tero, rub, break, thrash, bray, wear, waste.

[1] The main point to be kept in view in regard to *s*, is that it equals *h*, and often disappears entirely — that, besides, it is allied with *c*, *e*.

ETYMOLOGY. 177

Terra, earth. *t* = vowel often, or disappears.
Tergum, ridge, G. *rück*.
Tepeo, hot, tp, ht.
Testis, G. *Zeichniss*, evidence, show, de-sign.
Texo, weave, knit, net, (t, w), web, make.
Timeo, fear, dread, t, f, v.
Tollo, lift, S. *tul*, G'k *talaō*.
Tond-eo, S. *tud*, cut, shear.
Tono, sound, thunder.
Torqueo, twist, turn, writhe, S. *dhurv*, curve.
Torreo, toast, roast, parch.
Trabs, beam, tree, G. *baum*.
Tract-o, treat, touch, tact.
Trado, (= do), give, trd, d.
Traho, draw, drag, bring, force, stretch, wrest, drink.
Trepidus, tremble.
Tristis, harsh, cruel, dark, sorry, Go. *gaurs*.
Trudo, thrust, push.
Tueor, see, look, view.
Tutus, safe, total, whole, sound.

Vacuum, void.
Val-ens, able, force, 'vail.
Veho, (*ve-yo*), carry, draw, drag, (go, cause-to-go).
Vello, pull, pluck, tug.
Venio, come, go, went, v, c.
Venor, hunt. v, h.
Verto, turn, borrow.
Vestis, G'k *esthos*, *ge-wand*.
Vetus, past, old.
Video, see, view, vision.
Vigil, waking, watch, see.
Vincio, bind, tie, v, b.
Violo, force, vl, fr.
Vir, (man), first, former, fore, as man = one, hero.
Vireo, fresh, green, strong.
Virtus, virtue, force, courage, heart, value.
Vita, life, v, l.
Vivo, live, dwell, v, dw.
Unguis, nail, claw, ng, nl.
Volo, will, fly, wish.
Uro, burn, grieve, tease, Sans. *us*, *pr-us*.
Vultus, look, face.

We have selected from among the most difficult words for comparison, and we have taken a large share, but by no means all of them. Few words can be found in Latin which are not represented in the English and German languages. In most instances, the variation is very slight, often none at all. Of instances where the differences are greatest, illustrations have just been given in our parallel columns. It is worthy of note that all, or nearly all, of the endings, case, personal, adjective, verbal, and noun, are generally the same in Latin, German, and English; so, too, are the compound verbs, as they are called (really those which have developed representatives of prepositions in their initial letters), made of like elements. Even where the difference between two words is great, yet having the same meaning, as *ignis* and *fire*, *somnus* and *sleep*, *audio* and *hear*, *pello* and *drive*, *ago* and *do*, those words have still, in English, forms like them in some other parts of speech, as *somnolent*, *audience*, *compel*, *igneous*, *act*. These latter words have been claimed to be Latin words, but they are no more Latin words than nine tenths of the English — they are English words as much as there are such. We hence deduce the inference, that though we may not often find the parallel so clear in the precise equivalent of the Latin, we will generally find it in some related word.

Greek Etymology.

579.
A-bolos, foal, colt.
Aga-mai, awe, adm-ire.
A-gath-os, good, (kal-os).
A-gallō, brilliant, light.
A-geirō, crowd, herd.
Agelē, herd, flock, g, h.
Agē, awe, l-ook.
Agē, b-reak, wave, g, v.
Agkalē, (elbow), ankle, arm, branch, crook, break.
Agk-os, cr-ack, cleft.
Agkur, h-ook, anchor.
A-glaos, (agallō), gleam, brilliant, Ger. *glanz.*
Ag-mos, br-eak, bank.
Agn-os, G. *rein,* cl-ean.
A-greō, grab, (aireō).
Aguia, way.
Angkō, squeeze, strangle.
Ago, lead, go, Latin *veho,* go, br-ing.
A-dinos, dense, thick, thin.
'Ados, joy, L. *gaudium.*
Adros, mature, ripe.
Aeirō, raise, b-ear, c-arry, air = high.
Azē, heat.
A-zēlos,[1] zealous, jealous.
Athl-os, battle.
Aideo-mai, awe.
Aithō, heat, (burn).
Ail-inos, ail, wail-ing.

Aima, blood, L. *sanguis,* flow, str-eam, *cruor.*
Aimulos, mild, (*ai* prefix).
Ainē, fame, l-aud.
Ainos, (deinos), dire.
Aix, goat, *hæd-us.*
Aiolos, fleet.
Aipos,[2] height, d-eep.
'Aireo, g-ripe, rob, take, kill, r, l, de-stroy, G. *sterben,* (airō).
Aissō, rush, w-ax.
Aiskos, shame, (*ai* prefix).
Aiskunē, shame, ab-ash.
Aiteō, s-eek, ask.
Aitia, c-ause, c-ase, Lat. *ratio,* Ger. *r-ath.*
Aiōn, L. *evum,* time.
A-kan-os, thorn, pin, spin.
Akē,[3] point, edge.
Akē, silence, L. *t-aceo.*
A-kouē, sound, still, k, s.
A-kouō, L. *audio,* hear.
Aktin, light, fl-ash.
Alalē, howl, yell.
Ala-os, b-lind, 'look.
Ala-omai, walk, Fr. *aller.*
Algos, ache, anguish.
A-legō, reckon, read, l, r.
Aliō, ro-ll.
Alkē, strength, l, r, valor, force.
Alla-ssō, alter.

[1] Note that *a* is in Greek a very common prefix, or augment, without force.

[2] Note that *os, on, ē, ō, mai,* and others, are endings that with us are generally suppressed.

[3] *Akis, aktē, akōn, akron, akonē, akōkē, akmē, aichmē,* are forms of this *Akē,* and they give a good idea of the manner in which derivative forms arise generally.

ETYMOLOGY. 179

'*Allo-mai*, leap, L. *salio*.
Alukē, trouble, anxiety.
Alukros, luke-warm.
Alassō, walk, (escape).
Amaxa, wagon, w, m.
Amuō, hcap, cumu-late.
Ama-uros, dim.
A-mblus, blunt, mbl, bl.
A-melgō, milk.
A-mergō, press, urge.
A-milla, mill, battle.
Amnos, lamb, Fr. *agneau*.
Amos, sand.
A-munō, de-fend, L. *munio*.
A-nagke, need, anxious.
Anēr, man, one.
An-uō, finish, end.
Ara, prayer, curse.
Arkeō, ward, care.
Ar-ma, car, chariot.
Arn-os, ram, lamb.
'*Arpazō*, rob, ravish.
Arrat-os, hard, harsh.
Arrēn, brave, (male).
Artios, right, ready.
Archē, origin, first, Sans. *arh*, power, L. *rex*.
Aulē, hall, yard, fold.
Aulos, flute, hollow.
Auxō, wax, grow, augment.
Ach-os, ache, pain.
Bath-us, deep, bt, dp.
Bainō, (*Baō*), go, pass.
Ballō, fling, kill, fall.
Barus, grievous, heavy, br, gr, force, strong, harsh, grave.
Baptō, dip, b, d.
Basis, pace, base, gait, foot, beat, tread, (G'k *bēma*).
Belos, dart, L. *telum*, (*ballō*)
Beltiōn, better, Sax. *bet-ra*.
Blax, flaccid, loose, lax, sluggish, dull, silly.
Blaptō, stop, dam-age.
B-lepo, look, live, light.
Bauō, bubble, swell.

Boē, roar, shout, bawl.
Bombeō, bombast, hum, rumble, grumble, buzz.
Bo-skō, feed, fodder.
Boton, cattle, beast.
Boun-os, mound, mount.
Bradus, tardy, heavy.
Bra-ssō, stir.
Brach-us, short, crash, break, rattle, clash.
Brechō, wet, sprink-le.
Brithō, burden, press.
Brimē, rage, force, br, fr.
Brontē, thunder, roar.
Bruō, bubble, bud, bloom, flower, (*bluzo*, *bluo*, *fluo*).
Buthos, deep, bottom.
Bōlos, ball, lump, globe, clod.
Gaiō, rejoice, L. *gaudium*.
Gameō, marry, woman.
Gan-os, shine, sheen.
Gauros, proud, gr, pr.
Gaō, be, bear, born.
Gelaō, laugh, smile.
Gen-os, birth, be-gin, (been), Sans. *jan*, young, family, nation, race, g, r.
Gemō, stem, hem, hold, Sans.
Geneion, chin, jaw. [*yam*.
Geran-os, crane, bird.
Geuō, taste, gustable, chew.
Ge-phura, bridge. (Notice that *g*, *ge*, is often a prefix as
Gi-gnō-skō, know. [in Ger.)
Glax, (*glak*), milk, L. *lac*.
Glauk-os, blue, yolk, yellow.
Glassō, glance, shine.
Gluk-us, sweet, Latin *dulc-is*, *gluk* = *duk*, *dulc*, G. *süss*.
Gluphō, hollow, scalp, carve, grave, G'k *graphō*.
Glōssa, tongue, L. *lingua*,
Gnēsios, native, L. *natus*.
Goēs, cheater, 'chanter.
Graphō, write, L. *scribo*, grave, carve, score, sketch.

G-riphos, riddle.
Grup-os, stoop-ed, curv-ed.
Gual-on, hollow, vault.
Grōnē, grotto, rock.
Gnion, hand, knee.
Gur-os, circle, gyre.
Gōnia, nook, angle, corner.
Daizō, cut, tear, divide.
Daiō, burn, torch, *ar-deo, dah.*
Dak-nō, sting, stick, bite.
Dakru-on, tear.
Dap-to, hack, dev-our.
Das-os, thicket, dense.
Deidō, dread, awe.
Deikō, show, say.
De-ma, string, tie.
Dēleō, deal, split, kill.
Demō, build, timber.
Dēl-os, plain, dl, pl.
Dēris, (*eris*), strife, quarrel.
Dik-aios, just, right,   d, j.
Dips-os, thirst, dry.
Dmaō, tame.
Dok-eō, think, seem.
Don-eō, wind, bend.
Doru, tree, spear, dart, trunk.
Draō, do, serve, S. *trag.*
Drepō, break, tear, strip.
Dro-mos, run, course.
Dōma, house, a-bode.
Dō-ron, gift, dower.
Dōs, gift, dow-ry.
Deo-mai, need, want.
Derō, strip, bare.
Deuter, t-other, other.
Deuō, dew, wet, soak.
Dexios, right, just,   d, r.
Egeirō, arouse, stir.
Edra, seat, throne, chair.
Eikos, like, just.
Eilō, roll, whirl.
Eirgō, ward, guard.
Ela-unō, im-pel, drive.
E-lachus, little,   k, t.
'*Elkō*, pull, haul, draw.
En-timos, es-teemed.

En-tonos, tend, strain.
Epeigō, push, quicken.
Ep-os, speech, word, S. *ab.*
Eraō, love, friend, de-sire.
'*Erpō*, creep, S. *sarp, serp*'.
Erg-on, work, task.
Ereikō, break, split, bruise.
Ereuna, search, track.
Eruō, draw, tug.
Esthēs, L. *vestis*, dress.
Eur-us, broad, wide, far.
E-phedra, sitting, seat.
Echur-os, secure, firm.
E-pseō, seethe, boil.
Zaō, live, blow, L. *vivo.*
Zeug-os, yoke.
Zel-os, zeal, jeal-ous.
Zēmia, damage.
Zēteō, seek, search.
Zōnē, girdle,   z, g.
Zōros, pure.
Ege-omai, head, lead.
Ed-omai, pl-ease, glad.
Edus, sweet, delight.
Ekō, come, go.
Elakatē, stalk.
El-os, nail.
'*Epar*, liver.
Epiaō, appease, soothe.
Er, spring, early, fore.
'*Essōn*, less, weak.
Thakos, seat, chair,   th, s.
Thalassa, ('*als*), sea, salt.
Thallō, bloom,   th, b.
Thamb-os, awe, dumb.
Tham-nos, stump, stem.
Tha-omai, see, (wonder).
Thapō, stup-ified.
Tharros, courage, dare.
Thau-mazo, es-teem, search, see, seem.
Therm-os, warm, ardent, rash, fresh, tepid, hot, Sa. *tap*, Greek *tuphō*, warm, dry, burn, (*therō*).
Theō, run, go, L. *itu.*

Thēgo, whet, edge.
Thigō, touch.
Thlaō, (*thrauō*, *klaō*, *traō*), thrash, bruise.
Thrasus, brave, hardy, dare, courage, rash.
Throcō, up-roar, dis-turb, ter-rify.
Thusan-os, tassel.
Iallō, (*ballō*), fling, roll.
Ia-omai, heal.
Iaptō, L. *jactō*, throw.
Iacheō, shout, ch, t.
Idios, fit; *Idiō*, sweat.
Idnoō, bend, dn, nd.
'*Idruō*, sit, seat.
'*Ieros*, holy, r, l.
'*Ik-anos*, fit, equal.
'*Ikanō*, come.
Ikmios, wet, moist.
Ikria, deck.
'*Ikō*, come, go.
'*Ilaos*, mild.
Ilē, troop, group, l, r, ball, roll.
Ilus, filth, dirt, l, r.
Ipn-os, oven.
'*Ippos*, L. *equus*, horse, p, r.
Ichthus, fish.
Ichnos, track, foot; *i* often = *f*, or some similar conso-nant in English.
Kaiō, burn, cook.
Kak-os, bad, wick-ed.
Kal-os, well, belle.
Kamptō, bend, cramp.
Kardia, heart, L. *corde*.
Karp-os, kernel, fruit.
Karter-os, strong, force.
Keirō, shear, bore.
Keimai, lie, rest.
Keleuō, im-pel, mp, k.
Ken-os, empty, vain.
Kent-ron, point, thorn.
Kenō, pin, pick, k, p.
Keuthō, hide, coat, S. *kut*.

Kephalē, head, L. *caput*.
Kēd-os, care, sad, d, r, dear, trouble.
Kēleō, calm, heal, charm.
Kēlē, swelling, coil, boil.
Kēr, scarce, want, dearth.
Kērux, herald, crier.
Kēt-os, (whale), fish.
Kik-us, vigor, k, v.
Kithara, harp, thr, rp; *k* is often *h, v, w*.
Ki-neō, in-cite, stir.
Kind-unos, danger, k, d.
Kichō, catch, reach, fetch, at-tain, find. (*ch* in G'k has the power of *k*).
Kis, weevil, worm.
Klaggē, clang, clatter.
Klaiō, wail, weep, de-plore.
Klaō, clip, break.
Kleiō, close, lock, key.
Klinō, lean, bend, kneel.
Kluō, hear, listen, S. *slu*.
Kogchē, concave, shell, conch.
Koilos, hollow, coil.
Koinos, common, n, m.
Kolla, glue.
Kopis, dagger, knife, cut.
Koptō, cut, kpt, ct.
Korax, crow, raven, croak.
Kor-os, boy, *puer*, born.
Kotulē, hollow.
Krainō, reign, rule, kr, r.
Krater', hard, cruel, strong, brave, force, Ger. *kraft*, gripe.
Krauros, dry, hard, brittle.
Krekō, strike, knock, crack.
Krēnē, (well), spring.
Krizō, creak, shriek, sqk, cry, squall, bawl, shrill.
Krino, part, cut, kr, pr.
Krouō, crush, strike.
Kruptō, hide, coop, kr, h.
Kru-eros, cold, fresh, freeze.
Kta-omai, get, ob-tain.

Kteinō, kill, cut, S. *han*.
Kukl-os, coil, circle.
Kull-os, coil, circle.
Kupē, hollow, cup, goblet.
Kuptō, stoop, bend.
Kur-ios, sir, G. *herr*, k, h.
Kut-os, cavity, cup, hump.
Kuōn, dog, *canis*, G. *hund*.
Lagaros, laggard, slack, lank, lean, thin, flaccid.
Laios, left.
Lakeō, rack, rend, lacerate, tear, tatter.
Lakk-os, tank, pit.
Laleo, talk, prate, prattle.
Lampō, light, shine.
Laos, folk, G. *leute*.
Lasios, bushy, leafy.
Laō, see, look.
Le-go, say, spea-k, tell.
Leipō, leave, left, rest.
Lept-os, sleek, lank, thin.
Lep-os, peel, hull, husk, strip, rind.
Lethō, hide, (*keuthō*).
Liar-os, warm, clear, bright, (*ch-liaros*).
Lith-os, rock, L. *lapid'*.
Litos, little, fine, thin.
Log-os, ta-lk, word, speak.
Luk-os, wolf, Sl. *vulk*.
Lupē, grief, lp, rf.
Lusis, loose, free.
Mak-ros, long, much.
Malak-os, L. *mollis*.
Mall-os, wool, m, w.
Math', (*manth*), teach, L. *doceo*, (*m* prefix).
Marainō, burn, parch.
Marpō, grasp.
Mussō, touch, mash.
Mast-euō, wish.
Me-gairō, grudge.
Me-gas, great, m-uch.
Melos, verse, member.
Men-os, might, mettle.

Mer-os, part, turn.
Mesos, middle, mean.
Mig-numi, mix, join, yoke.
Mēlon, (sheep), wool.
Mik-ros, small, little.
Mnēmē, mind, memory.
Molos, toil, mill.
Mogos, misery, toil.
Moth-os, battle, tumult.
Naiō, dwell, live, stay.
Neatos, next, last, new.
Neikeō, bicker.
Nemō, deem, G. *nehmen*.
Neō, go, move, swim, spin, net.
Nēros, wet, G. *nass*.
Nikē, victory, n, v.
Noeō, know, see.
Niptō, wet, wash, dip.
Nussō, push, spur.
Zeō, shave, scrape.
Zēros, torrid, arid, dry, parch, sober.
Ziphos, sword, cut, shave.
Zuron, razor.
O-gkos, hump, bulk, hunk.
O-dazō, stick, pick, bite.
O-dous, tooth, (*odazō*).
Od-os, road, way.
Odunē, pain, sad, d, p
O-zos, shoot, sprout, shrub, G. *ast*, R. *sulc*.
Oikos, house, tent.
Oiō, see, think.
O-kazō, squat, crouch.
O-ligos, little, small.
'*Omilos*, family.
Onux, nail, hoof, Fr. *ongle*.
O-xus, sharp, a-cute, cut.
O-pisō, post, back, (*o* prefix as it often is).
Opē, hole, open, hollow.
O-ptaō, roast, bake, parch.
Opō, look, (*oraō*).
Orgē, ire, anger.
O-regō, reach, stretch.
O-rthos, right, straight.

ETYMOLOGY.

Ormaō, urge, rouse.
O-ros, rock.
'Oros, goal, mark, shore.
Ossa, voice, (*ops*).
Oud, n-ot.
Oura, tail, rear.
Ouros, guard, ward.
Ochos, L. *veho*, wagon, coach.
Pagios, fixed, bind, S. *pac.*
Pais, boy, L. *puer.*
Pateō, beat, tread, path.
Pauō, pause, cease.
Pachus, thick, fat, (*tachus*).
Peithō, obey, faith.
Peira, try, proof, peril.
Pempō, bend, p, s.
Penō, pains, do, penury.
Peptō, cook, bake.
Petaō, spread, e-xpand.
Pikros, bitter, piercing.
Pinax, plank.
Pi-pto, fall, (L. *cado*), pitch.
Plax, plank, plate, table.
Platus, flat, broad, wide.
Plekō, plait, fold.
Plēssō, flog, strike.
Pleō, fly, ply, S. *plu*, sail.
Pneō, blow, breathe, wind.
Polla, (many), full.
Por-os, ford, ferry, *fahren.*
Potē, flight.
Prassō, do, form, practice.
Praos, friend, *philos*, San. *kar*, L. *paro.*
Ptaiō, strike, beat, fall.
Pter-on, plume, bird.
Ptux, tuck, pucker, fold.
Pugmē, fist, fight, box.
Puthmēn, bottom.
Pulē, door, port, pl, dr.
Purgos, tower, p, t.
'Rabdos, rod.
'Ragos, crack, cleft, flaw, rent, crevice, chink.
'Rainō, rain, wet, drop.
'Raiō, break, ruin.

'Rakos, (*'ragos*).
'Rachis, ridge, back.
'Rach-os, crag, rock.
'Rētos, said, G. *reden.*
'Rinos, rind, skin.
'Ripto, throw, rip.
'Roē, stream, current.
'Ruma, stream, run.
'Rōmē, force, robust.
'Rōx, rock, c-rag.
Sagma, saddle.
Sairō, grin.
Sagis, sack, pocket.
Saos, safe, sound, whole.
Sattō, saddle, seat.
Seiō, shake, toss.
Selēnē, moon, L. *luna.*
Selas, light, lustre.
Sēma, sign, omen.
Sigaō, silent, g, l.
Sitos, wheat.
Skairō, skirt, leap, skip.
Skallō, scratch, scrape, rake, grub, hoe, scull.
Skoptō, dig, scoop, shave.
Skaphē, scoop, trough.
Skellō, wilt, wither.
Skepō, cover, pro-tect.
Skēnē, tent, shed, hut.
Skirtaō, skirt, skip, leap.
Skotos, shade.
Skul-on, spoil, peel, shell.
Skuph-os, cup, bowl, scoop.
Sobeō, shove, move.
Sophos, sage, wise, sp, sw.
Span-os, scant, scarce, span, spare, rare.
Spendō, spend, pour.
Stegos, deck, cover, *tectus.*
Steibō, step, tread, track.
Stenos, narrow, G. *eng*, want, penury.
Stereos, strong, hard, firm.
Stereō, strip, rob, de-prive.
Stēlē, pillar, prop, Ger. *stuhl*, (*stellō*), style.

Stonux = *onux*.
Strephō, (*trephō*), turn, twist, torture, G. *treffen*.
Stupos, stub, stock, club.
Sphēn, wedge, sp, w.
Schēma, shape, form.
Tagō, take, stretch.
Taker-os, soft, tender.
Talant-on, balance.
Talaō, en-dure, dare, Lat. *tuli*, G. *dulden*, bear, child.
Tarbos, terror.
Tarassō, stir, disturb.
Tachus, quick, swift.
Teggō, tinge, stain.
Teinō, strain, stretch.
Teirō, rub, wear.
Tek-mar, token, sign.
Tek-os, chick, child.
Teuch-os, G. *Zeug*, tool.
Tiktō, be-get, chick.
Tillō, pull, pluck, tug.
Tiō, pay, atone.
Tolmaō, L. *tollo*, bold, dare.
Topos, space, spot.
Toreuō, bore, pierce.
Treō, tremble, terror.
Trugē, fruit.
Truō, rub, bore, wear.
Tukō, do, make, fact.
Tuchē, luck, chance.
Ugros, watery, weak.

ʼ*Ulaō*, howl, yell.
ʼ*Ulē*, wood, L. *sylva*, G. *holz*.
· ʼ*Upsē*, weaving, woof.
ʼ*Ups-os*, high, up, heap.
ʼ*Uō*, wet, rain.
Phainō, view, show, fancy.
Phalar-os, clear, flare.
Phan-os, clean, G. *rein*.
Phaos, day, light, see.
Phaō, say, show, shine.
Phaul-os, small, foul, bad.
Phenō, kill, wound.
Phtheir-ō, de-stroy.
Phthoggē, tone, sound.
Phial-os, vial, bowl.
Phil-os, friend, kind, phr, fr, S. *pal*, Ger. *pflegen*, Lat. *placeo*.
Phleō, flow, pour, boil.
Phlegō, flame, blaze.
Phloiō, flay, strip.
Phra-zō, pray, say, phrase.
Phulē, file, tribe, folk.
Chalkos, copper, lk, pp.
Chaos, chasm, gap, yawn.
Charis, grace.
Cheir, (hand), arm, grasp, force.
Chēlē, claw, (hand).
O-kus, swift, quick.
O-lenē, elbow, *ulna*.
O-ruō, roar.

This list, like the others, is selected from the most difficult words. When we keep constantly in view the particular laws which the Greek follows in orthography, the different letters with which many of our own are represented there, besides the peculiar combinations which they sometimes make, we shall not find the Greek etymology doubtful or difficult. We must keep constantly in mind, also, that any single letter or combination of letters gives character to, or decides the whole word; that if we find a particular letter, or combination of letters, at the beginning of a word, for example, that letter may be taken as the basis of the whole, since all the remaining letters must be cognate with it. Occasionally we have brought together the like letters at the end of the line, with a comma between them; but generally we leave the learner to bear in mind that when

ETYMOLOGY.   185

we bring a word which is Greek along side of one or more which is English, it is because the letters of the two words are alike or cognate, and that they may be replaced, the one by those of the other; thus, *pateō*, beat, tread;—*pat* and *beat* are easy; *pat* and *tread* are also easy, when we remember that $p = t$, and $t = tr$. It is a safe rule, one which is important and universal, that, in etymology, a letter is always equal to those with which it is found combined, or it is equal also to the combination of which it forms a part; thus, that $str = r$, or t, or s, or st; that $mp = nd$, because $n = m$, $p = d$, or $m = b = p$; that $k = sq$, because $k = q$; that $pl = f$, because $p = f$; that $pt = pl$, because $p = p$, and $t = l$, both t and l being combined with the same letter p. Take also *kuptō* = stoop — $k = t$, also *st*, $pt = p$, since $p = p$; and *lakeō* = rack, because $l = r$, also *rend*, since *k* (of *lakeō*) $= d$ and t, also *tear*, because l (of *lak*) $= t$, and $k = r$; and *kteinō* = kill, since $kt = k$ and $n = l$; *thermos* = warm, since $th = w$, and the same equals *ardent*, since *th* may be dropped, and $r = rd$, or $rm = rd$, — *ardeo* = burn, where the b again represents the w of *warm*, *th* of *therm*; *karp-os* = fruit, since $k = f$, and $rp = rt$. Understanding these things, we shall find Greek etymology easy. Then, we have to remind the student again, that many of the Greek words have their initial letters, which, compared to those of our own words, are mere prefixes or augments. Taking the basis we have just established, the Greek can be easily made familiar. Very many words, and those the most common and characteristic ones, are alike in Greek, Eng., and German; and in those where the difference is greater, we can, in most instances, easily explain it, and trace the connexion. In conclusion, we may remark that the orthography of Greek is much more German than is usually conceded.

French Etymology.

580.
A-beille, bee, It. *ape*.
A-bord-er, to board, (*er* is inf. ending).
A-cheter, buy, get, *kauf*.
Agneau, It. *agnino*, lamb.
Aigre, sour, severe, acrid.
Aile, wing, fly, L. *ala*.
Aller, walk, alley, It. *ando*.
A-mas, heap, mass.
Ame, L. *anima*, mind.
Ami, L. *amicus*, friend.
Annee, year, n, r.

Aout, August.
Appui, prop, help.
A-rbre, tree, L. *arbor*, br, tr.
A-rene, sand, gravel, r, s.
Atre, hearth.
Aune, elder, au, el.
Aussi, so, as, also, G'k *ōs*.
Baiser, buss, kiss.
Balai, broom, l, r.
Baisser, bow, a-base.
Balayer, sweep, balance.
Bas, base, low, bottom.

Bassin, basin, pan, vase.
Bateau, boat.
Batir, build, baste.
Baton, stick, beat, bat.
Beau, L. *bonus*, good.
Beche, spade.
Benet, ninny.
Berceau, cradle, bower.
Bete, beast, cattle.
Beurre, butter.
Bien, well, L. *bonus*.
Bile, choler, gall.
Blanc, clean, white, *albo*.
Boire, drink, b, d.
Bois, wood, b, w.
Bon, good, kind, b, k.
Bourru, morose, cross.
Bout, button, tip, end.
Brillant, bright.
Briller, shine, sparkle.
Briser, break, bruise.
Bris, wreck, break, b, w.
Broult, gruel.
Bruire, roar.
Bruler, broil, boil, flask.
Brute, rough, brute.
Cachet, cover, hide, c, h.
Carr-eau, square.
Cayer, quire.
Caveau, cave, cellar, vault.
Caver, hollow, hole.
Chancre, cancer, sore.
Chateau, castle, seat.
Chaud, hot, warm.
Chauve, Ital. *calvo*, Ger. *kahl*, bare, bald.
Cheminee, chimney.
Chef, head, chief, f, d.
Cher, dear, L. *carus*.
Cheveu, fibre, hair.
Chez, with, L. *cum*, *que*.
Chien, dog, L. *canis*.
Chose, thing, L. *res*, cause.
Ciel, sky, shine, clear, Germ. *himmel*, hell, Lat. *celum*, Greek *helios*.

Cire, seal, (wax).
Cite, city, L. *civitas*, state.
Cle and *Clef*, Lat. *clevis*, Ger. *schlüssel*, It. *chiave*, key.
Cœur, heart, core.
Coi, quiet; *Coin*, corner.
Col, neck, G. *hals*.
Compter, count.
Couler, flow, melt.
Coup, cuff, blow, fit.
Courbe, curve, crooked.
Courir, run, L. *curro*.
Cout, cost.
Couture, suture, seam.
Crainte, fear, cringe.
Cramoisi, crimson.
Crete, crest, t, st.
Crepu, crisped, p, sp.
Creux, crucible, grave.
Croc, crook, hook.
Croire, credit, trust.
Croit, in-crease, growth.
Croupe, crop, top.
Cruche, crucible, mug, Germ. *krug*, crock.
Cru, grow, ground.
Cueillir, cull, collect, gather.
Cuire, cook, bake.
Cuisse, thigh.
Cuve, cup, tub, coop.
De-bat, de-bate, battle.
Debile, feeble.
Dedain, disdain, Ital. *sdegno*, deign.
De-border, leap, board.
De-lit, fault, L. *delict'*.
Devoir, duty, debt, need.
Di-re, say, tell, L. *dicere*.
Doigt, toe, L. *digit*.
Doit, ought, should.
Dol, fraud, Latin *dolus*, cheat, dl, fr.
Dos, back, ridge.
Douce, sweet, L. *dulcis*.
Dress-er, straight, dress, Fren. *drap*; *De*, (of), the, to.

Droit, straight, right, just, It. *jure, eretto*, direct.
Duit, lead, L. *ductus*.
Eau, water, L. *aqua*.
E-carter, s-catter.
E-chelle, s-cale, shell.
E-clat, clap, lustre, splendid.
E-corce, bark, L. *cortex*.
E-couter, hear, G'k *a-kouō*.
E-crit, w-rit, L. *script*.
E-cu, shield.
E-cueil, shoal.
Effet, fact, deed.
Egare, error, wild.
Eglise, church, gl, chr.
E-lan, leap, rapture.
E-leve, raise, lever, Lat. *altus*, lift, tread, (pupil).
Elire, elect, L. *e-legere*.
E-loge, eulogy, laud, *lob*.
Elu, elect, chosen.
Email, enamel.
Emoi, anxiety, G. *mühe*.
Em-pecher, push, stop.
E-mu, moved, angry.
En-ceint, fence, close.
En-cre, ink.
En-droit, place, part, region.
E-pais, thick, L. *spissus*.
Epingle, pile, pin, It. *spillo*.
Epoque, epoch, era, p, r.
Esquisse, sketch.
Etage, stage, de-gree, story.
Etient, extinct, quench.
Eteule, stalk, stubble.
Etoile, star, L. *stella*, e=s.
Etonner, astonish, stun.
Etrier, stirrup.
Etroit, straight, strict, ex-act.
Ex-torquer, ex-tort, wrest, turn, twist.
Facile, easy, free.
Facher, vex, anger.
Fa-ire, do, make, L. *fa-cere*.
Fait, fact, feat, deed, act.
Faux, false.

Faut, fault, want, defect.
Fer, iron, sworn, L. *ferrum*.
Feu, fire, G'k *pur*, L. *focus*.
Feuille, leaf, foliage, foil, Ital. *foglia*.
Fief, fee, feud.
Fier, trust, faith.
Fierte, pride, fierce.
Filet, thread, string.
Fin, end, aim.
Fils, child, son, L. *filius*.
Flot, wave, L. *fluctus*, flow.
Forain, foreign, alien.
Forer, bore, drill, pierce.
Fort, stout, strong, firm.
Fosse, pit, dig, grave.
Foule, throng, troop, many.
Fouler, tread, follow, fall.
Fournir, furnish, afford.
Foyer, focus, fine.
Fragile, frail, feeble.
Frere, L. *frater*, brother.
F-ripon, rogue.
Froid, frigid, fresh, cold.
Frotter, rub, friction.
Fuir, flee, L. *fugere*, g, i.
Furie, fury, passion, bear.
Gage, pawn, pledge.
Gager, en-gage, hire, wages.
Gagner, gain, win, earn.
Gant, glove, gantlet.
Gateau, cake.
Geler, freeze, 'geal.
Genou, knee.
Gorge, throat, gullet, gulley.
Guere, s-carce, spare,
Gorge, G. *hals*, channel.
Goutte, jot, drop.
Gras, fat, greasy, G. *gross*.
Grave, serious, severe.
Grele, shrill, slim.
Griffe, claw, grab, paw.
Gris, gray, brown.
Haut, height, tall, *altus*.
Heurter, hurt, hit, butt.
Ile, island, isle.

Jambe, limb, leg, G'k *kampē*, knee, j, l.
Jaune, yellow.
Jeu, game, jest.
Jet, cast, L. *jacto*.
Joie, joy, de-light, j, l.
Joli, pretty, belle.
Jour, day, L. *dies*, clear.
Jurer, swear, j, sw.
Lever, lift, raise.
Libre, free, bold, loose.
Lier, league, tie, bind, join, ligature.
Lievre, L. *lepus*, G'k *lagōs*.
Lit, bed, L. *lect-us*.
Li-vre, book, L. *liber*.
Macule, spot, stain.
Maison, mansion, main.
Mal, ill, e-vil, harm.
Mari, (husband), marry.
Mauvais, bad, (mal).
Mat, mast.
Meche, match, wick.
Meler, mix, blend.
Mer, sea, water, *aqua*.
Mettre, put, set, m, p.
Moeurs, manners, ways, mode.
Moins, less, more.
Moitie, half, middle, *meson*.
Montre, show, monitor.
Mordre, bite, carp, cut.
Mort, death, murder, kill.
Mot, word, note, speak, say, verb, G. *melden*.
Moudre, mill, mould, grind.
Mu, moved, stirred.
Mur, mature, ripe.
Mur, wall, G. *mauer*.
Moudre, mill, mould.
Muge, mullet.
Naitre, born, spring, *natus*.
Noir, black, niger.
Nuage, mist, L. *nubes*.
Obeir, obey, bend.
Oeil, eye, L. *ocul-us*, auge.
Oisif, lazy, idle, L. *otium*, easy.

Oiseau, It. *uccello*, fowl, bird, G. *vogel*.
Ongle, nail, claw.
Or, ore, gold, old = or.
Oreille, ear, *auris*.
Orme, elm.
O-ser, dare, bold.
Oubli, oblivion.
Ours, bear, L. *ursus*.
Ouvert, open, free, (*liber*).
Ouvrer, work, operate.
Pais, patria, It. *paese*.
Paitre, feed, pasture, graze.
Paon, peacock, L. *pavo*.
Pareil, pair, e-qual, like.
Parer, parry, ward.
Parler, parley, prattle, talk.
Purtir, depart, start, go.
Patte, foot, paw, flap.
Peler, peel, pare, bald.
Pencher, bend, pinch, 'cline.
Peser, weigh, ponder, think.
Peu, few, little, L. *paucus*.
Peur, fear, dread, terror.
Perte, ruin.
Petit, petty, little, few.
Peuple, folk, L. *vulgus*.
Pierre, drain, L. *lapis*, stone, L. *rupes*, rock, s-par.
Poids, load, weight, L. *pondus*, ponder.
Poisson, fish.
Poivre, pepper.
Poli, gloss, polish, glass.
Pour-voir, pro-vide, fore-see.
Puce, flee, It. *pulice*.
Pousse, shoot, push.
Prendre, take, grab, prize.
Priere, prayer, It. *preco*.
Racine, root, radix.
Raie, ray, streak, stroke.
Roide, stiff, rigid, steep, stubborn, rapid.
Rouge, red, ruddy, It. *rubro*.
Rouler, roll, rumble, rove, reel.
Sa-voir, see, know, sage.

Sage, L. *sagus*, G'k *saphês*, G. *sehen*, S. *suc*.
Saut, leap, jump, *salio*.
Semble, seem, re-semble.
Soie, silk, Ger. *seide*.
Soif, thirst, wish.
Solde, pay, L. *solvo*, soldier.
Suivre, Lat. *sequor*, seek, San. *saik*, see, go.
Songer, dream, think.
S-ouvent, often.
Taille, tally, cut, tailor, S. *dal*, split, deal, divide.
Teint, taint, dye, tinct.
Temps, time, L. *tempus*.
Tendre, tend, ex-tend, go.
Tete, top, L. *tectum*, head, sense.
Tige, s-tock, stalk.
Timbre, stamp.
Tirer, draw, pull, tug.
Tomber, tumble, fall, drop, ex-tract, re-quire.
Tondre, cut, tome, shear.
Tour, tower, rock, turn.

Trait, trace, dart, draught, treat, touch.
Troupe, troop, herd, crowd.
Trouble, thick, dull.
Tuer, kill, slay, die.
Tuyau, tube, pipe, tunnel.
Val, valley, vale, dale.
Valoir, worth, value, 1, r.
Veillir, wake, watch.
Vendre, sell, vend.
Venir, come, go, went.
Verge, rod, yard, wand.
Verser, turn, pour, fill.
Viand, food, meat.
Vetu, clad, vest.
Vif, alive, active, quick.
Vil, vile, mean, low.
Voeu, vow, vote.
Voie, way, means.
Vollee, flight, volley, brood.
Voute, vault, arch.
Vrai, true, right, Ger. *wahr*, very, mere, L. *verus*.
Verre, It. *giara*, jar, vessel.

The foregoing list constitutes a large share of such French words as differ very materially in their form from English and German. The great body of the French scarcely differs from those languages in orthography. It has strong hold, it is true, on the Latin, but its general appearance is decidedly German, if for no other reason, for the total absence of case, gender, personal and other endings, or at least their existence in a blunted form.

The French orthography is particularly useful in showing how one letter is equal to any development of that letter into two or more; as, *d* for *ld*, *t* for *st*, *f* for *fl*, *t* for *ext*, *ege* for *i*, in *legere* = *lire*. Even many letters, following the principle of one letter equal to several like letters, which appear in print, are not sounded in speaking; thus, *temps* is pronounced as if written *tem* (even *m* is reduced to a mere vowel), and so it identifies itself with our *time*, much nearer than the Latin *tempus*. This is all because *mps* is a development of *m*, or *p*, or *s*, and quite equal to either one of them; so *bris* = *bri*, *i* = *is*; *depot* = *depo*, *ot* = *o*, just as we in so many instances do, as in *blow* (*w* silent), *lamb* (*b* silent), *calm* (*l* silent), *psalm* (*p* silent), *debt* (*b* silent), *back* (*c* silent), *receipt* (*p* silent), *charm* (*r* nearly silent), *gist* (*s* silent), *oblique* (*ue* silent).

The principle is the same in all languages; no letter is entirely silent, but some letters become so like others that they cannot be distinguished by the ear, any more than one double letter can from another. In fact, there is a perfect identity between the double letters, i. e. the vowel united with consonant, or the consonant with consonant; *hiss, hiis, hist;* the two *s*'s are as much distinct as *i* from *s*, or as *s* from *t* in *hist*—and we constantly find different consonants, as *st*, becoming double, as *ss*, or one becoming a vowel, as *is*. We see this in *tall* for *talt*, *full* for *fuld*, *evil* for *ill*, *writt* for *script*.

We notice, again, that only like letters come together, and vowels are equal to the consonants with which they are found. Letters are never dropped, they are only merged with others, as sounds are lost in sounds which are in harmony with them.

Russian Etymology.

581.[1]
Agnez, lamb, Fr. *agneau*.
Bagor, purple, g, r.
Bazan', wash.
Bania, G. *bähen*, bath.
Baya, say, G'k *phaō*.
Beregu, be-ware, G. *sparen*.
Bereg, border, shore.
Beru, brat, bear, carry, *tragen*, brought.
Blazhu, 'plaud, praise.
Blyad, bleach, *blass, bleich*.
Blesk, look, *blick*, glance.
Bliacha, *blech*, plate.
Bobr, *biber*, beaver.
Biene, beating.
Bob, *bohne*, bean.
Bog, God, Bo. *Buh*, b, q.
Bogatch, rich.
Bodu, stick, pick, beat.
Bozhu, beg, *an-beten*.
Bo, battle, war.
Boltayo, beat, *plaudern*.
Bol, pain, smart, L. *dolor*.
Bormotchu, grumble, *brummen, trommeln*.

Baroda, brada, beard, *bart*.
Botaio, beat, strike.
Boyo, fear, *bange*.
Brat, brother, friend.
Brov, eye-brow.
Brayo, shear, barber.
Briatchu, rattle.
Bu, fool.
Burtchu, rush, roar, German *brausen*.
Butchu, bucking, *beuch*.
Buik, buck, ox.
Byo, bet, beat, strike.
Byagu, flee, L. *fuga*.
Byada, pity.
Byalenie, bleach, *bleich*.
Byas, base, wicked.
Vaga, hazard, wage.
Vakshu, wax, *wichsen*.
Valki, wag, *wankend*.
Val-ias, fall.
Valiayo, roll, *walken*.
Vanna, fan, *wanne*.
Varya, brew, boil.
Vaiayo, hew, dig.
Wergayo, throw, *werfen*.

[1] Let it be understood that words not English and not otherwise marked are German.

ETYMOLOGY.

Vgoniayo, hunt, vg, w.
Vgrebayo, dig, *graben*.
Vdova, widow, *wittwe*.
Vedu, lead, head, guide.
Velitchu, 'plaud, flatter.
Velyo, be-*fehlen*, fail, will.
Verbuyo, earn, *werben*.
Vertchu, turn, L. *verto*, bore.
Vetchi, old, L. *vetus*.
Vetcher, vesper, evening.
Vesh, thing, L. *res, sache*.
Vid, view, see, L. *video*.
Vzval, throw, *wälzen*, Greek *ballō*, vzv = vvv = w.
Vilki, fork.
Vino, wine.
Vishu, hang, wave, hover.
V-kratchia, short, *kurtz*.
V-kushayo, *kost*, cost.
V-lagayo, lay, place, vl, pl.
Vleku, drag, *schleppen*.
Vmalia, small, bald.
Vnov, new, (*v* is prefix).
Vnuk, ankle.
Voda, water.
Vzgliad, look, *blick*, vzgl = vvvl, wl, bl, as G. *schreiben* equals *reiben*.
Voshu, boss, *führen*.
Vozmog, might, vozm = vm.
Volk, wolf, L. *vulpes*.
Volna, wool, *woge*.
Volia, will.
Voron, raven, crow.
Vopros, ask, Lat. *rogo, frage*, vopr = vpr, vr, fr, r.
Vorota, port, door.
Vremia, time, L. *tempus*.
Vosk, wax, *wachs*.
Vpad', fall, Lat. *cado*, Greek *piptō*, vp, p, c, pp.

Vyadayo, know, L. *video*.
Vper', bring, vp, p.
Vyas, weight.
Vi-dyao,[1] give, L. *do*, vd, d.
Vyashu, wage, *wägen*.
Vya-zhayo, say, vyz, s.
Viazhu, bind, press, fast.
Gadayo, say, *rathen*.
Gas, gauze, gaze.
Gvardia, guard, gard.
Gir, weight, L. *gravis*.
Grasni, red, scarlet.
Gero, hero, held.
Glaba, Bo. *klava*, head, chapter, G'k *kephalē*.
Glagol, word, L. *lego*, gl, l.
Glazh, flat, *glatt*.
Glaz, (eye), glance, gaze.
Glas, voice, call, loud.
Glub, deep, gl, gi, d.
Gluchi, deaf, hear, gl, h.
G-liazhu, look, see.
Gnetu, bind, press, knit.
Gnu, bend, knee.
Gnyzado,[2] nest.
Goboryo, say, *sprechen* ; gobor, gbr, br, pr, pray.
God, year, L. *annus*, d, v.
Golo, bald, *kahl*.
Golos = *glas*.
Golub, dove, L. *columb'*.
Gora, rock, *berg*.
Gordo, proud.
Gorlo, gurgel.
Gorki, sour, bitter.
Gorod, (*grad*), state, de-gree, *burg, dorf*.
Gorgo, warm, burn, g, w.
Grabezh, rob, grab.
Gradar, gardner.
Gradus, grade, grad.

---

[1] The Russian shows most clearly the transition from initial letters to prefixes; in such cases as *vi-dayo*, we have a prefix without force, and the word is not different from *dayo*.

[2] See how often *g* = *h* is a mere prefix, or is lost in the following letter.

Grad, hail, Lat. *grando*, Fr. *grele*.
Granitchu, fence, *gränzen*
Gran, grey, *grau*.
Gran, corner.
Greblo, rudder, oar, row.
Greza, dream.
Grob, grave.
Groza, threat, *drohung*.
Grozd, grape, *traube*.
Gromko, strong, loud.
Grom, roar, rumble, thunder.
Gruda, group.
Grud, breast, bosom.
Grubi, hard, coarse, *grob*, rude, rough, *derb*.
Gruzki, L. *gravis*, hard, heavy, *schwer*.
Grunt, ground, *grund*.
Grusha, pear.
Grushu, grievo, sorry, *trüben*, *trauern*, gloomy.
Guliayo, walk, go.
Gryadu, go, L. *gredior*.
Gunia, *lumpen*, trumpery.
Gurt, herd.
Gusar, hussar.
Gusto, tight, thick.
Gus,[1] goose.
Dal, far, long, dl, fr.
Dayo, give, L. *do*, *dabo*.
Dver, door, port.
Dvigayo, move, *be-wegen*.
Dvor, court, *hof*.
Dek, deck, cover.
Den, *dna*, day, L. *dies*.
Derebnia, town, *dorf*.
Derevo, tree.
Derzayo, dare.
Deru, tear, *zerreissen*.
Dlan, palm, hand.
D-lin, long, far, Fr. *loin*.
Dob-ro, good, d, g.
Dolgo = *dlin*.
Dolg, *pflicht*, guilt.

Dol, deal, *theil*, part.
Doma, home, house.
Doroga, road, way, dr, w.
Dorogo, dear.
Doska, desk, *tisch*, table.
Dotch, daughter, *tochter*, Boh. *dcera*.
Dragi = *dorogo*.
Drug, friend, dear.
Drebo = *derebo*.
Drob, scarf, *scherben*.
Drotchu, thresh.
Duga, bow, d, b.
Dumayo, deem, think.
Dura, fool, *thörin*.
Durno, bad, worse.
Duch, ghost, gas, *dunst*, *ruch*, G'k *thuos*.
Duyo, blow, *hauch*, *dunst*.
Dsher = *Dolch*.
Duim, steam, *dampf*.
Dyalo, deal, done, deed.
Delayo, do, deal, make, Boh. *dilo*, equals done, work.
Dyayo, equals *delayo*, do.
Edinyo, unite, *vereinigen*.
Emez, man, *mensch*.
Emlyo, take, L. *emo*, *nehmen*.
Eres, heresy, *ketzerei*.
Eshe, yet, *schon*.
Zhar, warm, fire.
Zhgu, stick, bite, burn.
Zhalko, *kläglich*, clamor.
Zhal, harm, *schade*.
Zhdu, wait, dure.
Zhezl, stick, stab.
Zhelayo, wish, will.
Zhelt, yellow.
Zhena, woman, queen, zh = z = g, G'k *gunē*.
Zhibu, live, L. *vivo*.
Zhidki, thin, shad, G. *schlank*.
Zhmu, press, L. *premo*.
Zhilo, dwelling, live.
Zhru, greedy, *fressen*.

---

[1] *G*, in Russian, has principally the force of a strong *h*.

ETYMOLOGY. 193

Zhuyo, chew, *kauen*.
Zamok, lock, castle.
Zima, winter, L. *hiems*.
Zvon, sound, *schall, klang*.
Zvuk, shout, *schall*.
Zvyar, deer, L. *fera, thier*.
Zdo, dach, thatch.
Zelen, yellow, green.
Zemlia, L. *terra*, earth.
Zizhdu, build, *stiften*.
Zlo, ill, *schlecht*.
Znak, sign, mark, zn, s.
Znayo, know, Gr'k *gnō*, z, g.
Zobu, call, *rufen*, L. *voco*.
Zlui, slim, *schlimm*.
Zol = zlui.
Zoloto, gold, yellow, z, g.
Zrak, look, *blick*.
Zryo, see, G'k *oraō*.
Zug, tooth, *zahn*, z, t.
Zitchu, hiss, sigh.
Zialo, very, far, *sehr*.
Igo, yoke.
Igra, play, sport.
Idu, go, L. *itum, it*.
Ima, imeni, name.
Inok, monk, *mönch*.
Is-chod, out-going, ex-odus.
Is-klyotch, ex-clude.
Ishu, seek, wish.
Iere, priest, G'k *hieros*.
Kazanie, sign.
Kareta, coach, chariot.
Kad, cot, coop, *kufe*.
Ka-zhu, say, show.
Kalyo, glue.
Kam-en, stone, km, stn.
Kamera, chamber, room.
Kandil, candle.
Kapayo, drop, trickle.
Kapral, corporal.
Kara, correction, *strafe*.
Kit, whale, L. *cœtus*.
Klada, log, *klotz*.
Kladu,[1] lay, place, load.

Klad, load, last.
Klas = kolos.
Klegtchu, call, screech.
Klik, call, clang.
Klok, lock.
Kniaz, prince, king.
Kniga, book, Sem. *kitab*.
Knut, peitsche, whip.
Koza, goat.
Koleso, wheel, *rad*.
Kozha, coat, skin, hide.
Kolo, circle, wheel.
Kol, pale, *pfahl*.
Kom, heap, clump.
Konez, finish, end, point.
Kon, pony, horse, *ross*.
Kopa, heap, cumulate.
Kopoyo, scoop, ditch.
Kora, bark, L. *cortex*.
Koren, root, *radix*.
Korga, crow, L. *corvus*.
Korzina, korb.
Korma, stern.
Korova, krava, cow, kr, k.
Korol, (karl), king, Latin *rex*, Bo. *kral (= k-rege)*.
Kortchag, cup, *krug*.
Kotel, kittle, *kessel*.
Kosha, korb, curb.
Koshka, cat, *katze*.
Kradu, steal, G'k *klepō*.
Kra, rind, brim.
Krapayo, drop.
Krik, creak, shriek.
Kritchu, screech.
Krob, roof, cover.
Kroma, crumb.
Kroyo; cover, bury.
Krug, round, circle.
Krupa, grit, *graupe*.
Krupno, grob, coarse.
Krut', strong, gross.
Kryap, force, *kraft*.
Krotki, kind, soft.
Kupa, heap.

[1] *K* in Russian, is for us generally a prefix.

Kupuyo, buy, *kaufen*.
Kusayo, kiss, bite.
Kuknia, kitchen.
Layo, yell, bellow, low.
Lgu, lie, *lügen*.
Lev, lion, L. *leo*.
Legki, light, *leicht*.
Legkoe, lungs.
Led, ice.
Ladno, one, (*l* is prefix).
Lezhu, lie, L. *locus*.
Len, linen.
Let, flow, flight.
Liver, lever, (hever), heaver, raiser.
Lizhu, lick, *lecken*.
List, leaf, *blatt*.
Lize, look, gaze, face.
Lovl, claw.
Lozhe, lay, lodge, Latin *lectus*, place, bed.
Lokon, lure, *locke*.
Losk, look, glance.
Luna, moon, L. *luna*.
Lyavo, left.
Lyas, wood, L. *lucus*.
Lyoblo, love, *lieben*, like, long, S. *luh*, (*lyobov*).
Lyod, *leute*, folk, Bo. *lid*.
Malo, small, little.
Manyo, wink, *mahnen*.
Maslo, butter, sl, tr.
Mat, mother.
Mayo, *ermüden*, *ab-matten*.
Mgla, *nebel*, veil, L. *nubes*.
Med, honey, L. *mel*.
Melyo, mill, *mahlen*.
Mezh, with, *mit*, twixt, mid.
Metch, sword, *messer*, mace.
Merknu, murky, dark.
Mir, *friede*, *froh*, peace.
Mir, world, L. *mundus*.
Mleko, milk, L. *lac*.
Mnogo, much, many.
Mnu, *kneten*, knead.
Mnyo, mean, believe.

Mogu, may, might.
Mokro, moist, mucky.
Moloko = *mleko*.
More, see, *meer*.
Moroz, *mraz*, frost.
Motchu, moisten.
Motch, might.
Mrak, dark.
Mru, murder, die.
Mucha, fly, Fr. *mouche*.
Myalki, small, *klein*.
Myasto, spot, place, state.
Myaryo, measure.
Mias', meat, flesh.
Muzh, man, *mensch*.
Na-chozhy, in-go, in-vent.
Nag, naked, bare.
Nizki, be-neath, deep.
Novo, new.
Noga, hoof, foot, Fr. *ongle*.
Nozh, knife, *messer*.
Nora, hole, *grube*.
Nos, nose.
Noshu, L. *veho*, bring, push.
Nuzhu, need, press.
Obost, *obst*.
Ovza, L. *ove*, sheep, ewe.
Ogon, *ogn*, L. *ignis*, fire.
Orda, horde.
Orel, eagle, *adler*.
Oryo, L. *aro*, harrow.
Okno, window, look, see.
Ostrui, sharp, L. *acer*.
Padu, fall, G'k *piptō*.
Pa, part.
Parad, *pracht*, parade.
Paryo, burn, parch.
Pashu, *wehen*, wind.
Piita, poet, *dichten*.
Pishu, paint, write.
Pitie, drink, L. *pino*.
Plam, flame.
Plod, fruit, pl, fr.
Plug, plow.
Pluivu, swim, sail, *pleo*.
Polnoe, full; *pulia*, ball.

ETYMOLOGY. 195

Prabilo, law, rule, straight, line, true; law = *lex* = *rex*.
Petch, stove, bake.
Ptiza, bird, Boh. *ptak*, Greek *petomai*, fly.
Pravo, right, de-praved.
Rabot, work, *arbeit*.
Rab, serve, slave.
Rvu, tear, *rupfen*.
Razum, reason.
Rdyayo, red.
Rebro, rib, *rippe*.
Rad, joy, *froh*.
Rov, grave.
Rod, kind, art, way, (road).
Rog, horn, rock.
Rota, oath.
Ryatch, word, *rede*.
Rubez, *riefe*, furrow.
Ruka, hand, arm, G'k *cheir*.
Riba, fish, rb, f
Ryaka, river, run.
Riad, row, rank.
Rul, rudder, helm.
Sazhayo, set, place.
Salo, tallow.
Svinia, swine.
Solnze, sun, Bo. *slunce*.
Svara, quarrel, *streit*.
Svishu, whizz, whistle.
S-dayo, give-up, (*s* prefix).
S-doryo, strive, *streiten*.
S-dirayo, tear-off.
Sladki, sweet, G'k, *glukus*.
Shiroki, broad, spread.
Semia, family.
Serdze, heart, s, h.
Sizhu, sit.
Sila, strong, sl, str.
Sito, sieve.
Siayo, shine, light.
Skatchu, skip, spring.

Skoro, short, hurry.
Skrbu, scrape, shave.
Slabi, slack, *schlaff*.
Slava, glory, laud.
S-lagayo,[1] lay-up.
Sliva, plum.
S-lovo,[2] word, G'k *logos*, *sylbe*, syllable.
Sluch, hear, ear, *gerücht*, S. *sru*, G'k *kluō*.
S-mert, death, murder.
S-myalo, bold, m, b.
S-myach, s-mile, laugh.
S-nimayo, *ab-nehmen*.
So-bak, dog, bk, dg.
Sotchu, catch, take.
Sol, salt.
Stari, old, strong.
Stebel, stalk, *stengel*.
Strogi, strict, straight.
Son, sleep, Lat. *somnus*, Fren. *songe*.
Spat, *splyo*, sleep.
Stablyo, stable, *stellen*, stall, stand, stay.
Stan, stand, station.
Stez', stop, step, path.
Stol, table, *stuhl*.
Stop, foot, step.
Stoyo, stand, L. *sto*.
Stroenie, structure.
Struyo, stream, pour.
Stuk, stick, strike, *stoss*.
Suzhu, judge.
Suk, coin, twig.
Su-rovi, rough, coarse.
Suchi, dry, L. *siccus*.
Sushi, sure, certain.
Strana, tract, stretch, *strich*; land = tract, as line = rule, *rect*.
Schod', go, scud, scatter.
Syaku, hack, cut.

[1] Through all Russian, strike off the ending *yo* as a mere person ending.
[2] *S* is a prefix identical with *g*, *h*.

Syayo, sow, spread.
Sad, garden.
Tvoryo, work, *tragen*, born.
Telia, calf.
Temno, dim, dark.
Ternie, thorn.
Tkan, web, tissue.
Tna, dim, darkness.
Tolpa, troop, L. *turba*.
Torg, trade, handle.
Tonkie, thin, fine, tiny.
To-vare, wares.
Truba, trumpet, L. *tuba*.
Trud, tired, trouble.
Trutchu, press, *drücken*.
Tupo, dumb, stump.
Tyalo, body, *corpus*, tl, cr.
Tyok, pack, ball.
Tianu, ex-tend, *dehnen*.
U-bozh', poor, pov-erty.
U-gol, angle, *winkel*.
U-gol, coal.
U-met, mist.
U-tchu, teach, L. *doceo*.

Chvala, praise, *lob*.
Chozhy, go, walk, seek.
Cholodno, cold.
Chotchu, wish.
Chud, bad, worse.
Zyal, heal, whole.
Tchado, child, *kind*.
Tchad, vapor, steam.
Tchernie, black, *schwartz*, dark, tawny.
Tcherta, stroke, chart.
Tchislo, cipher, *zahl*.
Tchisto, just, chaste.
Tchitayo, read, re-cite.
Tchlen, member, *glied*.
Tchudo, wonder, awe.
Tchuyo, hear, L. *audio*.
Tcherv, worm, L. *ver*.
Tchas, time, *zeit*.
Tchin, rank. (*Tch* is one letter).
Iazuik, tongue.
Uzki, narrow, *eng*.
Um, wise, d-eem.

To this we will add only a limited number of Bohemian words, such only as present important forms, since the great mass of Bohemian words, as well as the rest of Slavic, are substantially the same as in Russian.

Bohemian Etymology.

582.

Klobouk, hat, cap, head.
Dum, house, home.
Pilny, diligent, *fleissig*.
Sely, whole, *ganz*.
Velke, great, much, *viel*.
Stul, stool, table.
Sin, deed, done, *thun*.
Uci, learn, teach, L. *doceo*.
Idou, go, L. *itu*, *it*.
Pri-sel, came, walk.
Hoch, boy, *knabe*.
Kosar, coach, carriage.
Mnoho, much, many.
Rad, willing, ready, rather.

Bydli, dwell, a-bide.
Stin, shadow, dim.
Imeno, name.
D-louhe, long.
Kapr, carp.
Muz, man, *mensch*.
Klis, key, lock, L. *clevis*.
Leto, year.
Zivot, life, L. *vivo*, G'k *zaō*.
Ia-zyk, tongue.
Miluj, love, G'k, *philos*.
Psar, writer, painter.
Iehla, R. *igla*, needle.
Bitva, battle.

Ko-sile, shirt.
Kuze, hide, coat.
Zluc, gall.
Kost, bone, L. *os.*
Cekoti, wait.
Hirati, sport.
Volati, call, L. *voco.*
Loviti, hunt, *laufen.*
Di, say, L. *dico.*
Brati, bere, bring, take.
Psati, write, *scri-psi.*
Prati, strike, bring.
Cnu, be-gin.
Chci, will, choice.
Miti, have, *habeo*, (*ti, iti, ati* is the infinitive ending).
Ziti, cut; *diti*, do.
Ctu, read, re-cite.
Strůhu, shear, strip.
Rici, say, L. *reo*, pr-each.
Chleby, (bread), loaf, G. *laib*, Go. *chläbs.*
Bily, white, bleach, L. *albus.*
Zeply, warm, tepid, hot.
Verny, true, L. *verus.*
Plny, full, L. *plenus.*
Husty, thick.
Chudy, poor, bad.

Drah, dear.
Mil, friend, G'k *phil'.*
Kriv, curve, *krumm.*
Mrtev, dead, mort.
Prost, free; *tvrd*, hard.
Znam, known, sign.
Zichu, still; *tuhy, steif.*
Tmavy, dark, dim.
Svaty, holy, saint.
Ruchly, quick, rush, rapid.
Hezky, pretty, *hübsch.*
Zimni, winter, L. *hiems.*
Zadost, joy, L. *gaudium.*
Noc, nos, night.
Kratke, short.
Ouzkost, anxiety, *angst.*
Lez, lie, *lüge.*
Dluh, debt, *schuld.*
Pero, feather, *feder, fer.*
Olovo, lead, *blei.*
Piti, drink, im-bibe.
Stribro, silver.
Svire, steer, *thier*, L. *fera.*
Neve, heaven, L. *nubes.*
Krk, neck, *hals.*
Pes, dog, bite.
Bor, wood, for-est.
Vlk, wolf, L. *vulpes.*

Slavic Etymology.

583. Enough words have been given as examples, to show the peculiar cast and appearance which Slavic words present, when brought into comparison with Latin and German words. The list which has been given is pretty comprehensive, and it embraces a large share of the most common and leading words to be found in a language. With all their peculiar dress, the words of Slavic can with certainty be identified with those of the Latin, Greek, and German class. It bears, when properly viewed, a close relationship with each of these languages — few words being found in Slavic which cannot, even at the present day, be easily identified with those of Greek or Latin, or German and English.

We have selected chiefly from the Russian, with only a few from the Bohemian, as it was of little use, as a matter of etymology, to bring more dialects into the comparison. Very few words could be found, in the related dialects, which do not appear uniform with either those of Russian or Bohemian. There is indeed a remarkable identity, making allowance for letter changes, found in the forms of words in the whole Slavic class. After passing from the Bohemian and Russian, we should find little that would be particularly new or important in the orthography of the words.

The most striking appearance in the forms of words in the Slavic, is the accumulation of consonants without intervening vowels. In this respect, it greatly resembles the Semitic class. We here find letters united which with us are separated by a vowel. And, in this prevailing character of the Slavic, as well as of other languages, we find renewed proof that the prefixes, so called, of the verb are not a distinct part of it, but rather inseparably united with the body of the word at the beginning, having, as we may say, grown upon it and from it. We have found in Slavic, as elsewhere, many of these prefixes existing only as a single letter, not divided from that which follows by a vowel, but united with it to form one single growth or element. Our own *direct, straight*, Fr. *droit, right*, furnishes a good illustration of this principle. We are wont to call *di* a prefix, because it is separated from *r* by a vowel, but it is plain that *dir, str, dr*, and *r*, are all equal, and that *st*, or *d*, is just such a prefix as the *di*, and, again, that they are no more prefixes than any other initial letter. The Slavic has left out this connecting vowel of the prefix so often, that its dependent existence is clearly proved. We have done the same thing in thousands of words; as in *w-rong*, compared with *right*, *p-lace* with *lay*, L. *locus*, in *k-now, k-nee, st-rip, sc-rub*. It need not be answered that *these* prefix letters have no meaning, for what meaning has *de* in *de-light, de-fer*, which is acknowledged to be a genuine prefix preposition? Most prefix prepositions, and we think all, have no more of an individual meaning than this *de*, or the letters *p, sc, k*, which have been pointed off.

It cannot be too well borne in mind that those accumulated consonants, as *mn, zv, zvy, dl, vgr*, in Slavic, are really to be taken as one letter, or as repeating elements like our $vv=w$; besides, in several instances, we are obliged to represent their single letter by two or three of ours, as in *tch, shtsh, ia, zh*.

It must be noted, too, that the prodigious growth of endings in Russian, and often when we have none at all, tends greatly to obscure the real resemblance — instance *blyad-ni*, German *blass*, our *bleach*. We have occasionally left off, or marked off these endings in the list, and where we have not, they should always, in etymological comparisons, not only in Russian, but in all, be struck off or disregarded.

We may as well remark here as elsewhere, and once for all, that our lists are only etymological comparisons, and they cannot by any means be relied on as giving the true definition of the word, as we have often found it proper to give some related rather than direct meaning. Besides, considering that a word never loses its original force by becoming a new part of speech and developing endings, we have, for instance, used *faithful* = *faith*, *wise* = *wiser*, *amo* = *amare*, *true* = *truth*.

Gaelic Etymology.

584.[1]
A-bairt, speech, preach.
Abhar, cause, L. *res*, G. *rath*, from *reden*, speak.
Abhaist, habit, fashion.
A-bhra, dark, b, d.
Achd, except.
Achd, case, state.
Achiar, tart, sharp, L. *acer*.
Acht, deed, statue, act.
Acht, claw ; *Ad*, water.
Adh, law, s-et.
Adhm, know, L. *video*.
Aedh, eye.
Agh, awe, battle.
Aghaisach, easy.
Aicim, ask, be-seech.
Aid, c-old.
Aigein, ocean.
Aighe, hill, high.
Ail, will, while.
Aill, place, course.
Aille, praise, laud.
Ailt, house, dwelling.
Ailidh, white, blank.
Aiminn, smooth.
Aimsir, time, season.
Aine, joy.
Ainninne, anger, ire.
Ainn, ring, L. *annus*.

Air, arise.
Airc, straight.
Aircann, certain.
Aird, quarter.
Airde, height, *arduus*.
Aire, servant.
Airghe, herd.
Airg, prince, *rex*, arch.
Airri, tyrant.
Ais, bashful.
Aisc, ask, re-quest.
Ait, stead.
Aith, quick, active.
Al, stone, flint, G'k *laas*.
Al, horse, Fr. *cheval*.
Aladh, malice, skill.
Allaidh, wild.
Alon, stone.
Alt, brook, valley.
Am, time, season.
Amail, evil.
Amha, man.
Anac, wound.
Anal, breath, L. *animus*.
Anam, life, L. *anima*.
Anachuram, anxiety.
Ang, r-ank, str-ing.
Aoi, island, hill.
Aoide, youth.
Aoil, mouth, G. *maul*.

[1] It will be constantly noticed that the Gaelic, and the other Celtic words, when compared with ours have the appearance of abbreviations. The initial letters of our words are for them mere prefixes, and we may consider them as silent.

Arad, strong, brave.
Aran, bread.
Arc, dwarf.
Asam, do, make, L. *facio*.
Ata, hat, cap.
Ba, good, L. *bonus*.
Ba, death, b, d.
Bac, hook.
Bad, bunch, tuft, bush.
Bagh, bind, bond, tie.
Bail, place, (see *aill*).
Baine, milk, b, m.
Bair, game, battle.
Bais, water.
Ballog, blot.
Ban, wan, pale.
Banna, band, troop.
Bar, bread, Sem. *bara*.
Bar, son, born.
Barr, top, head, first.
Bata, stick, staff, French *baton*.
Batham, die, faint.
Be, life, L. *vita*.
Beali, broom, l, r.
Beac, bee.
Bean, woman, queen.
Bearg, ire, anger.
Bearr, short, brief.
Beas, sure, G. *ge-wiss*.
Beirt, burden, birth.
Beo, alive, L. *vivo*.
Beo, cattle, beef.
Bothach, beast, wild.
Bes, custom, way.
Bi, bit, small, piece.
Bian, skin, hide.
Bil, blossom, flower.
Bil, good, Fr. *belle*.
Big, little, L. *paucus*.
Bid, hedge.
Bill, fool.
Binn, sweet, voice, sound.
Bior, water.
Bir, brief, short.
Bith, being, G. *welt*.
Bith, ha-bit, house.
Bla, village.
Bla, pale, yellow, blue.
Bladh, flat, smooth.
Bladh, flattery.
Bladhm, brag.
Blas, flavor, taste.
Blath, clean, white, blank.
Bo, cow, bull, L. *bos*.
Bocan, hook, crook.
Bochd, poor, want.
Bog, soft.
Boidhad, beauty, pretty.
Boile, ire, bile.
Bolg, bag, belly, swell.
Bolg, bellows, swell, blow, gulp, bowl.
Bor, pride, swell.
Borb, fierce, cruel.
Bord, board, table.
Bord, border, brim, brink.
Borg, burg, borough.
Borr, boss, burr, knob.
Borral, proud, swell.
Bos, base, low.
Both, booth, house.
Brac, arm, branch.
Bran, poor, black, rock.
Braos, gape, br, g.
Bras, brisk, active.
Brath, betray, treachery.
Breas, prince, reign.
Breisg, brisk, quick.
Breog, weak.
Bri, wrath, word.
Briar, prickle, thorn.
Brin, dream, Fr. *reve*.
Brog, sorrow, brogan.
Bru, bank, brow, brim.
Brug, burg, borough.
Bruighe, farm, G. *bauer*.
Buas, belly, pouch.
Buas, breach, rout.
Builgam, swell, boil.
Bunn, work, done, been.
Bur, swelling, ire, anger.

Bus, mouth, snout, Latin *os*, buss, kiss.
Ca, house, L. *casa*.
Cab, head, cape, gap.
Caban, cabin, cab.
Cad, high.
Cadall, battle.
Caec, blind, L/ *cæcus*.
Cagar, whisper.
Cai, way, road.
Caidh, chaste.
Cail, shield.
Caill, call.
Caimis, shirt, Fr. *chemise*.
Cain, rent.
Cairc, fur, hair.
Carraic, crag, rock.
Cairthe, chariot, cart.
Cait, sort, kind.
Calb, head, Sl. *glaba*.
Cala, hard, callous.
Call, veil, con-ceal.
Cam, sham, de-ceit.
Canam, sing, L. *cano*.
Canaib, hemp.
Caobh, bow, branch.
Caoimh, kind.
Caol, slim, small.
Caraid, friend, near.
Carbh, barge, car.
Cas, foot, c, f.
Casag, coat.
Cath, battle.
Ce, earth, G'k *gē*.
Ceal, heaven, Fr. *ciel*.
Cealam, eat, Sem. *chul*.
Cealg, malice, beguile.
Cean, favor, kind.
Ceangail, bond, L. *cingo*.
Cearb, silver.
Cearn, man, L. *vir*.
Ceasna, ne-cessity.
Ceill, sense, will.
Ceilg, de-ceit, L. *celo*.
Ceird, trade.
Ceisd, question.

Ciach, fog.
Cian, long, far.
Cine, kind, L. *genus*.
Cing, strong, bind.
Cior, hand, G'k *cheir*.
Cith, mist; *clab*, lip.
Claidamh, sword, L. *gladius*.
Clarach, clear, bare, bald.
Cleir, clergy.
Clioc, hook, clan.
Cloth, praise, laud.
Cluas, hear, ear, G'k *kluŏ*.
Cnag, knob, peg, snag.
Cneadh, wound.
Cneas, neck, (c is a prefix equal to *g*, *k*).
Cno, nut.
Coill, wood, L. *sylva*.
Coimde, custom.
Coin, hound, L. *canis*.
Coinnead, candle.
Coir, right, correct, crt.
Coire, cauldron.
Cois, foot, hoof.
Coll, ruin, fall.
Colum, dove, *columba*.
Con, sense, dog, *canis*.
Cor, twist, turn.
Cor, corner, near.
Cosg, cease, stop.
Corrbham, carve, grave.
Coth, meat, victuals.
Crann, tree, branch.
Craptha, warped, curved.
Creas, narrow, straight.
Criobh, trifle.
Criodh, heart, core.
Criosd, quick, swift.
Crogan, crock, G. *krug*.
Croc, horn, L. *cornu*.
Cromh, worm.
Cron, time, G'k *chronos*.
Cruadh, hard, crude.
Cruan, red.
Cruimam, thunder, grumble.
Cruog, need, press, crush.

Cuala, heard.
Cuirsam,[1] tire.
Cuire, throng.
Cuisne, ice, frost.
Cuison, wise.
Cul, chariot, coach, guard, custody.
Cum, combat, G. *kampf.*
Cumas, can, strength.
Cur, power.
Cutha, rage, G. *wuth.*
Cust, coat, skin.
Cuth, head, cap.
Dae, man.
Dagham, singe, burn.
Dail, deal, part, lot.
Daith, quick, active.
Daigh, fire, pain, hot.
Dan, work, done, poem.
Daoirse, dearth, scarce.
Dabh, coach, cab.
Dartan, herd, drove.
Dath, dye, paint.
Deachair, follow, after.
Deadla, dare, bold.
Deaith, wind, L. *ventus.*
Dealg, thorn, needle.
Deanam, do, done, work.
Dear, daughter.
Dearbham, try, prove.
Dearc, grave, cave.
Dearnam = *deanam.*
Deas, right, just.
Deas, neat.
D-eigh, ice.
Deilchead, ill, bad.
Deim, want, dearth.
Deir, say, L. *dico, dire.*
Deo, breath, G'k *pnco.*
Deolaidh, aid, help.
Det, food, victuals.
Di, want, G'k *dcomai.*
Diachair, sorrow, care.
Dibeail, dumb, mute.

Difir, difference.
Digham, come, go.
Dile, love, G'k *philos.*
Dioliochdadh, delight.
Dimeas, con-tempt.
Dinn, hill, deep.
Diouch, divine, L. *deus.*
Diog, dyke, ditch, pit.
Dioghais, high, tall, deep.
Diolas, true, dear.
Diro, tribute.
Dith, want, defect.
D-leachd, law, p-lace.
Dluth, near, tight.
Dob, stream, flow, go.
Doid, hand, Fr. *doigt.*
Doire, grove, thicket.
Doite, quick, active.
Dol, space, distance.
Donn, dun, brown.
Dorr, wrath, L. *durus.*
Dothar=*dob*, con-duit.
Drab, spot, stain.
Drabh, draw, cart.
Dragh, trouble.
Dream, tribe, family.
Drean, wren.
Droch, evil, bad, wrong, right, straight, *droit.*
Du, just, due.
Du, land, G'k *gē.*
Duchas, visage, face.
Duille, leaf, fold, *folia.*
Dulbhar, doleful, dark, gloomy, direful.
Dur, hard, water, *durus.*
Each, horse, L. *equus.*
Each, any, each.
Eacht, feat, act, state.
Eadh, time, season.
Eag, death, go.
Eagar, order.
Eaglais, church, Fr. *eglise.*
Ealang, fault, flaw.

[1] That mark *s*, which we so often elsewhere find as the sign of future, is found in many Celtic words.

Ealg, excellent.
Eallach, load.
Eang, year, L. *annus*.
Earb, offer.
Ear, head, ere, crane.
Earunn, share, portion.
Easba, want, absence.
Earr, grand, noble.
Easc, water, whiskey.
Eide, cloth, G. *kleid*.
Eifeacht, effect.
Eighi, science, art.
Eirigh, rising, arise.
Ell, flock, herd.
Ell, battle.
Er = earr.
Ette = eadh, age.
Eug, death.
Eugas, likeness.
Eun, bird, hen.
Eulogh, escape, flight.
Fabhar, favor.
Fachaim, fact, reason.
Fadail, delay.
Faghaim, find, catch.
Faigham, speak, L. *for*.
Faime, hem, brim, border.
Fair, watch, guard.
Faith, heat, fire.
Fallain, health, whole.
Fan, wander.
Fang, raven, vulture.
Faoil, deceit, L. *fallo*.
Farran, force, anger.
Fas, void, vase, hollow.
Fas, growth, wax.
Feach, see, view.
Feadhb, widow.
Feal, bad, ill, e-vil.
Feal, treason, villain.
Fear, man, L. *vir*.
Fearg, warrior.
Fearb, word, L. *verbum*.
Fec, weak, feeble.
Feathal, bowl, vessel.
Feis, pig, swine.

Fen, wain, wagon.
Fes, mouth, face, L. *os*.
Fiadh, land.
Fiamh, fear.
Fiar, crooked, warp.
Fine, family, L. *genus*, nation.
Fioch, wrath, G. *wuth*.
Fion, few, small, fine.
Fionach, old, ancient.
Fionn, white, blank.
Fior, true, L. *verus*.
Fios, science, L. *video*.
Firsi, power, strength.
Fis, dream, vision.
Fiu, worth.
Flaith, flower.
Flan, red, flame, blood.
Flur, flower, blossom.
Flock, lax, soft, flaccid.
Foairn, swarm, herd.
Focal, vowel, word.
Foghar, voice, sound.
Fois, rest, quiet.
Folg, fleet, active.
Follas, plain, clear.
Fonn, tune, song.
Foras, old, R. *stary*.
Forcam, learn, instruct.
Fortan, fortune, found.
Fortil, hardy, L. *fortis*.
Fot, giant.
Frag, woman, G. *frau*.
Fraoch, rage, fury.
Fras, ready, active.
Froghim, wrong.
Fuach, word, vocal, sound.
Fuar, cold, chilly, freeze.
Fuascraim, fright, fear.
Fuatham, hate.
Fuil, blood, gore.
Fuigam, leave, flee.
Fulla, false, lie.
Furtachd, comfort.
Gabhail, spoil, catch.
Gabhal, fork, G. *gabel*, gore.
Gath, dart, want.

Gag, chink, cleft.
Gail, kill.
Gaillian=gath, L. *telum*.
Gaid, father, dad.
Gair, cry, laugh, Fr. *rire*, rejoice, L. *gaudium*.
Gal, battle, L. *bellum*.
Garbh, rough, coarse, *grob*.
Garam, warm.
Garg, rough, fierce, firm.
Gasun, boy, Fr. *garçon*.
Ge, *geadh*, goose.
Geal, clear, fair, white.
Gean, favor, G. *gunst*.
Gearr, short, curt.
Geilt, wild, mad.
Gen, wound, knife.
Gion, will.
Giulam, follow.
Glacam, take, G'k *lab*.
Glaedh, broad, L. *latus*.
Glam, shout, clamor.
Glan, clean, pure.
Glas,[1] lock, *schloss*.
Glas, grey, pale, glass.
Gleann, glen, valley.
Gleire, elect, Fr. *elire*.
Gleith, clean, pure, neat, white, G. *rein*.
Gleas, order, class.
Glic, wise, G. *klug*.
Glinn, light, sky, gleam.
Glib, glide, slide.
Gloir,[2] glory, take.
Glor, noise, speech, yell.
Geal = glor.
Gna, mode, way.
Gnae, woman, G'k *gunê*.
Gneath, born, L. *natus*.
Gnic, know.

Gno,[3] note, known, fame.
Go, sea, water, L. *a-qua*.
Gabhar, goat, G. *gnwl*.
Goic, joke, scoff.
Goirt, sour, bitter, tart.
Goor, light, ore.
Gort, hunger.
Gradh, charity, L. *gradus*.
Graig, herd, drove.
Grata, great, noble.
Grian, ground, G. *grund*.
Grinn, garrison.
Grith, skill.
Grothal, gravel, sand.
Guala, shoulder.
Gubha, combat.
Guin, pain, dart.
Gul, wail, weeping.
Gus, anger, an-guish.
Guth, voice, vowel.
I, island.
Ial, light.
Iar, dark, black, bird.
Iath, land; *ibh*, drink.
Ic, cure, eek.
Idh, use, L. *utor*.
Idna, weapon.
Il, well, plenty, much.
Inhear, marble.
Im-lan, full.
In-shiocas, choice.
Ingne, nail, Fr. *ongle*.
Inntin, mind.
Iolar, eagle, G. *adler*.
Iomdha, many much.
Iomhadh, envy.
Ionga, nail, claw, hoof.
Ionnraic, upright.
Ionn-samhuil, same.
Ir, anger, ire.

[1] *G*, like other letters in Celtic, is often for us a prefix.

[2] We shall constantly notice, in Gaelic, the tendency of its orthography to identify itself with French.

[3] *G* is a prefix precisely as in Greek and German; we see also the suffix *c* = L. *que*, at the end of the Gaelic words, like Latin *hin-c*.— there are other suffixes, or common endings; as, *am*, *s-am*.

Iris, friend; *irr*, rear.
Itheadh, eating.
L-abhairt,[1] say, speech.
Lachd, milk, L. *lacte*.
Ladron, thief, L. *latro*.
Lag, weak, lag, lax.
Laibh, clay, lime.
Laith, many, G. *leute*.
Lamh, hand.
Laoghar, claw, toe.
La, day, l, d.
Laom, blaze.
Lan, full; *lasd*, load.
Lath, youth, lad.
Labe, bed, L. *lectus*.
Le-abham, read, *lego*.
Le-abhar, book, *liber*, (so that L. *liber* is equal to *say*, read.)
Leas, reason, L. *res*.
Lear, clear.
Leathan, broad, wide, L. *latus*.
Leigam, let, leave, allow.
Leimam, leap, jump.
Leus, light, look.
Lia, stone, G'k *laas*.
Liach, spoon, ladle.
Liobham, smooth, glib.
Liu, follow.
Loc, place, Fr. *lieu*.
Lom, lean, bare.
Lonn, strong, force.
Lot, wool, L. *lana*.
Luach, price, G. *lohn*.
Luan, moon, L. *luna*.
Luath, fleet, foot.
Lub, loop, hoop.
L-ubhra, work, opera.
Luch, mouse.

Luchd, equal to *laith*.
Long, ship, sail, p-low, G'k p-loion, *pleo* equal to sail.
Luth, strength, power
Mac,[2] son, born, *natus*, Go. *magus*, maid.
Mad,[3] hand.
Maiddin, morning.
Main, day, G'k '*emera*.
Madh, field, mead.
Mal, king, L. *reg*, Sem. *mal*.
Maoin, love, mind, think.
Maon, mute, dumb.
Maol, bald, blunt.
Marbham, murder.
Marc, horse, mare.
Meall, ball, blunt.
Meogal, medley, mix.
Mil, honey, L. *mel*.
Milis,[4] sweet, L. *mel*.
Mios, mouth, L. *mensis*.
Mir, part, bit.
Mogh, man.
Moin, mount.
Mois, mode, L. *mos*.
Mor, great, much.
Mort, murder.
Mucag, mug, cup.
Muill, delay.
Muinam, teach. L. *moneo*.
Mul, multitude.
Mur, wall, L. *murus*.
Nabadh, neighbor.
Naoi, ship, L. *navis*.
Namh, enemy.
Nath, science, note, know.
Nathair, adder, snake.
Neal, cloud, L. *nubes*.
Neamh, heaven, *nubes*.

[1] *Abhairt*, with the prefix *l*, corresponding with Ger. *lesen*, read, L. *lego*.

[2] We find also *macgim* equal to bear, carry; so *mac* has the same origin as *son*, in all languages equal to *born*, L. *natus*, L. *puer*.

[3] The forms *mad*, *man*, and *lamh*, are all equal to Latin *manus*, our hand.

[4] Prefix *mi* = *mis*, and *un* = not, bad, is common in Gaelic.

Neasta, just.
Neip, turnip.
Ni, not, thing.
Nim, do, make.
Nos, know, mode.
Nuall, noble.
Obair, work, opera.
Og, young, twig.
Ogh, whole, ear.
Oir, shore, border.
Olan, wool.
On, gain.
Ong, fire, L. *ignis*.
Ord, order, series.
Pais, passion.
Paiteog, butter.
Peall, horse, Fr. *cheval*.
Plosg, quick, G. *plotz*.
Porc, pig.
Rac, king, L. *rex, rege*.
Racan, noise, racket.
Racht, arose, arrive.
Rag, wrinkle, rugous.
Raith, ent:reaty.
Rang, rim, border.
Raon, green.
Read, thing, G. *rath*, L. *res*.
Rad-ham, say, G'k *reō*.
Readh, rage, fury.
Raith, went, ran.
Reim, troop, band.
Reo, frost.
Rith, arm, bracket.
Rodi, rotten, shrunk.
Roid, race.
Roth, wheel, L. *rota*.
Ruchd, room.
Rus, wood, brush, grove.
Sacham, at-tack, set.
Saisde, sage.
Saor, free, s, f.
Sar, very, G. *sehr*.
Sasat, L. *satis*.
Scib, skiff, ship.
Sdaid, state.
Sdair, story.

Sdeud, steed.
Sean, ancient, L. *senex*.
Searbh, sour, L. *acer*.
Scarg, seared, dry.
Searr, horse, colt.
Seis, skill; *sga*, sake.
Sgail, shade, sg, sc, sh.
Sgaol, scatter.
Sgeil, skill.
Sgille, quick, agile.
Sglata, slate.
Sgroibam, scrape, scratch, write, grave.
Sguabam, sweep.
Silam, drop, distil.
Sion, chain, bond, tie.
Slan, sound, healthy.
Sliogam, sleek, smooth.
Smuid, smoke, vapor.
Sochd, silence.
Sodan, joy, L. *gaudium*.
Spre, sparkle.
Sread, herd, troop.
Sreamh, stream.
Srian, strain, rein.
Stain, tin, Fr. *etain*.
Suil, eye, sun.
Sur, search, in-quire.
Tabhair, give, L. *dabo*.
Tai, deaf, silent, L. *taceo*.
Tais, wet, dank.
Talamh, soil, L. *terra*.
Tarmadh, dwell, tarry.
Teagh, house, sty, *tectum*.
Teith, hot, toast.
Tiag, sack, G. *tasche*.
Time, fear, timid.
Tig, go, come, L. *it*.
Tin, be-gin.
Tioncam, at-tend.
Tir, ground, L. *terra*.
Tiug, tight, thick.
Toid, whole, total.
Tor, lord, sovereign.
Torg, de-stroy.
Tread, herd, drove.

Trean, strong, brave.
Treotam, trot, come.
Trom, heavy, L. *gravis*.
Tuile, flood, deluge.
Tur, dry, bare, torrid.
Ugh, egg; *Uige*, wise.
Uidh, care, heed.
Uir, fire.
Uisge, water, whiskey.
Una, hunger.
Ur, earth.
Tlachd, delight.

We have noticed, in thus reviewing the Gaelic etymology, a striking tendency to the French and German forms of words. The words are very short; in comparison with the Latin and Greek languages, there are here but very few of what may be called formative syllables or letters. It is not alone the absence of gender and case endings, of endings to denote the persons of the verb and the agreement of the adjective; there are very few of what in other languages we understand by derivative forms—that is, forms developed by the appearance of new syllables. Thus, we find *borg* for *borough*, *bla* for *yellow*, *cearb* for *silver*, *cealg* for *be-guile*, *cleir* for *clergy*, *fis* for *vision*, *ba* for Latin *bonus*, *difir* for *difference*, *duil* for *delight*, *fec* for *feeble*. We find, also, many instances where one consonant, or vowel, in Gaelic, represents two or more in our own language, as *c-am*=*sh-am*, *a-it*=*st-ead*, *ei-de*=*clo-th*, *oir*=*sh-ore*.

The comparison of Gaelic words which we have made with those which follow them, will easily be understood. The words which are given as Gaelic equivalents, are equal to each other as well as to the Gaelic term itself; and the letters of the Gaelic are supposed to correspond with those of its definitions; as, in *cail*=*shield*, *c*=*sh*, and *l*=*ld*; *bran*=*black*, *br*=*bl*, and *an*=*ack*; *bord*=*brim*, i. e. *brd*=*brm*; *bosd*=*boasting*, *d*=*ting*—as *ting* is only a development of *t*; *bearr*=*short*, *b*=*sh*, *rr*=*rt*, (brief=short).

Bearing in mind the peculiar representatives or correspondents of letters in Gaelic, and Celtic, when compared with other European languages, we find but very few words there which cannot readily be placed along side some equivalent in English, German, Latin, French, or Greek. Indeed, it is almost as easy to identify Celtic orthography with these, as it is to identify English with German, provided that we proceed in the right manner.

We might add, also, that the number of Celtic words identical with Semitic, or nearly so, should not escape the notice of any inquirer, as it is really striking.

Welsh Etymology.

585.
Chaled, hard, callous.
Bran, crow, raven, black.
Cwmwl, cloud, L. *cumul'*.
Merch, girld, maid.
Ffenestr, window, *finster*.
Bryn, hill, brow.
Dyn, man, d, m.
Golwg, look, sight.
Porsa, pasture.
Adar, birds.
Melyn, mellow, yellow.
Coch, red; *Casglu*, gather.
Go-sod, set, place.
Fremin, king, *rex*, first.
Gw-lad, land.
Cryf, strong, G. *kraft*.
Awdl, ode.
Plygu, bend, fold.
Cwn, dog, G. *hund*.
Pechod, sin, wicked.
Miar, briar.
Wyn, lambs, Fr. *agneau*.
Bachgen, boy, *mac*.
Sefyll, stand.
Geffyl, horse, Fr. *cheval*.
Arth, b-ear, L. *ursus*.
Llyfr, book, L. *liber*.
Milwyr, soldier, L. *miles*.
Cadpen, captain.
Llythyr, letter.
Ddinas, city, town.
Peth, thing, L. *res*.
Amser, time.
Ddear, terra, earth.
Plwm, lead, plumb.
Chleddyf, sword, L. *gladius*.
Hiechyd, health.
Hebog, hawk.
Hwch, swine, hog.
Mwygl, muggy.
Posiaw, pose, puzzle.

Troed, foot, tread.
Esgyrn, bone, L. *os*.
Pwmp, bump, lump.
Crim, crimp.
Cic, foot, kick.
Peled, bullet.
Llwyar, ladle.
Gwyfr, wire.
Gwn, gown, G. *ge-wand*.
Gwalt, welt, hem.
Crwt, crust.
Mwg, smoke.
Plyg, plait, fold.
Llimp, slim, slender.
Colpo, cuff, Fr. *coup*.
Stang, tank.
Chweg, sweet.
Saffwn, shaft, staff.
Swmwl, stimulus.
Gwylt, wild, L. *velox*.
Curwf, G. *bier*.
Dewr, strong, L. *vir*.
Haul, sun, L. *sol*.
Ser, star, L. *stella*.
Llyn, lake.
Prynu, buy.
Marw, dead, *morte*.
Chwerw, bitter, sour.
C-loff, lame.
Caer, wall, G. *mauer*.
Enw, name.
Tref, town, G. *dorf*.
Gafr, goat, L. *capra*.
G-raig, rock, crag.
Gwr, L. *vir*.
Tra, very, L. *verus*.
Cnoi, bite, gnaw.
Bach, little, L. *pauc-us*.
Tywyll, dim, dark.
Clywed, hear, G'k *kluó*.
Chwant, want, wish.

Sufficient has been given of Welsh to show what forms our words have when they appear there, and, besides, enough to give some idea of the way in which Welsh compares with Gaelic.

ETYMOLOGY.   209

Semitic Languages.

Our selections will be first and mainly from *Hebrew*.

We shall notice continually in Semitic, and in Hebrew particularly, that certain initial letters are pure augments, or prefixes, for us, and if we would compare them with European words we must cast them off entirely. The letter *a* in Hebrew we shall find often to be such an augment.

A-bir, strong, force, *vir*.
Ae-ben, stone, Sl. *ka-men*.
A-bag, bind, ball, wick.
Agam, ignite, burn.
A-gan, go, gone, tread, G'k *bainō*.
A-zan, ear, hear, *akouō*.
A-zal, walk, glide, go.
A-gar, gather, collect, G'k *ageirō*, our *herd*. We find the related forms *ye-gar*, *gur*, *garar*.
A-chal, eat, chew, San. *gal;* to compare with our *eat*, we must strike off the *l*, *al*, which is often a suffix, like several other letters; Alb. *cha*.
A-dam, red, Ger. *roth*.
Adomo, bottom, G. *boden*.
Aeder, *Adir*, wide, (*r* suf.)
Ahab, *aab*, love, G'k *agapaō*,
Ahal, G. *zelt*, folk, *oel*. [L. *amo*.
Av, *au*, L. *vel*, wish.
Aud, wood, brand.
A-val, oval, fool.
Aid, strong, might, as we see by the form *meodh* equal to *might*,—*ail* is a cognate form, l, d; this *ail*, *el*, shows that *Aloa*, *Alla*, God, means power, the Almighty.
Aor, light, aurora, G'k *oraō* equal to see, *stare;* *ore* equal to *bright*, *shine*.

Aoth = *aor*, sign, show.
Azad = *Azal*, Ar. *zal*.
A-chaz, catch, L. *capio*.
A-char, after, follow.
A-mal, weak, G'k. *amalos*—other forms, *malal*, *mala*, *malaq;* wilt.
Ametz, might.
Ae-mesh, night, L. *nox*, evening, G. *abend*.
A-mar, *o-mer*, word (m, w); mr, pr, spr, pray, Gael. *abhar* equal to speak, say.
A-phal, veil, G. *verhüllen;* forms, *aphil*, *afaf*.
Aphen, *ofen*, time, *temps*.
Aphes, pause, cease.
A-phar, G. *fahren*, fare, form, *pharar*, Ar. *farak*, Ger. *sprossen*, sprout.
A-qqo, G. *bock*, goat.
A-rag, string, right, strong, firm, force.
Arrar, stick, arrow.
Aerez, earth, *erde*.
Aesh, ash, fire.
Ashur, G. *schritt*, tread, *ashar;* Chal. *atar*, tread.
Atha, *ata*, Celt. *aeth*, L. *it*, go, come, went.
Aenosh, *ensh*, G. *mensch*.
Baar, bury, G. *graben*.
Beer, G. *brunnen*, spring.
Baash, Ar. *baus*, Ger. *böse*, base, bad.

27

Bad, part; *badal*, G. *theil*, divide—other forms are, *bad-ad*, *bad-aa*, *bad-aq*, *bad-ar* (bdr, brd, spread) —showing l, d, a, q, r, to be equivalent suffix endings. These are letters which we shall often meet with as mere endings.

Balal, G'k *ballo*, pour, throw, Fr. *meler*, blend.

Bazar, spread, strew.

Bo, *boa*, G'k *baino*, go.

Bus, tread, foot, *fuss*.

Bur, *bor*, G. *forschen*, *fragen*, break, bury.

Bosh, bash, shame.

Baz, booty.

Baza, Ger. *spotten*, mock.

Baz-aq, piece (*q* suf.)

Bata, *batal*, hollow, empty, bottle, *bauch*.

Biyn, *deem*, b, d, L. *video*, G'k *phaino*, mean, medium, think.

Biyra, burg.

Bayith, *beth*, dwell, house, a-bode.

Bacha, weep, G. *weinen*, G'k *dakru*.

Bal-aq, pour, spill; *bal-a*, *bal-al*, *bal-ag*.

Bal-am, swell.

Bana, build, G. *bauen*.

Bead, a-bout.

Baat, beat, tread, walk.

Baar, burn, brand.

Baal, boil, flow, swell.

Baqa, split, stream, brook, G. *bach*, break; *baq*, *baqaq*, gush, pour.

Boqer, early, morn; so we use break in day-break, dawn.

Bar, boy, born, L. *puer*.

Bara, *barad*, *baraz*, stick, stab, brad, dart; *pare* equal to *cut*; *barach*, break, is a related form.

Bara forms, S. *kar*, L. *paro*, part, break; *barar*, cut, part.

Gad,[1] go, come.

Geeh, high, G. *hoch*.

Gav, heave, high, heap, cave, bow, back, ridge, hollow —all founded on the idea of concave = convex. So we find the *gee*, slightly varying, representing all those meanings; forms, *gav*, *gav-av*, *gav-ah*, *gav-al*, *gav-ach*, *gav-ar*, *gav-ash*. We see here one of the · principal means of multiplying derivatives in Semitic, that of varying the final letter, with a corresponding variation in signification.

Ge-bor, force, strong, German *ge-walt* and *kraft*.

Ga-bal, belly, G. *gauch*.

Ge-ber, *ge-ver*, L. *vir*, man.

Gadal, allied with *gab*, *gav*, heap, means great; gdl = gld, grd, grand.

Gadaa, cut, hew. The whole family of words meaning cut, pierce, part, shear, shave, etc., etc., are identical in Greek, Ger., and Sem., as a slight inspection will show.

Gadar, hard, grd, hrd.

Gubh, *guv*, hew.

Gur, draw, deer, *thier*.

Ga-zar, shear, cut, pare.

Ga-cheleth, coal.

---

[1] *G* is a prefix in Hebrew which is very common, identical, too, with the *g* of Europe.

ETYMOLOGY. 211

Giyl, Ar. *hal*, coil, G. *hohl*, cylinder, G'k *kuklos*.
Giyr, corner, short, curt.
Galab, clip, G. *glatt*.
Galgal, galal, roll, wheel; Russ. *kolo*, G. *kreis, circa*.
Galah, walk, wallow.
Galach, G. *glatt*, callow.
Gam, heap, high, cumu-late, aug-ment.
Ga-mal, ga-mar, mass, much, *multns, viel*.
Gaph = gam.
Ga-nab, knab, steal.
Garad, scratch, grate.
Gaph-an, heap, curve.
Ga-rah, raise, e-rect.
Gerah, corn.
Ga-ral, rough, raise, ran.
Ga-raph, grave, tear, rent, rip.
Garar, turn, G. *kehren, scharren*.
Gash-am, harsh, fast.
Da-bar, speak, pray (= *amar*), word, Gaelic *la-bairt* = speak.
Dagah, dagal, deck, clothe,
Dor, dur, tarry, during. [d-gl].
Dachah, stick, tap, beat — all the family of beat, strike, press, bind, etc.
Dal, door.
Diyn, deem, doom, just.
Dalah, L. *tollo*, bear.
Dam, blood, Fr. *sang*.
Damah, like, same.
Dapaq = dachah.
Darag, tread, Gr. *trecho*.
Darer = darag, turn.
Darash = darar, thrash, search, *fragen*, break.
He-bel,[1] blow, breath.
Hadah, lead, guide.
Ha-dar, draw, break.

Havah, Ar. *huach*, Ger. *hauch*, puff, breathe.
He-vah, be, was.
Hor, G. *berg*, rock, R. *gora*.
Halak, walk, go.
Halal, Ar. *hal*, clear, hell.
Hamas, mass, gather.
Zeban, gain, win.
Ze-bul, dwell.
Zid, seethe, cook.
Zul, guide; *zur*, press.
Zakar, think (r suf.).
Zal-al, eat, feast, *gal*.
Zam-ar, song, sing.
Zem-an, time.
Zaak, squeak.
Zara, strew, spread; *zaraq, zarar*.
Cha-bal,[2] bind, ball; related, *cha-bar, cha-bash, cha-bad, cha-bab*, (notice l, b, r, sh, th, m, q, are the common suffix letters).
Cha-bath, bake.
Chad-ad, cut, L. *acer*, axe.
Chul = giyl.
Chomah G. *mauer*, wall.
Choph, coast, brim.
Chur, hole, r, l.
Cha-za, see, L. *video*.
Cha-zon, vision.
Cha-zaq, fast, G'k *ischus*.
Chaya, live, G'k *zaō*.
Chaka, wait, watch.
Cha-kam, G. *kennen*, sage.
Chalal, wound, kill.
Cham, warm.
Cham-ar, scum, foam.
Chen, kind, favor.
Cha-sah, shun.
Chatab, cut, hew; in Ar., *kitab* = book, piece; writ = carved, graved, cut.
Chasaph, G'k *skapto*, shave.

[1] *H* is a common prefix.
[2] *Ch* (one letter) is often a prefix.

212   PHRASIS.

Chapha, cover, cap, deck.
Chaphar (krf), grave, carve.
Chereb, sword, b, d.
Charah, char, burn.
Charath, G'k *karatto*, grave.
Char-ash, chore, work, Ger. *arbeit*; *raa, char-ab, char-at*.
Cha-sah, silent, *sigaō*.
Tus, toss, G. *stossen*.
Tov, tob, good, t, g.
Taphash, fat, G'k *pachus*.
Taraph, tear.
Ye-or, river, run.
Yaal, fool.
Ya-al, go, Fr. *aller*.
Ya-bab, G. *rufen*, babble.
Yabal, G. *jubeln*, L. *jubeo*.
Ya-bal, stream, flow, go.
Ya-bash, a-bash.
Yaga, yoke, bind, press.
Yagabh, G. *ackern*.
Yaga, L. *ago*, act, work
Yagar, fear, horror.
Yadah, throw, L. *jacto*.
Yadaa, know, *oida*, L. *video*.
Yom, day, G'k *ēmera*, year.
Yach-adh, yoke, *eka*, oue.
Yacham = *cham*, warm.
Yain, wine, G'k *oinos*.
Ya-kol, can, could, Cel. *gal*.
Ya-ladh, L. *latum*, born.
Yeled = child, brought, born.
Ya-sadh, *ya-sab*, set, place.
Yaan, yearn, G. *gierig*.
Ya-za, go; Ar. *ja* = go.
Ya-zar, form, S. *kar*, zur.
Ya-qabh, scoop, cave.
Ya-qar, G. *schwer*, L. *gravis*.
Ye-qar, worth, dear, Latin *carus*.
Yaru, throw, *werfen*, arrow.
Ya-shar, straight.
Ka-bad, heavy, G. *bar-us*.

Ka-bash, wash, tread.
Ka-baa, bend, bow.
Kabar, great, G. `grob*, Ger. *heben*, heave, high; *kabrb*, *gabab, gabar*.
Kad, G'k *kadus*.
Kadar, gather, L. *tur-ba*.
Kava, G'k *kauō*, char.
Kul, hold, G. *halten*.
Kum, high, heap, cumu'.
Kun = *kum*, stand-up, raise, Arab. *kan* = be, stand.
Kus, ball, cocoon, *kuklos*.
Kur, roll, turn, ball.
Kush, heap.
Kid, G. *keil*, dart.
Kokar, circle, G. *kreis*.
Kol, all, whole.
Ka-labh, G'k *lab*, grab.
Keleb, whelp, L. *vulpes*.
Kalaa, full, complete.
Keliy, fasten, hold.
Kal-am, call, speech; Ar. *kal* = say, *kul* = voice.
Kalaph, *kalaa, kalabh*, grab, G. *greifen*, claw, club, G'k *kolapto*.
Ken, when.
Kemo, L. *quomodo*, how.
Kau-am, wound.
Kaph, cave, heap, hollow.
Ka-phal, fall, fold.
Kaphaph (kff), G'k *kampo*, *cumbo*, bow, bend, cramp, scoop, hollow; forms, *ka-pha, qabab, ya-kav, ka-vah, ku, na-qab, gav*.
Kaphar, cover, scoop.
Ke-phath, fasten.
Kar, L. *aries*, G'k *kar*.
Kor, G'k *koros*.
Karah, grave, carve.
Kerem, garden.
Karar, turn, G. *drehen*.

¹ *I* or *Y* (*ya*) is a common Semitic prefix.
² *K* is often a prefix.

ETYMOLOGY.

Karath, cut, part.]
Keter, G'k *kitaris*, crown.
Katuth, contusus.
Katal, chain, G. *kette*.
Kat-am, cut, stick.
Kuton-eth, coat, G'k *kitōn*.
Laat,[1] L. *lateo*, hide.
Leom, G'k *laos*, folk.
Laam, L. *ligo*, bind, tie.
Laba, *lava*, lion, L. *leo*.
Lab-ab, *laq*, love.
Laban, white, L. *alba*.
Leb-ush, c-loth.
Laab, flame, lamp, light.
Laha, languish, *lechen*.
Laat, *laab*, burn.
Lava, bind, L. *ligo*, *lego*.
Lucha, light, L. *luceo*.
Lachach,[2] *lqq*, G, *lecken*.
Lach-am, a variation of *lach-ach*, lick, and of *akal* = eat, showing *l* to be prefixed, and to be divided, *l-ach-am*, m, am, being suffix, and *ach* = eat; it equals comb-at, G. *kampf*, *la-cham*.
La-kadh, catch, G'k *lab*.
La-tash, tap, thump.
Lamadh, learn, beat, Greek *math*; *l-ama-dh*.
Laag, speak, L. *lego*.
La-path, wind, pack.
La-qach, catch, take.
La-qat, gather, co-llect.

La-shon, tongue, L. *lingua*.
La-shadh, suck, lick.
La-thaa, bite, tooth.
Ma-amar = *amar*.
Ma-boa, in-go, entrance.
Me-golla, roll, volume.
Ma-gan, give, *geben*.
Me-gamma, heap, *gam*.
Mo-debar, drift, drive.
Ma-dad, G. *denen*, stend, tend, mete, measure.
Mo-deyan, *zank*, wrangle.
Mc-dar, tarry, dwell.
Ma-halach, walk, go.
Mug, m-ove, go, mog.
M-ora, fear, horror.
Muth, die, *mors*.
Mazag, mix.
Ma-zah, G. *saugen*.
Mo-zah, fear, quake.
Me-zomma, sin.
Mo-zem-or, sing, song.
Me-chiyr, hire, price.
Me-tah, extend.
Malea, fill, whole.
Mo-lla, word, *logos*.
Malach, salt.
Me-lech, *rego*, *lego* (r, l), Gael.
mal, king, *rege*.
Ma-lal, speak, talk, *laleo*.
Maraq, G. *amergo*, rub.
Marar, turn, press, force, run, sour.
Ma-shal, rule, *herr*.
Maat, smooth, *glatt*.

---

[1] *L* changes with *n*, as *lachaz* and *nachaz*; with *r*, as *alu*; with *d*, as *rad* and *ral*; it is often introduced — besides being suffixed, as we have seen before.

[2] The *cha-ch*, *qq*, is one of the many instances of double letters at the end, showing clearly that as a universal principle in Semitic, words grow by repeating the final letters. These doubles again vary, as double letters so often do, and instead of *lechch*, *lqq*, we might have *lqr*, *lqt*, *lqk*, *lxm*, *lqsh* — those *qr*, *qt*, *qk*, *qm*, *qsh*, being double as much as *kk*, *qk*, *qq*.

[3] *M* is pretty uniformly a prefix, few words occurring with this initial where it has not clearly this office.

Naa, raw,[1] n, r.
Naad, wet, G. *nass*.
Naam, G'k *muo*, roar.
Na-bal, fall, flow, fool.
Na-gad, go, gad, R. *chod*.
Nagiyd, guide, prince.
Nag-aa, flog, strike ; forms *nag-on, nag-aph, nag-ach*,
Na-dibh, give, L. *do*. [*nag-as*.
Nubh, heave.
Nua, nod, G'k *neuo*.
Num, sleep, L. *somn-us*.
Nur, fire, G. *feur*.
Na-chal, hold, *halten*.
Na-zal, glide.
Nu-tal, L. *tollo, talah*.
Na-tar, na-zar, be-ware, L.
Nasas, sick, *nosos*. [*tueor*.
Naar, boy, L. *puer*, new.
Na-phach, G. *fachen*.
Na-qaph, cuff, Fr. *coup*.
Na-shak, bite, G'k *dak*.
Na-shal, fall, slide.
Na-tibh, G'k *tribos*, tread.
Na-zar = L. *tueor*.
Na-than, give, *ge-than*.
Na-thar, G'k *treo*, tremble.
Na-qar, bore, carve.
Saba, G. *zechen*, suck, drink, L. *bibo*.
Sa-gad, L. *cado*, fall.
Sa-gar, grab, hold.
Sadar, order, rank.
Sus, horse, L. *e-quus*.
Suph, L. *sumo*, shave.
Sak-ach, deck, thick.; forms sk-r, sk-th, sk-l, sk-n.
Salaa, sileo, silent.
Salach, walk.
Saman, sign, G'k *sēmain*.
Saphar, scrape, scribe; *sipher* = book, scrip, bit, — L. *liber* belongs with it.

Seren, prince, ezar.
Abhad,[2] oper-ate, *ergo*, G. *arbeit*, S. *kar*.
Adar = *sadar*, order.
Aeder, herd.
Aud, wind, wood.
Aod, again, L. *iterum*.
Aun, G. *wohnen*, dwell.
Aez, G'k *aix*, goat, *ziege*.
Air, gir, fire, warm.
Auph, guph, cover, fly.
Ala, high, L. *alta*.
Alaz, G'k *alalazō*.
Am, L. *gens*, G'k *dēm-os*.
Am-ar, L. *mergo*.
Ana, answer.
Amad, stand, *qam*.
Aphal, gaph, hill, swell.
Aphar = *chaphar*.
Atsabh, G. *schaffen*, shape.
Agal, agar, turn, *kehr*.
Aepher, heifer.
Arag, L. *rugio*.
Ara, bare.
A-rach, aram, G. *rüsten, richten*, -rect, raise.
Araph, strip.
Asah, L. *facio*, act, *ago*.
Atah, age, L. *aetas*.
Peah, face, mouth, L. *os*.
Paga, L. *pugna*, beat.
Pucha, blow, L. *pneo, ruch*.
Pur, part, lot.
Pa-zar, spread, strew.
Pachar, paar, bake, parch.
Pala-a, pala-h, pal-ad, pal-ag, pa-lach, split.
Peleg, flood, L. *fluss*.
Pal-at, pal-az, pala-th = *pal-ad*.
Palath, flow, fleet.
Pasas, pause, piece.
Pasach, pass, *pas-ag, pas-al*.

---

[1] *N* is generally a prefix, and is identical with *m;* it changes too pith r, y, i.

[2] The letter *ayin*, which we will represent by *a*, is closely related to *g*.

Paa-l, G'k *poieo*, *facio*, *kar*, Ar. *faal*, *gaal*.
Paam, beat, vanish.
Parad, spread; forms, *par*, *par-as*, *par-am*, *par-az*, *par-aq*, *par-ach*, *par-at*, *par-ah*, *par-ar*, *par-ag*.
Perach, G. *spross*, sprout.
Pash-at, *pash-aa*, *pash-ash*, *pash-ar*, are other forms of *parad*, where sh = r, meaning break, split, spread.
Patah, L. *pateo*, o-pen.
Patal, battle, beat.
Paar, ap-pear, *pareo*.
Ts-aba, go, G'k *baō*, war.
Tse-baa, will, wish.
Tsadh, side.
Tsa-diq, just, G'k *to-dikaion*; in Syr. *adaq* = right, just.
Tsa-hal, G. *hell*, glance.
Tsa-har, G'k *oraō*, ore.
Tsovah, L. *jubeo*.
Tsalal, yell, G. *schall*.
Tsur, turn.
Tsa-adh, go, *itu*, G. *steig*.
Tsaag, squeak, cry.
Tsaphah, show, G'k *phan*.
Tsachaq, joke, laugh.
Qabar, grb, G. *be-graben*.
Qadal, cut, G'k *kedaō*.
Qava, wish.
Qol, voice, *glas*, call.
Qum, raise, be, been.
Qat-ab, *qat*, *qat-al*, cut.
Qat-an, little, bit, cut.
Qal, light, G. *schnell*, a-gile.
Qat-al = *gal*, L. *levis*.
Qa-mal, wilt.
Qaph-ah, heap, cover.
Qaraa, call, cry, *kraz*.
Qanaz, hunt.
Qa-zer, short, kurt, cut.
Qeraa, cry, call, read.

Qarebh, G. *krieg*, war.
Qarobh, proach, near.
Raah, see, G'k *o-raō*, L. *reor*, think.
Resh, *res*, head, L. *rex*; in Corn. *ruy* = *rex*; in Ar. *ras*, *res* = prince, first, fore.
Shem, name.
Rabha, gross, G. *grob*.
Ragal, rd, tread, go.
Regel, foot, tread, Wel. *troed*.
Radah = *regel*, tread.
Raat, ruz, run.
Rucha, G. *hauch*, Ger. *ge-ruch*, spirit.
Rum, raise, a-ram, high, *qum*.
Ribh, riv, strive.
Rakabh, d-rive, ride.
Raphah, rap, G'k *rap*.
Raq-aq, strike.
Sa-gabh, high, = *gav*.
Such, shoot, stock.
Sum, set.
Sur, shear, part, cut, strive, rub, G. *herr*.
Sachaq, joke, laugh.
Sachah, see, seek, *sak-al*, *kal* = light, look.
Saar, rough, raw, hair.
Sa-phaq, pick, peck, strike.
Saraph, burn, scorch.
Sar, sarah, czar, prince, G. *herr*, sir, *res*.
Shaa, see, show.
Shab-ab, cut, saw.
Shebet, staff, stock, scepter.
Sha-bal, G. *wallen*.
Sha-bar, break.
She-beth, dwell, *beth*.
Shir, sing, sang, speak, L. *reor*, cry.
Shith, set, lay.
Shakach, seek, wish.
Shalach, G. *schicken*, *stellen*.

[1] *S* is prefix.

Shelet, G. *schild*.
Shalal, spoil.
Shamat, smooth.
Shamaa, hear, R. *slu*.
Shena, sleep, L. *somnus*.
Shaar, shudder, fear.

Shaqaa, sink, drink.
Tama, wonder, G'k *thauma*.
Taph-aph, tap, rap, tup.
Tur, turn, ring, *drehen*.
Tuph. G'k *tupto*, tap.
Taph-aph = *tuph*.

587. The style of orthography is essentially the same in Syriac and Arabic as in Hebrew, and we will content ourselves with but a few words from these two — taking first the *Syriac*.

Garo, arrow, dart.
Gudo, crowd, troop.
Acho, brother,
Atho, go, L. *it*, Celt. *aeth*.
Anosh, man, G. *mensch*.
Apha, face, over.
Gunio, shame.
Galaph, grave, sculp.
Zan, kind, L. *gentus*.
Zaq, call, L. *voco*.
Chiro, free.
Chob, debt, owe.
Chado, joy, L. *gaudium*.
Chaya, life, G'k *zaō*.
Chor, see, stare, *cer-no*.
Z-uro, rock, G'k *or-os*.
Tam, taste,
Taraph, strike.
I-laph, learn, take.
Kus, cup.
Karyo, sorrow, sorry.

Lubo, liver, heart.
Machor, morrow.
Ma-tho, go, come, (*m* prefix).
Ma-lo, word, G'k *logos*.
Mazo, may, might.
Mora, mister, sir, G. *herr*.
Sar, S. *kar*, make, *schaffen*.
Rabo, grow.
Ragam, stone, rock.
Rucho, wind, breath.
Aktho, hate.
Azar, treasury.
Bish, base, bad.
Baruk, break, knee, bend.
Gabo, choose, heap.
Gua, common.
Da-mar, ad-mire.
Gur, form, fi-gure.
Adar, aid.
Chusa, love, ek, k, l.
Cha-za, saw.

Very few words can be found in the Hebrew list that cannot be easily recognized in Syriac, as well as in Arabic; besides, there are a great many words in Syriac so nearly like Greek, that they are erroneously thought to be borrowed from that language.

The following are from Arabic.

A-zar, power, force.
A-far, fare, go, G. *fahren*.
A-fal, full.
A-kil, rex, kar.
A-mar, say, word, *mando*.
Ansan, man, *nas*.
Aal, folk, Heb. *am*.

Awzz, goose.
Aad, hard.
Baga, begin.
Bara, form, make, free.
Barad, frigid, freeze.
Baq, back, rest.
Bar, per-ish.

ETYMOLOGY. 217

Gaal, kar, make.
Gamal, collect, cumulate.
Gaz, go, went.
Harr, burn, warm.
Hasan, handsome.
Hall, L. *solvo*, loose.
Halu, L. *dulcis*.
Har, L. *curro*, run.
Hat, watch, wait.
Karaj, e-gress.
Hazir, horror.
Kan, sham.
Kal, false.
Daa, daga, talk, call.
Dall, tell, L. *dico*.
Zara, L. *creo*, grow.
Zarab, sharp.
Zall, vile, ill.
Ra-gaa, go, re-turn.
Ra-gal, foot, walk.

Ra-gib, wish, L. *cupio*.
Ruh, rest, G. *ruhig*.
Raa, g-row.
San, tooth, L. *dens*.
Sall, schall, yell.
Sanaa, do, G. *thun*.
Sar, form, *kar*.
Tal, long, tall, Sl. *dal*.
Alam, ilm, know, teach, learn, Heb. *lamadh*.
Ala, high, L. *alta*.
Amm, gam, common.
Uud, wood.
Fana, vanish.
Qadar, could, *val-eo*.[1]
Qa-sar, short.
Qal, call, say, (*kal*).
Qam = *kan* = stand.
Kalaz, collect.
Laqat, L. *legit*, -lect.

589. NOTE.—Liable as we necessarily are, in a work new and peculiar as this is, to be misunderstood, or not understood at all, we may with propriety add a few words here to explain and justify the positions we have taken.

It has been objected, that we pay too much attention to the growth of words, that we do not sufficiently regard the decay which always accompanies growth, or follows it—and the exception is perhaps well taken. It must be confessed that there is no more universal or important law in language than this, that words decrease or decline by decay, quite as surely and constantly as they increase or grow by development. This is the law of nature everywhere. But we have not thought it proper, here, to go into an extended discussion, such as would be necessary to point out the line of distinction between words which have become degraded by decay, and those, on the other hand, which have increased by development. Generally, with the data so far at the command of philologists, it is almost impossible to decide whether in a certain form which we find, a word has become reduced by decay, like the withering plant, or is in the first stages of development, as the tender germ. Again, it is often difficult to decide, in reference to two words, which is the older; thus, we have regarded the Greek *math* and *lab* as older than *manth* and *lamb*, the latter having grown from the former by development; but Dr. Lewis contends, and perhaps with as good reasons as we could bring to the contrary, that the

[1] Sound *q* as *k* in Semitic.

reverse is true, that *math.* and *lab* are the later forms, arising by reduction from the others.

But whether it is difficult or easy to draw the lines in question, we have found it sufficient for our purpose to show that it is a law in nature that words, that languages, do live and grow, as the vegetable and the animal (and hence must necessarily decay also), without making the least attempt to show what words are decaying, and what words, again, are increasing by growth. And, in very many instances where we have said that a certain word is a development from some shorter form, if some one should claim that they have rather arisen by decay from forms still longer and fuller, we should not object to it.

590. To those who would feel alarmed at the evil tendencies of some of the doctrines of this work, or, at least, at the gross absurdities they must inevitably lead to, we have only to call to mind the fact, or phenomenon, known to every true thinker, that philosophizing on any subject, when carried to extremes, will *always* lead to absurdities; that, if you would try the great ocean of thought, you must be content to keep close to the shore, resting assured that if you venture beyond your depth, you are certain to go down, and be buried in the depths of its dark and silent waters. He who has not had this experience, wherever may have been his path of inquiry, has surely never pursued thought very far.

591. It is no objection, again, that the reader may know something to be true which is quite contrary to some proposition in this work, and that what is found in one part of it may not seem to be exactly consistent with what is stated in some other part; a great many very different things may be true of one and the same subject—counting, mark you, from different stand-points; thus, a man six-foot-eight is very tall (high) compared with common men, but by the side of a respectable liberty pole he would be called quite the opposite. The question should be, as we understand it, *whether the proposition is in itself true;* are the facts such as they are stated to be; are the conclusions from them legitimate? No matter about the consequences, or about the other things that, no doubt, are likewise true.

592. And, finally, we ask those who complain that we identify and confound all things in language, to reflect and inquire, and see if they do not find that the identification of the unknown (which we examine) with the known (with which we are familiar) is the sole business of all inquirers, and if that identification is not all there is of progress in science. He who sets about showing you that the splendid locomotive is but a development of the tea-kettle (on wheels), that the law by which the planets revolve in their orbits is the same as that by which the

apple falls to the ground, that the pretty flower with all its variety of sepals, petals, stamens and pistils, is simply a leaf again and again repeated in all its changes of shape and coloring, busies himself solely with that identification which constitutes the basis of this work.

PART II.

HISTORY OF LANGUAGES.

CHAPTER I.

THE ENGLISH LANGUAGE.

593. When we treat of the English, we must also treat of the Anglo-Saxon, for the English takes its origin from the Anglo-Saxon, and there is no definite dividing line to distinguish the one from the other. Somewhere between 450 and 550, we cannot be precise about the time, England was invaded and settled by tribes from Germany. The foothold they gained was never wholly lost; they received accessions from time to time, and thus became the prevailing and fundamental people of the British Isles. Who it was that they replaced, what was the language of these aborigines, are problems that carry us too far back in the darkness of ages yet to be solved. Whatever was done, or whatever existed before the arrival of these German tribes, (Jutes, Angles, and Saxons, as they have been termed), relates to a people without history and without record; we must be content to remain in passive ignorance of these ancient days, or to amuse ourselves with mere fanciful conjecture.

594. For us, as philologists, we must start with the Anglo or the English-Saxon. As might be expected for history that dates back from us at least 1300 years, much of even this is questionable and uncertain. It is agreed that German is the basis of the English, that the Anglo-Saxon is German re-formed add re-wrought, and hence we are certain that German people are the stock out of which or on which has grown the English people; indeed, philology can prove all this without the aid of history; but the German people were, like all rustic and aboriginal people, a nation of tribes. It is not probable that one tribe alone made and maintained its settlement in England; indeed, we find different dialects in England, and these dialects could not have had one and a common base.

595. Three names are common in history as denoting those tribes which, or parts of which, are said thus to have left their homes to settle in England, the Jutes, from Jutland, the Saxons,

from Saxony, and the Angles, supposed to have been located in northern Germany. But all this is called in question; it has been claimed that Jutes and Saxons were not different, and that such a people as the Angles, from whose name that of the English is claimed to have come, never existed, or at least never had a "local habitation." But all these are points we gladly pass over; they afford little amusement, less profit, and infinite trouble.

596. From about the latter part of the 8th century, the Danes and other Scandinavian people made frequent incursions into England, often for the mere purpose of plunder, but again with the apparent design of a permanent settlement. Under Canute and his sons, the Danish was used as the court language; but as the Danish or Scandinavian settlement and mastery of the country was of comparatively short duration, it does not appear that their language had any material effect upon the development of the Saxon-of-England. The precise, or even approximate, value of that influence has not as yet been ascertained.

597. A more important, because more lasting, influence was that of the Norman French. The period of its introduction usually dates from the victory of William of Normandy, at the battle of Hastings, in the year one thousand and sixty-six. But Norman French was introduced, though we may not say fixed, in England many years before this. Edward the Confessor was a Frenchman by education, and, inspired with a love for Norman customs and Norman language, he never ceased in his endeavor to make them popular and predominant. The effort to root out the Saxon and put Norman French in its place was, however, under William, carried on in a more persistent and systematic manner. This French was not alone made the court language and the language of the higher classes of people; it was ordered to be taught in the schools; it was the language in which the laws were written, and in which legal papers were to be drawn. Yet with all these efforts, carried on for years, sustained by all the power of kings and their nobles, the English still remained a Saxon, that is a German language. And those very kings were compelled themselves to turn from teachers of French to learners of Saxon; so hard is the way of him who undertakes to destroy or change the spirit of a language, instead of being content to cultivate it as it is, or, at most, with changing its direction.

598. This Norman French has been the means, no doubt, of introducing many French terms, but it has no more changed the true character and inherent spirit of the language than has the Latin in those European countries where it was used as the language of science. But we must bear in mind, finally, that

the Norman French in its native land bordered on the German, and that even there it has much that is identical with German; and, if we find the English in the end somewhat assimilated to it, we must conclude that it was because of the original likeness in their natures.

599. Some there are who endeavor to give the very year (1356 and 1362 have been named) from which the English, as opposed to the Anglo-Saxon, is to date its existence; but we shall content ourselves with treating the English and the Anglo-Saxon as one and the same language, wearing different dresses, and presenting a different appearance in the various periods of the world and stages of its existence.

600. We will illustrate the nature of these two languages, or two forms of one language, by giving numerous examples, commencing with the Anglo-Saxon, and giving the age, when we happen to know it.

601. We will start with the Lord's Prayer in Anglo-Saxon, of about the Ninth century, (called also Dano-Saxon):
*Fäder ure, thu the earth on Heofenum
Si thin Nama gehalgod ; To be cume thin Rice
Gewurthe thin willa on Eorthan swa swa on
Heofnum. Urne ge dägwanlican. Hlaf syle us
to däg, And forgyf us ure gyltas, swa swa we
forgyfath urum Gyltendum.
And ne gelädde thu us on Costnung. Ac alyse
us of Yfle.*

Ure, our; *thu*, the, thou, that, or who; *on*, in; *si*, be (Ger. *sei*;) *ge-halgod*, is our hallowed, holied; *ta-be-cume*, impera. come, with prefix *to* and *be* ; *rice*, rick, Lat. *regnum* ; *ge-wurthe*, Ger. *werden*, be, become ; *swa-swa*, so-so, so-as ; *urne*, our, ouren; *ge*, every, or as a mere prefix ; *däghwanlican hlaf*, daily loaf, or bread ; *syle*, send, Ger. *stellen* ; *gyltas*, guilt, Ger. *schuld*, debt, should ; *gyltendum*, owing-ones ; in *gelädde*, lead, *ge* is prefix ; *costnung* has, in other dialects, the form *corung*, *koring*, *k* being a prefix, the word being equal to wrong, error, correction, try, peril, prove ; *a-lyse*, loose, Lat. *liber*, *a* being prefix ; *of*, from.

In the forms of other dates, we find *swilc* for such, so; *for-lete*, let, let-off; *halyed* for hallowed ; *als it in Heaven y do*, as it in heaven is done, *y* being the Ger. prefix *ge*; *uch*, every, each. The prayer form of English in 1160 differs scarcely from the one which we have given. In the form of 1370, we find *come-to* for *to-be-come*, impera. come.

603. The following lines are from the Saxon chronicle: *And thry Scottas cwomon to Aelfrede cyninge on anum bate*. And three Scots came to Alfred king on (or in) a (one) boat. *Se bat waes ge-worht of thriddan healfre hyde.* The boat was

wrought of third half hide, that is, two and a half hides, a Ger. expression. *He cwaeth that he bude on thaem lande northeweardum with tha west sae.* He quoth (says) that he bide (dwell) in the land northward with (against) the west sea.

604. And the following from the laws of Ethelbert; *Gif Cyinng his leode to him ge-hatath, and heom mon thaer yfel ge-do* — if king his people (Ger. *leute*) to him citeth (hight), and him one (any one) there evil do; in the last clause, *do* is brought last, as in German, while we say *do him evil*.

605. We take the following from an Anglo-Saxon poem:
Tha mec on-gan hreowon — then me 'gan (it) rue,
Thaet min hand ge-weorc — that my hand work
On feonda ge-weald — in fiends' power (Ger. *ge-walt*)
Feran sceolde — should fare (go), (fare should).

606. We find this in another poem, marking the transition of Anglo-Saxon to English:
He heom leofliche bi-heold — he them lovingly beheld,
Lithe him beo drihten — merciful (to) him be Lord,
Fethenen he nom mid fingre — feather (pen) he took with fingers,
And fiede on boc-felle — and wrote (paint) on book-skin.
And tha sothe word — and the true word
Sette to-gadere — set together.

The verb pretty uniformly in Anglo-Saxon, as in German, comes last; thus, *Hwaet do ic thaet ic ece lif age* — what (shall) do I that I eternal life have (may have); *sam hit monnum god thince* — whether it (to) men good seem (think); *heo hine axode h-lafes* — they (of) him asked loaf; *sceolde his Drihtne thancian thaes leanes* — should his Lord thank (for) this favor (lend, loan, Ger. *lohn*.)

607. *He witeth and wialdeth alle thing* — knoweth, wieldeth.
He i-scop alle sceafte — shapes all (things) shaped.
He wrohte fisc on ther sae — wrought, on the sea.
And fogeles on thar lefte — fowls, loft (air.)

These last last lines belong to the language in its later stages.

608. We give the following quotations of English in its earlier stages, principally illustrative of the peculiar forms of certain words, as well as the style of expression:
John highte that oon and Aleyn highte that other,
Of oo toun were thei born that highte Strother,
Ffer in the North, I cannot tellen where,
This Aleyn maketh redy an his gere,
And on an hors the sak he caste auoon.

Highte, a common word in old English, is *cite, called,* and it is here used as part. for pass. verb; *that oon,* the one; *thei,* they; *ffer,* far, over; ready all his gear — *gear* is apparatus.

John knewe the weye — hym nedes no gide.
And atte melle the sak adown he layth.
Him needs no guide — obj. pronoun for nominative, or we may treat needs as passive; at the mill down he lays the sack.

And therefore is I come and eek (also) Aleyn,
To grynde oure corn, and carye it ham agayne.
What wol (will) ye done (do) while it is in hande?
I is (am) as ille (ill) a meller (miller) as are ye.

This John goth out and fint his hors away,
And gan to crie, harrow, and wele away.
Goes out and finds; began to cry, hullo, and wail.
Whilke way is he goon? Which way? Ger. *welcher.*
The foregoing lines are from Chaucer, who was born in 1328, and died in the year 1400.

Then waxes his herte (heart) herde and hevye,
And his heade grows febill and dyssie (dizzy),
His gast (soul) then waxes sek and sair (sick, sore),
And his face rouches mair and mair (more) — lines from Northumbrian dialect of 15th century.

The following lines are from the piece "Havelok the Dane":
We haven (have), loverd (Lord), alle gode (goods),
Hors, and neth (cattle), and ship on flode (afloat, flood),
Gold and silver, and michel (much) auchte (else),
That Grim ure (our) fader us bitawchte (betook, gave).
 But hise (his) children alle fyve (all five)
 Alle weren (were) yet on live (a-live).
Bi-leve her (live here), loverd, and all (shall) be thin (thine).
Tho (thou) shalt ben (be) loverd, thou shalt ben syre (sire).
And we sholen serven the and hire (they, your, their),
Ne (nor) wantede (was) there no god mete (meat).

The following is from the York dialect of the 14th century:
In erthe (earth) is treys (trees) and gres (grass) to springe,
Bestis (beasts) and foulys (fowls) bothe gret (great) and smalle,
Fysschis (fishes) in flode; all othyr thyng
Thryffe (thrive) and have my blyssyng alle.

In hevyn er (are) angels fayre (fair) and brighte,
Sternes (stars) and planetis yar (their) curssis to ga (go).
Ye mone (the moon) servis on to ye nyght,
The son to lyghte ye day alswa (al-so).
 To swylke (so like) a lorde in all ye degre,
 Be evirmore lastande lovynge (loving, praising).
 Yat tyll (to) us swylke a dyngnite (dignity).
 Has gyffyne before alle othyr thynge (has given).

These two lines are Northumbrian:
Wha es he (who is the) *king of blisse? Laverd strang* (strong),
And mightand (mighty) *to fight, Laverd mightand lang.*

Here follow miscellaneous selections:
A wark ets fit (work that's fit) *for nin* (none) *but parson et dea* (to do, at do).

Thou that art to comynge (to come, a-coming).

Thynges that been to flien (are to flee, to fly from),
For suche men that ben vilayns (that are villains),
Be so thei mighten come a-londe — if that they might come to land (Gower, 14th century).

In Douglas, born in 1475, we find *gers* = grass, and in Gower *brydde* = bird.

The quhilk (which) *Juno nowthir lang dayis nor gyeris, nor nane diuyne sacrifice may appeis* (appease), — neither long days nor years, nor no (none) divine sacrifice; *and fatis war hir contrare* — and fates were (to) her contrary (Douglas). The is often left out, and $u = v, w.$

Quhither thay war livand — whether they were living,

And that gye knaw at quhais instance I tuke — ye know at whose instance I took; *gyit ne-the-les I aucht louit to be* — yet none-the-less I ought praised to be (Ger. *loben*, our *laud* (Douglas.)

Tyl she gan asken him howe Hector ferde — till she began (to) ask him how fared (how he did.)

Ful wel I thank it God, sayde Pandarus,
Saue in his arme he hath a lyttle wounde.

Full well, very well; I thank (for it) God — save, a little wound (Chaucer.)

Gif luf be vertew, than it is leful thing — if love be virtue, then it is lawful (Douglas.)

Yeoven (given) *under our signet* (sign, seal).

Take penne in hande and shape him a ful and plaine answeare — take pen in hand and shape (make, Ger. *schaffen*) a full answer.

Les sum (lest some) *historie, subtell worde or ryme,*
Causis me (to) *mak degressioun sum tyme* (some time.)

Withouten (without) *noyse or clatteryng of belles,*
Te Deum was our songe and nothing elles (else.)

Him behoueth serue himselfe that has no swayn.
Or els he is a fole (fool) *as clerkes sayn* (say) — Chaucer.
It behooves him to serve, he must serve.

Thah mi tonge were mad of stel (though my tongue),
The godness myht y (might I) *never telle.* 1307
With face bolde they shullen hem selue (them selve) *excuse,*
And bere (bear) *hem doun that wold* (would) *hem accuse.*
But rede (reed) *that boweth down for euery* (every) *blaste,*
Ful lyghtly cesse (cease) *wynde, it wol aryse* (will arise) —
if the wind ceases. (Chaucer.)

That sche (she) *might haue* (u = v) *the copies of the pretendit writingis giuen* (u = v) *in, quhilkis* (which) *they haue diuerse* (u=v) *tymes requirit of the Quene's maiestie* (i=j) *and hir counsel, suppois* (supposing) *thay haue not as git* (yet) *obtenit the samin* (same) (Mary, Queen of Scots.)

From hens to wĕnd (go, went) *full fer into exile,*
And ouer (over) *the braid sey sayl furth mony a myle,*—
From hence to go — far into — the broad sea (Douglas.)

Quhat (what) *auenture* (u=v) *has brocht the leuand hidder?* —
thee living hither (Douglas.)

Bot athir towart uthir turnis, but mare
And can behold his fellow in a stare, —
But other (one) toward the other turns, but more.

If that I speke after my fantasy (fancy)
As taketh not a grefe (grief) *of that I say.*

For myn (my) *entent is not but to play, sithe* (since) *ye ben* (am) *as gentyl borne as I.*

For neuir syne (never since) *with ene* (eye) *saw I her eft* (after). (Douglas.)

Al shulde I dye — although I should die.

Take rewarde (regard) *of thyn owne valewe* (value).

And certayne he was a good felawe (fellow),
Ful many a draught of wine had he drawe (drawn.)

Plesance of God (pleasure); *governance,* (government); *I wote well,* (wot well, know well); *outcept* Kent, out-take (Ger. *aus-nehmen*), ex-cept; *out-taken one,* excepting one; *hic up in the lyft,* high up in the loft, sky, (*lyft, luft,* is German, and so we find many German words in old English which do not occur in the present language.)

For as the fisshe, if it be drie,
Mote (might) *in defaute* (default) *of water die* (Gower.)

In the 14th century, we find *criand* for crying (the *and*=ung of German), *plesand* for pleasing, *sayande* for saying; and in 1528, *makand* for making.

609. We find *a* and *on* occurring often as a prefix to this part. or gerund (like the *to* of our inf., the *de* of French, and

the *ge* of German); as, *on hunting*, a hunting, in hunting; also, sound *on sleep*, asleep. We may notice also that some letters which we unite with a word, as the *a* in *alive*, are in old English separate prepositions — hence, again, we infer the identity of prepositions with prefixes and initials. To a very late day we notice, too, the existence of *y, i*, in place of German prefix *ge* of part.; as *y'taught* for taught; in the 15th century, we find a *child that is i-boryn* (born) *to us*, and a *sone i-gevyn us*, a son 'given us; also *ge mowe i-leven*, ye might believe (*be=i, ge, y*); in the 14th, we find *alle beth i-turned of cristale*, all be (were) turned of crystal.

610. We find also the *en, in*, of German inf. occurring very late in English, as, in a manuscript of 1400, we find, *he schal lovin* (love)*no man but for hiis* (his) *owne profyt* (own profit). And still later occurs the final *e* in the different parts of speech, which we have lost; thus, *keuerid* (kivered, covered) or *clothid with a cloude* (cloud); also, *unproperlicke sayde*, improperly said; *bryddes shall ete* (eat) *thy bodye* (body); *braste on peces smale*, burst in pieces small; *the brid is flowe*, bird is flew, flown; *as she was bode* (bid) *to say*.

611. The instances where participles differ not from verbs, (after the Celtic manner), and where the tenses and persons are not distinguished, are very numerous in old English; as, *the evill spirytes that ben* (been, be, am, are) *in the regyon* (region); *that she must gon* (gone, go); *up is she go* (gone); so, German *thun*=do is our *done*.

That char is char'd, chore is chored (Sans. *kar*, do); *I haue wel leuer* — I have well rather (liever); *frende steige heiger* — friend step (mount) higher; *whanne* (when) *he was dreynt* (pressed, Ger. *drücken*, throng, drive) *with a grievous sleep; sekynge fruyt*, seeking fruit; *was to takynge*, was to take.

612. We proceed next to notice some of the phrases and expressions of the different dialects of England, of which there are several. Some would be inclined to pass them by as spurious or vulgar, and hence unimportant; but it must be observed that there is nothing spurious in language, that the colloquial idiom of the peasantry is just as much a form of language, and just as valuable to the philologist, as the more refined expressions of the court and nobility.

In a Cheshire poem we find :
Hym (for him) *hade bene* (been) *better, in good faye,*
Hade (if had) *spared oyntmente that daie,*
For wracken (wreak) *I will be some waie*
Of waste that was done thier (there).

613. In Cornwall :
Arrear then, Bessy, ly aloane the backy (leave, tobacco).

Sty (stay) *here a tiny bit, and let us talky* (talk).
Ay but I've more to say; this isn't ale (all),
You deanc'd wy (with) *Mall Rosevear 't a sartin bale;*
She toald me so, and lefts me wy a sneare (with sneer).
Ay you, Pengrouse, did dance wy Mall Rosevear.

Hire (hear) *me, I says, and thou shat* (shall) *hire the whoale.*
I hires some mizzick at an oald bearne (barn) *doore.*

614. In Cumberland:
Then I'll sit down and wail
And greet (weep, re-gret) *aneathe a tree,*
And gin (if) *a leaf fa' i' my lap,*
I's ca't (I'll call it) *a word frae thee,*
Wi' sec (such) *thoughts i' my mind.*

615. In Derbyshire:
Becoz (cause), *mester, 'tis zo cood* (cold) *I conner* (can't) *work wee the tachin at aw* (all). *Why dunner* (don't) *yo mend meh shoom* (my shoen, shoes).

And I said if they were frunted (affronted) *wee Hester, they mid* (might) *be frunted wee mee.*

Hester hanner (haint) *bin a charrin* (choring) *there sin* (since).

616. In Devonshire:
Let's tell o'zummet (of something) *else; and you warent* (wont) *hear me; iv I say is, if I say yes; iv thee disnt* (doesn't) *zay thee wid* (will) *ha* (have) *me.*

I be a bit vrightened, but let us bide yerr (stop here.)
A urning (running) *along like a hoss upon wheels.*
Us was fools to come yerr and to urn (run) *into danger.*

617. In Kentish:
And one of theym cam into an hows (house) *and axed for mete* (meat), *and specyally he axyd after eggys* (eggs); *and the goode wyf* (wife) *answerde that she could speke no Frenshe. Loo, what sholde a man in thyse dayes now wryte, egges or eyren. Certaynly it is hard to playse every man, bycause of dyversite and chaunge of langage.*

618. The following is from an extract of 1340:
He answerede thet (that) *he com vram* (from) *the ze* (sea) *huer* (where) *he hedde y-mad* (made) *manye tempestes, vele* (full, many) *ssipes to-broke* (ships break), *and moche volk* (folk) *adreyct* (drown, drink). *The maister acsede ine hou* (in how) *long time. He zayde, ine zuo* (so) *moche time hest* (hast thou) *zuo lite* (little) *y-do* (done)? *Manyc werren and manye vigtinges* —many wars and many fightings; *thet he hedde grat thing y-do* (Ger. *ge-than*)—that he had great thing done.

619. In Lancashire:

Then I opp'nt (the) *dur* (door), *on whot te dule dust think—* and what the devil dost (thou) think; *l took her for a hoo* (high) *justice, hoor* (her) *so meety* (mighty) *fine. I axt hur of Mr. Justice wur o* (at) *whoam ; hoo* (she, he) *could naw* (not) *opp'n hur meawth* (mouth) *t-sey eigh or now* (to say aye or no).
Thirs nawt like thryin (there's not like trying. *Dunnos* (dont) *be fyert* (fraid) *us aw* (as I) *sed ofore* (before), *but ston* (stand) *up for wots reet* (right) ; *so aw mun lyev awt moor ut aw av to say—* so I must leave out more what I have to say. *Wayn* (we've) *helpt Kobdin, un wayn 'elp yo* (you) *if yoan* (you'll) *set obeawt* (about) *yur wark gradely.*

620. In Somersetshire:
Hem (he, me) *war nation avear* when *tha vuss put him in
Ta the grut ooden box, maust sa big's a corn binn ;
T'had two gurt large winders, wi' 'oles vor tha glass ;
Tha locked tha doors, an' there hem were vass* (fast)—

Afeard when they first put him (me) in—To the great wooden box, most so big—It had two great windows, with holes—They locked the doors.

*Us war glowing right at hem, ta zeen who hem coud find,
But avore hem coud look tha war a mile behind—*

We were staring to see who him (me).

*Nif Mr. Guy war hirch avaur,
A now war hircher still—*

If Mr. Guy was rich before, he now is richer still.

621. In Westmoreland:
Es aw (as I) *was a-sa'ing, me sweethart Nanny went ta Lunnen ta be a laddies* (lady's) *made, en aw sud* (should) *like varra weel* (very well) *to see her et times. By gum, if aw thout* (if I thought) *he'ed been breken t' seals ov my letturs es* (as) *aw sent ta Nanny, first time aw met him aw wad* (would) *giv him sic* (such) *a thumppen es he niver gat in his life befowre.*

622. In vulgar Cleveland dialect:
She ommost flyted an' scau'ded me oot o' my wits (almost blowed (chided) and scolded). *She war't t' arrantest scau'd 'at* (that) *ever I met wi' i' my boorn* (born) *days. She had sartainly sike* (such) *a tongue as never war i' ony woman's head but her awn* (own).

623. The next is Craven :
He nepped a lile wee nooken on't (nipped a little wee corner (nook) of it), *not t' validum o' my thoum naal* (thumb nail), *an' spluttered it out ageean, gloaring* (glaring) *gon he war puzzom'd* (staring as if he were poisoned).

624. The next, from the Lancashire dialect, is rather long, but its amusing character will warrant its insertion here. The subject is a newly discovered hedgehog:

He whoaved his whisket owr't (hov-ed, heaved his basket over it), *runs whoam* (home), *an' tells his neighbours he thowt in his guts 'at he'd fund* (found) *a thing 'at God newer mede eawt* (never made out); *for it had nother head nor tele, hond nor hough* (hoof), *midst nor eend. Loath to believe this, hoave* (half) *a dozen on em woud geaw* (go) *t' see if they coud'n mey shift to gawm it* (make shift to game it, make it out); *boh it cap't em aw* (but it capp'ed them all); *for they newer a won on 'em e'er saigh* (saw) *th' like afore. Then theyd'n a keawnsil* (had a council), *an' th' eend on't war, 'at teydn fotch a lawm, fawse, owd felly* (they'd fetch a lame, false, old fellow) *het* (called) *an elder, 'at coud tell oytch* (any) *thing, for they look'nt on him as th' hammel scoance, an' theawt he'r fuller o' leet* (thought he are fuller of light) *than a glow-worm's tele. When they'dn towd* (told) *him th' kese* (case), *he stroaked his beard, sowghd* (sighed), *an' order'd th' wheel-barrow wi' th' spon* (span) *new trindle* (wheel) *to be fotch't. Twur done, an' they beawld* (bowled) *him awey to th' urchon* (urchin) *in a crack. He gloared* (stared) *at 't a good while, droyd* (stroked) *his beard down, an' wawted it owr wi' his crutch.* "*Wheel me abeawt agen o' th' tother side,*" said he, "*for it sturs* (stirs) *and by that su'd be whick*" (should be quick, alive). *Then he dons his spectacles, steared at 't agen, and sowghing said,* "*Breether, its summot* (something); *boh feather Adam nother did nor cou'd kerson it* (christen it). *Wheel me whoam agen.*"

625. We will conclude our notice of English, by giving a still further selection of Anglo-Saxon sentences, taken from the gospels.

Tha com thaer an wif of Samaria wolde water feccan—then came there a wife (woman) of Samaria, (who) would water fetch; *tha cwaeth se haelend to hyre, gyf me drincan* — then quoth the Lord to her, give me (to) drink.

Tha answerede se haelend and cwaeth to hyre (then answered the Lord and saith to her), *gif thu wistes Godes gyfe* (if thou knowest God's gift), *and hwaet se ys he cwaeth to the, sele me drinken* (and who (what) that is who says to thee, give (*sele*) me to drink). *Witodlice* (then) *thu bede hyne thaet he sealde the lyfes weater* (thou (would) beg him that he (should) give thee living water); *thu hafst nan thing mid to hladene, and thes pett ys deop*—thou hast none thing with (which) to draw (lade), and this pit is deep.

626. Let us observe, once for all, that all translations given under this head, as well as under the heads which follow, are, with very rare exceptions, meant to be word-for-word, following the precise order of the text.

CHAPTER II.

THE GERMAN LANGUAGE.

627. On the German language we shall dwell longer than upon any other; it is important, not only by the number of persons who speak it, and the number of minor languages which are related to it, but more especially by the extent and variety of its literature, and the peculiar manner in which its thought is expressed.

628. The English is, as said before, a German language, and yet between the English and the German there is a great difference, one far greater than is generally supposed. The words in one, it is true, have their undeniable representatives in the other, and yet we put these German words in a very different place, and apply them in quite a different manner, from that which would meet the choice of a true German. The German thought is different from the thought of any other people, and as we might expect, it is clothed in a corresponding garb. They, the Germans, have the same grammar as we; it is easy for us, English as we are, to recognize their moods, their cases, their nouns, their adjectives, their pronouns, their particles; and yet they do, in some way, manage to work up those very same elements in such a novel yet true German style, that we find it hard to bring it home to us. It takes time to master the language — let the student bear that in mind. He may get a smattering in a far less period, he may learn the meaning of the words from the lexicon, he may get some little conception of the import of what he reads; but, nevertheless, he has not mastered the idiom, the style, the thought of the German people. It takes years for an Englishman to do it, hard labor and long months with that. But when it is done his toil will be well repaid. He has then mastered, if he be English, all the idioms of Europe, save the Latin and what belongs with it. And if, having the English and the German at command, he also be master of the Latin expression, there is no idiom of Europe that he will not easily understand. He may study the Slavic, the Finnish, the Celtic, the Scandinavian languages, and he will find little in their style of expression that is peculiar or strange to him. The idiom is the soul, the essence, of language; when we have mastered that, and not before, all flows along with us easily and smooth. The following selections will serve to illustrate the German idiom and peculiarities—with translations word-for-word.

629. *So scheint* (shines) *wirklich nichts beständig* (standing)

ewig (ever) *und des-namens-princip-würdig zu sein, denn* (than) *allein die materie*—so seems really nothing (nothing seems) lasting, eternal and of-the (*des*) name principle worthy to be, than (save) alone the matter (of-the-name-principle-worthy, is one adjective, referring back to *nichts*, nothing).

Es kann eine kraft (power) *so wenig ohne einen* (an) *stoff existiren, als ein sehen ohne einen seh-apparat*—it can a force so little without a stuff exist, as (*als*) a seeing (*sehen*) without a see-apparatus (a force can so little exist).

Geht man auf (upon, up) *den grund, so erkennt man bald* (soon) *dass es weder* (neither) *krafte noch* (nor) *materie gibt*— goes one down to the bottom (ground), so knows (perceives) one soon (one soon sees) that it neither force nor matter gives (*es gibt*, there gives, is).

Indem (in-that)· *der ver-fasser die feder* (feather) *er-greift* (grasps)—when the author the pen takes; *um sich mit einem vor-wort* (fore-word) *zu der binnen wenigen* (few) *monaten nöthig* (needy), *ge-wordenen dritten auflage* (edition) *seiner " Studien" an* (on) *das* (the) *publikum zu wenden*—for (in-order-to) self with a preface to the within few months necessary become third edition (of) his " Studies " to the public to turn (apply to); (for to turn (*sich-wenden*), or go, to the public with a preface to the-within-few-months-become-necessary-third edition). The long adjective belonging to *auflage* (edition) is one of the striking peculiarities, very common, in German. The *sich*, self, often cannot be rendered in English—often being a mere article.

Geschrieben wird (are) *der accent nur zum* (for-the) *unter-schied* (distinction) *verschiedener formen und ab-leitungen* (off-leadings) — written becomes the accent (it is written) only for-the distinction (of) different forms and derivations.

Was die bis-her (to-here) *be-kannten* (known) *Samoiedischen sprach-proben* (speech-proofs) *be-trifft*—what the to-here (now) known Samoidish specimens concerns (what-concerns, as concerns).

Den winter lang werde (will, were) *ich fische fangen*—the winter long (all winter) will I (am I) fish catch.

Ich weiss (wot, wit), *das die menschen zu hause* (house) *sind* (are)—I know, that the men to home are.

Was W. Humboldt, in seinen (his) *geist-reichen* (spirit-rich) *werke über die Kawi sprache, gelegentlich über die aus uralter* (early-age) *zeit her-stammende* (here-coming) *ver-wandtschaft der Malayisch-Polynesichen mundarten* (dialects) *mit dem Sanscrit merkt hat*—what W. Humboldt, in his ingenious work over (on) the Kawi language (speech), opportunely over the-out-(of)-early-time-originating relationship of the (*der*) Malayo-Polynesian dialects with the Sanscrit, remarked has. (What W. Humboldt has remarked, in his work on Kawi, incidentally on the relationship of, etc.)

Wäre das Gothische für uns ver-loren ge-gangen — were (if it were) the Gothic for us lost gone (go-lost = lost).

Gott ist das un-ab-hängige (un-hanging), *selbst-ständige wesen, welches* (which) *keines* (no) *andern wesens* (essence) *zu seiner existenz be-darf, folg-lich* (follow-ly) *von und durch sich-selbst ist* — God is the independent, self-standing essence, which (of) no other essence to its existence needs (has need of no other), con-sequently of (*von*) and through itself (it) is.

Der von (from) *der schranke des theismus freie Kant, ist Fichte* — the-from-the-limits-(of)-the-theism-free (free-from-theism) Kant, is Fichte.

Was nicht ge-liebt wird (are), *nicht ge-liebt werden* (be, were) *kann* — what not loved is, not loved be can (cannot be loved).

Wird man sich so-dann (so-then) *die frage zur* (to-the) *klaren ent-scheidung* (de-ciding) *bringen müssen* — will one self then the question to-the clear decision (separation) bring must (if one will must bring, i. e. if one will bring, the question).

Ich habe deinen bruder diesen morgen ge-sehen — I have thy brother this morning seen (I've seen him).

Ich bin schon zehn yahre in Amerika — I am (have been) already ten year in America; *ich muss ihn sprechen* — I must (to) him speak. *Ein stein fiel mir* (to-me) *auf* (up) *den kopf* — a stone fell (to) me up (on) the head.

Das buch ist keinen (no) *thaler werth* — the book is no (none) dollar worth.

Was ist aus ihm geworden — what is out (of) him become?

Ich sehe dich (thee) *als meinen freund an* — I see you as my friend on (look on thee as a friend). The separation of the *an* from *sehe* is a very common feature in German — and often they are far wider separated.

In einem (one) *tage lässt sich viel thun* — in one day lets self much do (may much be done).

In zwanzig jahren werde (am) *ich ein greis sein* (be) — in twenty years will (am) I a gray (old man) be.

Wenn ich nicht sinnen und dichten soll, so ist das leben mir (to me) *kein leben mehr* — when (if) I not muse and think shall, so is the life (living) to-me no life more (if I should not muse).

Er wusste nicht, sollte er (he) *gehen oder nicht* — he wist (knew) not, should he go or not (whether he should).

Ich schäme mich, dass ich es vergessen habe — I shame me (am ashamed), that I it forgotten have.

Ich habe niemals (no times) *in seinem hause mit ihm* (him) *wein ge-trunken* — I have never in his house with him wine drunk (drunk wine).

Ein hund stahl dem (from-the) *koche ein stück* (piece) *fleisch aus der küche, und ent-floh damit* — a dog stole (from) the cook a piece meat (flesh) out the kitchen, and away-flew there-with.

Und sprach: "den alten sultan (a dog's name) *schiess* (shoot) *ich morgen todt, der ist zu nichts mehr nütze;"* the old sultan shoot I (to-) morrow dead, who (the, he) is to nothing more use (I will shoot him to-morrow, he is of no more use).

Sie nehmen ihr (their) *kleines kind mit* — they take their little child with (them).

Alles licht unserer atmosphäre geht von (from) *der sonne aus* — all light (of) our atmosphere goes from the sun out.

Nehmen wir an — take we on (if we take on, claim); *wenden wir* (we) *diese analogie auf das licht an* — turn we this analogy up (on) the light on (we turn it to the light).

630. We may observe here that, in pronunciation, German $ie = ee$, $ei = ii$, $u = oo$, $au = ou$ in *our*, $a = ah$, or as *o* in *on*, $i = ee$ (short), $e = a$ in *ate*, *o* mostly as *u* in *up*, or long $\bar{o}$, j is always as our y; *e* final is always sounded; $v = f$, $w = v$, or *vw*, $th = t$. Thus, (very nearly) *die* is pronounced *dee*, *mein* = *mine*, *um* = *oom*, *haus* = *hous*, *man* = *mon*, *mir* = *meer*, *mehr* = *mayr*, *kopf* = *kup-f*, *so* = *so*, *je* = *ye*, *habe* = *hah-buh*, *vater* = *fahter*, *was* = *vwas*, *thun* = *toon*, *schein* = *shine* (sch = sh).

Forms of German.

631. The selections which we have so far given belong to the literature of the present standard German. But there are many forms, branches, and dialects of this language; that is, the term German may be applied to a great many varieties of the old Teutonic idiom, and we must endeavor first of all, to understand the application of the particular names which these varieties assume.

632. The first important division is that of High German and Low German, and alongside of these is usually placed another parallel class, the Gothic, called also Mœso-Gothic, or the Gothic of Mœsia.

633. The High German is again divided into sections, corresponding with its age: the old or ancient High German, or the earliest stage of High German known to us, Middle High German, or the same as it appeared in the 12th to 15th centuries, and the present or modern High German. The old High German, in different dialects, was spoken up to about the 11th and 12th centuries in southern Germany, in Switzerland, in Bavaria, Suabia, and Franconia — the name Francic, or Alemannic, is also applied to it, or to a particular stage of it.

634. The present German, or modern High German, is properly the written language of Germany, dating from the time of the introduction of Luther's Bible; as a spoken language, it is best represented in Saxony, Hanover, and Prussia—but at present, as well as in past times, the language spoken by the people greatly varies in the different portions of Germanic Europe.

635. The Low-German class is large; besides including the Anglo-Saxon and the English, the Old Saxon and Old Frisian, there is also belonging to this class the modern Dutch, and the Low German proper. The latter term, as a subdivision, applies to the dialects of the Elbe, Ems, and Weser. Grimm speaks of old Low German and middle Low German (or Netherlandish). The old Low German writings are found between the 8th and the 11th centuries, and the middle Low German between the 11th and 16th. The modern, or new, Low German (also called Modern Saxon) has ceased to be written as a dialect, since the 16th century, being replaced by the present High German. The Low German which is now spoken on the shores of the Baltic, differs very materially in sound from the ordinary German.

636. The following are early specimens of German (Francic), belonging, perhaps, somewhere between the 6th and 8th centuries — these selections also very well represent old Anglo-Saxon:

Fader ist usa firio barno; thu bist an them hohen himilo rikie; giuuihid si thin namo uuordu gihuilicu; cume thin craftiga riki; uuerthe thin uuilleo obar uuerold; alla so samo en erdu, so thar uppe ist an them hohon himilo rikie. Gib us dage gihuilices (whole) *rad, drohtin thie guodo, thina helaga helpu*—Father is our (of us) men born (sons of men, mortals; *firio*=Lat. *vir*, a man); thou art (be'st) on the (*them*) high heaven kingdom (*rikie*, rick); blessed be (*si*) thy name word all (every word); come thy powerful kingdom; become (German *werden*) thy will over world; all so same on earth, so (as) there up is (as it is up there) in the high heaven rick. Give us day every (each day) bread, Lord the good (one), thy holy help. (It must be constantly kept in mind that *uu = w*).

Thu bist thie uuaro, quat Petras, uuialdendes suno, libbiandes Godes, the thit lioht gi-schop (shaped), *Crist cuning euuig* (ever) — thou be'st the true (*waro*), quoth Peter, pre-vailing son (of the) living God, that this light (*lioht*) made (made this light), Christ king eternal (*ewig*).

Hluttro habis thu an thinan herton gi-lobon— sincere have thou on thy heart belief (Ger. *glauben*); *gi-frumide mid uuordun endi mid uuercun*—formed (performed) with words and with works; *endi* (and) *mid iro handon scriben an buok*—

and with their (*iro*) hands (to) write in book; *helagna* (healing) *gest* (ghost) — holy spirit.

The liudi stuodun unbi — the people (German *leute*) stood around (by); *hie gi-sah thar after* — he saw there after (*gi, chi, ge*, is often found with the past tense as a prefix here, while it belongs to the part. alone in German); *hie sprak him mid is uuorden tuo* — he spoke (to) him with his words to; *ik is engil beon* — I his angel am (been); *thina dadi sind* — thy deeds are; *thie guodo gumo* — the good man (Lat. *homo*).

So uuit an uncro juguthi — so we (two) in our youth: *hel uuis* (was) *thu* — hail be (was) thou; *thu scealt furi allon uuesan uuibon giuuihid* — thou shalt (be-) fore all be (was) wives blessed (before all wives); *huo mag that gi-uuerthan so* — how may that be-come so; *gi-sahan endi gi-horean* — (to) see and (to) hear; *thit ist mahtig thing* — this is mighty thing.

Dhuo ir (he) *himilo garuuida dhar uuar ih* — when he heaven pre-pared there was I; *chi-chundit* = known, acquainted, *chi-scaffanes ist* = created is (shaped); *chi-holan ist fona manno angom* — con-cealed is (it is) from men's eyes (*chi* = *ge*-); *chiburt* = birth, *chi-boran*, born; *Got chi-scuof mannan* — God made man; *chi-frumida dhen* — (he) formed him; *chi-deda* (did) *mih* — made me.

Gotes gheizt ist sprehendi dhurah mih — God's spirit is speaking through me; *vuip, obe thu vuissis* — woman (wife) if thou wist; *vuielih Gotes gift ist* — what God's gift is; *veiz ih daz du war* (true) *segist* — know I that thou true sayest.

Unde dir sinemo (his) *boden, vuanda ih sundic bin, ioh in ge-dahidon ioh in vuorden* — and (to) you his messenger, since I sinning am, both in thoughts and in words; *ih chi-sah*, I saw; *ih gi-sahi, gi-herte*, I said, heard; *so waz so ih uuidar gotes uuillen gi-tati*, so who so (what-so-ever) I against God's will did (*widar* = Latin *iterum*, our with = against).

Nu auh huuer mac dhesiu stimna uuesan (be) — now of who (whose) may this voice be? *ih quhimu* — I come; *chi-sendit*, sent; *chi-deda*, made; *chindh uuirdit uns chi-boran, sunu uuirdit uns chi-gheban* — (a) child (Ger. *kind*) becomes (to) us born, (a) son becomes (to) us given; *suueri bi Gote* — swear by God; *dhine daga ar-fullide uuerdhant* — thy days fulfilled were; *themo selueme cide* — (at) the same time; *thuruhc salichedi selu sineru* — through (for) health (safety) (of) soul his (his soul).

Athe vane andern thie theru selvern vuizzidi leven theru er selvo levitt — or (other) from others that (*thie*) (by) the same (self) law live (by) which (*theru*) he (him-)self lives; *thaz er habe allicha gi-lauba* — that he have all-like (catholic) belief (*gi* = be).

637. Much of what we have now given would be classed with

the old Saxon, but we must observe that it is difficult to draw a line between old Saxon and old High German. There is a great resemblance in the orthography, the words being often identical. We notice the following differences; the German person endings are *-u, -is, -it; -ames, -at, -ant*, but in Saxon they are *-u, -is, -id; -ad, -ad, -ad;* Ger. inf. ending is *-an*, prest. part. *-ant-er*, past part. *-an-er*, but Saxon inf. *-an*, part. *-and*, part. *-an';* the case endings do not materially differ.

638. It is worthy of remark, that in both these languages (or dialects) the endings of nouns and verbs resemble those of Latin much more than the endings of the present German do, and they have, besides, more words like Latin, and English, in orthography; thus, in old High German we find *hreini*, pure, serene; *kiri*, greedy; *reiti*, ready (L. *pa-ratus*); *lindi*, s-lender, thin (L. *le-nis*); *peraht*, bright; *klao* (L. *callidus*) skillful; *klat* L. *laetus*), glad; *vruot* (L. *prudens*), prudent; *luoken*, to look; *spreitan*, to spread; *tueljan*, dwell, delay; *scolan, scal*, shall; *scolta*, should; *chnahan*, to know — and the corresponding German words are *rein, gierig, be-reit, klein* and *schlank (klar), klug (froh), (vor-sichtig), (sehen), breiten, ver-weilen, sollen, sollte, kennen.*

639. From the old Saxon, we may introduce the following: *scado*, shade, Ger. *schatten; wac',* watch, Ger. *wach; hard,* hard, Ger. *hart; ward*, guard and ward, Ger. *wache* and *wehr; water,* water, Ger. *wasser.*

Ecid, acid, L. *acet-um;* Ger. *essig; sweban*, L. *somnium*, dream and sleep, Ger. *traum; heru*, sword, L. *gladius* (gld = hrd), Ger. *schwert; wiht*, (some-)thing, L. *quid*, Ger. *et-was.*

Mikil, much, L. *magnus*, Ger. *manche; thimm*, dim, Ger. *dunkel; scip*, ship (c = h), Ger. *schiff; lith*, limb, L. *memb-rum,* Ger. *g-lied; worold*, world, Ger. *welt*, L. *mundus* (m = w); *toth,* tooth, L. *dens*, Ger. *zahn.*

Lud, look (face), Ger. *ant-litz; gumo*, man, L. *homo*, Ger. *mensch; juguth*, youth, L. *juventus, juvend* (Ger.); *cumbal,* cymbal, L. *signum*, Ger. *zeichen; brastjan*, burst, Ger. *bersten; muth*, mouth, Ger. *mund; dad*, deed, Ger. *that*, L. *fact-um.*

Wapan, weapon, Ger. *waffe; seola*, soul, L. *(anima)*, Ger. *seele; wreth*, wrath, L. *iratus*, Ger. *wuth; mester*, master, L. *magister*, Ger. *meister* (e = a = ag = ei); *suet*, sweat, L. *sudor,* Ger. *schweiss; hlot*, lot, L. *fors*, Ger. *loos; grot*, great, Ger. *gross; bom*, beam (tree), Ger. *baum*, o = ea, au.

Hobid, head, L. *caput*, Ger. *haupt* (o = ea, a, au, and *bid, put, pt = dd, did, d*); *gruri*, horror (g = h), Ger. *grau-en*, gray, hoary, (also Ger. *schauer*, shower, shiver, shudder, dread); *hliop*, leap, Ger. *laufen*, L. *curro* (cr. = hr = h); *simnen*, ever, L. *semper*, Ger. *immer.*

Wurt, root, L. *rad-ix*, Ger. *wurz-el*; *ertha*, earth, L. *terra*, Ger. *erde*; *morth*, murd-er, Ger. *morden*; *thiob*, thief, Ger. *dieb*; *hros*, horse, Ger. *ross*; *her*, cl-ear, Ger. *hell*.

Quic, quick (q-vick), L. *vivus*, Ger. *leben* (lb = vv); *garu*, ready and prepared, L. *paratus*, G. *bereit*, *gar*; *kuth*, ac-quainted, L. *notus* (for *gnotus*), Ger. *kund*; *suot*, sweet, Ger. *süss*; *suar*, severe, L. *gravis* (sur, svr, vr = grv, rv, vr), Ger. *schwer* (s-ch = s-k, s-g).

Blithi, b-lithe, L. *lætus*, Ger. *lustig*; *crumb*, crumb and crimp, L. *curvus* (cr-v, cr-vm, cr-um, cr-imp), Ger. *krumm*; *cvic*, quick, L. *vivus*; *suepu*, sweep and brush, L. *verro* (su = s-v, v), Ger. *fegen* (fg, vg, vp).

Hropu, call, L. *clamo*, Ger. *rufen* (hrp = clp, clm; h-rp = rf); *radu*, per-suade, L. *suadeo*, Ger. *rath*; *faru*, fare, (go), L. *fore*, were, L. *vado*; *skaku*, shake, L. *quatio* (skk, shk = kt, kk, qt), *schütteln*; *gripu*, gripe and grasp, L. *arripio* (arr = gr), Ger. *ergreifen*.

Writu, write, L. *scribo*, Ger. *schreiben*; *scridu*, L. *gradior*, stride, Ger. *schreiten*; *hnigu*, kneel, L. *in-clino* (cln = nl, knl), Ger. *knien*; *luku*, lock, close, L. *claudo*, Ger. *sch-loss*; *tiuhu*, tow, L. *traho* (tr = t), Ger. *ziehen*; *biddu*, beg, bid, L. *peto*, Ger. *beten*, *bitten*; *deljan*, deal, L. *dividere* (dlj = dlv, dv), Ger. *theilen*; *hlinon*, incline (hl = cl); *copon*, get, Ger. *kaufen*.

640. We will next give the following specimens of old German poetry. They will afford a fair idea of the way the ancient Germans, in common with the whole of northern Europe, expressed their thoughts, and an idea, too, of the peculiar vein in which those thoughts are found to run. The lines are taken from a poem supposed to belong to the 9th century.

Einan kuning uueiz ih — A king knew I,
Heizsit her hluduig — called Herr Ludwig,
Ther gerno gode thionot — that willing God tend (served);
Ih uueiz her imos lonot — I know he him reward;
Kind uuarth her faterlos — (while a) child were he fatherless.
Thes uuarth imo sar buoz — this was (to) him soon redressed;
Holoda inan truhtin — favored him (the) Lord (did),
Magaczogo uuarth her sin — (his) leader became he his;
Gab her imo dugidi — gave he him virtue (he gave)
Fronisc githigini — and noble servants (people);
Stual hier in urankon — (a) throne here in France,
So bruche her es lango — so use he it long (time);
Thaz gideilder thanne — that divide-he then (he did)
Sar mit karlemanne — soon with Carloman,
Bruoder sinemo — (a) brother (of) his,
Thia czala uuunniono — the (a) great joy (to both).
* * * * * * * *

Koron uuolda sin God — try (him) would his God,
Ob her arbeidi — whether he labor
So iung tholon mahti — so young bear might (could bear it);
Lietz her heidine man — (then) let he heathen man
Obar seo lidan — over (the) sea come (lead).
This is considered a specimen of old High German.

641. We add a few extracts from another Old German poem, called "*Der Nibelunge Not.*" Its great resemblance to old English will be easily observed; indeed, its style is not German.

Do wuohs in Niderlanden — there grew (wax) in Netherland
Eins richen küneges kint — a rich king's son (child);
Des vater hiez Sigemunt — the father (was) called Sigemunt.
Sin muoter Sigelint, — (And) his mother Sigelint,
In einen bürye riche — in a (one) burg rich (a rich one),
Witen wol be-kannt — wide, well known (ac-quaint)
Niden bi dem Rine — Down (neath) by the Rhine,
Diu was ze Santen genant — It was to Santen named.
* * * * * * *
So bin ich dines willen — So am I (of) thy will
Waerlichen vro — Truly (verily) glad
Und wil dirz helfen enden — and will thee (it) help accomplish
So ist aller beste kan, — So I all best can (the best I can),
Doch hat der künic Gunther — Though has the king Gunther
Vil manege hoch vertigen man — full many (a) valiant man.
* * * * * * *
Welt ir den künic vinden — Will you the king find,
Daz mac vil wol geschehen — That may full well happen (be);
In jenem sale witen — in that hall wide
Han ich in gesehen — have I him seen,
Bi den sinen helden — By the his heroes;
Da sult ir hine gan — There shall you (to) him go.
* * * * * * *
"*Das tuon ich,*" *sprach Hagne* — "That do I," said Hagne,
Zeinem venster er do gie — (To) his window he then went,
Sin ougen er da wenken — His eyes he there (let) waver,
Zuo den gesten lie; — To the strangers (he) let (them);
Wol behagte im ir geverte — Well pleased him their trappings,
Und ouch ir gewant — And eke their garment (pleased).
Si waren im vil vremde — They were (to) him full strange
In der Burgunden lant — In the Burgundy land.
* * * * * * *
Ir ros diu sint schoene — Their horse they are shiny (pretty),
Ir kleider harte guot — Their clothes hard good;
Von swannen sie koment — From whence they came,
Si sint helde hoch gemuot — They are heroes (of) high mind.

Also sprach do Hagne — So spoke then Hagne,
"*Ich wil des wol verjehen* — I will this well confess,
Swie ich nie mere — So (though) I never more
Sivriden habe gesehen — Sivriden have seen,
So wil ich wol gelouben — Yet (so) will I well believe
Swie ez dar umbe stat — so (that) it there of stands,
Daz ez si der recke — That it is that hero
Der dort so herlichen gat — Who there so lordly goes."

The words are pure German, but with a tendency in orthography to the simplicity of the old English.

642. FRIESIC.—The old Friesic was spoken a long time since by the Frisons of the Rhine, extinct since about the 16th century. It very closely resembles the Anglo-Saxon, and was intimately related to it, as well as to the Icelandic and old Saxon.

There is the modern Friesic, still the language of a portion of the German race, in Friesland and elsewhere; even this is again divided into different sections or dialects.

643. Under the term Netherlandish, may be included two forms, varying slightly, of one and the same dialect of the great German language — the Flemish, or Flandrish, and the Hollandish, or Dutch. They constitute a class running parallel with the Friesic, and identical with it in almost every essential point — save variation in orthography. A brief notice of the Dutch will suffice to give a general idea of the peculiarity of the whole.

644. Notwithstanding all the similarity between the Dutch and German in their natures, there is yet considerable difference in the appearance they present. The Dutch construction and composition of words is entirely German, but the orthography is as decidedly English, rather English, however, in its older days — what of the Dutch is not either German or English, is a very small portion of it; so that for an English scholar understanding German, the task of acquiring the Dutch is very short and easy, not to say pleasing also.

645. A few examples will illustrate these facts: *Voorts meen ik, insgelijks, als regel te kunnen stellen* — further think (mean) I, likewise, as (a) rule to can give (that I can give as a rule); *ge-lijk-ook de daarvan af-ge-leide* (off-lead) *naam-woorden* — like also (*ook*, eke) the therefrom derived name-words (nouns). *Om het bepalend lidwoord in het Makassaarsch uit te drukken* — for the limiting (be-paling) article (limb-word) in the Maccassar out to press (for, *to press out* (express) the limiting article).

Dikwijls ook treft men zelfstandige naam-woorden an — thickwhiles (often) also meets one (one meets, hits) independent (self-standing) name-words on (*treffen-an = an-treffen*, strike on, hit).

Het onderscheid tuss-chen beide formen — the difference (under-cut, sever) twixt both (*beide*) forms; *dat er een zekere nadruk op het woōrd valt* — that there (*er*, Ger. *gar, dar*) a (an) certain (secure) force (strike, blow) up (on) the word falls; *hetzij door aan-hechting van letter-grepen* — it-be (al-beit) through on-fixing of syllables (letter-groups).

Ook tot beteren ver-stande der oude schryvers is de kennis der dialekten hoogst ge-wigtig — and for-the (*tot*, to, till) better understanding of-the (*der*) old writers (scribers) is the knowledge (of) the dialects highest important (weighty).

De enkele consonanten klinken zoo als men ze uit een zuiver nederlandschen mond hoort — the single consonants sound (cling) so as one them (*ze*) out (of) a pure (sure, sober) Netherlandish mouth hears (sound as one hears them from a). *Het scheelde weinig of hy was dood ge-weest* — it wanted (lacked) little but (or) he was dead been (as we would say, a little more and he had been dead, or killed).

Ik zal 't hem doen doen — I shall it him make do (do do = make do); *hy zal hem nooit konnen doen werken* — he shall him never can (be able) to-make work (never make him work); *de gene die ons kwamen zien* — the ones that (the, which) us came to-see (came to see us) (*gene*, written *geen*, is Ger. *kein* = none, our *any, one* — it has the force also of *which*).

Zie of (if) *hy dat ge-daan hebbe* — see if (whether) he that done has (has done that); *Ik doe het eens-deels om de vriendschap te onderhouden, en ander-deels om niet leeg te zitten* — I do it partly (one-parts) for-to the friendship to uphold (underhold), and on-other-hand (other-parts), for-to (*om*) not idle (Ger. *ledig*, void, lazy) to sit (for not to sit idle).

Zo gy my (me) *de eer wilt gunnen u altemets te zien* — so (if) you (thou) me the honor will grant (give), you alltimes (sometimes) to see (to see you sometimes). *De ziekte is erger* (worse) *dan men denkt* — the sickness is worse than one thinks. *Het ys boog* (bow-ed) *onder onze voeten* — the ice bend-ed under our feet (foots).

One single example (John xx, 2) will suffice to compare the Dutch and German, as to appearance — and first the German: *Da läuft sie, und kommt zu Simon Petro, und zu dem andern jünger, welchen Jesus lieb hatte, und spricht zu ihnen: Sie haben den herrn weggenommen aus dem grabe; und wir wissen nicht, wo sie ihn hingelegt haben.*

(Dutch): *Zij liep dan, en kwam tot Simon Petrus, en tot den anderen discipel, dien Jezus lief had, en zeide tot hen: Zij hebben den Heere weggenomen uit het graf, en wij weten niet, waar zij hem ge-legd hebben.* (Translated): Shé ran (leap) then, (Ger., then leaped she), and came to Simon Peter, and to the other disciple, that (*dien*, the, which) Jesus dear had (held dear), and (*en*) said to them: They have the Lord way-taken out (of) the grave, and we wot (know) not where they him laid have (have laid him).

646. SWISS IDIOM.—We will next dwell briefly on the Swiss form of the German. It is spoken in the greatest part of Switzerland, and is found in several dialects. It is particularly interesting from some of the peculiar forms which its words present. It is evidently German, but German with a ruling tendency to identify itself in orthography with the English. The German article *ein* is here reduced, as with us, to one letter, *e*, *a*; *I* is *i*; *em* and *im*, Ger. *ihm*, our *him*; *e* is acc. of our *he*; our, Ger. *unser*, is here *use*, *euse*, *eus*, *us*; from-us is *von-us*, prep. united with pronoun, as we often find it elsewhere; *you*, in the oblique cases, is *ech*, *uch*, *uwe*, Ger. *euch*—in the nom. of this pron., we find the forms *der*, *er*, *ier* (*i-er*, as if we said *ye-r*, Ger. *ihr*); *de* is for Ger. *den* and *der*, our *the*; also *da*, as *da stier won-i g-chauft ha*—the (that) steer which-I (*wo* = which) bought have (which I bought); *mi*, Ger. *mein*, our *my*; *wele*, Ger. *welcher*, L. *qualis* and *ille*; *de ma won-i gseh hab*—the man whom-I seen have;—there is a general tendency to slight the final *n* and *m*, as in *ma* for *man*.

Er hed, he has, Ger. *hat*; *mer hand*, we have, Ger. *haben* and *habend*; *i ha g-ha*, I have had (G. *ge-habt*); *mer si*, we are, G. *wir sind*; *i bi g-si*, I be (am) been (G. *ge-wesen*); *si*, be, G. *sein*; *i will*, or *i wolt*, I will, or would; *give* is *ga*, or *gah*, G. *geben*; *mer gend*, we give, G. *gebend*; for *go*, with *I*, we find the forms, *gan*, *ga*, *gah*, *goh*, *gange*; *er gat*, and *er gohd*, or *geit*, he goes (he go-ed); Ger. *kommen*, to-come, is here *cho* = *go*; *i bi cho*, I be gone, have gone (go).

647. We notice, here, many beautiful illustrations of the fact that every part or person of the verb presents one of its simple forms, and that the form which we find with one application in one language, is found in a very different place in another; thus, here, *er leit* (or *lait*), he lies, in form equals *he laid*; *er seid* (or *said*), he says (said); *i gan* (or *gange*), I go (gone, going); *i wott*, I will (would); *i bi*, I am (be); *er lobt*, he praises (praised); *gang*, impera. go (going). So we see, again, that the past tense, or any other part of the verb, is quite identical with the present.

This language presents, too, many excellent illustrations of one letter representing two or more condensed, latent; thus, *ch-o*, (go) = Ger. *k-ommen*; *i ligge* (G. *liegen*, lie), and *er lit* (li-es), hence *lit* is for *liggit* (iggi, iyyi, iiii, i); so Ger. *haben* is *ha* (*aben*, *aven*, *auen*, *aee*, *a*); *er git*, he gives, Ger. *giebt* (ieb = i) (give = go).

648. We will next add a list of a few of its most peculiar or instructive words:

A and *aa* (brook, river), Ger. *b-ach*, L. *amnis*, Icel. *aa; auw, ow*, L. *ovis*, our *ewe, sh-eep; baa, pa,* Ger. *vater*, father; *däsig*, tame, still, L. *taceo ; dolen,* L. *tollo*, Icel. *dol*, G. *dulden*, *en-dure; trant* (course, step), train, Du. *trant* = pace, tread, tramp, Ger. *schritt ; dur,* through ; *engen,* alone, one, Ger. *ein; eppis,* (something), Ger. *etwas ; eren,* Ger. *ackern,* acre, ear, L. *aro* = till; *gell*, yell, G. *schall; glaren,* to glare, g-lance, look; *gropp,* crop, top, head, Ger. *kopf; lüpfen,* lift, heave, L. *levo*, Dan. *lofte* (loft); *lustig*, lovely, lusty ; *lützel*, little, Du. *luttel*, Go. *leitil*, Ger. *k-lein ; mar* and *mor*, Dan. *mor*, Fr. *meur* and *mur*, L. *maturus* (*matur* = *maur, mur*).

649. There are, besides, many other forms, or dialects, of German as it is now spoken in Europe; but to notice fully their many instructive features, would require a moderate-sized volume. Many of them differ from the present standard German but slightly, and others vary from it as much, perhaps, as the Swiss form just noticed. There are, among others, the Bavarian, Austrian, Tyrolese, Thuringian, Transylvanian, and Jewish.

650. The following is from the dialect of Augsburg: *Fother onser, daehr* (Ger. *der*) *duh bischt em Hemmel; Gehoyligt weard deih nahm; zua ons kumm daih Raich; Daih will g-scha wi em Hemmel, atz och auf earde; Onsär deklich broad gib ons heint* (Ger. *heute*); *Ond vergiab ons onsr schuld, als wihr vergäba onsärn schuldigärä; Ond führ* (Ger. *führ*) *ons nitt ind versuachong; Sunderän er-loas* (loose) *ons vom ibel. Denn dain ischt däs raich, ond dia krafft, ond dia härlikoit in ewikoit*—Father our, who (the) thou be'st (art) in Heaven; holied were (be) thy name; to us come thy kingdom (*rick*); thy will be (Ger. *ge-schehen*) as in heaven, as also upon (*auf*) earth; our day-ly (daily) bread give us to-day (this); and forgive us our guilt, as we forgive our debtors; and lead us not into (*ind*) temptation; but (Ger. *sondern*) free us from evil. For thine is the rick, and the power, and glory in eternity (ever).

651. In the Bavarian form, we find, *keiligt werd*, holy, hallowed, be; *zu-kumme uns*, come (to) us; *gihw uns heind*, give us to-day (*heute*); *unsre schulln* (our shalls), our debts, guilts; *von alln ihblamm*, from all evil (blame). In Transylvanian: *zau-kom aus deing rekch* —to-come (come) us thy kingdom; *deing uell ge-schey aff* (*auf*) *jerden*—thy will be on earth; *briut gaff aus heigd*— bread give us to-day; *auser schuld,* our debt; *mier fergien* — we forgive; *fier aus net*— lead us not; *erlüs aus von dem üwell*— loose us from the evil.

These are as great differences (from common German) as we usually find in these dialects, and we easily see they are confined to mere orthographic variations.

652. GOTHIC.—The Gothic is a German language, but German in a somewhat peculiar form. It may be placed alongside with the other two branches of the great German family, the High German and the Low German, not running parallel and independent of them, but rather in a line converging with them the farther back we press into the shades of antiquity. Grimm takes the Gothic as the base of German, but it is only so because it is older than the rest, or that we have learlier records of it. It stands nearer to the High and Low German (with which, especially the former, it is easily compared) than to the old North, or Scandinavian.

653. It was the language spoken by people known in history as the Visigoths, the Ostrogoths, and the Moesogoths. Gothic is a very indefinite term—as the Goths are, for us, a very indefinite people. Goth was a favorite name with the Romans, to apply to wild hordes to the north of them. These Goths seem, too, to have been especially a progressive, a moving people. They made their settlements not only in the whole south of Europe, but we in time find Goths in Spain and in Italy. In later times, they seem to be more particularly located in the north of Europe. Indeed, it is claimed that the Germans and the Scandinavians belong to the Gothic stock, that they are descendants, that is, a continuation, of the Goths, or that they have commingled with them, the Goths. The term Gothic, finally, is often used as a convenient word to denote the German and Scandinavian combined.

654. The Moeso-Goths have the greatest importance for us, they being by far the best known to us by their writings; Moeso-Gothic is often (generally) denoted by the term Gothic alone, it being the Gothic with which we are acquainted—it has been considered by some, and with some plausibility, as being the original of High German.

655. The oldest specimen not only of the Gothic, but older also than any other Germanic idiom, is the Gothic translation of the gospels by Ulfilas, the bishop of Moesia, supposed to have been made about the year 370. Some specimens from that translation will best illustrate the character of that language, as compared with our own and with other German tongues.

656. First, the beginning of the 7th chapter of John: *Jah warboda Jesus afar thata in Galcilaia; ni auk vilda in Judaia gaggan, unte sokidedun ina thai Judaieis usqiman*—and walked Jesus after that in Galilee; not for (for not) would (he) in Judea go (*gang*, going), for (and) (they) sought him (*ina*), the Judeans (did), to-kill (him), (*us-qiman*, over-come).

Thanuh quethun du imma brothrjus is—then quoth (said) to him brothers his (his brethren); *us-leith thathro jah gagg* (*gang*) — depart (out-lead) hence (thither), and go (*gang*). (So the Scotch say, where are you *gangen?*)

Ni mag so manaseths (the world) *fijan izvis* (you), *ith* (but) *mik fijaith*— not may (cannot) the men hate you but me (it) hateth (men hate me, not you); *thatuh than qath du im, visands in Galeilaia*— this when (he had) said to them (*im*), being (dwelling, as he did) in Galilee (when he had said these things to them); *ith ik kann ina, unte fram imma im, jah is mik insandida*— but (and) I know (*ken*, acquaint) him, for (*unte*) from him (I) am, and he me sent (me).

Vas Johannes daupjands — was John dipping (he was baptizing); *at-gibans varth*— up-given were (were given up); *qemun than motarjos daupjan* — came then publicans to-baptize (to be baptized) (prest. inf. often for pass.)

657. There are, as has been already suggested, strong likenesses between the Gothic and High German, as well as between the Gothic and Low German; and yet, notwithstanding the impossibility of measuring quantity in such cases, we feel constrained to say, in comparing these tongues, that the Gothic is more like the Low German, the Saxon, the English, than the High German, the literary German of the present day.

658. First, the style, the expression, is rather Low German than modern German. From Mark i. 8, we take the following: *Aththan ik daupja izvis in vatin, ith is daupeith izvis in ahmin veih-amma* — And (for) I dip you in water, but he dip-eth (dips) you (*izvis*) in (the) ghost holy (I baptize, but he will with holy ghost). In German it reads: I dip you with water, but he will you with the holy ghost dip (baptize); 11th verse, *jah stibna qam us himinam; thu is sunus meins sa liuba, in thuzei vaila galeikaida* — and (a) voice came out (*us*) heaven: Thou art (is) son (of) mine the (be-)loved, in whom (that) well (I am) delighted. In German: There was (came) a voice from heaven, thou art my dear son, on whom I well-pleasing have.

Jah suns sa ahma ina ustauh in authida — and soon the spirit (Fr. *ame*) him drove (out-towed, out-lead), into (the) wilderness (Ger. *wüste*). In German: and soon drove him the spirit (did) into the waste (wilderness).

659. And next we find many words which are more like English, for example, than German, as the following list will demonstrate—1st Goth., 2d Ger., 3d Eng.: *aftu, nach,* after; *aibr, gabe,* offer; *air, fruh,* ere; *airtha, erde,* earth; *aivs, zeit,* age, L. *ævum; akvila, adler,* eagle.

Baurd, bret, broad; *beitan, beissen,* bite; *bugjan, kaufen,* buy; *dags, tag,* day; *deds, that,* deed; *dails, theil,* deal; *divan,. sterben,* die; *diups, tief,* deep.

Dumbs, stumm, dumb; *d-vola, naar,* fool; *fairra, fern,* far; *fotus, fuss,* foot; *fodeins, speise,* food.

Gaits, *ziege*, goat; *karan*, *sorgen*, care; *hairto*, *herz*, heart; *halts*, *lahm*, halt; *hauhs*, *hoch*, high.

Lamb, *lamm*, lamb; *letan*, *lassen*, let; *liban*, *leben*, live; *leiks*, *gleich*, like; *lithus*, *glied*, limb; *lukan*, *schliessen*, look.

Man, *mensch*, man; *managei*, *menge*, many; *maurthr*, *mord*, murder; *mikils*, *viel*, much; *raihts*, *recht*, right; *rums*, *raum*, room.

Sair, *schmerz*, sore; *silan*, *schweigen*, silent; *skadus*, *schatten*, shade; *sleps*, *schlaf*, sleep; *sliuthan*, *gleiten*, slide; *suns*, *bald*, soon; *svistar*, *schwester*, sister, (suister).

Taikns, *zeichen*, token; *triu*, *boum*, tree; *tungo*, *zunge*, tongue; *tunthus*, *zahn*, tooth; *van*, *mangel*, want; *viljan*, *wollen*, will; *vothis*, *süss*, sweet; *viko*, *woche*, week.

We must, of course, strike off the final *s*, as the representative of the Latin gender ending, *us*, *a*, *um*. To this list we add the following interesting forms, without any particular reference to the question in view.

660. *Airzis*, err, German *irre*; *aithei*, mother; *aiws*, *aiwus* (horse), L. *equus*; *alev*, oil; *ana-leiko*, Ger. *ähnlich*, like, one-like; *anda-vaurdi*, answer, Ger. *ant-wort* (on-word); *ansts*, Ger. *gunst*, *gnade*, grace, thank; *ara*, Ger. *adler*, eagle; *augjan*, show, Ger. *zeige-n*, and *augo* = eye,—hence we see *eye* = see, look, show; *auknan*, wax, (grow), L. *augeo*; *aurahi*, g-rave; *aurkeis*, Ger. *k-rug*, c-rock; *auths*, Ger. *wüst*, waste; *avi*, ewe, sh-eep; *awa*, *w-asser*, L. *aqua*.

Bai, both, Ger. *beide*; *bairan*, Ger. *tragen*, drag, carry, bear; *bairhts*, bright; *baitrs*, bitter; *balvs*, evil, base; *batan* (good), better; *bi-aukan*, w-ax, in-crease.

Faur-thei, fear, Ger. *furcht*; *fra-liusan*, Ger. *ver-lieren*, lose (*fra* = from = *ver*); *freis*, free, fresh; *frijonds*, friend; *friks* (greedy), L. *a-varus*.

Hnaivs, be-neath, Ger. *niedrig*; *hropi*, Ger. *ruf*, report; *in-veiten*, *an-beten*, in-vite; *juk* = yoke, and *jiukan* = fight, con-quer — so we say to *join* in battle, to match (G'k *makomai* = to fight), to equal, and we get the idea of strife, contest, from that of union, joining; every union implies two things united, as well as contest, fight, does.

Kas, cask, Ger. *gefäss*; *kaurs*, Ger. *schwer*, L. *gravis*, heavy; *kavtsjo* is the way they spell *caution*.

Laigaion is their orthography for *legion*; *laisjan*, Ger. *lehren*, learn, L. *doceo*, teach, d = l; *leisan*, learn, lesson; *luban*, (love) = hope.

Magus = boy, Celt. *mac*, maid; *mais*, more, L. *majus*, *magis* (*mayis*); *meljan* = write, Ger. *malen* = paint; *mins*, Ger. *wenig* (less); *nagaths*, naked, Ger. *nackt*; *new* = near, Ger. *nahe*.

Qums (comes), Ger. *an-kunft* (on-come), arrival; *reiks*, prince, L. *regis*; *sa-wazuh* (the-what) = each, *s-was* in old Ger., *et-was* in Ger.; *siggqan*, sink (gg=ng); and *siggvan* is sing (and read); *silubr*, silver; *sinthan* (= go), send; *sitts*, Ger. *sitz*, seat, saddle, Ger. *stuhl* (*situhl*); *siuks*, sick, Ger. *sch-wach*, weak, s = w; *skath*, Ger. *schaden*, scath; *s-kevjan*, go, scud; *slavan*, still, (sly); *snivan* = go, come; *staiga*, way, st = w; *s-vers*, worth. *Triggvs* (*triuuvs*) true; *thiuth*, good; *th-vahan*, wash; *vaihts* (thing), what, Ger. *et-was*; *vair*, man, L. *vir*; *vaurd*, word, Ger. *rede*, read; *vcitan* (see), L. *video*; *vitan*, wit, know; *vizon*, live, L. *vivo*; *vopjan*, whoop (call); *v-raton*, ride (go).

We must not omit to observe that there are also many Gothic words which are German and not English.

661. SCANDINAVIAN: The Scandinavian (or North) language constitutes a large and important part of the great German or Gothic family. The three leading branches of this division are the Icelandic, the Danish, and the Swedish; indeed, if we count in the dialects of these, especially of the two latter, we shall have, substantially, all there is of Scandinavian.

662. These languages did not become individualized until after the 14th or 15th centuries; before that time, they were merged in what is called the Old North; or, turning to the descending side, the Old North gave birth to these modern dialects. The best representative of that old idiom is the Icelandic. Living far away on their distant island, the Icelanders have been little affected by the culture of the continent, and have scarcely yet, as makers of language, been warmed into life. It may not be amiss to remind the reader of the great resemblance between the Icelandic and our own, especially the old English, and the parallel which we can draw between it and the Gothic. It is claimed as a matter of history, and it is certainly very probably from the location, that the ancestors of these islanders were Norwegian colonists. Certain it is, the Norwegian, or a great portion of it (for it, too, has its varieties), is a dialect very closely connected with the Icelandic. Taken as a whole, the Norwegian has a distinct character as compared with the Danish or Swedish, and differs from them considerably; yet that difference lies chiefly in the variation of orthography—the grammar being the same.

The language of the Faroe Islands is a dialect with some distinguishing peculiarities.

663. We will treat more fully of the Swedish and Danish, and after them the Old North, and that will suffice to give a general idea of the Scandinavian peculiarities.

664. To the student who is acquainted with both English and German, the acquisition of Danish and Swedish is exceedingly

easy, so little does he find in them that he does not readily recognize as either English or German. The general appearance, the cast, of Swedish and Danish, is rather English, rather Saxon, than modern High German; the style, the idiom, with some exceptions, is not German but English. Yet, notwithstanding the orthography of the language is decidedly English, when considered generally, there are many words which are as decidedly German and not English, as the following forms will illustrate :

Angenäm, angenehm, agreeable (first Swed., next Ger.); *anlete, antlitz,* countenance; *begär, begierde,* desire; *befäl, befehl,* command (befail); *be-röm, ruhm,* renown; *betala, bezahlen,* pay; *bo, wohnen,* dwell (hide); *fara, ge-fahr,* peril; *fogel, vogel,* bird (fowl); *färdig, fertig,* ready; *knappt, knapp,* scarcely (tight); *kropp, körper,* body; *öyonblick, augenblick,* moment (eye-look).

665. A few specimens of the language will give something of an idea of its character, and we take up first the Swedish:

Jag önskar dig den gladjen, att se dina barn lyckliga — I wish thee the gladness, to (*att*) see thy (thine) children (thy born) lucky (prosperous); — *barn* is singular; one of the Swedish declensions has singular and plural alike.

Den soldat högaktar jag, som vågar (wages) *sitt liff för fäderneslandet* — the soldier high-respect I (*jag*), who risks his life for fatherland (I much respect him); *han älskar honom såsom sin egen son* — he loves (likes) him so-so (so-as) his (*sin*) own son.

Det blifver fyra år (year) *i morgon sedan* (sithen) *jag sjuknade* — it becomes (leaves, is) four year to (*i*, in) morrow since I sickened; *jag har lemnat dem ett nöjaktigt svar* — I have (*har*) given (let) them an (the) accurate (satisfactory) answer; *jag på-minner mig den omständigheten* — I remember me (be-mind me) the circumstance.

Jag såg henne kommande — I saw her coming; *det är fara om lifvet* — it are (there is) danger about (the) life; *vi sälja efter vigt* — we sell after weight; *jag tror, att du kan göra det* — I trust, that you can do (chore) it; *han kom gåendes* — he came going (on foot); *jag bad honom* (*att*) *låna mig sin bok* — I bade him (to) lend me his book (in Ger. (to) me his book to lend, while the Danish is precisely English). *Få personer hafva varit* (been) *begåfvade med så utmärkta* (out-marked) *själsförmögenheter* (souls-for-might-hood-er, soul-power), *som* (as) *Gustaf Adolph* — few persons have been endowed (begifted) with so remarkable soul-power as Gustav Adolph; *jag har köpt en häst* — I have bought (got) a horse, (in Ger., I have a horse bought).

666. DANISH : *Det var* (were) *en löverdag morgen, og netop den förste September, da den unge Russer meget tidlig rejste sig fra sit leje, i den hensigt at gaa* (to go) *ud, for at optage et par skidser af Albanersöens meest romantiske partier.*—It (*det*) was a Saturday morning, and (*og*) just (neat) the first September, that the young Russian much early (timely) raised (him-)self from (*fra*) his bed (L. *lectus*), in the view to go out, for to take (off-take) a pair (couple) sketches of Albanersen's most romantic parts.

En köbmand modtog (with-took) *en fem shillings-mynt, der ikke syntes ham at vaere* (to be, were) *aegte, og spurgde* (Ger. *fragen*) *derfor en sagförer, som gik* (*gang*, went) *forbi hans* (his) *butik, hvad han* (he) *meente om* (of) *den* — A merchant (buy-man) received a five-shilling-piece, that not seemed to-him to be pure (*aegte*), and asked therefore an attorney, that went by his shop (booth), what he thought (meant) about it (that).

I mange til-fuelde, hvor der i (in) *andre sprog vilde vaere brugt et adjectiv, bruges i Zulu sproget et substantiv* — in many cases, where there in other language would (*vilde*) be used an adjective, is-used (*bruges*, uses) in Zulu language a substantive.

Taelle (tell) *med fingrene, begyndende fra venstre haands, lille-finger, idet hver finger som er optagen i taellingen, raekkes ud* (stretches out)—count (they do) with fingers, beginning from left hand, little-finger, until (*idet*) every finger which (some) are (is) up-taken in counting, is-stretched out (*ud*);— *medens de övrige* (the overs) *forblive knyttede*—while the remaining (ones) leave (are left) knitted (shut); *ere ogsaa formede udaf* (out-of) *vedkommende* (with-coming) *begyndelser*— (they) are also formed out-of with-coming prefixes (beginners).

Skulle bruges—should (be) used; *tiderne kunne ind-deles* (deal, divide)—tenses can be-formed (can form, can form selves); *det er naeppe* (nip, Ger. *knapp*) *vaerd at se* — it is scarce worth to see; *jeg har et lille besög at gjöre i nabolauget*— I have a little visit to make in (the) neighborhood.

667. To show the great similarity between the Danish and Swedish, we will give the same verse used in German with Dutch. First Swedish :

Då lopp hon, och hom till Simon Petrus, och till den andra lärjungen, som Jesus älskade, och sade till dem; De hafwa tagit Herran bort utaf grafwen, och wi wete icke hwart de hafwa lagt honom.

Danish : *Da löb hun, og kom til Simon Peder, og til den anden discipel, hvilken Jesus elskede, og sagde til dem : De have bort-toget Herren af graven, og vi vide ikke, hvor de have lagt ham* — Then ran (leaped) she, and came to (till) Simon Peter, and to the other disciple, which Jesus liked, and said to them,

They (*de*) have taken Lord forth (away), (Dan. forth-taken) out-of (Dan. off, *eaf*) (the) grave, and we wot not (*ikke*) where they have laid him.

668. OLD NORTH: Speaking approximately, we may say that the Old North has the same relation to the modern Scandinavian languages, that the Anglo-Saxon, or Old English, has to the present English, or that any old language has to its living descendants. The Old North is abundant in its relics, both poetry and prose. Poetry, in the early centuries, of course predominates, and it possesses all of that laconic and quaint style which characterizes so preëminently the earliest productions of all northern Europe. Its mythological impress is also a striking fact; its tales of gods and of the deeds of gods, suffer not, in beauty and interest, in comparison with the long-admired history of the divinities of Rome and of Greece. This impress, which we have noticed, is one of a hundred forcible evidences that connect and combine the German of the North with the Classics of the South.

669. The oldest monument of the German-North languages, is the poem entitled "*Vaulu-Spa*," of a date uncertain to history, but supposed to belong between the 5th and 8th centuries. A few selections from it will give some idea of the features of composition in Old North, and some idea, too, of the comparative form of the words it contains:

Aund thau ne attu, oth thau ne hafdo — mind (L. *anima*), they not had, sense they no had; *lae ne laeti, ne litu gotha* — motion nor hearing, not face (look) (Ger. *antlitz*) good; *aund gaf Othinn, oth gaf Haenir* — mind gave Odin (he gave), sense gave Haenir; *lae gaf Lothr ok litu gotha* — motion gave Loder, and face (*litu*) good (also).

Ask veit-ek standa, heitir ygg-thrasill
Har-bathmr, ausinn hvitom auri;
Thathan koma dauggvar, thaers i dali falla;
Stendr aei groinn yfir Vrthar-brunni —
Ash knew-I (to) stand, hight Odins-horse,
Hair-tree, strewed (with) white dust;
Thence come dew (rain), that in dale fall,
Stands (it) ever green over Urthar-brunni.

Thrisvar brendu thrisvar borna,
Opt ok osialthan, tho hon enn lifir
Heithi hana hetu, hvars til husa kom —
Thrice burned (they) thrice born,
Oft and unseldom, though she yet live.
Heithi her (they) call, where (whose) to house come (to whose she came).

Ein sat hon uti, tha hinn aldni kom,
Yggiongr Asa, ok i augu leit;
Hvers fregnith mik, hvat freistith mik
Alone sat she out, there the old come
(The) king (of) Ases, and in eye (of him) looked;
What ask (you) me, why try (thou) me (of me?)

The following is a verse of another style, taken from another poem:

Fraemr mun ek seigia — farther will (mean) I say (tell)
Effirdar theigia — if (the) men (L. *vir*) (be) silent;
Fragom fleira — (we) learned more
Til frama theira — to (of the) journey (of) theirs;
Aestust undir — (were) made wounds (they were made),
Vith Jofurs fundir — by king's arrival;
Brusta brandir — strike (the) swords (did),
Vith blar randir — with (against) blue shields.

670. A selection from Freysgode's Saga:
Hrafnkell reid upp eptir Fljotsdalsheradi, ok sa hvar eydidalr gekk (went) *upp af Jökulsdal; sa dalr syndist* (seemed) *Hrafnkell byggiligri, enn adrir dalir, their sem hann hafdi adr set; en er Hrafnkell kom heim, beiddi hann födur sinn fjarskiptis, ok sagdist hann* (he) *bustad vilja reisa thar. Thetta veitir fadir hans hanum; ok hann görir boe i dal theim, ok kallar a Adalboli. Hrafnkell fekk* (took) *Oddbjargar, Skjaldulfs dottur, or* (out) *Laxardal; thau atta tva sonu: het* (hight) *hinn* (the) *ellri Thorir, en hinn yngri Asbjörn.*

En tha er Hrafnkell hafdi land numit at Adalboli, tha efldi hann blot mikit (much); *Hrafnkell let göra* (make) *hof mikit. Hrafnkell elskadi ekki annat* (no other) *god meir* (more) *enn* (than) *Frey, ok hanum gaf hann* (he) *alla hina beztu gripi sina* (his) *halfa vid sik. Hrafnkell byggdi* (dwelt, bide) *allan dalinn, ok gaf mönnum lond, en vildi tho vera yfirmadr theirra, ok tok godord yfir theim. Vid thetta var lengt nafn hans, ok kalladr freys-godi* — *ok var ujafnadarmadr mikill, en menntr vel.*

671. (Translated, word-for-word). Hrafnkell rode up through (after) Fljots-dals-pass, and saw (sa) that (where) (a) wastedale went up from Jökulsdale; that (the) dale seemed (to) Hrafnkell (more) dwellable, than (enn) other dales, those that (which) he had before (ere) seen (set); and when Hrafnkell came home, asked (bade) he father (of) his (for) goods-division (to divide the property), and saidest (that) he (his) dwellingplace (abode) will move there (would fix his abode there). That grants (the) father his (to) him (the father gives); and he made (a) dwelling (a bye) in dale that (one), and calls (it) to Adal-

boli. Hrafnkell married Odd., Sk's-daughter, from Lax.; they had two son; called the older Th, and the younger Asb.

And when there Hrafnkell had land taken at Ad, then (would) make he (an) offering (a) great (one). (H. let make offer-place (*hof*) great (one). Hrafnkell loved no other god more than Frey; and (to) him gave he all the best property (of) his half with self. Hrafnkell settled all (the) dales, and gave men land, and would then be (were) over-man (of) theirs (their governor), and took office-of-overseer (*godord*) over them. With that was long name (of) his (from that came his surname), and (is) called Freysgodi; and (he) was (an) unfair-man (very) much, but brave much (very brave, able).

672. A few lines of Danish will show how it compares with the above : *Hrafnkell red op gjennem Fljotsdalsherredet, og saa at en ode Dal gik op fra Jokulsdalen ; denne Dal syntes ham beboelligere end de andre dale, han jör havde seet. Men da han kom hjem, bad han sin Fader om at skifte Godset med sig, og sagde, at han vilde opslaa* (strike up, move) *sin Bolig hist.*

673. We conclude the subject of German languages by remarking, that to the philologist the most important members of the whole class are, besides the German proper, the Dutch, Danish, and Swedish, as they contain much of value, on the subject of his inquiry, which he will not find translated.

CHAPTER III.

CELTIC LANGUAGES.

674. The Celtic class of languages readily falls into two leading divisions : the first composed of the Welsh or Cymric, of Wales, the Cornish, of Cornwall, now extinct, and the Celt-Breton (Armorican), of Brittany, a province of France; and the second embracing the Scotch, or Gaelic, of the Highlands of Scotland, the Irish, or Erse, and the Manks language, of the Isle of Man. The term Cymric, or Welsh, is often used to denote the whole division to which that language belongs ; so, Gaelic is used to denote Scotch and Irish together; Erse is used in the same way by some; Erse is also applied to Scotch.

675. These two divisions have important features to distinguish them, and yet when we become thoroughly acquainted with them, we readily see that they are simply strongly-developed dialects of one and the same tongue. The Celtic idiom is, to the philological student, a subject of great interest. With all

the odd dress it wears, and the peculiar lines of direction it is sometimes found to take, we have only to become thoroughly acquainted with its true character and spirit, to perceive that it is not so strange as we have been wont to conceive it. We find that there is, after all, often cloaked in its own Celtic fashion, a remarkable identity with the English, French, and German idioms.

676. The most striking feature which impresses us on our first acquaintance with Celtic, is the strange orthography into which it shapes not alone its own but foreign words, and we have only to master that peculiar fashion which it has, in order to make the Celtic appear to us a very common and familiar idiom. The oddities of arrangement in its sentences, when we keep French as well as English in view, are by no means great. We find, it is true, particles piled on in greater profusion than we that are English might expect, though not so much greater than we find in many other languages which are not Celtic. We find the adjective, as in French and Semitic, very generally after the noun, though by no means uniformly in any of the different forms of Celtic, nor in all of them equally. The nominative is often after the verb, while it is generally before it with us. There are many other important differences, but which we must pass by entirely, or which will be observed in the selections which we are about to give. There is one very noticeable point, however, which we will dwell on here, a feature not by any means peculiar to the Celtic, for we find it well defined in French, in German, in Greek, and in many, if not, indeed, in all others — though perhaps nowhere so prominent as in Celtic; we refer to the change which a word undergoes (to adopt the current idea) to correspond with some other word connected with it, and either preceding it or following — thus, in Greek, *apo*, from, before some words, is written *aph*, and *kata*, *kath*; and *sun*, with, connected with a following *k* or *g* sound, becomes *sug* by assimilation. It is on this same principle that we find, in Celtic, *pen*, a head, alone and with *eu*, as *eu pen*, their head; but, with *dy*, as *dy ben*, thy head, *pen* changes to *ben*, and with *fy*, my, as *fy mhen*, it changes to *mhen*; and we find *ei phen*, her head; also, *brawd*, a brother, *dy frawd*, thy brother; *fy mrawd*, my brother; also the forms, *troed*, *droed*, *nhroed*, *throed*, (foot); and *ci*, *gi*, *nghi*, *chi* (dog) — according to their connections.

677. It will be observed that all these changes or mutations, are mere variations of cognate letters, that these variations are on the same principle as those which occur in compound words, or in the different parts of the same word. All variations in the end of words, in all languages, to denote tense, person, case, etc., arise from this same principle of assimilation between cog-

nate letters; it is regarded as certain that these mutations in Celtic may be taken as representations of the case relation, or case variation. We nowhere find stronger proof than this which we find in Celtic, of our position that all the letters of a word, all the letters of compound words, of words coming together in any way, are of the same nature, and continually tend to assimilate.

678. The following selections will serve to illustrate the character of the Celtic languages, and we take first the Welsh: *Prynodd y dyn geffyl*— bought the (*y*) man (did) (a) horse (Fr. *cheval*); *y dyn hwn* (this)—the man this (one). *Cododd y milwyr yn-erbyn eu cadpen* — rose the soldiers (did) a-gainst their (*eu*) captain. *Darllenwyd eich llythyr i-r aelodau* — was-read your (*eich*) letter (was) to-the members. *Pa* (what) *derfysg sydd yn y ddinas* — what disturbance is (Ger. *sind*, are) in the city (town); *gwelais ef*— I-saw him (*ef*); *a-welsoch chwi ef neu hi* — a-saw you (did you see) him or her?

Y gwr a-i wraig a-ddaethant — the man and-his (a-i) wife a-came (*a* is a common verb prefix, like the Ger. and G'k augment). *Galloch chwi a-ch* (and-your) *gwraig fyned* — can-you (you can) you and your wife go (mount, *fyned*); *daeth efe*— came he; *daethant hwy*—came they; *deg llyfr*— ten book; *Gwelais geffylau, a phrynais hwynt* — I-saw (some) horses, and I-bought them. *Yr-wyf yn credu ei bod yn gwawrio* — there-am (I) in believing (*i. e.* I believe) it is (be, *bod*) in dawning (it dawns) (*yr* is a prefix, like our *there* in *there is*, and like Ger. *es*, Scand. *er*, and we may regard *yr-wyf* as double *be*, for *yr* = are).

Gwelais y milwyr a-r carcharwr yn myned i-r llys — I-saw the soldiers and-the (*r* = *yr*, the) prisoner in going (a-going) to the (*r* = the) hall; *fel nas gellaf ei chredu*—that not I-can its (*ei*) believing (cannot believe it). *Pe lladdai efe fi, eto mi* (I) *a-obeithaf ynddo*—though (*pe*, what) kill he me, yet I (will) a-trust in-him (*ynddo*). It is a prevailing feature in Celtic, to find the pronoun and preposition united, as in *yn-ddo*, or according to our view, to see the preposition, as *to*, develop elself into the representative of pron. and prep., as *to-me*.

Yr oedd y dyn yn ddoeth —there was a man in knowing (the man was wise (knowing); adjectives like in-wisdom, for wise, are common); *mor drwm a phlwm*— as heavy (drag) as (and) lead (L. *plumb'*); *y fenyw yr oeddych yn ei gweled*— the woman there (which) were (you were) in her seeing (the woman which you saw). *Fy mhen, fy mraich, fy nhroed*—my head, my arm, my foot. *Paham yr ydych yn ceisio fy lladd* — why there are-you (*ydych*) in seeking my killing—seek to kill me (*yr* must be counted as an augment).

Myfi yw y bara bywiol, yr-hwn (the-this) *a-ddaeth i waered o-r nef* — I (I-I, my-self) am (is) the bread living, which a-came to down from-the (*o-?*) heaven (L. *nubes*). *Yna y cy flawnyd yr-hyn a-ddywedasid* — then there (was) fulfilled the-this (what) (was) a-spoken; *llef a-glybuwyd* — voice (was) a-heard (*a* is prefix); *ac wedi ei gyfodi* — but after his hearing, *i. e.*, when he heard; *y gelwid ef* — there (shall-be)-called, he, *i. e.* he shall be called.

Ac yn y dyddiau hynny y daeth Joan Fedyddiwr, gan bregethu-yn niffeithwch Judea — and in the days those (*y* augment) came John (the) Baptist, with preaching in (the) wilderness Judea.

679. CORNISH: Little can be said that is peculiar to the Cornish, when compared with Welsh. We notice our form of passive: *a-n nef of danfenys* — from-the heaven I-am (*of*) sent; *bos rewardyys* — be rewarded; *an gorhel my a-n gura* (wórk) — the ship I it (will) make; *me a-s ygor an* (the) *darasow* — I (for) them (will) open the doors.

680. CELT-BRETON: The Celt-Breton has greater and more important peculiarities, not only orthographic but grammatical, as the following examples will show: *Ann douar ho tigemero goude ho maro* (death), *am gwelo o vervel, hag enn han e vezinn douaret* — the earth (L. *terra*) you (it) will-receive after (*goude*) your death (which receives you after), me (it) will-see (*gwelo*) to die (in dying) (see me die), and in it (*e* augment) I-shall-be (*vezinn*) earthed (interred); *it gant* (with) *hi* — go with her; *evid mond e bro* — for (to) go into (the) country, *gand he c-hreg hag he zaou vab* — with his (*he*) wife (Welsh *wraig*) and his two sons (*bub*, Ger. *knabe*); *he zaou vab a-oa hanvet* — his two son a-was named; *ead e bro* — go into (the) country; *Noemi a-lavaraz d-ezhi* — Noemi a-said (*a* augment) to her (*hi*).

681. A few more words must suffice to give an idea of the orthography: *Kaloun*, heart (*l = r*); *eva*, drink, L. *bibo*, beverage; *mad*, good, L. *magnus*; *mor*, sea, Fr. *mer*; *an or*, the door; *chatal*, cattle; *gar leg*, arm, G'k *cheir* = hand; *lech*, place, L. *locus*.

Melen, yellow, mellow; *moal*, bald; *nerz*, force, nerve; *niver*, number; *paz*, all, G'k *pas*; *penn*, head, L. *caput*, mount, point; *ti*, house, sty, L. *tectus*; *teod*, tongue; *deiz*, day, L. *dies*.

Breach, arm, L. *brach*; *iach*, health; *choad*, wood; *war*, sure; *gwarek*, arc; *gwir*, true; *uhel*, high, hill; *fall*, e-vil, bad; *kaer*, pretty, L. *pul-cher*; *braz*, great; *mean*, stone; *dour*, wa-ter; *breur*, brother, Fr. *frere*.

Koulm, Fr. *colombe*, dove; *paotr*, boy, L. *puer*; *hano*, name; *tan*, fire; *kelch*, circle; *env*, heaven; *ali*, bird, L. *avis*, l, v; *tra*, thing, L. *res*; *avel*, blow, wind, Fr. *vent*; *wel*, look.

Ki, dog, Fr. *chien; baz,* stick, beat, Fr. *baton; gwell,* better, well, Fr. *meilleur; gwenn,* white, Fr. *blanc,* L. *can'; biz,* digit, Fr. *doigt; he zourn,* his hand, G'k *cheir; piou,* who; *c-hoar,* sister, Fr. *soeur.*

Kresk, grow, Fr. *crois,* increase; *digor* (learn), L. *disco; ro,* give, L. *do,* r, d ; *kred,* Fr. *crois,* credit, trust; *laka,* put, place, L. *locus.*

Kar, love, dear, care; *lavar,* (speak), L. *lego; kav,* Fr. *trouv* (find), re-trieve; *gall,* can, will; *gwez* (know), sage, wise; *dont,* come, gone, d, g; *mont = dont,* mount, went; *kea,* go, Fr. *va; gan,* sing, L. *cano; dale,* delay.

Ober, work (make), L. *opere; ra,* do, *rann,* done, r, d ; *gra,* do (g prefix); *sevel,* raise, Fr. *lever; kaout,* have, k, g, h; *krenn,* round, Fr. *rond, kr = r; glin,* in-cline, knee, Fr. *genou; den,* man, Fr. *gens* (plur. of *den* is *tud,* Ger. *leute,* folk).

Lagad (eye), look ; *geo,* yoke, Fr. *joug; enk* (straight), Ger. *eng,* narrow, anxious; *garrek,* rock ; *trouz,* Fr. *bruit* (noise); *bran,* raven.

These, and very many more which we might give, comprising a large portion of the language, are easily seen to be variations of French and German words.

682. GAELIC: Our next selections we will take from the Gaelic proper, or Highland Scotch : *Agus a-deirim ribh* — and I-say unto-you (*a* is an augment); *agus ri m-shearbhant, dean so, agus ni se e* — and to my-servant (I say), do that, and doeth it he (he does it); *nach d-fhair mi creidimh co mor as so* — not (have) found I (*mi*) faith so great (*mor*) as that (I have not found) — *d',* for *do,* is the prefix or augment for the past tense.

Thigaedh (infin.) *do rioghachd* — come thy kingdom (Ger. *rick,* L. *regnum*); *deanar do thoil air an talamh, mar a-nithear air* (on, in) *neamh* — (be) done thy will (*thoil*) on the earth (L. *terra*) as a-done (as is done) in heaven (*a* augment); *chualas guth an Rama* — (was) heard (G'k *kluō*) voice in Rama; *agus an uair a-chunnaic iad* (they) *an reult* — and the hour (*i. e.* when) a-saw they the star (when they saw); *bha a chulaidh* (clad) *aig Eoin* — (then) was the raiment to John (John was clad, clothed); *thubhairt e ris* — said he to-them ; *oir ata* (is) *e scriobhta* — for is it written (it is written); *am pobull a-bha 'nan suidhe an dorchadas* — the people a-was (was) in sitting (was sitting) in darkness; *ag imeachd da Josa* — in walking (coming) of Jesus (*i. e.,* Jesus while walking).

Agus bha e an-sin gu (to) *bas Heroid* — and was he there (the-there) until death (of) Herod ; *anns na laithibh sin* (those) *thainig Eoin Baiste, a-searmonach am fasach Judea* — in the days those (those days) came John Baptist, a-preaching in wilderness (of) Judea — *agus ag-radh*, and a-saying (in saying, *radh* (Ger. *reden*).

Agus bhaisteadh iad leissam (by-him) *ann an Jordan, agaidmheil am peacanna* — and (were) baptized they (were) by-him in the Jordan, a-confessing (admitting) the (their) sins; *chum gu-m biodh e air a bhaisteadh leis* (*le* = by) — for that be he (for him to be) in (*air*) the baptizing by-him (baptized by him) — *a* is a prefix; *chaidh* (*goed*, went) *e air ball suas as an uisge* — went he (e) on (the) spot (*i. e.* immediately) up out the water. *Is e so mo* (my) *mhac gradhach, am bheil* (Slav. *byl*) *mo mhor thlachd* — is he that (this is he) my son (*mac*) beloved, (he) is my great delight — *am* is prefix.

Chum gu-m biodh e air a bhuaireadh (try, proved, *b-r-d*) *leis an diabhol* — for that be he (he be) on the (*a* is prefix) tempting by (*leis*, by-him) the devil (to be tempted); *oir teachd do-n bhuaireadair* — on coming of-the tempter, *i. e.*, when he came; *an sin thug an diabhol e do-n bhaile* (ville) *naomha* — the then (then) took the devil (did) him into-the city (the) holy (one); *Leanaibh mise* (my-self), *agas ni* (make) *mi iasgeirian* (fishers) *air daoinibh dhibh* — follow-(ye) me, and make I (I will make) fishers of men (of) you (*dhibh*); *lean iad esan* — follow they him.

Cha-n fheudar baile a ta air a shuidheachadh air sliabbh 'fholach — not can (*a*) city which (*a*) is (*ta*) on a sitting (which sits) on (a)hill hide (be hidden); *ni h-ann a sgaoileadh a-thainig mi, ach a choimhlionadh* — not for the destroying (to destroy) a-come I (do I come), but the fulfilling — (the *a* here may be treated as *the, to*, but it is as much a part of the verb as any prefix is; so, in the sentence before, *a*, which was called *which* is so much a part with *ta*, that in Irish it is written *ata*).

Chuala sibh gu-n dubhradh, Suil air son sula, agus fiacail air son fiacla — heard ye (ye have heard) that say (it is said), eye (L. *occul-us*) for sake (of) eye, and tooth for sake (of) tooth; *tabhair* (L. *dabo*) *do-n ti* (the, that) *a dh-iarras ort* — give to-the he (to the one) who asks of-thee — (*dh* is prefix, *iarras*, ask); *buailibh an dorus, agus fosgailear dhuibh* — knock (blow-ye) the door, and (it shall be) opened to-you; *o-ir gach uile neach a dh-iarras, glacuidh e* — for each all one (every one) who asks, receives he (does); *lean cuideachd mhor e* — followed multitude great him (followed him).

683. The idiom and grammar of the Irish is so nearly identical with the Gaelic, which we have illustrated thus copiously, that we will not stop to select expressions from the Irish. We will next give a comparative view of the Gaelic, Irish, and

Welsh, using, in this case, the verse in John already taken for a similar purpose.

Gaelic: *Ruith i an sin, agus thainig i gu Simon Peadar, agus gus an deisciobul eile a b-ionmhuinn le h-Josa, agus a-deir i* (she) *riu: thug iad leo an Tighearn as an uaigh, agus cha n-eil fhios againn c-ait an do chuir iad e —* run she (*i*) the then (then she run), and came she to Simon Peter, and to the (*an*) disciple (the) other, who w-dear (was dear) to h-Jesus, and a-said she (she said) to-them (*riu*): Took they (have) away the Lord out the grave, and not is (not) knowing to-us (*aga-inn*) where that (*do* pref.) laid they him (we do not know where (the place) they have laid him).

684. The same verse runs in Irish thus: *Uime-sin* (therefore) *do-rioth si* (*do* is prefix, *si* = *i*), *agus tainigh si mar* (where) *a-raibh* (was) *Simon Peadar, agus an deisciobal eile, noc do-b* (who was) *ionmhin le Hiosa, agus a* (pref.) *dubhairt si riu, Rugh-adar* (they took) *an Tighearna leo as an dt-uama, agus ni* (not) *bhfil* (is) *a fhios aginn gha-hait* (what-place, where) *ar* (pref.) *chir-eadar e* (is laid he, they laid him). We notice that *they* (*iad* of Gael.) is here represented by the ending *-adar*, and we see the prefix *do* = Gael. *a*, our *to*.

685. And next we give the Welsh: *Yna* (then) *y-rhedodd hi, ac a-ddaeth at Simon Pedr, a-r disgybl arall* (other) *yr-hwn* (who) *yr-oedd* (*yr* = there, prefix) *yr* (to) *Jesu yn ei garu* (in his care, love), *ac a-ddywedodd* (a-said) *wrthynt* (to them): *Hwy* (they) *a-ddygasant* (took) *yr Arglwydd ymaith o-r bedd, ac ni wyddom ni* (not we-know not) *pa le* (what place) *y-dodasant ef* (him).

686. The Irish is written with letters of its own, an alphabet of eighteen characters, differing considerably from the English or Roman.

The amount of writings in Irish is very large, and in point of time they range between the 8th and 14th centuries. Those of the Gaelic are not so abundant as the Irish, nor do they bear a date by any means so ancient.

687. In conclusion, we may remark on the Celtic languages, that though they present many features in a new form or new light, they are still much nearer the German and Latin class of languages than is generally supposed. When once we fully understand the nature of their orthography, and their system of prefixes, or augments, we shall find few words and few points in grammar, that cannot be compared with the English or French.

CHAPTER IV.

LATIN LANGUAGES.

688. The Latin, long since an idiom without a living people to speak it, is represented still by these three important families: the Italian, the Spanish, and the French — and with these we may count the less prominent Portugese, Wallachian, and Provencial. There are, indeed, many other members of this great Latin family, which we may either regard as branches of these late living languages, or as themselves independent dialects. Such of them as come within our scope, will be noticed in the course of the review. The old Latin itself we treat of sufficiently in another place, and it remains to speak briefly of the main points observable in its descendants. We will introduce the French first.

689. We may with propriety divide the French into a northern and a southern dialect, as we divided the German into High and Low German. For practical purposes, we may say the Loire marks the separation of two idioms very easily distinguised. The oldest, and once the ruling one, as a cultivated language, was the southern, to which the comprehensive term Provencial is applied, as well, too, as the name Langue d'Oc. The northern is the source of our present modern French, the written language; the names Langue d'Oïl and Norman French have been applied to it. Besides these two leading sections of the French spoken language, in both north and south there are other subdialects, more or less defined and extensive in point of area, but we have not the space to dwell on them here. Suffice it to say, that several of them present some very interesting and instructive features, when compared with the modern standard French.

690. Of these two leading divisions we may say further, that, as we might expect, the northern, coming constantly in contact with the German culture, has received a German impress, while the southern, intimately associated with the Latin languages, has been affected in its growth by their pressure, or, in other words, one presents a phase more or less German, while that of the other is quite as much Latin.

691. It should be noticed, with regard to the names Langue d'Oc and Provencial, that they are sometimes used without distinction, as denoting the southern languages of France; still, the names are used in a narrower sense, to denote the idioms of two different localities in Southern France; or, again, Provencial is used as the comprehensive name of the old idiom of South France, of which the Langue d'Oc and others are now dialects.

692. A few examples selected from French authors, with the explanations belonging to them, will give a better idea of the leading points in this language than any abstract remarks.

De meme que (which, as) *Kepler* — of same (the same) as Kepler (*de* is called a prep. equal to *of*, but it often, as here, takes the place of our *the*, with which it agrees in form also); *l'homme* (*l'* = the) *qui se sert du* (of-the) *microscope parle* (speaks) *de grossissements, et s'imagine pouvoir a leur* (their) *aide connaitre mieux les objets* — the-man who self serves (serves himself with) of-the microscope speaks of enlargements, and imagines self (*s'* = self, a pure article, or pref.) to-be-able (*pouvoir*, power, L. *potis, possum, It. podere*) by (*a*) their aid to-know better the objects.

Peut encore nous conduire — can yet us conduct (can conduct us); *une derniere fois nous l'avons* (*l'* = it, the) *pressé sur notre cœur* — one (*a*) last time we it-have pressed upon our heart (have pressed it); *il est*, it is, there is, *nous avons vu que* — we have seen that; *ce corps se trouve* — that body self finds (finds self, is found); *de cette maniere* — of that (in that) manner; *une partie en est dissoute dans le suc* — one (*a*) part of (it) is dissolved in the juice (*s* = *j*).

A dû jeter — has ought (due) to-throw (*has ought* is good French and German, if not English); *de donner* — of giving, to give (*de* = to); *de plus en plus* — of more in more (more and more).

L'etude de la structure intime — the-study of the structure intimate (adj. follows); *et meme de l'homme* — and same of the-man (even of man).

Comme ils (they) *le sont in effet* — as they it (*le*) are in effect (are it = are); *il a egalement* — it has (there is) equally; *d'une* (an) *maniere tout opposée* — of (in) a manner wholly opposed.

Rien de solide — nothing of solid (nothing solid); *le monde animal suit les plantes* — the world animal follows (pur-sues) the plants; *sans dire* — without to-say (*i. e.*, saying, without saying); *dit il* — says he; *mais ce principe unique de la vie, comment Barthez l'a-t-il concu?* — but that principle unique of the life (of life), how Barthez it (*l'*) has-he conceived (how has he conceived it, Barthez)? The French use generally this surplus *it* in questions — *t* between *a* (has) and *il* (he) is the usual connective letter.

Je l'ai deja dit — I it (*l'*) have already said (*dit*) — already said it, for already said that; *il faut de plus considerer* — it must of (the) more to-consider — there is need of more considering; *Etre roi proprement, c'est avoir* (to have) *des subjets et n'avoir point d'amis* — to be king properly that-is (*ce-est*) to-have of-the subjects, and not (*n'*) to-have none of (*d'*) friends (not to have friends)—the *of*, and *none*, are some of the many words, or particles, which the French employ, and which we have no use for; *lui dis-je*, to-him said-I (*je* = I); *l'un et l'autre*, the-one and the-other *i. e.*, the both, or both; *ils se poussent l'un l'autre* — they self push the-one the-other, *i. e.*, they push each other; *je viens de recevoir* — I come to (of) receive, come to receive, *i. e.*, have received.

Donnez-moi ce livre-la — give-me that book-there, *i. e.*, give me that book; *cette femme-ci* — this woman-here (as we say, this 'ere woman); *elle se brula la main* — she self burnt the hand, she burnt herself the hand, *i. e.*, on the hand. This *self* is very common in French, and in German and other European languages; in many instances, it has the force of an article, or a simple prefix, and generally it has no equal in English; *vende-m'en un* (one) — sell-me of them (*en*) one (one of them); *parle-lui-en* — speak him-of-it, speak to-him (*lui*) of-it (*en*); *de lire* — of to-read, of read, of reading; *dites-lui de venir* — say-him (to him) to come (*de* = of, with inf.); *il ne fait que son devoir* — he not does only (*que*, which) his due (duty) (*ne* = *que*, not that, only).

693. There are many other idiomatic expressions in French as important and interesting as those just given, but there is not space to go further here; it should be noted, however, that, strange as these expressions may seem to us, they are very common forms, in Europe, in other languages besides the French.

694. The principal difference between the Provencial and the French proper, is one of orthographic dress — though that is not the only difference; we often find one using a word, French though it be, in a place and in a manner not common to the other. A few examples will illustrate the difference in orthography:

695. First, Prov., next, Fr.: *Nouastre, notre,* our; *noum, nom,* name; *crespa, crêpe,* crape; *cagar, chier ;* *chin* and *can, chien,* L. *canis,* dog; *cabra, chevre,* L. *capra,* goat; *espigat* and *espade, epee,* spade and sword; *espina, epine,* spine and pin.

Espes, epais, thick; *aigua, eau,* L. *aqua,* water; *grat, gre,* will; *goust, gout,* taste; *jaire, gesir,* lie; *camba, jambe,* leg, limb; *abri, ivre,* drunk; *hort, jardin,* garden; *juni, jeune,* junior.

Lach, lait, milk; *luec* and *loc, lieu,* L. *locus,* place; *liame* and *lianc, lien,* lien; *liech, lit,* L. *lectus,* bed; *ligible, lisible,* legible; *man, main,* hand; *boutar, mettre,* put; *neou, neige,* snow; *negre, noir,* black.

Pes, poids, weight; *pourpre, poulpe,* pulp; *prochi, pres,* near and 'proach; *prest, prêt,* ready; *pregar, prier,* pray and preach;

rabi and *ragea, rage,* rage; *garri, rat,* rat; *ren* and *ves, rien,* L. *res,* thing; *buou, taureau,* stier and bull.

696. It must by no means be supposed that the above may be taken as the proper measure of the difference between French and Provencial; they are selected from the very few of their like— the vast majority of words varying but little, or not at all, from the French; and it is to be noted, too, that the variation of the Provencial which we have seen above, is in almost every case a variation in agreement with Latin.

697. The changes of words in Old French, in its gradual growth into the late or new French, presents some interesting facts which may be noticed here. The older these forms are, the nearer they approach to Latin: *acheter,* to get, has the different forms *acapter* (L. *capio,* catch), *acater, achepter* (c = ch, pt = t); *donner,* give — *dorrai, dourai, doint, doing; parler,* speak — *paroler, paraut, aparlui, mes-parler; trouv,* retrieve — *troz, truis, troeffe.*

Courir, course and run — *escourre, sequeur* (L. *sequor), keurt, corre, se-cor; dormir,* sleep — *dort, dorge, devorge; ouvrir,* open, overt — *aouvert, apert* (apart), *overt, uevrir, ubrir; tenir,* retain — *tieignent, tieg, tigne, tendrai.*

Faillir, fail, false and fault — *faldra, faulra, faura, fara; ouir,* hear, L. *audio — oyr, oyt, et, orra, oon, oues; voir,* see, view — *verrai, voyrras, veoir, vehoir, vehu, veir, vcois, veoid, vir, vinrent, varout.*

Boire, drink and beverage — *beurai, burez, beivre, boif; connoitre,* know, ac-quaint — *cognoistre, conistre, quenoist, conuistre, cognehu, conusier, conissies; dire,* say — *dict, dient, dioms, dixons, desis, dites; ecrire,* write, scribe — *escripre, scripsi, escripvi, ecrivi.*

698. The *Gascon* is an important dialect of the French. There is, too, in Switzerland, besides others found there, a form of French approaching near to the Latin, and called by the different names of *Romanic, Rhaetish,* and *Celto-Romanic.* It runs parallel with the other Latin languages in every essential particular. We find such variations in orthography as these, comparing Romanic, Latin, and French: *els, illi, les,* the, those; *madem,* Fr. *meme,* It. *medesmo,* same; *tschel, quis* and *ille, celle,* which and that; *jou* and *eug, ego, je,* I; *fova, fui, fus,* was; *sunt, sum, suis,* am; *ean, sunt, sont,* are; *filgs,* L. *filii,* sons; *ilg,* Fr. *il,* L. *ille,* he.

Un hum veva dus filgs; Fr. *Un homme avait deux fils* — a man had two sons; *schet alg bab,* Fr. *dit a-son* (to-his) *pere* — said to-the (*alg*) father; *mi dai la part,* Fr. *donnez-moi* (give me) *la part* — me give (*mi dai*) the part (give it to me); *a*

parchirar ils porcs, Fr. *pour* (for-to) *paitre les pourceaux* — to feed the porks (swine).
Mo nagin lgi deva — but none (to) him gave (Fr. *donnait*); *a jou miei* (die) *d'fom*, Fr. *et je meurs de faim* — and I die of famine (hunger); *jou vi lavar si, ad ir tier* (Fr. *irai vers*, go to) *mieu bab* — I will raise self (rise), and go to my father; *jou hai faig puccau ancunter (contra) ilg tschiel* (Fr. *ciel*) *ad avont tei* — I have done sin against the heaven and before (Fr. *avont*) thee; *ilg qual eis* (is), the which art, who art (Fr. *qui es*); *tieu raginavel* (L. *regnum*) *vengig* — thy kingdom come, (Fr. *ton regne vienne*); *nou tiers* — us to (to us); *tia velgia du-ventig* — thy will be-come.

In the different forms of this idiom, for there are several sub-dialects, we find for *da-ventig* (be-come), *daventa*, *d'vaint, dvainta; naun proa*, for *nou tiers; houtz*, Ger. *heute;* for debts, we find *dabitts, dbits; culpants*, L. *culpa*, Ger. *schuld*. We see that this Romanic is French, with a strong tendency to the German, with which it is associated.

699. The Walloon and Flemish (or Flandrish) are two kinds of French, possessing the form and spirit of the French, varying from it not by any striking differences of orthography, and yet so pressed by the German people, among which they have been located, that they have received much of the German finish. The Walloon and Flemish have much in common with each other, whole sentences being translated from one to the other in almost identical words. Both are interesting and valuable to the philologist, but more especially so the Walloon.

Other forms of French we must pass by without notice.

700. ITALIAN: The Italian is a language spoken by a people known to be direct descendants of the Latins, and occupying to-day the very country which was the central part of the once proud and powerful Roman Empire; and yet, take it all in all, the Spanish is a closer imitator of the Latin than the Italian is. Still, the parallel between the Italian and Latin is very regular and exact. Its words are like emigrants, which, however far they may have wandered away, never seem to forget their nativity, and point constantly homeward.

It seems to have pretty much the same history as the French, and is more like it than any other language. Were they spoken in more limited localities, and by a people less strongly defined, they would easily be taken for dialects of the same language. It is common to French and Italian, that though they use the Latin word, somewhat varying in its form, they often give it a different place, and generally a different meaning. We select the following examples:

701. *Pochi giorni dopo la battaglia di Waterloo* — (a) few

days (Fr. *jour*) after the battle of Waterloo; *non avete un instante da perdere* — not you-have a (one) instant to (of) lose (*da* = to, of); *i momenti sono preziosi* — the moments are precious.

Ma gli uomini degli (of-the) *altri partiti cominciarono allora contro di lui* (him) *una crociata, che fu poi* (L. *post*) *causa principale di sua grandezza* — but the men of the other parties commenced then against to him a crusade, which was (*fu*) afterwards (the) cause principal of his greatness; *che cominciavano a temere dell' influenza, che poteva* (*pot* = could) *esercitare il nome di lui, lo ammisero con diffidenza al consesso loro* — (they) who (*che*) commenced to (*a*) fear of-the influence, which could (*poteva*) exercise the name of him (his name could exercise), (they) him sent, with distrust, to-the (*al*) assembly (of) theirs (their assembly).

Palla di cannone — ball of cannon (cannon ball) — as it is uniformly, too, in French; *il suo porto* — the its port (its port); *i nostri libri* — the our books (our books); *egli non si limito a far* (L. *facere*) *conoscere il effetto* — he (did) not self limit (limit himself) to make (*far*) know the effect (to publish the effect); *e la sua fantasia ando inflammando 'si* — and the his fancy went (on) inflaming (it) self (went inflaming); *in che si gioceva* — in which self laid (he was placed); *lo faro* — it (I) will-do (I will do it); *dite-lo* — tell-it; *e cerca* (search) *di ritornare a vita il poverello* — and seeks to restore to life the poorone (poor-little); *che credeva perduto* — which (he) believed lost (perished).

Rispose-gli — responded he; *per esprimere* — for (to) express; *con cui una sillaba viene pronunziata a preferenza dell' altra* — with which one syllable comes (is) pronounced in (to) preference of-the other. The personal pronoun is very often not expressed where we would find it indispensable; *viveva* — lived, i. e., there lived; *era* — was, i. e., there was; *finita la commedia si ballo* — (being) finished, the comedy, one danced (they danced); *piu ricco di mi* — more rich of me (than me); *voglio parlar-vi di questi affari* — (I) will (wish) speak-you of these affairs.

La citta ha fatto construire un pònte — the city has made construct (has had constructed) a bridge; *al lato di* — to-the side of (near); *che che sia* — what that be (= whatever); *nel modo che* — in-the manner that (= how); *fin a quando* — till to when (= till when); *quando vuol ella* (she) *mandarmi il paniere* — when will you send-me the basket; *vuole dar-mi del pane* — will (you) give-me of-the bread (some bread); *li ho* (I-have) *avuti* — them I-have had; *non mi* (myself) *lamento* —

not me (do-I) lament, lament myself, lament; *far dei progressi*
— to-make the progresses, to make progress.
E ella ricca ? lo sono — are you rich? it I-am (I am it, *i. e.*,
I am), (she is used for you); *l' aiuto a far-lo* — him I-aid to do-
it, help him do it; *egli è più dotto ch' io non credeva* — he is
more learned (taught) than I not believed, *i. e.*, than I believed;
io me lo procuro — I me it procure, I procure it (for) me, *i. e.*,
I procure it; *noi veniamo amati* — we come (= are) loved ; *le
quali andarono fallite* — the which went failed, which failed
(as Ger. *go lost*).

702. In conclusion we may say, there is not a single important feature in the Italian idiom that is not French as well.

703. Like the French, the language of the Italians may be divided into northern and southern classes, influenced by different forces, and taking directions, hence, somewhat varying. As standing between the two, we may count the Tuscan and Romish. Other dialects are the Genoese, Milanese, Tyrolian, Venitian, Piedmontese, Bolognish, Sabine, Tarentian, Friulan, Neapolitan, and a few others, besides Sicilian and Sardinian. These are dialects pretty well distinguished, and having their own books — yet all plainly starting from the Italian, or Latin, as a base, and departing more or less from it.

Of the Sardinian it must be said, it has more of the Spanish than of the Italian cast.

704. SPANISH : To the Spanish, or Castilian, we come next. For the English and Latin scholar, this is one of the easiest languages in the world to acquire. It is a Latin language in every respect; it has not departed from the mother tongue so far by any means as the French, or even the Italian — but so far as it has gone, that has been in a direction in common with them. To use a figurative expression, it has been somewhat squeezed out of shape, but the body is Old Latin none the less. It has been pressed, hard pressed, on the south by Moors, or Arabs, from Africa, and on the north it has been subject to incursions from the notorious and powerful Goths. The Moors left a lasting impression ; they added many words; they changed, too, in a measure, the style of the native. Indeed, the Moors were masters of Spain for something near eight hundred years. They did not destroy or change the spirit of the tongue, but they did warp its form and mar the finish.

705. The following will illustrate some of its peculiarities compared with our own idiom :

Tuvo la boca grande — (he) had the (a) mouth large (a large mouth) ; *quiero los ojos grandes* — (I) like the eyes large (large eyes) ; *casa de ladrillo* — house of brick, *i. e.*, a brick house ; *coluna de piedra* — column of stone, *i. e.*, stone pillar (Span. as well as Fr. and It.); *es tan noble como tu lo decias* — (she) is so noble as (how) you it said (as you said it, as you said); *una nacion vencida* — a (one) nation conquered, *i. e.*, a conquered one; *la dijo* (also *dijo-la*) — (to) her (he) said, *i. e.*, said (to) her (*la* = the, her); *yo me he cortado el dedo* — I me have (he) cut the finger (*digit*) — cut for me the finger, *i. e.*, cut my finger; *un hombre rico* — a man rich, *i, e.*, a rich man.

Yo mismo (Fr. meme, same) *lo vi* — I same (myself) it saw; *ella le echó los brazos al cuello* (L. *collum*) — she him (*le*) threw the arms to-the (*al*) neck — threw around him the arms, *i. e.*, threw her arms around his neck; so again, *el caballero* (cavalier) *le besó* (bussed) *las manos* — the knight (for) her kissed the hands; *no sabe lo que quiere* — not (he) knows the which (what) (he) wants (re-quires); *este quiso* (-*quire*, wish, qu) *sujetar* — this (one) wished (to) subject (some one); *nada se ha hecho* — nothing self has done (done self, been done).

Se dice — self says, *i. e.*, is said; *no tiene razon de decir esto* — (you) no have reason to (*de*) say (inf.) that (*no tiene*, not it-has, has not, is not); *he de salir* — I-have to (*de* = of, to) go, must go out (*salir*, our walk); *esta leyendo* — is reading, *paseando*, walking (passing); *tiene de hacer-lo* — he-has to do-it; *entraron cantando* — they-entered singing; *lo iran* (run) *diciendo a todos* — it (they) will-go (*iran*) telling to all (go telling it).

Quiere que lo haga yo — (he) desires (-*quire*) that it do I (that I do it); *hoy* (has) *mucho que hacer* — there-is (*hay*) much which to-do — much to do; *mis hijos é hijas vinieron todos hoy para ver-me* — my sons (L. *filii*) and daughters came all (*todos*) to-day (Ger. *heute*) for (to) see-me (*ver-me*); *yo amo aun a mis enemigos* — I love even to my enemies (I love them). An extra preposition is very common in other languages).

Fue asolada — was d-esolated; *es estimado* — is esteemed; *todos mis cartas estan por escribir hoy* — all my letters are for to-write to-day — must be written to-day; *pero no le he hablado jamas* — but not (to) him have-I (*he*) spoken never — never spoken (to) him (double negatives are common in Europe); *todo esto se hizo* — all this self did, *i. e.*, was done, did self; *esto es de mi hermano* — this is of my brother — it is my brother's.

706. The Catalan, or Catalonian, and the Valencian languages in Spain, are built upon the Spanish basis, and are Spanish throughout, but they have received, from their locality, much of the French touch; there are those who think them more French than Spanish. In the Catalonian is especially observable the ending *-it* for the past part., as in Old French; as, *esta possehit* — is possessed; *haveu llegit* — have read; *havent ohit* — having heard (L. *audit*). While the idiom is purely Spanish, the lan-

guage is chiefly interesting from the peculiar orthographic forms in which Spanish words appear here.

707. The Castilian has several minor dialects, not particularly known to philology, and which we cannot here dwell on.

708. The PORTUGESE is spoken by a people having a separate nationality, but so far as difference in written language is concerned, it varies from the Spanish no more than one dialect does from others of its class. Its nature is purely Spanish; it is true, the pronunciation of the words as written differs considerably from that of the same words in Spanish. Its orthography presents us with forms of much interest.

709. We will give here a comparative view of four of the languages related to the Spanish, taking first the Italian, John, xx, 2:

Laonde ella se ne corse (therefore she self then ran) *e venne* (went) *a Simon Pietro, e all'* (to-the) *discepelo, il qual* (the which, who) *Gesu amava* (loved), *e* (and) *disse loro* (to-them): *han tolto* (have taken) *dal* (from-the) *monumento il Signore, e noi* (we) *non sappiamo ove* (where) *l'* (him) *abbian posto* (have put).

710. French: *Elle courut donc* (then) *trouver* (to-find) *Simon Pierre, et l'autre* (l', the) *disciple que Jesus aimait* (loved); *et elle leur* (to-them) *dit, on a* (one has) *enlevé du* (from-the) *sepulcre le Seigneur, et nous* (we) *ne* (not) *savons* (know) *ou* (where) *on l'a* (him has) *mis* (put) (where one has put him).

711. Catalan: *Y corregue* (and she-ran), *y vingue a* (to) *Simo Pere, y a aquell* (that-which) *altre* (other) *deixeble amat* (loved) *de* (of, by) *Jesus, yls* (to-them) *digue: Sen han portat* (carried) *lo Senyor del* (from-the) *sepulcre, y no sabem* (not we-know) *ahont l' han* (him-(they)-have) *posat* (put).

712. Portugese: *Correo pois* (then), *e veio* (went) *a Simao Pedro e ao* (to-the) *outro discipulo a quem* (to whom) *Jesus amava, e disse-lhes* (said-them): *Ao* (to-the) *Senhor tomarao do* (from-the) *sepulcro, e nao* (not) *sab-emos onde* (where) *o* (him) *pozerao* (they-have-put).

713. And, finally, one of the dialects of Romanic (low Eugadina): *Per il qual* (for the which, therefore) *ella currit, e venn pro Simon Petro, e pro* (to) *l'auter scular il qual Jesus amava, e diss ad els: Haun els* (have they) *tut dal* (from-the) *monumaint il* (the) *Segner, e nus nun* (not) *savain* (know) *ingie l'hajan tschanta* (placed).

714. BASQUE LANGUAGE: There is a language of Spain, known to philology under the name of Basque, and sometimes called Iberian — an idiom somewhat celebrated, but certainly not well understood. The Basque, with some kindred dialects

is the present language of the people of Biscay and Navarre, and is the representative of an ancient language, now extinct, and of a people once powerful and prosperous, but long since departed and forgotten. There is reason to believe that it was once the idiom of all of Spain, or nearly all, besides of a large portion of southern France.

715. It has been supposed, and with good reason, that the Basques, and their family, belonged in their connections with the Celtic people. There is, indeed, much in the general cast of Basque orthography that reminds one of Gaelic or Cymric, but in the grammar there are many strong points of difference. With the limited knowledge we now have of the Basque, we would prefer leaving it to stand as some solitary monument, alone. It is not enough to say that all of its points of construction and grammar have something similar to them in other languages; that many, no doubt most, of its words can be traced back to a relationship with words in the European or Asiatic languages; the road we have to travel is far too long to allow us to call this connection and relationship a family likeness. Its very marked character can never be changed, though it is of course probable that time will make us more familiar with its peculiar features, and bring it nearer to some languages with which we are better acquainted.

716. The language is found in Spain (and that is the only reason why it is introduced under the head of Latin Languages), but it is quite as different from Spanish as Irish is from English. We will proceed now to give some idea of its prominent points:

717. The article, so-called, is here found suffixed, as we find it in Scandinavian and elsewhere; thus, *gizon*, man; *gizona*, the man; *gizonak*, the men; *gizonbat*, a man — *bat* is the numeral *one*, used for *a*, *an*, as we everywhere find it. The cases are formed by varying the endings, as in Latin; thus, *aita*, father; *aitaren*, of the father, or father's; *aitari*, to the father. This genitive *aitaren* (the father's = that of the father), may undergo another change, or may be used as a base on which to form a new genitive; thus, *aitaren-arena*, that-of-that-of-the-father, and the latter form again as a new base, going on so without limit, just as we may say, that-of-that-of-that-of, indefinitely.

718. What we use as prepositions, they use as post-positions, placing them after the noun, and generally united with it at the end; as, *ogi-gabe*, without (*gabe*) bread; *jauna-gatic*, through (*gatic*) the (a) Lord; *jauna-re-kin*, with (*kin*) the Lord; *aita-gana*, to (*gana*) father; *ceruaren contra* — heaven against; *gu-gana* — to us (*ga*).

719. The adjective is found after the noun; as, *guicon on*, man good; *abre on*, good (*on*) animal. Not only are adjectives compared by a change of endings, but nouns are compared in the same manner; thus, *bide*, way; *bideago*, more way; so can participles be compared; as, *edertzen da*, improving he is; *edertzen-ago da*, more improving is he.

720. In verbs there are two ways of conjugating, one the simple and older form, and the other compounded or circumscribed by the use of participles with auxiliaries — the simple form being used only with a few verbs. Verbs which are used in the simple can also be used in the compound form; as, *nator*, I come (from *etorri*), and *etorten naz*, coming I-am (*naz*). It is particularly noticeable that not only are nominative pronouns developed at the end of verbs, but, also, the objective (acc.) and dative occur very generally in connection with the verb; as, *dut* (*dot*, *det*) I have him, or it. Here *d* is the representative of the object *him*, *u* of the verb-root, and *t* the pronoun I; so *du* is he has him, or it — here the mark of *he*, the subject, is not so developed as to be distinguished from *u* of the verb-root. It will be remembered that the marks of the third person very commonly lie latent. Again we find *dugu*, we have him, or it; *duc*, thou hast it; *natzatzu*, I am to you — where *n* marks *I*, *atz*, root *be*, *a* is connecting letter, *tzu* marks to-you, dat.

721. Speaking generally, the auxiliaries *be* and *have*, as we find especially evident in Turkish, are the basis of the verb, and are in fact the only real verb in Basque — to form the usual tenses of the verb, we must attach the participle to these as a base. The auxiliaries, as in other languages, are placed last; thus, *maitetuten dot* — loving him-have-I (*d-o-t*), I loving have him, love him; *maitetuten naz* — loving I-am (*naz*). The auxiliaries play a very conspicuous part in Basque, as we shall see by the examples we are about to give, and they are often too numerous for us to dispose of in the translation. We find many elements united into one word, which we regard as distinct in our own and other languages, and, as we have seen in *dut*, those elements are often so little developed as to have only single letters to represent them. Examples will best illustrate further the character of the Basque :

722. *Eta hitz-aren ministre içan* (been) *diradenec* — and the-word's minister been being (having been), *i. e.*, who were ministers of the word (*hitz*); *hats-etic fin-erano* — beginning-from end-to, *i. e.*, from beginning to end. *Herodes Judeaco regueren egun-etan cen Zacharias deitzen cen* (G'k *gin*, been) *sacrificadore bat* — in-the days (*egun-etan*) of-Herod of-Judea, the-king (of-the-king, *regue-ren*) was (there was, *cen*) sacrifizer one (a certain one, *bat*) named (who was named, *deitzen cen*) Zacharias.

Eta haren (his) *emaztea cen Aaron-en alab-etaric* — and (*eta*) his wife was (*cen*) Aaron's daughters-from-the (one from the daughters of Aaron); *iai-quiric ioanen naiz* (be, will) *neure aita-gana* — rising, go (*ionanen*) will-I my father-to (to my father); *eta errancn draucat* — and say will-I; *ethor cedin* — come has, has come; *ikus cecan* — seen has; *hil eçaçue* — kill do-ye; *ecen ene seme haar hil cen* — for my son this (one) dead (killed) was.

Hi bethi ene-quin aiz — thou be me-with (with-me) ever (art ever with me); *ceren hire anaye haur hil baitzen* — for thy (*hire*) brother this (one) dead was; *ene gucia hire duc* — my all (*gucia*) thine it-hast-thou (thou hast (it) my all).

Ecen ikussi dugu haren icarra Orientean — for seen it-have-we (*d-u-gu*) his star East-in (his star in the East we have seen); *trubla cedin* — troubled was, had trouble; *ezaiz Judaco gobernadoren arteco chipiena* — art-thou-not (thou art not) Judea's governors among (*arteco*) the least (art not the least among).

Scribatua duc — (is) written thou-hast-it (hast written); *enganatu içan cen* — mocked been was, had been mocked; *erran içan cena* — said been being, having been said; *io ceçan haren famac Syria gucia* — gone (*io*) has his fame Syria all-through (through-all, *gucia*); *cuec carete munduco arguia* — ye are the-world's light; *eznaiz ethorri abolitzera, baina complit-zera* — I-am-not come to-abolish-for (for-to-abolish), but complete-for (to complete). The present part., used like ours, ends in *-ic;* as, *itzir-ic*, leaving.

723. Here we introduce, for further illustration of the character of the language, a list of some of its words : *aditu*, hear, L. *auditum ; andia*, grand (*a =* gra) ; *aurra*, fore, ere ; *beguia*, eye, Ger. *auge* (*be* is pref.); *beroa*, warm ; *biar*, morrow; *bidea*, way, path; *burua*, head; *chiloa*, hole, ch, h; *cillara*, silver; *cerua*, heaven, Fr. *ciel*, r. l.

Deitu, call, L. *dico; doya*, just, G') *dikè ; eann*, when ; *echea*, house, case; *esan* and *erran*, say, G'k *reō ; edo*, or, other ; *eguin*, make, do, L. *ago* and *egi ; eguna*, day, Fr. *jour*, g, d ; *eman*, give, L. *dono ; ez*, not, G'k *ouk*, Ger. *kein*.

Zaca, save, without, Fr. *sans ; gacia*, acid ; *gan* and *goan*, go; *gosna*, cheese ; *gauba*, night, g, n ; *goia*, high, g, h ; *gucia*, all, Ger. *ganz ; guero*, near, g, n ; *gura*, will, Ger. *gierig*, gr, wl ; *guti*, little, bit; *hiru*, three ; *iboya*, river.

Mintza and *hitza*, word, Fr. *mot ; icena*, name ; *icasi*, teach ; *icusi*, see, look; *il*, die, kill ; *igan*, go, Ger. *st-eigen ; igil* and *isil*, silent; *jan*, eat; *lo*, sleep, l, sl; *lora*, flower; *lurra*, earth, L. *terra*, l, d, t.

Mendia, mount; *mia*, mouth, tongue, word; *obe*, better (notice that many letters in Basque are prefixes for us); *sendoa*, sound; *sua*, fire, s, b.

Tipia, bit, little; *ucitu*, cut, deal; *zaldia*, horse, Fr. *cheval;* *erre*, burn; *ikuo*, see, l-ook; *al*, can; Celt. *gall*, our will; *arria*, (stone) rock; *bicia*, life, L. *vivo;* *choria*, bird.

Egon, be, stand, do, L. *ago;* *izan, ucan*, Ger. *sein*, be — *i* is in Basque commonly a prefix, as, also, in *igo*, for our go; *mola*, L. *multus*, many, Ger. *viel;* *ona*, good, L. *b-ona*.

724. WALLACHIAN LANGUAGE: The last language of the Latin class which we come to, and the most of all different from it, is the Wallachian. It is unquestionably built on the Latin basis; its whole framework is Latin; but it must not be forgotten that it is Latin as it has grown up in a Slavic atmosphere, and under Slavic influences. What there is of it that is not Latin is Slavic — speaking generally, of course. While a vast majority of its larger words are almost identical with Latin, there is enough of the smaller words and particles so un-Latin as to divest the text of very much of its Latin cast — especially so; when we find find it, as we often do, written in the Cyrillic, or old Slavic alphabet.

725. The Wallachians call themselves *Romani*, and their language is spoken in Wallachia (a country in Austria), in Moldavia, in Transylvania, in Bessarabia, and in parts of Hungary. It is divided into a northern and a southern branch.

726. Among the prominent features of this language, we notice the suffixed article *il, le*, L. *ille;* as, *cane-le*, the dog; *serpe-le*, the serpent; *ceriu'l*, the heaven; and we find the feminine article *a;* as, *mente-a*, the mind; *flore-a*, the flower — all of them, it seems evident, a pure development of the ending *-us, -a, -um*, of Latin nouns and adjectives; as, *bon-us, -a, -um*. This suffixed article takes a dative and genitive form in *ui;* as, *socru-l*, the father-in-law (L. *socer*); *a socru-lui*, of the father-in-law (L. *soceri*); *frate-le meu*, the my brother (L. *frater meus*); *a frate-lui meu* (L. *fratris mei*, gen.), of the my brother; *pre frate-le meu* (L. *fratrem meum*, acc.), to the my brother — *pre* is a mere sign of the accusative, a mere inseparable prefix, and is not translated in English; and *a* performs the same part for the genitive; *de la frate-le meu* (L. *a fratre meo*, abl.), from the my brother. Conclusive proof we find in these facts, that the prepositions are mere prefixes, and the articles, pronouns, case endings, and the like, are simply developments of the endings of nouns. In the plural, we find *a fratilor mei* (L. *fratrum meorum*, gen.), of the my (*mei*) brothers.

727. Other features will be best understood by the examples which we are about to give:

Cicero oratoru-l quelu mare — Cicero orator-the which great (one), that great, the great one, or who (is) great (Cicero the great orator) ; *fa' casa' de lemnu, nee de petra* — make (L. *fac*) the-house from (*de*) wood (L. *lignum*), not from stone; *calul' quelu suru mi 'l dede* — the-horse (Fr. *cheval*) that cerulean (one) (to) me it (*'l*) given (he has), has given it, the horse, to me (this superfluons *il*, as well as many other superfluous particles, we find in other Latin languages as well); *quare-le* (the-which) *au* (has) *datu legi poporu-lui Romanu* — who has given laws (to) the-people Roman (to the Romans); *se chiama* — self calls, calls self, *i. e.*, is called.

O fera mi s-au (self has) *aratat in visu* — a beast (to) me hasself appeared (has appeared) in sight (to my vision) — showself = appear; *se vede* — self sees, is seen; *leul' au invinsu preursu* — the-lion has vanquished the bear — call *pre* an unmeaning prep., or the sign of acc.; *omu cu intelepciune mare* (L. *magnus*) — (a) man with intelligence great, man of great intelligence; *judecatoriu cu direptale* — judge with justice, a just judge; *casa aquesta e buna* — house this (this house) is good. We find the leading character of the Latin family here, the adjective after the noun. It will be observed that all the features which strike us in the modern Latin languages, are only developments of what we may also find in the old Latin.

Este de vendutu — is to (*de* = of) sell, *i. e.*, to be sold ; *nu e tempu si giaci* (L. *jaceo*) *in patu* — not is time (it is not time) that you-lie in bed, time not *to lie* in bed — this *si* = that, may be treated as *the* or *to*, and we shall always find *the*, *that* and *to* used to perform one and the same office ; the Wallachian language continually reminds us, by the identity of form, of the identity of prepositions with articles and pronouns; witness the prepositions *la*, *de*, *din*, *a*.

Vedu-l' io — see-him I, I see him (*l'*) ; *io l'asi* (him-that) *lauda* — I him might-praise (*asi* = that is merely sign of subj.); *cedru-l este arboru-l quel* (which) *mai tnaltu* (L. *altus*) — the-the cedar is the-tree that (the) most high, highest tree (we see in *in-altus* the addition of prep. *in*, not found in other idioms, and we find very many like instances — this shows that there is an *in* undeveloped in L. *altus*); *da-mi* — give me, to me; *june* (L. *juvenis*) *albu* (blank) *la facia* — (a) young (one, a youth) white to face, *i. e.*, with a white face (*la* is preposition with force of article); *tener* (tender, young) *ayer la mente* — (a) youth acute (*ager*) to mind, *i. e.*, in mind; *gradina nostra* (our) *cu* (with) *doa iugere este mai mai mare de* (from) *quat'* (from what, from as-much) *a-vostra* (your) — (the) garden ours by (with) two acres is more more great from what yours (is), *i. e.*, greater by so much than yours is ; *greu* (*gravis*, grievous) *de suitu*, difficult to ascend.

Fiiu-ti este aquestu? — son-you (to-you, *ti*) is that, *i. e.*, is that thy son? *stele-le quele mari* (great) *noui* (us) *se in-paru a-fire mici* (much and mite) — the-stars which great (the great ones) to-us self show (appear) to-be small; *que voiu* (will) *face* (do) *qua si* (subj. sign) *me mentuescu* — what shall-I do that (*qua*) me(-self) I-may-save (may save myself); *da-mi dare* (there-fore) *una dintre* (de-inter) *quele* — give-me there one from them; *'a-mi pare* — to me (it) 'pears (ap-pears to me); *me dore capu* — me it-pains (in-the) head (L. *caput*).

728. There is very little else in Wallachian that is sufficiently peculiar to justify further notice here. We will next introduce the 2d of the 20th John, so as to compare it with the rest of the family:

Deche au alergat, si au (has) *venit' la Simon Petru, si la chela* (*quela*) *lalt ouchenik* (disciple), *pre karele iuvia Jesus, si au-zic lor* (to-them): *Au luat pre Dmnul din mormunt, si nu* (not) *sciu ounde l-au* (him-have) *pus'* (put) — afterwards (she) has run (*i. e.*, she ran), and has come to (*la*) Simon Peter, and to that other disciple, whom (*pre-karele*, which) loved Jesus (did), and has-said them (to-them): (they) have removed the (*pre* sign acc.) Lord from grave, and not I-know where (*unde*) him-they-have put (have put him).

729. Here follows a list of some important and interesting words, with Latin and English counterparts: *peptu, pectus*, chest; *chidu, claudo,* close; *cetate, civitas,* state: *dosu, dorsum,* back; d, b.

Foame, fames, hunger, f, h; *geru, gelu,* cold, r, l; *nopte, nox,* night; *quelu, ille,* he, Ger. *welcher; tunu, tonitru,* thunder, and tone, sound; *porumbi, columbæ,* doves; *reu, malus,* worse.

Puntea, pont, bridge; *pruncu* (born), *puer* (boy); *plopu, plebs,* and *popul-us,* people; *spunu* and *espunu, expono,* expose; *scriu, scribo,* write; *angeru, angelus,* angel; *santu, sanctus,* saint; *sore, sol,* sun.

Ghiacia, glacies, ice, gla, ya, i; *delu, collis,* hill; *neue, nix,* s-now; *ochiu, ocul-us,* eye, Ger. *auge; chiae, clavis,* key; *gaiina, gallina,* hen, gal, gai, hai; *scurtu, curtus,* short, s prefix.

Cercu, quaero, search and seek, cr, sr, qr; *gatu, paro,* get, g, p; *scapu, fugio,* es-cape; *saru, salio,* spring, walk, sr, spr, and sl, wl.

Tocu, tango, touch; *tragu, traho,* drag, g, h; *jude, judex,* judge, d, dg; *diori, aurora; golu,* (*nudus*), bald, bare, g, b.

Micu, s-mall, mite; *mane,* morrow, morn (maun); *afundu,* profound, a, pro; *naltu* (for *inaltu*), L. *altus; amu,* have (our am); *atingu,* L. *tango,* at, t; *astemperu,* L. *tempero,* ast, t; *asunu,* L. *sono,* as, s; *sbatu, quatio,* quash, shake, sb, qu, qv; *spariu, terreo,* sp, t.

CHAPTER V.

SLAVIC LANGUAGES.

730. We pass next to the language of that extensive and powerful race, the Sclaves. These people were the last to come into notice on the theatre of European civilization; but, once organized, they have ever been active, and their march has been constantly onward. Their course has exhibited the unchangeableness and majesty of the moving mountain. They stand as an ever-enduring monument of our Asiatic ancestry; they afford us a living demonstration of the transition from the wild and monadic Tartar to the proud and polished citizen of enlightened Europe.

731. While we call to mind again the fact, that all classifications are more or less arbitrary, and that, particularly, subdivisions in language cannot stand the test of critical examination, we will yet, on the ground of convenience, and because even unjust classification is far better than none at all, divide the Slavic idioms into the following usually recognized families.

732. First, the Lettic, or Lithuanian class, composed of the Old Prussian, the Lithuanian, in its forms of Lithuanian proper, Samogitian, and Pruss-Lithuanian, and the Lettic or Livonian, together with its several dialects; the line of distinction between this family and the rest of the Slavic, is very clear and striking.

733. Next, the Russian, comprising, again, Great, Little, and White Russian; and the Illyrian, or South Slavic, comprising, or used as synonymous with, Servian, Slovenian, and Croation — the Slovenian having the minor dialects of Carinthian, Windian, Carniolan, and Styrian. This constitutes the south-eastern branch of Slavic.

734. And, finally, the western portion; being the Polish, Bohemian, and Sorbian, or Wend.

735. There is, besides, the Bulgarian and the Polabian, quite distinct from any of the above.

736. Having given this brief notice of the classification of these languages, we will now take the Russian and describe it more particularly, as the representative of the whole Slavic class. The Russians are the leading and ruling people of the whole Slavic race; Russia is the literary center, too, of the Slavic territory; the Russian language contains the works which will be found by far the most important to the philological student.

737. In passing to the Russian, and to the Slavic generally, you find, together with much that is Latin or German, a great deal besides that is peculiar to it. It takes some time to become acquainted with and accustomed to its strange orthography, its consonants piled upon consonants, and its comparative scarcity of vowels;—in Russian, too, though not in most others, you must learn to know its peculiar, though not very difficult, alphabet. When you have once fully mastered these obstacles, your task, if you properly direct your efforts, is half done. Learn well its orthography, and you will find its prepositions, its pronouns, its conjunctions, and its adverbs, all familiar to you; you will find they have all their easily recognized relatives in Greek, in Latin, or in German. Personal endings, participle endings, and lastly, though less plain, the case endings, all those seeming little marks which when really mastered leave but little of our work yet to be accomplished, will be easily made familiar, from the resemblance which they bear to similar marks found elsewhere.

738. The idiom of the Russian, and of the Slavic generally, the arrangement of its words, is to an Englishman exceedingly easy. There are, it is true, important differences, but they are very few; and without assuming to have counted the points of likeness or unlikeness in any two cases, we have a feeling that the order of the Russian, and of others of its class, is more like the English than the order is of any other language of Europe. One cannot but be struck at every step, especially in Russian, with this remarkable identity. Russian is also strikingly Greek in many of its features, particularly in orthography; after Greek, it is German.

739. The only real and lasting difficulty (and that one occurs in most foreign languages, particularly so in Greek) is in the difference between the root given in the dictionary, especially in verbs, and the derivatives in the text which are assumed to come from it. No quick, or far-sightedness can provide against these obstacles, and so long as our dictionary system remains as it is, those derivatives must be learned as a mere matter of memory. The science of etymology can aid some, but it can do no more than help us.

740. We give now the following examples in Russian, remarking generally that the points illustrated, in nearly every instance, are points equally the same in most or all of the other Slavic idioms.

Ia dam vam trech tchelovyak — I (will) give (to) you three man. The Russian numerals are followed by the genitive singular after 2, 3, and 4, and the genitive plural after other numerals — some few nouns are used in the nominative singular with numerals, as we say 20 foot; *dva glaza*, two (of) eye (two eyes); *kogda* (when) *bi vi mnya ne dali* (given) *pozvoleniya, to ya bi ne prishel*—if that (*bi*) you (to) me not (had) given permission, then (*to*) I would not (have) come—*bi* has the force of *would*, but it is a simple particle *that*, sign of subjunctive.

Skolko naidu ya podobnich miast—how-many (would) find I like places (how many like places would I find); *svoi pogryashnost strogo nakazivat dolzhno*—(one's) own faults strongly (*strogo*) (to) reprove (one) must (one should reprove his own faults); *ti polytchil ot nego pismo*—thou (hast) received from (out) me (a) letter. There are no articles proper in Russian, nor in Slavic generally; *gdya ymershii pogreben* (be-graved) *bit chotchet*—where the-dead (one) buried be will (will be buried); *ne mozhno dumat tchtob vsya cii* (these) *obriadi zavedeni bili takim narodom, kotorii*—not (is it) possible (to) think that all these ceremonies performed were (*bili*) by-such-a (*takim*) people, which—

Tam vidyal gori nad soboyo—there saw (I) rocks over self (over me).

Ti beri u nas zlato, serebro
Ti i nas vozmi vo riadi svoi

(Do) thou take from (*u*, to) us gold, silver,—
Do) thou also (*i*) us take into covenant (of) self—
also take us into thy covenant; *i ni kakich zanimatelnich predmetov v glaza ne popadaet-sia*—and not any interesting object to (*v*) eyes not presents-self (*sia* is suffix self) (no object presents itself to the eyes). This extra negative *not* is common in Russian, as elsewhere; *y vorot zapisali nashi imena*—at (the) gate (they) wrote our names; *na paradnom myastya protiv dvorza ytchila's* ('*s* = self) *gvardiya*—on (the) parade place opposite (the) palace (*dvorza*) exercised-selves (the) guards (did).

V bolshoi ulizya mnogo velikolyaphnich domov—in (the) great street (are) many (of) magnificent houses (gen. plur. after *many, mnogo*). A leading feature of the Russian is the general absence of the verb *be*, in cases where we find it indispensable; in this matter, Russian is by no means alone.

Zanimoyot'sya soldatami—(they) occupy 'self (by) soldiers, *i. e.*, are occupied—this form of passive is very common. In the expression of case relation by varying the endings, and without the use of prepositions, Russian is very much like Greek and Latin; *mi mogli siskat ego*—we could (might) find (infin.) him; *drug-drug*—other (the) other, *i. e.*, each other.

Moskva dolgo budet krasovat-sya vo glavya gorodov Russkich—Moscow long will (*budet*, be) shine-self (shine) at (the) head (*glavya*) (of) cities (of) Russia; *soldat etot sluzhil dolgo, i* (and) *visluzhil pensiyo* — soldier this (one) has-served long, and has-received (a) pension ; *za eto ega nagradili ordenom* — for that him (they) rewarded (with a) decoration (he was rewarded with) ; *Rossiya obitaema mnogimi narodami* — Russia (is) inhabited by-many nations ; *Ia vas utchu, zhelaya vam dobra, i nadayas tchto vi* (you) *uspyaete v naukach* — I you teach, wishing (as I wish) you good, and hoping-self (as I hope) that you (will) progress in (*v*) (the) sciences.

Odna vdova imyala (had) *dvuch dotchere* — a (one) widow had two daughters ; *tchto ia vizhu* — what (do) I see ? *gdya ti tak* (so) *dolgo bila* — where thou (*ti*) so long (hast) been ? *i onya brosili's bit .menshuyo dotch* — and they (Ger. *jener*) ranselves (ran) (to) beat (the) little girl (child, daughter).

741. It may not be amiss to remind the student that *l, il, li, la*, as endings of verb, mark the past, and equal our -*ed;* that *t, it, at*, are infin. endings ; that *am* marks dat. plur. ; *om*, and *em*, instrum. sing. ; *ach* marks instrum. plur., and *ich* marks gen. plur. of adjectives. We must note, too, that *ya, ia, yo, tch, sh*, and *zh*, we use as representatives each for a single character in Russian.

742. It must be observed, finally, that the examples we have given here, as elsewhere, are those which contain some peculiarity of expression, while, as a general rule, the Russian order scarcely differs from ours. The number of idiomatic expressions is not very large.

743. BOHEMIAN : The Bohemian possesses the general structure of the Russian, as well as of the other Slavic languages, with, however, several strong points of difference. The orthography, while it possesses thoroughly the Slavic character, is yet considerably different from Russian — there are many words common to both, and many words, again (in the two languages), with equal meanings, have very different forms.

744. The Bohemian has an extensive literature, and some of it dates back several centuries. Bohemia, it will be remembered, is a country of Austria bordering on the German States — the people call themselves Tchezki, and number between seven and eight millions. It is spoken, too, in Moravia and Hungary ; the *Slovak of Hungary* is a leading form of it. There are several dialects of the Bohemian, which we cannot notice here.

745. A few examples will be given from what would strike us as peculiar :

Muj bratr narozen jest (is) *v Praze* — my brother born is (was) in (*v*) Prague ; *to mesto kde jsem* (am) *prava studoval* — that (the) town (place), where (I) am (have) (the) rights (laws) studied ; *slove Viden*, calls (self) Vienna, *i. e.*, is called ; *jak jste star* — how (much) are (you) old, *i. e.*, how old are you ; *cisare samcho jsem videl* — (the) emperor (czar) himself (the

same) have (am) (I) seen, *i. e.*, I have seen him; *slysim ho çisti*
— (I) hear him read (inf.); *jeho syn byl ucitelem* — his son
was (for) teacher, *i. e.*, was a teacher. This is a common form
in Slavic — the dative (instr.) after *be*. So, again, *bude se jeden-
krate jmen-ovati nasim cisarem* — (he) will self some-day (one-
time) name (for) our czar (he will be named as our czar); *bude
se — jmenovati*, will himself name = will be named. This separation of *self* from the verb is very common in Slavic, as well as
in German; and the use thus of reflexive for passive is very
prevalent.

Kolik jest hodin — what is (it) hour, Ger. how much clock
is it; with us, what time is it? *narodil ysem se* — born (I) am
self, I have born self, *i. e.*, I am or was born; *chodilo se* — it
went self (there went); *hlas w (v) Rama slyssan gest* — (a) voice
from Rama heard is (was heard); *bily jako snih* — white as
snow; *coz mam ciniti* — what have (I) to-do (what shall I do);
to nemuze byti — that not-may (cannot) be; *chci meho bratra
navstiviti* — (I) will my brother visit. The persons being well
indicated in this language, as in Russian, the pronouns are
mostly left out, as in Latin.

Kdo vam to rekl — who (to) you that (has) said; *ne-verte
mu nic* — (do) not-believe him nothing; *to je zly clovek* — that
is bad man; *on mluvi cely den* — he speaks all day; *mluvilo se
o vojne* — (it) spoke self of war, *i. e.*, they spoke.

Mrtvola, ktera se v lese hledati mela, byla na silnici nalezena
— (the) body, which self in (the) wood seek (inf.) had, was in
(the) street found (*se-hledati mela* — has to find itself, was expected to be found, Ger. should be found); *myji diteti ruce* —
(I) wash (for the) child (the) hands; *kdy-bych-om byli* (was)
meli zizen — when-that-we had (was) had (*meli*) thirst; *ptak
ktereho jsem vcera chytil, dnes uletel* — (the) bird which (I)
have (am) yesterday caught, to-day (has) flown; *co to mas v
oku* — what that (thou) hast in eye, *i. e.*, what hast thou in eye;
pilny syn jest ve skole — (the) diligent son is in school; *sel k
tobe* — (he has) gone to thee, Ger. he is to thee gone; *Muj kun
ma* (has) *dlouhe nohy* — my horse (pony) has long feet; *chlapec*
(Ger. *knabe*) *nema* (*ne* = not) *sve knihy* — (the) boy not-has
his books; *kdo sil tuto kosili* — who (has) made this shirt, Ger.
who has this shirt made.

746. POLISH: The Polish is the language of a people once
the most powerful and important of the Slavic race; but for
many years past they have been the mere vassals of Russia. A
people distinct in character, and distinct in language, they have
been merged, for all practical purposes, in the race that has
mastered them. The Polish has many points of likeness with
the Bohemian, with which we, with others, have classed it; but

it has, too, many points that place it parallel with the Russian. We leave the examples given to afford some idea of the relation between the three. It must be observed, too, that Polish, as we might expect from its location, has reflected very much of the German hue.

747. *Bielsza od sniegu*—whiter from (than) snow ; *uczyc sie*— (to) learn self (to learn) ; *kiedi nie chcecie* (will) *sluchac, to bedziece* (will) *czuli*—when not (you) will hear, then will (you) feel (felt)—*czuli* is really a perfect participle, or tense. *David zabil Goliata kamienem*—David slew Goliath (with a) stone (the prep. denoted by ending *em*); *malo chleba*— little (of) bread (little bread); *powiem ci* (thee) *co nowego*— (I) will-say (to) you something (anything, what, *co*) of-new (tell you something new); *daj mi chleba*— give me (of) bread (loaf), *i. e.*, me some bread ; *nie moge ci prawdy powiedziec* — (I) not may you (to you) truth say (not tell you the truth); *nie zlac to rzecz* — not bad (ill) that thing (L. *res*) (is), *i. e.*, it is not bad.

Ma byc w (in) *domu*—(he) has to-be in house, Ger. he should be, *i. e.*, they say he is in the house ; *slonce swiecace*— (the) sun shining (shining sun) ; *list napisany*— (the) letter written (written letter); *idac do kosciola spotkalem mego przyjaciela*—going (as I went) into (the) church met-I my (*mego*) friend ; *ide swoia droga* (road)—(I) go own way, *i. e.*, my own way; *zjadlszy wstal od stolu*—having-eaten (he) arose from (the) table ; *wiele do czynienia*—much for doing (much to do); *juz slonce weszlo*—already (has the) sun risen ; *ja slyszalem, ze umarl wczorajszej nocy*—I (have) heard, that (he) died yester night.

Tys (thou-est) *swoje przedal*—thou-has own (*i. e.*, thy own) sold (in *ty-s* we find only the person endings joined to *ty*, thou, for thou art; and *my-smy*, we-are, *we* and person ending of 1st plural); *my-smy* (we-are) *widzieli jego* (his) *pismo* — we-are (have) seen his writing ; *slucham*, I hear, and *wy-slucham*, I will hear, or listen — *w* and *wy* is a mere prefix, like the *ge* of German, here used as sign of future ; *mam czytac*—I-have to-read, I shall read; *stal sie panem*—(he) became self (stood self) for-(a) lord, became a lord; *kto ma wiele*—(he) who has much; *ja wiem* (wit, Ger. *weiss*), *czemu* (for-what) *sie pytam*—I know, why self I-ask, *i. e.*, why I ask.

There are several minor dialects of Polish, but none of them present features of any great importance.

748. ILLYRIAN : The Illyrian stands at the head of a family possessing the form and spirit of the Slavic in every part, yet with such other marks, made by the neighboring German and Latin, as render it particularly distinguishable from the rest of

the great class of which it forms a part. The modern Illyrian, it will be noticed, is separated from Venice and northern Italy, by the dividing line of the Julian Alps; the limits of ancient Illyria are not well understood, but there is every evidence to lead us to believe that the Illyrians were once a people far more numerous and more powerful than the modern Illyrians now are.

749. The words are nearly all Slavic, but with a strong tendency to the Latin and German methods of orthography. As compared with the rest of the class, it is particularly noticeable that this family forms its past or perfect tense by the ending *ah*, *ach*, or *ech*, in place of Slavic *l*, or our *ed*; thus, Polish *czytal*, read (past), Illyrian *citah*, read (past) — and so, Illyr. *bi-ah*, Pol. *b-yl*, Servian *b-ech*, our *w-as*.

750. Illyrian compares with Bohemian thus: *Otce nas koji* (who) *jesi na nebesih*; (Boh.) *Otce nas, jenz jsi na nebesich* — father of-us (our) who art in (*na*) heaven (*jenz*, Ger. *jener*, that = who); *Sveti se ime tvoje*; (Bo.) *po-swet se jmeno twe* — hallowed (saint, holy) be name thy (*sveti se*, hallowed self, for be hallowed, reflex = pass). (In Boh. *po-swet* compared with *sveti*, we see *pos* = *s*, or that prefixes are developments of initial letters, and add nothing in any case to the original or base word); *pridi kraljevstvo tvoje*; (Bo.) *prijd kralowstwi twe* — come kingdom thy (*pridi* = *pr-idi*; *pr* is a prefix, and *idi* = go, L. *ivit* and *it*).

Budi volja tvoja kako na nebu tako i na zemlji; (Bo.) *Bud wule twa jako w nebi tak i na zemi* — be will thy so (*kako*) in heaven so and (as) in earth; *kruh svagdanji* (daily) *daj nam danas*; (Bo.) *chleb-nas wezdejsi dejz nam dnes* — bread (Bo. bread-our, our bread) daily give (*daj*) to-us to-day (*dnes*); *nego izbavi nas iza zla*; (Bo.) *ale zbaw* (see *iz-b* = *izb* = *zb*) *nas od zleho* (ill, evil, *z* = *v* = *i*) — but (G'k *alla*) deliver us from (out) ill.

751. We cannot resist the temptation to introduce here some Illyrian words, to show their departure from the northern and eastern Slavic style of orthography, in words clearly identical; we will introduce some words, too, which are more or less peculiar to Illyrian.

Ako (when), L. *ac*, and, at; *bar* (at least), bare, barely; *Becs*, Vienna; *bel* (white), blank, bleach; *berz* (quick), hurry; *biber*, pepper, It. *pevere*; *bodni*, poiut (bodkin); *bolse*, well, better, It. *meglio*, L. *melius*; *brada*, beard; *brebir*, beaver; *brek*, (dog), bark; *brek*, burg; *brod*, boat, br, b; *buha*, It. *pulce*, flea, uh, ul.

Car, czar, L. *rex* (king); *carkva*, church; *carn*, dark (black), It. *nero*, L. *niger*, Ger. *schwartz*, n, schw; *cel*, whole; *cepati*,

Ger. *spalten*, It. *spaccare*, split, cep, cp, sp; *cerv*, worm, It. *verme;* cia = cil, whole, Ger. *ganz;* *cipela*, It. *scarpa* (cpl, srp), shoe; *civ*, tube; *csa*, It. *cosa, che*, what; *csedo*, child, Ger. *kind*, cs, c; *csela*, bee; *csep*, It. *tapo*, stopple; *csesto*, It. *spessa*, oft, st, sp, ft; *csez*, with, G'k *meta* (through); *csin*, done, deed, cs, s, d; *csredo*, It. *greggia*, herd, gr, hr — mark that the *cs* of Illyr. is very clearly only a kind of *s*, or a kind of *c*; *csud*, sense, Ger. *sinn*; *csudan*, wonder, cs, *w*; *csutti*, It. *udire* (*cs* prefix), It. *sentire* (hear); *csuvar*, ward (*csuv, csv, sv, w*), guard; *csverst*, force, strong, Ger. *stark*; *cucak*, It. *cane*, Ger. *hund*, (dog) — *ak* is a common noun ending of Illyr.; *cukro*, sugar, c, s; *cura*, girl, G'k *kore*.

Dabar, beaver; *dar*, dower (gift); *darvo* and *drevo*, tree (wood); *davati* (give), L. *past, dabat* (gave); *debeo*, thick, dense; *decs-ak*, It. *giovine* (young), child, d, g, ch.; *desan*, and *desna*, It. *destro* (just, d, j), right, d, r; *diliti* (*iti*, Illyr. inf. ending), deal, divide, It. *s-partire* (*ire*, inf. ending), separate, dvd, dl, spt; *dim*, It. *fumo*, steam, d, st; *dlakka*, It. *pelo* (pl, dl), hair; *dreti*, tear, It. *stracciare*, strip, Ger. *zerreissen*, dr, str, zerr — see Ger. prefix *zer* lost in the Illyr. *dr*; *dug*, due, It. *debito*, Ger. *schuld*, sch, d; *duha*, o-dor, Ger. *ge-ruch*, r, d; *dvor*, court.

Frigati (*ati*, inf. end.), It. *friggere*, fry, parch (bake); *Gark*, Greek; *Gjuro*, George, gj, ge, g; *glas* (sound), Ger. *laut* (*gl* = *l* or *g* pref.), loud; *gled*, look (*g* pref.), Ger. *blick* (*b* pref.); *gluh* (deaf), G'k *kluō* = hear, as It. *sardo* (deaf) = heard; *godina*, year, gd, yr; *gorje*, worse; *gorki* (bitter), sour; *gavor* (speech), word, verb (*ga*, pref.); *grabiti*, L. *rapio*, rob, gr, r; *gravran*, raven, It. *corvo;* *gredem* and *grem*, go (gr = g), L. *gredior;* *griem*, warm; *grih* (sin), error (go, wander).

Haran (thank), It. *grato;* *hit*, jet, (throw), It. *gittare;* *jablan*, apple; *jagnje*, It. *agnello*, l-amb; *jaje*, egg, Ger. *ey, ei*, It. *uovo;* *jedin*, union, join, one (*d* suppressed); *iskatti*, seek, search — *is* is treated as prep = *iz* = out, but it is our *s* in seek, isk, sk; *Ivan*, John, It. *Giovanni;* *izfrigati* = *frigati*, izf, f; and *izgrabite* = *grabiti*, izg, g.

Kcsi, daughter; *kerv*, gore (blood); *kip*, Ger. *bild*, pict-ure, fig-ure; *kisel*, acid; *kljucs*, key, Ger. *schlüssel;* *klup* (bank), cliff; *kola*, car, r, l (wheel); *koleno*, knee, (-cline, bend); *kost*, bone, It. *osso;* *kralj*, royal, kr, r; *krepost*, force, Ger. *kraft;* *krics*, cry; *kriva*, wrong, curve, -prave, It. *reo;* *krov*, roof — Illyr. *k* is often for us a prefix; *kroz*, through, -cross; *krupan*, gross, robust, rp, rb (*k* pref.); *krut*, rude, c-rude, hard; *kucha*, house, cage; *kuhan*, cook; *kupiti*, Ger. *kaufen*, It. *comprare*, buy — so we see *k* of *kaufen* is com of *comprare*, or pref. *com* becomes lost in the word; and this is only one illustration of the universal law; *kus* (bite), *kiss*.

Labda, ball, lbd, bl; *lagak*, light, It. *leggiero* (strike off *ak* generally as mere ending); *mek*, meek, weak, Ger. *weich*, It. *molle*; *mil* (deal), G'k *phil-os*, L. *a-micus*, It. *a-mabile*; *mir*, Ger. *friede* and *ruhe*, joy, fr, j; *mlad* (young), lad; *moch*, might, may; *mraz*, ripe; *mriti*, die, r, d (*m* pref.)

Nag, naked, nude; *narav*, nature; *nauka*, doctrine — *na* is Illyr. pref., but it is our *t* of teach and *l* of learn; *na-ucsan*, taught, L. *doctus*, n, d; *nechjak*, It. *nipote*, nephew; *nem*, dumb, mute; *nemogu*, not-may (cannot), *nem* = nm = m; *nor*, fool, Ger. *narr*, ig-nor-ant, ign = gn (know); *nuglo*, a-ngle, Ger. *eck*, nick, nook.

Ocsi, eye; *odkrit* (*od* pref.), discover (dscover), It. *scoperto*, Ger. *ent-deckt* (decked) — *krit*, covered; *odpert*, o-pen, German *o-ffen*, It. *a-perto*; *ogled* (o = od), (object) look, glook; *opad*, full (p, f), L. *cado*; *ov* (this), L. *ubi*, Fr. *ou*.

Pal, fall; *penna*, foam, It. *schiuma*, scum; *pokrit*, covered (*po* pref.); *posobnost*, substance (*po* pref.); *pot*, sweat, It. *sudor*; *po-znan*, known, Ger. *be-kannt*; *prav*, right, -prave (*p* pref.). L. *verus*; *pridi*, L. *gredior*, come, go, L. *it* (*pr* pref.) — so *pri-chi*, come, go (*pri* pref.); *pri-lika* (*pri* pref.), likeness; *pri-pek*, burn, bake; *puk*, folk, people.

Rabiti, work, Ger. *a-rbeiten*; *rasti*, g-row, L. *c-resco*; *rat*, war, Ger. *k-rieg*; *razbor*, reason, It. *ragione*; *razdel* = *del*, deal, and *razgovor* = *govor*, word — *raz* is prefix; so *raz-krivati*, cover; *raz-lika*, un-likeness; *red*, order.

Sam, sole, some; *san*, sleep, It. *sonno*, s, sl; *sarce*, heart, It. *cuore*, core; *sbitti*, beat (*s* pref.); *sirov*, rough (*si* pref.); *skerb*, care, It. *cura*, Ger. *sorge* (we see Ger. s, our c = k, both used in Illyr. as sk); *skrovan*, secret (s-covered); *skuhati*, cook (s-cook); *slava*, glory; *smart* (death), L. *mors*; *smok*, sap; *sneg*, snow, It. *neve* (s-neve); *spor*, spare, It. *parco*; *suh*, dry (s, dr), It. *secco*; *sur* (s, g), gray, It. *grigio*; *svet*, world, Ger. *welt* (sv = vv = w).

Tat, thief, It. *lad-ro* (l, t); *tvard*, hard, It. *duro*; *tvor*, work (tv = vv = w); *ud*, limb, Ger. *gl-ied*; *ugal*, angle, Ger. *eck*; *vart*, gard-en; *voz*, wagon; *vrata*, port, door (p, d).

Xiv, live, It. *vivo*; *zanak*, knot (z, k), It. *nodo*; *zanat*, -quaint, Ger. *kunst*, know; *zima*, frigid, winter, L. *hiems*; *zvir*, Ger. *thier*, It. *fiera* (beast).

752. SERVIAN: The Servian subdivision is easily classified with the Illyrian; they run parallel in every essential point; they are evidently closely related dialects of one original tongue. Indeed, Illyrian is used as a comprehensive term for the Servian taken in connection with Slovenian and Croatian.

753. Servia extends west to the Adriatic; and on the south, merging into Bulgaria, it extends to Albania and northern Greece. The Danube separates it from Wallachia on the north; further towards the west, taking in the Illyrians, it crosses that river, and the Save, and extends to the southern limits of Hungary. The Servians number over five millions. Speaking generally, Servia is the northwest portion of Turkey.

754. There are, of course, many forms of Servian; two leading forms, after the Illyrian portion, are the High and Low Wend, or High and Low Lusatian. The term Wend is used by the Germans often as synonymous with Servian. The High Lusatian is spoken in the country about Budissin, Reichenbach, Kaimenz, Bautzen, Loebau, and Muskau; and the Low, in various dialects, in the region about Cottbus.

755. The following selections are from the High Wend: *To czini, so mamy wustojneho a pilneho sahrodnika* — that makes (Ger. *thun*), that (so) we-have (a) clever and (a) diligent gardener (s = g); *wone budze dre skoro* (shortly) *czass* — it (will) be very soon time (*wone* = one, Russ. *on*, he); *to moze byez* — that might be; *pol punta zokora* — half pound sugar (of sugar).

Schto moze to wedziez — who (*scht* = w) may that (*to*, the) know (Ger. *wissen*); *ja bdu 'mu tuhlej njeschto na-pissacz* — I will (be) him here (of-this) something write (*na*-write, *n*-write).

A tejz to ssym ja sesnal — and also that am (have) I known; *schtoz* (what) *ja newjem* (*ne* pref.) — what I not-know; *chzecze* (choose) *dacz* — will (you) give (*dacz*).

756. It is well to observe that these Lusatian dialects are often treated apart from the Illyr.-Serb., and placed in the Bohemian class, under the name of Sorbian, Sorabian, or Wend. The term Servian for a language is like Servian to denote a people, anything but definite.

757. Croatia lies between the Drave and Save rivers; Croatian is spoken, too, in western Hungary. The Croatians, or Croats, are also named High Slavonians. The language is eminently Illyrian; it also very much resembles the Bohemian. Compared with these two, nothing particularly important can be said of it. The orthography presents very few peculiarities. It has, however, several forms, or sub-dialects.

758. There is yet an extensive family, called the South Wends, who belong with the Illyrian race, or may be classed with it. Their language is called, also, Slovenian and Corutanian, and is spoken in Styria, Carinthia, Carniola (Carniolan or Krain), countries above the north Adriatic — also in a portion of Illyria and in Hungary.

759. The following from the Hung-Wend (Lord's Prayer) will show how it compares with Illyrian or Servian: *Otscha nasch, ki ssi* (who art) *vu nebesay; ssveti sse* (hallowed self) *ime tvoje; pridi* (be) *uola tvoja, kako* (as) *je* (it-is) *vu nebi, tak i* (also) *na semli; krucha nasega* (our) *vszakdenesnyega* (daily, each day) *daj* (give) *nam ga dnesz* (to-day).

760. We may notice here briefly the North Wend, or Polabian. This dialect represents a language once, beyond doubt, prevailing in different dialects, to a large extent, in northern Germany. We hardly know where to class it; it is neither German nor Slavic, or it is both, as you like. A very large proportion of the words are German and not Slavic; again, there are many others which are Slavic and not German. The following, from the Lord's Prayer, presents one of its forms:

Nos holya wader, ta toy (that thou) *chiss* (art) *wa nebisgay; sjunta woarda* (holy be, were) *tugi geima* (name); *tia rik komma; tia willya schingot* (be) *koke* (so) *nebisgay kokkak* (as) *no sime* (earth).

This language has been extinct since about the eighteenth century.

761. BULGARIAN: Here we may speak also of the Bulgarian. Bulgaria is a country in the northern part of Turkey. The language is clearly Slavic in its form and spirit, easily classed with the Servian or Illyrian, but having much stronger evidences of Greek relationship than any other Slavic tongue. The alphabet, differing somewhat from the Russian, may, like that, be called a form of the Greek, or, the three may be all forms of a common original.

762. The following are selections: *Oni mu rekocha* — they (to) him said; *e pisano*, is written; *otrotche to* — child the; *zashoto videchme zvyadza ta negova* (of-him) *na vostok* (east), *i doidochme da mu* (him) *ce poklonime* — for (we) have-seen star that (the) of-him in East, and (we) have-come that (to) him self worship(-we) — that we may worship him, worship-self = worship.

We notice here the *ch* = *k*, sign of past tense, like Illyrian, which may be looked upon as standing nearer the *ka* of Greek perfect, and the *ed* of English, than does the *l* of other Slavics. We find here the article, or demonstrative, *ta, te, to,* following the noun, as we find possessives and relatives doing in the other dialects.

Dum-ashe — (and) said; *veshe* — was; *govoreshe* — he said; *she ti dam* — will (to) thee I-give, *i. e.*, I will give thee (will is used separate to form future here, as in Illyrian); *retchenno to* — spoken the (the (thing) spoken); *da bude vola ta tvoa* — then be will the thy, *i. e.*, be thy will; *i sitchko to-ti* (and all the-thy) *tyalo* (body) *she da bude svyastlo* — and all the-thy body shall then be lighted (*svyastlo*) ; *da ne sudeni budete* — that not judged (ye) be (that ye be not) ; *she da retchesh* — will then (thou) say (thou wilt say); *i kato videcha narodi te* — and when saw (they) people the (people saw).

Dade, L. *dedi,* gave; *vide,* L. *vidi,* saw; *koito* (which) *ce naritcha* — who self called (was called); *ste,* (ye) are; *tchuli ste zasho e* (is) *retcheno* — heard (ye) are that (it) is said (have heard, it has been said); *ne mozhete da rabotite na* (to) *Bga i na mamuna* — not ye-can (may) that ye-serve to God and to mammon (ye cannot serve); so, *will that I deny,* for *I will deny ;* and *I have come that I destroy,* for *come to destroy.*

763. *Da* is a prefix (separate) used before infinitives and imperatives, equal to our *to, do* of Celtic, and the *da* of other Slavics — it is used also for *that,* and it shows very clearly what augments may become by development. We have nothing to add that is peculiar to the language, so thoroughly is it Slavic, not only in its form and grammar, but also in its orthography.

764. The Bulgarian is an interesting and valuable language, and it is greatly to be regretted that it has not received greater attention from philologists.

765. LITHUANIAN: The most interesting, in a philological point of view, of all the Slavic families, is the Lithuanian, sometimes called German-Slavic. It is intesesting because it shows the transition of the Slavic to the German, or of the German to the Slavic. The leading members of the family are the Old Prussian, the Lithuanian, with its branches, Samogitian, or Shamaitish (called also Pol.-Lithuanian), the Pruss-Lithuanian, which, too, has several minor dialects, and the Lett, or Livonian, which, again, has at least five recognized divisions (one of which is Semgallian). These languages constitute a well-defined family, possessing uniform features, and alike distinct, as an individual, from both the Slavic and the German, while they are yet each and all made up of elements common to one or the other of the two.

766. The Old Prussian we will take up first: it is, of all the family, the nearest to the German. This was once, it is agreed, the language of a numerous people, divided into different tribes with corresponding difference of idiom. They dwelt in northern Germany. Of the language, extinct since the seventeenth century, very little remains to us, and we know less of it than could be desired. With all its German or Gothic orthography, it is still essentially Lithuanian. Some examples will best show what it is :

767. *As quoi stesmu ainan po-galban teckint* — I (*as*) will (to) him an (a) help make (give) — (*int* is one of the inf. endings); *stwi billa stas smunents* — then spoke the (Ger. *das*)

man; *turri gerdant*—shall say; *turri* = have and shall, is like Lith., and connected with Ger. *soll*, shall, l = r; *laikuts wirst*—held becomes (is held); *kai stai ismukint masi*—that they (to) learn (inf.) may (may learn); *tou ni-turri*—thou not-should (shouldn't); *ka ast sta billiton*—what is that said; *-on, -ats, -ints, -ts, -ton*, are pass. part. endings; *-ans, -uns*, are of the act. part.; *-twei, -ton, -int, -ut, -it, -t*, are infinitive endings.

Ains dilants ast waisei (his) *algas werts*—a worker is (of) his pay worth (worthy); *kai erains labban segge*—what every-one good does; *bhe prei wiran billa Deiws*—and to (the) man spoke (tell) God; *quoi warein kirsa* (over) *din turri*—which power over him has (*turri*) (has power over him).

768. We may notice the following orthographic forms besides:

Adder, other; *a-nimts*, Ger. *ge-nommen* (taken); *arwis*, true, right; *astin*, thing (a form of *stas* = the); *ausins*, car. *Billa*, say, tell; *buttas*, house, a-bode, Semitic faith: *dilas*, works (dl = dr); *druwe* (believe), trust; *eit*, goes, L. *it; gannan*, woman, queen; *garrin*, tree; *giwan*, life, L. *vivo*, g, v, z; *gurins*, poor, g, p; *ilga*, long.

Kaekint, to catch; *kawids*, which (*ka* pref.); *kermens* (body), L. *corpus; kird'*, hear; *kittan*, other (*k* pref.); *labs* (good), Slav. *dobry*, d, l; *laukit*, seek, look(-for).

Maldai (young), small; *mylis*, love (*my* pref.), L. *a-micus; packe*, peace; *per-eit* = *eit* (go); *per-gimmons* (born) = *gimmons*, G'k *ginomai; po-lygu*, Ger. *g-leich*, like (*po* pref.); *po-simma*, Ger. *be-kenne*, know.

Schlusi, serve (*schl* = sr); *sidons*, sitting; *sparts*, Ger. *stark*, strong; *stas*, Ger. *das*, the, st, d; *teiku*, do, Ger. *thun*, make; *urs*, old; *wyrs*, L. *vir*, hero, man, force.

A very large portion of the words of this language are decidedly Slavic.

769. Lithuanian proper is spoken by a people not very large in numbers, nor possessing any particular national importance. They are found in Prussia and in Russia, and number, with the Letts, perhaps two millions. We proceed immediately to illustrate some of the features of the language:

770. *Kas tur ausu* (ears) *klausyt*—who hath ears to-hear—in Samogitian, *ant klausimo*, for to-hear; *su juni*—with him; *jie at-sake jam*—they to-said (said) to-him; *ir jis kel-es, nakcze eme* (took) *waikeli* (*wkeli*, w-child)—and he (*jis*) arisen (having), by-night took (the) child; *bet girde-dams*—but hear-ing (Samo. *iz-girdes*, heard); *jis bus* (be) *wadinnams*—he (shall) be called; *tary-dams*, saying; *asz sakau jums*—I say (to) you; *sakyti*—to say; *gal prickelt*—can raise-up (*pri* pref.) (*gal* for

can is common — our *shall*, Welsh *gal*); *wandenimi* — with water; *ugenimi* — with fire; *isz wandens* — out (of) water.

Kad jo kriksztijams butu — by him baptized to-be (*butu*); *ir tu ateini pas mane* (me) — and thou comest to me; *pa-kriksztitas* — (being) baptized (*pa* pref.); *gundinams butu* — tempted to-be; *jey essi* (art) *Diewo sunus* — if (thou) is God's son; *poto wede ji welnas i szwenta miesta* — then took him (*ji*) (the) devil (did) into (the) holy city (place); *ir state ji ant* — and stood him on; *tai wislab du-su taw* — these all (I) will-give thee (Samo. *wistag duosin tau*). See the *s* mark of the Greek and Irish future — it is common in Lith. Notice also the pasts with suppressed endings, like L. *dedi* and *feci*, in the forms *sake*, said, *wede*, took, *state*, stood.

Jus este swieto szwiesybe — ye are (the) world's light; *ne atejou paniekint, bet iszpildit* — not (I) come to-destroy, but to-fulfill; *sakyta esant* — said being (being said); *eit wiena myle* to-go one mile; *eik su jumi* — go with him (*su* = G'k *sun*, L. *cum*); *butumbit* — may be.

Niekz ne gal dwiem ponam szluziti — no-one act can two masters serve (none can); *jey nori* (L. *nolo*) — if (thou) wilt (this *will* is used with future also); *busit wedami* — (ye) shall-be brought, (Samo. *busite wadziuti*); *ne turrit dumati* — not (ye) have to-think (not to think, shall not); *pa-duti yra* — given are (*pa* pref.). Prefixes in the way of meaningless augments are very common.

Zinnotumbit — ye may know (had known), (Samo. *zinotumet*); *kasgi tadda gal iszganytas buti* — who then came saved be; *zinnote* — ye know; *kas daryta yra* — which done is (*dar* = *kar*, chore); *zmogus* — man (*zm* = m); *lygi yra* — like is.

771. After the examples given in Lithuanian, little need be said of Samogitian; for the two are much alike. The Samogitian often changes the form, but seldom changes the principle. These few examples will suffice:

Ejo pirm ju — (it) went before them; *ey-kite* — go ye; *kur bowo* — where was (L. *cur* = why); *ineje* (*in* pref.) *ing namus* (L. *domus*) — coming (they) in (the) house; *idant ji nuzuditu* — for (-to) him destroy (*itu* is a common supine ending); *tardamas* — saying; *kas ira pa-sakati* — what was said; *ira girdetas* — is heard; *norejo buti palinksminta* — will be comforted; *isz-girdes* — having heard; *buwo nuwestas* — was lead; *palayminti* — blessed; *bus wadinti* — shall-be called; *priesz zmonies* — before men, L. *homines; noriu* — I will (L. *nolo*); *idant mokitu* — for (to) speak (preach); *walgans ir gierans* — eating and drinking: *kur turejo Christus uzgimti* (*uz* pref.) — where should (has) Christ (be) born.

772 The Lettish is spoken in Livonia and in Kurland. It

has considerable literature, and some of it goes back as far as the thirteenth century. We give only a portion of the Lord's Prayer of one of the forms of Lettish : *Muhssu tehws debessis* — our father (in) heaven ; *sswetihts lai tohp taws wahrds* — sanctified let be thy word (this *lai* is the prefix *da* we have seen elsewhere); *lai nahk pee mums tawa walstiba* — let come by us thy kingdom ; *muhssu deenischka maisi dohd mums schodeen* — our daily bread give (*dohd*) us this-day (to-day, *heute*) ; *peedohd* = *dohd*.

It bears a strong resemblance to the other Lithuanian dialects, but it has also several peculiarities of its own.

773. We give here the Lithuanian form of the 20th John, 2, and will follow it with the other Slavic tongues, for comparison with it and with each other :

Tay ji bega (then she ran), *ir ateit* (came) *pas Simona Petra, ir pas* (to) *ana kitta mokitini* (disciple), *kurri* (whom) *Jezus mylejo, ir sako jiem dwiem* (to-them two); *ateme* (they have taken) *Wieszpati isz kapo* (out the grave), *ir ne zimmome* (we-know) *kur* (where) *ji* (him) *padejo*.

774. In Samogitian :

Nubego tada (came-she then), *ir atejo pas Simona Petra, ir pas kita mokitini kuri milejo* (loved) *Jezus, o sakie jems ; ateme Wieszpati isz grabo, o nezinome kur ji padejo* (they-have-laid).

775. In Bulgarian :

Otortcha protchee, i doide (came, *do* pref.), *kod Simona Petra, i kod drugiat* (other) *outchenik, kogoto* (whom) *obutchashe Jisus, i retche* (and said) *im ; zeli* (taken) *Gda o grobat, i ne znam* (we-know) *gdya sa* (have) *go* (him) *polozhili* (*po* prefix).

776. In Bohemian :

I bezela (and she-ran), *a prissla k* (to) *Simonowi Petrowi a k druhemu* (other) *ucedlnjkowi tomu* (this) *gchoz* (which) *milowal* (loved) *Gezjs, a rekla* (G'k reõ) *gim : Wzali Pana z* (out) *hrobu, a newjme* (not-know-we) *kde* (where) *geg polozili* (placed-they, *po* = *p* of place).

777. In Hungarian Wend :

Bezi zato i pride (ran then and came) *k Simon Petri i k tomi* (that) *drugomi* (other) *vucseniki, steroga je lubo Jezus, i ercse* (said) *nyima ; odneszli* (taken-they, *od-ne* pref.) *szo Goszpoda z groba, i neznamo, kama szo* (to) *ga djali* (him placed).

778. In the Polish :

Biegla tedy (therefore) *i przyszla do Symona Piotra, i do drugiego ucznia* (disciple) *ktorego* (whom) *milowal Jezus a rzekla im ; wzietoc Pana z* (from) *grobu, a nie wiemy gdzie* (where) *go po-lozono*.

779. And last, in Russian :
I tak (and then) *byazhit i prichodit* (comes, *pri* pref.) *k Simonu Petru, i k drugomu utcheniku kotorago* (which) *lyobil Jisus, i govorit im ; unesli Gospoda iz groba, i ne znaem* (we-know) *gdya polozhili ego* (him).

780. (We may make the general note here, that the contents of parenthesis, in the text, generally gives the meaning of the word that precedes that ; occasionally it only suggests some related word. In the selections from John just given, we have only given the meaning of a few words, the rest being sufficiently determined by the translation known, or from comparison with the others accompanying it. The order and number of words in our translations will uniformly correspond with the text, and when the meaning is not sufficiently clear it is explained in parenthesis. Generally, words in parenthesis, in the *translations*, are meant to be only explanatory and suggestive. Through the whole work, be it marked, letters and groups of letters are meant to denote actual equivalents when placed side by side, with or without the sign of equality).

781. In concluding our remarks upon the class of Slavic languages, we may review some of its peculiarities. We notice, especially, the great abundance of prefixes and augments, not so developed as to affect the meaning of the root; or, as we may otherwise express it, we find them representing our initial letters by groups of letters, as *gov* for w, *pol* for p, *mil* for l — also many separate adverbs used as augments, as *da ;* the existence of a dual, as in Greek — but not so prominent; the tendency to put the possessive pronouns after the noun, which show themselves as suffixes in Hungarian, and which are like the following article in Bulgarian ; the use of the singular after numerals ; the absence of personals with verbs, and the medium between the particles of Greek and those of German ; also the common use of the reflexive (G'k middle) for either the passive or active ; the use of gerunds as a sort of transition between verbs and participles ; the strong development of case endings, and endings of all kinds, placing the class much nearer to Greek and Latin than to German ; the absence of an article such as German has, and the continual tendency to develop it from the numeral *one* and the demonstrative *this, that* — seen more strongly in some members of the class than in others; as, in the Wend, *ta, to, ton,* Greek *to* and *ton.*

CHAPTER VII.

FINNISH LANGUAGES.

782. The Finnish languages proper, the Hungarian or Magyar, and the Turkish, are usually put together as one family; but while we leave the classification so, it is with the observation, that there is a greater difference between the three than is usually found between members of the same family. The Finnish languages, embracing a large number of distinct dialects, are sometimes denominated Uralic, being found originally in the region of the Ural Mountains. The Voguls, Ostjaks, and Hungarians, constitute the Ugric branch of the Finnic languages.

783. We will treat first, and principally, of the Hungarian. There is, evidently, a closer relationship between this and Slavics, than is generally supposed; and so there is between Finn and Slavic. There is not a feature in one that we cannot recognize, somewhat changed, in the other. The pronoun is not exactly suffixed in Slavic, as in Finnish, but it is one of the leading marks of Slavic to find the possessive following the noun — and in Bulgarian the article also.

784. The suffix preposition in Finnish strikes us as peculiar, but we find it even in German and English; as, *dem-nach* (that-after), *wo-mit* (where-with), where-in, there-after, where-to, there-on; so, Ger. *meinen-freund an* — my friend on, *i. e.*, upon my friend; *ist keinen thaler werth* — is no dollar worth, *i. e.*, not worth a dollar; we say, read a book *through,, i. e.*, through a book; the suffix *nach*, after, is very common in German; as, *der sprache nach*, the language after, *i. e.*, after the language, *dem umfange nach*, the extent after; also, but, as *he but*, for *but he*, as we say *he however*, for *however he*.

785. But we find, in the family in question, prepositions before as well as after, and those that follow are not different from the case endings of Slavic, except that they are more developed than those of Slavic. The verb system is about the same in both; and in orthography they have much in common.

786. The Hungarian is Eastern, but Slavic is Eastern too. The following illustrations will give the best idea of the character of the language:

Az atyak — the father (Ger. *d-as*); *a'kalap* — the hat (*a = az*); *szep estve* — (a) beautiful evening; *hazat epiteni* — (a) house to-build; *a'hegy-en embert* (man) *lattam* — the mountain-on (on the mountain) (a) man I-have-seen (*en* is suffix prep. = on). Prepositions uniformly follow in Hungarian, save in some instances of pronouns; *egy* (one) *Balsorai kiraly* — a Balsora king (king of Bals.); *derek egy ember* — excellent a man; *szena gyujteni ment* — hay to-collect he-went; *ez a' könyv a' gyermekeke* — this the book (is) the children's, *i. e.*, belongs to them. The final *e* in the last word takes the place of the possessive sign; *a' ki magae lehet* — the who (*i. e.*, who) his-own (*i. e.*, own master) can-be.

Nagy-obb volt mint — greater was as (greater than); *mas Europai nemzet* — (an) other European nation; *ezen a' fa'n sok alma van* — this the tree-on (on this) much (many) apple is; *beteg volt* — sick was; *betegek voltak* — sick were; *vettem lovat de nem igem szepet* — I-bought (have) (a) horse, but not very (*igen*) beautiful (*t, et, at*, are accusative endings; *nak*, gen. and dat.; *k, ak, ok*, plural sign).

The adjective, when standing before the noun, is not changed for case, number, and gender; as, *a' nagy varos* — the great town; *a' nagy varos-nak* — the great towns — but after the verb *be* it suffers changes.

Lov-aim igen kicsinyek — horses-my (are) very little (*ek* is plural sign of adjective taking place of verb — poss. pronouns uniformly suffix); *legerös-ebb a' negylabu allatok közöt* — (the) strongest the four-footed (*lab*, foot) among (prep. following separate, frequently).

The use of personal is very limited in Hung. — possessives are never found separate; *kaptam levelet, de meg nem olvastam* — I-received (have) (a) letter, but yet not (have) I-read (it); *az en hazam, nem a' tied* — the I house-my (*i. e.*, my house), not the thine (this double personal *I* is very common — it is emphatic, like *I myself*); *az ö hazok* — the she house-her (her house) — we would say his house, John's; house of him, John; *szavam*, my word; *szavad*, thy word; *szava*, his word.

Boldog az a' fiu — bulky this the son (is); *o magat dicseri* — he self (same) praises; *a' világnak teremtö-je* — (of) the world (gen.) its-creator (the world's creator). This superfluous *its*, the ending *je*, and the like, is common, as our *the man his house*; *az ember elete* — the men life (for men's) — as we say *goose quill*, for *goose's quill*; *a' mi-rol szolok* — the what-of (where-of, of which) I-speak (say); *mellyet ma lattunk* — which to-day (*ma*) we-seen (have) (*unk* = we); *a' micsoda jo lo-nak tudom annyit meger* — the what (-ever) good of-horse I-knew (*tudom*) so-much worth (it is) (as far as I know); *a' mi-m van* — the my-what is, that what is to me, what I have; *a' mid van* — what you have (what is to you, yours).

Latok (I see) *valakit a' kert-ben* — I-see some-one the garden-in (*ben* = in); *ki ir, ki olvas* — who (the-one) writes, who (the-other) reads; *tudom hogy nemelly itek szegeny* — I-know that many of-you poor (are); *a' könyvtarba valo konyv-ek* — the in (*ba*) library being (belonging) books; *kezdek szolni* — I-begin to-speak (*ni* inf. ending).

A' tanulo gyermek — the learning boy; *egre kialto vetek* — (a) heaven-to (to-heaven) crying sin; *setalvan az oramat elvesztettem* — walking (*i. e.*, as I walked) the my-watch I-lost (in *oramat*, *m* = my, and *at* is acc. sign); *varva vartam* — waiting I-waited (have), *i. e.*, I have long waited (in *vartam*, *t* is sign of past tense, the ending also of past part., and *m* = I); *irva van* — writing (it) is = it is written, the pres. part. used as passive; *varalak* — I expect you; *kivan-lak latni* — I-wish-you to-see; *egy reszt igen szeretem* — (to) a part (*i. e.*, partly) very (much) love-him-I (partly love him much); *ezt mondjak* — this one-says (they say this); *mikor pedig szuletett volna* — when but (but when) been-born was (had been born).

Es mikor lattak volna — and when they-saw was (when they saw, or had seen). We find prepositions before the pronouns; as, *bennem*, in me, *benned*, in thee, *benne*, in him, *rajtam*, on me, *rajtad*, on thee; *kelj fel* — rise up; *fel-kelvan* — up-rising, *i. e.*, rising up; *meg-hallatott* — is-heard (*meg.* pref.); *meg-holt volna* — dead was; *ö nekünk atyank* — he (is) to-us for-father (we have him for father).

Negyven nap — forty day; *mind ezeket neked adom* — all these to-thee I-will-give; *mondatnak* — they-shall-be-called (*nak* denotes *they*, and *at* the passive *mond*, Ger. *mund-art*, say, speak); *ti vagytok e' földnek savai* — ye are-ye the earth's salt; *ne ölj* — not kill (kill not); *valaki ølend* — whoever killing, *i. e.*, that shall kill; *mi Atyank ki vagy a' mennyek-ben* — we father-our who art the heaven-in, *i. e.*, our father; *senki nem szolgalhat ket urnak* — no-one not can-serve two master (no one can).

787. We here furnish a list of Hungarian words, to show the form which German and Slavic terms assume there:

Szek, stool; *kar*, arm, branch, G'k *cheir*; *has*, meat; *ser*, beer; *nap*, day, sun; *torony*, tower; *elet*, life, el, l; *lo*, horse, colt; *o*, old; *so*, salt; *szo*, say, word, L. *os*.

Ko, stone, Slav. *ka-men*; *szu*, heart, Slav. *serdze*; *fi*, son, L. *filius*; *sok*, much, Ger. *sehr*; *folyo*, flow, river; *uj*, new, *uj* = *nu*; *de*, and, but, G'k *de*; *juh*, sheep, L. *ovis*, ewe; *arany*, gold, L. *aurum*.

Ev, Slav. *nev*, sky, heaven; *kez*, hand, claw; *tuz*, fire, heat; *iras*, writ; *legy*, fly; *keves*, little, Ger. *wenig*; *hev*, heat; *jeg*, ice; *szel*, wind, blow (*sz* is used here, as in Slavic, as the equal of w, v, u, b).

Ut, r-oad, L. *it* = go; *viz*, water; *okor*, ox; *alom*, sleep, al, sl; *etek*, food, eat; *bereg*, worm; *halom*, hill; *jarom*, yoke.

Olom, lead, L. *plumb'*, ol, pl; *sir*, grave; *in*, nerve, Ger.

sehne; iz, limb; *Gyula*, Julius; *droga*, dear; *vastag*, thick, L. *spissus;* vas, iron, Ger. *eisen;* ercz, earth, metal.

Ferfi, man, L. *vir;* penz, money, pence; *pedig*, but; *kard*, sword; *het*, week, seven; *hang*, clang; *mod*, mode; *ev*, year, L. *aevum*, age; *hurt*, horn.

Gomb, know; *resz*, part, L. *res* = thing; *csillag*, star, L. *stella;* hal, go, walk, Fr. *aller;* lab, foot, c-law; *szem*, see, eye; *barat*, friend; *leang*, daughter, l, d; *szo*, voice, sound.

Fal, wall; *hany*, how-much, L. *quot;* erdo, wood, Ger. *wald;* jus, just, *tanul-ni*, to teach; *ir-ni*, to write; *erdem*, work; *keres-ni*, to seek, search; *lop-ni*, to steal, G'k *klep;* te and *tesz*, do; *hi* and *hiv*, call, Ger. *rufen;* akar, after, either.

Ad-ni, to give, L. *do;* allani, to stand; *ar*, river; *azon*, that; latt, look; *embert*, man, L. *vir (mber);* Becs, Vienna, Ger. *Wien;* biz, true, Ger. *wahr* and *ge-wiss;* csata, battle, Ger. *schlacht;* csinos, clear, shine, Ger. *rein.*

Edes, sweet, G'k *edus;* egesz, whole, Ger. *ganz; ej*, night; *el-ni*, to live, be; *er-ni*, to reach.

Fed-ni, deck; *fejer*, white, fire; *fel*, half, Slav. *pol; fö* and *fey*, head, f, h; *föld*, land, field; *Görög*, Greek; *gyönge*, weak; hajo, ship, L. *navis;* hatra, after, back; *halloni*, hear, l, r; hegy, high, rock; *hir*, hear, Ger. *ruf*, report; *hit*, oath; *hon*, home.

Idö, time, tide; *igaz*, true, Ger. *wahr;* ivas, drink, L. *bibo; jor-ni*, go; *jut-ni*, go, L. *itum;* kis, little, Ger. *klein; kimen-ni*, go, come; *kora*, early; *kota*, note; *köz*, common; *körül*, circle, around.

Me-gholt, killed, dead; *me-gint*, a-gain; *myack*, neck; *on*, tin; ok, cause, Ger. *sache;* rossz, bad, worse.

Teljes, full; *ten-ni*, do, Ger. *thun; tett*, deed, Ger. *that; tor-ni*, break, twist; *tud-ni*, know, L. *video; ut-ni*, beat (b-eat); *vad*, wild; *ver-ni*, strike; *viadal*, battle.

Zöld, yellow, Slav. *zelen;* zseb, sack; *level*, leaf, letter; *ur*, sir, Ger. *herr;* arok, grave; *nyil*, nail, dart, Ger. *pfeil; fond*, pound, Ger. *pfund.*

Zsido, Jew, Ger. *Jude* (yude); *nep*, folk, people; *ver*, gore, L. *cruor;* azon, that, Ger. *jener, das;* ar, price; *bö*, wide and rich; *elso*, first, l, r; *hives*, be-lief; *igy*, so; *ki-tör*, out-turn (ki pref.); *köt-ni*, bind, knit; *köröm*, claw, r, l.

Lang, flame; *len-ni*, be, been, l, be; *miv*, work; *mivel-ni*, build (*mi* pref.); *nev*, name; *ott*, there, Ger. *dort; öreg*, old, Slav. *stary; ven-ni*, take, Ger. *fang-en;* veg, end, L. *finis.*

788. The fact particularly noticed in Magyar, is the shortness of the words, the condensing, if you please, of two or more letters of ours into one of theirs; thus, we often find that our initial letters are entirely suppressed; as, *ut* = b-eat, *ar* = price, *on* =

tin. Prefixed, prepositional, verbs of all kinds, are well developed in this language.

789. FINNISH: The Finnish class proper is as interesting and valuable as it is peculiar and beautiful. It has all the prominent features of the Magyar; the two stand very nearly related in many particulars; and yet the Finnish, and especially some of its forms, possesses the whole Slavic structure, only developing some of its features in an unusual manner. The Finnish must stand as an invaluable light to show us the path that leads from Magyar to Lithuanian and the Slavic, or the reverse. All the endings and prefixes of Finnish, the verb *be*, all the pronouns and particles, all the participles and tense forms, manifest a strong tendency to identify themselves with Slavic, and indirectly with German and Latin. Hence, the acquiring of the language is quite easy, and always full of interest. The Finns, as a whole, are not an organized people, though some portions of them are highly cultivated and possess many men of learning; for example, those of Finland proper. They are divided into many sections, with their dialects each peculiar to them.

790. There is an east and a west Finnish group, with considerable marks of difference; the tribes or sections are, the Suomi, Esthnish, Syryanish, Wotjak, Mordvin, Tcheremish, Ostjak, and Wogul. We regret that there is not room here to speak of some of their most interesting peculiarities, especially in the structure of the verbs.

791. We will give but few examples, sufficient only to give a rough idea of Finnish orthography and structure:

Koska he olit kuningan kuull-et — when they (*he*) had (was) (the) king heard (*ol* of *olit* is the *byl* of Slav. *was*); *syndy-män piti* — born shall-be (shall be born — *puti* is Slav. *budu*, be, the sign of future); *syndy-nut oli* — born was (was born); *sen* (that) *kuuli* — (he) that heard (heard that). Pasts are formed like Latin perfects, *dedi, feci, rexi*, with vowel endings; *nousi ja otti*, arose and took; *nouse ja ota*, rise and take; *on kuulu-nut* — is heard; *tämä* (same) *on se* — this is he (that one); (*tuli*), went; *jonga minun kansaani pitä hallitz-eman* — who my people shall rule (*pitä* = be, shall); *minä sanon te-ille* — I say to-you (*mine* = 1); *Isa meidan* — father our.

The case endings are heavy — prepositions follow, either suffixed or separate. Poss. pronouns are developments of noun endings not separated; *ou prophetan kautta kirjoi-tettu* — is prophet by written (written by the); *on tulewa* — is to-come, will come; *menit he* — went they; *huoneseen* — house-in; *he tähden nä-it* — they (the) star saw; *he olit mennet* (went) — they had gone; *Egyptistä kutzuin minä* (I) *poik-ani* (boy-my)

Egypt-out called (have) I son-my (called my son); *joka sanoo* —which says.

Sanottu oli— spoken was; *Rham-asa on ääni kuulunut*— Rama-in is (a) voice heard; *joka kutzutan*—which (was) called; *wedellä* — with-water; *tulella*— with-fire; *kastetta häneldä*— to-(be)-baptized him-by; *he kastettin*— they (were) baptized; *kastan teitä* — baptize thee; *hän kastaa*—he (shall) baptize; *ei ihminen* (L. *hominem*) *elä*— not man (shall) live (*e* pref.); *asetti hänen* — set him (*a* pref.).

Jos sinä olet— if thou art; *ja osotti* (show, *o* pref.) *hänelle kaikki* (all) *mailman* (Ger. *welt*, L. *mundus*) *waldakunnat*— and showed to-him all world's kingdom (of the world); *nämät kaikki minä annan* (give) *sinulle*—these all I (will) give to-thee; *silmä on* (is) *ruumin walkeus* — (the) eye is body's light (of the body); *silmä silmästä*—eye for-eye; *kuollet* — the dead (killed); *seura minua*— follow me; *se sana*—that word (that = the), say; *joka tehty os*—which did is (made); *hänesä* (in-him) *oli elama*— in him was life; *he kysyit*—they asked.

792. It would be a very easy task to show a multitude of Finnish words agreeing substantially with correspondents in Hungarian, and, with suitable allowance for their style of orthography, we might identify a large majority of its most common words with German and Slavic, particularly Lithuanian—but we can barely touch upon this question here; thus, we notice *elä*, live, Hung. *el-ni*; *tunde-nut*, knew, known, H. *tud-ni*; *mene*, go, H. *menni*; *tul*, fire, H. *tüz*; *poja* and *pa*, head, H. *fo*; *jalg*, foot, H. *lab*, lg, lb; *wesi*, water, H. *viz*; *ssilme*, eye, H. *szem*; *ssu*, mouth, H. *szaj*; *kasi*, *ked*, *ki*, hand, H. *kez*; *nait*, saw, H. *nez-ni*; *kuollet*, dead, killed, H. *holt*; *puu*, tree, H. *fa*, p, f; *ihminen,* man, H. *ember*; *voj*, night, H. *ej*; *anna*, give, H. *ad-ni*—and every one of these words can be identified with German or Slavic.

793. We give, next, the 2d of John 20, to compare with Hungarian:

Nun hän juoxi ja tuli Simon Petarin tygö, ja sen opetuslapsen tygö jota Jesus rakasti, ja sanoi (said) *heille: he owat Herran ottanet pois haadasta, ja en me tiedä, kuhunya he hänen* (him) *panit*— then she ran and came (*tuli*) Simon Peter to (*tygö*), and that disciple to (to that one) whom Jesus loved, and said to-them : they have (are, *owat*) (the) Lord taken away grave-from, and not we (*me*) know, where they him put (have).

794. In Hungarian:

El-futa azert es el-mene Simon Peterhez, es ama masik tanitvanyhoz, a' kit Jezus szeret (cherished) *vala, es monda* (said) *nekik: El-vittek az Urat a' koporso-bol, es nem tudjuk hova tettek ötet* — then (*azert*) she-ran (*el* pref.) and came Simon

Peter-to (-ez), and that other disciple, the whom (*kit*) Jesus loved had (was, *vala*), and said to them: taken (they have) the Lord the grave-from (*-bol*), and not know (I) where (*hova*) laid (they have) him (*öt-et*).

795. The Syryan deserves this especial notice: In it we find *muna* (mount), I go; *muny*, went; *munly*, has gone; *muna*, will go; the verb *be* has em (am) for all persons singular, and *emos* in the plural — a fine proof that any person of a verb may represent all the persons. We find *me völy* (will), I was; *syja völy*, he was; *vony*, been, be. In a form of this language, we find *vyjym* = em, showing e = vyjy, yyyy, eeee.

796. LAPP: The Lapp language, of the Laplanders, is most undeniably a Finnish language; it is, if anything, nearer the Magyar than the Finnish itself. It has by no means received that attention which its numerous points of interest justify us in saying it deserves — and this has arisen from the political insignificance of the Laplanders as a people, numbering, as they do, less than thirty thousand. A single example must serve to give a comparative view of its features. Same verse as above:

Wiakei sodn tabbelt ja pati Simon Petru-sen kaik, ja tan mubben appetesalman kaik, juob Jesus etsi, ja jatti sonnon: Sije läh eritwaldam Herrab gruoptest, ja epe tete, kosa litjeh piäjam so — ran she therefore and came (*pati*) Simon Peter to (*kaik*), and (*ja*) (*tan mubben*) that other disciple to, whom (*juob*) Jesus loved (*etsi*), and said to-them: they have (are, *lah*) taken-away (the) Lord grave-from, and not-we know (*tete*) where they-have put him.

Attjes kuoren — father-his near (by his father); *mo-kum*, me-with; *mon etsetowap* — I loved-am; *sotn etsetowa*; he loved-is; *sije läh etsetowomen* — they are loved-been; *mije lepe etsetowomen* — we are loved-been (are loved); *etset*, to love.

In Suomi, *ovat* = *owap* is used for *are*, and *ova*, more or less varied, is a common ending for verbals in the Finn languages — it is the ending, too, of active tenses; as, *antavat*, they give; *tulevat*, they come; *tulivat*, they came. In Lapp, we find *lei*, or *li*, for was; and *orrat* for be (are, L. *eram*); it is not different from *ol*, *lei*, *li*, of past. Lapp verbs have a dual form.

797. The Serenian is the language of a Finnish tribe, on a Finnish basis — but having strongly developed the Slavic tendencies of the family. There are many points where it is Slavic and not Finn, and as many others where it is Finn and not Slavic. It is found written in the Slavic letter.

798. The Karelian is another Finnish language, with a Slavic finish. It is written in the Russian letter.

799. SAMOIDISH LANGUAGES.—The Samoidish languages constitute a family located in the north of Russia and in the north and centre of Asia. They are connected, on one side, with the Finnish, and, on the other, with the Siberian family. Many of the leading features of the language are Finnish; there is a strong tendency, however, to the peculiar North-Asiatic stamp.

800. The following translation of Samoidish composition will give some conception of the manner in which they tell their stories:

The woman goes; the servant goes; the woman (to) father came, into house went, father up-raised, father old; two man sit, three brother stand — those two bad (are), those two sleep: woman sits, (to) servant says, back go, (to) him say, "two man came"; servant back went. Other (one) man got up, out went, bow sounds, servant (he) killed; man (into) house came, (with) selves they talk, laughing go-to-sleep; morning get up, from-around folk came, "thy servant killed" (-is, they say); woman sits, sleep, woman wakes; one-has-stolen-her (*tualambadat*), two men came (in-)boat, take-her (*tadaret*).

801. This gives us an instructive lesson on what language is in its infantile style or state — it shows how particles and endings and fixes are the result of growth out of fundamental words. The ancient poetry of northern Europe has advanced farther than this towards our present complicated style, but evidently by traveling the same road as this.

802. ALBANIAN LANGUAGE. — The Albanian, we do not hesitate to say, is to be classed as one of the remote forms of Greek, especially of modern Greek. Philologists are at a loss where to place it, partly from the little knowledge they have of it, and partly, too, from the peculiar phase the language presents. But we feel confident that the more we become acquainted with it, the nearer we shall find it to Greek. It has not the character of an ancient language — it is essentially modern; it has the article, compound tense, passive on the reflexive and with *to be*, the declining appearance of endings, and the like.

803. It has many points that are Celtic, if not Greek, as the abundance of augments and little meaningless particles, and adverbs; it has many more that are Slavic, others, again, that are particularly French, such as the adjective following the noun, and the orthography of some of its words. But all these points of agreement do not necessarily prove it related to these languages in particular; it rather shows that they have all traveled the same way, and have the same history.

804. Albania proper belongs in Turkey; it lies north of Greece, and between the Adriatic sea and Bulgaria.

805. The language presents little that is really strange, little that we have not already seen in some other language. A few examples must suffice for it:

Me mirre — more good (better); *me* is scarcely more than a prefix; *fort poukoure* (L. *pulcher*, pretty) — very pretty (most, super.); *ti me dese* — thou me lovest; *doua te skruoaig* — I-will that (to, the) I-write (will write); *douame te skrouageme* — we-wish, etc; *difioig, difion* — I, he, hears; *chap* — I open (gap); *thom, thote* — I, he, says, th, s; *dall* — go, Fr. *'aller*; *pat skrouare* — he-had written; *pat bdekoure* — he-had died.

E i pirri (L. *puer*) *i dot atig* — and the son he said to-him (*atig*) (you may also call the *i* before *dot* an augment); *se este kioutet i mpretit* (prince) *se mad* (*magnus*) — for (it) is town that (the one) (of) king the great (that of the great king); *bete mpe stepi* (stoop) *te Petrit* — I-go into (*mpe*) house that (of) Peter (*bete* = went) — *te* here may be called a suffix article, indeed our own relatives *that* and *which* are not more than post-positive articles; *i lioutem perntise* — (to) him I-pray to-God, *i. e.*, I pray to him, to God (or call *i* an augment).

Po ou thom gioubet — but (to) you I-say to-you, *i. e.*, to you I say to you (or call *ou* an augment). Such difficulties we have seen often before, and the student must be reminded that all the words of a sentence, when traced far enough back, prove to be duplicates like these; *ai ke seste me moua* — the (who) who not-is with me (as we say *he who*); *se kouig pirri im* — for this son (of) mine.

Si kountre este skrouare nte profêter, na oune derfoig eggeline tim perpara phakese sate, ate-ke do te dertoge oudene tente (thy) *perpara tege* — so again (contra) it-is written in (*nte*) prophets, behold I (*oune*) send angel the-my (*tim*) before face (of) thine, the-which shall (*do* = *te*) prepare way (road) thine before thee; *e si thurri nie gka kopigte, e pieti tzdo te gene* (been) *keto* — and so (he) called one (*nie*) from servants, and asked (Ger. *beten*) what that be (been) this, *i. e.*, what it was (*te* augment), or what it may be.

E tha: nie (one) *nieri kis di dgielm* — and (he) said: a man (G'k *anēr*) had two sons (child); *giati ine ke ge mpe kiel* — father our which thou-art (*ge*, be) in heaven; *pas* (*post*) *gio* (G'k *ouk*) *soume* (some) *ditet* (*dies*) — after not many days.

806. There are still a few words which we must notice for their extraordinary orthography:

Skourtoig — to shorten; *skoig*, go (*s* pref.), scud; *ikeig*, go; *tzourare*, tear; *pounoig* (work), G'k *poieo*, Ger. *thun*; *krache* (arm), bracket.

Geiri (arm), G'k *cheir*; *mpe*, up, 'pon; *gkre*, right, erect; *si*, eye; *ched* (pour), gush; *giaste*, out; *pime* (tree), Ger. *baum;* *lis* (tree), L. *lignum;* *ourder*, order; *serpeig*, serve.

Feta, find; *lesoig*, louse (notice that *oig, aig, eig*, are endings of first per. singular, and that *-are* is a part. ending); *este* (bone), L. *os;* *xomple*, example; *thurra* (call), Ger. *rufen*.

Strome (bed), L. *stratum;* *lid* (tie), L. *ligo;* *mplioump*, plumb, Ger. *blei* (lead); *lioule*, b-loom, f-lora; *fiak* (blood), L. *sang-uis;* *kekia*, bad, G'k *kakos*.

Pouke (bread), bake — Ger. *brot*, bread, is allied to *braten*, roast, bake; *pris*, break; *ferre*, broad, far; *pirri*, bring, bear; *bela*, brother, l, d, t; *tzati*, L. *tectum*, roof; *tent*, thine.

Drod, turn, Ger. *drehen;* *streggoig*, stress, press; *de*, earth, G'k *gē;* *stere*, earth, L. *terra;* *arrig*, reach, Ger. *erreichen;* *tremp*, tremble; *pare*, first.

Chiri, carry, ferry; *zgiar*, fire; *fist*, finger; *pisk*, fish; *li*, flax, linen; *mise*, meat; *muze* (fly), *mouche;* *lioume* (river), flume; *froua* (wife), Ger. *frau;* *lephter* (free), left, loose; *faz*, peace, L. *gaudium*, L. *pax*.

Phriout, fruit; *phrike*, fear, fright; *fithe* (all), Ger. *ganz* — sound the *f* as *g*, as it may in all cases in Albanian; *dourim*, Ger. *ge-duld, -dure*.

Riziko, risk; *chapsa*, catch; *garaphe*, grasp; *gkrig*, freeze, gk, f; *musteri*, mystery; *spirt*, spirit; *litoure*, lettered; *sos*, L. *satis;* *dreigte*, straight, direct.

Poune, business; *nom* (law), G'k *nomos;* *phake*, face; *stat*, state, Ger. *ge-stalt;* *pesoig* (believe), faith; *ta-lich*, luck; *zere-miri*, grim; *berde*, verdant; *phound*, ground; *stepi* (house), L. *tectum;* *krie* (head), L. *cranium;* *sent* (holy), saint.

Bape, hot; *kemise*, Ger. *hemd* (shirt); *drou* (wood), tree; *ougia*, hunger; *re*, young, new; *niocha*, know; *ropa* (cloth), Ger. *rock;* *mount* (can), might, mought; *kake*, Ger. *kopf*, head; *sorra*, crow; *gete*, be, live; *doua*, love, d, l; *megges*, morning; *nate*, night; *more*, Ger. *narr*, fool.

Gkrigta, take, grasp; *kale*, colt, Fr. *cheval;* *phuti*, plant; *phlet*, read, Ger. *lesen, lego;* *sktad*, shade; *skoume*, scum, foam; *sioch*, see, seek; *bitorea*, victory; *mount*, sur-mount.

Kentoig, sing, L. *cano;* *stereos*, strong; *bdes*, die; *mpourr*, proud; *zog*, Ger. *vogel* (bird), fowl; *lao*, folk, G'k *laos*, Ger. *leute;* *bape*, warm; *ouge*, water; *phgiale* (word), G'k *logos*.

Seker, sugar; *be*, lay; *bichem*, become; *boub*, dumb, mute; *pise*, beast; *pout*, foot; *pri*, horn; *geni, genus*, kind; *giam*, am; *gio*, no, g, n; *giou*, you, your; *gkia*, wild, gk, w; *gkrig*, cry.

Fial (gial), like, *gleich;* *frik*, herd; *dex*, take; *drite*, bright (light); *eleuthero* (free), loose; *emere*, name; *zi*, black, Ger.

schwartz, dark, dim, z, d ; *thele* (deep), L. *altus* ; *thèke*, dagger; *thu*, swine, L. *sus*.

I-ken, gone, go ; *kàrre*, car; *kelk*, glass; *ken* (dog), L. *canis*, Ger. *hund;* *kies* (laugh), L. *ris-um;* *kipi*, heap; *koske*, L. *os*, Ger. *kno-chen*, b-one; *kourm*, L. *corpus*, body; *kous*, who, Ger. *was*.

Lebdoig, laud; *mole*, L. *malum, apfel*, Ger. *pfel, ppel, mpel, mel, mol ; monede*, money ; *mpareig*, bear, carry, Ger. *tragen ; nam*, fame ; *nemer*, number ; *ntgiek*, chase.

Xestra, cistern ; *oull*, star, L. *st-ella ;* *ourte*, prudent; *pgiel* (bear), beget; *pelouma*, L. *columba ; pgiese*, piece ; *pioul*, wood, Ger. *wald ; poune*, thing, done, p, t.

Ropa, rob; *skiat*, hat ; *skias*, glide, skip; *tzale*, halt ; *trap*, grave, t, g; *phemige*, family; *phle*, sleep; *phscch*, bedeck; *phscche* (thing), Ger. *sache ; choda*, go, lead.

This is but a small portion of words of the kind.

807. TURKISH LANGUAGE.— The Turkish is the last of the European languages which we shall notice; it stands on the very threshold of Asia, and we must pass over it to reach Asia. Thoroughly Eastern in its spirit and origin, it has yet developed itself in the atmosphere of European civilization. Born of Arab and Persian ancestors, it has been educated under the roof of the Greek and the Slave.

808. Very little need be said on this language here, for the reason that it has scarcely a feature that does not in a stronger, or at least in as strong a light, appear either in languages which we have already noticed, or, more especially, in the Tartar, Persian, and Semitic languages, which we shall notice hereafter. These few lines must suffice :

809. *Baba-muz ki sema-de sin*—father-our who heaven-in thou-art (*sin*) ; *mukaddes ola senin ismin*—sanctified be thy name ; *senin emrin olsun nitek i goj-de ojic jerde-de*—thy will be so in (*i*) heaven and earth-in; *illa chelas ojle bizi, fena-dan*— but free make us (*bizi*) evil-from.

810. We have already said that it is often grouped with the Finnish and Magyar, but we must also observe, that while it has several leading points in common with them, it clings as strongly to the Tartar as they do to the Slavic.

811. There are many forms or dialects in which Turkish is spoken by the people. Leading branches of the Turks are the Turkomans, Kirghis, and the Osmanlis, or Ottomans. The latter are the dominant people of the Turkish empire, and it is their language which is generally intended by the term Turkish.

CHAPTER VIII.

PERSIAN LANGUAGES.

812. One of the most interesting languages of Asia, or of the world, and to the philologist one of the most valuable, is the Persian. It gives evidence to us of the easy transition between the idioms of Europe and those of Asia, particularly Semitic. Its remarkable coincidence with the English, or German, not only in orthography but also in grammatical structure, is hardly what history would lead us to expect. We have been told, or rather it has been conjectured, that our ancestors were Asiatics, but not that they were particularly Persians or Semites. For aught we know, they might as well have been Tartars, or the people of India. Yet it must not be supposed that Persian is the only one of its neighborhood which is especially related to ours; it only stands in the front of that relationship. The Semitic and Indian first, and the Tartar languages next, manifest a strong tendency to identify themselves with the European — the Persian has only developed that tendency in a higher degree.

813. Let it be remembered that Persian, while it agrees so nearly with ours, is still, nevertheless, eminently a Tartar and a Semitic language. The number of words in Persian confessedly Semitic, particularly Arabic, is very large, and an expert etymologist could easily identify nearly all the words of the two classes — not only the words, but the grammar also. Those decaying *a*, *st*, *m*, *n*, *b*, prefixes of verbs and verbals, are forcible illustrations of the connection. And Hindostani, which may be called a form of Persian, has also a large supply of Semitic words. Persian is also intimately connected with the Indian and the Afghan.

814. The Persian which we treat of now is that of modern Persia. We have said that the Persian has the European style of orthography, and the grammar too of modern Europe, but, on the other side, the arrangement of the words and of the members of the sentences, the idiom, the thought, is not European but Asiatic. We are at the same time aware that others think differently. In fact, the leading difficulty in thoroughly mastering the Persian, after knowing its particles, its endings, and its irregular imperatives (on which some verb forms are based), is the, to us, peculiar nature of its compounds, its arrangement, its expression, its thought. Persian words are far from being fully

individualized (being like Sem. and Sans.). We find many words united together which with us are separate; thus, *one-part, not-is, my-head, who-is*. A limited number of examples, to illustrate, among other things, this peculiar thought, we will now give:

815. The article does not exist developed as it is in Europe, or even as it is in Semitic; there is a common ending of nouns, *i*, which, among other uses, performs the part of a suffixed *a* or *an*; thus, *kuh*, a rock, *kuhi*, a certain rock; *padishah*, pacha or king, *padishahi*, a certain king (G'k *basileus*). As we have seen often before, and will often see again, here the numeral *one* is often used to supply the place of *a, an*, and uniting with its noun as a prefix; so *an*, that (Dan. *han*, Slav. *on*), and *ain* or *in*, this, he, are used in place of the definite article, *the;* also uniting with the noun, as *im-ruz*, this day, the day, to-day, *im-sal*, this-year. Of course, there is nothing unusual in all this.

816. Noun endings are here in about the same stage of advancement as we find them in English; thus, *padar*, father, *padar-an*, fathers (*an* = en of children, oxen); *murgh*, bird, *murgh-an*, birds; *man*, I, *man-ra*, me-to, to me, *tu-ra*, thou-to; *zan*, woman, *izan*, of woman (the *i* coming from preceding word); *zan-ra*, to woman (acc. and dat.); also *ba-zan* (*ba* = to), *az zan*, from woman, *az zan-an*, from women; *dil-am*, my heart (-*am* = my), *padar-ash*, his father (-*ash* = his), *kitab-at*, thy book (-*at* = thy); also, *dili man*, heart-of me (*man*), *ani man*, that-of me, *i. e.*, the mine; *bah*, good, *bah-ter*, better, *bah-terin*, best; *ind az inglistan garm-ter ast*—India than (by) England warmer is (warmer than England).

Mah nicku-st — (the) moon splendid-is (all adjectives may thus develop *be* at the end); *rahi-st rah ashek* — (the) way-is (*st* = is) way (-of) love; *kah hich-esh kanarah ni-st* — that any-its (to it) end not-is; *ani kud* — that-of self, his own. They say *mai-ra nushidam* — the wine I-drank; but if indefinite, then the form is, *mai nushidam*, wine I-drank (so that acc. ending *ra* has sometimes the force of *the*); *in-zamin* — (at) this-time; *im-shab*, to-night; *dust-am*, or *dust-i man*, my-friend, friend-of me; *asp-i kud-ash* — horse-of his-self, *i. e.*, his own horse; *bira-dar-i kud-at* — brother-of thy-self (*at* = thy); *da-vidan*, to run, *davanidan*, to cause to run.

817. In the abundant capacity for such compounds as *fire-temple, rose-garden, mountain-country, lion-heart*(*ed*), *kub-awar*, pretty-voice(d), *nik-nam*, (of) good-name, *gul-afshan*, flower-scattering, *sar-afraz*, head-exalting, battle-seeking, hard-hearted, we know of no European language it so much resembles as the German. The Persians are very partial also to compound verbs,

made by a noun or adjective joined to *make, do, have, strike, come, sit, find, take,* like our *take-rest,* for rest, *sit-smiling,* for smile, *make-inquiry,* for inquire, *keep-watch,* for watch, *make-happy,* for delight.

818. *Asp-ra didi* — (the) horse did-you-see (*ra* sign of acc.); *dar kuab didan* — in sleep to-see (*i. e.,* to dream); *mard kah au-ra didam* — (the) man (L. *vir*) that him I-saw (*that* is another case of doubles), *i. e.,* the man I saw; so again, *an mard kah au gaft* — that man (the man) that he said (that-he = he); *parsidah shudah budam* — asked been was-I, *i. e.,* I had been asked; *ma-pars* — (do) not-ask; *tamam kardan* — complete to-make (to complete); *rujuu namudan* — returning to-show (to return); *dar amadan* — in to-come, *i. e.,* come in.

Prefix prepositions to verbs are common; *ba-daria dar* — in-sea in, *i. e.,* in the sea (double, like Lat. *ad homin-em*); *dikani bagi dasht* — a-husbandman a-garden had (the usual order is nom., obj., verb), (adjectives uniformly follow nouns); *padishahi takt-nishin* — the-king (the) throne-sitting (one), *i. e.,* who sits on the throne; *silah u* (and) *dirham dad lashkar-ash-ra* — arms and money gave-he (*dad*) army-his-to (to his army).

Au-ra guft kih na-kuaham kurd (eat) — to-her (he) said that (*kih*) not-I-will eat (we would rather say, that *he* would not eat; *kurd* is inf. less the ending); so we find, commanded that to-master robe and reward they-gave (*that they should give,* we would say); *bayad kah bizani* — it-must that you-beat, *i. e.,* you must beat; so, I-wish that I-go, for I wish to go.

Man (I) *igbar bi-didan-ash raftam w-abas* — I once to-seeing-his (to-see-him) I-went, and-only (once and only once) — *w* = and, pref.; *man kah man dashtam* — I that I had-I, *i. e.,* I-who had (thrice I, while we would have it only once). We need hardly remind the student again, that there is a tendency to such repetitions in all tongues — so we say, *of whom it was spoken of;* *1-had-I,* is taken as a new base, where the *I's* are quite absorbed and cease to be felt; *birun shud* — out he-was, went out (be = go); *gahi abi surk na-didam* (seen) — sometimes (*i. e.,* never) water-of (being) red not-seen (have I) (never seen water red); *baad az du ruz* — after from two day (after two days); *hama sarhai kahka zadah kandidand* — all (the) heads (*sarhai*) a-shout striking they-laughed.

Yaki ba-sanat-i kushti ba-sar amdah bud — one (a-man) in-art-of wrestling to-head (at-the-head) come was (*bud*), *i. e.,* stood first in the art; *dar-in* — there-in; *awardand* — they have brought (related, L. *fero,* bring = tell); *dar-u sih mahi shigaraf* — in-it three fish fine (ones), *i. e.,* three fine fishes; *kah Hut-i sipihr az rash-ki aishan bar ta-bah ghairat birian shudi* — so-that Hut-of sphere (*pisces*) by (*az*) envy-of them (*aishan*) on frying-pan-of (*tabah*) envy burnt might-be (was roasted on pan); *kada-ra shukar baid* (must) *bi-kanam* (*bi* pref.) *kih namat-i sihat bi-man* (on-me) *ita furmudah ast* (*est*, is)—to-God praise (it) must (that) I-make (I must praise) who (*kih*) blessing-of health on-me gift (*ita*) made has (*ast*) (who has bestowed).

819. The foregoing will give a fair idea of the peculiarities and difficulties of the Persian. Most of the difficulties are such as we find in all Asiatic languages; they did not, evidently, recognize the division of sentences in composition, and of words and phrases from sentences—at least not to the extent that we do. You do not find capitals, and periods, and commas, and such guide marks to steady you. The running of words together, or rather the non-development of terms or expressions into their word-elements, is a uniform Asiatic feature, a feature which places them all so far back toward the original or infantile character of language.

820. These compounds, as we are wont to conceive them, are the real *words* of the Oriental; and as long as we have dictionaries that have not these words, but rather their assumed elements, so long must the first day's travel of the Oriental student be "hard upon the weary way." Be it remembered, that our own words are not ultimates—there are no ultimates in wholes. Our own words have their parts, parts that we now recognize, and more yet that we some time hence shall recognize; and still we find the necessity of defining words aside from the elements.

821. Of the forms of the Persian we have this to say:

PARSEE is a name applied to the Old Persian; it has been extinct for long centuries. There is a modern form of this ancient idiom, that of the Parsees, and called by that name. The Parsees live in the southern province of Fars; and a larger number still dwell in a portion of India. The term Persian, as applied to a people, is very comprehensive; it includes the various tribes or people.which constitute the Persian nation. This Parsee was for a long time the prevailing language of Persia; but when the Persians were mastered by the Arabs and the Tartars, there grew up under their influence, from this Parsee, a new language, the modern Persian. This became the national language, and it left the Parsee, or ancient Persian, to grow along into a mere provincial idiom. Persian is spoken in a large part of India.; a form of it is the language of Bukhara.

822. The PEHLVI, called also Huzwaresh, and the ZEND, are names of old languages of Persia, closely allied to the Persian, and once more or less prevailing. The Pehlvi shows the transition of Persian to Semitic.

823. The Zend is admitted to be one of great age; it seems to have been a church language. It is not now much known,

though it is attracting the serious attention of philologists. Its identity with the Sanscrit, and, through it, with the Greek and Latin; is certainly remarkable.

824. An interesting and valuable language is the KURD. It is closely allied in form to the Persian, even so much as to appear to be a mere dialect of it. It, too, gives us many valuable hints on the connection between Semitic and Persian. It is the language of Kurdistan and Luristan, and exists in several different dialects. It is neighbor to the Armenian, and is much like it. It is without literature.

825. The BELUCHEES language is evidently built on the same basis as the Persian, but it has varied the Persian orthography very materially. There are two leading dialects.

826. It is here that we would remind the student, that a careful comparison of the different forms of Persian, must lead us to the belief in the identity really existing, in their origin, between the Semitic and the Persian families.

827. AFGHAN LANGUAGE.—The language of the Afghans is by no means well known, and its place in the family of tongues is not accurately defined. Some place it with the Persian, and others, again, put it in the Semitic division—and there are, of course, reasons for both conclusions. It is related to both, as they, too, are related to each other. It plainly possesses the foundation common to both, but there are many points, especially in the orthography, where it differs very materially from either. It possesses those marks which we should expect to distinguish the idiom of a rude and wild people from that of a comparatively intelligent and progressive people. We will briefly notice some of its leading features.

828. A prominent mark is the agreement of the transitive verb, in the past tense, with the object in gender and number, while the intransitive agrees with the nominative in gender. And there is reason in this. Their verbs, and, really, verbs in all languages, are true participles, and, as such participles, like adjectives, they have an agreement; the past tense is, especially, everywhere based on the passive or past participle. We have here a case precisely like that of French and Italian perfects, where the participle agrees with the object. So, *I struck him* = *I have him struck*, where it can well be seen that *struck* should agree with *him*. They, the Afghans, do still more — they put an objective or instrumental form where we put a nominative; as, *the striking of him by me*, rather than *I struck him*, *i. e.*, they make of it a case exactly like our passive expression. All this in Afghan has its counterpart elsewhere: by-the-man the-

woman (was) struck, the man the woman struck, *i. e.*, struck the woman.

829. The cases are clearly on the Persian system; so are the plurals. The adjective precedes the noun. The Persian comparative ending *ter* is found here, but attached to, or connected with, the noun compared with; many comparatives are made by doubling the positive.

830. The pronouns are decidedly Persian, and not Semitic: *haga*, he and him, reminds us of Danish *han*, L. *hac; d-ga, da, di*, this, the; *kum* and *kam*, whom; *zana*, some, any; *zah* = I; *ma*, me; *tah, ta* = thou, thee; *mung* or *muz*, we.

831. The Afghan has not only developed such endings as we find in Latin, and in nearly all other languages, as *zah aus-m*, I exist, *tah aus-i*, thou or you exist, but it has some peculiarities besides. These endings, with or without the separate pronouns also (as liked), may be used with intransitives, and with the tenses, not past, of transitive verbs also.

832. With transitive pasts they use the instrumental form of pronoun, as *by me struck* = I struck; or, more particularly, they adopt a form of pronoun, either prefixed or inserted, and not having an independent existence, which is different from the separate pronouns, and from the endings above noticed; thus, *mi kah* — I did; *di kah* — thou didst; *mu kah* — we did.

833. These pronouns, or prefixes, when used with verbs not transitive, denote the object or the possessive case. They remind us of the Semitic tense, where also the person endings are initial, and they must be explained in the same way. Their intimate connection with those augments which we find so prominent in Afghan (as *bi, da, u*), and which seem to characterize particularly the Semitic and Persian families, is undoubted. There are also pronouns, or prefixes, in Afghan used solely with the verb to denote the object.

834. We find the infinitive used for past tense, and the past for the perfect and pluperfect tense; indeed, it is very clear that all their tenses are but variations of participles and infinitives. Passives are formed as in English or Persian, compound, and compound tenses are found made like theirs.

835. The infinitive ending and those of the participle are Persian; so, evidently, are many of the particles. Taken as a whole, we might call the Afghan a remote form of the Persian.

CHAPTER IX.

CAUCASIAN LANGUAGES.

836. An important, though by no means well-known, family of languages, related to the Persian, is the Caucasian group. It includes the Georgian and Armenian, both more or less cultivated, and these we will treat of separately in their turn; but there are, too, belonging to this group, many little dialects, well defined as they are, but unwritten. The four chief divisions are Lesghian, Misjeghian, Ossete or Iron, and Circassian; and they, too, have their various forms or subdivisions.

837. That they are all of them Persian in their character, disguised by a strange orthography, we hold to be unquestionable. They bear a close relationship with the Finnish, Samoidish, and East Slavic; but it is only as they also are related to the Persian.

838. Compared with ours, their order of words is much inverted; though, if we place them along-side the Persian and the languages of Eastern Europe, we shall find almost nothing that is remarkable. Their sentences are short, disconnected, and emphatic; in a word, they possess the character of all uncultivated idioms.

839. We will introduce a few examples of their expression, and we will note some points that are peculiar:

In Lesghian: *Emen nedscher sovalda-ish bugewk* — father our heaven-in (thou) art; *bugabi chatir dur kin sov-alda hagadin ratl-alda* — be will thy (*dur*) so heaven-in like-as earth-in; *dur zar* — thy name.

To-God death not (is), *i. e.*, God dies not; *to-man life much not-lasting* (is), *i. e.*, man lives not long; *yet she sick* (is); *daughter by sits* (sits by), *weeps* (and weeps); *this man blind* (is), *his wife deaf is; from-us* (the) *speaking not-hearing is* (she), *i. e.*, (she) hears not the speaking by us; *little eats, little drinks, i. e.*, eats and drinks little; *nose* (of the) *face middle* (is), (in the middle of face); *tongue-and, teeth-and* (*and* is suffix); (on) *head hair grow; bones* (are) *hard stone like; moon great is star by, sun by* (it is) *small* (*large by a star*, larger than a star); (the) *hair long is, thin is*, *i. e.*, long and thin; *fire burn, we see smoke, flame* (and) *coal*. It may be well to mention that words in parenthesis are not in the text.

840. As an instance of the peculiar form our words take in this group, we note the numeral *one*, which is *zo, zis*, and *hos, z* equal to the *d* of the Slavic *one;* other dialects have *mi*, G'k

mia, and others still have *ert* and *art*, our erst and first; for *two*, we find *ki-go, go* being suffix, and *ki = ti*; in Circassian, we find *tu* = two; day has the forms *dge, ga, jogh, djaka, deni, toha, div* — all variations of one form equal to *day*, Fr. *jour*; we find also for *day* the form *ko*, which equals *ga = dge = da*. It would be interesting, had we the space to spare, to go through many other comparisons of this kind.

841. We come next to the Ossete, or Iron, the idiom of a people neighbors to the Circassians and the Georgians. It is without literature, and yet it is a language of great interest to the philologist, from the form in which it presents to us the Persian, and remotely the European in general. The orthography presents a very unexpected agreement with that of the Persian and the Eastern European, and even with the German.

842. *Mai stalutei istir-daru, choreitei kzill-daru* — moon of-star (than star) great-er (is), of-sun smaller (it is), *i. e.*, but smaller than the sun; *as* = I, *di* = thou, *ui* = he (*ho*, Per. *au*), *mach* = we (Per. *ma*, Slav. *my*), *smach* = you (Per. *shuma*, G'k *humeis*), *udon* = they (Slav. *yeden*, one, Sw. *eder*, Ger. *der* and *jeder*); *as dan*, I am, *de* = art, *isz* = is; *mach stem* — we are; *stut* = are-ye, *isti* = are-they. This *d* of *dan* (am) brings us back to the Turk. *idum*, Pers. *budam*. A better representative is found in the Ossete past, *uden, ude, udi*; plur. *udsimen, udsine, udseni; wod* (would) = be, was.

843. Many verbs are formed here, as we find in so many languages, by using *make* (*kanin*, Ger. *thun*, t = k, L. *paro*, Per. *kardan*), and noun or adjective as a base; as, *kar-kanin* — cry-make (to cry); *achur-kanin* — learn-make (to-learn).

844. Augments before verbs here play a prominent part — they are *fe, ni, ba* (forms of Pers. *bi*, and Sem. *n*). We find the perf. part. ending *nag* and *ag*; as, from *kus* or *qus*, hear, we have *qus-ag*, which we find varied to *qus-gond* (this *ag* and *nag* are clearly related to our *ing*, Turk. *mek*. The imperative has prefix *bai, bi*, as *bai-qus* — infin. *qus-en*. So in the Tushi, another Caucasian tongue, the present part. ends in *-in*, as *dagu-in*, eating, from *dago*, eat; and the perf. part. ends in *-no*, as *xac-no*, heard, from *xace*, hear. The prest. indefinite of Ossete scarcely differs from the infinitive.

The prepositions, adverbs, and conjunctions, are easily recognizable as either Persian or European.

845. A few selections will further illustrate its peculiarities:
Ui-thychei, ama man urnin chnzaw — this-for (for this), that I trust God; *zei-thychei*, Ger. *was-fur*, what-for; *ama kanin chors* — and do good; *za ui sidag dsinad sahi* — what his (*ui*) holy law command; *as kud fand-kanin chuzawei* — I as judgment-make of-God (as I judge of); *jul uni, jul kusi, jul soni* —

all (everything) sees, all hears, all knows; *kud* (how) *ui iss ud* (ghost) — as he is spirit.

Fid mach kazi de wol-arwi — father our who art (*dc*) in-heaven ; *sidag wond* — holy be (was, being) ; *ali andar chuson* all other things (Fr. *chose*); *zitkin dar da-fidi ama da-madi* — honor give (L. *do*) thy-father and thy-mother; *ma amar* (murder) — not-kill; *ma-zisah* — not-say; *e kawi* — his-dwelling (*e*, his) ; *dsul mach bonthy* (daily) *ratt machen abon* — bread our daily give us to-day (*abon*).

846. It is to be hoped that in time this remarkable idiom will come to receive more study than it has so far.

847. To the CIRCASSIAN the same general remarks will apply that were made on the rest of the family. A few examples must suffice for this :

Szie shad (Per. *shud*) — I was ; *arr shad* — he was ; *masar whagoh me nachjin-sh* — moon star by (*me*) greater-is (*sh* = is) — moon greater than star (*nach* = more, *jin* = great). The '*sh* is an *is* developing itself at the end of adjectives, as we saw in Persian — it is not really *is*, but a mark for it, and at the same time a part of *jin; hache*, dogs ; *ha-kode*, much dogs (*kod* = much); *sheh-kod*, much horses (a beautiful illustration, this, of the growth of adjectives from nouns, similar to diminutive endings); *sse unneh me ssoko* — I house to go (to house) ; *s-ab*, my father ; *w-ab*, thy father ; *r-ab*, their father.

Bdse-ma nna (eye) *iash, thakhuma eakom* (not) — fish-to (to fish) eye is, ear not (is) ; *my zugur naf-sh* — this man blind-is. The pronoun object of a verb is incorporated with it. We notice in this language, as everywhere, words assuming different forms according to their different connections.

848. GEORGIAN. — The Georgian is another language belonging with the group under consideration ; it has received some attention at the hands of philologists, but it has not been studied with any great amount of perseverance. It is only valuable in respect to its linguistic illustrations.

849. We will dwell but briefly on this tongue : *Me am tsigns gtser* — I this letter you-write (*g* is pref. = obj. you) ; *ak dids kalaks Pharizs mowcqith* — here (to-this) great city Paris (I have) come ; *mowedin supeva scheni* — come kingdom thy ; *puri tshweni* — bread our ; *da nu* — and not; *szeda* — earth-on ; *tzata* — heaven-in.

850. Postpositive particles, or prepositions, after the noun are here quite prominent. The comparative, marked by its ending, is followed by the genitive. The pronouns are easily referable to the Persian-German class ; their genitives are used as possessives. The demonstrative letters are $g = d$, $m = n$, and

s = *t.* The verb has considerable development in person endings; and prefixes, or augments, are prominent. The endings of the participle are well developed. A leading difficulty, in acquiring a knowledge of this language, is its exceedingly strange alphabet. It is only after careful search that it can be found to be connected, though remotely, with the European alphabets.

851. The ARMENIAN is the last of the class before us; and it is by far the most cultivated and the best known. There is much written in this tongue — going back even to the fourth century. The ancient Armenian is extinct. The alphabet is odd to us, but very handsome; and it is easily traceable to the Greek and Semitic alphabets. It has, like the Georgian, capitals as well as small letters. We notice, briefly, some of the features of Armenian:

852. In Armenian, and also in all the class, gender as a distinctive mark is scarcely developed. The *k* mark of the plural is so far Hungarian and Tartar. The objective here, as we so often see elsewhere, does not differ in form from the nominative; it has a prefix *z*, our *to, the*, and Heb. *eth*. The *ra* ending of some genitives reminds us of the *ra* of Persian cases; the dat. ending is *m*, the *am, em*, of L. accusative — the abl. ends in *e*. There is, besides, a dative prefix or augment, *i, z*. Many case changes are manifested by what are called inserted letters, but what is really a development of the letters in the word, as we term it, rather than at the end of the word as usual.

853. The pronouns, and the particles generally, are clearly recognizable. Pronouns are often found as suffixes to the noun, as in Persian. The verb is well developed, having its augments, endings, and participles. We find the active and the passive participles undistinguished. There are full sets of compound tenses, by the aid of *be* and *become*. The infin. ending is *el, al*, and the part. endings are a variation of it. The verb *be* is *el*, as in Amharic; it reminds us, too, of the Finnish and Slavic classes; *become* is *linil*, and this also reminds us of Hungarian and Finnish. The present participle ends in *og*, our *ing*, while the past or passive ends in *eal* = infin. *el*.

854. A few selections from the language we now give: *Hair mer or zergins ies* — father our who in-heaven art (is); *kam kho* (will thy) — thy will; *karoyr-n otevan norin woch evs hencher i tsayn yerkotz nora* — (the) cavern (*-n* = the, her) the-abode of-her (*norin*) not more (no more) resounded with (*i*) sound of-voice hers; *kosel*, to speak; *henchel*, to resound.

Ev linizi int orti — and may-come (be born) to-me (a) son (L. *puer*); *ergou ortil ant* — two sons are; *es em ortin ko* — I am son thy (thy son); *ev deseal ezna*—and seeing him; *ase z-na Zrouan*—said to-him Z. (did); *orowk ez-hasdn arner*—with-which sacrifice he-made; *z-Ormitz*, to-Ormiz; *orti nora*—boy his; *wasn oroh*—cause (of) which; *wasn-ko*—cause-thy; *wasn-im*—my cause; *z-or arnem*—which I-make (*z* pref.); *has-d arar*—sacrifice (he) made, *i. e.*, sacrificed.

Haindam esgsan Ormizt ev Arhmnen arn-el ararads—then began O. and A. to-make creatures; *im orti-n e*—my son is (*n*=the); *tou es*—thou art (L. *tu es*); *des-eal ez-na* (*z-na*)—seen him; *ev amenain ine zor Ormiztn arner pari er ev ougig* — and all that what O. made (*arn-er*) good was (are, were) and right.

Asei, I said; *asem*, I say; *asen*, they say; *kid-az*, knew; *iur*, his, her; *nma*, him, to him; *z-na*, him, that; *mek*, we; *mer*, of-us (our), *mez*, to-us, *z-mez*, us; *imk*, our; *touk*, ye, *tser*, of-you, your; *sir*, love (dear, cher-ish); present indic. *sir-em, zir-es, sir-e* ; plur. *sir-emk, sir-ek, sir-en*; imp. ind. *sir-er, sir-eir, sir-er* ; *sir-eak, sir-eik, sir-ein*; aorist *sir-ezi, sir-ezir, sir-eag*; *sir-ezak, sir-ezik, sir-ezin*; infin. *sir-el*, part. *sir-og*. The endings of the pres. indic. are almost identical with am, art, is, etc. (*em, es, e ; emk, ek, en*); infin. *to be* is *el*, part. *eal*.

And we may note here, that the uniform agreement everywhere of verb and participle endings with the forms of *be*, is not accidental, but it proves the fact that the verb *be* is only a development of those endings thrown off.

855. Of the verb *give* we may notice these forms: *dam*, I give (L. *dam', dem*), *damk*, we give, *dan*, they give; *dal*, infin.; *dou-ael*, part. aorist; *dou-og*, pres. part.; future part. *daloz*; impera. *dour*; imperf. *dahi*; *dou-eal linim*—given am (am given, become given); *pazeal linim*—openened (I) become (am openened); *kid-em*, I know, L. *vid-eo*; *gou-el*, to go (tsh =g); *lo-el*, to hear (G'k *k-luō*); listen; say, impera., is *asa*, aorist part. *asa-zeal*, infin. *as-el*—other participles, *as-og, aseloz*, and *asa-zog*; *e-dov* (*e* augment), have given, L. *dedi*.

856. Aside from the alphabet, the language is easy to learn, and when learned it will prove one of much interest, importance, and beauty. The idiom is by no means hard or unnatural. For an Asiatic language, there is much that is European. There are very many words which are clearly identical with words in Europe; the orthography of these is very interesting; we have space here only to instance such words, in addition to those already named incidentally, as these: *tun* (house), L. *dom-us*; *oskr* (bone), L. *os*; *air* (man), L. *vir*; *lusin* (moon), L. *luna*; *am* (year), L. *annus*, time; *mis* (flesh), meat; *dzarr*, tree; *djur*, water; *glouk* (head), Slav. *glava*; *amarn*, summer; *koz* (swine), L. *sus*; *hur*, fire; *div*, day; *agn*, eye, Ger. *aage*; *liezu*

tongue, L. *lingua;* odn, foot, G'k *pod-os;* adanm, tooth, G'k *odous.*

857. It is greatly to be regretted that this language has not been better studied, so well does it illustrate our own languages. The facilities for studying it are very limited, and the number of thorough Armenian scholars is very small.

CHAPTER IX.

TARTAR LANGUAGES.

858. That the Mongolian, Manchu, Tartar, and Turkish, constitute one great family of languages allied to each other by various and unmistakable marks, and that they belong also with the Semitic and the Persian, are facts beyond all doubt; and yet these positions have each been often questioned. As a whole, we may denominate them the Tartar class. Those people are by no means all Tartars; but as they are all closely related to the Tartars, and as the Tartars, if not the oldest, were at least the most prominent and most numerous branch of the family, the name seems fully justified. But let it be borne in mind, also, that Tartar as a name of a people or a tongue, is very indefinite. They, the Tartars, have at times conquered others, and have been lost with the vanquished; they have themselves in turn been overrun, and the limits that defined them have vanished in the darkness of the past. The Mongolians have absorbed a large share of them — they are themselves Tartars; but Mongolian, as a country name, has to a great extent taken the place of Tartar. The name Tartar is now confined to narrow limits, and is applied to that portion of the class most nearly connected with the Turkish. The term Ouighour is also applied to it, or to a form of it.

859. We may as well remark here, that the term *Turanian* is often applied to this class, taken in connection with Finnish and Samoïdish; the term *Arian,* or Indo-European, is opposed to Turanian; the Semitic is accounted a third class, distinct from both these — as to which we will see hereafter. What is not Semitic or Turanian (Tartar) in Europe and Asia, speaking generally, that is, all that has the European character, is Arian. The Chinese and Malay class have so far been compelled to take a place outside.

860. Tungusic and Manchu are names which may cover nearly the same limits, the one as the other; and yet Tungusic is used

in a narrower sense to apply to a subdivision of Tungusic, parallel to the Manchu, and indicating a people consisting of tribes in the north of Asia, principally in Siberia.

861. TARTAR: The Tartar (-Turkish) possesses those features which so strongly mark the whole class. And, first, we notice the strongly developed case endings, so far advanced as in the end to separate from the stem and become postpositions. The gen. mark is *ung, ing;* as, *bach-ung* — of-head (Slav. *-ego, -ych,* Hung. *-nek*); *de* and *den* are abl. marks, as *bach-de,* in-head (L. *de,* Per. *-ra,* and *der*) — besides these marks, separate postpositions are used. The suffix possessive pronouns appear here as we saw them in Finnish and Hung. The adjective is always before the noun, with which it unites so strongly that the latter only receives the case and number endings. The plural ending is *ler.* The absence of the article is a mark of the whole class, save that *bir,* one, is used for *a,* and *that* for *the.* A few illustrations, in the way of selections, may now be given :

862. *Chedjy nam karye* — Chedjy (by) name (a) village (a village called); *guicuz-um kan dolsa* — eye-my blood should-fill-with (if my eye should be filled with); *bu kiar-ing ferdjami* — that affair-of (of that affair) end-its (the end of that affair); *su buch-i* — water chief-its,, *i. e.*, head-water, the sea; *beyler-bey,* of beys-the-bey; *mutemed adem-isi guiel-ub* — faithful men-his arriving (his faithful men arriving); *kimi-miz* — who-your, *i. e.*, who of you, some one of you; *her birimiz* — every one-us (one of us); *kande baghtche* — where (is) garden. We find compounds as in the Persian style.

Beuiles-ini guieurme-mich idi — like-of-him (his-like) seen-not had-he (was) (had not seen ; *me* inserted = not); *benim bir baghtch-em var dyr* — to-me a (*bir* = one) garden-my is there (I have a garden of mine); *guieurduk-leri* — their-having-seen (*leri* = their), *i. e.*, what they had seen ; *guield-iguim* — my-having-come, *i. e.*, what I had come to; *bun-ing birle* — that of for (because of that); *bunler guibi* — those as (as those); *benim djins-im* — of-me race-my (my race of mine); *senung-ki* — of-thine that, *i. e.*, that of thine, thine (*ki*=that), like Ger. *deinige;* *yok-dur* — not-is, *i. e.*, there is not.

763. Besides the pronouns and particles of Tart.-Turkish, so easily reduced to European relationship, there are many other leading words, verbs and the like, which are by no means strange, if we bear in mind the laws of letter changes. In the case of verbs, we drop the *mek* of the infin. ; as, for *itmek,* we take *it* as the representative :

Bas, press, bind ; *var,* go, walk, L. *erro ; vir,* give, L. *fero,* bring ; *al,* take, G'k *el; geur,* see, peer, view ; *eul,* die, kill ;

kyl, Sans. *kar, l, r; gel,* go, walk; *di,* L. *di-co,* say; *it,* do, Ger. *thun; ara,* search; *ak,* blank, white; *oku,* read, L. *lego; sev,* love; *ko,* put, L. *po'; kara,* black, dark; *at* (horse), G'k *'ippos.*

864. MONGOLIAN: This has all the features characterizing the Tartar languages; but, more than this, it can with a slight effort be placed along-side the Persian and European. The pronouns, the participles, the structure of the moods and tenses, the form of the verbals, all these are quickly made familiar to us by their resemblance to languages known to us, not only Asiatic but European also.

865. The leading sections of the Mongolians are the East and West Mongolian, the latter being again named Kalmuk. They are closely related dialectic forms.

866. MANCHU.— This refers particularly to the language of the people of Manchuria. It is in all respects a Tartar language, but Tartar which has been pressed by the Chinese. It serves well to mark the transition of Chinese to Tartar.

867. As a language of the class, we find little in the grammar to remark as peculiar. The plurals (for living beings only) end in *sa, ta,* (the *k* of other forms); *i* is the gen. sign, *de* is dative, *be* is acc., *tchi* is abl. We find an ending *ngga,* our *ing* of verbals, which is seen in all Tartar; also, *miningge,* mine, and *siningge,* thine (Ger. *deinige*). As we find in the whole class, so here we find no proper relative. We find, between the root of the verb and the infinitive ending, *bu* as a pass. mark; *ako,* Turk. *me,* is the negative mark, joined to the verb (*k m*). Many of the particles are easily connected with the Greek.

868. We will give a few examples of its peculiarities: *Ere gisun-be niyalma tome kitchetchi atchambi* — this word (*be* is acc. sign) man all to-inquire ought (all ought to inquire, consider). The genitive, like the adjective, is always before the noun: *emke emkei*— one to-one, one after another; *emou niyalma, i-ni dchoue niyaman imbe bandchifi* — one man, his two parents him bearing (whose two parents have borne him).

Oubabe dchafafi gisouretchi — this assuming (if we) speak (*ou-ba* is a double *this, be* is acc. sign, *fi* pres. part., *tchi* is conditional mark — verbs have not developed personal endings, and the persons are often neither indicated nor expressed); *touba-de* (dative mark) *bitchi*— that-in (there) (he may) be. *i. e.,* he may be there (*bi* = be); *toumen dckaka* — all thing; *mini beye* — my body, my self; *terebe we same moutembi* — that (-thing, acc.) who (*we*) to-know might (who might know); *men-de emou sain sargan dchoui bi*— us-to a (one) good girl daughter be (is) (we have a beautiful daughter); *geneme*, to go, gone; *geno*, go; *gen-ere* — will go (Fr. *irai*); *sa-mbi* — I, thou, or he know (Fr. *sais*); *sar-ko* — know-not (*ko* = not).

Kake keke — husband (and) wife (*and* is omitted, as it is uniformly — conjunctions are scarcely yet developed here); *banin keseboun sere dchoue kergen* — nature (and) fate (so) called two words (two words, names, nature and fate); *dergi edcheni bandchiboukangge* (of or by) supreme lord being-been-born (*bandchibouba*, has created, or borne); *moukchan dcheingge-i warangge* — (with) staff (or) sword slaying; *emou ikan-be bakatchi* — one (a) ox (if you) receive (receive one ox, *i. e.*, if you receive).

Si aika sain-be yaboutchi — thou if good (you do) do; *tatchire-de* (teach) *amourangge* — to-learn loving (*i. e.*, loving to learn); *bov touketchibe* — house fall, *i. e.*, although the house fall, Ger. *wohnen*, a-bode; *bandchiboure wemboure sekiyen tede bi* — (of) bearing (and) dying (the) fountain (in) him (*tede*) is (be), *i. e.*, their fountain is in that; *biya chun-i* — moon sun-with; *goa koungtse-i barou khend-ouke* — one Confucius before said (one said to C.).

869. A few parallel lines will give some idea of the comparative form of Tartar, Mongolian, and Manchu:

Tartar: *Atha wisum chy kok-ta sen* — father our who heaven-in art; *wer wisum gundaluch otmak* — give (bring) to-us daily bread; *wou-gun* — this-day; *garta wisni geman-dan* — free us evil-from.

870. Kumanian: *Bezom atta-masz* — to-us father-our; *kem-ko* — who-art; *kik-te* — heaven-in; *sze-lezon szen-ad-on* — holy-be (*lez*) thy-name-thine.

Kalmuk, or West Mongol: *Atshiga mani octorgi-du baiktshi* — father our heaven-in being (who art); *tani naratani* — thy name-thine; *mani odor* — our day; *tani gar-tu amai* — thy hand-in am (is) (in thy hand it is).

871. Tungusic: *Aminmun mungi avagu negdavgidadu* — father-our (of) us (thou) art heaven-in; *gerbish singi* — name thine (word); *on singi bisin* — for thine is (be-st, Ger. *bist*); *on neg-da-du do endra-du* — as heaven-in so earth-in.

872. And, finally, Manchu: *Abka-de thege megni ama* — heaven-in (there) dwell our father; *sini kebu enturinge okini* — thy name (word) holy be (Arab. *kan* = be); *na-de* — earth-in.

873. The Mongolian and Manchu have both an alphabet peculiar to them, though the two have a clear reference to each other, and are supposed to have been built on the same basis. They are written in lines downward, proceeding from left to right. These alphabets are syllabic, and are evidently related to the Chinese; and they have the character, too, of the Sanscrit.

874. The leading point which we notice in these languages, and in those of Asia generally; is that words here, where so many are connected together, are not yet individualized as they are in Europe: they are not yet old enough to be detached from the parent stem — as is particularly the case, also, in Sanscrit and Semitic.

CHAPTER X.

CHINESE LANGUAGE.

875. Our knowledge of the Chinese language is commensurate with our knowledge of the Celestial people. There is more than one point of obscurity in both. Still, the study of the Chinese character and Chinese idiom has many able devotees, and we are flattered with the assurance that we are daily becoming more enlightened in respect to this portion of the history of the "Central-Flowery-Kingdom."

876. It is not many years since we were taught that the Chinese were a people without another with which to compare them, and that their language was without a parallel or connection in the whole wide world. But time and labor have made us wiser. We now know for a certainty that the roots of both the language and the nation extend far back into the great Tartar class, in the north and west, and into the Malay and Indian, in southern Asia — thus proving that here, at least, we do not find an exception to the great truth, that nothing is found in this world without its kind, its like, its homologue.

877. All things considered, the Chinese is to be ranked among the most infantile and uncultivated idioms so far known to us. Speaking generally, we may say the language has all the characteristics of a wild people, and that it lacks those which mark the idioms of enlightened men. There is almost a total absence of those derived forms of adverbs, adjectives, verbs, case, number, and gender forms, besides those of tense, mood, and participle — an absence of everything that is properly inflexion and derivation. The parts of speech and their subdivisions are not distinguished by appropriate forms, but, rather, by their connection, and by the relative place they occupy. There is much in all this, and more that might be mentioned, that is Polynesian, that is even African. We have, here, says one author, only to do with naked stems or roots.

878. The genitive is a pure adjective, and as such it is placed

before the noun. It is placed thus without any variation from the noun form, as we do in our *iron*-horse, horse of *iron*; or, the genitive is followed by a sort of suffix prepostion, *ti* or *chi*, *i. e.*, of, or of the; as, *wa-ti*, I-of, of me, or my; *ta-ti*, he-of, or his. Other cases are marked by prepostions placed before or after. The plural may be expressed by the singular, marked by some word equal to *much, all*; also by suffix *mun* (= other). It is expressed also by the well-known mode of repetition.

879. For all persons, all tenses and moods, all participles, it may be said that the same unchanged and bare form of the verb is used, *i. e.*, the Chinese mind is scarcely conscious of these distinctions. They know only live and dead, or full and empty words — meaning by the former verbs and nouns, and by the latter, particles; beyond that, they are uncertain, unconcerned. The persons they distinguish by the context, or they use pronouns before the verbs; as, *wo yu kin* — I have gold; *ni yu kin-sha* — thou have gold-dust. The tenses are either not distinguishable, or auxiliary particles are used as in English.

880. There is, in these respects, a great difference between the ancient and modern Chinese: in the former, there is an absence of these particles and auxiliaries — the sentence being here one unresolvable whole (while the other form shows the result of development). The modern is again divided into the Pekin and the Nankin dialects, having considerable differences; and, besides this, the written form varies greatly from the spoken language.

881. The words of Chinese are chiefly of the simplest kind, such as we find in Polynesian and African — but they are not all monosyllabic. Not only is there an absence of derivative forms, but we scarcely find what we may call true compounding — unless we may consider every noun with adjective, or indeed the sentence itself, as a commingled mass or compound. Others, looking at it from another stand-point, decide that there are many compounds in Chinese. They, to say the least, are compounds of a character very different from what we consider compounds in our languages.

882. From the absence of derivative forms, we find many instances where the same word, if we look to the form alone, is applied to several different objects — or, as we express it, one word has several different meanings. Generally, we either use different words, or words which have varied their form to correspond with the new application; as, *price, prize, praise;* also *rise, rose, raise, raised, raiser, raising, rising*. But the Chinese has no capacity for such variation. In spoken language, they distinguish by nice variations of tone or accent, precisely as we do, to a limited extent, in *prem-ise* and *pre-mise*, *read* (present)

and *read* (past), *man* and *men*. All changes of vowels, and, more remotely, all changes of the word, are the workings of this variation of tone, found so prominently in Chinese. The Chinese carry the principle much farther, and they have many shades of tone not perceptible to us — these changes of sound being incipient to a change of form, and in a measure representing it.

883. A very fruitful source of new words, or terms, in Chinese, is found in the associating of two words of similar meaning — an application of the universal principle of doubling or repeating words to form new elements. Their words having each a great variety of different applications, their meaning must be fixed in some way. They take two words having each one meaning like one of those of the other, and thus use one to determine the other. Our compound *stage-coach* will serve to illustrate this system in Chinese. The word *stage* applies to a great many different things, besides to a certain kind of coach, and so does *coach* apply to many other kinds of car besides that used in staging; but put them together, and we know with certainty the object intended.

884. In this and like cases, both *stage* and *coach* denote the very object pointed out by *stage-coach*, but also so many other things as to be indeterminate. We see here, again, that the part really includes the meaning of the whole, that it is equal to the whole. This affords an instructive lesson on the origin of new words.

885. *Chinese Writing.* — There are no letters in Chinese, such as we find in European tongues. Their words are represented by characters which are known only as one sign, *i. e.*, the parts have no separate existence, more than the parts of the figure 4. But, more generally, the representatives of ordinary words are made up of two individuals, having each a separate value, somewhat as in our fractions 1-3, 2-5 — or even of three parts, as in our complex fractions 2-3-5.

886. What may be considered the base of this Chinese word-sign, is the so-called radical, of which there are about 214 in the language. These radicals, or keys, are themselves words, referring to elementary ideas.

887. The other part of the word-sign is called the phonetic part; it, too, is a separate word, as the 3 of 1-3 is a separate number. The phonetic alone gives the name to the whole character, as the fraction is called 4ths, 5ths, from its denominator alone. That is, as we understand it, generally the Chinese words or names are all adjectives, as indeed the case is everywhere, and the radical is the base noun which becomes obscured or lost in pronunciation, as we say the *good*, for *good men*, the *senior*, for *senior one*, a *level*, for *level ground*. This, we think,

is the precise principle in Chinese. So the words sea, river, lake, in Chinese, have for their key or base the element *water*, *i. e.*, they are certain kinds of water; the *kind* alone is expressed (the adjective), and *water* as a sound (but not as a sign) is lost. So the sign composed of the parts *shui*, water, and *cing*, blue, is called *cing*, and it means clear or pure.

888. Some of these sound-giving signs have lost their meaning, and are mere characters, while others are proper words. Chinese word-signs have at least one radical, and some have more; they are hence all compounds, as *Egypt-land*, for Egypt — in which *land* is not sounded. It is a very extensive application of that principle of determinatives, or radicals, which we notice in the Tartar, Malay, and other Asiatic languages; just as if we said, *gold-metal* for gold, *America-land* for America, *Persian-man* for Persian, *male-man* for male, *city-place* for city, *king-ruler* for king, *speech-make* for speak, *walk-go* for walk.

889. The Chinese word-characters have parts, as our own words have, but not so many recognized as we have. The Tartar and Sanscrit write their letters after the same principle as we find in Chinese. There is no doubt but that the origin of these Chinese characters will be found in hieroglyphics. A few examples will best illustrate some of the peculiarities of the language:

890. *Ngo fu* — I father, my father; *s-in sin* — man heart, heart of man; *sin sin* — man man, each man. The pronouns are, *wo*, I; *ni*, thou; *ta*, he; *wo-mun*, we (*mun* sign of plural); *tamun*, they; *wo yu*, I have; *wo sien-shi-yu* — I had; *ta sien-shi-yu* — he had; *wotsiu yu* — I will have (the words before *yu* being used as signs of tense — but even these auxiliaries are not used in the written language); *wo mu yu* — I not have; *wo-ti ta-shan* — I-of coat, my coat.

Na, which; *shui*, who; *tung-si*, thing; *na-ko*, the, that; *che-ko*, this; *che-ko ma*, this horse; *ji ji*, day day, every day; *kau-ti*, high; *twan-ti*, short (*ti* gen. or adj. sign); *ki to*, how much; *chi*, only; *kin nien* — this year; *kin ye* — this night, to-night; *wo shi* — I am; *ta shi*, he is; *yu*, there is, has; *shi-ti*, right (*ti*, the, of); *lai*, come, *ku*, go; *ta lai* — he come; *wo-mun lai* — we come; *wo lai-liau* — I came; *ku-liau*, went; *ta tsiang lai* — ho will come; *tso*, do; *tso-yuen-liau* — done.

891. The following translations will exhibit some other features of this idiom :

(The) folk (is) quiet (adjective used as verb, *is* being suppressed); *fu hai, seu san* — (his) *luck* (is a) *sea*, (his) *life* (-length) *mountain*, *i. e.*, his-fortune (is) *great-as-sea*, his-life-length (length of life) like that of a mountain. All those qualifying words are not expressed in Chinese, or they lie latent in the words *luck, sea, mountain*: they regard the points only of a sentence.

Heaven (and) *earth* (are) *blue* (and) *pale* (remember that all words in parenthesis are not in the original text); (in) *that land much mountain* (is); (to) *men all deep eye* (and) *high nose*, *i. e.*, they all have deep eyes; *body* (and) *face* (were) *broad*. (The tense is known by context, and *broad* is a real verb in its office); *mun prince* (*sin kiun*) — a man (who is) a prince; *cold come heat go* — (when the) cold comes (then the) heat departs.

I seu — has taken (several verbs are used, as with us, with other verbs to denote past or complete action, as *i, yu, ke*). The noun before another noun is uniformly the adjective, and the noun before the verb is the subject; *je ming* — *night sing*, *i. e.*, in-the-night ho-sings; *not can* (he) *far fly*; (the) *prince why* (he) *grieve?* (in) *name-report under Kuang very far* (was he), *i. e.*, in reputation (was he) far under Kuang; *thou come already long*, *i. e.*, hast long been here.

Place-place, every place; *he saw water suddenly came*, *i. e.*, saw it come; *he was a man he possessed*, *i. e.*, who possessed; *middle-land hear it* (but) *not believe it*, *i. e.*, China heard but did not believe (all those conjunctions and particles so used with us, are left out in Chinese); *thou where see him*, *i. e.*, thou whom you see; *I where have money*, *i. e.*, money which I have.

892. Adjectives, as *great, good*, can be used not only for *is-great, was-good*, but also for transitive verbs, as *make-great, consider-great* ; as, *ta* = great, *chi* = it, *ta-chi* = increase-it, *i. e.*, make-great it. Adjectives not before the noun are, as with us, adverb, participle, or verb; as, we say *great* in all, being great in all; *formerly say Chin-tu*, *i. e.*, formerly they said Chin-tu; *India-of man*, *i. e.*, Indian man, Indians; *different country different use*, *i. e.*, (for) for different countries (are) different usages; *from-far to-cite*, *i. e.*, to cite from far; (to) *express* (what) *they it beautiful*, *i. e.*, what they think *it* beautiful (here, *mei, beautiful*, is used causatively or transitively = to-think-beautiful).

Man it love — what men love; (if) *king say how for good I* (of my) *empire* (must I act) (then) *great man say how for good I family* — *i. e.*, if the king says how (must I act) for my country's good (then too will the) great man say how for (that of our) families.

893. We conclude the Chinese with the remark, that there is nothing there that is not found, at least in the germ, in other languages. The time will yet come when it will not be thought amiss to compare European words with those of Chinese.

CHAPTER XI.

SEMITIC HISTORY.

894. The Semitic languages constitute a large and distinctly marked class. From the peculiar phases in which they present language, they are to the philologist of the utmost interest and importance. They are very properly located on the confines of Asia; their character and history affords us the transition from what is European to what is Asiatic. It affords us another illustration of the truth that languages uniformly belong where they are geographically located.

895. The Hebrew, Syriac, and Arabic, constitute the main body or branch — they are what we generally have in view when we speak of the Semitic languages. The Ethiopic is located in Abyssinia, and has been so long and so far removed from the fatherland in Asia, as to receive, on a Semitic basis, an impress peculiarly its own. The Egyptian is Semitic too, but it differs from the original family even more than the Ethiopic does.

896. The Hebrew is without doubt the oldest of the family; certainly, at least the oldest written monuments are found here. Like its near relative, the Syriac, it is now, and long since has been, for all practical purposes, an extinct idiom. Hebrew, as well as Syriac, is still spoken in some form or other by the scattered remnants of the old Hebrew family; but it is rather, like Latin, when spoken in its purity by the students of Europe, as a language that once was, but now is not. It is a language only of literature; it is, and in so far like the Sanscrit, a sacred language, one appropriated to the church. The Hebrews no more exist as an organized race, or people; they were first swept down by the Syrians, and they in their turn were vanquished by the Arabs, a people that have long since absorbed all that was either Hebrew or Syriac in Asia. Scattered as the Hebrews now are over the broad face of the earth, they readily yield to the influences of the people that adopt them.

897. Among the dialects or forms of the Hebrew, we may name the *Rabbinic*, which is Hebrew and Chald. in its features, and the *Samaritan*. The latter may indeed be called a dialect, but nevertheless it has several leading characteristics of its own. The Rabbinic alphabet is Hebrew slightly varied. The Samaritan alphabet is Hebrew very much changed — it is old Hebrew (it has no vowel points). The number of Samaritans still living is very small; their language ceased to be a living one several

centuries ago, but it is still written and read, like the Hebrew, as a church language. It is now replaced, as a vulgar tongue, by the Arabic.

898. The *Phœnician* runs closely parallel with the Hebrew, with several distinctive features however. It yielded much to Greek influences. Very little in the way of specimens of the language, and those inscriptions only, have come down to us, and hence our knowledge of it is very imperfect. The Phœnician has an alphabet — it is old Greek also.

899. The Chaldaic with the Syriac constitute a branch of Semitic called Aramaean. The former is mostly Syriac in its features — but it has some, too, which are not Syriac, but Hebrew. It is written in the Hebrew alphabet.

900. The *Sabien* is an obscure form of Semitic, noticeable for its peculiar kind of alphabet. We might name also the *Assyrian*. But little is known of it; it is, however, attracting some attention. It is known to be essentially Semitic.

901. If the extent of territory which it covers, if the number of people by whom it is spoken, and the extent of its family connections, render a language worthy of study and attention, then, certainly, *Arabic* ranks among the very first in is claims upon us. Of ancient Arabic we have little that remains to us, and little that can be said of it. One of the forms of Old Arabic, Southern Arabic, is the *Himyaritic*, of Yemen. It differs very materially, however, in a dialectic way, from the Arabic now known to us. It is known by inscriptions, and much is yet to be learned of it. It was spoken in Yemen as late as the fifteenth century. Another form of old Arabic is known as the *Koreish*.

902. Unlike the Semitic idioms already spoken of, the Arabic is a living, progressive language. The Arabs as known to us are by no means an ancient people; they do not seem to have begun to have an individualized existence until some centuries after Christ.

903. There is a difference between the literal Arabic and the vulgar or spoken language; and the spoken language has differences also, according to the region where it is spoken.

904. The *Ethiopic*, as we find it, is supposed to have had its origin in an Arabic colony. *Amharic* may be called a modern form of Ethiopic, one modified by African influences. The latter is now become practically a sacred language; in its true form, it is no longer spoken.

905. Ethiopic literature embraces about two hundred works, mostly translations from Greek and Arabic — the oldest repository of Ethiopic is a copy of the Bible. About the fourteenth century, it began to cease to be spoken. The *Tigre* is a language

similar to Amharic, and holding about the same relation to Ethiopic.

906. The *Egyptian* we notice next; the connection between this and Semitic is undoubted. But it has a peculiar form nevertheless, which we shall see when we come to treat briefly of its character. The *Coptic* is properly modern Egyptian — it is the language spoken by the Christian portion of Egypt. The Coptic alphabet, in form, is a modification of the Greek letters. The Coptic has three dialectic forms, differing from each other but slightly, and called, respectively, the Theban, Memphitic, and Basmurian.

907. The *Maltese* is a Semitic (Arabic) language, greatly modified by European touches, or, if you prefer, by European admixtures. The *Berber* is the last of the class which we shall name.

908. SEMITIC LANGUAGES. — The peculiarities that characterize the style of any one of the Semitic idioms (Hebrew, Syriac, Arabic, and Ethiopic), speaking generally, characterize the others also. So, we will dwell at length upon the idiom of the Hebrew; and we shall after that have little that need be said on any feature belonging exclusively to any one of the remaining tongues.

909. The difficulties in acquiring the Hebrew, or any of the class, do not arise from the unusual position and strange combination or order of the words; for there is in all this, making due allowance for the simplicity of the language and its expression, much that is quite natural to us. There is, however, a great uncertainty, often, arising from the absence, to a great extent, of inflexion, or variation of the forms of words, to indicate that one word belongs with another, and from the absence, too, of those marks or auxiliaries which point out to a nicety the different shades of mood and tense. We have to depend much upon position, and more upon the context; there is much of latent or unindicated meaning in Semitic terms. But to the uninitiated learner, there is yet a greater and more embarrassing difficulty — that of finding in the lexicon the words which shall denote the meaning of the word which he finds in the text; for he finds one form of word, a sort of root, in the lexicon, and a very different, more intricate, form in his reading. His grammar informs him that some parts of the word which his text offers are ending or prefix, to denote the pronoun, subject or object, the gender, and to some extent, the case; that each verb has its derived forms or conjugations, which have developed new letters, either prefixed or infixed; that there is a large number of prepositions and adverbs, or conjunctions, welded to

the word at the beginning, or incorporated with it, in a manner that is quite foreign to most of the European languages.

910. It takes time, considerable time, before we can at a glance, as if by intuition, separate the formative letters (the prefixes, suffixes, and infixes) from the body of the word, and turn without hesitation to the very root or base-form which we should look for in the lexicon. The student of Greek can well understand these difficulties, but he must mark this difference: in Greek, it is the irregularity of a few words, while in Semitic it is the irregularity of the whole system. It is with great effort, too, that we become familiar with the Semitic alphabets, and with the oddity of reading the words (save the Ethiopic) from right to left.

911. Nearly all the characteristics of these languages which seem so strange to us, are those which are more or less common in all the languages of Asia; for instance, the union of particles and pronouns with the main word. So we see, that in Semitic, also, words are not individualized to the extent that they are with us. We offer now selections from Hebrew composition, as the best method of pointing out the peculiarities of the language:

912. *U-legach-tiy-cha* — and-I-have-taken-thee (u = and, *tiy* = I, *cha* = thee, and *legach* is the root or base-form of the verb, found isolated in the third person present); *legache-ta-nu* — (hast) taken-thou-us (thou has ttaken us) (nu = us); *be-malech-o* — in-reigning-his (*malech* is the infin. or verbal noun, be = in, pref. prep., and o, or u = his, meaning when or while he reigned, or he reigning; this *be* is, without doubt, only a modification of the participle prefix m, as well as of the *bi* of Persian verbs); *achal* — he-ate; *be-achele-nu* — in-eating-our, *i. e.*, when we eat, or ate (inf. is *achol*); so, we find *and-in-speaking-my*, *i. e.*, in my speaking; *le-shachen-iy* — for-dwell-my, *i. e.*, for me to dwell, that I may dwell; *u-be-yade-cha* — and-in-hand-thine, *i. e.*, in thy hand (*yad* = hand).

The-voice-thine-heard-I-in-garden (thy voice I have heard); *given-I* (I have given) *to-thee the-all* (given thee the whole); *all-these* (were) *drawers* (of) *sword*. The verb *be* in all its forms is very generally omitted, *i. e.*, the nouns and adjectives are real verbs here; in the last example, *sholephey* is a participle = the drawing (ones), the drawers — the word for sword, *charebh*, is really a part of the participle, though separate from it, *i. e.*, they (were) sword-drawers.

And-not shall-be-they (*yo-hey-u*) *to-thee, i. e.*, there shall not be to thee, you shall not have; *give-to-us water and-shall-drink-we* (that we may drink); *fruit-of greatness-of heart* (*i. e.*, boasting) (the mark of the genitive being, in Hebrew, put on the word governing it, when two nouns thus unite); (it was) *heavy* (the) *famine in-land, i. e.*, there was a heavy famine (*heavy* = a verb).

913. The infinitive form, as that of *to-know*, equals a noun, as *knowledge;* many participles and verbal forms are used, without any change, as real nouns. We find, comparatively, but few adjectives, but rather nouns and verbals with preposition used instead of them; thus, we find *ark of wood*, for wooden ark; *with-power*, for powerful.

914. As we find the prepositions, or case fixes, placed at the beginning of the word, so we find also the article; as, *ha-yom* — this-day, the day; *ha-aaretz*, the-earth. In the use of the articles, we find such instances as *men the-war, i. e.*, the war men, those-of-war; *the-city the-great* (one); *the-place the-that*, that place; *honest* (are) *we; thou he king mine, i. e.*, thou art my king (*he* taking the place of *be*). The possessive suffixes are used to denote objectives also; as, *wrong mine, i. e.*, my wrong, wrong to me; so, *fear his, i. e.*, his fear, the fear for him; *daughter* (of) *who, i. e.*, whose daughter; *which to-him, i. e.*, to whom; *which in-it* (in-there), *i. e.*, wherein.

915. We find verbs repeated, one of them being infin., and the other acting as adverb with it; thus, *ask he-asked, i. e.*, he asked much, or urgently; so, *he went going, i. e.*, he continued to go (like L. *contendit ire* = goes to-go, starts to-go — so, in Ger. *come-going, come-walking*, our *came-running;* hence, we see how one of them becomes an auxiliary, which gradually changes its form and meaning, and in the end the repetition which really exists becomes obscured). The infinitive is used, too, in the place of a full verb, as, *we-have-rebelled and turned*, instead of *we have turned* (really, we do the same when we say *we will go and see*, where *see* is only an infinitive); *water for the people to drink*, in Hebrew is *water for-the-drinking of-the-people*.

916. In general, we may say that the infinite is used in most cases as a finite verb. The participle does not distinguish time, and may be used, according to context, for any tense; so, *nophel* is used to denote *one falling*, or *having fallen*, or *who will fall*.

917. *God perfect* (is) *way-his* (his way is perfect); *the-people removed he them* (it); (a) *light* (a) *great* (one), *i. e.*, a great light — the adjective follows the noun; *sin* (is) *bitter very* (very bitter); (the) *spirit and-soul* (are) *of-God* (pref. prep.); *of-ten year was-he* (ten years old was he); (a) *woman* (being) *good loves-she the-Jehovah* (she loves God); *placed-he, Jehovah* (did), *to-Cain* (pref. prep.) (a) *sign* (God placed a sign).

They-caused-to-err the-people-mine by-boasting (caused them to err; here is used simply the causative of the verb err, *ta-gah*, just as *qatal*, to kill, *hi-qetiyl*, cause-to-kill — which form, again, has its persons, like the original *qatal*; we can see by this how such verbs as *cause, make, do*, etc., grow out of other verbs; *he-made, God* (did), *the-two* (of) *the-lights, the-great* (ones), *i. e.*, God made the two great lights.

918. If Hebrew, and the rest, prove anything conclusively, it is the independence of the nominative from the verb to which it is supposed to be joined, and the independence, also, of the adjective from the noun to which it is supposed to belong.

Behold we (are) *binding sheaves* (part. = verb); *carrying*, masc. form, = *he* (is) *carrying*, he carries; *two* (and) *ten* (of) *lion* (are) *standing-they there, i. e.*, twelve lions are standing there. This participle is used precisely as if L. *amantes* (they-loving) be taken for *amant* (they love) — showing very clearly that the verb is a participle, and *vice versa*.

919. The potential *may say, can say*, etc., is expressed by the future, *will say*; *go for-meet Moses* (to meet); *this* (is) *the-man who fears the-Jehovah*; *for not has-obeyed-she* (she has not); *wonders* (are) *thy testimony* (wonderful); *and-have-said-we*, for we will say; *go* (going) *hast-gone-thou from-with-me* (go-gone = hast gone); (the) *doors* (of) *brass I-will-break* (them); *the pride* (of the) *man it-shall-humble-him*; *with-the-God walked he, Noah* (did); *saddled-they-him* (for him) *the-ass*, (and) *rode-he* (he rode) *upon-it*; *I I-will-comfort-you*.

920. Short and disconnected sentences, we observe, prevail. One example more, illustrating repeated words, will close the Hebrew: *dachoh de-chiy-ta-niy li-nephol* — to-thrust hast-thrust-thou-me for-to-fall, *i. e.*, thrust at me that I might fall (*ta* = thou, *niy* = me, *li* = foe, to, like our sign of infin. — we have here the double verb *thrusting he-thrust*, simply he thrust).

921. The Syriac we find, in character, but little different. The following are selections, translations: *came-he set-he against Acco*, *i. e.*, he came to besiege Acco (*he-set*, used for *to-set* — so, he began he opened, for he began to open); *arose-they went-they* — they arose to go, *i. e.*, they went; *all* (every one) *who shall-drink from this water again he-shall-thirst*; *he-shall-come to-me and-he-shall-drink*, *i. e.*, let him come to me and drink; *that-he-shall-go and-shall-see*, *i. e.*, he might go and see (future = sub. and potential); *entreat-they with-him that-he-shall-be* (shall remain) *with-them*, *i. e.*, they entreat his remaining (this future *shall-be* has the Syriac prefix *d*, a true augment, with the force of *that, the*; we find this *d* frequently with the infin. and part., and it is evidently a variation of the Hebrew and Arab *l*, and the *m* of verbals); *who shall-say*, *i. e.*, can say; *not shall-fear*, *i. e.*, fear not (future for impera.); *sought-he that-he-shall-kill*,

i. e., he sought to kill (*d* being prefix to the future, equal to *the, that,* and indicating the true gerund.

Blessing I-will-bless, i. e., I will greatly bless; *going not went-he, i. e.*, he did not go at all; *sought-he for-catch, i. e.*, (for-catching) he sought to catch; *the-knowing* (ones) (of the) *law, i. e.*, those knowing the law; *and-saw-he* (a) *company* (a) *great* (one) *which-coming* (the-coming (one), who came) *to-him* (the *which* before *coming,* or *came,* is denoted by the prefix *d,* already noticed); (he-shall be) *rising brother-thine, i. e.*, thy brother shall rise (part. for future). Speaking generally, it may be said that the participle and infinitive may be used for the different moods and tenses.

Thou but (but thou) *what* (why) *judge thou brother-thine* (why judgest thou thy brother); *I I, i. e.*, I am (pron. = be); *ye in-me ye* (are), *i. e.*, ye are in me; *against-him* (the) *tyrant; I he* (am) *Jesus; in-it in-field* (in the field); *to-it to-law* (to the law) (this extra pronoun is common).

I I (I am) *Joseph that-sold-ye-me* (*i. e.*, whom ye sold; for *that, whom,* we find, again, that prefix *d*); *but that-of-he* (his) *that-sent-he-me* (his who sent me — both *thats* are represented by prefix *d*); *which-created God* (did) *in-the-making* (it) (*which* is represented by prefix *d, in* by *l,* prep., and *the* by *m* verbal pref.); *queen that-of-south* (queen of the south, *d = that* here is sign of genitive); *sorrow-thy and-conception-thy, i. e.*, sorrow of thy conception, *and* (*u*) having place of *of; da-bnay-nosho —* of-sons-men (of sons of men — that *da,* the *d* above, has the force of a preposition).

922. Prepositions are not prefixes to verbs in Semitic, but, in Syriac particularly, we find them as suffixes to the verb, though separate; as we say *speak-of, wonder-at, drink-from.* The tendency in all Semitic is to bring the verbs first, and adjectives and participles after the noun. Comparisons are made thus, *dear before* (the) *queen, i. e.*, dearer than.

923. In Arabic there is very little that is not Syriac first, and Hebrew afterwards. We will notice only the following features:

Proposed-he to-them what commanded-he-the-Mamun, i. e., showed them what Mamun had commanded; (it) *was went-he, i. e.*, he had gone; *was-he not doing, i. e.*, he did not. In Arabic, *l* is a common prefix, identical with our *that, to, the,* and the Syriac *d*; it may be termed the article of the verb, and it is often a mere unmeaning augment; *f, u,* is used as a prefix, in the same manner — it is not different from the Semitic prefix *u* = and; *that-go-I* = that I may go (*that* is prefix).

924. Those double verbs, one being participle or infinitive, which we noticed in Syriac and Hebrew, are also common here.

From the verb *give-you-it*, having suffix pronouns, we get the participle, (the one) *giving-you-it*, *i. e.*, the giver-to-you-of-it. We find *and* = with; thus, *what* (is) *to-you and-Zeid* (with-Zeid); *not to-me* (there is) *father and not-mother* (I have not, etc.); (there is) *dead to-me* (a) *brother, i. e.*, my brother is dead; *the-creating-thee*, the one creating (he who creates thee); *that-aid-I* = that I may aid; *I* (am) *going* = I go; *we* (are) *going* = we go; *to-us* (it is) *long time not* (have) *seen-we-you* (it is long since we have seen you).

Business-thy what (it is) *thing now?* *i. e.*, what is thy business? *one from the-animals, i. e.*, some animal, an animal; *time-time* = from time to time. The genitive scarcely differs from the nominative; *Y-amur-u-kum* — shall-command-he-you, *i. e.*, shall command you (*y* is sign of future, *kum* is suffix pron. *you*, and *u* may be taken as equal to *he*, or as part of the root); *fa-mala-u-hunna* — and-filled-they-them (they filled them), *fa* = and, *u* = they, and *hunna* (fem.) = them.

El-ma = the water (*el*, *'l* is the prefix article); *el-m-asiru* = the-returning (*el* is article, *m* or *ma* is the augment of participles or verbals, common in Semitic).

925. SEMITIC RELATIONS. — It is very generally claimed, even to-day, that the Semitic is an anomalous and distinct class. We will, however, examine briefly some of the leading features of the class, with a view to show that they are not so extraordinary as they have been considered, and that we may find clear parallels to them in the European and related languages.

926. That the pronouns, particles, and numerals can be identified with those with which we are familiar, is a truth which no one will dispute who understands the forms that are found in Semitic — we will at least pass them by without any special consideration.

927. One of the most striking points of resemblance between Semitic and European, is the strongly developed prefix article. It is true that in Semitic it is associated with the noun, or united to it; but we must remember that in European, also, though printed apart from the noun, it is in conversation treated as an inseparable part of it. The Arabic article *el, il*, reminds us of the Latin *ille*, Fr. *le; a* and *ha* of Heb. points to Lat. *hi, hae*, G'k *ê, ò* — and the Syriac prefix *d*, used in so many different capacities, is a clear representative of Ger. *die, der*, Semitic *ze*. In Egyptian and Coptic, we find the articles *pe, te* (the), *ne*. In Ethiopic, the prefix *ma* is a demonstrative akin to the articles of the other Semitic tongues, though used in them more as a relative.

928. We may call attention to the fact, also, that the noun

endings *n* and *t*, so well developed in the formation of Syriac nouns, also the *i*, *ai*, *et*, of Ethiopic, are evidently related to the suffix article of the Scandinavian class, and to that of the Albanian — as well as to the gender endings of Greek and Latin.

929. Not only do we find the prefix article, but also, as in English and other European tongues, we find prefix prepositions (not separate, as with us, but united with the noun or pronoun). But it is a very common thing in Europe to find the preposition unite with the article or pronoun, as in Ger. *beim*, for *bei dem*, and our own *to-em*, for *to them*; in Celtic, it will be remembered, the union of preposition with pronoun is a very prominent feature, as in Irish *agam* = with me (*ag* = with).

930. All these Semitic prepositions are, without doubt, only a variation of the article *el*, *il*, *l* — indeed, one of the most common Semitic prefixes is *l*, and another is *ch* or *k* (clearly pointing to the *ch*, *k*, *q*, which we find everywhere marking either the relative or demonstrative). Another is *m* (also demonstrative); a fourth is *b*. This *b* is identical with *m*, as well as with the Syriac *d*, used as article, relative, conjunction, and preposition. We might add to these *eth*, *th*, *t*, our *to* and *the*. The very common prefix *u*, though a conjunction equal to *and*, is to be classed with these, and is evidently identical with the prefix *b*; the prefix *f* = and, in Arabic, is another form of the *u*, *v*.

931. But by far the most common of all the prefix letters of the Semitic languages, is *m*. It compares almost perfectly with the German *g* and *ge*; it is used not only as the prevailing mark of the participles and the infinitives, but it is, like the Ger. *ge*, *g*, also a common mark of nouns and adjectives — just as we find *ge-sicht*, sight, face, from *sehen*, to see, and *g-lück* = luck, *g-leich* = like, a-like, Fr. *e-gal*, equal. As there is no doubt that the Ger. *ge* is closely allied to the various prefixes and inseparable prepositions of the language, so, too, there is quite as little doubt that the Semitic *m* is closely allied to all the prefixes and articles of that class of languages. It may be even convenient to consider this verbal prefix *m* as identical with the article *l*, and the two as the bases of all the other prefixes in the class. We find this *l* not only used as a prefix preposition, but it is also, like this *m*, used as a prefix to verbs, a mere augment, particularly in Arabic.

932. The identity of the prefix prep. *b* with the *m* is shown, among many other ways, by *b*, as well as *m*, being used in Persian as an augment before the verb, and at the same time as prefix preposition. Even *m* itself is used somewhat with the force of a preposition in those abstract or verbal nouns, with prefix *m*, denoting place where (and equal to *in*), and the instrument

(equal to *by*); as, in Arabic, *katab*, write, and *ma-ktab*, (a place) for-writing.

933. We must not forget that the Syriac prefix *d*, in its double force of relative, or article, and preposition, is also a good representative of this *m*. The Egyptian participle prefix *nt*, *t*, = who, which, also represents Semitic *m*. In Ethiopic, the participle prefix *m*, *ma*, has the force of *the*, as *ma-ammes* = the-wrongdoer.

934. To understand the nature of this *m*, we must bear in mind that one of the most common pref. preps. is *m*, and that *m* is a prominent relative or demonstrative letter (and Coptic *n* = *m* is one of the articles).

935. But *m* has still other very important representatives or connections in Semitic. We find it, varying its form and taking that of some related letter, used as the mark of certain forms of the verb. In the form of *n* (known to be equal to *m* the world over) it marks in Hebrew the reflexive; as, *qatal*, kill; *ni-qetal*, kill self (and in some Hebrew verbs, it marks the passive; in others it is a simple active). Welsh has the same prefix for the same purpose; as, *plygu*, bend, *ym-blygu*, bend self; in Cornish, it is *em*; in Armoric, it is double, *en-em*, thus, *en-em-wiska*, to dress self (*wiska*, to dress), *en-em-wiskomp*, (we) dress selves.

936. Among other proofs of the identity of this *n* with the *m* treated of, we notice that while the participles of other forms of the verb are marked by *m*, the participles of this reflexive-pass. form is marked only by this *n*, *i. e.*, the participle form practically identifies with the tense form, *niqetal*, above.

937. In Arabic, this *n*, *ni*, has the form *an*; in Syriac, *eth* takes the place of *an*, *n*, *ni*; the Ethiopic *as* (as well as *an*), the Arabic, Amharic, and Ethiopic *ast*, are other forms of *eth* = *en*. In Amh. and Eth., *as* = *ast* is chiefly a causative mark — in Arabic, it indicates a wish; as, *ilm*, know; *ast-ilm*, or *ast-alam*, desire-to-know.

938. But *n* is by no means peculiar to such forms of the verb; it is often used, like other augment letters, to begin verbs (and other words) with, and then it seems to have no special office; thus, we have *na-tal*, to raise (G'k *tlao*, L. *tollo*), in Heb., and the form *talal* besides; so, *na-shal*, slip, fall ($s = f$), also *na-than*, *na-tan*, give, L. *dono* ($t = d$). It is a prefix letter also in Per., as *ni-shan* = sign, *ne-zr*, see, peer. It is used, too, as a mark of persons in the future tense. Again, it is not only the mark of many other things besides passives and reflexives, but, on the other hand, many of these are made by using other marks, and others again are found without any prefix letters at all; thus, in Heb., *qittel*, kill, massacre; *quttal*, be killed, massacred.

939. In concluding upon this letter, we may notice that the

prefix *eth*, *est*, is so strongly developed as to well represent *is*, *be*. Is there any doubt that these passive forms, thus marked with prefixes, are anything more than participles with the prefix *m* developed?

940. We find, in Heb., the prefix *hith* = Syriac *eth*, another prefix to indicate the reflexive, and *hath* or *hoth* to indicate the passive. This *hith*, *ith*, equals *is* and *the*. This same *hith*, reduced to *hi*, becomes a causative mark; as, *hi-qetiyl*, cause-to-kill; it is identical with Syr. and Ar. *a*, Syr. *sh*, and Ar. *t*, *an*. We must notice that these forms, commencing with *hi*, as well as those with *ni*, do not take an additional *m* in the participle, but change the *hi* to *m*, showing that *hi* = *m* (but forms with *hith* have *m-ith* in the participle).

941. In Arabic, *t* is a very common prefix to verbs. It is used to mark the passive and reflexive, and is plainly identical with *a*, *an*, *ast*, as well as Heb. *hith*, Syr. *eth*. In Amhar. and Eth., we find the prefixes *nt*, *ant*, showing that *n*, being associated with *t*, is equal to it; and hence *t* = *n* = *m*. This *t* is found in many other places besides passives and reflexives; among others, in the form of *th*, it marks person forms, as a prefix, in the future.

942. We must add to this, that we find in Persian this same *m*, *a*, *an*, *ast*, *t* (among others) as prefix to verbs, nouns, and adjectives, and having precisely the same office as our prefixes or augments *be* in *be-wail*, *per* in *per-form*, *re* in *re-cess*, Ger. *ge* in *ge-sicht*, our *a* in *a-live*.

943. So we easily come to this conclusion about the verb-forms in Semitic: that these prefixes are developments of *m*, being all identical with each other; that while they do appear in these verb forms, they are by no means peculiar to them, being found not only in the original form of the verb, but also as initial letters of parts of speech which are not verbs; and we conclude, finally, that these prefixes, as well as others, are identical with the inseparable prefixes and augments of our own and other languages.

944. And we must remark, also, by the way, that no class of languages is so valuable as the Semitic to point out the history and character of prefix letters, to show that they have all one common origin, and that they all diverge from one and the same point; and again that there is no class of languages so valuable to prove that all particles, pronouns, and auxiliaries, are developments of initial (or final) letters, which in the end separate from the stem and become individualized.

945. We now perceive that, contrary to the general opinion, the Semitic languages have inseparable prepositions before verbs. They are not used to the same extent, and not always in the

same manner, that they are in all European languages; but we can find parallels for them, in Europe, for every office which we find them performing in Semitic. Not alone in Celtic do we find prefixes used to play such parts, but even in our own we find them; thus, in en-*large*, make-large; en-*trap*, take in a trap; Ger. *ein-kleiden*, en-clothe, to dress; *er-lauben*, give-leave — we find *en, ein, er,* used precisely as the Semitic causative *a*. (And, if we mistake not, the form *is-gone, is-left, is-taken,* is a fair representative of the Semitic passive form). We might refer also to *s-lay* = cause to lay, G'k *ste-llō* = cause to go (from *elō*); Ger. *sch-icken* = cause to go (from *gehen, ging, gick*).

946. So the Greek reduplicated forms, as *pi-piskō* = cause to drink, may be taken as forms similar to the Semitic. And the Slavic languages use their prefixes of verbs in a manner, if not identical with, very similar to, that of Semitic. They are there used as signs of tenses (particularly future); also to denote completed action. And the prefix *m* we know has its representative, as a mark of infinitive and participle, in more than one of the languages of Europe.

947. There is no single instance of importance where we shall find the Semitic verb system differing from that of Europe. We have thus far seen prefixes play an important part in the making of new forms, but it is far more common to find new forms arising not by assuming these augments, but by changes in the body of the word — just as we get *sung* and *song* from *sing, rose* from *rise, written* from *write, men* from *man*.

948. A very prominent way of deriving new forms of verbs, is by doubling some of its consonants, as we have *fat* and *fatten, gleam* and *glimmer, beat* and *battle,* Ger. *leiden,* past *litt,* part. *ge-litten* (suffer), *mix* and *mingle, ng* = *gg, wag* and *wiggle.*

Many new forms are made, again, by inserting letters (as it is said), just as we have L. *dicto* from *dico, fundo* from *fudo,* G'k *tuptō* and *tupō, esthlos* and *ethlos, thapsō* and *thapō.*

949. There are but two simple tenses in Semitic, and there are no more in any language. These two are made to supply the places of our usual compound tenses, just as we use the present sometimes for the future, and the past for the perfect and pluperfect. The past tense of Semitic has developed endings in full, as they are in Latin and others, to denote the persons. But the tense called future has the apparent peculiarity of developing the initial letters to indicate the pronouns, instead of the final letters as usual. We consider this subject one of sufficient importance to entitle it to special notice here.

950. We remark, first, that so far from being peculiar, it is precisely as we form all our tenses; thus, he-says, we-say, thou-sayest — with this difference only, and that not real, that with

us the pronoun is printed apart from the verb, though in conversation it is closely united to it.

951. To enable us to understand what these initial letters in Semitic are, we give them as follows:

1st sing.,	a	for Heb., Syr., Ar.			1st plu.	n	for Heb., Ar., Syr.		
2d "	th	" " " "			2d "	th	" " " "		
3d "	y	" " Ar., Syr. n			3d "	y	" " " Syr. n.		

952. In Coptic, we see what the initial letters are by noticing the persons of *mer*, fill; thus, sing., *t-mer*, *k-mer*, *f mer*; plur., *tn-mer*, *tetn-mer*, *se-mer*. The 2d singular, *k-mer*, is masculine; *te-mer* is feminine. The Amharic and Ethiopic present nothing peculiar compared with Hebrew, Arabic, and Syriac.

953. There are several facts which we must now notice. All except *y* are letters which we have already seen to be verbal prefixes or augments. But this *y* or *i* is also a very common prefix. That it is identical with the others, as they are identical with each other, is a fact not to be doubted. That it is equal to *n*, is seen by *n* replacing it in *Syriac*; that it is equal to *f* and *s*, is shown also in Coptic; that *a = t*, we see by *t*, *ti*, of Coptic 1st singular.

954. It is not in the least to be doubted that these future initials are the ordinary prefixes of the verbs, and that they may be considered as a variation of the prefix *m*. The basis of the future is the infinitive, in other languages; and, in the Semitic class, it is known also that the infinitive is the basis of the future; but the infinitive we know also has the prefix *m*. It is one of the plainest laws in natural history, that *the same member in different animals may be developed in a very different manner and put to very different uses;* thus, the fore feet of quadrupeds, the wings of birds, and the fins of fish, are known to be homologous. In the Latin, for example, it is the ordinary endings of participles that we find representing the persons. And, if we notice the Semitic future final letters, we shall observe that the future has the same person element as the past tense, though not so fully developed as in the past.

955. We may with equal propriety consider the future as a participle having the article prefixed, as we find it in Arabic; thus, *the knowing* (ones), the knowers, for *those who-know*, shall know. This transformation of participle with prefix article into a verb with pronoun nominative, is most clear in Coptic.

956. It is important in this connection to notice that in one of the forms of Arabic, that spoken in modern Syria and Egypt, an *m* is prefixed before the first person plur. future, and a *b* before all the other persons — showing that such prefixes do change for the persons. This *b* and *m* is in place of the *l* which

we find so constantly, in ordinary Arabic, united to the future in some of its applications (that *b* and *m* is prefixed in addition to the usual person letters, as well as the Arabic *l*).

957. The whole history of the Semitic future shows that it is really a dependent form; it is the exact counterpart of the Lat. subjunctive, in application as well as in origin. Both are alike identical with the infinitive, and both from mere usage are transformed sometimes from a dependent, objective expression, to one which is independent, indicative, as opposed to subjunctive. Dependent, or objective, as we know the Latin infinitive to be, it is still often used as an indicative.

958. It is over and over again, particularly in Arabic and Syriac, that we might replace their future by a participle or an infinitive—and the Syriac uses the gerund or participle, with the prefix *l*, where the Arabic uses a future. Where we say, *he went to sow*, the Arabic has it *went that-he-shall-sow* (future); instead of saying he desires *to aid*, it is, in Ar., desires that *he shall aid*. The imperative, with its prefixes *a* and *l*, is one of the forms of the future.

959. To all this we may add, that, in all instances where relatives occur as subjects of the verb, we have a parallel to this Semitic future; as, I speak of him *who-does* it, *i. e.*, the-doer of it, the one-doing it; the word *which-was-spoken*, *i. e.*, the word the-spoken (one)—the relatives being developments of prefix articles, as we may assume.

960. To continue the parallel of the Semitic and the European languages, we must remind the reader of an auxiliary which, in Semitic, has the office of our *be*, and which is clearly identical with it. In Arabic particularly, we find this auxiliary *be* used to form compound tenses as in Europe. We learn, too, in Semitic, that this *be* is only a variation of *he, she, it*—they being often used for *be*.

961. And Coptic teaches us that this *be* is, in Semitic at least, a development of the ordinary prefix letters. Thus, we find *ai*, I was, or have been, and *ai-me*, I have loved (*me*, love); and *nei*, I was, *nei-hmoos*, I sat (*hmoos*, sit); *eie*, I shall be, *eie-mou*, I shall die (*mou*, die). Other forms of *be* are prefixed to denote *may, might, would*. The infinitive has the prefix *e, n, m,* and participles the prefix *e, et,* and we may with propriety consider the auxiliaries above as developments of these prefixes.

962. Having thus disposed of the apparent anomaly of the tenses, we may add, further, that as far as regards the assumed peculiarity that Semitic roots are composed of three letters, we have only to remark that, by a proper method of reduction, we can bring the number down to two, or even one, and, on the other hand, if we insert the vowels, the *h* of aspirates, and dou-

ble letters, we shall increase the number considerably beyond three.

963. There is an almost entire absence of such compounds as we find in the nearly related Persian — yet we must consider, at least, that every case where two nouns are united, one of which is genitive, is a true compound.

964. Endings such as the *tas, ia, um*, of Latin, are not very prominent in Semitic; still we begin to find them pretty generally and clearly in Syriac and Ethiopic, as well as in Arabic; thus, we find such verbal endings as *o, ot, an, ta, na, av, avi*.

965. EGYPTIAN.—The Coptic, and Egyptian, while it is emphatically a Semitic language, as said before, still has developed some Semitic features in a peculiar manner. So far as stage of life is concerned, it is considerably in advance of the common Semitic, with a strong hold, nevertheless, upon its embryonic structure. Not only the alphabet is not Semitic, but rather Greek, but the orthography too, as we might infer, is not Semitic. There is the same system of prefixes that so strongly characterize the others of the class, but they are strongly developed, and are often strangely applied, while the old uses, such as that of prefixes for verbs, are often nearly or quite lost sight of.

966. There is here the Semitic pref. article, but it is no longer *al* and *ha*, as there, but *pe, te*, approaching nearer to our own; it is *ne* in the plural, like the Persian *an*; thus, the vowel being eclipsed, *p-noute*, the-God, *n-rome*, the-men. We find also the double *na-p* = the-the = that-the, that-of. We find here derivatives formed by change in the word, as opposed to fixes so prevalent in the other Semitics. Compound terms, which are rudimentary in the rest, are here more common.

967. And, after the pure Semitic style, we find derivatives thus, *mat*, to-love, *met-mai*, the-love, or loving (*met* is the Sem. pref. *m*). We find, as we have seen elsewhere, the pref. *ma* to denote the place where. As in the rest, cases are denoted by prefixes and prepositions; *nte* marks the genitive case, *ha* the dative, *e* the acc.; *ngi* = the, is the sign of nom. Derivative adjectives are formed by prefixes, that same part. prefix modified. We find compound adjectives as in Persian.

968. The pronouns are strictly Semitic, and they readily become suffix with particles; poss. pronoun is suffix as in Semitic. Double pronouns are common, as *pe-k* = the-thy, for thy. Imperatives have the prefix *ma* of Semitic; so has the infinitive. Tenses and moods are formed by augments or prefixes, as in Semitic. Among the many compounds of Coptic, is that of the genitive following its noun, and identical with the construct case of the other Semitic languages.

969. The following selections will also illustrate the language:

Pi-koudgi ebol oute ni apostolos ter-ou—the-small from among the (*ni*) apostles all-these (*ter* = all), *i. e.*, the least of the apostles all; *tei-hime* — this-woman; *pe-et* — he-who. The articles are used for verb *be*; as, *pe* = he is, *te* = she is, *ne* = we are; *ank-pe* — I am; *anan ne* — we are; *p-hoout ta-pe pe nte-s-hime* — the-man the-head is of-the-woman; *nt-af* — of-him (in Celtic, *ef* = he); *ou* = what, *ent* = who, *esh* = what (Sem.), *nim* = who; *shat* = to cut, *shent* = to be cut; *talo* = to offer, *taleout* = to be offered; *ko* = place, *ke* = be placed (see active = passive).

Pen iot et khen ni pheoui — our father who (*et*) in the heavens; *pen oik nte* (gen. sign) *rasti meif nan m-phoou* — our bread tomorrow give us (*nan*) this-day; *n-etero-n* — our-debts (the-debts-our); *ethrefi* (*e-thre-f-i* — *e* = to, *thre* = make, *f* = him, *i* = go, come) to-make-him-come (see how one word develops itself into several of ours).

In *pek ran* = thy name, *p-e-k* is composed of at least three parts, *p* = the, *e* = his, *k* = thy; so also in *p-e-n iot* = our father; *ro k* = face-thy, thy face or mouth; *ro-i* = face-my; *akteif* = *a-k-tei-f*, thou hast given him (*a* = past augment, or *have*, *k* = thou, *tei* = give, *f* = him, to-him); *oube-k* = against-thee, *oube-f* = against him; *neme-i* = with-me (*nem*, with); *pe-dsh-an* = we say, may be considered as having the elements (at least) *pe-dsh-an* = the-say-our, the-saying-of-us (these elements may be again divided).

970. While the Persian exhibits the Semitic as taking one direction, and having a certain phase, the Coptic, or Egyptian, exhibits Semitic as taking another direction and assuming another phase. We learn from Coptic many important facts, among these, that pronouns and particles may be developed from either end of the word; that one and the same element, with or without variation, may perform the office of pronoun, particle, and auxiliary; that the letters of a word represent an accumulation of repeated elements, which in the end come to represent individual words (and that even these letters have their elements in turn).

971. ETHIOPIC: The Ethiopic and Amharic are so thoroughly Semitic that very little need be said of them now. The Amharic, especially, shows a very strong development of endings, to correspond with our *-ous*, *-ness*, *-ing*, etc. — proving again that the germ of such endings really exists in Semitic, and is suppressed in some of its forms. Many derivatives are formed by prefixes also, and we find the very prefixes of the Sem. conjugations, such as *t*, *a*, *m*, *as*, *ast*, the initial letters of nouns as well.

Nouns are derived by infixing, as well as prefixing, such letters; also by reduplication of letters.

972. The auxiliary *be* here plays a conspicuous part. It is placed (in form of *al, hal,* identical with Arabic article *al*) after the verb, as it is in Lat. *amatus est* = loved is. In Ethiopic, we find it used with the ordinary future, before it or after, and separate from the main verb. When the auxiliary is thus used, we have an expression equal to *he-will-come he-will*, for he will come; also, *it-was he-came*, for he came (as in Arabic).

It is in the Amharic that we find the peculiar *constructive mood*, a transition, as it is, between verbal, or infinitive, and verb, but still possessing more or less of the nature of a verbal noun. It will yet be found to be identical, in its character, with the Semitic future.

973. BERBER.— The Berber language, spoken by people living in North Africa, must be considered a very rude form of Arabic.

974. The Berber verb is full of interest. The language may be said to have but one individualized tense, and that the past; but this is so far like the Semitic future, and unlike the Semitic past, that it has initial letters varying for the persons. Thus, we find *askar*, imperative, make (Sans. *kar* = do); past tense, 1st person, *seker-agh*, 2d *te-seker-ad*, 3d *i-sker;* 1st plur. *n-esker*, 2d *te-sker-em*, 3d *seker-end ;* so also the persons of *be* (*il*, Arab. art. *el*), *ell-igh, te-lli-d, i-illa ; n-ella, te-lla-m, ell-ant*. We see besides the variation of the prefix letters, also the regular changes for person endings ; so, we are taught that in the Semitic future the former are not to take the place of the latter ; also that these prefix changes are not confined to the future (indeed those endings *id, am, ant*, must remind any one of the person endings *it, am, ant,* of Latin).

975. The future, and present, is made by prefixing *ad* = d to the tense already given (just as *l* and *d* in Semitic, which letters *ad* equals, as well as Persian *bi*). Thus, *ad-isker* = he makes, *ad-nesker* = we make. Possessive pronouns are developed at the end of nouns, as in Semitic.

976. The tendency in all Semitic to discard real adjectives, abstract terms, and individual conjunctions, has gone in Berber almost to their entire absence. Hence, its sentences are very short and disconnected; thus, *he-eats he-goes*, he eats and goes. There are evidently many points of interest in the idiom, but there is much yet to be learned in regard to it. It is chiefly valuable in showing how Semitic languages may have European orthography.

CHAPTER XII.

INDIAN LANGUAGES.

977. None of the family tongues of Asia are at present receiving greater attention, or are studied with greater interest, than the languages of India, and of these, especially the Sanscrit. The Europeans have made permanent settlements in Southern Asia, and a knowledge of these languages is the more valuable on that account. But more than this, the Sanscrit, the type, if you choose, of the family, is found to be a great repository of ancient philosophy. This has been one of the impulses to the study of Sanscrit, but there is yet one more. There has been unexpectedly found a remarkable identity in the words and structure of the Sanscrit and European, and of the European, particularlythe Greek and Latin.

978. The SANSCRIT is an ancient language, with all the characteristics of one which has grown old and gone down. It has not been a spoken language for many centuries; it has become a mere repository of literature, laws, and particularly of religion; running in this respect a course very much resembling that of the Latin. To what extent it has given rise to the modern idioms of Southern Asia, is not at present accurately determined. It is certain they have replaced it, but not it alone. There is reason to believe it was not the only language of India. One thing is certain; the languages of India which we shall notice hereafter, all bear a close connection with the Sanscrit, and seem beyond doubt to have the relation to it of a modern to an ancient tongue.

979. The Sanscrit is written in an alphabet peculiar to it and to its cognate idioms. Neither the Semitic nor Greek alphabets, at first sight, bear any resemblance to it; though, on closer inspection and careful study, we find it has a basis in common with them. If we look at the grammatical structure of the Sanscrit, and even to the form of many of its words, we shall be forced to confess that it has a greater resemblance to Greek than any other Asiatic language. But this we do not understand proves that the Sanscrit has, as often is claimed, in respect to origin, a so much closer relationship to Europe than the Semitic does, or the Persian, or the Tartar. It has only developed, exhibited, germs and features which, to a greater or less extent, lie latent in those less cultivated idioms. Hence we see that the modern

languages of India are far more Persian first, and next Tartar and Semitic, than Greek, or Latin, or even Slavic.

980. And mark still further; notwithstanding this remarkable parallel between Sanscrit grammar and Greek grammar, and Sanscrit orthography, to a certain extent, and Greek orthography, a fact which must be surprising to every student, yet the style, the thought, the idiom, the soul, of Sanscrit, is not Greek or European, but rather Asiatic, and not only Asiatic but Indian. It is hard estimating values in such cases, as said before, and yet we feel constrained to say, that in these latter respects, the Persian, and even the Arabic, is more European than even the Sanscrit is.

981. So little do we find peculiar in the Sanscrit grammar, in the case and person endings, in the forms of their comparatives, their pronouns, their particles, their moods, and their tenses and participles, when compared with Greek and Latin, we shall need but little space for it here. Its forms worthy of remark we notice elsewhere. The striking and characteristic features of the language are the size and number of its compounds. We had particularly noticed this principle at work in the Persian, but the Sanscrit has carried it much farther. We do not look upon this phenomenon as a simple union of two or more individual words. It indicates, rather, that in Sanscrit the words are in many cases not individualized; it is in this respect far behind the languages of Europe. The words had not so far grown to maturity as to be able to separate from the parent stock. This same feature we find in all ancient languages; we find it in Latin and Greek, in their moods and tenses, their cases, their participles, and prepositional verbs — and, to a limited extent, in their compounds.

982. One class of compounds is made by the non-development of *and*, and the union of two words or more which we could connect by it; as *sun-moon*, for *sun-and-moon; song-music-dance* (and dance). These elements unite as a single unit, the last alone taking the case-sign; just as we say, *Peter-the-Great's* (not Peter's). It is clear in all these compounds, that of their being made of elements the Sanscrit mind was quite unconscious; so, we find *pretty-brow-nose-eye-hair*, for having a pretty brow, etc., or *pretty browed, nosed*, etc.; *this-shape, i. e.*, this-shaped, shaped like this; *lance-hand, i. e., lance-handed*, lance-in-hand (having). In all the compounds of Sanscrit, we shall find united only such as belong together in all languages; the principle is the same in all languages, and it only works in Sanscrit on a grander scale.

983. One single selection must suffice to give a little idea of Sanscrit composition : *Asti Magadha-dese Champakavati nam-*

aranyani. Tasyam chiran mahata snehena mriga-kakau niva-satah. Sa cha mrigah swechchhaya bhramyan hrishta-pushtan-gah, kenachit srigalenavalokitah. Tam drishtwa srigalo chin-tayat: ah, kathan-etan-man-sam sulalitam bhakshagami — (there) is (in) Magdha-land (*dese*) Champakavati (a) name-large-forest (a forest called Ch.); there (in-it) long (in) great (*mahata*) friendship (a) deer-crow (and-crow) dwell (the two did); (he) the also (*cha*, L. *que*) deer (the deer also) at-pleasure roaming gay-fed-body (by a) certain jackal-seen (-*avalokitah*, part. seen) (*i. e.*, the deer was seen roaming at will); him (*tam*) (having) watched the-jackal (he) thinks (thus): oh, how-this-flesh delicate (shall I) eat (how can I get it).

984. Here follows a list of some of its most important fundamental or root words:

As, be, Ger. *sein; an* (live), animal, mind; *ah*, say, *spr-echen*, Ger.; *ag*, near, Ger. *eng; ag*, move, go, Ger. *wegen*, shake; *agh*, fl-og, Ger. *sch-aden; ac*, respect, Ger. *ächt; av*, will, wish, love; *am*, honor, L. *amo; ab*, speak, G'k *epō; ab=ag; ap*, have, hold, L. *c-apio; arh*, power, G'k *archō; arj*, work, Ger. *arbeit.*

Svan, sound, tone; *saik*, go, seek; *sagh*, saw, cut; *süc*, see, sage; *sarp*, go, creep; *sar*, go, run, spring; *da*, give, L. *dono*, do; *da*, divide, deal, Ger. *theil; dah*, burn, L. *ardens, ar-dens; duh*, draw, tug, L. *duco; dic*, show, say, digit; *dar*, tear, break; *dra*, run, G'k *draō; dal*, split, deal, Fr. *taille; dha*, put, L. *do, po.*

Tan, tend, extend; *tag*, take, touch; *tvac*, deck; *tap*, burn, tepid; *tur*, move, turn; *tars*, torrid, toast, parch; *trag*, go, drag; *tul*, bal-ance.

Stigh, step, steep; *star*, strew, spread; *iks*, see, look; *ir*, run, go, L. *erro; il*, go, Ger. *eil-en*, walk; *yam*, hem, hold; *han*, kill, G'k *kteinō*, wound; *hi*, pour, gush; *har*, grasp; *hal*, hollow; *hul*, veil, conceal.

Cvid, white; *ci*, lie, G'k *keimai; cau*, hew, L. *cavus; car*, bore; *cru*, hear (*sru*); *gal*, eat, swallow; *jam*, been, born, kin, G'k *genaō; jna*, know; *jna*, bend, knee; *jiv*, live, L. *viva.*

Ghas, chew; *kan*, sing, tone, L. *cana; kup*, hope, desire, L. *cupio; kruc*, screech; *karp*, break, L. *carpo; kal*, yell, call; *cad*, shine, L. *candeo; khya*, say, L. *lego; ksur*, shear.

Us, burn, L. *us-tum*, from *uro; ul*, flame, Ger. *stralen; va*, go, L. *venio*, Fr. *va; vid*, know, L. *video; vac*, speak, voice, L. *vaco; vil*, di-vide, Ger. *theilen.*

Ma, measure; *man*, think, mean, mind; *moth*, move, L. *mitto; mar*, kill, murder; *bal*, live; *bhi*, fear; *bhar*, bear, L. *gero*, wear, carry; *pa*, hold; *pa* and *pi*, drink, L. *pi-no; pad*, go, foot, path; *pac*, pack, bind; *pu*, pure, Ger. *rein; parth*, spread, part; *pri*, love, friend; *prach*, preach, speak; *pil*, press, tread, walk, fly.

S-par, breathe, L. *spiro;* *arch*, go, G'k *erchomai;* *radh*, work, G'k *redō;* *rat*, read, speak; *ri*, run, flow; *ruj*, break; *raph*, break, force, ravish; *lut*, read, L. *lego;* *luh*, love; *laks*, look; *lubh*, love, will, wish; *laip*, leave, run.

985. These, it must be observed, are the elements of the language; they do not generally occur in this crude form, but rather with the additional development of pre- and suf-fixes, like our own *pel*, in the form ex-pel or ex-pelling, *fer*, in pre-fer-ence, L. *fero*, *rog*, L. *rogo* = ask, in pre-rog-ative.

986. It will be noticed, also, that the above forms given are greatly reduced, *i.e.*, many of their letters have not developed into two or three, as with us and elsewhere; compare *an* and mind, *ac* and look, respect, *arh* and force, power, *da* and deal, divide, *ab* and speak. We observe, also that they represent our letters by very different ones, but, as we shall find elsewhere, always in accordance with the law of letter changes; thus, $d = sp$, $t = b$, $g = v$, $j = v$ and l, $h = g$, gr, $jn = kn$, $p = h$, d, etc.

987. MARATHI: The following is a short list of words from the Marathi, a modern Indian language: *Asan*, seat; *avaz*, voice; *ehede*, one; *uga*, quiet; *umer*, age, Ger. *immer;* *upar*, over, upper.

Katir, severe, hard; *kad*, edge; *kar*, do, form; *kal*, time, Ger. *mal;* *kul*, all; *kir*, dirt; *kaid*, catch, capture; *kith*, castle; *khali*, hole; *khara*, salt, r, l; *khali*, hollow; *khed*, dig.

Gat, gang, band; *gat*, fate; *gam*, compassion; *gaman*, giving; *garami*, warm; *gaya*, cow; *ga*, sing, *ca-no;* *guha*, cave; *gira*, fair; *ghar*, house, yard; *ghe*, catch (the infinitive ending *ni* in all cases left out).

Chal, walk; *chir*, tear; *chain*, sound; *chap*, stamp; *jan*, live; *jad*, join; *jalad*, quick, L. *celer;* *jor*, force, L. *vir*.

Tar, trick; *dail*, form, style; *tamam*, all, Ger. *zammen;* *tar*, wire, t, w; *ter*, great; *dam*, breath, Ger. *damp*, steam; *dar*, per; *dad*, just, G'k *dikē;* *das*, slave, tie, bind; *de*, give.

Nanga, naked; *nak*, nose; *nad*, noise; *nav*, boat, L. *navis;* *nir*, water; *pad*, foot; *par*, through, L. *trans;* *pun*, again; *pus*, ask; *per*, boy, L. *puer;* *phar*, very; *phir*, turn.

Bara, well, very; *bin*, without, L. *sine;* *beli*, talk, old Prus. *bill;* *bhala*, well, L. *bonus;* *bhal*, bear, l, r; *bhed*, view; *mis*, meat; *mus*, mould.

Metha, great, L. *magnus;* *ran*, war, rattle; *rang*, rank, row; *raza*, king, L. *rege;* *vach*, read, L. *lego*, voice; *vap*, vapour; *vara*, air; *vir*, hero; *vel*, time.

This is only a few of the very many words which we might cite as familiar in this language. Many are Sanscrit, many more are Semitic and Persian; and then, besides, there are large numbers of words almost identical with those found in European tongues.

988. BENGALI: The two most important languages of modern India are the Bengali and the Hindostani. The former is spoken by perhaps over thirty millions of people, and the latter, in its dialects, is spoken by fifty millions.

989. The Bengali is perhaps the most Sanscrit, but slightly varying from it. Case endings are well developed, and postpositions are also common. The adjective with the noun forms a compound, and hence it takes no case or number signs; it is compared by *-tara* (our *-er*) and *-tama* (our *-est*, L. *-timus*). The verb seems to be built up after the Turkish manner, with a participle for base, and *be*, in its tenses, for auxiliary. The pronouns, particles, and endings, are all familiar. A few examples will best illustrate the character:

990. *Si balakke amara-nikat ana* — the boy me-to (to-me) bring (bring to me; *si=that*, used as *the*). This language abounds in compounds, as in Sanscrit, which may have an indefinite length; as, *the-beauty-of-shoots-fruits-flowers-clusters-and-buds.* A standing rule in arrangement, in Bengali, is to put the nominative first and the verb last, bringing the object before the verb. This may be peculiar to us, but it is a common Asiatic feature. The adjective goes before the noun.

Amra tanhar tara dekhite paiyachi — we his star (*tara*) seeing have-got (have-seen, *pa* = get); *tahate tahara kahila* — then they said; *ei mat likh-ita ache* — it thus written is; *takhan se uthiya shishu o tanhar mata-ke* (*ke* acc. sign) *la-iya Ishrael-deshe aila* — then he ris-ing (the) child and his mother tak-ing (*la-iya*), Israel-land (into) went (he), *i. e.*, taking them he went.

Prachar kar-iya kahila — preach making said (he), *i. e.*, he preached (compound verbs of all kinds are very numerous); *ei amar priya putra* — this my dear son (is); *Johan dwara* — John-through (by-John); *tini uttar karilen* — he (this-one) answer made (answered); *kebal rut-ite manushya banch-ibe na* only bread-by (by-bread) man shall-live not (not by bread alone).

Not only the noun comes first (the nominative), but also all that belongs to it as an adjective; the rule is the same with regard to the object and all that belongs to it.

Tumi jadi ama-ke — thou if me (if thou me); *ami si sakal toma-ke diba* — I this all (to) thee will-give (*diba*); *tanhar seba kar-ite lag-ila* — him service to-do (they) began (another compound, they-began-to-make-service = they serve); *jaite-jaite*, going-going, *i. e.*, while going (double words of this kind are very common); *upadesh dite-dite* — (his) teaching making-making, *i. e.*, making-teaching, *teaching* simply; *prachar karite-karite* — preaching making-making, simply *preaching*. (Our possessives, as *his*, *its*, are rare — so also *him, it, them*, as the object of verbs); *tomar ichcha swargete jeman hauk* — thy will heaven-in so be.

Se giya tomar-agre path prastut karibe — he going thee-before (thy) way prepared shall-make (shall-make-prepared, shall prepare); *Jardan nadite baptaijit haila* — Jordan in baptized (they) were; *pashchat-pashchat-gaman-karila* — (to) follow-follow-going-he-did (*karila* = he did), *i. e.*, did go following, he *followed* simply; *raja jini janmi-yachhen tini kothay* — (the) king who was-born he (this-one) where? *i. e.*, where is he who; *bhar-er sahit* — (their) load-s with.

991. A leading peculiarity of Bengali is the inversion in the order of clauses, from the fact already noted, that not only the object, but all that belongs to it, must come before the verbs — thus, we find, I which man I saw this (is) that (one), *i. e.*, this is the man whom I saw; he my desire (if he) grant does, I satisfied shall be, *i. e.*, if he grants my desire.

992. HINDOSTANI: To this language we come next. It is written in the Persian (Arabic) character. It is this form of Indian that shows most forcibly the connection with Semitic and Persian.

993. Here, as in Afghan, we find transitive verbs in their past tenses agreeing with their objects — the nominative appearing in an ablative or instrumental case. It is really using a passive form thus, *by-me he was struck*, for *I struck him* (in Hin., it would be *me-by the man-to the-striking* (was).

Alone, the language is the most interesting of its class, but compared with what we have already noticed, there is little that is new, being, as it is, mostly Bengali or Sanscrit, as well in arrangement as in orthography and grammar. Much of it is Semitic also.

994. Hence very little must suffice as a specimen of the language: *tu kis tarah janta hai* — thou (in) what manner known hast (is)? (how hast thou known); *aur kaha ki is larke-ko tarbiyat kar* — and said that this boy (*ko* acc. sign) instruct make (do instruct, *i. e.*, instruct him; he told him to instruct the boy); *ek bat men ja* (go) *nikla* — a wood into gone coming (or wandering), *i. e.*, wandering into a wood; *wise wahan aur to koi na nazar aya* — (to) him there other then some not (nothing) sight came (came to him), *i. e.*, he saw no other sight; *puchha, ate-ho kahan-se aur* (and) *ja-oge kahan* — asked (he), (you) coming-

are where-from and go-will (you) where (he asked whence come ye and where will ye go).

995. An older than the Hisdostani, but one closely resembling it and the Sanscrit, is the HINDEE. Another one of the ancient languages of India, and long since dead, is the PALI. It is closely connected with the Sanscrit, but in what precise relation as to origin is not yet determined. There is also the PRACRIT, a form of Sanscrit. There are other languages in Southern Asia belonging to the Indian, or more or less related to it, and more or less important, but all these we must pass by here.

996. We can only name the TELINGA as belonging to the Sanscrit family, and partaking largely of its characteristics.

997. The TAMIL is a language of considerable interest. It belongs to the Sanscrit and Indian class, and so little is there in it that we have not already noticed in these languages, we will scarcely dwell on it here. It is the leading member of the class which includes also the *Telugu, Malayalam,* and *Canarese.* Its literature is considerable.

998. Prepositions, adverbs, and conjugations, are all rare; the relative is absent. The whole verb system is plainly built on participles, or verbal nouns, from which are developed personal and tense endings. What few prepositions do exist are real nouns, or adjectives, and are placed after.

999. The BIRMAN is a language of Southern Asia, which is very instructive to the philologist, but by no means well known. Many of its essential characteristics are those of the language of Thibet, but in simplicity and lack of development it is, perhaps, most like the Chinese. It may be said to be destitute of inflexion — a want which is compensated for by compounding. Many parts of compounds have no separate or individual existence.

1000. In the structure of sentences, the relations of words are indicated by particles. The adjective and noun constitute a compound. The verb, in all its forms, is nothing but a participle. As we might expect, the parts of discourse are scarcely distinguished. Intonation here, as in Chinese, plays a conspicuous part. Like the people of Southern Asia generally, they rather sing than talk.

The languages of Siam and Anam are classed with this.

CHAPTER XIII.

MALAY LANGUAGES.

1001. From the Indian we naturally pass to the Malay languages. This class, from the peculiar and new phase in which it presents language, is very important as well as very extensive. Its roots plainly extend far into the Indiam idioms, but as an individual growth, it has much to distinguish it from its neighbors. The whole family is decidedly infantile in structure; yet some of its members are more so than others. The leading members of the class are the Malay proper and the Java tongue. We will start with the Malay, and notice the others in the order in which we come to them.

1002. One of the most striking features of the Malay is the inordinate growth of inseparable particles, often where none exist in other languages; but the character of those particles, prefixes, and suffixes, are like those of all tongues; thus, from *ada* = be, they get *ka-ada-an* = existence; *me-mukol* = to beat, from *pukol*, strike — *p* changing to *m* after *me*.

1003. We find here, too, in a strong light the variation in the forms of words according to what they are associated with. At the same time, with the great growth of the particles spoken of above, there is an absolute want of what should correspond to the Latin case, gender, and person endings — of everything that belongs to inflexion. We find double or repeated words very common; as, *radia-radia*, for princes (L. *reges*); *kata-kata*, word-word (words), (Fr. *mot*). And we should remark, that much as the members of these duplicates seem to resemble each other, they are still very distinct and different, and one is used as a mark or determinative for the other; this is clearly established in Chinese.

Orang laki-laki — person (man) male-male, *i. e.*, a male man, a male; *ka-pada rumah* (L. *domus*, room) — to-wards (the) house; *deri-pada rumah* — from-away (the) house (double, and even treble, prepositions are common, like our *down-along-side*, *away-from*, *from-beneath*); *dengan tulong nabi* — by aid (of) prophet (genitive without sign); *pukol akan andieng itu* — strike to dog that (one) (*akan* is often used as a mere sign of acc., and *itu* as a sort of suffix *the*); *mata hari* — eye (of) day, (*i. e.*, the sun); *hamba punia ouang* — I (= my) own silver.

Mati = dead; *ka-mati-an* = death; *boat* = to do; *per-boat-an* (a) work; *baier* = pay; *pem-baier* = payment; *peng-ikut* = follower (*peng* is prefix); *kawal*=to-guard; *peng-awal*= (a) guard; *sama-sama*, together, Ger. *sammen*; *ber-sama-sama-an*= union; *kuda* (colt) *putih* — (a) horse white (adj. generally after); but, *putih kuda radia* — white (is) horse (of) king. The verb *be* is generally left out, or it is represented by pronouns, as in Semitic, as *I that* = I am.

Lebeh manis deri-pada (by-with) *gula* — more (*lebeh*) sweet by (than) sugar; *ter-ladiu*, very-rapid; *ter-lebeh tua*, very great old, very old; *ka-mana* (to-where) *tuan hendak pergi* (L. *perge*) — where (do) thou (prop. master) wish (to) go? *apa tuan man* (must) *maka* — where thou must (will thou) eat (or eating); *marika-itu* — those-there, they; *aku punia* — I (my) own; *mata-mu* = eye (of) yours; *anak-kau* = son-thy (thy son); *kapala-nia* = head-of-his (*nia*, his).

Prefixes to verbs are common; *di-puka-nia* = his striking, he strikes, or struck (*di* is a mere augment); *yang baik* — which (is) good; *itu*, the, that, L. *id*; *ini*, this, L. *hinc*, Slav. *on*; *si-apa* =the-which, what; *orang mana itu* — man what that? (what man is that); *yang am-punia ruma* — who (whose) the-own house, *i. e.*, to whom belongs the house; *ia-itu* = this-that, that is.

Ada is used for *be*, and *di-adi* = become (*ada* with augment); *ada-lah pada hamba* — (there) is to me (I), *i. e.*, I have (*lah* is not person ending); *hendak ada* — will be (*ada*, Fr. *ete*, Turk. *idum*, our *the* and *that*); *orang ada maka* — man be eating, *i. e.*, the men are eating, they eat; *dia diadi kaia* — he becomes rich.

Men-diadi-kan radia — to-make-be king (causative of *diadi*—*kan* is often for infinitive ending, but not for that alone); *ter*, like Ger. *ge*, is pass. part. sign, as *ter-tulis* = written, *ter-bunoh* = killed; *bri*, give, bring; *pergi*, go (thou); *mari-lah*, come; *kata* and *burkata*, speaks, says; *apa kata kamu* — what say you.

Di-tidar-nia = he slept, or sleeps (*nia* = his); *tidar* = sleep (thou); *dia akan tidor* — he (is) to sleep, *i. e.*, will sleep; *ada tidor* — is sleeping (see the absence of person and verbal ending); *sudah tidar*, or *telah tidar*, having slept (*sudah* and *telah* are both used for *have* and *having*, but they are called adverbs — so *lagui*, yet, now, is used in place of *is*); *ber-tidor* = to sleep; *ka-tidar-an*, also *ber-ka-tidar-an*, sleeping, in sleeping (see the growing particles, like our accumulated consonants at the beginning of words, as *strip*, for *rip*, *dispense* for *spense*, *secede* for *cede*; *dialan* = to walk; *kamu sudah dialan* — thou hast walked; *telah bur-dialan* — have walked.

1004. Most of the prepositions, adverbs, and conjunctions, are rendered familiar by keeping in view the forms of the Indian languages; *s-ini, s-itu, s-ana, m-ana,* and many others, are compounds, *the-this, the-that,* for *here, there, then;* so the prepositions *dalam,* Fr. *dans,* in; *arah,* around; *ka,* to, *k* = t — conj. *dan* = and.

1005. Prepositions have pronouns as a sort of affix; as, *pada-ku* = to-me (*ku*); *pada-nia* = to-him; *bumi dan languit* — earth and heaven; *kuda-ku* (*ku* = my) = my horse; *kuda-mu* = your horse; *anak manusia itu* — son (of) man the (one) (suffix art.); *itu-lah dunia ini* — is world this (the) (is this world); *gigi ganti gigi* — tooth for tooth; *kata-nia* = saying (*nia* is a verbal ending, as well as pronoun); *ber-kata-lah ia* = said he; *kamu telah munungar* — ye have hear (heard); *bapa-mu yang ada dishorga* — father-our who (he, that) be (art) in-heaven.

Sagala fihak fihak — all part part (all parts); *ka-rumah-mu* = to-house-thy (thy house); *dosa dosa-mu telah di-ampuni* — sin sin-thy (thy sins) are forgiven (*te-lah* = is, the, that); *buat-lah ini maka di-buat-nia itu* — do this and (*maka*) doeth-he it (he does it); *akan di-bri* — shall give, for giving, *i. e.,* shall be given; *te-lah mati* — is dead; *telah ber-bang-kit deri-pada* (up-from) *mati* — was risen from dead; *telah datang* — is come.

Kata kamu aku ini — say you I (am) this. It seems to be a leading feature of Malay to develop a verb *be* from *he, the, this,* or *that.* Malay only thus illustrates a universal principle; *ini-lah aku handak buat* — this I will do; *sudah mati* — was dead; *telah hidop* — is alive; *yan ber-nama Yahya* — who by-name (named) John (was named).

Subab tiada di-kunal-nya (*nya* = his, he) *akan* (the) *suara orang-orang-asing* — for not knew-he the voice (of) man-man-stranger (strangers, or strange ones; *akan* is sign of acc.); *orang-itu* = man-the, the one; *aku burkata pada-mu* — I say (*bur* is prefix) to-you (*mu* = you); *aku ini-lah pintu* — I am door (*ini* = this, and it has *lah* the verb ending); *aku-lah gombala yang baik itu* — I-am (*lah* verb end.) shepherd which good the, *i. e.,* I am the good one; *mum-bri* (*mum* is pref.) *jua-nya ganti domba itu* — (he) gives life-his for sheep the (the sheep); *angkau ini-iya itu-dia* — I this-he (am) that-he, *i. e.,* I this-here (am) that-there, for *I am he.*

1006. We notice a great abundance of conjunctions, for which we can find no place in translation; just as we say, now-when-therefore he went, for *when he went.* We have given this large amount of space to the Malay, to illustrate some of its many peculiarities. The order of words is remarkably natural to us — but their form and composition are often strange. Besides this, the features which we have noticed are common, more or less, to all of the class, and they will not need to be noticed again.

1007. JAVAN: The Java idiom runs closely parallel with the Malay. We find, here, the same absence of proper inflexion, of case, number, gender, and person ending, the same duplication of words, the same abundant growth of inseparable prefixes and suffixes, particles which have not yet gained an independent existence. The prefix *si* represents an undeveloped article. Not only are many new terms formed by doubling, but the initials are often doubled after the manner of the Greek reduplication. Personal pronouns are not used for lifeless objects; we find suffix pronouns, as *aku tuku omah-mu* — I buy house-your.

1008. One of the most common prefixes of the verb is *ma*, so often seen in Malay and Semitic. The prefix *ha*, seen often in Malay, is used, among other purposes, as a sign of past participle, like *ge* in Ger. *ge-sehen, ge-macht*. Tenses are marked not by developed endings, but, as in Malay, by proper adverbs or auxiliaries. New words are formed by compounding or uniting different words, as well as by doubling or repeating the same word.

There is so little in the grammar of the Java idiom that is not Malay, that we need not dwell on it farther. The orthography alone is somewhat different. The Java alphabet is peculiar, while the Malay is written in Arabic.

1009. MACASSAR: One of the Malay class is the Macassar, a leading language of the island of Celebes. We find the same prefixes here in like abundance as in Malay, and very nearly every feature found in Malay and Javan, is found here also, and but little more. In this, as in all the related languages, there is great want of individuality in the words; they have all a strong tendency to run together.

1010. In this language there are no relatives, and possessive pronouns are suffix. Derived verbs are formed by doubling, and by using the prefixes *a, ma, ni, ta, pi, ka, pa-ka,* and *si*. We find the ending *ang* very common; it is the Malay *an*, our *-ing, -ion*, as in per-form-ing, per-form-ance. It is clear that all these prefixes and endings have their representatives with us.

1011. Many verbs are made by compounding two different words, as *akanatodjeng* = to true-word (make), *i. e.*, to make an oath, *a* being prefix, *kana* = word, *todjeng* = true. These compounds are treated in all respects as simple verbs, and as such they receive the ordinary fixes. The prefix *ni*, Malay *di*, elsewhere *ri*, is used, like *ge* in German, for pass. part.; as, *ni-yalle* = (been) taken, *alle*, take; *ni-buno* = killed; *ni-gau* = become blue, make blue; and *ta*, Malay *ter*, is used also as participle prefix.

1012. We find here, as in Javan, (it is) *true his-word, i. e.,* his word is true; *inakke asare* — I giving, *i. e.*, I give, gave, have given, should give, etc.; *ikatte asare* — we giving, etc.; *inakke ni-sare* — I (am or was) given; also, *ku-sare* — I give, gave, etc.; *ki-sare* — we give; *na-sare* — he give (pronoun united with verb as prefix — a Semitic feature); *asare-ya* = give I, *i. e.*, I give, gave (it also means *give me*); *asare-dj-a* = give-ever-I, *i. e.*, I ever give, am giving; *asare-s-a* = give-once-I; *asare-kang* — give-we, *i. e.*, we give (give-us).

1013. These added or inserted adverbs, so called, are plainly the result of a tendency to develop auxiliaries, precisely as L. *am-ab-am* = loving-was-I, loving-did-I, I loved. As we might expect, it tends to develop obj. and subj. pronouns, like Semitic, at the end. Adverbs are, as in Malay, used to denote time as auxiliaries; as, *lebah*, past, done; *leba ku-sare* — already-I-give, *i. e.*, have given; or the personal, as with our auxiliary, unites with the adverb, so called, as *leba-ka asare* — already-I give, have-I given, did-I give.

The alphabet is one of its own.

1014. KAWI: The Kawi was once a language on the isle of Java, and no doubt on some of the neighboring islands. Its precise relation to Javan and Sanscrit is not yet determined. It has the grammar of the Javan, but many of the words are Sanscrit. It represents, no doubt, an ancient growth of the Malay class, which has been long since dead. It evidently stood nearer to Indian than the modern Malay idioms do.

1015. Its article is *sang*, Malay *yang*, who, and the *si* and *se* of others; *ka*, Ger. *ge*, is not only passive sign, but it is often used elsewhere; *sa* = one, the, is a prefix denoting the singular; *ma-nama*, by-name, named — this is the common Semitic and Malay prefix, used for adjectives as well as verbs.

1016. Here, as in all the class, it is a prominent feature to find the verb a mere verbal noun, and the nominative pronoun in the poss. or instrumental case; as, my giving, or giving by me, for *I give;* my seeing (was) star = *I saw star*. As we might expect, we do not find a real passive in these languages. All the passive we find is made by the use of verbal nouns with *be* omitted. A word without the least change may be used as verb, noun, and adjective.

1017. HAWAII LANGUAGE: Still more infantile in structure than any we have so far noticed is the Hawaii, or the language of the Sandwich Islanders. It is one of the members of the Polynesian branch of the Malay languages, a branch which may be said to represent Malay, and indeed language in general, in its least advanced stage. The Polynesian idioms are those of a savage people, with the usual features of savage idioms, but with a greater tendency to develop itself, and far greater inherent power for that development, than we find in the languages of the wild Americans. The numerous members of this Polynesian class are unmistakably connected with each other, and more remotely with the Malay.

1018. In these languages, differentiation in classes of words has gone but a little distance; there is scarcely to be found either clauses or accent; even our individual words are hardly distinguishable in the molten mass. This is the history of all wild or uncultivated languages. It is worthy of remark, too, that there is a great predominance of vowels over consonants. Vowels are clearly earlier than consonants.

1019. In all savage idioms, speech has but few variations, few notes; there is much of singing about it, but it is mostly like the singing of infants, merely an up and down, up and down.

1020. Inflexion we find, of course, at zero. We give the following illustrations: *wahine maikai* — wife good, wife (is) good, or good wife; *wahine kane-make* — wife (of) man-dead, *i. e.*, a widow (we have here separated the words, but they are found united together); *haawi*, to-give, *haawi-ia*, be-given (*ia* is pass. ending, it is the Malay *iya*). Duplicates are numerous; *keiki*, child; *keiki-kane*, male-child, *i. e.*, son.

1021. There is, as in Malay, much of prefixes, and some, as *ke, ka, na*, are called articles; *ke-kanaka* — the-man; *ka-mea* — the-thing; *kuu mea* — my thing; *keia mau mea* — the some thing, *i. e.*, these things; *kahi*, one, *ke-kahi*, the-one. The singular is often used for the plural; *o* = the; *o na mea* — the these things, *i. e.*, the things.

He is used for the article and for *be*; *he aina maikai o Farani* — be (is) land good the France (good country France is); *he maka no ka maka* — be eye for an eye; *o ka moku nui Nu holani o na moku a-pau ma ka honua nei* — the this island great (one) New Holland (of) the those (*na*) island the-all (*a-pau*) in (*ma*) the earth here (largest of all islands); *ia* (he) is used for preposition.

I kei la — on this day; *kana hana* — his deed; *kana olelo* — his word; *o-ke keiki hipa* — the (*o-ke*) child (of the) sheep (lamb); or, *a-ka hipa* — of-the-sheep; *ko* is article and preposition also; *ko Aigupita* — to Egypt; *na lima* — the hand (hands); (*no* = *the* and *of*); *no Perusia* — of Prussia; *ma* = *in* and *where*, really a pronoun (it is in this language that we particularly see prepositions and *be* identical with pronouns).

Io makou nei — to us here; *au* and *wau* = I (Mal. *aku*); *oe* and *oukou* = thou, you (Mal. *kamou*); *ia* and *na* = he (Mal. *iya, nia*); all these pronouns have prepositions corresponding with them, and these again unite with these pronouns; thus, *na-na* = of him, his, *o-na* = to him; *ko wahine* — thy wife; *kela,* that; *nei,* here and now; *lakou nei* — see here (look); *ia kanaka la* — the man there, that man; *wai,* who, which; *ka inoa wai la* — the name which there? (what name); *ia-wai* = whom? *o-wai* = whose? *me* = with, as, and how; *me ka lima* — with the hand; *poepoe ka honua* — round the earth (is).

1022. As we have seen in the languages before, verbs are not properly varied with inflexions such as we have, but they develop particles or auxiliaries like prefix prepositions. They are properly augments; *e, mai, o,* for the present and future, *i* for the past, as ε in Greek; *ke* is used like *that* — indeed, all these augments are clear pronouns.

Ana, which we found in Malay equal to *-ing,* is here also; *ke ola-na,* the living; *ai* = *be,* have, shall, and pass. sign — the *iya* of Malay; *aloha,* loves, *aloha-ia,* is-loved; *ike,* see, know, *ikeia,* seen, known; *ho-ike,* let-see (caus.); *ike-ike* and *ho-ike-ike,* see often; *e* = by, *ia* = to; *oia ka mea au e-haawi aku nei ia-oe* — this the thing (is) (which) I (by-me) give there now to-you (*e* is present sign; *ia* is dat. sign) (the thing which I give you). Mark the abundance of adverbs.

Ka-u keia i-haawi aku ia-oe — I (by-me) this gave (giving, with past mark *i*) there to-you; *e-haawi ana aku* — giving there him (*e* and *ana* are both present or continuing signs); *ka mea e-haawi-ana aku* — the one giving there, *i. e.,* the giver (*mea* = thing, one); *ka haawi-ana* — the giving; *o oe no ke Akua nana i-hana ka-lani* — the thou art the God he (who, by whom) made the-heaven (*no* = indeed, but it has the place of *be*); *na-na* = by-him (*ka* is article or acc. sign, *i* is past sign).

1023. The simplicity of this language is its difficulty for us. There are many other points which it illustrates, and we regret to be obliged, for want of room, to stop here. Its relation to the Malay, through all its variations, is never lost; very many of the words are clearly Malay — and others can be discovered with a little effort. Through the Malay we connect the Polynesian with Sanscrit and European. Nothing could be more interesting than to compare with European the forms of many related elementary words in Malay and European, but there is no space for it. We should find many surprising identities. Pronouns, numerals, and all particles, are easily traced back to those with which we are familiar.

1024. All the Polynesian languages, particularly the Eastern, as the New Zealand, Fejee, Tonga, Tahitian, and Marquesian, have the general characteristics of the Hawaii. We find augments to denote tenses, particles or prepositions as signs of cases, the same abundance of adverbs, and the use of one and the same word for present, adverb, pronoun, auxiliary, and augment or prefix (proving the common origin of these parts of speech and elements, here at least). As in all the Malay, except Tagale, the adjective follows. Here we may give some of the forms of the pronouns as we find them in Malay, Jav., Bugis, Mad., and Tag., in order: I, *aku* and *ku*, *haku*, *iyak* and *idik*, *zao* and *ahou*, *aco* and *co ;* thou, *angkau* and *kau*, *kowe* and *ko* and *iko*, *ano* and *no*, *ica* and *iyo* and *tayo ;* he and the, *iya* and *yang*, *hiya*, *yatu*, *izan*, *siya* and *niya*.

1025. MADAGASCAR: An interesting language of the class, and possessing the usual characteristics of the Malay proper, and Javan, is the Madagascar. Here, all verbal prefixes begin with *m : soulon*, a change, *ma-noulon* (n for *s*), to change; *foutsi*, white, *ma-moutsi*, to whiten. The prefix *de*, the *di* of Malay, is very common here, and, though an augment, it has the real value of *be*, *is*. The passive (or intransitive) is used in preference to the active; so, *rehefa hita-ny ny Petera izany* — as see-he (his) by Peter this, *i. e.*, Peter he-saw this (*-ny* = his); *mitady*, he seeks; *nitady*, has sought; *hitady*, will seek; tenses are formed by a change of initials, as well as by augments or adverbs.

Izany no sorata-ny — this is write-his (he), he writ this, is his written; *ary no ny efa nilaoza-ny ny Devoli izy* — and was the been (*efa*, past sign) leaving-he (by-him, his) by (by-the) devil he, *i. e.*, he was left by him the devil, the devil left him (*ny* = his, the, by, and by-the).

1026. TAGALE : Another important Malay language, of the Phillippine class, is the Tagale. The words do not vary by inflexion, but, as in others, they use particles separate and fixed. Its verb is perhaps the most complete of the Malay class. It has, like others, a fondness for passive in place of active. A peculiarity, which we find, too, in Malay, is the insertion, so called, of *in* and *un* after the initial consonant. We find something like it in Semitic; but we regard it rather as a new form of the initial than the insertion of a new element; so, from *bating*, cut, cutting, we get *b-in-ating-an*, cut-been, been-cut (*in* being inserted, and *an* the passive end.); *can-in mo ito* — eaten-been by-you (*mo*) this, *i. e.*, eaten or eating by you, or you eat, will eat, this; *i-bigai mo* — given by-you, you give (there are three styles of passive — *i* as prefix, *an* as suffix, and *in*); *in* is future and impera. sign ; from *sulat*, writing, *s-um-ulat*, to write. Prefixes *ma*, *mag*, and *man*, are very common; *ma* is intrans. and passive sign. Reduplication of initial syllable, as in Greek, prevails here; it is used in the present.

CHAPTER XIV.

THIBETAN LANGUAGE.

1027. The transition from the Indian languages and the Malay, to the Thibetan, is both easy and natural; Thibet lies to the north of India, and the idiom has evidently much of its history in common with the Sanscrit and its related tongues. It is already conceded that there are many points of resemblance, and it is certain that as we become more acquainted with it, we shall find it built on the same foundation as the Indian languages — and hence, too, the same as the European. It is, indeed, a very different growth from any European or Indian language; but the elements, the base-forms, are the same as in them.

1028. There are the pronouns, the reliable index in all cases, *nga*, I, L. *ego*; *khyod*, thou, you (*khy* = *ty* = *y* in *ye* — or transpose *khd* to *dkh*, Ger. *dich*); *kho*, he, who; *hde*, this, the, there, *h* being prefix; *sou*, who — also *chi*, Ital. *che*, our *that*.

A little examination renders the numerals familiar; there is *djug*, six = sigs; *dun*, seven — other forms, *chet* and *sayt*; *gad*, eight — other forms, *payt* and *pet*; *gu*, nine, *g* = *n*; *dju*, ten, = two; *la*, five — other forms, *nya* and *nam*; *fschi*, four — also *pou*; *ssum*, three — alse *sam* and *thum*; *nniss*, two — also *so*, *hait*; *djig*, one, a, an — also *nin*, *noo*. These are easily compared with European and allied forms.

1029. Then take, besides, such leading words as *dje*, tongue; *sso* and *fan*, tooth (fang); *lag*, hand, also *me*, *ma*, Fr. *main*; *nawa*, nose; *bu*, go; *hou*, head; *ma*, mother; *pa*, father; *ssa*, earth, L. *terra*, G'k *gê*; *la*, moon, L. *luna*; *me*, fire; — then the verb and the verbal endings, which we notice elsewhere; also the particles.

1030. As we have found in so many other languages, we find here also a great abundance of prefixes; but they are yet so feeble, in most instances, that though they exist in writing, they are mute in pronunciation, exactly as our *p* in psalm, or *h* in hour. It is clear that these are as much prefixes as those in the Thibetan — and so in all other cases where words begin with a consonant. There are endings like those of Latin; they, too, are not of strong growth; they are often silent or but feebly expressed. This language presents the Chinese feature of small words — generally mere monosyllables reduced to the smallest possible; as, *va*, fox, *na*, malady, *kha*, snow, *na*, fish, *sa*, earth, *djo*, master.

1031. In inflexion, it has much of the Malay character — everything is expressed by particles, so called; they represent inflexion in its earlier stages. There are endings following nouns and adjectives, corresponding to suffixed articles, and grown into gender endings, like the *-us, -a, -um,* of Latin. So we find *mi-vo,* the-man (*vo* = the); *mi-mo,* the-man (fem.); *lag-pa,* the-hand (*pa* = the). Sometimes we find double endings; as, *byed-pa-po* — the-doer, *i. e.,* do-er-the (*pa* = -er). Cases are expressed by preposition endings, such as *hi* and *gi* for gen., *la* for dat. We look upon these endings, as with those of Latin, as the development simply of the suffix articles just noticed.

1032. In regard to the adjective, we notice that when it is placed before the noun, it takes no case particles, or it assumes the genitive form, just as in Latin we use the same unvarying form *ejus,* of-him, his, for the full number of cases of its noun; as, by his (*ejus*) act, his (*ejus*) act, his (*ejus*) acts. But when the adjective follows, it, and not the noun, takes the case endings, just as we place the preposition before the adjective alone, as *for all times* — and for like reasons in both cases, that the whole unites as one unit.

1033. The verb is pretty well developed for an Asiatic language. The present participle ending is *pa,* corresponding to our *-ing;* a variation of this, *par,* is the infinitive ending. Auxiliary verbs are used in the formation of tenses. The past part. has the same ending, *pa,* as the present, but on a new base, apparently just as we find in Latin two infinitives, *esse* and *fuisse.* Such aux's as *do* and *make* are often used; as, *do go* for *go.* The perfect is only a past part. used as a tense; we find augments also. The future is formed as in German, *be go,* or *become go,* for *will go.* The imperative takes sometimes the dative form, as our infinitive *to go;* we find this so in several other languages. Pronouns are used before verbs just as we use them; taking one form of the verb for all pronouns, there being no variation for number and person.

1034. The arrangement of the words is somewhat peculiar. The verb is placed at the end of the sentence. The use of the instrumental, or ablative, for nominative, is favored; we find it before transitives and passives, and the nominative before intransitives.

1035. The passive is a mere verbal noun, and so is not distinguished from the active, except in the use of the instrumental pronoun; thus, *ngas khyod rdoung-bar byed-do* — by-me thou striking (inf.) make (*byed-do,* make-do, do-make), *i. e., I strike thee,* or *thou art struck by me.* Another important point is the making a participle by adding the particle *jing* to the verb; as, *smra-jing,* bay-ing.

1036. There are many points of interest in the language, but none of importance that have not been illustrated under other heads. The alphabet is peculiar to it, and is after the Sanscrit style; we also find letters connnected together and placed one above the other.

CHAPTER XV.

JAPANESE LANGUAGE.

1037. The Japanese has many of the characteristics of the Thibetan, but it is perhaps nearer related to some forms of the Chinese than to any other. Here, as in other Asiatic idioms, we find but three parts of speech are recognized by the Japanese themselves; they are noun, verb, and particles. They seem to be conscious of no other classes, and indeed they are all that can be said to properly exist in these idioms.

1038. There are suffix gender signs, and, as in Thibetan, suffix articles and case signs; as, *fito-va*, man-the, or a man; *fito-no*, of-man; *fito-wo*, man (acc.); *fito-ni*, to-man; *fito-bito*, men. The genitive, like the adjective, precedes. As in all Asiatic tongues, we find much of the so-called determinatives, base-words of a compound; as, Egypt-land, for Egypt, Paris-city, for Paris. We may notice the pronouns *ware* and *waga*, I; *nandzi*, thou; *ano-fito*, this-man, he; *ko-re*, *ko-no*, this; *so-re*, *so-no*, that; *ta-re*, *to-no*, who, which; *a-re*, *a-no*, he, this. In the verbs, there are no person endings, and the tenses are based on the participle, and compounded after the usual manner with *be*; thus, *ware aro*, I am; *are aro*, he is; *ware atta*, I was (has). The subj. ends in *ba*, as *ware areba*, that I be. We find verbals with *koto* = thing as ending; *aro*, to be, *aro-koto*, be-thing, being; *atta-koto*, been-thing, been-being, or being-been.

1039. The past tense is a participle. The passive ending is *rare*, as act. *age*, pass. *age-rare*. Doubling is very prevalent. Prepositions follow. The progress of inflexion here is indicated by the following: *koro*, (Fr.) le noir; *korosa*, noir-ceur; *koroki*, noir, noire (black); *koroko*, black-like; *korosi*, is-black; *koro-moro*, noircir; *koromo*, se noircir (blacken). The use of pronouns is rare.

1040. The Japanese writing is much simpler than the Chinese, but is evidently connected with it. They write down in perpendicular lines. The language exists in several different forms or dialects.

CHAPTER XVI.

AFRICAN LANGUAGES.

1041. If we except the country north of the Great Desert, where we find Arabic in some of its forms, and also Egypt and the country of the Ethiopians, where we find other idioms of the Semitic family, we may say that Africa presents us with a wholly new and peculiar class of languages. They are the tongues of people wild and little known to us, and we find the language untamed and uncultivated. Our progress towards an acquaintance with them is very slow. However, one by one, at intervals more or less long, a grammar of the idiom of some new tribe or nation appears, and we are gratified with the consciousness that our sphere of vision is becoming more and more enlarged, and that the data on which we are to found our conclusions, are becoming daily more and more extensive.

1042. Yet we must not suppose that these wild tongues, however peculiar they may seem, are without their relatives, in Asia at least. The idioms of Eastern Africa are neighbors to the Malay class, exhibiting strongly its leading features; while the idioms of Southern Africa are evidently also connected with Malay or Semitic. Through these southern idioms we may connect those on the western coast with the languages of Southern Asia.

1043. As a people, all the tribes of Africa are too insignificant, too ill-defined, and too little known, to admit of any labored account of their idioms. Speaking generally, we may say that most of the chief characteristics of the great Malay class also prevail here in the African languages.

1044. The first thing that impresses itself upon us, more in some than in others, but strong in all, is the prefixes or augments. Many of them are used to perform the usual office of prefixes in other languages—but very many more have not developed themselves into any individual significance. We see these prefixes in great abundance in the Herero, a language of the western part of Southern Africa. We find here such prefixes as *omu*, *e*, *oku*; as, *omu-ndu*, man; *omu-ko*, region; *oku*, which is really an infinitive prefix, like our *to*, is used also as an ordinary noun prefix; *oku-oko*, arm; *oku-ripam-bu*, pride.

1045. Many of these prefixes clearly identify themselves, in use, with the Malay articles. Many of them are doubled, or receive a new pronominal element with them; such are the double prefixes *in-di*, *im-ba*, *in-ga*. We find others thus, *omu-*

na-vita = the-with-hating, *i. e.*, the hating one, the enemy (*an* = with).

1046. The common origin of these prefixes with demonstratives, or pronouns, in the first place, and with prepositions next, is proved over and over again in these tongues. We notice in all these languages an entire absence of all that labored system of case, gender, and person ending, which characterizes the Greek and Latin and others of their class. And yet we find in all these languages, in some more than in others, an evident tendency to develop this very system of inflexion. Hence, we find a general absence of those marks which with us, and others, distinguish the noun, adjective, and verb from each other, and the same form unchanged may be used to perform the office of any one of them.

1047. In the Namaqua or Hottentot, in South Africa, we find the pronouns take the place of a suffix article and case ending; as, *koie*, the man; *koi-na*, the men; *kois*, thou man; *koi-da*, we men — proving the identity of pronouns, case-endings, and articles. So we find *ba* here as a dative ending; thus, *koi-ba*, to man — this *ba* is a clear demonstrative, and we shall find it also with the verb; *di* is in like manner used as a genitive sign. In Akra, or Ga, we find *tse*, among others, as a sort of determinative, or ending; thus, *man-tse*, *sien-tse*, friend; *dien-tse*, self.

1048. In all these languages, we find diminutives more or less developed; as, in Zulu, a form of Caffer, in South Africa, *inja* = dog, *injana* = little dog; *inlu* = house, *inlwana* = little house. In this tongue, we find nouns derived from verbs, distinguished by a certain prefix, as *im* in *im-bazo* = an ox (from *baza*). So, in Suaheli, from *soma* = to read, we have *m-soma* = reader (showing that this *im*, *m*, is the Semitic prefix *m* of verbals). Infinitives are used as nouns, retaining their prefix *uku*; as, *uku-hamba*, going.

1049. The plural is not generally well distinguished, but in Zulu, as in others, we find it varying thus from the singular: *umuntu* = man, *abantu* = men; *inlu* = house, *izinlu* = houses — being a change in prefix.

1050. The adjective generally, in the African languages, follows the noun, showing its participial or verbal character. Comparisons are expressed by different contrivances; as, in Herero, *mountain this goes above that*, *i. e.*, is higher than that; *honey this very fine by that*, *i. e.*, is finer than that. In the Ewe language, of West Africa, adjectives formed by reduplication are very common; as, *dso-dsoe* = right, *ko-ko*, holy. In short, reduplication appears everywhere in the African languages. In them, too, we find the adjective used as verb, just as if we should use *wise* for *is-wise*, *was-wise*.

1051. In Zulu, we find adjectives of elements like this, *the-with-strength*, for strong; as, *umuntu u na-manla* — man the with-strength (*na* = with); *umuntu o na-manla* — man who (is) with-strength, *i. e.*, who is strong. The absence of *is* in African tongues is general. Verbs as well as nouns can be used as adjectives, with the affix *jo*, and that, too, not only in the present but the past; as, *inkosi e lungile-jo* — king the good-being, *i. e.*, being good, the good king; *umuntu o hama-jo* — (the) man the wandering, *i. e.*, who wanders; *izinto e ngi zenzile-jo* — (the) thing the I heard, *i. e.*, which I heard. In all these cases, the verb is turned into a true participle, and *e* and *o* are used as augments = the, who.

1052. We notice particularly of the Zulu adjective, that it is preceded by prefixes which vary according to the initial of the noun preceding it; as, *umuntu om-kulu* — man great, *i. e.*, great man (*kulu* = great); *into en-kulu* — thing great; *isika esi-kulu* — tub great. Properly speaking, the real adjective hardly exists in African, and it is rarely used. In some of the tongues at least, the attributive adjective varies in form from the predicative, as *de* and *dew*, *den* and *denen*. In some cases, the single adjective is used in one application and the duplicate, or double, in the other.

1053. In the African class generally, the pronouns *thou* and *I* exist independent, but the demonstratives, and hence the personals *he*, *it*, and *she*, tend to identify themselves with prefixes and suffixes of nouns and verbs, and they are generally found as such. In Zulu, this is particularly evident; there, as in Herero, the personals of the 3d person and demonstratives seem to have a very close connection with the noun; they are mere forms of the noun prefix, and vary according to the prefixes of the noun they are associated with; as, *jena* for *he*, when the noun prefix is *um* or *u*, and *sona* when it is *isi* — also *kona* when it is *uku*. So we find *le in-doda* — the husband (*le* with prefix *im*). All this shows that the personal and demonstrative are mere duplicates of the noun and verb augments.

1054. Here, too, the interrogative is to be referred back to the demonstrative, and questions are made thus: *ini loku na* — what this here? *ini na* are used together equal to *what*, but both are demonstratives; so, again, *into ini loku na* — thing what this here? *i. e.*, what thing is this? *leli ilike li jini* — that (the) stone it what (*jini*, what that), *i. e.*, what stone is that? *lo umuntu u jini* — that man he what, *i. e.*, who is that man?

1055. Relatives here are only demonstratives of a certain kind, varying according to the noun they are found with; for example, *ilizwe eli-mkaulo u kude* — (the) land which-limits (whose-limits) it far (are far) (*di* is noun prefix, *eli* is relative prefix, really

= *a*, *the that*, but here *which*, *whose*); *umuntu ili-zwe lake li na-manla* — (the) man the-word his it mighty, *i. e.*, a man whose word is mighty; *ikaki u li tandajo* — (the) horse thou it hold, horse thou hold which, *i. e.*, which you hold; *amadoda e ngi bonile wona* — (the) men which (*e*) I seen them, or which I have seen; *o ngi kuluma ku je* — whom (*o*) I speak to him (*je*), *i. e.*, whom I speak to.

1056. The use of pronoun for verb *be* is also common; thus, in Herero, *oami Jehova* — I (am) Jehovah; *oeie imb-a* — we (are) this. Here, too, the separate personals used as object are before the verb; as, *ami me ku tono* — I, I thee strike, or I will strike thee. The superfluous pronoun is very common; as, *the man he speaks*, for *the man speaks*; *ami ami ani* — I, I who, I who am I.

1057. In Namaqua, the personals are all demonstratives; so is the interrogative. The pronouns of this and other African languages, are easily referable to those of Semitic and South Asiatic; for instance, in Akra, *ene* and *no*, the, this; *le*, the; *ni*, who. Here, too, all the augments, prefixes, and auxiliaries, are seen to be pronouns, or it is seen that pronouns are not different from these augments. The same thing is seen very clearly also in the Oji. In the African languages generally, we may say that pronouns, in all their kinds, are found both separate and as fixes; the relative, like conjunctions, being usually absent or represented by demonstratives.

1058. With regard to the verb of African tongues, we notice, generally, that regular forms for tense and mood are not found, but that they are indicated by augments and auxiliaries. So, in Namaqua, *koiba ma*, man gives; *koiba go ma*, man has give (*go* perf. sign). We find, here, *tita ma* — I give, or *ma-ta*, give-I; so, *ma-ta go*, give-I have, have given. The imperative and infinitive here are the root; there is a participle ending *ia*, as *ma-ia*, giv-ing; *ge* and *a* represent the verbs *be* and *have* (really they are pronouns); *tita ge koita*, I be man; *koib ge ma*, man be give, does give, gives.

1059. As an instance of that repetition, that superfluity, so often found in uncultivated languages, we instance this in Namaqua: *tita ge ra ma* — I be do give, *i. e.*, I give. The passive in this language is a form of the active; as, *tita ma-he* — I am-given (*he* being passive sign). In Zulu, the passive differs from the active, thus, *loba* (active), *lokwa* (passive); *tanda*, love, *tandwa*, be loved; *bubisa* and *bujiswa*; to form causatives, they use *is* or *isa*; as, *hamb-isa*, from *hamba*, to go; *gi hamba*, I go; *ga hamba*, I went (change in *gi*, the pronoun); *go hamba*, I shall go (pronoun changed); *gi hamb-ile*, I have-gone (ending *ile*).

1060. The help-verbs are *ba* (be), *ja* (go), and *za* (come); *gi nga hamba*—I can go. In Akra, *e* is the augment of the perfect, as in Greek; as, *fo* = to do evil, *efo* = has done evil. We find here a great many compounds of two verbs, one of which grows into a simple auxiliary; as, *go-see* (go and see), for see; *take-show* (take and show), for show; *he walks and goes Ga, i. e.*, he goes to Ga; *read this story show me, i. e.*, read to me this story.

1061. In Herero, as in Caffer, there are many derivative forms of verbs; as, *suta, sutisa, sutika, sutira*, having causative, reflexive, and other meanings. Here, as in Zulu, tenses and moods are indicated by augments and auxiliaries. In Herero, *ri* = be, *rira* = become. In Oji, *mi-ko*, I go; *wo-ko*, thou go; *o-ko*, he goes; *ma-ko*, I (have) gone; *wa-ko*, thou (hast) gone (change of pronoun, as in Zulu); *mi-be-ko*, I will go; *wo-be-ko*, thou wilt go. It is hardly necessary to remark that in all these languages, the participle and its class are scarcely developed.

1062. In Ewe, as in all West Africa, there is a great heaping of verbs to express a single idea—all but one being a pure auxiliary; thus, *he brought* (a) *sheep come give me, i. e.*, brought a sheep to me; *he took his boy* (to) *go* (to) *stand up, i. e.*, stood him up. Many of these form-, or help-verbs grow, in some languages, to be conjunctions and prepositions, and their origin is thus shown.

1063. We find in all the known languages of Africa, conjunctions, prepositions, and adverbs. The last are more numerous, being mostly pronouns, nouns, adjectives, and verbs, used adverbially, just as we find in other languages. Conjunctions especially are rare, and so are prepositions. Sentences and clauses are detached, or they are connected as the elements of our compounds without a conjunction. In Herero, it is said, there are only four real prepositions, *mu* = in, *pu* = by, *ku* = up and on, *na* = with; all of which are pronominal in their character. Many others are compounded from these, taken with some noun or pronoun, like our *in-stead*, *in-front* = before.

1064. But in many instances where we use prepositions, they express the relation by the verb alone. The conjunctions in Herero are almost identical with those four prepositions already named. We find here, as in all languages, but particularly in Semitic, nouns used as prepositions; as, in Ewe, *ta*, head, *dsi*, cover, *gbo*, side. In Namaqua, the prepositious are principally to be referred back to a verbal origin, and stand regularly after the noun.

1065. We notice particularly in these languages, a scarcity of abstract terms, and a multiplication of words by reduplication. We find many points of resemblance in orthography, not only between the languages themselves, but between them and the languages of Europe and Asia. We find reduplication, or repetition, to express frequency of action, plurality, etc.; but we notice often a slight variation in one of the duplicates, just as we find with us. We might remark that all our cases of verb with kindred objects (or any other) are also duplicates; as, *dream a dream, ask a question, talk a talk, see a sight;* also, *one-by-one, here-and-there.*

1066. A very noticeable peculiarity of the South African, is the clacking, geese-like sound of their talk; in short, it may be remarked that in all the rudest languages the talk partakes more and more of the character of the clacking, chirping, or even the singing of birds.

CHAPTER XVII.

AMERICAN LANGUAGES.

1067. The aborigines of the New World, the Indians, present us with a class of uncultivated languages, differing considerably from those we have already noticed; yet the more light we get on them, the more do we perceive that they are built on a basis precisely similar to those of the Old World. As they have no literature of their own, that is, as their language is not tangible and we are left to the uncertainties of oral discourse, we can make but a slow and unsteady progress towards an acquaintance with these American idioms. Using such information as we now have upon the subject, we will notice a few of the features of some of the languages coming under this head. The *Greenland* tongue we will notice first.

1068. It possesses that leading character which marks the American languages generally, namely, long words and few of them; every word is here properly a whole or condensed sentence. The pronouns are developments not yet detached from the noun or verb; thus, *igdlua* = his house, *igdlut* = thy house; *takuva*, he sees it; *takusava*, he will see him; *takuvat*, thou see it; *terianiak takuva* — (the) fox he-saw-him (he saw the fox).

1069. In the noun we find developed endings like the Latin case endings, and equal to them; *nunane*, on land; *nunamit*, from land; *nunakut*, overland. Interrogative form of verb, *takuvauk*, saw he him? *takulerpa*, begin to see him (a variation of *takuva*). In fact, we find generally in these idioms much that partakes of the nature of inflected forms—especially a great variety of forms of verb like the Semitic.

1070. The demonstratives are familiar to us; *ma*, here, *tass*, there, *uv*, here; *manga*, from here, *mana*, this, *na* that and what; *kina*, who, *suk*, what, *kikut*, which; *nuna-ga*, my land, *nun-et*, thy land, *nuna-mit*, of land, *nunaunit*, of my land.

1071. Nominative and objective forms exist; as, *nuna*, land (obj.), *nunap* (nom.); so, *tasek* (obj.), *tatsip* (nom.). Even the particles are developed at the end like the Latin *-que*, *-ve*, *-ne*; *pitsut*, the poor, *pitsutdle*, but the poor; *kavane*, in South, *kavanilunit*, or in South. Some particles are separate; *tokuvok angunito*—he-is-dead his-father-also, *i. e.*, he and his father are dead; *angune tokungmat*, *uterpok*—his-father-when he-was-dead, he-came-back (when his father died); *kitornanut tuniupa*—to-his-child he-gave-it; *kajak issiyara ornikatit*—(a) kajak I-saw-him he-comes-to-you, *i. e.*, I saw a kajak who came to you.

1072. Many of these particles which we use, are not expressed, or they lie latent in the verb, showing, as we understand it, that every sentence, with its pronouns and particles, is a pure growth of the verb of that sentence; so, in *naparssimassup misigilerpok*—he-began-to-mark that-he-is-sick—the first being a growth of the verb *mark*, and the latter, of the verb-adjective *sick* (a fine illustration of the growth of the parts of a sentence in all languages.

Nuna-vtinit kanipok—by-our-lands he-is-near (he-near). All adjectives in this and other American idioms, are real verbs or participles; as, *nuna panertok*—land the-dry, being dry, which is dry; they develop endings, as *I-great* = am great, *he-great* = is-great; *igpagssak kikia-lia-ra*—yesterday my-made-nail (*kikiak* is *nail*, *liak* = *lia* has the force of *made*, *ra* = my).

1073. Participles, infinitives, and moods, have their own endings; tenses are not much distinguished. Prepositions follow the noun. We notice here and throughout the class, that a different object makes a different verb; so, they might have the word *wash* in *wash-hands*, and another verb to express *wash-face*, *i. e.*, they do not always generalize as we do. What we consider as the same kind of action, known by one common name, they may look upon as quite different, and on the other hand, for very different things, they have names which can hardly be distinguished, that is, they generalize often where we particularize or separate.

1074. The absence of abstract, insensible, ideas exists everywhere in the American class of languages; they can think of *this tree* and *that tree*, *my tree* or *his tree*, *beech tree* or *pine tree*, but not of *a tree* in general, *i. e.*, of no particular tree at all. We notice in all these Indian tongues, that they do not see things as individuals, but always as being somewhere and belonging with something. Their sentences are not made up of words, but they seem to be struggling to grow words out of sentences.

1075. In Dakotah (Sioux), we find a suffixed article, *kin*; *wicaxta-kin* — the man. The adjective follows the noun; as, *maka waxta* — land good; from which we judge that the adjective is a true verb or participle. Poss. pronouns are prefixed; as, *ta-wa* = his God; *ta-wala* = his ship. So the persons are known through prefixes; as, *wakaga* = I make, *ya-kaga* = thou makest, *kaga* = he makes; *wa-ni*, I will, *ya-ni*, thou will, *ni*, he will; *ni kta* = he make will, will make; *waya* = I am; *yaya* = thou art; *ya* = he is. Prefixes are prominent in this language; as, *na-ron* = hear, *na-pa* = flee, *na-jin* = stand; in like manner the prefixes *ana, ko, o,* etc. There are many verbs with ending *ya*, the verb *be*; *cante-ya* = love; *iye-ya* = make. The passive, infinitive, moods, tenses, and participles are hardly differentiated here; they are either indicated by particles, or known by connection.

1076. There is a general tendency in all these languages, as well as elsewhere, to conjugate all parts of speech, that is, to treat them as verbs. It should be borne in mind, by the way, that when we put a noun, adjective, adverb, etc., after *be*, we treat it as participle, *i. e.*, as a verb; thus, *is here, is on, is a man, is good*. So they also take the word *man* in the sense of being a man, and from or on this develop the pronouns; as, *he-man* = he-being-a-man, or *he is a man*, all a development of man. This is not strange, when we bear in mind that with us *go-er* = one-who-goes, and this latter expression contains no more than *goer-one*, the *who* being represented by the development *er*.

1077. In the Lenapi (Delaware) language, we find the adjective and noun united; as, *chingo-teney* = great village (*chingue* = great, and *oteney* = village. Indeed, in all the wild tongues, we can say that the parts of the sentence, short and frequent as sentences are, constitute one undistinguishable mass.

1078. *Ki-soghen-injenin* = I take you by the hand (one word, or the growth of one) (of this, the part *sogenaut* = take, grasp, *oninjima* = hand, *ki* = thee); *soginikenin* = take-by-the-hand-him (*nininj* = my hand, *kining* = thy hand). In these conglomerations of words, we do not find the full form of the separate elements, but only a part of them, indicating that those parts are not full grown. We find this mutilation of elements in the compounds of other languages not American. In the first example *take-by-hand* is plainly a growth on *hand* as a basis — and we may call to mind our own *handle*, from *hand*, which may be used for take-by-the-hand. And the moment it gets to be a verb, it may of course also develop nom. and obj. pronouns, like any verb.

1079. Let us take one term more : *quita-gischg-ook* = serpent which fears the day (and lives in the earth); the first part indicates *quitameu* = to fear; *gischgu* = light, day; *achgood* = serpent (a fear-light serpent). We find in this language, as in others, many prefixes. Here, as elsewhere, the person signs of verbs are prefixes to them ; as, *n-pendame* = I understand, *n-pendaxi* = I am understood.

1080. We will dwell a moment on the Huron, one of the most instructive of these wild idioms. They have neither derivative nor compound forms as we have. No noun is found without its pronoun — not *father* alone, but his-father, my-father, etc. They are without the use of pure abstract terms. Their adjectives are pure verbs. They do not speak of *good* and *bad* alone, but they always use those words as a verb ; thus, *he is good, you are bad*. And if they do not have separate adjectives, they neither have separate verbs, as *walk, go, cut*. Active verbs are found only with their objects ; as, *cut-wood, cut-head-off*. The same is true of the Mexican verb. To take the verb away from its object or subject, is an abstraction unknown to them. They have no prepositions or conjunctions. They do not have distinct forms to denote *act, actor, acting*. Tenses hardly exist. Such are some of the points in the account given of the Huron. It accords with our notion of what a language most infantile would be in these respects.

1081. There are many points of identity which we find between the different and even remote American idioms, especially the prevailing *n* for *I*, *k* for *thou* (as in Semitic). In the Peru tongue, *ca-ni* = I am, *ca-nqui* = thou art, *can* = he is, or they are ; *mamay* = my mother, *maman* = his mother. In Mexican, *ni-auh* = I go, *ti-auh, j-auh* = he go ; *mo-ma* = thy hand, *mo-ca* = you with, *no-ca* = me with ; *ni-ca* = I am, *ti-ca* = thou art, *ca* = he is. This language and that of Peru seem more elevated than the other Indian idioms.

1082. The importance of any of the American tribes as a people is not sufficient to justify here any extended review of these idioms. We have given only briefly a few points in which they particularly instruct us. They are languages embryonic and more or less chaotic. They give us positive proof of what embryonic language is. In so far, and only so far, are they valuable at present.

CHAPTER XVIII.

ABSTRACT PHILOLOGY.

Reduplication.

1083. No feature is found more universally in language than reduplication. It is found in all idioms, but it is most prominent in the wildest and rudest tongues. It is in these languages that we see most clearly that doubling is the leading and original source from which new terms are got—doubling not only of syllables but of words. This phenomenon continually impresses itself upon us, meeting us everywhere, at every step and at every turn, forces us to conclude that language in its whole growth and in the growth too of its parts, is a mere result of the working of the principle of repetition. That language is in the likeness of a living organism, following the laws of a living organism, is a fact admitted by all intelligent philologists of the present day. The proposition itself is not denied, but the notion of it is crude and imperfect; it needs time and thought to enable us to feel and see that language does live and grow.

1084. But if language does live and grow, it must live and grow as the animal, the plant, and the crystal, for all things grow alike. And what is the fundamental law of their growth? It is development by repetition; this is plainest in the lowest orders of creation, and it grows dark as we reach the organism which is more perfect, more intricate. In the plant we see the leaf, even the twig, the branch, repeated hundreds of times. In the lowest animals, which are still far above plants, we see the same arm, the same foot, the same segment, repeated, with scarcely any perceptible difference, over and over again. As we rise higher in the scale of being this likeness of parts, this doubling, becomes obscured. The highest animal has just as many parts or organs as the lowest, but they have become differentiated, so that in quadrupeds, for example, what things we find so much alike as to be called by one name, we find again in man so much unlike that we call one set arms and hands, and the other set legs and feet.

1085. But even in the highest organism, as man, there are certain parts of the structure that evidence this duplication principle most clearly; there are the two ears, two eyes, two feet, the fingers, the hairs of the head, the teeth, and the like. Go where you will in the living creation, you will find all increase to be a continuous repetition of one model, as one cell followed by a like cell, one bud followed by another bud, one segment by a like segment, one arm by another arm. And if when the being is arrived at maturity, we find the highest parts differing from the lowest in character, the skillful naturalist can show you where this difference is apparent and not real, and that the two most remote parts of the body are yet repetitions of one type. No new part is ever created; one structure has as many and the same parts as every other structure. To repeat illustrations given elsewhere, the elephant has a trunk and tusks, but they are only a developed nose and teeth; the wings of the bird and bat, the fins of fish and the claws of the crab, are only developed arms and feet; the shell of the tortoise is but the internal framework of bones of other animals, here grown upon the outside. In chemistry we find the same evidence; a few simple elements lie at the base of all things, that is, all things are made of the same ingredients repeated over and over again. (Even the number of these few elements is becoming less and less, as we become acquainted with their character).

1086. The picture we have given of the living creation is the picture as well of language and its parts. We need only take a comprehensive view to perceive this truth; in fact, we may use language to illustrate growth in nature generally. The Eight or Ten parts of speech are the development of one type, and we can easily trace them all back to that common ancestry. The different letters which we find in the alphabet are the growth of one single letter, or at least of a very few; and it is the repetition of this one, or these few, which constitutes the framework of so many thousand words. Words repeated or words growing upon words make new terms; these new terms by doubling again produce new terms of a higher scale, as leaf follows leaf and twig follows twig. Terms make phrases, phrases make sentences, and these again make composition, and all by growth, all by the repetition of like elements. There is no true compounding, no putting together of old parts; all being one from the other or on the other, as we find budding in plants and the lower animals.

1087. We have seen elsewhere that the letters of the word are duplicates, as the hairs of the head are duplicates; the words of every term, as that from adjective and noun, of every phrase or sentence, are repetitions of words having meanings in fact alike, without which likeness they would not grow together. The cause gives character to the effect, the parent cannot beget that which is not in harmony with its nature. When we say *the fisher fishes fish with a fishline* (fisher), every one sees the repeated words, and yet the same kind of repetition exists in every sentence. When we say *the man catches fish with a hook*, we use *man* = fisher, *catches* = fishes (a particular kind of fishing), *hook* = fisher, fishing-thing (sometimes used in fishing).

1088. But then there is about this term and idea of repetition, something to be borne in mind, in natural history as well as in philology. Nothing is properly repeated; it is only that imaginary thing, the form, that is thus repeated. The *b* of book is as different from the *b* of boy as *o* and *y*, or *o* and *k*. However much alike any two doubled words or doubled letters may be, they are yet besides as unlike, as distinctly individual, as any two other words or letters. So, again, in living beings, similar as may be our two eyes, two ears, two hands, they are nevertheless, too, very distinct, very different, things; one never does and never can take the place of the other.

Interrogative Expressions.

1089. The difference between interrogative and affirmative amounts, when carefully sifted, to nothing. We know indeed that we use the relatives *who, which,* and *what,* as interrogative without any change of form and meaning; we know, also, that we can take an affirmative expression, as *you spoke,* and make a question of it by adding the interrogative sign, thus, *you spoke?* Again, the very form which we commonly denominate interrogative, as *does he speak?* is not peculiarly such; we use it in cases not interrogative; as, does he speak, (then) all listen, *i. e.,* if he speaks. Every subjunctive expression is one which contains a question, and is hence interrogative. Our ordinary question forms, as *what (did) he say?,* imply another part which is commonly suppressed, as *I ask what did he say,* or *what he said?*

1090. Every question is a dependent form, like a subjunctive expression, governed by some such verb as ask, wish-to-know, etc.; thus, *can he read = I wish to know (if) can he read,* or *tell me (if) he can read.* Hence, we must insist that our questions are subjunctive, questionable, doubtful, and not, as grammarians say, indicative. While our question-form differs often from the indicative, we must bear in mind that, in very many languages, there is commonly no difference at all in the arrangement. In many cases, a particle is used with the form to indicate doubt or question, like our *if* he speaks, *does* he speak, *whether* he reads, *perhaps* he reads = does he read? All such words or particles in any language indicating doubt or question, are pure interrogative marks.

1091. *Negative* forms are closely related to interrogatives. We can say equally *can he read?,* or *can he not read?, will you take this?* or *will you not take this?* It is as true in philology as it is in philosophy generally, that the negative is a form, a growth of the affirmative, or that both are different developments of the same form; thus, *ignorant* denotes *knowing*, but a particular kind of knowing, *i. e.* knowing nothing or little; so, *un-successful* is a kind of *successful*, and the former is a growth of the latter by a development of the prefix *un*, just as *wrong* is a form of *right*, and *there* a form of *here*.

1092. We must identify negatives with opposites; the opposite of *heat* is *cold*, and we may call one the negative of the other, and still one is just as positive, as real, it is as much something, as the other is—so, taking is as positive as giving, minus is as positive as plus, low as high, empty as full, bad as good.

1093. The idea should be forever banished that a negative is a nothing, a nonentity; that *nothing* is not a thing as well as *something* is. We have more than once had occasion, etymologically, to identify what are usually considered the most opposite terms, as *big* and *little*, *one* and *none*, *few* and *many*, *to* and *from*. We have noticed in other languages a regular class of negative verbs; based on the affirmative, they are merely a departure from it, as our *cant* from *can*, *mistake* from *take*, *undo* from *do*—just such verbs as *de-bar*, *in-lay*, *dis-cover*.

Compounds.

1094. Every instance where an adjective is joined to a noun affords us an example also of a compound; and we must bear in mind in this connection that the case of one noun joined to another to denote a single object, is one precisely that of an adjective joined to a noun—every adjective being a real noun in an oblique case, and always to be so considered.

1095. But the real question under this head is, how two names usually denoting each one thing, can come to be so united as together to denote but one object. It occurs to us that these two names, however much we may endeavor to unite them, never do cease each to denote their own object, though it may be true that one is more or less slighted, as *road* in *rail-road*. Expressed in other words, we are using two names to denote one object, with the design of being more specific or definite, exactly on the same principle as we say a *tall-old-oak-tree*, one which is tall, old, and of oak. That the name *rail* may be used to denote the object known as a *rail-road*, may be seen by such expressions, as *goods sent by rail, travelling by rail*.

1096. Another kind of compound is found in such expressions as *Clayton-Bulwer treaty*, *i. e.* the treaty of Clayton and Bulwer, the *South-Atlantic ocean*, *i. e.* which is south and Atlantic.

1097. So that we conclude any two or more words joined together by any connective, as *tall and straight, men and women, better than that, men of talent, nails with heads, iron for wheels*, constitute a true compound, and just such a one as *talented men, headed-nails, wheel-iron.* It will be remembered that in the Eastern languages the great body of compounds were found to be words thus connected. We now understand that there is a reason for such expressions, in Hebrew, as *the choice of thy valleys,* for *thy choice valleys, the strong of shields,* for *strong shields,* and a reason why we say *the fashion of the place,* for *the fashionableness of the place.*

1098. Compound sentences are as much compounds and just such compounds as we have found in words—they are made up of two or more inseparable parts, elements, and yet the compound is practically a unit, a single sentence. How two sentences as *this is the man, whom I saw, i. e. this is the man, him I saw,* can ever become one sentence, is just as incomprehensible, for it is the same question, as how we should ever come to consider one thing as being two, or two things one. It is the identical question of the idea of number, and one not so easily solved.

1099. It will have been observed long before this, that the linguistic system of this work is based not on the current doctrine that two things unite and form one, but, reversed, that one thing develops, grows, and manifests the new elements not as real, separate individuals, but as formerly latent, covered, folded parts now becoming visible. This idea is illustrated and repeated in the history of every living, growing thing. The majestic oak now with its thousand leaves and scores of boughs, once emerged from the ground a simple, single, stem, with all its parts folded, compressed, encased. It has displayed its innumerable parts, but all the while it remains in number simply one, an oak. So it is with words that grow into parts, and so it is with the sentence also.

1100. In the sentence named above, if we take the idea of one sentence, we must consider *whom I saw* as an adjective, or rather participle, belonging to *man;* that is the relation it now holds to the main body of the sentence. The word *whom* as a relative is known to be an adjective; it has a tendency to become independent, just as the personals, originally adjective pronouns, are now become individualized;—in this respect, the relative stands as a sort of transition from the adjective to the personal. As before suggested, *whom-I-saw* is a true participle = *the-seen-one-by me;* indeed we say, he is the man *seen by me,* he is the man *I-saw* (me-seen, my-seen). It is very clear that *whom* is not the object of *saw,* that it is the mere development of a participle prefix, like *the* in *the-seen-one.* We have no doubt that all adjective expressions like these in compound sentences, are the growth of participles at first suffixed to the main verb in a rude state.

1101. All other compound sentences are to be referred back to the relative class as the original one, especially those made by connectives, as *and*, *as*, *when*, all of which are pronouns, and more than that, relatives also; thus *as* = *sk-os* = *as* = *who;* Fr. *que* = *which* = *and, as;* *when* = which; *if* = L. *ibi, ubi, where, which.*

Imperative.

1102. After having discussed the other moods as we have, little need be said of the imperative. In all languages, it has a history in common with the infinitive first, and with the future and the subjunctive next — all of which are often used for the imperative, though they may differ from it considerably in form. With a uniformity remarkable, in the different languages, the imperative is the shortest, barest, form of the verb — so much so as to give us often what is called the root of its class.

1103. Indeed there is very little of the verb about the imperative; it is a mere term of exclamation, and partakes most of the character of an interjection. When a man exclaims in terror, a tiger! a tiger! he uses an imperative as much as if he said see! see! If I say *roam where we will*, I use *roam* as a mere abstract noun = *a roam be it where we will*, or *be the roaming where we will.*

1104. The imperative, being identical with the infinitive, is a dependent, objective, term always governed by some implied verb, as *I wish that*, or *ask that*, or *demand that* you do this, for *do this*. Hence, we easily understand how it tends to identify itself with the form of an oblique case; thus, in Latin, *rege* = imp. rule; is identical with *rege* = by a ruler; and *audito* = hear thou, and hear him, also *auditu* = with hearing; and *ama* = love thou, *audi* = hear thou, have the form of an ablative singular. G'k imperatives have case endings; witness *on-tōn* = gen. plur.

1105. It is worthy of remark that the simple form of the Latin imperative, as *ama* = love, is condensed for *amat*, for we find another form of the same, *amato;* besides, it is often seen that the imperative is a mere departure from the 2d sing. prest. ind. (or subj.) *amas, ames*. But *amato* may perhaps better show the supine in the abl. case. In G'k, too, *tupte* (imp.) = *tuptet*, as one of the forms is *tupteto*. The old L. *estud* = be (imper.) also shows the ablative.

CHAPTER XIX.

WORDS IMPLIED.

1106. We frequently speak of words being understood or implied; we seem to imagine that a word expresses or indicates more than it does express or indicate, that a word means more at one time than it does at another, more when it stands alone than when accompanied by other words. Thus, we say that in the expression *the wise are esteemed*, *wise* means wise men, or wise people. The point which we must first settle in discussing this question is, what is the difference between *the wise are esteemed*, and *wise men are esteemed?* There is certainly a difference in the forms of these expressions, and is there not an equal difference in their value and nature? In the first case, *wise* presents to the mind one idea, that of a certain and distinct class, *the wise;* in the next, there is an attempt made to direct the mind to two objects, two classes, at the same time, *men* and the *wise* of men. But as it is impossible for us to think of two objects at the same time, when we turn to one, we must lose sight of the other; we think of *the wise* or of *men,* according as we emphasize, or accent, the former or the latter. It is a mistaken idea that *wise* is not as much the name of *a class* as *men* is, and that one is not as much adjective or noun as the other. All such terms made by the adjective and noun are compounds, two independent words united, precisely as in any other compound;—as in *stone-house, hammer-handle*.

1107. But more than this, in all such cases, when we mean to speak of *wise men* as a class of men, distinguished or marked by their wisdom, the adjective, so called, is the real principal, and *men* is the real adjective, the cipher. It is not men that are esteemed, it is a class, a part, of men; it is the wisdom, and not the manhood. Nouns following adjectives in this way are the determinatives, the radicals or general terms, which prevail in the Asiatic languages. They are the kind of thing named, but the adjective points out the *what* of that kind. The denominator of the fraction represents the noun, while the numerator, which tells how many or what, is the adjective. And just as the numerators, and coefficients, are alone added, subtracted, and divided, leaving the denominator, the thing named or numbered, to follow along as a valueless and unnoticed element, so it is precisely with the adjective.

1108. The *point* always lies in the adjective; that is the real subject. When we say we like *good* men, or *tall* men, or sweet *apples*, or *sour* wine, it is not the men, or apples, or wine in general, that we like; it is only a certain *kind* of these classes; it is the goodness, the tallness, sweetness, sourness, that strikes us so favorably. When we say *ten books will suffice*, we have no reference to *what* will suffice, the thing, the kind, but rather how much, or how many, and that point lies in the word *ten*. Hence *ten*, we apprehend, is the real and only subject — *books* being parenthetical, adjective, valueless. If we say *ten* of books have, the *ancient* of poets have, *much* of money has, *this* of business has (all which are common and prevailing forms in other languages), no one would for a moment doubt that the adjective is the subject, and that the noun is the real adjunct or adjective. Why is not the fact the same in the equivalent English expressions, *ten books, ancient poets, much money?*

1109. But if the point does lie in the adjective, if that is the real and only subject, of what use is the noun following it? Of the same use as the denominator, the thing numbered, in Arithmetic — this and no more. But numbers are alone considered in Arithmetic, while the thing numbered is continually lost sight of. This is exactly the case in language. When we speak of a certain *kind* of thing, denoted by the adjective, we lose sight of the thing to which the kind belongs; and though the kind is not dropped in print, or in conversation, it is so disregarded, so slighted, in pronunciation as well as in thought, that we leave it unaccented, and it passes along for a mere cypher. In language, as in mathematics, as soon as the subject of thought or conversation is named or known, we need not have it repeated again; we deal after that only with adjectives, with marks that point out *who, what, what kind*, exactly as in mathematics we deal only in numbers, or marks which indicate how many. Thus, speaking of John, we say: he (or John) *rises* early in the day, *prepares* himself for its labors, *and sets* about performing them; at night (he) *may turn* back and *see* what (he) has accomplished. Observe that the subject appears but once for all these verbs; and should it be named before each one, it would be none the less a mere cipher.

1110. We now begin to see how one word may represent several words, as is often said, and we see what the real state of the case is when words are said to be implied. We say *the wise* are esteemed (instead of *wise men*), because the point lies only in the adjective, and the noun falls off as useless. (It is usually said, in such case, that the adjective stands for a noun. This is not correct, for *wise*, if it stands for anything, stands for *wise men*. But is there not a palpable absurdity here, when *wise* is assumed to stand for, or be equivalent to, itself and something more?)

1111. We observe still further, that in the expression *wise men are esteemed*, *wise* and *men* both of themselves indicating a class, one or the other, in the thought, must be eliminated, for we cannot speak of the *wise* and of *men* also. If we give the adjectives the force, we wish to distinguish the wise from the foolish (nothing said or thought of *men*); but if we give the force to *men*, we wish to distinguish men from those who are not men (nothing said or thought of *wise*, or any other class of men).

1112. The student cannot be impressed too thoroughly with the idea that nouns point out a kind of thing, to distinguish from some *other* kind of thing, precisely as the adjective does; that a noun may be or is understood after every noun, just as much as after *wise* in the expression *the wise are esteemed*. There are *book* things, *men* persons, *house* property, *table* articles, exactly as there are *good* things, *wise* persons, *this* property, *that* article. We speak of servant, and that is a pure noun; but servant is a serving one,—it is really the Latin form of our *serving*, and no more. Our words, senior, level, walker, wader, youths, a black, a gray, we see clearly are adjectives, and only adjectives;—other nouns are just such adjectives, though their history may not be quite so plain. And as no one thinks that any noun is understood after such nouns, so no one should think of supplying a noun after adjectives used alone as these nouns are.

1113. The sooner we come to understand that many words stand unquestionably alone and independent, the sooner we shall find language a simple and easy thing. It is perhaps unnecessary, so often has it appeared already in the course of this work, in different ways, and yet we reproduce it, and remark, that not only some adjectives have no nouns with which to be connected, but rather that no adjectives have such nouns, in the sense in which the proposition is usually understood; that they each stand independent of the other, and are wholes in themselves, bearing latent, each in its own individuality, the essence of the whole clause. We see this most strikingly in the Chinese tongue, where there is no connection or agreement, and where every word stands apart from the others and independent of them.

1114. And the difficulty which we so often experience when we undertake to dispose of adjectives in which we assume that something is understood, lies in the fact that we start upon this wrong basis, namely, that every adjective must belong to some noun. We all know that many adjectives do occur where it is impossible that any word should be implied; such as, in *vain*, at *least*, at *first*, besides all pronouns and adverbs (which we know to be adjectives in origin). There are also those cases where the adjective follows the verb; as, is *glad*, grows *warm*, looks *fine*, stands *erect*, was *mine*: who would say that it is *glad something*, or *erect something?* Just as much as in the expression *he is an orator*, it is *orator something*—just as much and no more. So in the case of participles, as *he is walking*; here we are wont to call *walking* a participle, *i. e.*, an adjective, and to say it belongs to *he*. But it is well known that *walking* is as much a noun as any one can be which follows a verb in this way, and hence it need not have, any more than such a noun, another word to belong to. The original form of such expressions, it must be remembered, and that form still exists in many languages, was *he is a walking*, at or in walking,—in which the noun character of the participle cannot be mistaken. Again, we speak of the Germans, the Romans (L. *Romani*), and never think of putting *people* after them; so in tropics, blacks, ones, skeptics.

1115. But this fundamental error which we have spoken of, is not confined to adjectives. It is also wrongly assumed that every verb must have a nominative, while in fact many verbs have none (if any do). Thus, John reads a sentence, reflects, and understands (it). The subject is named but once, and it need not be repeated. The point is not *who*, but *what*. What does John do?—Answer, *reads a sentence, reflects, and understands* (it). Will any one insist that those verbs ought to have nominatives? It is at least certain they *do not* have any. Again, what is John engaged in?—answer, reading, reflecting (or reflection), and understanding. Do these nouns need to have nominatives forced upon them? No. But all words are developments of just such verbal nouns as these; and in their application, they never get to be more than verbal nouns, never have any more of expression or affirmation than they do. In other words, to insist that every verb must have a nominative, whether it will or not, is to assume that every infinitive, every participle, must have one; it is to insist that every verbal noun, or one derived from a verb, as addition, reception, government, and the like, must also have one. We need not, then, say that many verbs have no nominatives, but that they do no more have them than all nouns and adjectives do, those derived from verbs at least.

1116. In other languages much more generally than in this, verbs are without nominatives, it being assumed, as in Latin, for example, that the endings (which we have elsewhere shown to be a mere development of participial endings), represent nominatives. Again, in all our cases where pronouns are assumed to be the nominative, we may say the verb really has none. When we say *John writes and he reads*, the *he* is valueless; it is nothing but an augment or prefix. We have shown elsewhere that a *he, she, it,* and *they,* are only forms of *the,* an article which we know to be a meaningless prefix to the word that follows it. We have seen in more than one language, *they reading, the reading* (ones, plur. form of part.), get to be *they read*, or represent it. We have proved over and over again that the verb in all its moods, tenses, and persons, is only the participle wrought up into different shapes. So when we say *it rains, there goes, they say,* there is really no nominative; it is not meant to say who or what goes, says, rains, but merely that there is a going, saying, raining (verbal nouns and no more).

1117. In conclusion, we claim that words should always be treated as what they are, and not as what we would assume or wish them to be.

1118. We turn next and consider, in this connection, the subject of abbreviated words. Is there anything implied in an abbreviated word? To use a paradoxical expression, is there anything in it that is out of it? By what right do we assume that Rob., or Bob, is a shortening of Robert? We say a part is left off in the case of Rob. (-ert); hence, it is only a part of a word, only a part of Robert. Is that true? Only a part of a word! Is not Bob a whole word, a real name, as much as Robert itself? We might as well claim that *rise* is a shortening of *rising,* or *faith* of *faithful,* or *bit* of bite. Words are not parts of words, or less than a word, because they are short; *a* is as much a word as *and,* and as much a whole word. So we apprehend that *par, kath, meth,* and *aph,* are just as much forms of Greek prepositions, and independent forms, as *para, meta, kata,* and *apo,* from which they, the former, are assumed to be derived.

Radicals.

1119. In looking over the Asiatic languages, we are struck with the unwonted abundance of general terms. They are wanting in that luxurious growth of endings which we find in European languages, and among other substitutes for these endings, they employ general or generic terms which are lost with us; thus, they would say male *man*, for male, London *city*, for London, walk *go*, for walk, Persian *man*, for Persian, preach *make*, for preach, stranger *man*, for stranger, white *metal*, for silver, great *water*, for ocean. These general terms are known as *radicals,* or *determinatives.*

1120. The Chinese radicals or keys belong in this category.

Every Chinese word has at least one of these generic or common names as an element. These radicals have so little force, are so abstract and ethereal, that, although found in the written character representing the word, they have no part in the sound of the word when spoken; they are unaccented — mere ciphers. They play a part exactly as the ending of our words, such as *-ous*, in joyous, *-er*, in worker, *-ment*, in treatment, and we consider the two classes parallel in every respect. Some of these endings of ours grow into distinct individuality, and being detached, become themselves words. So in Chinese, of these keys, or radicals, some are found as separate words, while others, again, exist only as component parts of the word-sign. That these generic terms, these radicals, have grown out of or on the other part, the sound-giving and accented element, of the word-sign, just as *ous*, from joy, and *er* from work, we believe is capable of demonstration.

1121. But it must be remembered that while those Asiatic languages which thus abound in these general and apparently superfluous terms, are by no means destitute of common endings, our own languages are quite as far from being destitute of common radicals. Every time we say *go* lost, for lost, *go* walking for walk, *take* a sleep, for sleep, *keep* watch, for watch, *stand* talking, Delaware *state*, Albany *city*, *negro* men, for negroes, loving *ones*, for lovers, ten *heads* of horses, for ten horses, we are using those very same meaningless, valueless, terms which we think characterize the Asiatic tongues. Our auxiliaries, such as *do*, *be*, *make*, *go*, *keep*, etc., belong here—so do our pronouns and particles.

1122. Prefixes may also be referred to in this connection; they also are meaningless marks, having a general and abstract character, similar to those radicals under consideration. That they have no more value than these radicals, is seen by the numberless instances where the word which is found with the prefix in one language is found without it in others; as, the Latin *pello* = expel, re-pel, *paro* = ap-pear, *paro* = prepare, *porto* = trans-port, Fr. *partir* = depart.

INDEX.

THE NUMBERS REFER TO THE SECTIONS.

Abbreviations, explained, 157.
Adjectives, what they are, 12; when found after verbs, 13; they have the nature of verbs, 14; their degrees, 15; numerals, 17; adj. and noun make a compound, 142, 143; they are developments of noun endings, 144; like verbs, 152; after nouns they are adverbs, 153; how adj's and nouns agree, 154.
Adverbs, 41; what they are, 42; their forms and history, 196; those of clear pronominal origin, 196, 197.
Afghan lang., 827 to 835.
After, its forms, 206.
African lang's, 1041 to 1066.
Albanian lang. and specimens, 802 to 805; forms of words, 806.
American lang's, 1067 to 1082.
Amharic lang., 904.
And, its forms, 201.
Anglo Saxon lang., its history, 593 to 599; its forms and specimens, 601 to 607, and 625.
Aorist, 104: in Greek, 408; 1st Aorist of Greek, 410 to 413.
Arabic, Etymology, 588; its forms, 901; selections, 923.
Armenian lang., 851; selections, 854.
Articles, what words, 17; forms, 172.
As, its forms, 202.
Augsburg dialect, 650.
Augments, defined, 109.

Back, its forms, 207.
Basque lang., or Iberian, its features, 714 to 721; specimens, 722; forms of words, 723.
Bavarian dialect, 651.
Be, the verb; in Gothic, 474; Ang. Sax., 476 to 478; Old Germ., 479; French, 480; Italian, 481; Celtic, 482 to 487; Slavic, 488 to 493; Albanish, 494; Wallachian, 495; Hungarian, 496; Finnish, 497; Mongolian, 498; Persian, 499; Arabic, 502; Greek, 503, 504.
Beluchees lang., 825.
Bengali lang., 988 and 989; selections, 990.
Berber lang., 973 to 976.
Birman lang., 999.
Bohemian, etymology, 582,; lang. and specimens, 743 to 745, and 776.
Bolognish dialect, 703.
Bulgarian lang., and specimens, 761 to 764, and 775.
But, its forms, 208.
By, its forms, 230.

Case, what are case forms, 8; names of cases, 9; in Latin, 51; names and forms in Latin, 54, 55; in Germ. and Ang. Sax., 9; in Latin, case-forms a variation of gender-forms, 57; they vary to correspond with verbs governing them, 58; oblique, 59; more than six in some lang's, 107; endings of case, history and forms, 111 to 131; common ending for nom. case, 112 to 118; endings of all cases a mere variation of one type, 118; Greek cases like Germ. and English, 119, 120; endings disappear in mod. Lat. lang's; Slavic case ending, 122; every genitive a plural, 133; identical with personal endings, and a variation of suffix articles and demonstratives, 129; adverbial endings belong with those of case, as well as verbal and part., 129; case endings in Polish, 123; in Bohemian, 124; they are a growth to represent prepositions, they add nothing to the word but grow out of it, 125.
Catalan lang., 706; specimen, 711.
Causatives, 520 to 525.
Caucasian lang's, 836 to 857.
Celtic lang's, history, 674; features, 676 and 687; Celtic mutations, 676 and 677.
Celt Briton, specimens, 680; forms of words, 681.
Chaldaic, 899.
Cheshire dialect, 612.
Chinese lang., 875 to 893; writing, 885; specimens, 890 and 891.
Circassian lang., 847.
Clacking sound of African lang's, 1066.
Cleveland dialect, 622.
Comparison, of adj's in Latin, 61; not peculiar to adj's, 146 and 147; compar. a form of positive, 147; every adj. a comparative, 148; really no degrees in quality, 149; and none beyond comparative, 150; superlative endings, 151.
Compounds, all duplicates, 145; all made of like elements, 194; discussed, 1094.
Conjunctions, what they are, 43; the list, 44. (See Particles.)
Cornish lang., 679.
Cornwall dialect, 613.
Craven dialect, 623.
Croatian lang., 757.

Dacotah lang., 1075.
Danish, etymology, 577; its words and Germ., 664; specimens, 666 and 672; compared with Swedish, 667.
Demonstratives, 173 to 177.
Derbyshire dialect, 615.
Derivatives, 526.
Desideratives, 519.
Devonshire dialect, 616.
Dutch, etymology, 576; lang., 644; specimens, 645.

Each, and any, their relatives, 187 and 188.
Egyptian, 906; lang. and specimens, 965 to 969.
Eight, its forms, 259 to 261.
Endings, defined, 108; of case, 111 to 131; personal, 337 to 345.
English lang., its history, 593; Old Eng. specimens, 608 to 611, 618; specimens of Eng. dialects, 612 to 624.
Ethiopic, 904; lang. and character, 971 to 972.

Etymology, separating words into parts, 528; separating letters into parts, 529, 530; that of Germ., showing the form which certain words of ours assume there, 576; that of Dutch, 576; Danish, 577; Latin, 578; Greek, 579; how its words identify with ours, end of 579; of Russian, 581; Gaelic, 584, note on same, end of 584; of French, 580—Fr. Orthography shows one letter equal to several, end of 580; Welch, 585; Hebrew, 586; Syriac, 587.
Every, its relatives, 186.
Even, Evor, forms, 209, 210.
Ewe lang., 1062.

Faroe Islands, lang., 662.
Feminines, 137; agree with plurals, also fem's and abstracts, 139; fem's and 2d person agree, 141.
Finnish lang's, 782 to 798; Finn. proper, 789; divisions, 790; and specimens, 791 to 793.
Finite, what it is, 40.
Five, its forms, 253 to 255.
Flemish lang., 643 and 699.
For, its forms, 232, 233.
Four, its forms, 250 to 252.
Forms of words, any case-form or person-form is a form of a word, 237 to 139.
Frequentatives, 510 to 514.
French lang., its forms and history, 689 to 691; specimens, 692 to 710; Old French forms, 697.
Friesic lang., 642.
Friulan dialect, 703.
Future, in Latin, 430; in Pol., etc., 431; Wallachian, 432; Albanish, 433; equals pres't ind. and subj., 434; in Goth., 435; in Illyrian, 436; modern Latin, 437.

Gaelic, etymology, 584; specimens, 682; compared with Irish, 683.
Gascon dialect, 698.
Gender, what it is, and the kinds, 4, 5, 6; endings in Latin, 52; its true nature, 136.
Genoese dialect, 703.
German lang., its history and character, 627, 628; specimens, 629, end of 645; pronunciation of Germ. letters, 630, note, page 157; forms of Germ., 631 to 635; Old Germ., Francic, specimens, 636; Old H. Germ. endings, 638; and its poetry, 640, 641; dialects of Germ., 649; etymology, 575; their compounds like ours, end of 575.
Gerund, what in Latin, 71.
Georgian lang, 848 to 850.
Gothic lang., 652 to 655; specimens, 656 to 658; forms of words, 659 and 660.
Greek lang., idiom like Latin, 104; comp'd adj's, 105; articles, 104; Greek etymology, 579—how words identify with ours, end of 579.
Greenland lang., 1068 to 1073.

Hawaii lang., 1017; specimens, 1020, 1021.
Hebrew, etymology, 586; difficulties, 909; selections, 912 to 920.
Herero lang., 1056 and 1063.
Hindostani lang., 992; selections, 994.
Hindee lang., 995.

Hungarian, lang. and specimens, 783 to 786, 794; forms of words, 787.
Huron lang., 1080.

If, forms, 211.
Illyrian lang. and specimens, 748 to 750; forms of words, 751.
Implied words, 1106 to 1118; adj. and noun form a compound, in which one or the other must be lost, 1106; the adj. is the real principal, 1108 and 1109; the noun following adj. is like the denominator in arithmetic, 1109; nouns have nature of adj's, 1112; adj's stand independent, 1113 and 1114; all verbs do not have nominatives, 1115.
Impersonal verbs, 505 to 509.
Inchoatives, 515 to 518.
Indefinite pron's, 186 to 192.
Indian lang's, 977.
Infinitive, in Latin, common ending, 69.
Instrumental case defined, 107.
Interrogatives, 23; compared with affirmatives, 1089 to 1090.
Intransitives, 31.
Irish lang., compared with Gaelic, 684; letters, 686.
Italian, its character, 700; specimens, 701; like Fr., 702; dialects, 703.
Japanese lang., 1037 to 1040.
Javan lang., 1007.

Kawi lang., 1014 to 1016.
Karelian lang., 798.
Kalmuk, 870.
Kentish dialect, 617.
Kumanian, 870.

Latin, grammar, 50 to 79; selections, 80 to 101; its etymology, 578; how easily it compares with Eng., end of 578; Latin lang's, 688.
Lancashire dialect, 624.
Lapp lang., 796.
Laws; the working of one thing into different results, without losing identity, 130; that addding letters to a word gives no new sound, but indicates an old one, 539.
Lenapi lang., 1077.
Lesghian lang. with specimens, 839.
Letters, the latent parts, 531; syllabic, 535; vowels implied in consonants, or latent, 535 to 539; the base stroke or key of consonants, 540 to 543; our words like Chinese letters, 543; marked and single letters really double, 544 to 546; assimilation of letters, 547, 548; the form and value of the letters of the alphabet, showing the connection of each, 549 to 566; the order of the alphabet in Heb., Greek, and Russ., 567 to 571; other alphabets, 571; vowels, related to each other, 572; they unite in diphthongs from harmony, 573; what vowels for ours, in Old Germ. and Lat., 574; letters never lost nor silent, end of 580; their harmony, note, page 184.
Lettish lang., 772.
Lithuanian lang., 765 and 769; specimens, 770.
Locative case, 107.

Macassar lang., 1009 to 1013.
Madagascar lang., 1025.

INDEX. 381

Malay lang's, 1001 to 1016; selections, 1003.
Maltese, 907.
Manchu lang., and specimens, 866 to 869.
Many, its relatives, 189.
Middle, form of verbs, 104.
Milanese dialect, 708.
Mongolian lang., 864, 865.
Moods, what are they, and the names, 36.

Namaqua lang., 1047, 1058, 1059.
Neapolitan dialect, 703.
Negatives, allied to interrogatives, 1091; and opposites, 1092; not a nothing, 1093.
Neuters, objective in character, 138; neut. plur. and abstract, 140.
New forms, any oblique case may be base for such, 128.
Nine, its forms, 262, 263.
North (*Old*), 662; history, 668; specimens, 669 to 671.
Nominatives, after be, 27.
Nor and Not, forms, 213, 214.
Notes, about all reduced to identity, etc., 155; explaining the meaning of equality, 195; on decay of words, 589; all philosophizing leads to absurdity, 590; explaining translations, 780; it is no objection that one proposition does not agree with every other, 591; on identifying all things, 592.
Nouns, defined and divisions, 3; their history, 110.
Number, in Grammar, the kinds, 7.
Numerals, their history, 240; those over twelve, 272 to 275; letters used for them, 277; are only marks of order, 278 to 280.

Oblique cases, what are they, 59.
Of, Off, their forms, 234.
Often, its forms, 216.
One, its forms, 240 to 242.
Only, its forms, 217.
Or and nor, forms, 212, 213.
Order of words—words belong where found, in Latin, 80 to 101, 89.
Ossete (or Iron) lang. and specimens, 841 to 846.
Other, its forms, 190.
Out, its forms, 227.

Pali lang. and Pracrit, 996.
Parts of Speech, how many, 47; no distinct line to mark them, 48.
Parsee lang., 821.
Parts of words, their development, 229; part as great as whole, 531.
Particles, their history, 193.
Participles, what they are and the kinds, 38; used like adj's, 40; used for verbs in Latin, 106; their history, 283; German, 284 to 288; Celtic, 290 to 293; Slavic, 294; Hung. part's, 302; Finnish, 303; Turkish, 304; Albanish, 305; Persian, 306; Hindostani, 307; Bengali, 308; Manchu, 309; Semitic, 310; Malay, 312; Greek, 313 to 318; part. in urus, 319 to 326, 439; other points in German verbals, 327 and 328; Old Eng., 609 to 611.
Passive, in Latin, 438 to 443; Slavic, 444 to 446; Hung., 447; Albanish, 448; Wall., 449; Celtic, 450 to 452; Latin past pass., 453; Greek, 454; Greek past, 455; Greek perfect, 456, and p. perf.,

457; Greek future, 458; Bengali, 460; other points in Greek passive, 461.
Past tense, in Latin, etc., 401 to 404; in Greek, 405 to 407.
Persian lang's and specimens, 812 to 819; forms of, 821 to 823.
Pehlvi lang., 822.
Person, what it is, 37.
Perfect tense, in Latin, etc., 414 to 419; Greek, 421 to 426; Mod. G'k, 427.
Philology, abstract, 1083.
Phœnician lang., 898.
Piedmontese dialect, 703.
Pluperfect tense, in Latin, 420; in Greek, 428; in Albanian, 429.
Plurals, connected with fem's, 134, 135; identical with genitives, 132; not different from sing., 133; a noun in gen. case, 281.
Portugese lang., 708; specimens, 712.
Polish lang. and specimens, 746, 747, and 778.
Polabian lang., 760.
Polynesian lang's, 1024.
Possessives, 10.
Preformatives defined, 109.
Present tense, in Latin, etc., 399 and 400.
Prepositions, what they are, 45; growth by doubling, 231.
Pronouns, personals, 18, 19; compound, 20; relatives, 21; compound, 22; interrogatives, 23; pron's equal adj's, 23; in Latin, 62; their history, 156; they have arisen by growth of noun and verb endings, 156; personal, I, 158, 159; it is a demonstrative, 162; plural, we, 160; poss., our, 161; personal, thou, 163; in plural, ye, 164; poss., your, 165; those of the 2d person identical with the 3d; the different cases of pron's all variations of the same form, 166; personals of 3d person, 167 to 171; he and it, 169; she and it, 170; they and their, 171; demonstratives, 173 to 177; relatives, 178 to 185; indefinites, 186 to 192; the parts or elements of pron's, 191, 192.
Provencial lang., forms of words, 695.
Prussian (Old) lang. and specimens, 766, 767; forms of words, 768.

Rabbinic lang., 897.
Radicals, in Asiatic lang's, what they are, 1119 to 1121; prefixes, 1122.
Reduplication, 422; words grown by repetition of like elements, as plants and animals, 1083 to 1088.
Relatives, 178 to 185, 21.
Repetitions, the sentence is made up of them, 103, 126, 127; repetition or doubling in adverbs, 198, 199; in compounds, 194.
Romanic, or Rhaetish, dialect, its words and specimens, 698, 713.
Root, or base, defined, 108.
Russian etymology, 581; lang., 736 to 739; specimens, 740 to 742, 779.

Sabien lang., 900.
Samaritan lang., 897.
Samoidish lang's, 799.
Samogitian lang. and specimen, 771, 774.
Sabine, Sicilian, and Sardinian dialects, 703.

INDEX. 383

Sanscrit lang., 978; alphabet, 979; list of words, 984; compounds, 982; specimens, 983.
Saxon (Old), differs from Old H. Germ., 637; forms of words, 639.
Saxon (Ang.), see English.
Scandinavian, its branches or forms, 661.
Semitic lang's, 908; history and forms, 894 to 907; relations and peculiarities, 925, 964; prefixes, 932 to 964; tenses, 949; Semitic etymology, 586.
Sentence, what it is, 1, 2.
Servian lang., 752.
Serenian lang., 797.
Seven, its forms, 258.
Since, its forms, 218.
Six, its forms, 256, 257.
Slovenian lang., 758.
Slavic etymology, 583; lang's, 730 to 781; its forms, 732 to 735; its peculiarities, 781.
So, its forms, 203.
Soon, its forms, 215.
Spanish lang., history, 704; specimens, 705.
Still, its forms, 220.
Subjunctive, in Lat., 462, 463; modern Lat., 464; Slavic, 465; Celtic, 466; Greek (and optative), 467 to 469; in German, 470 to 472.
Suomi lang., 796.
Supine, in Latin, what, 72.
Swedish, specimens, 665; compared with Danish, 667.
Swiss idiom, 646, 647; list of words, 648.
Syrian lang., 795.

Tagale lang., 1026.
Tamil lang., 997.
Tartar lang's, 858 to 874; Tart. proper, 861, and spec., 862.
Telinga lang., 996.
Tenses, what are they, 32; in Latin, 64 to 68.
Ten, its forms, 264, 265.
That, its forms, 204.
Thibetan lahg., 1027 to 1036.
Though, its forms, 220.
Three, its forms, 246 to 249.
Through and across, 236.
Tigre lang., 906.
Till, its forms, 220.
To, at, in, on—their forms, 235.
Together, forms, 221.
Transitives, what are they, 26, 28.
Translations, are word-for-word, 626.
Turanian, 859.
Tungusic lang., 860.
Turkish lang., 807 to 811.
Tuscan lang., 703.
Twelve and eleven, 266 to 271.
Two, its forms, 243 to 245.
Tyrolese, Thuringian, and Translvanian dialects, 649.

Up and upper, their forms, 228.

Valencian lang., 706.
Venetian dialect, 703.
Verbs, what they are, 25; trans. and intrans., 26; reg. and irreg., 25; history, 333; do not peculiarly affirm, 334 to 336; in Latin, 63; Turkish verbs, 347 to 357; Finn., 357; Mongolian, 358; Persian, 359; Afghan, 364; Hung., 365 to 370; Slavic, 371 to 383; Bengali, 384; Hind., 385; Celtic, 386 to 397; Greek and Latin, 398.
Verbals, what are such, 40; verbal endings, 329 to 332.

Wallachian lang., 724; features, 726; specimens, 727 and 728; words compared with Eng. and Latin, 729.
Walloon lang., 699.
Welsh, etymology, 585; specimens, 678; compared with Gaelic, 685.
Wend, language and specimens, 754, 755; Hung. Wend, specimens, 759 and 777.
Westmoreland dialect, 621.
With, its forms, 224, 225, 226.

Yet, its forms, 219.

Zend lang., 823.
Zulu lang, 1051.

www.ingramcontent.com/pod-product-compliance
Lightning Source LLC
Chambersburg PA
CBHW030346230426
43664CB00007BB/553